Controversies in Revelation

A Comparative Analysis of Premillennial Interpretation

Controversies in Revelation

A Comparative Analysis of Premillennial Interpretation

Copyright © David Criswell 2003

Second Edition © David Criswell 2012

David Criswell

FORTRESS

ADONAI
PRESS

Dallas, TX

Controversies in Revelation

A Comparative Analysis of Premillennial Interpretation

David Criswell

ISBN NUMBER 978-0615591841

Cover Design by David Criswell
Photo and art by David Criswell

FORTRESS

ADONAI
PRESS

Dallas, TX

Printed in the United States of America

Dedication

For all those whom I wish I could have known better, but hope to know in eternity.

"Know this first of all, that no prophecy of Scripture is *a matter* of one's own interpretation, for no prophecy was ever made by an act of human will, but by men moved by the Holy Spirit spoke from God" (2 Peter 1:20-21).

Preface

The book of Revelation has been the subject of debate for thousands of years. The popular interpretation thereof has shifted dramatically over the centuries. "Chiliasm," the belief in a literal second coming of Christ to reign for a thousand years, was the well accepted and attested view of the early church fathers but was slowly replaced by "amillennialism" in the Middle Ages. According to amillennialism, Revelation was an allegory whose passages should not be taken at face value. Chiliasm was even outlawed in the High Middle Ages as the Catholic Church sought to suppress all opposing views. Some dissenting Christians, known as Joachimites, attempted to resurrect some of the literal applications of the early church fathers while still being legally compatible with the official amillennialism of the church. The Joachimite view came to be known as "historicism" and eventually became the dominant view of the Protestant Reformation. Nevertheless, once the Reformation Church had purged themselves of Catholic control, it became more obvious that Augustinian influences, including amillennialism, were no longer needed. The later Reformation scholars slowly began to return to chiliasm, now known as "premillennialism."

With these wide variety of views held throughout history the average Bible reader is left to ponder the vast array of interpretive methods utilized in Revelation. Too many readers feel overwhelmed and give up. The purpose of this book is to allow the reader, whether he be a scholar, student, or layman, to better be able to compare, evaluate, and debate various interpretations within a school of thought. Nevertheless, even this requires certain choices to be made. What school of thought? What scholars will be cited?

In regard to the first question, the answer is "chiliasm" or the "premillennial" school of thought. Of the three main schools of thought (which are discussed in Appendix F) only "premillennialism" has shown itself to use a consistent methodology and to reach back to the church fathers. Amillennialism arose under Eusebius and Augustine hundreds of years after Revelation was written and postmillennialism did not truly appear until after the time of the Reformation, although it is a spiritual descendant of amillennialism. Only premillenialism can be traced back to chiliasts such as Tertullian, Irenaeus, and Victorinus of the early apostolic age. This book will, therefore, discuss variant interpretations within the premillennial school of thought.

The next question is what scholars will be cited from this school. This was certainly the most difficult question to answer in the preparation of this work. This book has divided the scholars of the ages into five categories. These are the church fathers, the medieval scholars, Reformation scholars, post-Reformation scholars, and modern evangelicals. The division is made for several reasons. First, there is a clear distinction in the views of each age. The medieval scholars were forced to improvise their views of Revelation in order to avoid persecution. The Reformers inherited the medieval Joachamite views. However, by the late 18th Century, and particularly the 19th Century, the "post-Reformation" scholars had sufficiently discarded Augustinian, and other medieval influences, and were returning to the chiliasm of the early church. It is my wish to distinguish between these scholars and those of the modern evangelical church.

From among these five categories of scholars I chose the most influential and popular of expositors. Still, even this choice created many new choices. Among the church fathers, every father is quoted who speaks on the issues. Unfortunately, few writings of the church fathers survived and even fewer that deal explicitly with Revelation. The writings of Irenaeus, Tertullian, Hippolytus, Victorinus, Ephream, and Lactantius are cited whenever possible.

The medieval scholars created a far more difficult problem. Of the medieval chiliasts, only Adso of Montier's works survived. Unfortunately, his work itself is a general expostion of prophecy and offers little in the way of the exegesis of Revelation. In order to afford the medievals a greater voice in this work I have chosen to include occasional references to Joachamite scholars including Joachim himself, Pierre d'Olive, and the Catholic supporter, Nicholas of Lyra. Although few in number, their works represent medieval thought as a whole. Since these later scholars were not true chiliasts or premillennialists, their works are included largely to show continuity. It was through the "historicists" vessel that God permitted chiliasm's roots to be carried through the persecutions of the Middle Ages. The medieval "historicists" (see Appendix F for a detailed discussion of "historicism") brought certain literal applications of Revelation back into the allegorical school of thought that was dominant at the time. It would, however, take many centuries before the allegorism would be shed completely as the Reformers themselves continued the Joachamite historicist tradition.

It is with the Reformers that my most difficult task was set forth. Most of the Reformers were clearly historicist of the amillennial school of thought. However, some scholars, such as Joseph Mede and Isaac Newton, slowly returned to the premillennial school of thought while retaining the "historicist" framework. I was faced with the issue of whether or not to include the large school of historicists within my book. I chose to reject all but the most influential historicists, and then only those who were clearly premillennial. This leaves only a handful of Reformation scholars, among whom the most prominent are Joseph Mede and Isaac Newton. Since most other premillennial scholars of this time merely mimiced Mede's work, I felt this was a sufficient answer.

Within the latter two ages are the majority of premillennial authors. I have cited every major commentator or prophetic scholar with one reservation. They must have written a commentary on Revelation. Occassional quotes by those who did not write a commentary may occur, but will by no means be commonplace. The "post-Reformation" scholars are composed largely of the ninteenth century scholars from John Nelson Darby to Joseph Seiss and Robert Govett. The "modern evangelicals" are composed of scholars from the twentieth century.

The reader will notice that the medieval and Reformation age scholars are relatively poorly represented. This is highly regrettable, but since chiliasm was a persecuted minority at this time, the lack of balance is a necessity. The views of the medievals have been almost completely rejected as inadequate and antiquated. They are included for both continuity and out of respect for the vehicle through which God carried the Word in the difficult times of Romanist subjugation. Appendix G gives an extensive biographical details on all "historical witnesses" cited in this volume as well as a more detailed explanation of which authors were omitted and why.

With the vast array of scholars cited within this book, it is hoped that the reader will be able to gain a better grasp of the meaning of Revelation. The reader is encouraged, however, to examine the Appendices before plunging headlong into the book itself. This is because this book is written on several levels. It is prepared in part as a college textbook. Charts are furnished at the end of nearly every chapter showing the main perspectives and the strengths and weaknesses of each view. Nevertheless, because the book assumes a basic knowledge of prophetic interpretations, those who are unfamiliar with the basic premises and presuppositions of premillennial theology, and the various schools of thought within the interpretation of Revelation, should begin *first* with Appendix F which gives a brief summary of each of the major interpretive method discussed within this book.

The final issue that needs to be addressed here is the question of what passages in Revelation are to be examined. A complete comparative analysis of every single passage in Revelation would be far too great and tedious a tasks for most students. Therefore, I have decided to address only the major interpretive issues and passage. This does encompass the majority of Revelation, excluding only chapters one through five and chapter fifteen. Those chapters are generally agreed upon and do not have a relatively large content of prophetic material. They were, therefore, left out in order to reduce the volume of this work. The chart below identifies the specific passages and where they may be found in this volume.

Passages	Brief Description	Discussed in Chapter
Revelation 1	The introduction to the prophecies of Revelation.	Not discussed in this book.
Revelation 2 & 3	These chapters are composed of seven letters to seven churches. The letters are not generally considered prophetic in content (with a few exceptions).	Not discussed in this book.
Revelation 4 & 5	These chapters introduce the vision of Christ in heaven and the preparation for the coming judgments.	Not discussed in this book.
Revelation 6	The first seven judgments, or seals, of God are unleashed.	Chapter 3 : The Seven Seals.
Revelation 7	An interlude between the judgments, this chapter discusses the 144,000 sealed of God.	Chapter 4 : Israel and the Church.
Revelation 8 & 9	The resumption of God's judgments with the sounding of the seven trumpets.	Chapter 5 : The Trumpet Judgments.
Revelation 10	A second interlude which discusses the "little scroll" and the "seven thunders."	Appendix C : Misc. Issues in Revelation.
Revelation 11:1-2	A continuation of the interlude discussing the Temple and the Holy City.	Chapter 4 : Israel and the Church.
Revelation 11:3-19	The prophecy concerning the two witnesses.	Appendix C : Misc. Issues in Revelation. and also referenced in Chapter 4 : Israel and the Church.
Revelation 12	The woman clothed with the sun and the dragon's persecution of her.	Chapter 4 : Israel and the Church.
Revelation 13	The vision of the beast from the sea and the beast from the earth.	Chapter 6 : The Beasts of Revelation.
Revelation 14	A continuation of the previous interlude with a vision in heaven in preparation for the final judgments.	Vs. 1-7 referenced in Chapter 4 : Israel and the Church. Vs. 8 referenced in Chapter 8 : The Whore of Babylon. Vs. 9-11 referenced in Chapter 6 : The Beasts of Revelation Vs. 14-20 referenced in Chapter 7 : The Bowls of Wrath.
Revelation 15	The final part of this interlude shows heaven's final preparations for wrath.	Not discussed in this book.

Passages	Brief Description	Discussed in Chapter
Revelation 16	The final series of judgments are poured out in the bowls of wrath.	Chapter 7 : The Bowls of Wrath.
Revelation 17 & 18	The final interlude is a vision of the Whore of Babylon and the fall of Babylon.	Chapter 8 : The Whore of Babylon. Rev. 17:8-13 also referenced in Chapter 6 : The Beasts of Revelation.
Revelation 19	The second coming of Christ is described.	Referenced in Chapter 9 : The Millennial Kingdom.
Revelation 20:1-10	The Millennial Kingdom is described.	Chapter 9 : The Millennial Kingdom.
Revelation 20:11-15	The Great White Throne Judgment.	Appendix B : The Resurrections and Judgments.
Revelation 21-22	The New Heaven and New Earth described along with the doxology.	Referenced in Chapter 9 : The Millennial Kingdom and Appendix B : The Resurrections and Judgments.

This volume before you is the product of nearly two years of research and over a year of writing. It was a three year labor of love. It is my sincere hope that this book will provide a good resource for those just learning prophecy, as well as for those who are already familiar with it, who are seeking a more complete survey of premillennial thought.

David Criswell, November 2003 / January 2012

"Know this first of all, that no prophecy of Scripture is *a matter* of one's own interpretation, for no prophecy was ever made by an act of human will, but men moved by the Holy Spirit spoke from God" (2 Peter 1:20-21).

Table of Contents

1

Introduction

The two most controversial books in the Bible are, not surpisingly, the first and the last. Genesis and Revelation are the beginning and the end of the Bible and it is little wonder that these books create such controversy for the validity of everything that falls between them rest upon the foundation and the consumation of the Bible. Destroy the foundation, and the building will fall. Destroy the consumation, and the marriage is annulled and the courtship meaningless. The course of human history itself rest upon the hope of the consumation of all things with God. This is of what the book of Revelation speaks.

Any student of prophecy will immediately be struck by the vast and diverse opinions that occur in the interpretation of Revelation, even *within* the same hermeneutical approach. Students are taught that there are only three basic approaches to Revelation; premillennial, amillennial, and postmillennial. He is then introduced to various approaches within each of these groups; preterists, futurists, idealists, and historicists. Unfortunately, once one goes beyond the basic hermeneutical approaches, he does not have any solid tool to help him view and interpret the vast diversity with that hermeneutic group.

I first became interested in prophecy in high school. Since that time I have continued to study prophecy. When I received my Ph.D. from Tyndale Seminary, it was in the field of prophetic studies. Among the various approaches (defined and discussed in Appendix F), premillennialism is the one that seemed to show the most respect for prophecy, but throughout all this study and interest I found that there was no one source or commentary that adequately addressed the various interpretations and differences *within* the premillennial exposition. As a result, readers of Bible commentaries may be led to believe that there is either no issue to be debated or he is provided with a straw man argument, resulting in a reader who has no substance to his belief and cannot defend them properly.

Ultimately, the purpose of this book is not to provide a commentary or to list every different interpretation that has ever been given for a specific passage. Rather this book is compiled to show, and fairly evaluate, each of the interpretations that have been put forth in various aspects of Revelation by premillennialists. These aspects ultimately have bearing upon how one reads and interprets the individual passages. In short, this book is not to "give" the reader the correct interpretation of each and every verse in Revelation, but to show, and expound, to the reader each of the major issues and interpretations that effect how he interprets Revelation. Careful attention will be made to various approaches to the 70th week of Daniel, the chronology of Revelation, the Rapture question, the identification of the Whore of Babylon, and the identification of the seven heads of the Beast, as well as highlights from various interpretations of individual passages. The hope is that the student of prophecy, whether he be a scholar, student, or layman, may be able to better understand the issues, and formulate a position that gives honor and glory to God rather than being based upon a blind obedience to a particular commentator.

Certainly critics of premillennialism will scoff and say that such a book only proves that premillennialists cannot even agree among themselves as to the correct meaning of Revelation. It should be pointed out, however, that there is *far less* diversity in opinion among premillennialists than in *any* other interpretive method. This is because premillennialism is the only methodology that attempts to have a consistent and methodical approach. Ultimately, all other views *must* rely on allegorical interpretation that places the interpretation in the imagination of the reader. In fact, many readers may have heard of the alleged distinction between prophecy and "apocalyptic" literature. Even many evangelicals have adopted the term "apocalyptic" to explain the prophecies of Revelation and Daniel. This, however, creates confusion, for such a distinction arose not so much from an attempt to classify the subject matter of Revelation, as to create a new classification of prophecy that could be interpreted differently, and more freely, than tradition prophetic passages.

Is Revelation "Apocalyptic" Literature or Prophecy?

What then is "apocalyptic" literature? The exact definition of "apocalyptic" literature varies depending on the author. For the evangelical, the main difference is simply in subject matter of apocalyptic literature which focuses on the "end times" or "last days." If, however, this is the only real distinction between traditional prophecy and apocalyptic literature, then one may well ask why there is a need to distinguish it at all. The answer is that many evangelicals have naively adopted the term as a form of convenience when discussing various literature, including extra-Biblical literature, about the end of the world which flourished shortly before and after Christ. Unfortunately, the use of the term does little to clarify anything but does serve to confuse those who are familiar with "apocalyptic" literature's true origins.

It is not entirely clear who first created this classification. Some of those who advocate this category of prophecy attribute it to ancient Greek and even Babylonian origin.[1] That pagan influences would give inspiration to Biblical prophecy is not only without historical foundation, but reflects upon the assumptions from which these scholars proceed. The truth is that, regardless of who invented it, this classification was popularized, particularly among evangelicals, by George Ladd.[2] Ladd was an evangelical theologian who tried to bridge the gap between 19th century liberalism, which viewed the Bible as "historical myth," and the evangelical community, which treats the Bible as the inerrant Word of God. Ultimately, to achieve this futile goal, he argued that the theology of the individual authors changed over time. Alleged contradictions were looked upon as a shift or change that had occurred in the apostle's theology. One could understand God's inspired words *if* he understood the historical evolution of the apostle's theology. In prophecy he argued that apocalyptic literature evolved.[3] Ladd saw apocalyptic literature as a form of literature whose basic premises and ideas were formed by culture and people, not by direct divine inspiration. Ultimately, Ladd saw the theology of the New Testament, and particularly of prophecy, as an evolution of ideas that changed over time. One author, inspired by Ladd, even suggested that alleged conflicts between passages of Christ's second coming, such as those used to support a pretribulational rapture position, can be explained by the evolution of Pauline or Petrine theology. "It is entirely probable," he says, "that perspectives changed with the passing of time. No doubt Paul's expectations about whether he would live until the Lord's return changed as he grew older."[4] Another author even suggested that Peter's proclamation that "a day is as a thousand years to the Lord" (2 Peter 3:8) is a "rather unsatisfactory" attempt to resolve the complications that he and the apostles had themselves created![5]

It is easy to see how such a philosophy can easily be manipulated to pick and choose what aspects of Scripture to take seriously and which aspects may be "safely" ignored. Indeed, taken at face value one may conclude, as David Wenham has, that there is a "chasm" in the New Testament "with Paul being the founder of Christianity as we know it and *his religion* being *radically different from that of Christ*" (emphasis added).[6] Another example is from George Caird's popular commentary on Revelation. Caird continuously argues that John used "a greater artistic freedom"[7] to represent *his* theology and says that John "wrote as an artist,"[8] thus turning Revelation into a work of artistic fiction. From such statements, found in textbooks used in evangelical seminaries, it is not hard to understand how these designations can create chaos in interpretation.

If such a distinction truly exist then what is the difference between true prophecy and "apocalyptic" literature? Many authors fail to give any clear definitions of the distinctions. Most of the "definitions" are vague, such as "dualism," "rigid determinism," and even the alleged "esoteric" character of Revelation.[9] Ray Summers has done the best job of these authors in trying to give a clear definition. He claims that the distinction between these two is primarily that "apocalyptic" literature contains verses about an immediate and dramatic ending to the world and a New Heaven and a New Earth.[10] Nonetheless, his argument also falls apart upon close examination.

First, he has argued that "apocalyptic" literature created the idea of a New Heaven and New Earth but one need only look to Isaiah 65:17 which reads, "For behold, I create new heavens and a new earth; and the former things shall not be remembered or come to mind." This passage is a parallel to Revelation 21:1,4 which says, "I saw a new heaven and a new earth; for the first heaven and the first earth passed away ... for the former things have passed away." Now Ray Summers acknowledges that Isaiah is a book of prophecy. Indeed, to suggest otherwise is to decimate the most explicit and literal prophecies of Christ. Isaiah 53 is held up by most all Christians as proof that the Messiah was to come and suffer for man's sins. If Isaiah is rejected as prophecy, then it becomes impossible to explain the many passages of Isaiah that were fulfilled literally in the New Testament. Certainly, before their fulfillment many Jews may have looked at Isaiah and sought allegorical interpretations, since they could not understand it, but once the prophecies were fulfilled, it became obvious to all believers that the prophecies were intended to be understood literally, just as they had been fulfilled. So we must understand Isaiah 65 and 66 in the same light. This, however, clashes with "apocalyptic" interpretation, which sees these events as spiritual allegories and not future historical events.

Summers also suggested that a cataclysmic end to the world is part of the nature of "apocalyptic" literature. This, too, is inconsistent with other passages of Scripture. Jesus Christ Himself expressly foretold of the cataclysmic end of the world. "For then there will be a great tribulation, such as has not occurred since the beginning of the world until now, nor ever shall. And unless those days had been cut short, no life would have been saved" (Matthew 24:21-22), for in " ... the tribulation of those days the sun will be darkened, and the moon will not give its light, and the stars will fall from the sky, and the powers of the heavens will be shaken, and then the sign of the Son of Man will appear in the sky, and then all the tribes of the earth will mourn" (Matthew 24:29-30). Is Summers to classify the book of Matthew as "apocalyptic" literature that must be interpreted differently from gospel of John?

Yet another proof of this fallacy is the testimony of Revelation itself for John specifically calls Revelation "prophecy." In the introduction it reads, "Blessed is he who reads and those who hear the words of the *prophecy*" (Revelation 1:3). In Revelation 22:7 also says, "Blessed is he who heeds the words of *the prophecy* of this book" and promises are given to those who heed the words of prophecy while curses are promised to those who do not. "I testify to everyone who hears the words of the prophecy of this book: if anyone adds to them, God shall add to him the plagues which are written in this book; and if anyone takes away from the words of the book of this prophecy, God shall take away his part from the tree of life and from the holy city, which are written in this book" (Revelation 22:18-19).

Revelation and Daniel must be considered prophecy, indistinguishable from any other form of prophecy, and utilizing the same methods of interpretation. Unfortunately, many premillennialists and literalists have erroneously begun to utilize the terminology of "apocalyptic literature" which can only lead to confusion. Prominent premillennial author, John Walvoord, who rejects allegorical and esoteric interpretations, has made comparisons to apocryphal books, such as the *Assumption of Moses*, the *Book of Enoch*, the

4

Apocalypse of Baruch, and the *Apocalypse of Adam*,[11] which only serves to lend credibility to the idea that "apocalyptic" literature was a new invention which evolved from non-Biblical sources as Ladd and others have suggested.

Evangelicals would be better served ignoring the topical differences in Revelation and Isaiah and clarifying that they are both a part of the same prophetic literature that must be interpreted by the same basic methodology. If one accepts that Revelation is a distinct type of literature from that literature used in Ezekiel, Isaiah, Joel, and many other Old Testament books (all of which contain prophecies of Jesus Christ and his first coming), then one would have to view the prophecies about Jesus as being allegorical and call into question the historicity of the New Testament. That scholars who truly accept "apocalyptic" style of literature must ultimately reject a true literal interpretation is admitted by Robert Mounce, a "historic premillennialist" who admits that apocalyptic literature gives "free rein to the imagination [and] symbols of the most bizarre sort become the norm."[12] Clearly, one cannot reject the prophetic nature of these books without rejecting Christ Jesus Himself. To attempt to split prophecy into separate types of literature, which require separate types of interpretations, is to destroy the prophecies of Christ and His first coming along with those of His second coming. One may not arbitrarily choose which prophecies to take literally and which ones to take figuratively. This is an inconsistent hermeneutic that results in chaotic interpretation.

Literal premillennialists do not deny the existence of symbols; they deny that Revelation is allegory. Symbols, by definition, have specific, literal, meanings. Where they have no specific literal meaning, they cease to be true symbols, but merely become a Rorschach inkblot where the reader sees whatever he wishes to see. In literalist interpretation there are distinct rules of interpretation that are used to decipher the meaning and message of Revelation without giving in to subjective interpretations. These rules must be same as all other books of prophecy and must be consistent with the interpretations of those books. Only then can we understand what God would have us to know.

Premillennialism and the "Literal" Interpretation

So what exactly is premillennialism? And what is the consistent methodology of which I speak? Premillennialism takes its name from the belief that Christ will literally return to the earth to establish a thousand-year reign as described in Revelation 20. Hence, the name itself means Christ returns before ("pre") the "millennium" (thousand-year reign). This interpretation is synonymous the so-called "literal interpretation" of Revelation. *So what exactly is the "literal interpretation?"* Having been born and raised in a liberal Methodist Church, I was always taught that "literalism" meant that some fire-breathing dragon would come and eat people in the last days. I was told that such absurd reasoning was the doctrine of Baptists and other "fundamentalists."

5

In fact, the term "literalism" originated in response to the liberal high allegorical interpretations that became prominent among the nineteenth century liberals (and as such they called themselves). The liberals of that era believed that science had disproven the existence of miracles, so they began to reinterpret the miracles of the Bible to suggest that these were merely allegorical stories intended to tell us a moral or lesson. These scholars denied the historicity of the Scriptures and denounced those who believed in its historicity as naive. In response to the growing popularity of this view, some Bible believing Christian theologians gathered a systematic response to this doctrine. They stated, in essence, that the view held since the beginning of Christendom is that the events of the Bible are historical, literal, and true. They held that symbols, which no one denies exist, have literal meanings that should not be arbitrarily taken as allegory.

In short, *literal interpretation means that the Bible speaks about literal historical events and symbols, where they occur, have literal meanings* that cannot be interpreted by free style Rorschach inkblot mentality. In prophecy, this means that the Bible is speaking about literal events that will occur in the future and the symbols cannot be taken as broad allegories. This is the only consistent methodology that does not rely on the speculative imagination of the reader.

Deciphering Symbols in Revelation

When one drives by a large building with a giant cross upon it, he does need to ponder the great mysteries of the symbol. He recognizes, without hesitation, that the cross upon a building symbolizes one thing; a church which professes to be Christian. Given a specific context, the cross may have a slightly different meaning. If it is Christmas time, a person may simply be expressing his faith. If one is watching a bad horror movie, the cross may take on Gothic meanings. Nevertheless, the meaning of the cross is apparent to the average person with little or no explanation. *Symbols have specific meanings.* When one rejects this notion, he finds that it is not only impossible to arrive at any definitive answer, but ultimately finds there is no real use in *trying* to find one.

There has always been a profound difference between symbols and allegories. While allegories are a type of symbol, not all symbols are allegories. Like the old saying, "a Ford is a car but not all cars are Fords." Allegory is, by definition, fictional. It is a story which represents something else, whereas a symbol is a word or phrase that represents something else. A symbol, as opposed to an allegory, must be interpreted literally. When the Bible speaks of a parable, it specifically defines it as a parable and gives the meaning of the parable. Where the Bible does not define a story as a parable, we must accept it at face value, as intended. Any symbols utilized in the stories must be interpreted systematically, and not haphazardly.

6

The first thing that must be taken into consideration when deciphering the symbols of Revelation according to a literal approach is to look for one of several things before discarding the natural meaning of the word. In the book of Revelation symbols usually take one of several forms.

1. The Bible should itself be examined for the answer. In some cases the meaning of a symbol is explicitly given only a passage or two later. Despite this, there are those that ignore the explicit definition of a symbol for one of their own liking. Not only should the book of Revelation be scoured for definitions to its own symbols, but many symbols have common usages throughout the Scriptures. The entire Bible must, therefore, be referenced.

2. Context must be thoroughly examined itself. Sometimes the meaning is obvious by the context, but ignored by those who want to read something into the passage that is not there.

3. The history and culture of the writer should be examined. Many words have a clear symbolic meaning to one culture, but lose that meaning in another culture. A cross in 33 B.C. meant death. A cross in 33 A.D. meant life eternal. The meaning of the word in the author's culture may be of great value in determining the meaning of a symbol.

4. Finally, if none of the previous appear to clear up the problem, then it may be that John is not using a symbol, but merely trying to describe, in words he could best use, things that he could not himself understand. For example, in Joel 2:30, the prophet saw something he did not understand. He could only describe it as a "column of smoke." However, the Hebrew word for "column" here is taken from the word for "palm tree." It is a specific type of column with the ornamental furls, like a palm tree, at the top. Joel may have been referring, not to a column, but a "palm tree of smoke." If this is so then he was seeing a "mushroom cloud," something he could not put into words. This is usually where commentators are in disagreement and where the most controversy exists.

By following these principles, the reader of prophecy will find his task far more enriching. This book will endeavor to help the reader to examine the prophecies of Revelation in this light and to compare and contrast the various views of premillennial authors throughout history. With God's help, this book will help the reader to better understand His Word without dictating the author's own personal opinions. Remember the words of the apostle Peter when he said, "know this first of all, that no prophecy of Scripture is *a matter* of one's own interpretation, for no prophecy was ever made by an act of human will, but men moved by the Holy Spirit spoke from God" (2 Peter 1:20-21).

2

The 70 Weeks of Daniel

Biblical prophecy is sometimes like a jigsaw puzzle. Certain passages will give you a couple of pieces but it is hard to be able to see where all the pieces fit unless you have a picture to go by. This is the book of Revelation. By itself Revelation cannot give a full picture of the end times. Indeed, the failure of some to account for parallel prophecies in other books of the Bible is one reason that some reject or misconstrue the prophecies of Revelation. Revelation gives the big picture but the specifics are sometimes found in other prophetic passages. Matthew, Luke, 1 and 2 Thessalonians, Ezekiel, Joel, Isaiah, Malachi, and Zechariah are just a few of the books that need to be scoured for parallel passages, but the one that seems to be the most closely connected to Revelation is the book of Daniel. Daniel helps to establish many of the events and circumstances that occur in the book of Revelation. That Daniel is closely related to Revelation is attested even by those that reject the reality and literalness of the prophecies in Revelation.[13] Consequently, before analyzing the various interpretations of Revelation it is necessary to devote a chapter to one of the more important sections of Daniel. In Daniel 9:24-27 it was foretold that the nation of Israel would be given a specific amount of time before its sins would be atoned for and before the Messiah would rule over them. This passage, not surprisingly, has become one of the greatest controversies in the study of Biblical prophecy for it, in one prophecy, spells out the entire historical framework for God's plan of redemption. How one interprets it will impact, or be effected by, one's view of Jesus Christ as savior, one's view of the end times, and one's view of the nation of Israel. That this is case can be easily shown by a look at the origins of some of the views. Rabbinic Jews, who do not accept Jesus as Messiah, interpret the events as culminating in Maccabean revolt while anti-Semites who despise Israel claim that the prophecy was fulfilled in full in the first century so that there will be no promised future for Israel. These verses are, as Stephen Miller states, "the most controversial verses in the Bible."[14] Walvoord declares that they are "one of the most comprehensive and yet concise prophecies to be found in the Bible."[15] Therefore, if we are to truly understand Revelation and God's plan for the ages, we must first understand what God has put forth without predetermined answers.

Daniel's Seventy Weeks

"Seventy weeks have been decreed for your people and your holy city, to finish the transgression, to make an end of sin, to make atonement for iniquity, to bring in everlasting righteousness, to seal up vision and prophecy, and to anoint the most holy *place*. So you are to know and discern *that* from the issuing of a decree to restore and rebuild Jerusalem until Messiah the Prince *there will be* seven weeks and sixty-two weeks; it will be built again, with plaza and moat,[16] even in times of distress. Then after the sixty-two weeks the Messiah will be cut off and have nothing, and the people of the prince who is to come will destroy the city and the sanctuary. And its end *will come* with a flood; even to the end there will be war; desolations are determined. And he will make a firm covenant with the many for one week, but in the middle of the week he will put a stop to sacrifice and grain offering; and on the wing of abominations *will come* one who makes desolate, even until a complete destruction, one that is decreed, is poured out on the one who makes desolate" (Daniel 9:24-27).

This passage begins by declaring that at the end of seventy "weeks," or literally "sevens," there will be an end to "the transgression," an "end to sin," "atonement for iniquity," and "everlasting righteousness." It goes on to state that sixty nine "weeks" are also declared to begin with "the issuing of a decree to restore and rebuild Jerusalem" and to end with the Messiah who will "be cut off and have nothing." Various interpretations have been applied to this verse but this passage does make clear that there are several things which must occur. A breakdown of the events is as follows:

1. A total of seventy "sevens" (490 years) are prophetically decreed for the nation of Israel. Once these years are complete there will be "an end of sin," "atonement for iniquity," and "everlasting righteousness."
2. After a total of sixty-nine "sevens" (483 years) "the Messiah will be cut off and have nothing."
3. "After" sixty-nine "sevens" (483 years) a man will make a covenant with Israel for "seven" but he will break the covenant and desecrate the Temple in the middle of that "seven." At the end of this last "seven" God's wrath will be "poured out" on the man and he will be destroyed.
4. These prophetic "sevens" will begin with "the issuing of a decree to restore and rebuild Jerusalem" with "plaza and moat."

The Shevim

Before interpreting these difficult verses, we must begin by defining several terms. The actual Hebrew word translated "weeks" is merely "sevens." According to virtually all scholars the "weeks" represent not days but years. Despite the widespread acceptance of this view, it is efficacious to justify this presumption. Dwight Pentecost indicates that "since Daniel had been thinking in terms of years (v. 1; cf. Jer. 25:11-12; 2 Chron. 36:21), it would be most natural for him to understand these 'sevens' as years."[17] Alva McClain clarifies this position better saying:

> "The Jews had a 'seven' of *years* as well as a 'seven' of *days*. And this Biblical 'week' of years was just as familiar to the Jews as the 'week' of

days. It was, in certain respects, even more important. *Six years* the Jew was free to till and sow his land, but the *seventh year* was to be a solemn 'Sabbath of rest unto the land' (Lev. 25:3-4) ... Daniel also knew that the very length of Babylonian captivity had been based on Jewish violation of the divine law of the Sabbatic year. Since according to II Chron. 36:21 the Jews had been removed from off the land in order that it might rest for *seventy* years, it should be evident that the Sabbatic year had been violated for 490 years, or exactly seventy 'sevens' of years."[18]

Thus a week was a unit of seven, or a *shevim*, in Israel. The Jews also a *shevim* of years, similar to our decade, but composed of seven years. Now critics may respond that every other usage of *shevim* or "sevens" in the Bible is appropriately translated "week" and refers to a week of days. Nevertheless, the week of years is not unusual in Jewish literature. It is found in Jewish writings outside of the Bible including the apocryphal book of Enoch.[19] Moreover, "*shavua'* [the singular of *shevim*] literally means a 'heptad,' or 'unit of seven,' and has no intrinsic reference to time periods of any sort. Support for this may be seen in three appearances of *shavua'* with *yamin* ('days'), the addition indicating that *shavua'* alone was not sufficient to show that a period of seven days was meant (cf. Ezekiel 45:23; Daniel 10:2-3). The fact that two of these three combinations occur in Daniel 10, immediately following the 'Seventy Weeks Prophecy,' may be a signal to the reader that a different sense of *shavua'* is now intended."[20] Further proof is in the parallel to Revelation's chronology where "time, times, and half a time" (12:14) is synonymous with "1260 days" (11:3).

A final proof is in the historical interpretation of Daniel. That these *shevim* or "weeks" have been accepted as "weeks of years" is an attestation that the view is not peculiar. Even the ancient Qumran communities before Christ accepted the weeks as years.[21] This view was supported by the early church fathers[22] and continued to be promoted down to the Reformation[23] and in modern times with no general criticism.

The Sixty-Nine Weeks

Now according to the prophecy sixty-nine "weeks" of years (or four hundred and eighty-three years) would begin with the "decree to restore and rebuild Jerusalem" and end with the Messiah being "cut off." Various scholars have offered four possibilities for the starting point of this prophecy. These are four different decrees issue by Persian kings to Israel. One of these four decrees must be the *terminus a quo* or starting point for the prophecy. They are shown below.

Decree	Date	What it permits
The decree of Cyrus	Sometime after October 29, 539 B.C.	Decree allows Jews to return to Jerusalem.
The decree of Darius	Circa 519 or 518 B.C.	Confirms previous decree.
The decree of Artaxerxes to Ezra	457 B.C.	Decree permits civil authority and Temple.
The decree of Artaxerxes to Nehemiah	Early March, 444 B.C.	Decree allows the building of fortifications.

The Decree of Cyrus

The first possibility is the decree of Cyrus the Great which was given sometime after the fall of Babylon on October 29, 539 and which allowed Jews to return to Jerusalem. Its strength is that the edict permits the rebuilding of the Temple for, as Edward Young states, "it is not justifiable to distinguish too sharply between the building of the city and the building of the temple."[24]

The drawbacks of this theory, however, are many. First, he must *assume* that the decree to rebuild the Temple allows for the rebuilding of fortifications, or rather the "plaza and moat," specifically mentioned in verse 25. Without these fortification the city is not independent, and remains a Persian province. The decree only allows Jews to return to the city and to build a Temple but nothing else. Jerusalem was still a captive city subject to Persia. This is clear by the fact that Ezra and Nehemiah both had to write the Persian King to clarify what they were and were not permitted to do. It was these requests that brought forth new proclamations and decrees.

The second, and greatest, problem with this view is that the termination of the sixty nine weeks is highly ambiguous. Nathaniel West begins the seventy weeks with Cyrus and ends it with the birth of Christ.[25] However, in order to make the numbers come out correct he must create an interval of some fifty odd years. He notes that the seven weeks are differentiated from the sixty-two weeks which make up the sixty-nine, but in his scheme he places an interval of fifty-seven years, not between the seven and the sixty-two, but rather in the middle of the seven weeks, by dividing the seven into three weeks and four weeks![26] Edward Young concurs with West that the sixty nine weeks end with "the time of Christ,"[27] but rejects his chronology. Since four hundred and eighty-three years from 539 B.C. takes one to only 56 B.C., Young argues merely that the dates correspond "roughly"[28] to the periods in history. Prophecy, however, is not based on "rough" estimates but precise prophetic fulfillments. It is for this reason that the view is suspect and a minority view.

The Decree of Darius

The second starting date for the sixty-nine weeks is the decree of Darius in circa 519 or 518 B.C. This decree, however, merely reaffirms the decree of Cyrus and is not a new decree at all, but rather a confirmation of the older decree of Cyrus. This view also lacks in the same areas as the former theory and has fewer advocates. Matthew Poole list it as a possibility[29] but is noncommittal and most modern scholars do not take this option seriously.

The Decrees of Artaxerxes

The last two decrees are the best choices and the most popular among modern evangelicals. Both of these last two decrees were given by Artaxerxes, the Ahasuerus of the Bible. The first of these designates the decree of Artaxerxes to Ezra in 457 B.C. The second is the decree of Artaxerxes was to Nehemiah in March of 444 or 445 B.C. This latter decree specifically permits the building of fortifications while the former does not. Miller, who holds to the 457 date, admits that in the decree "there was no specific command to rebuild the city of Jerusalem"[30] but Gleason Archer argues that even though no such statement was made, permission was given in "Ezra's mind."[31] Harold Hoehner, however, holds to the latter decree based on the following:

> "First, there is a direct reference to the restoration of the city (Neh. 2:3,5). Second, Artaxerxes wrote a letter to Asaph to give materials to be used specifically for the walls (2:8). Third, the Book of Nehemiah and Ezra 4:7-23 indicate that certainly the restoration of the walls was done in the most distressing circumstances, as predicted by Daniel (Dan. 9:25). Fourth, no later decrees were given by the Persian kings pertaining to the rebuilding of Jerusalem."[32]

That the facts seem to support the decree to Nehemiah should appear obvious but in reality it is not the *terminus a quo,* or starting point, that determines scholars interpretation of the prophecy but the *terminus ad quem,* or ending point that ultimately determines which view is taken. Daniel states that the sixty-nine weeks continue unto the coming of the Messiah. He then states that "after the sixty-two weeks the Messiah will be cut off and have nothing, and the people of the prince who is to come will destroy the city and the sanctuary" (Daniel 9:26). This passage is very controversial for those who take the decree to Nehemiah universally end sixty-nine weeks with the crucifixion of Christ whereas many, of those who accept the decree to Ezra believe that the sixty-nine weeks end with the consummation of Christ's ministry.[33]

Archer has argued that the sixty-nine weeks end only with the "appearance" of the Messiah, indicating that crucifixion occurs "after" the weeks end.[34] Miller also contends that "Christ's crucifixion ("Anointed One ... cut off," v. 26) and the subsequent destruction of Jerusalem in A.D. 70 (v. 26) would occur *after* the sixty-ninth seven, but *not during* the seventieth seven (v. 27), revealing a gap between these sevens."[35] Indeed, all dispensationalists (see Appendix F for a detailed discussion of dispensationalism) agree that the seventieth week is separated from the sixty-nine but the issue of the Messiah's death is a controversial one and appears to be tied to the question of chronology,[36] more than exegesis.

The Calendar Year

The crux of the problem is that using the normal Gregorian calendar of today 483 years would take the reader to either 27 or 39 A.D. If one adopts 457 B.C. as the *terminus a quo* then 27 A.D., which some believe is the inauguration of Christ's ministry,[37] becomes the *terminus ad quem*. On the other hand 39 A.D. is obviously far too late for the crucifixion date. However, this is based on faulty chronology. It has long been an accepted fact of history that the ancient Jews did not use 365 day calendar years. Those who hold to the decree to Nehemiah point out that 360 day years were common at that time and recalculate the "prophetic years" which, in turn, are said to take the reader to the exact week of Christ's crucifixion,[38] as shown below:

Hebrew/Chaldean Calendar (360 days)	Gregorian Calendar (365 days)
483 years x 360 days = 173,880 days	173,880 days / 365 days = 476.38 years

483 years x 360 days = 173,880 days
 	
Edict given in early March 444 B.C.
 	
Christ crucified April 3, 33 A.D.
	Specifically:
	    173,740 days = 476 Gregorian years
	+ 116 days in leap years
	+ 24 days between early March (when edict was given) and early April (when Christ was crucified)
	= 173,880 days or *exactly* 483 Hebrew years
	                  from the edict to the crucifixion!

483 years x 360 days = 173,880 days Edict given in early March 444 B.C. Passover week begins March 30, 33 A.D.	Alternately shown as: 476 x 365.24219879 days per year in the Gregorian calendar = 173,855 days + 25 days between March 5 and March 30 = 173,880 days or *exactly* 483 Hebrew years from the edict to the crucifixion!

This view has created a flurry of controversy. Critics of the view argue that 360 days years were not common,[39] that the view was invented by Robert Anderson,[40] and that "the Lord may not make things to complicated."[41] In reference to the last remark it should be pointed out that such a view is only "complicated" to modern scholars. To Jews who used 360 day calendars it would have been the simplest and best view.

Although some have argued that the 360 day calendar theory has "seemingly insurmountable problems"[42] this view was neither created by Robert Anderson nor is it untrue. A cursory examination of calendar years proves that the current calendar did not come into existence until centuries after Daniel. The earliest cultures used a calendar year based solely on the lunar months. This created twelve months of alternating 29 and 30 day months totaling 354 days. The ancient Jews had used this calendar at one time,[43] while the ancient Romans had a 355 day calendar.[44] The Assyrians also used a similar calendar with a leap month to correct the conflict with the solar year.[45] Nevertheless, this method of calculation created too much a disparity between the lunar calendar and the solar calendar. The ancient Chaldeans, or Babylonians, in turn created that 360 day calendar that remained in effect for centuries.[46] This same 360 day calendar continued to be used by the Persians when Cyrus conquered Babylon, at the time Daniel still lived.[47] The first Greek to attempt to institute a 365 day calendar was Thales[48] whose calendar would become the standard for Julius Caesar when he created the Julian calendar,[49] later amended by Pope Gregory the Great; hence the Gregorian Calendar.

Critics, however, have made much over the fact that many of the ancients, particularly Egypt, made adjustments to the solar calendar.[50] Nevertheless, this is both misleading and irrelevant. According to Egyptian historians Egypt's "population had adopted a year of twelve months of thirty days each, with an additional period of five intercalary days to avoid too great a variation from the true solar year."[51] Now the use of five intercalary days *did not* create a 365 day year as claimed by critics. On the contrary, for the Egyptian seventy-two years was just that, seventy-two years. It was *not* seventy-three years because they no more took into account the intercalary days for historical purposes that modern historians calculate our leap years to date the past. When referring to an event in the year 545 modern historians *do not* say "1461 years ago," calculating the 365 leap years as an extra year, but rather "1460 years ago." Likewise, not one of these critics has declared that the Jewish exile in Babylon lasted 48 years, rather than 49, as one would expect if they used intercalary days to date historicial events![52] So it must be stated finally that history proves that *all* the ancients used between 354 to 360 day calendar years until the time of the Greeks, or more accurately until Julius Caesar altered the calendar. In short, there is no logical reason to expect that the ancients would have *anticipated* the Gregorian calendar and, therefore, no reason to believe that the years prophesied in Daniel would have reflected a calendar which did not yet exist.

Anderson himself pointed out "that the prophetic year is not the ordinary year is not a new discovery. It was noticed sixteen centuries ago by Julius Africanus in his *Chronography*, wherein he explains the seventy weeks of the (*Jewish*) lunar years."[53] In that third century epistle Julius Africanus places the *terminus a quo* with Artaxerxes decree to Nehemiah and calculates the date using the ancient "Hebrew numeration."[54] Even the great Isaac Newton, nearly two hundred years before Anderson, calculates the seventy weeks using "Jewish Luni-solar years."[55] He then clarifies the issue as follows:

"The ancient solar years in the eastern nations consisted of 12 months, and every month of 30 days: and hence came the division into 360 degrees. This year seems to be used by *Moses* in his history of the Flood, and by *John* in the *Apocalypse*, where a time, times and a half time, 42 months and 1260 days, are put equipollent."[56]

He further notes that the Luni-solar years were used by "the *Chaldeans* long before the times of Daniel"[57] and "even from their coming out of *Egypt*."[58] It is, therefore, clear that Robert Anderson did not "introduce"[59] the 360 day "prophetic year" but it was a recognized fact long before the modern era and is confirmed by history. Still, the strongest argument for the 360 day calendar year is from the Bible itself, and not only from Revelation but in the non-prophetic books as well.

The book of Revelation clearly uses a 360 day calendar for, as Isaac Newton alluded to,[60] John clearly calls 1260 days the equivalent of three and a half years but this would equate only to 360 day years, not 365. Moreover, Genesis also appears to use a 360 day calendar for Genesis 7:11 declares that the flood began on the seventeenth day of the second month and ended on the seventeenth day of the seventh month, "*150 days*" later (Genesis 8:3-4). This is exactly five months of 30 days. Thus the Bible itself affirms the use of the 360 day year. It is, therefore, not surprising that while critics appear to have an answer for just about everything they seem unusually quiet concerning the use of 360 day years in the Bible. Miller merely implies that the Biblical numbers are "rounded off"[61] while Archer merely considers the Revelation passage "about" three and a half years and calls it "slender support."[62] Both ignore the passage in Genesis.

The fact is that the ancient Jews did use a 360 day calendar. This is even admitted by Nathaniel West who rejects Anderson's thesis.[63] Thus it is correct to say that "the Lord may not make things to complicated,"[64] but how much more complicated would it be for Jews who used a 360 day a year calendar to calculate the coming of the Messiah using a calendar which wouldn't even exist for another three hundred years! The usage of the ancient Chaldean calendar cannot be ignored.

Still, one final criticism offered is that Christ was not crucified in 32 or 33 A.D.[65] However, this is based on a faulty assumption. Because most scholars believe that Christ was born three or four years earlier than originally assumed, they also assume that the crucifixion must also have been three to four years earlier. Nonetheless, the date for Jesus' crucifixion is not based on its relation to His birth. Nowhere does the Bible say that Jesus was 33 years old when He was crucified. Even the popular verse often quoted says only that Jesus was "about" thirty when He began His ministry (Luke 3:23) and nowhere is there a definitive answer as to how long His ministry lasted. The three and a half year ministry, which may or may not be true, is based partially on tradition and partially on circumstantial evidence. That Jesus was crucified on passover of 33 A.D. (see *Controversies in the Gospels*) is well attested by archaeology, history, and even astronomy.[66]

So it should now be obvious that Daniel's prophecy of sixty-nine weeks ended with the crucifixion of Christ. What then of the seventieth week? This discussion has been prolonged because it is essential to prove that Christ's death and resurrection fulfilled only the first sixty-nine weeks, and not the seventy as amillennialist Edward Young argues.[67] Young's thesis cannot work for he is forced to argue that "the *terminus ad quem* was not regarded as possessing particular importance or significance."[68] If this so then the prophecy itself would have no "particular importance." On the contrary, the prophecy is vital and the *terminus ad quem* for the seventieth week has not occurred. This is the "missing week" that is found in Revelation. This is how Revelation is connected to Daniel and why most premillennialists beleive that Revelation speaks of this "seventieth week" of Daniel.

The Missing Week

The subject of the missing week is crucial to the promise to the Jewish people and the nation of Israel. Amillennialists like Young suggest that the seventy weeks were fulfilled at the destruction of the Temple in Jerusalem in 70 A.D.[69] but the "transgressions" of the Jews can scarcely be said to have passed away in 70 A.D. when even the extreme Zealots declared that God was punishing them for some unknown sin. Eleazar on Masada said to his people before killing themselves "God hath brought this decree against the whole Jewish nation"[70] and "God himself hath brought this necessity upon us."[71] Truly the "transgressions" of the Jews can never be finished until they have accepted and received the Messiah, whom we know to be Christ Jesus. Some would deny the salvation of Israel, but this event remains to be fulfilled in the future. In fact, there is no legitimate way to allegorize the seventieth week or make its historic fulfillment in the past. This seventieth week, and Israel's salvation, remains to be fulfilled in the future.

Jim Combs states "an interregnum or hiatus takes place between the 69th and 70th 'week,' during which the Dispensation of Grace, geared primarily for the salvation of Gentiles, takes place."[72] Concerning this interval Dwight Pentecost says, "this interval was anticipated by Christ when He prophesied the establishing of the church (Matt. 16:18)."[73] As further proof of this interval Randall Price notes "the sixty-ninth week has already been set off as a distinct unit comprised of the seven and sixty-two weeks. This would imply in itself that the events of the seventieth week are to be treated separately."[74]

In summary, "the truth of a parenthesis is implied in Matthew 24 where the present age is described as preceding and intervening between the cross and the sign foretold by Daniel 9:27 (cf. Matt. 24:15)."[75] Daniel itself confirms such

17

an interval. As Walvoord states, "the anointed one, or the Messiah, is cut off after the 69th week, but not in the 70th. Such a circumstance could be true only if there were a time interval between the two periods."[76] Even nondispensationalists like Gleason Archer have reluctantly admitted that the sixty-ninth and seventieth week must be separated. Says Archer, "if the seventieth week finds fulfillment at all, it must be identified as the last seven years before Christ's return to earth."[77] Thus the "missing week" of Daniel's prophecy remains to be fulfilled in the future whereas the other sixty-nine weeks have been fulfilled in the past.

It is this "missing week" that provides the clearest connection to Revelation. Both the timetable and the events spoken of in Daniel correspond directly to Christ's prophecies concerning last days and the book of Revelation. An examination of these events is prudent to show the connection.

Concerning the end of these seventy weeks Daniel says:

> "Its end *will come* with a flood; even to the end there will be war; desolations are determined. And he will make a firm covenant with the many for one week, but in the middle of the week he will put a stop to sacrifice and grain offering; and on the wing of abominations *will come* one who makes desolate, even until a complete destruction, one that is decreed, is poured out on the one who makes desolate" (Daniel 9:26-27).

In Matthew 24:15-21 Christ specifically speaks of this abomination as a future event in the last days. He says:

> "Therefore when you see the abomination of desolation which was spoken of through Daniel the prophet, standing in the holy place (let the reader understand), then let those who are in Judea flee to the mountains; let him who is on the housetop not go down to get the things out that are in his house; and let him who is in the field not turn back to get his cloak. But woe to those who are with child and to those who nurse babes in those days! But pray that your flight may not be in the winter, or on a Sabbath; for then there will be a great tribulation, such as has not occurred since the beginning of the world until now, nor ever shall. And unless those days had been cut short, no life would have been saved; but for the sake of the elect those days shall be cut short."

The apostle Paul also speaks of this abomination as preceding the second coming, saying, "with regard to the coming of our Lord Jesus Christ ... let no one in any way deceive you, for *it will not come* unless the apostasy comes first, and the man of lawlessness is revealed, the son of destruction, who opposes and exalts himself above every so-called god or object of worship, so that he takes his seat in the temple of God, displaying himself as being God" (2 Thessalonians 2:1-4).

How can the anti-Christ take "his seat in the temple of God" when the temple was destroyed in A.D. 70? This leads to the inevitable question of the rebuilding of the Temple in Jerusalem. The Temple is destroyed in verse twenty-six of Daniel's chapter but made desolate in verse twenty-seven. Obviously its existence in verse twenty-seven implies that the Temple has to be rebuilt, a fact which any literal reading of Paul's statement also affirms. Therefore this verse is in itself justification for a gap between the sixty-ninth and seventieth week. A gap during which the Temple would have to be rebuilt, or at least during which the Temple would not exist.

That the Temple must be rebuilt and the Jews must return to Israel, as they did in 1948, was accepted even by the ancient Christians. Irenaeus, who lived a hundred years after the Temple fell, states that the future anti-Christ shall sit in the one true and literal temple of God and declare himself Christ.[78] Hippolytus, not long after, declares that when the anti-Christ comes he "shall build the city of Jerusalem and restore the sanctuary."[79] But these church fathers were not the only ones to espouse this view for Joseph Mede, of the Reformation, while not accepting the return of a Jewish state, believed that Revelation was about the repentance and redemption of the Jewish people. He says "when the fulness of the Gentiles should come in, that Israel should be received again to mercy."[80] This was the view stubbornly held by dispensationalists until the prophecy was fulfilled in part in 1948. Still, many maintain that Israel has no role in Revelation.[81] They continue to reject the belief that Daniel's seventieth week is reflected in Revelation.

Nonetheless, dispensational premillennialists believe that Israel's restoration is no mere accident but a harbinger of things to come. The Jews are back in the land precisely because the seventieth week has yet to be fulfilled. Revelation speaks of this missing seventieth week.

A Review of the Positions

Some evangelicals, including a few premillennialists, maintain that the sixty-nine weeks of Daniel's prophecy begin with the edict of Artaxerxes to Ezra in 457 B.C. and ends with the baptism of Jesus in 26 A.D. This view is often held by those of a non-dispensational position, such as covenant theologians (see Appendix F for a discussion of this view) who deny Israel's place in end times prophecy. Some of these scholars will even go so far as to suggest that it is Christ, not the anti-Christ, who is spoken of in Daniel 9:27. They further argue that the destruction of the Temple by the Romans in 70 A.D., over 35 years later, fulfills the prophecy. The latter arguments are easily discounted. First, the prince who comes and makes the covenant *clearly* comes after the initial destruction of the Temple which is mentioned in the preceding verse. Moreover, the prince is obviously connected to "desolation" and "destruction." This is not Jesus Christ, but rather the one Jesus Himself spoke about in Matthew saying, "So when you see standing in the holy place 'the abomination that causes desolation,' spoken of through the prophet Daniel—let the reader understand—then let those who are in Judea flee to the mountains" (Matthew 24:15-16). If Jesus Himself quoted Daniel's prophecy as a future event surrounding end times, then it is unacceptable for a premillennialists to accept it any other way.

On the issue of the sixty-nine weeks, this view is also weak. To begin with, four hundred and eighty three years does not take you to 26 A.D. but 25 A.D. because there is *only one year* between 1 A.D. and 1 B.C., *not two*. Moreover, the Baptism of Jesus was probably not 26 A.D. as argued by this group but 29 or even 30 A.D. This, however, enters a debate about chronology and beyond the scope of this work.[82] All that needs be said is that the assumption that Jesus was born four years earlier than we originally thought (4 B.C.) *does not* *change* the date of his crucifixion in 33 A.D. Even if Jesus did begin His ministry in 26 A.D., the advocates of this view fail to take into account the single year interim between 1 B.C. and 1 A.D.

The second problem is that while the edict of Artaxerxes to Ezra did permit civil authority and Temple worship, it did not allow for the building of a "plaza and moat" (vs. 25) as provided for in Daniel. It was not until the final edict of Artaxerxes to Nehemiah that Israel was recognized as a Jewish province of Persia and allowed to "rebuild and restore Jerusalem" with military fortifications which would *have* to be a part of the decree in order for Israel to truly be restored. If it were not fortified then it would remain a captured nation and not an independent province.

Finally, this view fails because it cannot adequately explain the prophecy which states that after sixty-nine weeks of years "the Messiah will be cut off and have nothing" (vs. 26). How does Christ's baptism signify a cutting off? How can the beginning of Jesus' ministry be equated with Jesus having "nothing?" This is the critical flaw of this view. If "the Messiah will be cut off and have nothing" (vs. 26) then this can only refer to Christ's crucifixion, not his baptism.

The view most often accepted by premillennialists that the sixty-nine weeks of years begins with the edict of Artaxerxes to Nehemiah in March 444 B.C. and ends on Passover week of 33 A.D., the very week that Christ was crucified on the Cross. It has been shown that the prophecy works out to very *day*. Four hundred eighty three years in the ancient Chaldean calander is exactly 173,880 days. From March 444 B.C. to Passover week 33 A.D. is exactly 173,880 days. While critics argue that this conversion of Chaldean, or "prophetic," years is a "tampering" with the text, any student of history knows it is just common sense. More importantly, such "tampering" would still not explain the amazing "coincidence" which is created by converting the years to days. This view is the correct view because history has proven it to be true. Christ was "cut off" and "had nothing" on Passover 33 A.D., exactly 173,880 days, or 483 Chaldean years, after Artaxerxes' edict to Nehemiah in early March 444 B.C.

CHAPTER SUMMARY

Daniel 9 establishes the framework for the book of Revelation as follows.

1. Revelation describes a seven year period at the end of the age before the second coming of Christ.
2. This seven year period is various called the 70th week of Daniel, the Tribulation, or the time of Jacob's trouble.
3. This Tribulation begins with a peace treaty, or covenant, signed between the anti-Christ and Israel.
4. The Temple of Jerusalem will be rebuilt (before or after the treaty we cannot say).
5. This peace treaty is broken in the middle of the Tribulation when the Abomination of Desolation takes place in the Temple of Jerusalem.
6. War will erupt following the Abomination and a time of unparalleled distress will follow.
7. Christ will return at the end of the Tribulation and establish His kingdom.

Study Chart on the *Terminus Ad Quem* of Daniel's 69th Week

Messiah cut off at Christ's Baptism (26 A.D.)

Tenants of:

The seventy weeks of years begins with the edict of Artaxerxes to Ezra in 457 B.C. The sixty-nine weeks of years end in 26 A.D. the year that some scholars believe Jesus was Baptized by John the Baptists.

Strengths:

1) At first glance, it appears to be the most straightforward interpretation.
2) It terminates the sixty-nine weeks with Jesus Christ, albeit his baptism.

Weaknesses:

1) It ignores the *fact* that Israel used 360 day years.
2) It terminates the sixty-nine years at Christ's baptism, rather than His crucifixion as the verse implies.
3) It begins with a decree that did not fully restore Jerusalem as prophesied.
4) It uses an errant chronology for Jesus' life and ministry.
5) It ignores that there was only year between 1 B.C. and 1 A.D.
6) It is often used as a way of eliminating the need for the nation of Israel from Daniel's "seventy weeks."

Messiah cut off at Christ's Crucifixion (33 A.D.)

Tenants of:

The seventy weeks of years begins with the edict of Artaxerxes to Nehemiah in March 444 B.C. and the sixty-nine weeks of years ends on Passover week of 33 A.D., the week that Christ was crucified on the Cross.

Strengths:

1) It best fits the prophecy of restoration and the termination.
2) It acknowledges that Daniel was written to the Hebrews and not to those who use the present day Gregorian calandar.
3) It terminates on *the very week* that Christ was crucified.

Weaknesses:

1) It seems too complicated to some. They argue this is "tampering" with the text.
2) It is *alleged* that this view uses a faulty chronology for the crucifixion (but see *Controversies in the Gospels*).

3

The Seven Seals

Among premillennialists there is little controversy about the first five seals. Most of the debate among premillennial scholars is not in the general interpretation of the seals but in their nuances and technicalities. By and large the first five seals are regularly perceived in a like manner. With the sixth seal, however, there does begin to be a wide divergence of opinions. This chapter will examine the common conceptions of these seals among premillennial authors and explore the subtle differences in their convictions.

It should be noted that the first four seals are all of a like kind. Each refer to a horseman and each of the horsemen appear to relate to another in some manner. The first horsemen is the trigger for the second, who in turn triggers the third horseman who triggers the fourth and last of the horseman. This is why the first four seals are also referred to as "the Four Horsemen of the Apocalypse." This name was even used as the title for a classic silent movie about World War I. Because the four horsemen initiate a world war, and because the world had never known a world war before that time, many people living at the time speculated that World War I could be of what was spoken in Revelation. Certainly there were many similarities, as the reader may observe for himself, but ultimately World War I only proved that the events of Revelation could now happen quite literally and need not be viewed allegorically anymore. Although premillennialism existed from the earliest of times when the apostles still lived and their students, the church fathers, wrote, it was not until after World War I that seminary students and scholars began to be enamored by the study of Revelation. The "revelation" of World War I was that allegory was no longer needed in interpreting the book of Revelation and with this revelation premillennial research began to blossom and flourish to this very day.

The misinterpretations that some people made in World War I simply urged theologians and lay persons alike to know Revelation better so that they would not make the same mistake. This anecdote shows the importance of knowing what God has chosen to reveal to us ahead of time so that we will not be deceived. The seals represent the beginnings of the sorrows and tribulations of Revelation. With these, the rest of Revelation follow.

The First Seal

"I saw when the Lamb broke one of the seven seals, and I heard one of the four living creatures saying as with a voice of thunder, 'Come.'

And I looked, and behold, a white horse, and he who sat on it had a bow; and a crown was given to him; and he went out conquering, and to conquer" (Revelation 6:1-2).

Historical Overview

The first witness to the interpretation of this verse is the church father Irenaeus who identified the rider of this white horse as Jesus Christ Himself.[83] This view, or a variant of it, would become the predominant view for the next thousand years, although the absence of any complete exegetical commentaries before the allegorism of the Middle Ages leaves this open to doubt. Only one other Ante-Nicene Father mentions the white horse. This was Victorinus who took a derivative, and more allegorical, view that identified the white horse with the preaching of the gospel,[84] rather than with Christ specifically. This may also have been the view of Tertullian, but his allusion is to vague to be sure.[85]

Among the medievals Augustinian allegorism was predominant. They naturally took the Christ view, seeing this as the conquest of the gospel throughout the world, as seen in Bede's commentary.[86] Among the extant writings on the Middle Ages only Adso takes a truly literal stance though he and his colleagues were a minority. However, since Adso does not refer to the seven seals we can only examine the Joachimite writings, many of which continue to identify the rider as Christ.[87] Nevertheless, Nicholas of Lyra refutes the teaching that this white horsemen was Caligula indicating that some Joachimites were already teaching that the rider was a Roman Emperor.[88] Thus it is clear that by the Middle Ages, if not before, some historicists came to see the negative connotations of the rider, identify him with the Roman Empire or an emperor in his conquest.

It is only natural that if medieval historicists followed one of these two views, so would most Reformation age historicists. Many Reformers continued to identify the white horse of Revelation 6:2 with the white horse of Christ in Revelation 19. Other Reformers, however, saw negative connotations in the rider, equating him with various Roman dictators. This includes Joseph Mede and Sir Isaac Newton while Matthew Poole saw the rider simply as Rome itself.[89] These commentators saw a connection between the first seal and the seals that followed. For them, the first seal was not a victorious Christ but the beginnings of the sorrows inflicted by the succeeding seals.

Following this line of thought, the overwhelming majority of modern premillennialists have rejected the notion that the rider is the Christ, saying instead that this is a false Christ, or the anti-Christ. Although seemingly a dramatic shift in thought it is really only a slight revision, for the imagery of Christ (whether the true of false Messiah) is acknowledged by most all. The shift is predominantly because of the rejection of any form of historicism. As a result, the horse is not released until the end times, and, therefore, is probably not the gospel or Christ, but the ruler who will alter history in those last days. John Darby, Walter Scott, E. W. Bullinger, H. A. Ironside, John Walvoord, Tim

LaHaye, Dwight Pentecost, and Hal Lindsey (among many others) all taught that the horseman is not Christ, but the anti-Christ.

The Arguments and an Evaluation

Despite the fact that the Christ view held sway for some many centuries, this seems to be the weakest thesis. In terms of exegesis its main argument is based on the imagery of the white horse. George Eldon Ladd, one of the few modern scholars to support the position, lists many verses where white is used as a symbol for Christ or godliness in some form. He mentions that Christ's hair is white as wool (1:14) and that the stones given to believers are white (2:17) as are the garments given to them (3:4, 5, & 18), the twenty-four elders (4:4), the martyrs (6:11), and the multitude in heaven (7:9 & 13).[90] He also notes that Christ is seen sitting on a white cloud (14:14) and the Great White Throne bears this color (20:11).[91] The most obvious parallel, however, is with the white horse of Christ in Revelation 19:11 & 14. Nevertheless, the parallels end here. The image of a white horse could just as easily represent a false Christ as the true Christ. Moreover, many commentators have noted that a white horse was used by the Roman Emperors and others when they rode triumphantly into a conquered kingdom.[92] The white horse is then taken to represent triumph. As Walter Scott suggested, "a white horse represents victorious power."[93] We must, therefore, look beyond the color of the horse to identify the rider.

The problems with identifying the rider with Christ, or even the more generic gospel, are numerous. First, this position looses the apparent continuity between the first seal and the ensuing seals which bring war, famine, and death. In the preceding chapter only the Lamb was found worthy to open the seals. This appears to be because the seals contain the judgments of God. Indeed, the whole of the seals, trumpets, and bowls describe God's punishments meted out upon man. Consequently, the idea that Christ or the gospel would be contained in the first seal contradicts the context of both the opening of the seals and the entire scope of Revelation. Revelation is not about the ministering of the gospel to the lost but about the judgment of God on the ungodly. It is man's final chance to repent before the wrath of God is poured out completely.

Another problem is that the imagery does not really match Christ as closely as one might at first think. To begin with the rider is said to be a conqueror. Although it is fair to say that the gospel will prevail, the image of conquest does not seem to fit the ministering of the gospel very well. As Joseph Seiss illustrates this is not the image which fits "the patient and forbearing ministrations of grace."[94] "Neither is a victorious conqueror on a war-steed a fitting image of 'the foolishness of preaching,' or the work of beseeching men to be reconciled with God."[95] Moreover, "the Gospel, as now preached, is not, and in the present order of things never will be, triumphant"[96] until Christ returns in chapter 19. This then leads to the question of the parallel between the first seal and the return of Christ in chapter 19.

A close examination of Christ in Revelation 19 with the rider of this horse shows dramatic differences. Aside from the white horse, no true parallels can be found. In Revelation 19 Christ is described with the words, "His eyes *are* a flame of fire, and upon His head *are* many diadems (vs. 12)." The word diadems (διαδήματα) is different from the crown (στέφανος) *given* to the rider in the first seal. The mere fact that the rider in chapter 6 was *given* a crown implies that his authority was bestowed on him by God for a limited time whereas Christ wears *many* diadems which he merited by His death on the cross. Walvoord comments on this distinction saying, the rider is "given a crown, that is, the crown of a victor (Gr., *stephanos*), not the crown of a sovereign."[97] It is of interest to note that Robert Govett, who holds to view that this is Christ, refutes those historicists who identified the rider with a Roman Emperor by saying that the crown cannot be those of emperors for, "how do you interpret it consistently of the locusts, who have, as it were, crowns?"[98] Thus he rejects the idea that the crown is proof of the imperial dignity on the grounds that it is inconsistent with the appearance of demons who also wear the same crowns (στέφανοι). Nevertheless, such an insight (and true it is) also negates the idea that the crown proves the rider to be Christ. The crown merely indicates authority which we are specifically told the rider was "given" rather than earned.

Another problem with seeing this as Christ is that it is Christ who breaks the seal and yet some maintain that Christ is called forth out of the seal. Moreover, one of the living creatures specifically calls out the command, "come!" Does Jesus take orders from His angels? Why, if this were Christ is the command required of the living creature and why, if this were Christ, is Christ Himself required to break the seal? Has the gospel been withheld for two thousand years? Govett suggest that this is "not the going forth of the gospel of peace"[99] but Christ going forth to "wrest" his inheritance "from foes with sword, and with bow."[100] Certainly this is a more consistent interpretation than the ministrations of the gospel, but it still fails to take into account the other problems with assigning this rider to Christ.

The problems with associating the first seal with our Savior are not small. In fact, Joseph Seiss, who had a strong inclination toward the Christ/gospel view, saw it was inadequate to explain the context of the passage He therefore shifted the rider from the gospel of Christ to mass conversions which follow the *judgment* of Christ.[101] Specifically, he seems to equate this with the "translations of the saints" or rapture and the effects that this event would have on those "left" behind.[102] As a result, the victory of the gospel is manifested in the mass conversions which follow. At the same time Seiss sees the seal as a symbol of divine judgment. While the shift is preferable to the gospel theory it seems to have won few converts, perhaps because the whole of the seals, trumpets, and bowls represent the judgment and wrath of God. It does not seem reasonable to assign to one seal the designation which rightfully applies to all of them. Moreover, the question of the judgment of God does not necessarily relate to *mode* of that judgment. We see throughout Revelation that God *permits* demons and other evils to mete out punishment on man. Therefore, there is no reason to reject the idea that God will execute His judgment on man by releasing the anti-Christ whose authority, represented by a crown, is restricted to but a few short years.

His rapture theory is of more interest but it seems ill fitting the context of the passage. Seiss' commentary seeks to moderate between the popular Christ/gospel theory and the more natural meaning of the text, which indicates judgment in some form. Still others have attempted to reconcile this in a different manner.

Some take the view that this rider merely represents "conquest" in general.[103] This view is an open alternative which is similar in effect to another moderated view held by historicists; the idea that the rider represents the Roman Empire and/or its emperors. They argue that the ancient emperors rode forth on white horses whenever they entered a conquered city. The view has notable advocates such as Jospeh Mede and Sir Isaac Newton. Unfortunately, this view is the weakest of all. It relegates the prophecy to past history and, thus, is solely compatible with the preterist and historicist interpretations. It seeks to find in history the fulfillment of a conqueror but even the supporters of this view can come to no agreement as to what emperor it may have represented. Names have ranged from Caligula to Nero to Domitian or many others.[104] In fact, this view is really a historicist and preterist answer to the anti-Christ view for it recognizes the conqueror as a great enemy of the gospel whose appearance signals the release of the next three horsemen.

The logical answer to the similarity between this rider and Christ is not that they are one and the same, for the former is but a faint shadow of the glorious Christ, but rather that this is a false Christ, the anti-Christ. As E.W. Bullinger said, "how natural for the false and deceiving Messiah to go forth in a manner that will be most calculated to 'deceive many.'"[105] Nevertheless, some commentators have been reluctant to specifically identify the rider. John Nelson Darby merely referred to the rider as a "great conqueror" and noted the white horse represents "imperial or royal power in exercise."[106] Walter Scott compares the rider to a future Napoleon[107] and Sir Robert Anderson merely refers to the rider as "that terrible enemy of Christ."[108] In each case it is clear what it is implied. These authors are, perhaps, showing the better part of valor in refusing to explicitly name the rider, but there is no doubt that each of these men identify the rider as being the one who will bestow authority and power to the anti-Christ.

This view has become the dominant view of modern evangelicals with a few exceptions. It seems to be the best supported by exegesis. The most literal understanding is that this is a real historical figure who will arrive on the scene in last days with the purpose of conquest. His resemblance to Christ lends credibility to the belief that this is the anti-Christ for he is a counterfeit or false

Christ. Because he is followed by war (the second seal), famine (the third seal), and death (the fourth seal) it is reasonable to assume that it is this rider who initiates the war which follows for the four horseman all seem to have a cause and effect relationship to one another. The conqueror brings war which in turn bring about famine and death.

A more complex question is the meaning of the bow and quiver. Some authors have made much of the fact that no arrows are specifically mentioned. Watchman Nee suggest that the alleged empty quiver "indicates that the victory is not real."[109] This seems particularly odd since Nee holds that the rider is Christ. The fact that no quiver is mentioned should not be significant for this is an argument from silence. The Bible does not mention the arrows but neither does it mention whether the rider is wearing shoes. We must agree with Arthur Bloomfield that "if we say a man carries a gun, we assume the gun to be loaded."[110] Attaching too much significance to this omission is reading too much into the text. Indeed, some scholars have no doubt that the bow is strung with arrows already at hand. Robert Govett even says that the rider, whom he sees as Christ, "shoots His arrows from afar."[111] So there is no real reason to make too many assumptions about the failure to specifically mention the quiver.

Having said this, there is some merit in the idea that the conquest is not yet a violent conquest. Charles Ryrie has said it represents a "cold war,"[112] arguing that "peace is not been removed from the earth until the second seal is opened."[113] This viewed is echoed by many others. Walter Scott had said that the bow represented a "bloodless victory"[114] and Dwight Pentecost argues that the bow represents the establishment of peace by the anti-Christ.[115] These statements seems the more discerning since open war does not appear to break out until the second seal but the question must then be asked, "what is the rider conquering?" On this subject there can be no affirmative identification until the prophecy becomes history but it is logical to assume that what is described here is the conquest of the three kingdoms of the Revived Roman Empire by the anti-Christ. We are told in Daniel 7, a parallel passage to Revelation, that "out of this kingdom ten kings will arise; and another will arise after them, and he will be different from the previous ones and will subdue three kings" (vs. 24). The ten nation confederation (see chapter 6) will then be reduced to seven or eight nations (depending on whether or not one sees the anti-Christ as originally being one of the ten).

Now such a conquest does not seem consistent with the initial rise of the anti-Christ to power for the apostle Paul seems to indicate that there will be "peace and safety" when destruction falls suddenly upon man (1 Thessalonians 5:3). If, however, the anti-Christ seizes power by violence, it is hard to see how he can establish a treaty with Israel and promise "peace and safety." We know that in Revelation 17:16 when the Whore of Babylon is destroyed each of the ten kings are involved. This would mean that the conquest of the three kings by the anti-Christ has not yet taken place. This leads to the final question.

What are the chronological implications of the first seal? A more thorough discussion will occur in Appendix D, but a cursory examination of the judgments shows that this seal is not opened until the middle of the tribulation. If it were opened at beginning of tribulation then how could this be reconciled with the establishment of the seven year peace treaty? If there are to be three and a half years of "peace and safety" before judgment befalls man then this conquest begins at the midpoint of the tribulation after the "abomination of desolation." The ten kings will turn on the Harlot and the peace treaty will be broken. It is likely that it is at this time that the anti-Christ makes his play for supreme power and seizes the throne of three of the kings.

This view is at least partially supported by scholars like G. H. Lang who includes the subduing of the three kings in this initial "conquest."[116] Although his chronology differs in some respects, he realizes that the fall of the three kings is the signal that will lead to the final global conflict. What follows is all out war as described in the second seal.

The Second , Third, and Fourth Seals

> "And when He broke the second seal, I heard the second living creature saying, 'Come.' And another, a red horse, went out; and to him who sat on it, it was granted to take peace from the earth, and that *men* should slay one another; and a great sword was given to him.
>
> "And when He broke the third seal, I heard the third living creature saying, 'Come.' And I looked, and behold, a black horse; and he who sat on it had a pair of scales in his hand. And I heard as it were a voice in the center of the four living creatures saying, 'A quart of wheat for a denarius, and three quarts of barley for a denarius; and do not harm the oil and the wine.'
>
> "And when He broke the fourth seal, I heard the voice of the fourth living creature saying, 'Come.' And I looked, and behold, an ashen horse; and he who sat on it had the name Death; and Hades was following with him. And authority was given to them over a fourth of the earth, to kill with sword and with famine and with pestilence and by the wild beasts of the earth" (Revelation 6:3-8).

Historical Overview

The second, third, and forth seals may be discussed jointly for there is not great controversy among them individually. The last three horsemen of the apocalypse are universally agreed upon to bring war, famine, and pestilence. This is incontrovertible. Not a single commentator of any interpretive view debates this. Nevertheless, the specifics of the war, including its timing and role in Revelation have been debated.

Because the verses are self explanatory there is no debate on the central *meaning*, which is war, famine, and pestilence. Nevertheless, there has been speculation on *which* war, if any, constitutes the beginning of the fulfillment of these judgments. The early chiliasts offer no hint that the seals had experienced their fulfillment in history nor that they were living in the prophesied days of the second to fourth seals. All the church fathers saw these as future events in the end times. It is not until the Middle Ages that historicism's tenants began to flourish. Joachim argued that this referred to the pagan priests of Rome up until the time of Constantine[117] while the Joachimite Nicholas of Lyra identified Nero as the second rider.[118]

In the Reformation the historicist school of thought continued to seek the war in history as Joseph Mede and Isaac Newton identified these with the Roman wars from the time of Trajan to Hadrian.[119] Even a few modern futurists have hinted at a historical reference. Both George Ladd[120] and Alan Johnson have hinted that the imagery refers to ancient Roman and the wars that were fought in the days of the church fathers.[121] Nonetheless, as the church returned to futurism, the historical theories were dropped, in no large part because of the failure of historicists to come to an agreement upon what time frame was truly prophesied.

With the return of the predominance of futurism the fulfillment of these verses are held to be the future world war which will rage in the tribulation, sometimes called the "war of Armageddon." Hal Lindsey attempts to equate the war specifically with the invasion of Gog mentioned in Ezekiel 38 and 39[122] while others refuse to specify any particular battle.

The Arguments and an Evaluation
The red horse is said to "take peace from the earth [so] that men should slay one another." It is, therefore, no surprise that this rider is universally accepted as representing war. Whatever the nature of the conquest in the first seal the ultimate result is all out war, but what war? If the church fathers experienced the events of which the prohecies speak then one is bewildered as to how they could not see it. How could the church fathers have missed that they were in the prophesied days of the four horsemen? The obvious answer is that they were not. The prophecies were not about the past or present, but the future. Historicism arose in large part because chiliasm was outlawed. While historicism should be recognized as the vessel through which God carried the literal elements of Revelation in the difficult times of persecution during the Middle Ages, it was derived in no small part from an attempt to avoid persecution from the church. It errs in attributing the seals to the early church, a fact which the church fathers could not possibly have missed.

Nowhere is the failure of historicism more obvious that in its own failure to come to even a moderate consensus. Joachim, the father of historicism, placed the second seal in the time from Nero to Constantine, the third seal from Constantine to Justinian, and the fourth seal from Justinian to Pope Gregory VIII.[123]   The later Joachimite Nicholas of Lyra, however, identified the second seal with Nero, the third with Titus and the fall of Jerusalem, while placing the fourth under Domitian.[124]   Reformation commentator John Bale puts the second under the ten persecutions of ancient Rome, the third under the rise of heresy after Constantine, and the fourth under the establishment of the Catholic Church.[125]   Joseph Mede begins the second with Trajan, the third with Septimus Severus and the fourth with Maximinus.[126] Isaac Newton, who usually follows Mede's commentary, differs on the third and fourth seals. He begins the third with Gordian and the fourth with Decius.[127]

Still many others could be cited, but the point has been made. Even the historicist commentators could come to no consensus. How can futurists take seriously the tenets of historicism when even they cannot come to some better uniformity. Certainly they do not need to agree on all points, but neither should they all differ. The vast array of different interpretations among the historicists only proves that it is their imagination that is exegeting the Scriptures. Historicists cannot agree upon when this war occurred because the war has not occurred. It is a future war which will be initiated by the anti-Christ.

Of course, if these events occur in the future the obvious conclusion is that they will at some time become history. To this end there are some who have argued that they were living in the very fulfillment of the prophcies in the twentieth century. Among the more respectable of these was Norman Harrison. In Harrison's unique chronology (discussed in appendix D) he places the seven seals *before* the tribulation. He connected the first four seals seals with Jesus' Olivet Discourse, something accepted by many, and argued that the events spoken of by Jesus were but a *prelude* to the coming tribulation. Thus the war of the second seal he connected with World War I.[128] He then associated the third seal with the Great Depression and what followed.[129] He went on to even suggest that the trumpets may relate to World War II, but denies that events of Revelation have come to their conclusion.[130]   This sentiment was certainly echoed by many people in those days. Indeed, the two World Wars did much to prove that the events of Revelation could occur literally, thus discounting the long objections of allegorists who claimed that Revelation *must* be taken figuratively. Nevertheless, Harrison was a man of his time. He *assumed* without proof that the judgments of God were already being meted out on man. This was doubtless one reason that he created his midtribulational view. If the seals had already begun, the bowls could not be far behind.

Of course, the overwhelming majority of premillennialists accept that Revelation is future and that the seals have not yet been broken. So if it is agreed that Revelation speaks about the future then this war must also be future and it must be the direct result of the conquest initiated by the rider of the white horse unleashed in the first seal. This is the beginning of the final World War as the kingdom of the anti-Christ begins to crumble and open rebellion against his kingdom unfurls. This being agreed upon, some have attempted to fit specific prophetic events under this seal. G.H. Lang has associated the fourth seal with China's invasion of the Middle East.[131] Hal Lindsey, on the other hand, has attempted to identify the red horse specifically with the Russian Invasion of Ezekiel 38 (see Appendix C for a detailed discussion of the invasion). He says, "Russia, the rider of the red horse, snatches peace from the earth. With her Arab allies she invades the Middle East and attacks Israel."[132] Dwight Pentecost may also hold to this theory although it is unclear.[133] Since a good chronology of the second seal would appear to coincide with the invasion of Russia (see Appendices C & D) this remains a legitimate possibility although the verse itself cannot be defined with such specificity. The color red certainly represents the blood of war and not the now non-existent Communist flag. Lang's theory seem weaker.

The second seal should be recognized as representing the beginning of the final war of Armageddon, a war which begins in the middle of the tribulation, after the fall of Babylon and the three kings. It is also possible that the invasion of Russia (or more precisely Gog and Magog) occurs at this time, following the anti-Christ's betrayal of the Harlot and the three kings. Thus the prophecy of the four horsemen relate to one another. In the first seal, the anti-Christ attempts to subjugate those he distrusts. The time of peace is over. The abomination of desolation has apparently already occurred (but see Appendix D) causing a backlash which the anti-Christ will attempt to thwart by crushing the Harlot and the three kings, but this does not end his opposition. On the contrary, it antagonizes many of the anti-Christ's nominal subjects. Russia will probably launch an invasion of Israel at this time and the United Federation will become irrevocably at war with foreign nations in rebellion against it.

The Fifth Seal

> "And when He broke the fifth seal, I saw underneath the altar the souls of those who had been slain because of the word of God, and because of the testimony which they had maintained; and they cried out with a loud voice, saying, 'How long, O Lord, holy and true, wilt Thou refrain from judging and avenging our blood on those who dwell on the earth?' And there was given to each of them a white robe; and they were told that they should rest for a little while longer, until *the number of* their fellow servants and their brethren who were to be killed even as they had been, should be completed also" (Revelation 6:9-11).

Historical Overview
As with the last three horsemen, the only real controversy is surrounding the time of the seal and the identity of the martyrs. The church fathers did not attempt to define the martyrs. They were martyred believers, and for them there was no need to further define them. With the rise of historicism there was, of

course, the desire to relate the martyrs to specific victims in a specific time frame. Nevertheless, Nicholas of Lyra did not attempt to restrict the martyrs to one age but identified them as martyrs throughout the ages.[134]

In the Reformation John Bale specifically restricted the martyrs to those of the Middle Ages, even naming the Waldenses, Berengarians, and others.[135] Joseph Mede identified them with the martyrs of the Aurelian emperors[136] while Isaac Newton said they were the martyrs before Constantine.[137]

With the resurrection of futurism, the identity of the martyrs took on a slightly different tone. The opening of the seal is agreed to be in the future but the martyrs themselves are shown in heaven. So it is possible that the martyrs could be from the past, present, or future. Some modern evangelicals have argued that they represent all the martyrs of history[138] while others have specifically identified them with the tribulation saints who will die during the Great Tribulation.[139] Some say that these saints are restricted solely to Jewish believers,[140] while others maintain that all saints, be them Jew or Gentile, are included.[141]

The Arguments and an Evaluation

That the martyrs should be restricted solely to the Middle Ages or some other period in history should be rejected. The errors of historicism have been recounted already and will not be repeated here. However, inasmuch as these martyrs are in heaven, and already deceased, it is entirely possible that the martyrs of history are included. Does the possibility of their inclusion mean that they are what is envisioned here?

Revelation says that these were "the souls of those who had been slain because of the word of God." Was it, however, *all* the souls of those who had been slain because of the word of God? George Ladd believes that "John has in view all believers who have so suffered."[142] George Peters believes that these men constitute saints from all dispensations.[143] Edward Hindson also views this as all the believers of the church age adding that, "their cries may well be intensified as they see new converts being slaughtered during the tribulation because they are told that other 'brethren' will still be killed."[144] Jim Combs, however, goes one step further. Since the text does not specify Christ, but rather the "word of God," Combs says that the passage represents "the martyrs from Abel until the last martyr of the Tribulation."[145] Certainly the language tends to imply that all martyrs are present, for "those who had been slain" does not seem to restrict the number of martyrs to a select group of those slain. Nonetheless, there are reasons to reject these views.

A similar passage in Revelation 20:4 reads, "the souls of those who had been beheaded because of the testimony of Jesus and because of the word of God." Most all agree that "the souls of those who had been beheaded" is idiomatic and does not necessitate that the martyrs have been decapitated. If so, then "the souls of those who had been slain" could also be idiomatic and need not necessarily be taken as proof that *all* martyrs are included among these saints, but why not?

Those who believe that this represents only the saints from the tribulation base their argument on several factors. H. A. Ironside believes that the church cannot be present here because "the church is represented by the throned and crowned elders in Heaven before the first seal is broken."[146] Another says, "they are not the martyrs of the past ages, for those, by this time, already have their crowns, and are seated on their heavenly thrones."[147] Such an argument is logical but only if one agrees that the church is, indeed, what was pictured in that passage.[148] So that argument, in itself, is insufficient to prove that the church is not amongst these martyrs. Still another argument is that "the introduction of these martyred dead in heaven at this point immediately after the fourth seal seems to imply that these martyrs have come from the tribulation scene on the earth."[149]

The best argument, however, is made by John Walvoord. He says, "if the church has already been raptured, the dead in Christ have been raised from the dead before the time pictured here and those pictured do not include the martyrs of the present dispensation."[150] In other words, these martyrs are depicted as "souls" without bodies. If they had been resurrected, which occurs at rapture, then they would not be without bodies. The inescapable conclusion is that these are the souls of martyrs who have not yet been resurrected and, therefore, died after rapture. Of course critics will argue that this is based on a pretribulational assumption. In fact, even some pretribulationists disgree with this assertion. Arthur Bloomfield, for example, believes that *all* the martyrs depicted here died *before* the rapture.[151] Nevertheless, this explanation seems the best as it better fits the context of the seals. Seiss has noted that their cry indicates "that their murders are then still living."[152] Thus, it is logical to believe that these are the martyrs of the Daniel's 70th week. While the possibility of all martyrs, past as well as future, cannot be excluded, the context seems to imply tribulation saints.

Of course, the question of whether or not these martyrs are Jews, or a mixture of Jews and Gentiles, is also related very closely to the tribulation question. Robert Govett presents a dispensational argument which he believes excludes all "gospel-martyrs."[153] His defense begins with a discussion of the matryrs' cry for vengeance. This argument is echoed by E. W. Bullinger who states that "the church of God in this day of grace does not, and cannot, cry for vengeance. Indeed, it is expressly taught not to do so (Rom. xii. 19)."[154] Thus Govett and Bullinger believe that "these words are not appropriate to this present dispensation."[155] A similar argument is presented by Walter Scott who says that "*law* was the principle on which God dealt in Old Testament times. *Grace* is the platform of His present acts and ways. *Judgment*, in dealing with evil and evil workers, characterizes the future."[156] All these authors make comparisons of the cry of the martyrs in Revelation to the Psalms and Lamentation of the Old Testament.

Psalms 94:1-3 reads, "O Lord, God of vengeance; God of vengeance, shine forth! Rise up, O Judge of the earth; Render recompense to the proud. How long shall the wicked, O Lord, How long shall the wicked exult? They pour forth *words*, they speak arrogantly." It is easy to see the parrallel to the cry of the martyrs, "How long, O Lord, holy and true, wilt Thou refrain from judging and avenging our blood on those who dwell on the earth?" Thus Bullinger believes that this is "the cry of Israel represented as a 'widow.'"[157] However, the "widow" representation is not apparent in Revelation and Bullinger is merely assuming it based on a comparison to Lamentations 1:1 which speaks of Israel as a "widow."

A better argument procedes from Scott who points out that "the imagery" of the alter, sacrifices, and incense "is cast in Jewish mould."[158] He then states that the martyrs are "probably Jewish,"[159] but is not dogmatic. Scott's lack of dogmatism is probably the best approach. The imagery definitely follows Jewish imagery, but then so does much of Revelation. It has been called many times a "Jewish book," but does such a Jewish character necessarily expel the Gentiles?

Ironside has added another reason to believe that the martyrs are Jews. He maintains that "after the fullness of the Gentiles has come in – after the present dispensation has come to an end ... the blindness will pass from Israel."[160] Thus he says that these must be "Jewish believers."[161] While the statement is true, it does not prove that Jews alone will be persecuted or martyred in the tribulation. There is no doubt that Jews will be among the martyrs represented, probably in great numbers, but to say that they are Jews alone is to exclude any Gentiles.

Revelation makes clear that there are Gentiles saved during the early judgments. Man does not appear to have completely hardened his heart until after the bowl judgments are poured out. Certainly the restoration of Israel (see chapter 4) indicates that the Jewish believers will suffer great persecution, but so will everyone who do not have the "mark on their right hand, or on their forehead" (Revelation 13:16). The best conclusion is then that this fifth seal reveals the massive martyrs of the tribulation. They will include both Jewish and Gentile believers, although Jews will be the predominant victims of the anti-Christ's wrath. They are told by God to wait a little while longer "until *the number of* their fellow servants and their brethren who were to be killed even as they had been, should be completed," and they are comforted in knowing that God will mete out justice.

The Sixth Seal

"And I looked when He broke the sixth seal, and there was a great earthquake; and the sun became black as sackcloth *made* of hair, and the whole moon became like blood; and the stars of the sky fell to the earth, as a fig tree casts its unripe figs when shaken by a great wind. And the sky was split apart like a scroll when it is rolled up; and every mountain and island were moved out of their places. And the kings of the earth and the great men and the commanders and the rich and the strong and every slave and free man, hid themselves in the caves and among the rocks of the mountains; and they said to the mountains and to the rocks, 'Fall on us and hide us from the presence of Him who sits on the throne, and from the wrath of the Lamb; for the great day of their wrath has come; and who is able to stand?'" (Revelation 6:12-17).

Historical Overview

There is no greater controversy among the seven seals than that of the sixth seal. Opinions have been diverse and wide even among modern dispensational premillennialists. The destruction and devastation described is parallelled in the book of Joel 2:10, although some even dispute this.

The earliest of the church fathers took the approach that Revelation did not need expounding. The sixth seal was quoted with no attempt to define its meaning. The logical assumption is that they either could not understand it or believed it to be self explanatory. The latter is the better explanation for it was their practice to assume that such events were supernatural and would occur literally. Nevertheless, Victorinus strays from this and adopts a more symbolic interpretation. According to Victorinus the earthquake, falling stars, the shaken fig tree analogy, and the mountains moving under the quake all represented the persecution of believers in the last days.[162] The darkened sun he argued was the "brightness of doctrine obscured by unbelievers."[163] He then stated that the sky rolling up like a scroll was indicative of the church being taken away. [164]

Despite Victorinus' theory, which would find popular following in the many centuries to come, it was not immediately received. Lactantius maintained that the darkness, the color of the moon, and the "falling stars" should all be taken quite literally.[165] The same view was echoed by Ephraem the Syrian and probably Adso of Montier.

With the rise of Joachimite historicism, however, the literal approach was abandoned and the views of Victorinus were embraced. The Joachimites accepted the Victorinus theory, but most did not fit the prophecy into history as is the standard practice of historicist. They believed that the sixth seal represented the sixth age which they were rapidly approaching.[166] The "persecutions" spoken of were believed to be awaiting around the corner. Nonetheless, some Joachimites, like Nicholas of Lyra, refused to place the sixth seal in the future and maintained that it represented the victims of Diocletian's persecutions.[167] His interpretation mimiced that of Victorinus and the Joachimites save that he saw the men crying out to rocks as presenting God's anger "against his church"[168] and the falling stars were church leaders who fell by way of apostasy.[169]

36

The Reformers were also split on their interpretation. John Bale utilized much of Nicholas of Lyra's symbology but carried the logic and time forward. The darkening of the sun was specifically heresy blotting out the true word of the Lord, rather than persecution.[170] He also read the heresy of the medieval church into the sky rolling like a scroll, saying that it represented the word of God becoming hidden by an apostate church.[171] Thus, he shifted the symbology subtly from persecution to the promulgation of heresy. This view was taken up by Joseph Mede who attributed the prophecy to Constantine's day.[172] Isaac Newton placed the seal under the emperor Julian the apostate.[173]

With Darby and the post-Reformation age the prophecy was again brought back into the future and the last days, but the symbology was not entirely abandoned. Darby saw the earthquake as symbolic for "an overthrowing of everything"[174] and the sun being darkened he said represented the fading powers of the "supreme government."[175] This point of view was later represented by Walter Scott.[176] On the other side of the post-Reformation interpreters were those who returned the prophecy not only to the future, but also to its literal application. E. W. Bullinger, Sir Robert Anderson, Robert Govett, and Joseph Seiss all took the prophecy literally, applying falling stars to meteorites or similar phenomenon.

Modern evangelicals are equally divided. On the more literal side are William Newell, Arthur Bloomfield, Charles Ryrie, Tim LaHaye, Hal Lindsey, and Robert Thomas. Those utilizing a more symbolic approach or mixture of the two include George Ladd, Norman Harrison, and H. A. Ironside.

The Arguments and Evaluation of the Great Earthquake
If we examine the different aspects of the prophecy individually it will prove a far easier task than taking them as a whole. It may also serve to prove that those who prefer an allegorical approach do so from intimidation of the sheer magnitude of the prophecy. Taken as a whole there is no doubt that the sixth seal describes the most terrible of judgments yet meted out, although worse will follow. The sheer scale of the judgment intimidates many an expositor, but viewed one aspect at a time, it should become apparent that the judgment is real in all its aspects. It is not a judgment on Christians, and cannot be taken to refer to persecution of believers, but rather it is a judgment on the world.

Victorinus first presented the theory that this earthquake merely represented the persecution of believers. However, it should be apparent that the judgment is cast out upon the unbelieving world. The Bible is clear that "God has not destined us for wrath" (1 Thessalonians 5:9) and yet the sixth seal is expressedly said to represent the "the wrath of the Lamb" (vs. 17). It is inconceivable to attribute the prophecy to the persecution of the church or the rise of heresy, as if God metes out heresy. The judgment must properly be attributed to a judgment on the unbelieving world.

Darby recognized this flaw and attempted to shift the symbolic interpretation to the unbeliever. He claims that the earthquake is "an overthrow of everything."[177] Walter Scott also saw the powers that be on earth, or governing authority in the alleged symbolism. He said that the earthquake characterized "social and political revolution"[178] a view mimiced almost word for word by Henry Swete.[179] Even H. A. Ironside take this view saying "it should be evident from the balance of the book that we are not to take this as a literal earthquake."[180] Yet despite this statement he immediately procedes to admit that "our Lord's words in Matthew 24 show us that there will be such phenomena in various places, terrific in character as the end draws near."[181] So Ironside admits that earthquakes can and will happen in the last days but that this cannot be a literal earthquake because of the "balance of the book." Such is a weak argument from an otherwise careful scholar. There seems nothing in the context to deny the fact that the earthquake is literal. In fact, many scholars believe that the earthquake spoken of here is the exact same one spoken of by Jesus in the Olivet Discourse, which Ironside admits is to be taken literally.

Although it is not by any means certain that this earthquake is the same as that of the Olivet Discourse (see Appendix D), the connection is a popular one. G. H. Lang, Sir Robert Anderson, and Robert Govett are among the more notable to make the association. The correlation of this prophecy to that of Joel 3:9-16 has also been made. However, Wathcman Nee rejects that this is the earthquake of Matthew 24, but believes that this is the earthquake spoken of in Joel 3:16.[182] He reasons that the earthquake of Matthew 24 occurs during the Great Tribulation, but Joel's occurs *before* the latter half of Daniel's 70th week.[183] Such an theory is better left to a discussion of chronology (see Appendix D), but illustrates that the connection to Matthew is unsure. Jesus Himself refers to earthquakes in the plural, thus there is nothing to prove that these are the same earthquake. One thing that is sure, however, is that nothing in the text implies that this is not a literal earthquake.

The Arguments and Evaluation of the Sun and Moon

A more debatable topic is that of the prophecy of the sun and moon. Victorinus interpreted the darkening of the sun as the "brightness of doctrine obscured by unbelievers."[184] Nicholas of Lyra argued that the sun represented the word of Christ and its darkening was the supression thereof.[185] The moon's color of blood represented the blood of martyrs.[186] This line of thought was carried on until the days of Darby and the return of chiliasm. That Christ might be depicted as the sun is not untenable, but imagery is suspect for several reasons. First, it has been demonstrated that the church is protected from the wrath of God (1 Thessalonians 5:9) and the sixth seal is expressedly said to represent the "the wrath of the Lamb" (vs. 17). This is *a judgment of God*. When the martyrs were depicted in the fifth seal, the martyrs were comforted. They die in the tribulation, but it is not the fifth seal *which causes* their deaths. The sixth seal causes the destruction which is described and God does not cause the death of believers. He might *permit* it, but never *causes* it. Consequently, the idea that *God's* judgment suppresses *the gospel* is inacceptable.

Furthermore, there is a clear and direct association between this passage and the following passages; Matthew 24:29, Mark 13:24, Joel 2:10 and 31, Joel 3:15-16, and Isaiah 13:10. Each of these verses speak of the devastation of the Day of the Lord and each mentions that "the sun will be darkened, and the moon will not give its light." Even those who take an allegorical approach to Revelation often admit that the Olivet Disourse and the prophecies of Isaiah and Joel are to be taken literally. More importantly, none of these passages imply that the sun or moon are representative of the Messiah or his disciples. Consider Amos 5:20 and Zephaniah 1:15 , which also appear to parallel this passage, and, again, a cursory reading leaves no impression of the word of God suffering, but of wicked men. The context give no hint here of the symbolic appearance of God or the gospel within the image of the sun and moon.

Such insurmountable problems forced John Darby to take a new approach. He argued that the sun represented the governmental authority of the world.[187] Yet despite his generally strong appeal to the Bible itself Darby *nowhere* cites a single passage of Scripture where the sun is taken as a symbol for secular or state authority. Walter Scott and H. A. Ironside also fail to mention any verses to justify this symbology. Walvoord points out another flaw in this system. Pointing to the words of the kings and peoples of the earth in this passage he says that "it is questionable whether changes in government and in human affairs would have brought such a striking transformation in the hearts of these wicked people."[188]

Others who prefer symbolic or partially symbolic approaches also fail to provide a single illustration of this symbolic use in the Old or New Testament. George Ladd merely calls it "semi-poetic,"[189] but is forced to admit that it must describe some "real cosmic catastrophe."[190]

So if the allegorical or symbolic approaches fail to satistfy the text, then what does the "literal" interpretation mean. Certainly the image of the sun being darkened need not create too much controversy. Critics who take a hyper-scientific approach, thereby denying that the sun can be darkened, are frivolous. If the sun's rays are blocked by something, then the sun's light is darkened. While politicians and Bible critics use language as a means to confuse, true language is a tool to communicate. The sun can, and has been in the past, darkened. In Luke 23:44-45 we are told that the sun was darkened when Jesus was on the cross (cf. Matt. 27:45 and Mark 15:33). Exodus 10:22 also recounts a darkening of the sun. There is nothing to deny that a literally blotting of the sun's rays in not intended here. Scientist Henry Morris accepts the literal application of this verse and believes that the terrible earthquake of this seal will cause "volcanic eruptions, spewing vast quanitites of dust and steam and gases into the upper atmosphere ... that will cause the sun to be darkened and the moon to appear blood-red."[191]

Another theory of the sun and moon's alteration is put forth by Hal Lindsey who believes that both the earthquake and the darkening of the sun are set off by nuclear blasts.[192] The fallout is said to cause the darkening of the sun and the apparent color change of the moon.[193] Regardless of the cause, there seems little reason to take the darkening of the sun figuratively. Nothing in the text implies anything more than a literal falling of darkness upon the world, a view presented throughout both the Old and New Testament as the dawning of the Day of the Lord. Likewise, the illusion of the moon's turning to blood need not concern the reader either. If there is a "cosmic disturbance"[194] then there is no reason to believe that such a catastrophe, whether from radioactive fallout or volcanic dust, may cause the moon to appear red as blood. This passage must also be taken at face value.

The Arguments and Evaluation of the Falling Stars
The symbolic approach to the falling stars echoes that of the sun and the moon. Throughout the medieval and Reformation age the allegorical view took prominence arguing that the stars were church leaders falling from power. If these are understood to be faithful believers then the view is fraught with the same difficulties as aforementioned. This is God's wrath, not man's. If these are taken as false church leaders or heretics, other problems are presented.

The first problem is the relationship of these stars to the rest of the passage. It is has been demonstrated already that the sun and moon *cannot* be taken as references to the church or to governmental authorities. If this is not so then neither can the stars represent church authority. Stars do occasionally take on a symbolic meaning but only if the sun and moon also take on that meaning. Since the sun and moon have never been demonstrated to depict secular or religious authority, the authority symbolism must also be rejected for the stars. Secondly, if the stars are portrayed as figurative for church authority then the cause and effect relationship to the rest of the prophecy is obscured. How do falling church leaders cause men to cry out to the rocks? How does the fall of false prophets cause men to hide in caves? Did the fall of Jim and Tammy Baker cause distress to the world or did it merely give them cause to laugh and ridicule "Christians"?

Again, the figurative approach is insufficient to explain the passage. What then is the major obstacle to the literal view? George Ladd suggest that "in light of our modern knowledge of astronomy can we conceive of the stars falling upon the earth?"[195] Seiss courteously replies to such reasoning that "they are thinking only of the great and unknown bodies which shine in the vast fields of immensity. It remains to be proven, however, that the apostle had his eye upon stars of that character. Those heavenly orbs, of which astronomy tells, are not the only objects to which, in common language, the word *stars* literally applies."[196]   Indeed, the ancient Greek language makes no attempt to differentiate between solar stars and other astronomical objects. The Greek word ἀστέρες (*astares*) properly refers to any object from outer space, or even the sky. Thayer's Greek Lexicon lists "comet" as one possible meaning,[197] although it could also refer to meteorites or countless other objects. To attempt to apply modern twenty-first century scientific English to ancient first century Greek is an insult to the intelligence. Even to this very day the *common language* speaks of "falling stars" and "shooting stars." Again, lawyers uses language as a means to deceive, but the apostle is here using language to expound the truth. The stars spoken of here may be any astronomical object, or possibly even something of human origin which has fallen back into the atmosphere. They are "falling stars."

If this is so, then what? Many expositors, perhaps wisely so, make no attempt to specifically identify the objects. Most believe that they are meteorites. A few have suggested that they may be nuclear devices or similar man made objects. Those who believe that a meteor shower in envisioned, appeal to the natural meaning of the Greek. Joseph Seiss, Arthur Bloomfield, Charles Ryrie, Tim LaHaye, Henry Morris and Robert Govett favor this view, pointing out that meteorites are commonly called "falling stars."[198] Seiss says, "even science itself still popularly speaks of 'falling stars,' when it means simply meteoric phenomena."[199] Robert Thomas also includes the probability of comets among these stars.[200] Henry Morris believes that the impact from asteroids, or a meteor shower, may be the actual "trigger" for the earthquake mentioned at the beginning of the verse.[201]

At least one literalist deviates from this view. Hal Lindsey believes that "fractional orbital" nuclear bombs[202] may be depicted here. He argues that "when these missles streak through the air they'll look like meteors showering the atmosphere."[203]   Although often ridiculed for his sometimes wild speculation, there is nothing in the context to deny such a possibility. Hence, whether the verse speaks of meteories of some sort, or perhaps even man-made weapons, the earth will experience a showing of astronomical objects that will cause great devastation. The comparison to "a fig tree cast[ing] its unripe figs when shaken by a great wind" further illustrates the severity of the shower which cannot be interpreted lightly.

The Arguments and Evaluation of the Sky Split Like a Scroll
The most difficult passage to interpret is that which reads, "the sky was split apart like a scroll when it is rolled up." Those who reject literalism have been quick to seize upon this saying, "since we know that the blue vault of the sky is really an optical illusion, how can we imagine the heavens being rolled up like a scroll?"[204]   However, while "difficulties do not lie on the literal side only. Greater difficulties besiege the figurative interpretation." [205] Such difficulies are obvious in regard to the belief that the sky being rolled up like a scroll

represents the word of God being been hidden by the apostates.[206] Nicholas of Lyra's theory that the rolled up scroll implies that Christians are "hiding" from persecution also lacks merit.[207] Some the problems with this type of allegory have already been addressed. Likewise, the newer figurative theories also lack merit. Ironside believes that "the heavens, symbolizing the ecclesiastical powers of every description, will depart as a scroll when it is rolled up."[208] Walter Scott argued similarly that the removal of the sky like a scroll indicates that anarchy has begun[209] but nowhere can such an analogy be drawn from Scripture, nor Jewish tradition, nor the "apocalyptic" literature of later authors. It is purely speculative.

So what then of the "literal" interpretation? Asks George Ladd, "since we know that the blue vault of the sky is really an optical illusion, how can we imagine the heavens being rolled up like a scroll?"[210] Ladd envisions a mixing of symbolic and literal meanings but cannot himself come to a conclusion. Norman Harrison also argued that "in the Revelation narrative the literal and symbolic are largely interwoven"[211] but Robert Thomas reminds us that "the suggestion of mixing symbolic and literal is fraught with hermenuetical difficulties." [212] Consistency is the best answer. There is no doubt that John was seeing exactly what Isaiah saw when he wrote that "the sky will be rolled up like a scroll" (34:4). Like Revelation, there is no justification for taking Isaiah's words here as figurative language. Isaiah describes God's wrath upon the world and recounts many of the same events that John has envisioned. Isaiah declares that "the LORD'S indignation is against all the nations, and *His* wrath against all their armies; He has utterly destroyed them, He has given them over to slaughter. So their slain will be thrown out, And their corpses will give off their stench, and the mountains will be drenched with their blood. And all the host of heaven will wear away, and the sky will be rolled up like a scroll." (Isaiah 34:2-4) Here Isaiah is describing God's wrath against the nations, even as John is describing the wrath of God in the last days against the unbelieving world.

The language is clear. It is about the destruction of the wicked in the end times, but what exactly did John and Isaiah see? What did they mean when they said "the sky will be rolled up like a scroll"? The word "like" is the key. The Bible does not say that the sky *did* roll up like a scroll but that it was "*like* a scroll when it is rolled up." It is language of comparison, not allegory. Thomas says that it gives the "impression" of "the universe coming apart."[213] It is literal inasmuch as the sky will *appear* to roll up like a scroll, but how?

There has been much speculation on what the apostle John could have been describing. Clearly his language is one of comparison, as he was unsure of exactly what he was seeing. Robert Govett suggests a natural phenomenon arising from the same cause as that which caused the darkening of the sun. He says that John may be seeing the stars from the east being "swept from their places, the sky there becoming blank, and the unpeopling of the sky continuing, till it reaches the west."[214] Henry Morris lends some credibility to this saying, "the clouds of dust will gradually spread across the sky, making it appear that the sky is being 'rolled up,'"[215] but he notes that "the use of the graphic term *departed*,' seems to indicate something more spectacular even than this."[216] He contends that "the other possibility is that the earth's crust, highly unstable ever since the great Flood, will be so disturbed by the impacting of asteroids ... that great segments of [the geological plates] will actually begin to slip and slide ... those who reside in regions above such shifting crustal plates will observe the heavens appearing to move in the opposite direction, and it will seem as if they are being 'rolled up.'"[217]

Charles Ryrie takes an even more literal approach believing that heaven itself opens to give a brief "glimpse" to the world.[218] Hal Lindsey, in keeping with his nuclear holocaust theory, reminds the reader that when an atomic explosion occurs, "the atmosphere rolls back on itself."[219] This is technically true, and remains one of the strong points of his argument, although it is unsure if any of these things are exactly what John saw. Still, some have argued that this is a parallel passage to Peter's reference to the destruction of the heavens in 2 Peter 3:10.[220] In that passage Peter says that "the heavens will pass away with a roar and the elements will be destroyed with intense heat." However, a close examination of the text makes it clear that Peter is talking about the end of the Millennium when Christ will create a New Heaven and a New Earth (cf. 2 Peter 3:13, Revelation 21:1, Isaiah 65:17 and 66:22).

The best answer to believe that John saw something which looked *like* the sky was rolling up, but not to attempt to read too much more into it. Whether it be a cobolt bomb, as Lindsey suggest,[221] or a shifting of continental plates, the revealing of heaven, or merely an "optical illusion,"[222] will be known until that day has come and passed. We are merely to know that it will happen exactly as God foretells and we will understand it when it comes.

The Arguments and Evaluation of the Mountains and Islands

The last issue is that which reads, "every mountain and island were moved out of their places" (vs. 14). Again, many cannot see this as literal and argue that the mountains represent goodness being removed[223] or else graspe for some other symbolism. Henry Swete merely suggest that this is to be compared to Jesus' statement about faith that can move mountains[224] but in no way attempts to explain its meaning within the context of the passage. Darby merely says that the verses "are not to be taken literally"[225] but nowhere explains their exact meaning. Scott believes that the moved mountains describe an economic collapse,[226] but, again, does not provide any evidence of such a symbolic usage anywhere else in the Bible nor in any other Jewish literature.

Once again, figurative language is taken as an easy out for the difficult passages but if no meaning is found for the figures and symbols then it is pointless to call them symbols. God does not use symbols unless those symbols can be clearly understood. Ambiguous allegory was not used in the Bible. Nowhere can one honestly and justifiably prove that the Bible used such ambiguity. Even when Jesus spoke in parables (a kind of allegory) he often explained to His disciples the *exact* and *true* meaning of the parable (cf. Matthew 13:22-23, 15:15, 24:32; Mark 4:3-20, 4:34, 7:18-23, 12:12, 13:28; and Luke 8:4-15). Jesus was never ambiguous. Says Mark 4:33-34, "with many such parables He was speaking the word to them as they were able to hear it; and He did not speak to them without a parable; but He was explaining everything privately to His own disciples." Thus Jesus *explained* the parables because their was a *true and correct* meaning to the parables. They were not merely Rorschach inkblot tests, but had true meanings. Consequently, if those who accept figurative language for these passages cannot explain their meaning, we ought reject their speculative interpretations outright.

Once again, we are left with a literal meaning. Why is the idea of moving mountains and islands so strange? Is it that they are assuming the mountain must move at least 2000 feet per minute? Are they assuming that the island must move from one coastline to another? Do not the science textbooks themsevles admit that mountains do move, and grow, albeit at an indiscernibly slow rate? In fact, catastrophes of a far less nature than those described here have been known to move mountains and islands.

Robert Govett notes that the effects of the sixth seal "are natural enough"[227] for "similar effects have occasionally followed such convulsions of nature."[228] Indeed they have. Joseph Seiss recounts an event in his lifetime when a mammoth earthquake (and far greater ones have been recorded since) caused "islands [to be] moved in their places, mountains shaken, vast districts of shore engulfed in the sea, thousands and thousands of lives lost, and hundreds of millions of treasures destroyed."[229] At least one scientist accepts this prophecy in its most literal meaning. Henry Morris attributes the moving of mountains to his shifting plate theory[230] cited previously.

Once again, the literal view is the best. It suits the context fully, being the natural result of the catastrophes previously described and is not in any reasonable way untenable or unrealistic. Critics have suggested that the literal view must mean that the mountains and islands move tens of thousands of meters, but the text does not say that, and neither do advocates of the literal interpretation.

Conclusions
It has been demonstrated that the sixth seal can in no reasonable way be seen as figurative for persecution of believers. This is expressly stated to be the "wrath of the Lamb" (vs. 17). Since believers are not the subjects of God's wrath there can be no possible way to attribute the images here to Christians, be they Jews or Gentiles. The only other figurative approach offered has been unable to show a single passage where similar imagery is used in either the

Bible, Jewish literature, or any other ancient literature. Moreover, the idea that the sixth seal is speaking of the fall of governments on earth cannot justify the scope and nature of the prophecy. What could cause the kings of the world to cry out to the rocks, begging for death? As Walvoord reminds us, "it is questionable whether changes in government and in human affairs would have brought such a striking transformation in the hearts of these wicked people."[231] Such imagery cannot be justified.

Only the literal interpretation can adequately address the prophecy and its ramifications. A literal meteor shower, or similar catastrophe, creates a massive earthquake, the blotting out of the sun, and "fantastic changes on the physical earth."[232] So terrifying are these catastrophes that;

> "The kings of the earth and the great men and the commanders and the rich and the strong and every slave and free man, hid themselves in the caves and among the rocks of the mountains; and they said to the mountains and to the rocks, 'Fall on us and hide us from the presence of Him who sits on the throne, and from the wrath of the Lamb; for the great day of their wrath has come; and who is able to stand?'" (Revelation 6:15-17).

There are several factors to consider in this. Why did they flee to the mountains? Was it because they feared staying in the cities or was it because the cities were destroyed and in flames? Was the catastrophe man-made or caused by the direct intervention of God from heaven? Regardless of which is true, the people of the earth express two sentiments. First, they asks the rocks to fall on them, which is by all rights a death wish. They appear to desire death, but is seems to escape them. Such is the terror that appears on the earth in these last days. No allegorical explanation of the sixth seal can account for such terror, only the literal reality of a massive catastrophe. Second, the victims here do not question the existence of God. They do not doubt that Christ is the Lamb of God. They do not deny that they are being punished, but neither to they repent. They cry out that the great day of the Father and Son's wrath has come, but they do not offer repentance. Man is not ignorant of God, he is rebellious against God. In these last days man will either repent or harden his heart against the Lord. Even as all men by the time they die have so hardened their hearts or repented, the wrath of God in the last days will hasten that decision. No longer will man sit around for a lifetime delaying his inevitable choice. He must make his choice or be lost forever. This is what the passage literally tells us.

The Seventh Seal and Conclusions

> "When He broke the seventh seal, there was silence in heaven for about half an hour. And I saw the seven angels who stand before God; and seven trumpets were given to them" (Revelation 8:1-2).

45

The seventh, and final, seal is not mentioned until a chapter after the sixth seal is opened. It does not trigger any specific judgment but rather it signals the beginning of the seven trumpet judgments which are to follow. That the seven trumpets follow the seven seals is evident by the fact that the trumpets are handed out to the angels after the seventh is broken.

Some have commented upon the "silence in heaven." As one author put it, this silence "has made a good deal of noise in the world, especially among commentators."[233] Some scholars believe the silence indicates that the results of the seventh seal are secret and not made known. Historicists have suggested that it represents a brief period of rest for Christians between one of various persecutions to which they attribute the prophecies. Still others see it as a prelude to the millennium or even as the beginning of eternal rest for the saints.[234] Among those who take the prophecies at face value, there is less controversy. One says it indicates a time of meditation and prayer.[235] Another says it is "portending such ominous developments ahead it is an indication that something tremendous is about to take place."[236] Walvoord compares it "to the silence before the foreman of a jury reports a verdict."[237] In either case, it is an ominous prelude to the coming trumpet judgments. It is a prelude to those judgments to come. It is the eye of the hurricane; the calm before the storm.

Thus the seven seals have ended, but the wrath of God is far from finished. Seven trumpets are about to sound, and after them seven more judgments will follow. The seals were only the beginning and a small taste of the wrath to come on those who have hardened their hearts and murdered the saints.

CHAPTER SUMMARY

The seals are not opened until after the Abomination of Desolation in the middle of the Tribulation (see Appendix D for a defense of this position).

1. The first four seals are also called the "four horsemen of the apocalypse." The first of these horsemen is the white horse which is the anti-Christ riding forth conquering. It is likely, but not certain, that this is when the anti-Christ subjugates the three kings of Revelation 13 and Daniel 7:7 & 24 as well as the whore of Babylon (see Chapter 8).

2. The second seal represents war which follows the anti-Christ's play for power. His plan fails and open rebellion will result. This is a world war which will center around Israel and threaten the anti-Christ's power.

3. The third seal is famine which follows in the final world war.

4. The forth seal is the death which will take place on a massive scale during this final war.

5. The fifth seal depicts all the martyred dead crying out to God for justice. The Lord tells them that they must wait a little longer for more

are to be slain during the persecutions which will take place in these last days.

6. The sixth seal describes a catastrophe on a massive scale involving a great earthquake, meteorites of some form falling to the earth, and the shifting of geological formations, as well as the blotting out of the sun. The moon will appear red due to some sort of phenomenon and even the sky will appear to be shifting. These descriptions are similar to those described by Jesus in the Olivet Discourse.

7. The final seal unlocks the next seven judgments, which are trumpet judgments.

Study Charts on the First Seal

Leading Scholars

	Position	Interpretation
Irenaeus	Chiliast	White horseman as Christ.
Victorinus	Chiliast	The rider as the spreading of the gospel.
Joachim of Floris	Medieval Millenarian	Christ.
Nicholas of Lyra	Medieval Joachimite	Christ.
Joseph Mede	Historicist premillennialist	An emperor.
Isaac Newton	Historicist premillennialist	An emperor.
John Darby	Dispensational premillennialist	A great conqueror.
Nathaniel West	Futurist premillennialist	The anti-Christ.
Joseph Seiss	Futurist premillennialist	The judgment of God connected to Rapture.
Robert Govett	Futurist premillennialist	Christ coming in conquest.
E. W. Bullinger	Ultradispensationalist	The anti-Christ.
H. A. Ironside	Dispensational premillennialist	A warrior.
Dwight Pentecost	Dispensational premillennialist	The establishment of peace.
Norman Harrison	Midtribulational premillennialist	Spiritual war against anti-Christian ideology.
John Walvoord	Dispensational premillennialist	The anti-Christ.
George Ladd	Posttribulational Premillennialist	The spreading of the gospel.
Tim LaHaye	Dispensational premillennialist	The anti-Christ.
Hal Lindsey	Dispensational premillennialist	Anti-Christ.
Marvin Rosenthal	"Pre-wrath" premillennialist	Anti-Christ.

Historical Survey

	Position
Church Fathers	Only two witnesses testify, hence the view of the church fathers cannot be stated with impunity. The two witnesses identify the white horseman as Christ and the gospel respectively.
Medieval Theologians	Most appear to follow the Christ view. Some followed the belief that this is the Roman Empire or one if its emperors.
Reformation Scholars	Most Reformers followed the historicist view which identified the white horseman as either Christ, the gospel, the Roman Empire, or a Roman emperor.
Post-Reformation Scholars	With the rejection of historicism the white horseman came to be predominantly seen, not the Messiah, but as the false Messiah, anti-Christ.
Modern Evangelicals	A continuation of the post-Reformation view, the white horseman is predominantly seen, not as the Messiah, but as the false Messiah, anti-Christ.

Theological Breakdown

	Position
Premillennial Historicists	Historicists are generally split between seeing the first seal as Christ and seeing it as the Roman Empire, or similar variant. Most premillennials, however, lean towards the Roman Empire view.
Dispensational Pretribulational Premillennialists	Almost complete unanimity identifying the rider as the anti-Christ.
Midtribulational (and "Pre-Wrath") Premillennialists	Generally agreed that the first seal represents the anti-Christ.
Covenant Theologians and Postribulational Premillennialists	Usually seen as the anti-Christ but the leaning is not as strong as with pre- and midtribulationists.
Variant Premillennial views	Govett and Seiss take a variant of the Christ view but add "negative" elements. Govett sees Christ in conquest of earth while Seiss sees the effects of the first rapture signaling judgment to come.

First Seal as Christ or the Gospel
Tenants of:
This view sees the rider of the white horse as either Christ or a more generic presentation of the gospel.

Popular advocates from:
The Church Fathers : Irenaeus and Victorinus.
Medieval Theologians : Joachim of Fiore and Nicholas of Lyra.
Reformation Scholars : No premillennial authors but many amillennial historicists.
Post-Reformation Scholars : Robert Govett.
Modern Evangelicals : William Newell, Watchman Nee, George Eldon Ladd, Arthur Bloomfield, and Henry Morris.

Strengths:
1) The imagery of white usually refers to purity or goodness which is incompatible with the anti-Christ.
2) The imagery of a white horse seems parallel to Christ in Revelation 19.
3) Has the support of commentators throughout the centuries.

Weaknesses:
1) If the rider is Christ or the preaching of the gospel then why is God's permission required to open the seal? Is not the Great Commission sufficient?
2) The position looses continuity between the first seal and the seals that follow.
3) The imagery of conquest does not seem appropriate for the witnessing of the gospel and would be the only such analogy in the Bible.
4) Ignores the differences between Revelation 6 and 19.
5) If the horses in Revelation 6 and 19 are the same then does Christ appear twice in the tribulation?
6) Ignores the possibility that the white symbolizes not righteousness but counterfeit righteousness or authority, as in ancient Rome.
7) The view is predominantly compatible only with allegorism and historicism.

First Seal as the Anti-Christ
Tenants of:
The white horseman is seen as the anti-Christ coming to solidify his position of power. The possible apparent absence of a quiver and arrows is usually, but not always, taken as a "cold war."

Popular advocates from:
The Church Fathers : None known.
Medieval Theologians : None known (but see Variant Theories).
Reformation Scholars : No clear advocates (but see Mede & Newton under Variant Theories).
Post-Reformation Scholars : John Darby, Walter Scott, Sir Robert Anderson, Nathaniel West, James Brookes, and E. W. Bullinger.
Modern Evangelicals : C. I. Scofield, G. H. Lang, Watchman Nee, H. A. Ironside, John Walvoord, Dwight Pentecost, Charles Ryrie, Hal Lindsey, Tim LaHaye, Robert Thomas, and Marvin Rosenthal.

Strengths:
1) The first horseman is followed by war, famine, and death. Thus the first horseman should be consistent with the riders who follow.
2) The imagery of conquest is consistent with the rise of the anti-Christ who conquers three of the ten kings (cf. Daniel 7:7 & 24).
3) The first seal should contain something wicked since God's permission is required to release the rider.
4) The similarity of the white horse to Christ's in Revelation 19 is seen as a counterfeit.

Weaknesses:
1) The imagery of the color white must solely be taken as a counterfeit or as an authority symbol.
2) No extant commentators clearly supported this view until the modern era (but see Roman Empire Theory below).

Minority Variant Theories on the First Seal

1) Roman Empire Theory:

    A historicist view that recognizes the negative connotations of the seal. It was a shift away from the Christ/gospel view but draped in historicist viewpoint surmised that the conqueror was not the anti-Christ of the Revived Roman Empire but the Roman Empire itself or an emperor thereof. This is a variant of the anti-Christ theory.

2) Judgment of God/Rapture Theory:

    Joseph Seiss' commentary promotes another variant that is a merger between the Christ/gospel view and the anti-Christ view. He sees in the seal the imagery of God but also recognizes the negative aspects of the seal. He, therefore, depicts it as the mass conversions following the first Rapture event (he advocates Partial Rapture theory). He then calls this repentance brought on by the judgment of God. So the first seal is supposed to be connected to both the gospel and God's judgment.

    Others, although not connecting this to the rapture, also see the seal in a more ambiguous judgment context, sometimes identifying it simply as the beginning of conquest with no attempt to identify the rider.

Study Charts on The Identity of the Martyrs of the Fifth Seal

Victorinus	Chiliast	Makes no clarification of Jew or Gentile nor indication of time period.
Joachim of Floris	Medieval Millenarian	Says represents the medieval martyrs.
Nicholas of Lyra	Medieval Millenarian	Identifies them as Christian martyrs throughout all the ages.
Joseph Mede	Historicist premillennialist	Identifies them as martyrs under the Aurelian emperors.
Isaac Newton	Historicist premillennialist	Identifies them as martyrs before the time of Constantine.
John Darby	Dispensational premillennialist	Is not entirely clear on this. Expresses the time as tribulation but implies all saints may be invovled.
Sir Robert Anderson	Dispensational premillennialist	Connects the martyrs with the prophecy of Daniel 12:1, thus Jewish martyrs.
Robert Govett	Futurist premillennialist	Identifies them as Jewish believers matryred during the tribulation.
Joseph Seiss	Futurist premillennialist	Identifies them as tribulation saints with no distinction between Jew and Gentile.
E. W. Bullinger	Ultradispensationalist	Identifies them solely as Jewish believers matryred during the tribulation.
H. A. Ironside	Dispensational premillennialist	Identifies them as "Jewish believers" matryred during the tribulation.
Norman Harrison	Midtribulational premillennialist	Identifies them as both Jewish and Gentile believers matryred during or near the tribulation.
George Ladd	Posttribulational Premillennialist	Identifies them as Christian martyrs throughout all the ages.
John Walvoord	Dispensational premillennialist	Identifies them as tribulation saints only.
Hal Lindsey	Dispensational premillennialist	Identifies them solely as tribulation saints.
Robert Van Kampen	"Pre-wrath" premillennialist	Identifies them as "probably Jewish" tribulation saints.

Historical Survey

	Position
Church Fathers	Make no attempt to specify the identity of the martyrs, implying they made no distinction between Jew and Gentile. The time frame was apparently the future.
Medieval Theologians	Most attributed the martyrs to various times in history with a few indicating these were martyrs from all ages.
Reformation Scholars	Most continued to attribute the martyrs to various times in history with a few indicating these were martyrs from all ages.
Post-Reformation Scholars	Most of these scholars shifted the martyrs time frame back to the future but debated as to whether they are Jewish martyrs alone or a mixture of Jews and Gentiles.
Modern Evangelicals	Have continued to see the martyrs mainly as tribulation saints, with a few dissenting voices, and also continue to debate as to whether they are Jewish martyrs alone or a mixture of Jews and Gentiles.

Theological Breakdown

	Position
Premillennial Historicists	The majority of historicist attempt to place the martyrs in a specific time frame of history although there has been no consensus on the era.
Dispensational Pretribulational Premillennialists	Most, but not all, see these are Jewish tribulation saints. A fair number see them as a mixture of Jews and Gentiles, but still tribulation saints.
Midtribulational (and "Pre-Wrath") Premillennialists	In general agreement with dispensational authors although not as strongly leaning toward the sole identification of the martyrs as Jews.
Covenant Theologians and Postribulational Premillennialists	Usually see the martyrs as being from all ages.
Progressive Dispensationalists and other variant Premillenial views	No real variant views are put forth. Progressive dispensationalists tend to follow traditional dispensationalism save in that they lean toward seeing a mixture of Jews and Gentiles among the martyrs.

The Martyrs as Believers throughout the Ages

Tenants of:

This view argues that the martyrs seen in the fifth seal are martyrs through history.

Popular advocates from:

The Church Fathers : Possibly Victorinus.

Medieval Theologians : Nicholas of Lyra.

Reformation Scholars : No premillennialist cited.

Post-Reformation Scholars : George Peters.

Modern Evangelicals : George Eldon Ladd and Jim Combs.

Strengths:

1) Nothing in the text clearly differentiates between Jews or Gentiles.

2) There is nothing which explicitly defines the time in which the martyrs died.

3) The language does not specify Christ and could, therefore, include Old Testament age believers in the Lord.

Weaknesses:

1) The seal is opened immediately after the four horseman of the apocalypse indicating that the martyrs came out of time period.

2) Their cry implies that their persecutors still live.

3) If the rapture has already occured then the pervious dead have already been resurrected and cannot be depicted here.

The Martyrs as Jewish Tribulation Saints
Tenants of:
This view argues that the martyrs seen in the fifth seal are predominantly, if not exclusively, Jewish martyrs from the tribulation alone.

Popular advocates from:
The Church Fathers : Unknown.
Medieval Theologians : None known.
Reformation Scholars : No premillennialists cited.
Post-Reformation Scholars : Walter Scott, Robert Govett, and E. W. Bullinger.
Modern Evangelicals : H. A. Ironside and Robert Van Kampen.

Strengths:
1) The seal is opened immediately after the four horseman of the apocalypse indicating that the martyrs came out of time period.
2) Their cry implies that their persecutors still live.
3) If the rapture has already occured then the pervious dead have already been resurrected and cannot be depicted here.
4) The language of vengeance allegedly implies that the church is not present.
5) Revelation teaches that the 70th week of Daniel will be a time when the nation of Israel is converted, implying many of the converts of that age will be Jews.

Weaknesses:
1) Whether the church is present or not is irrelevant as to whether or not Gentile believers will be present.
2) Nothing in the text clearly differentiates between Jews or Gentiles.
3) Most of the Jewish converts will be protected by God and, therefore, may not constitute the majority of martyrs.

The Martyrs as Jewish and Gentile Tribulation Saints
Tenants of:
This view argues that the martyrs seen in the fifth seal are Christian martyrs, both Jew and Gentile, from the tribulation alone.

Popular advocates from:
The Church Fathers : Possibly Victorinus.
Medieval Theologians : None known.
Reformation Scholars : No premillennialists cited.
Post-Reformation Scholars : Joseph Seiss.
Modern Evangelicals : Norman Harrison, Charles Ryrie, Arthur Bloomfield, John Walvoord, Hal Lindsey, and Henry Morris.

Strengths:
1) The seal is opened immediately after the four horseman of the apocalypse indicating that the martyrs came out of this time period.
2) Their cry implies that their persecutors still live.
3) If the rapture has already occured then the pervious dead have already been resurrected and cannot be depicted here.
4) Nothing in the text clearly differentiates between Jews or Gentiles.
5) Most of the Jewish converts will be protected by God and, therefore, may not constitute the majority of martyrs.

Weaknesses:
1) The language of vengeance allegedly implies that the church is not present.
2) Revelation teaches that the 70th week of Daniel will be a time when the nation of Israel is converted, implying many of the converts of that age will be Jews.

Study Charts on the Sixth Seal

Lactantius	Chiliast	Says all should be literally understood but does not elaborate.
Ephraem the Syrian	Chiliast	Appears to take it all literally.
Victorinus	Chiliast	Earthquake as persecution. Sun darkened as supression of the gospel. Moon as blood called symbol of persecution. Falling stars as martyred Christians. Sky scolling as church being taken away. Mountains moving also seen as persecution.
Joachim of Floris	Medieval Millenarian	Generally follows Victorinus and believes the seal is the near future.
Nicholas of Lyra	Medieval Millenarian	Connects the seal with Diocletian. Follows Victorinus save that he reads heresy into the prophecy of the falling stars.
Joseph Mede	Historicist premillennialist	Follows Nicholas of Lyra save that he places the prophecy under Constantine's day.
Isaac Newton	Historicist premillennialist	Follows Mede save that he places the prophecy under Julian the Apostate.
John Darby	Dispensational premillennialist	Moves prophecy back to the future. Sees earthquake as destruction of governing authority. Sun darkened as fall of govenments. Other prophecies also seen symbolically as the fall of the worldly powers.
Sir Robert Anderson	Dispensational premillennialist	Takes the prophecies literally.
Robert Govett	Futurist premillennialist	Takes the prophecies literally.
Joseph Seiss	Futurist premillennialist	Takes the prophecies literally.
E. W. Bullinger	Ultradispensationalist	Takes the prophecies literally.
H. A. Ironside	Dispensational premillennialist	Follows John Darby in interpretaion.
Norman Harrison	Midtribulational premillennialist	Mixes literal and symbolical views.
George Ladd	Posttribulational Premillennialist	Mixes literal and symbolical views.
John Walvoord	Dispensational premillennialist	Takes the prophecies literally.
Hal Lindsey	Dispensational premillennialist	Takes the prophecies literally. Sees "cobolt bomb" as trigger for some of the events.

Historical Survey

	Position
Church Fathers	Most took the events literally save Victorinus who first began to take the events symbolically as the persecution of believers.
Medieval Theologians	The majority saw the events as symbolic for the persecution of Christians.
Reformation Scholars	Largely symbolical in approach, following medieval line of thought.
Post-Reformation Scholars	A mixture of views developed. Some were literal, some continued the medieval thought, and others took a new symbolic approach seeing the prophecy as a symbol of the secular govenments of the world falling.
Modern Evangelicals	A continued mix of views similar to the post-Reformation scholars but with a rejection of the medieval historicism.

Theological Breakdown

	Position
Premillennial Historicists	Predominantly see the passage as symbolic of the persecution of Christians in history.
Dispensational Pretribulational Premillennialists	Mostly literal but some see symbols for the fall of governmental authority.
Midtribulational (and "Pre-Wrath") Premillennialists	Generally a mixture of symbolic and literal interpretations.
Covenant Theologians and Postribulational Premillennialists	A mixture of symbolic and literal interpretations with a heavier leaning toward figurative language.
Progressive Dispensationalists and other variant Premillenial views	A mixture of symbolic and literal interpretations with a leaning toward figurative language.

The Sixth Seal as Persecution
Tenants of:
This view sees the events of the sixth seal as symbol for the persecution of Christian believers. The sun is usually taken as a symbol of the word of God being suppressed and the other images are interpreted in a like manner.

Popular advocates from:
The Church Fathers : Victorinus.
Medieval Theologians : Nicholas of Lyra and probably Joachim of Fiore.
Reformation Scholars : Joseph Mede and Isaac Newton.
Post-Reformation Scholars : No premillennialists cited.
Modern Evangelicals : No premillennialists cited.

Strengths:
1) The image of the sun, moon, and stars has been used to reflect individuals in certain contexts.
2) The color of blood on the moon could conceivably represent the blood of martyrs.

Weaknesses:
1) The sixth seal is expressedly said to have the wrath of the Lamb within it. Christians cannot be the victims of His wrath.
2) This view cannot explain the terror which the seal causes to the kings and people of the earth, especially if they are the instruments persecuting Christians.
3) Historicists cannot agree on what time frame this occurs.
4) The view did not develop until hundreds of years after the apostles.
5) Mountains and islands have never been used symbolically to represent the church.
6) The parallel passages all appear literal, including the Olivet Discourse.

The Sixth Seal as the Fall of Governments
Tenants of:
This view sees the events of the sixth seal as a symbol for the fall of the governments of the world. The sun is usually taken as a symbol of authority. The other images are interpreted in a like manner.

Popular advocates from:
The Church Fathers : None known.
Medieval Theologians : None known.
Reformation Scholars : No premillennialists cited.
Post-Reformation Scholars : John Darby and Walter Scott.
Modern Evangelicals : H. A. Ironside and J. Dwight Pentecost.

Strengths:
1) The imagery takes into account God's judgment upon the world.

Weaknesses:
1) There is nowhere in the Bible or other ancient literature where the sun, moon, stars, or islands are used as symbols for governmental powers.
2) This view cannot in any explain the terror which the seal causes to the kings and people of the earth.
3) The view did not develop until over a thousand years after the apostles.
4) The parallel passages all appear literal, including the Olivet Discourse.
5) It is unrealistic to take the sun, moon, and stars as all being symbolic for the same thing.

The Sixth Seal as Literal Catastrophes
Tenants of:
This view sees the events of the sixth seal as a description of actual literal catastrophes visiting the earth. The falling stars are usually seen as meteorites and the other images are interpreted as the natural effects of this disaster; the blotting out of the sun's rays, earthquakes, etc.

Popular advocates from:
The Church Fathers : Lactantius, Ephraem the Syrian, and probably others including Irenaeus.
Medieval Theologians : Possibly Adso of Montier.
Reformation Scholars : No premillennialists cited.
Post-Reformation Scholars : Robert Govett, Joseph Seiss, Sir Robert Anderson, and E. W. Bullinger.
Modern Evangelicals : William Newell, Arthur Bloomfield, Charles Ryrie, Tim LaHaye, Hal Lindsey, Robert Thomas, John Walvoord, Henry Morris, and Marvin Rosenthal.

Strengths:
1) Falling stars often refer to meteorites (or similar phenomena) throughout both literature and history.
2) The darkening of the sun is used many times in the Bible literally.
3) Earthquakes are mentioned in the Olivet Discourse and earthquakes have not been shown to be used symbolically in the Bible.
4) This view explains the terror which the seal causes to the kings and people of the earth.
5) The was the view of the apostle's disciples.
6) The parallel passages all appear literal, including the Olivet Discourse.

Weaknesses:
1) The image of the sky rolling up like a scroll is hard to imagine in literal terms.

4

Israel and the Church

Chapter seven of Revelation begins the first of several interludes in the book. It also begins one of the greatest controversies in Revelation. The question involves the nature and purpose of both Israel and the church, and their roles in the last days, if any. There are actually many verses in dispute, most all of which speak of Israel; either its nation or people. While many maintain that Israel is to be understood only symbolically, others insist that the literal nation of Israel and the Jews are intended.

The passages in question are Revelation 7, 11:1-2, 12, and 14:1-5. Since chapter seven properly begins an interlude, it is appropriate that this chapter will also serve as an interlude to the discussion of God's judgments. The next chapter will resume the judgments with the seven trumpets, even as chapter eight of Revelation resumes those judgments. It will, however, be necessary to deal with all of the verses in question since they generally relate to one another in some fashion. To address chapter seven without discussing chapter fourteen would be futile. So each passage will be addressed, first separately and independantly, and then collectively.

The Sealing of the 144,000

> "I saw four angels standing at the four corners of the earth, holding back the four winds of the earth, so that no wind should blow on the earth or on the sea or on any tree. And I saw another angel ascending from the rising of the sun, having the seal of the living God; and he cried out with a loud voice to the four angels to whom it was granted to harm the earth and the sea, saying, 'Do not harm the earth or the sea or the trees, until we have sealed the bond-servants of our God on their foreheads.'
>
> "I heard the number of those who were sealed, one hundred and forty-four thousand sealed from every tribe of the sons of Israel: from the tribe of Judah, twelve thousand *were* sealed, from the tribe of Reuben twelve thousand, from the tribe of Gad twelve thousand, from the tribe of Asher twelve thousand, from the tribe of Naphtali twelve thousand, from the tribe of Manasseh twelve thousand, from the tribe of Simeon twelve thousand, from the tribe of Levi twelve thousand, from the tribe of Issachar twelve thousand, from the tribe of Zebulun twelve thousand, from the tribe of Joseph twelve thousand, from the tribe of Benjamin, twelve thousand *were* sealed" (Revelation 7:1-8).

Historical Overview

The nature of the sealing of these 144,000 is universally agreed to be for protection. Some have taken the protection more literal than others, but all agree that the sealing is a divine form of protection. Two other issues remain. First, are these real Jews or members of the church? Second, are there literally 144,000 of these saints, or is the number mere symbolism, representing an indeterminate number of believers?

Many of the early church fathers accepted this prophecy both as literal in number and in the literal identification of them as Jews from the tribes of Israel mentioned therein. This view is expressedly stated by Victorinus, the more allegorical interpreter of the church fathers.[238] The view also existed in the early medieval church under scholars like Adso of Montier.[239] Nevertheless, it is little surprise that under the Augustinian allegory of the Middle Ages the literal view became combated. Joachim did not deny the conversion of Jews in the end times,[240] but did not specify who they were. Nicholas of Lyra openly said that the 144,000 were Gentile converts,[241] thus making the tribes of Israel an allegory for the church and the apostles.

Although the Reformation commentators usually followed the medievals in many of their interpretations, the identification of the 144,000 with the church was not universally accepted. John Bale clearly stated that they are literal Jews, noting that "the Jews must be sealed with the word."[242] In 1642 Robert Maton wrote a book entitled *Israel's Redemption or the Prophetical History of Our Savior's Kingdom on Earth*. Within that volume he outlines the importance of Israel in the prophetic scheme of God.[243] He was not alone in this as many Reformers were already returning to a more literal understanding of the passages. Nonetheless, even men such as Joseph Mede took the view that this was but "surrogated Israel,"[244] or Gentile believers.

The resurrection of chiliasm, or premillennial futurism, favored the literal interpretation, but did not entirely discard the figurative approach. John Darby accepted the 144,000 as a literal Jewish remnant[245] but, ironically, said that the number twelve was merely "symbolical."[246] Samuel Kellogg affirmed, with most premillennial scholars of the day, that "Jewish history was thus written in advance."[247]

Of the modern premillennial futurists, it seems as if only the covenant theologians (see Appendix F) reject the more natural meaning of the text. Men like George Ladd and Robert Mounce reject that literal Jews are intended even though Ladd admits "the most natural way to interpret them is to see them as the Jewish people."[248] Both see the number 144,000 as metaphorical for an infinite multitude.

The Arguments and Evaluation of the Number
The idea that the number should be taken symbolically for an indefinite number has circulated with infrequency throughout the ages. The justification for it seems vague. Even Darby suggest the number is symbolic, saying only that "it is the perfect number of those who escape of the remnant in Israel."[249] Norman Harrison contends that "the number 144,000 is a symbolic number, embodying

12, the basic number of the church ... [it symbolizes] the completeness of the Body of Christ."[250] This is also followed by Robert Mounce who asserts that the number is a "way of emphasizing completeness."[251]

George Ladd says, "the meaning of the number, 12 X 12,000 is not difficult. As usual in Revelation, the number is symbolic and affirms that the full number of people of God will be brought safely through the time of tribulation."[252] Such a statement only belittles dissenters; it scarcely proves the assertion. Ladd says "as usual" it is a symbol, but does not list a single verse where the number twelve is used to represent fullness or completeness. How do these men come to conclude that the number represents completeness? When pressed for answers they usually reply merely that there were twelve tribes of Israel and twelve apostles. Are they suggesting that there were an infinite number of tribes of Israel, or an infinite number of apostles? There were twelve literal tribes of Israel and twelve literal apostles. There were not eleven tribes or ten apostles. There were not thirty tribes and seventeen apostles. The numbers are literal in Genesis, Exodous, Matthew, and Luke. They are literal everywhere else as well.

How can we legitimately, without even a single Scripture verse to support it, take "a definite number for an indefinite"?[253] It is true that some numbers, such as seven, can have a certain symbolic value, but *not in themselves*. When the number seven is used, it is used literally, even though it may have a secondary symbolism. Certainly, God may have chosen 144,000 for symbolic reasons, but the number itself is literal, as is proven within the text itself. As Nathaniel West commented, even if we grant "that prophetic numbers are symbolic and schematic, *it does not follow* that they have no temporal value."[254] He reminds us that "we are not to explain the symbol symbolically."[255] This is common sense. The seventy years that the Jews spent in exile certainly had a symbolic purpose, but that does not negate the fact that they were *literal* years. In fact, if they were not literal, then the symbol looses its meaning, for the meaning of a symbol is inherent in its literal counterpart. Eliminate the literal, and the symbolism disappears. Consequently, to merely state that the number 144,000 is symbolic does not justify rendering it a myth.

Govett has noted that the number must be taken literally for two reasons. First, "by its standing contrasted with an *infinite* number"[256] presented in verses 9-17. Second, because "the items which go to make up the sum, are given in detail."[257] West adds yet another reason that they must be literally, saying that because these are sealed and protected from death by the anti-Christ, the number could not be taken as an infinite number,[258] for the Bible is clear that many will be martyred during the tribulation. Only those sealed are guaranteed protection. All three arguments are sound. It is illogical to constrast a number symbolic for infinity *with infinity*. One contrast a definite number with an indefinite, not indefinite with indefinite. Moreover, the detailed description of each and every tribe seems to fly in the face of figurative language. Finally, if there are to be martyrs in the tribulation, and such has been proven and is accepted by all, then how can the 144,000 be protected from martyrdom if, in fact, this is a symbolic number for all believers?

Nevertheless, there are those who believe that the 144,000 will be martyred. Martin Kiddle believes the 144,000 "represents that proportion of Christians who in the book of destiny are inscribed as martyrs"[259] Mounce argues that "there seems to be no place in Revelation for any believer who will not face martydom in the last days."[260] He believes that because the anti-Christ has authority to "cause as many as do not worship the image of the beast to be killed,"(13:15) this forbids any beleivers from being protected during the tribulation. This is not, however, a logical argument and even proves ironic. Although the text does not say that the anti-Christ is successful in causing the deaths of all these men (only that he has the authority to do so) Mounce takes a seemingly extreme literal view of this passage in order to justify an allegorical view of another. However, even he must admit that there will be believers alive when Christ returns. Thus, his attempt to make the 144,000 an indefinite number of Christian martyrs fails. While the issue of whether this is the church will be addressed separately, the numerical argument attached to it fails. "Israel has twelve tribes, but the church is one. How can the church be divided into twelve tribes?"[261]

The 144,000 appear to be just that. They are contrasted with the innumerable numbers in the ensuing verses and they alone seem immune the persecutions of the anti-Christ. The tribes are discussed in detail and no symbolic use of the number twelve has been proven which would deny the literal application. God may have chosen that number for symbolic reasons, but the number is real and literal. Twelve thousand from each of the twelve tribes of Israel listed are to be sealed and protected by God from the wrath of the Dragon.

The Arguments and Evaluation of the Identity of the 144,000
Far more controversial than the number of these men is their identity. The Bible appears clear on this issue, saying that they are "from every tribe of the sons of Israel." Nevertheless, some have claimed that the church is the "true Israel,"[262] citing Galatians 6:16, and, therefore, it is the church referenced in this passage. George Ladd, even goes on step further. He fully admits that "the most natural way to interpret them is to see them as the Jewish people,"[263] but then argues that the "true Jews" are the church![264]

The passage in question (Galatians 6:16) actually reads, to "those who will walk by this rule, peace and mercy *be* upon them, and upon the Israel of God." Note that the passage nowhere says that the church is the "Israel of God." In fact, they appear to be contrasted with the "Israel of God." It says "mercy *be* upon them, *and* upon the Israel of God." It does *not* say, "mercy *be* upon them, for they are the Israel of God." Where do the covenant theologians get this? Ultimately they take from Paul's assertion that being a Jew outwardly, does not make one a true Jew. Paul also notes that Gentiles, through Christ, are grafted *into* Israel (Romans 11:11-24), but nowhere does it say, as covenant theologians claim, that the church has replaced Israel once and for all time. They have arrogantly claimed that God's promises to Israel have been revoked and now fall upon the church and it is that unfounded assumption which they then read into Revelation. Consider Ladd's remarks. He correctly states that "there are men who are actually and outwardly Jews – literally Jews – but in reality they are not true Jews," [265] but he then immediately jumps to the false conclusion that the "true Jews" are the church.[266] In fact, as one author put it, "there is a sense in which a man may be a Jew outwardly, and yet not be one according to the spiritual calling of the Jews; and there is a sense in which even Gentiles, if they be true believers, are 'Abraham's seed;' but I know of no instance in which the descendants of the twelve tribes of Israel include the Gentiles."[267]

Are there any other passages from which the covenant theologians can draw their conclusions? Robert Mounce argues that "James addresses his letter to 'the twelve tribes in the Dispersion' (1:1) when writing to the Christians scattered throughout the Roman world."[268] However, Mounce is *assuming* the letter was written to Gentiles, but even Robert Gundry (who identifies the 144,000 with the church)[269] admits in his New Testament survey that James was writing "probably to Jewish Christians living outside Palestine."[270] This is affirmed by the fact that "the synagogue is mentioned as the place of meeting rather than the church"[271] as well as the address to "the twelve tribes in the Dispersion."

Still one other verse is presented as proof that the church has replaced Israel is John 11:51-52,[272] but once again, the passage says nothing of the sort. It reads, the "high priest that year, prophesied that Jesus was going to die for the nation, and not for the nation only, but that He might also gather together into one the children of God who are scattered abroad." No mention is made of Israel, nor technically even the church. It is a prophecy of Gentile salvation, nothing else. Certainly there is nothing that proves that the "children of Israel" should be properly understood as the church. As John Walvoord has said, "the word *Israel* is never used of Gentiles and refers only to those who are racially descendants of Israel or Jacob."[273]

Robert Govett offers nine proofs that this is Israel of the Jews. The seven best are recounted here. First, "by the express mention of each tribe."[274] Second, by their standing in contrast to the Gentiles of verses 9-17. Third, that the church recognizes no tribal order among themselves. Fourth, that the tribe of Judah is everywhere else taken literally. Fifth, the expression "children of Israel" is also taken literally everywhere else in the Scriptures. Sixth,[275] Revelation 9:1-12 describes the same event as Joel 2, but Joel expressedly says that it is Israel or the Jews who will escape their destruction. Lastly, "John, who needed to be instructed concerning the Great Multitude, needed no teaching concerning the twelve tribes. Why? Because they were literally taken."[276]

Each point is irrefutable. "The actual listing of each tribe would be irrelevant if they were not intended to represent the specific people of Israel."[277] The church has no tribes and are contrasted against these Israelites. As Ironside remarks, "there is not a Gentile among them."[278] That the 144,000 are Israelites should be "indisputable."[279] They are, as Victorinus said, "the number of those that shall believe, of the Jews."[280] It is only logical that "when John writes, '*children of Israel*,' he means 'children of Israel.'"[281] To attempt to read the church into Israel is to read covenant theology into the text. It does not come from the passage, nor does it flow from the context. The entire context, wherebeit literal or not, speaks of Jews, not Gentiles. As Seiss says;

> "Though all the prophets were Jews, and Jesus was a Jew, and the writer of this Apocalypse was a Jew, and all the Apostles were Jews, and salvation itself is of the Jews, and the Jews as a distinct people are everywhere spoken of as destined to continue to the world's end, it is regarded as the next thing to apostasy from the faith, to apply anything hopeful, that God has said, to this particular race."[282]

The Bible makes clear in Romans 11:25-29 that "a partial hardening has happened to Israel until the fulness of the Gentiles has come in; and thus all Israel will be saved ... from the standpoint of *God's* choice they are beloved for the sake of the fathers; for the gifts and the calling of God are irrevocable." So the "the gifts and the calling of God *are irrevocable!*" God has not cancelled His promises to the Jews, as a people. God does not and cannot lie. When Paul says that the Jews have experienced a "hardening in part" until "the fulness of the Gentiles" has come in, he is clearly stating that there will be a time when the veil is lifted from their eyes, *after* the time of the Gentiles has been fulfilled. This, by definition, means that the time of the Gentiles will pass away. Some would like the Gentile dispensation to continue forver, but the Scriptures are clear that "after the fulness of the Gentiles is come in, the scales are to drop from the eyes of Israel's blinded descendants, and a fresh current of salvation is to set in towards them."[283] This is the purpose and reason for the 144,000. They are Jews from the tribes of Israel.

The Arguments and Evaluation of the Tribal Omissions
There is one notable peculiarity within the list of tribes, and one which has created much controversy. It is the omission of the tribes of Dan and Ephraim. The list in Genesis is the same save that Manasseh, one of the sons of Joseph, replaces Dan. In Ezekiel there is another list in which Manasseh and Ephraim replace Joseph (thus giving Joseph's descendants a double portion). Why are there these differences? George Ladd says, "the prophecy in Ezekiel 48 tells of the final salvation of Israel and the eschatological division of the land of Palestine. If John means to reveal eschatological salvation of Israel, we would expect him to follow the list of Ezekiel."[284] He then insist that these differences

prove that the tribes are but symbolic of the church. Of course there are several problems with Ladd's assumptions, not the least of which is that no one has suggested that Israelites from the tribe of Dan will not be saved. Even Bullinger, an ultradispensationalist, openly acknowledges that Dan and Ephraim will be "restored in the future distribution of the land"[285] as recorded in Ezekiel. Walter Scott also mentions the restoration of Dan in Ezekiel's lists but believes that Dan and Ephraim are omitted from these elect 144,000 because of the sin of idolatry.[286] The question has nothing to do with the salvation of individual tribes.

The real question is why are Dan and Ephraim omitted? "Some have suggested that *Dan* was inadvertently copied as *Man*, which was later taken as an abbreviation for Manasseh.."[287] If true, this would explain both the double portion given to Manasseh (for he receives a portion under Joseph as well) and the omission of Dan. However, this but "conjecture unsupported by any solid evidence."[288] Indeed, only the Bohairic manuscripts replace Manasseh with Dan,[289] and the Bohairic manuscripts are translations dated many years after the original Greek copies were written and distributed throughout the Roman world.

Another possible answer, first popuarlized by Irenaeus, is that Dan is omitted because the anti-Christ will come from the tribe of Dan.[290] This is an ancient theory found in the apocraphal *Testament of Dan* where Satan is the prince of the tribe of Dan.[291] It is based on rabbinical tradition[292] which stems from Genesis 49:17 and Jeremiah 8:16. The Genesis passage reads, "Dan shall be a serpent in the way, a horned snake in the path that bites the horse's heels so that his rider falls backward." Jeremiah says, "From Dan is heard the snorting of his horses; at the sound of the neighing of his stallions the whole land quakes; for they come and devour the land and its fulness, the city and its inhabitants."

Both of these passages indicate a reason why Dan might be excluded from the list in Revelation, but it is certainly not clear that the passages indicate that anti-Christ would come from the tribe of Dan. In fact, many scholars believe that the anti-Christ will be a Gentile, and not a Jew at all (see chatper 6). Regardless, the medievals followed Hippolytus[293] and the church fathers in this tradition. Even those who believed the tribes were symbols for the church persisted in believing that the anti-Christ would come from Dan's tribe. Scholars ranging from Haymo of Halberstadt in the ninth Century [294] to Adso of Montier in the tenth[295] to Nicholas of Lyra[296] to Thomas Aquinas[297] all believed the anti-Christ would come from Dan. Because most evangelicals do not believe the anti-Christ will be Jewish (a derivation from the rabbincal teachings) they have by and large rejected this teaching, although some, like Hal Lindsey, believe that the False Prophet (see chapter 6) may be from Dan.[298]

If the anti-Christ does not come from Dan, then why is the tribe excluded? The predominant thought is that Dan and Ephraim are excluded because of the sins of idolatry. Judges 18:14-31 is the most cited passage in this regard.[299] Govett goes into great detailing discussing the idolatry of each of the two tribes.[300] So prominent has this theory become that even some who believe the tribes represent the church have begun to argue that Dan and Ephraim are symbols of "Christian idolatry."[301]

That idolatry is the probably reason for their exclusion here should not be denied, but at least one other theory deserves mention. Joseph Seiss had presented a truly unique theory, which also explains the order in which the names are given. He argues;

> "All Jewish names are significant ... Juda means *confession* or *praise of God*; Reuben, *viewing the Son*; Gad, a *company*; Aser, *blessed*; Napthalim, *a wrestler* or *striving with*; Manasses, *forgetfulness*; Simeon, *hearing and obeying*; Levi, *joining* or *cleaving to*; Issachar, *reward* or *what is given by way of reward*; Zabulon, *a home* or *dwelling-place*; Joseph, *added* or *an addition*; Benjamin, *a son of the right hand, a son of old age*. Now put these several things together in their order, and we have described to us : Confessor or praisers of God, looking upon the Son, a band of blessed ones, wrestling with forgetfulness, hearing and obeying the word, cleaving into the reward of a shelter and home, an addition, sons of the day of God's right hand, begotten in the extremity of the age ... Dan meaning *judging* ... but these 144,000 are not judges ... Ephraim means *increase, growth by multiplication*; but these 144,000 are a fixed company."[302]

So four theories have presented themselves. The first, that the omissions were made to key the reader not to take the passage literally, has been thoroughly refuted. The context, passage, and Scriptures make clear that the "children of Israel" are the "children of Israel." The second, that the anti-Christ is from the tribe of Dan, fails to explain Ephraim's omission and is based largely on rabbinical interpretation. The third, and best, is that Dan and Ephraim are omitted because of idolatry but will be restored in the Millennial Kingdom. Seiss' theory is presented for the reader's approval and deserves respect, although the third view remains the strongest.

The Temple of God

> "There was given me a measuring rod like a staff; and someone said, 'Rise and measure the temple of God, and the altar, and those who worship in it. And leave out the court which is outside the temple, and do not measure it, for it has been given to the nations; and they will tread under foot the holy city for forty-two months.'" (Revelation 11:1-2).

Historical Overview

Here in Revelation is the description and measurement of a temple which had been destroyed long before John wrote the apocalypse. That it appears, at least at first glance, to refer to the temple of Jerusalem is without question, but how are we to consider it? Is the Temple to be rebuilt before the last days are completed or is it a symbol of temple of the believer's body; i.e. the church?

The early church fathers were overwhelmingly of the opinion that the temple would be rebuilt and the Jews would return to the land. This is affirmed by Irenaeus,[303] Hippolytus,[304] Lacantius,[305] and Ephraem.[306] Victorinus, however, deviated from this and claimed that the temple was merely representative of the church.[307] In the medieval church Adso followed the earlier view, accepting the literal restoration of the Temple[308] while Nicholas of Lyra, along with the majority of medieval scholars, applied it to the church.[309] As was usually the case, most of the Reformation scholars continued in this line of thought, including Joseph Mede. Ironically, although arguing that the "holy city" should be interpreted as the church,[310] he then goes into great detail about the literal Herodian temple.[311]

Despite the seeming abandonment of the belief in a rebuilt and restored holy city and temple, the scholars of the post-Reformation began to see in the prophecy its literal aspects. Darby,[312] Kellogg,[313] Anderson,[314] Scott,[315] Bullinger,[316] and West,[317] among many others, returned the belief that the temple would be rebuilt, that the city of Jerusalem would be restored to the Jews, and the nation of Israel would again come to life. Each of these men lived between a hundred-fifty and two hundred years before Israel became a nation, but each believed it would happen; a testament to their faith and trust in the Word of God above that of men.

Despite the restoration of Israel in 1948, there are still some scholars who deny that the temple will be rebuilt. Chiefly among these are the covenant theologians, who see in Israel all things Gentile.

The Arguments and Evaluation of the Temple of God
The sudden appearance of the long destroyed temple in Revelation is not unique. The prophecy of Daniel's seventy weeks also presents this apparent problem, for in Daniel 9:26 it is prophesied that "the people of the prince who is to come will destroy the city and the sanctuary" but in verse 27 the anti-Christ is halting sacrifice in the very temple which was destroyed one verse ago. Chapter one has already discussed the prophecy of the 70 weeks. It was shown that a gap is accepted between the 69th and 70th week. It is apparently during this gap that the temple is destroyed and built again.

The allegorical application of the temple to the church need be only briefly addressed since many of the same arguments are used as were used in the identification of the 144,000 with the church. Still, there is a legitimate debate on some of the images found in this passage. Those who present the temple as a symbol of the church point out that the phrase "temple of God" is used of the Christian and of the church. 1 Corinthians 3:16-17, 2 Corinthians 6:15, and Ephesians 2:20-22 all speak of the believer as a temple of God. Ironically, this "symbolic" use is actually a very literal usage of the word, for the "temple" is properly the dwelling place of God. Since God dwells within the believer (2 Corinthians 6:16) he is properly, and literally, a temple of the Lord. Having said this, the application to Revelation 11:1-2 does not hold water.

The first problem is that "temple of God" is set against the backdrop of the "altar," "those who worship in it," the "court of the Gentiles," and the "holy city." If "temple of God" is to be understood symbolically, so must the altar, the worshippers, the court of the Gentiles, and the holy city. That this is not an idle difficulty is obvious not only by the vast diversity of opinions generated, but also by the fact that the worshippers and the "holy city" are also applied to the church. Mede, for example, reads "holy city" figuratively for the church.[318] Robert Mounce holds that the temple refers to the church but claims that the court of the Gentiles *also* refers to the church "from a different perspective."[319] If this were so then the passage would read that John is to measure "the *church* and the *church* within it which is in the city of the *church*, but the *church* is to be cast out."

Another problems is that the measuring is generally accepted to represent God's protection, but the "holy city" is said to be trodden under foot for forty-two months (vs. 2). Ironically, George Ladd has come to the defense of a more literal interpretation. He has said, "it is difficult to recognize here, as some do, a contrast between spiritual preservation in the midst of physical persecution and martyrdom."[320] He acknowledges that "the most natural meaning of Jerusalem is that it stands for the Jewish people,"[321] or perhaps one might add that Jerusalem stands for Jerusalem. In either case, Ladd is freely admitting the Jewish character of the passage and comes to the conclusion that the worshippers of the temple represent the faithful remnant of Israel.[322]

The most obvious and natural meaning of the text is that there will be a time when "Jerusalem will have been largely repopulated by the children of its ancient inhabitants, its temple rebuilt, and its ancient worship restored."[323] This view has been long promoted against the backdrop of jeers and mockery. The idea of a restored nation of Israel seemed absurd, but fifty years before that momentus day in history Nathaniel West said that "the day may not be distant when *literal Israel will be for us a light as brilliant on the Eleventh chapter of John's Apocalypse, as they are now upon the Eleventh chapter of Paul's letter to the Romans.*"[324] More than a decade before the creation of the Zionist movement and over sixty years before Israel became a nation, men such as Nathaniel West, James Brookes, Samuel Kellogg, and Sir Robert Anderson also declared that Israel must be restored. West said, "the Temple, laid in ruins, shall be rebuilt. The Outcasts shall be gathered to their home."[325] Brookes states that Christ "cannot come until the restoration of the Jews in large numbers to Jerusalem."[326] Kellogg declared that "sooner or later the world will witness the reinstatement of the Jewish nation in the land of their fathers."[327] Sir Anderson insisted not only that "the covenant people must regain their normal position,"[328] but also that "the restoration of the Covenant people precedes the 70th week."[329]

Brookes made an even bolder claim, in 1889, quoting Isaiah 66:8, he declared that "Israel, as a nation, shall be born at once - in one day."[330] Such is now history. Before the 70th week, in 1948, Israel became born in a single day on May 14, the only country in the world's history to do so. It survived a massive invasion by five sovereign Arab nations although it was outnumbered ten to one[331] and yet there remain men sceptical of the literal application of this passage. Yet this is not the only passage which speaks of a literal restoration. Speaking on Isaiah 11:11-16 Brookes says;

> "Here, the recovery of God's ancient people is said to be for 'the second time'; to consist, not of a few, but of the entire remnant that shall be left; to be composed, not of those carried captive into a single land, but of those gathered from various countries and from the islands of the sea."[332]

Thus, before there was a "first time," Isaiah prophesied of a "second time" when the Jews would be gathered from many lands across the world. It is bewildering how anyone could deny that these prophecies were fulfilled literally just over fifty years ago. Yet some continue to ask how God could "reject" the church for a people who have rejected the Messiah. To this answer, the scriptures are clear. There are "abundant prophecies a restoration or returning of the Jews to their land *in unbelief*"[333] (emphasis added). "The final evangelism of the world awaits the restoration of Israel."[334] If God forgave the pagan Gentiles, whose history included human sacrifice and cannibalism, will God not keep His promises and bring *His* people to repentance? While at least one scholar believes this is a reference to the temple in Heaven,[335] the natural and clear meaning is a literal temple in Jerusalem.

The Arguments and Evaluation of the Outer Court
In addition to the temple and Jerusalem, there is the question of the outer court of the Gentiles and the trampling which is said to occur for forty-two months. If the temple and Jerusalem are taken literally, then so too should the outer court.

Most agree that the trampling indicates Gentile occupation of Jerusalem during the last three and a half years of the tribulation, or at least extensive fighting and battles within the city, but what is the purpose of the explicit mention of the outer court of the Gentiles? Is there any special significance to John's being told to leave it out of the measurement? Seiss believes that the rejection of the court of the Gentiles represents the end of the present dispensation.[336] However, Hal Lindsey and others have proposed a more intriguing answer. Lindsey believed that the outer court was rejected because the Dome of the Rock would still be standing in the outer courtyard.[337] He argued that the temple could be built with Dome of the Rock still standing; a seeming impossibility to many minds.

The problem is that the Muslim shrine, the Dome of the Rock, stands where many believe the great temple of God once stood. Orthodox Jews would never accept the temple being built anywhere except upon the Temple Mount where God had told Solomon to build it. As a result, both Jews and Muslims revere the Temple Mount as a holy site. Since the mount is currently in the hands of the Palestinian authority, archaeological surveys have been limited, but some research has suggested that the temple may have been either to the north or south of the Dome of the Rock. If this is so, then it could be possible for someone (who many believe will be the anti-Christ) to arrange a pack between the Muslim and Jews which would permit the temple to be rebuilt without tearing down the Dome of the Rock.

There are currently three major theories regarding the location of the ancient temple of Jerusalem, and several derivations. The latest theories are variations on the belief that the temple was actually built to the south of the Dome of the Rock. In 1979 a Franciscan began to argue that the temple had been built on lower ground, rather than on the higher ground of the central and northern part of the Temple Mount.[338] The main argument lies in historical writings that imply that the temple could not be seen from certain locations. According to this theory, the temple could only be missed if it were built to the south.[339] Moreover, they note that the Mishnah places the temple closer to the southern gate than the Dome of the Rock is.[340] The problem is that the ancient Temple Mount was enlarged by Herod. Consequently, the current location of the southern gate is further south than it used to be. This would negate the force of that argument. Finally, the court of the Gentiles is known to have lain to the south of the temple. If the temple was in the south then there would be no room for the court of the Gentiles.

Two variants on this theory suggest that the current Temple Mount is not really the Temple Mount at all but the remains of the Fortress Antonia.[341] They propose that another mount used to exist to the south. One places the Temple Mount just to the immediate south while another places it over the springs of Gihon.[342] Unfortunately, these theories rest on questionable exegesis and lack archaeological support.[343] The latter confused the term "Zion" with the temple location and ignores much historical evidence as well. The biggest problem is that the southern steps, which exist to this day, are known to date back 2000 years. That would mean that an entirely separate Temple Mount would have to have existed at that time. Although archaeological diggings are not permitted on the Temple Mount by Arab authorities, they are allowed elsewhere, and no evidence of such an ancient structure exist.[344]

These southern theories, particularly the variants, are the weakest views. Most archaeologists subscribe to one of the remaining two views. The first is the age old belief that the temple resided where the Dome of the Rock now stands, and the other is the belief that the temple was actually built slightly to the north.

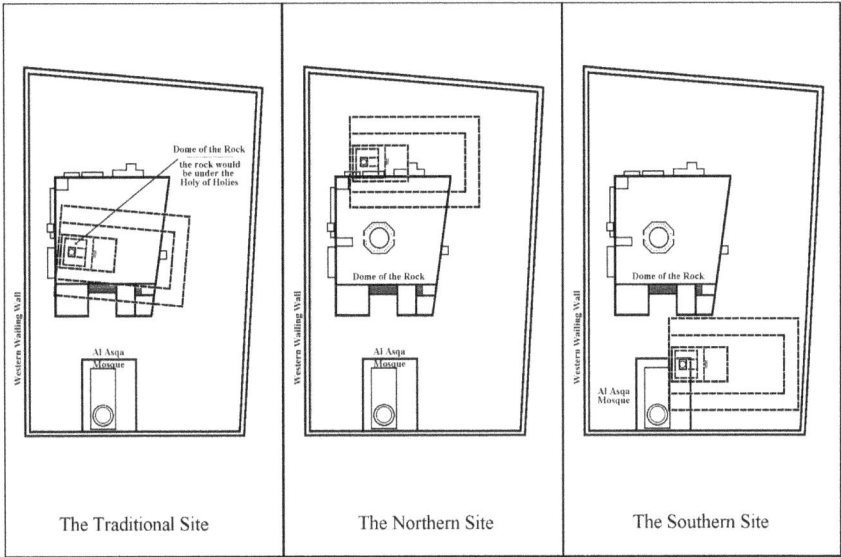

| The Traditional Site | The Northern Site | The Southern Site |

The traditional site for the temple of Jerusalem is exactly where the Dome of the Rock currently resides. This is the accepted view of most Orthodox Jews and was passed down through the ages. It also carries considerable archaeological support, considering the vast limitations placed on archaeology on the Temple Mount. According to this view, the Dome of the Rock was built over the very rock where the Ark of the Covenant once sat, in the Holy of Holies.[345] There are a number of slight variant views, including the belief that the rock was the Foundation Stone for the Temple,[346] but each view places the Temple over the Dome of the Rock. Recent archaeological support for this was presented by Leon Ritmeyer in the *Biblical Archaeology Review*. Since archaeological digs are not permitted on the Temple Mount itself, Ritmeyer examined the surrounding archaeological evidence to attempt to discover the original dimensions and area of Solomon's Temple Mount. This differs from the current Temple Mount because Herod is known to have expanded and enlarged it by almost double its original area.[347] Since the Second Temple was built on the foundations of the first Solomonic Temple, it is obvious that the temple must have been located within the boundaries of the original Temple Mount.

Ritmeyer deduced that various locations around the supporting Temple Mount structure were Herodian additions. Based on these observations he placed the original Solomonic Mount in roughly the south central area of the current Temple Mount. The temple would then have been placed in the northern section of that area, which is today the center of the Temple Mount, dominated by the Dome of the Rock.[348] This has been the accepted view of the

75

predominant number of archaeologists as well as the Orthodox Jewish community. However, in recent years it has been challenged by the views of Dr. Asher Kaufman, and promoted by evangelical Christians such as Hal Lindsey, Grant Jeffreys, and Chuck Missler.[349]

In 1983 Dr. Kaufman published the results of his own archaeological surveys and findings. Although his findings were quickly accepted by many evangelicals, Kaufman distances himself from the evangelical views and did not base his findings on any religious presuppositions.[350] Kaufman's thesis was based on the writings of the Mishnah (Jewish tradition) and other literary sources. According to the Mishnah the court of the Gentiles in the south was larger than the northern, eastern, and western sections of the Temple Mount.[351] He also noted the messianic tradition that the Messiah would enter through the eastern gate to gaze upon the temple,[352] but oddly enough the eastern gate, or Golden Gate, is located to the north, and would barely have even been within the location that Ritmeyer assigned to the original Temple Mount. Kaufman suggested that owing to these two factors the temple may have once been located to the north of the Dome of the Rock. He further noted that the Dome of the Tablets, a small Muslim shrine, was directly across from the gate and in perfect line with the Mount of Olives, which the temple was to be facing.[353] This Dome of the Tablets (also known as the Dome of the Spirits) rest atop a large rock. Kaufman suggest that the Dome of the Tablets may have taken its name from the tablets contained within the Ark of the Covenant.[354] Thus he places the Dome of the Tablets as the site of the Holy of Holies, rather than the Dome of the Rock.[355] He also found archaeological support for this in the surrounding area including the cisterns below the Temple Mount which could correspond to the temple above if it were in the location he suggests.[356]

Other arguments used to support this theory include the tradition that when the Caliph sought to build a Dome over the site of the ancient temple of Jerusalem, the Jew who led him to the spot where it once resided intentionally misled the Caliph because he did not want the sacred spot descrated by a Muslim Mosque.[357] Certainly, this makes sense. Jews believe that the spot where the temple and Ark once resided are sacred. Orthodox Jews fear even treading upon the sacred spot with their unsanctified feet. It seems odd that the Jews would have led the Muslim Caliph directly to the spot, so that he could build a Muslim alter over the site. This lends credibility to the belief that the Caliph was deceived.

The central, or traditional, theory and the northern theory are the strongest theories. However, without real archaeological diggings it will be impossible for either theory to be proven or falsified. Only time will tell if the Dome of the Rock will fall to make way for the temple or if the temple will be built in a different spot.[358]

If the northern conjecture is accurate, then the temple could be built without destroying the Dome of the Rock. The Dome would actually be standing outside the temple in the court of the Gentiles. Is this what John envisioned? Certainly it is a strong possibility, but others attatch no special significance to the rejection of the outer court. "Traditionally, Gentiles were allowed to enter the outer courtyard surrounding the temple but never into the temple itself. This area, therefore, was not to be included in John's measurement. That is, it was the judgment of Israel, not that of the Gentiles, with which he was to be concerned."[359] This is valid reasoning except for the consideration of the explicit statement that the court of the Gentiles "has been given to the nations." This cast doubt on the belief that the exclusion of the outer court was of no real significance and strengthens the view that the outer court is unhallowed for some reason.

Only time will tell for sure which of these beliefs is the true and correct one, but the current political situation in the Middle East proves that the temple of Jerusalem cannot currently be built without igniting a war. Many scholars believe that the seven year peace treaty, spoken of in Daniel (see chapters 2 and 6), brokered by the anti-Christ, will actually be for the purpose of permitting the building of the temple. If this is so then the Dome of the Rock could still be standing in the outer court of the temple. One cannot be dogmatic in this matter, but the pieces seem to fit very well. Another possibility, however, is that the Dome of the Rock could actually be destroyed by Muslim terrorists themselves! This seemed an extreme possibility until very recently. The Wahabi terrorist group believe that even Muslims who reject their own views are to be considered infidels and are objects of attack. In June 2003 the Wahabi even attempted a failed attack on Mecca, the holiest of Islamic sites. If they would be willing to attack Mecca, there is certainly no doubt that the Dome of the Rock could also be a target. In any case, whether by treaty, by building the temple next to the Dome, or by some act of terrorism, the Bible is clear that the temple *will* be rebuilt in the last days.

A Note on Bloomfield's Prophecy of the Restoration
On the prophecy of the restoration of Israel a unique interpretation was first presented by Arthur Bloomfield, based on some vague ideas which had circulated over the past century. Nathaniel West had made special note of the reason for Daniel's seventy weeks. Since the Jews had not kept the sabbath year (Leviticus 27:16-25) God promised in Leviticus 26:18 and 28 to punish Israel "seven fold" for their sins. 2 Chronicles makes this clear, saying that the Jews would be carried into Babylon "until the land had enjoyed its sabbaths. All the days of its desolation it kept sabbath until seventy years were complete" (36:21). Now West noted that in Daniel's seventy weeks there was "the *Sheba'* or Seven Times of Israel's national punishment" which "are the whole stretch of time in Israel's chastisement, from the smiting of Israel and Judah, as kingdoms, down to the '*Last Days*.'"[360] This is accepted by the majority of premillennialists, but Bloomfield saw in the then newly discovered Qumran (Dead Sea) scrolls some

interesting commentaries which led him to adopt a unique interpretation of Ezekiel 3-4.

Bloomfield says, "both Daniel and Ezekiel foretold the number of years the Jews would be scattered among the nations: Daniel has a period of 490 years, divided into three parts ... Ezekiel has two periods, one of 390 years and one of 40 years, making a total of 430 years."[361] In Ezekiel, the Lord prophesies the coming destruction of Jerusalem and orders Ezekiel to lie on his left side of 390 days to symbolize the "years of [Israel's] iniquity" (vs. 4). He is then told to lie on his right side for forty days to represent the years of Judah's iniquity. The passage is clear that there is "a day for each year" (vs. 6). Now most commentators to this day have troubles with the prophetic aspect of this passage. John Walvoord accepted these acts as representing the period of Israel and Judah's apostasy but attatches no special prophecy to the act.[362] Matthew Henry suggest that the first siege of Israel lasted 390 days.[363] Other commentators, particularly Jewish ones, believe that the 430 years of punishment were to run from the time of Jehoiachim's deportation in circa 597 B.C. to the Maccabean revolt of 167 B.C., during which the Jews threw off the Greek bondage.[364] However, Israel cannot truly be said to have become independant after the Maccabean revolts for the Romans soon followed on the heels of the Greeks and the puppet kings, like Herod, were in some ways worse than the oppression the Jews experienced under the Persians or the earlier Greek period.

Bloomfield believed Moses' warning, so aptly applied to Daniel's seventy weeks, should also apply to Ezekiel's prophecy. He argued that of the 430 years, only seventy were erased by the Babylonian exile.[365] This, he said, left 360 years which would multiplied by seven according to Leviticus 26:18.[366] He makes careful note that the Jews were never truly independent after the Babylonian exile. They were always under the domination of either Persia, Greece, Syria, or Rome, thus he calls this a "partial return."[367] Consequently, he believed that the prophecy of Ezekiel demanded an exile of 2520 years from the invasion of Israel by Nebuchadnezzar.[368] Unfortunately, Bloomfield failed to recognize, in both this prophecy and his interpretation of Daniel's seventy weeks, that the ancients did not use a 365 day calendar (see chapter 2). He, therefore, saw the years extending to 2004 and merely suggested that some unknown "event" would occur.[369] Had he realized that all historians grant that the ancients used a different calendar he would have made a far more convincing argument.

If we correct Bloomfeld's numbers for those of the ancient Chaldean calendar then the 2520 years become 2483 and ¾ years by the modern Gregorian calendar. Now according to some scholars Nebuchadnezzar first besieged Israel in the summer of 606 B.C.[370] Seventy Chaldean years later, sixty nine by the Gregorian calendar, the exiles began to return in the summer of 537 B.C., a few years after the famous edict of Cyrus. The critic will note that *Controversies in the Prophets* I prefer the dates of 605 and 536 B.C. Either date will do for the purposes of this debate for I am merely presenting the view which, when we examine the numbers, creates a curious coincidence; namely, that the prophecy would take us to when Israel became an independent nation for the first time since Israel fell.

Below is a chart showing these views in detail.

The prophecy in days as converted from the Hebrew/Chaldean calendar to the Gregorian Calendar.	2520 years x 360 days = 907,200 days (**Hebrew/Chaldean Calendar - 360 days**) 907,200 days / 365.25 days = 2483.778 years (**Gregorian Calendar - 365 days**)
From the month of Av (mid-July) 537 B.C. to December 31, 537 B.C.	Approximately 169 days
From the January 1, 536 B.C. to December 31, of 1 B.C.	195,770 including 130 leap year days Sub-total: 195,939 days
From January 1, 1 A.D. to January 1, 1948 A.D.	711,127 days including 472 leap year days
From January 1, 1948 to May 14, 1948, Israeli Independence Day.	134 days Sub-total: 711,261
From the month of Av (mid-July) 537 B.C. to May 14, 1948, Israeli Independence Day.	Total: 907200 days or 2520 Chaldean Years

Or alternately :

The prophecy in days as converted from the Hebrew/Chaldean calendar to the Gregorian Calendar.	2520 years x 360 days = 907,200 days (**Hebrew/Chaldean Calendar - 360 days**) 907,200 days / 365.25 days = 2483.778 years (**Gregorian Calendar - 365 days**)
From the fall 536 B.C. to December 31, of 1 B.C.	195,507 including 130 leap year days
From January 1, 1 A.D. to the spring of 1949 when armistice treaties were being finalized and Israel won its independence.	711,693 days including 472 leap year days
From the fall 536 B.C to the spring of 1949 when Israel won its independence.	Total: 907200 days or 2520 Chaldean Years

May 14, 1948 is Independence Day for modern Israel, but they did not truly achieve independence until July 20 1949.   After Israel declared

Indepenence they were invaded by five of their Arab neighbors. The war lasted over a year. The first armistice was signed on February 24 with Egypt and the last, with Syria, was signed on July 20.[371] Thus between February 24 and July 20 would be when Israel truly won its independence. If 536 B.C. is held to be the appropriate *terminus a quo* then the spring of 1949 would be the proper *terminus ad quem*. This is a strong possibility although it would be harder to determine the exact dates for these events as the Jews would not have begun to enter the land of Israel until several months after Cyrus' edict and the exact date of Israel's victory can only be said to be in the spring of 1949.

Ultimately this view is the most intriguing, but it does rest on dubious grounds. Should we really subtract the seventy years of Jeremiah from the 430? Should we really be multiplying those numbers by seven? Do the numbers come out exact (for no prophecy of God should be approximate, but precise)?

I will leave to the reader the answer to these questions. This view certainly has a strong appeal to the premillennial dispensationalist and will doubtless be mocked and despised by the replacement theologian who denies any future for national Israel. Its tenants, however, cannot be so easily dismissed, despite its questionable presumptions. The mere fact that the view was taught centuries before Israel's restoration should immediately silence the critic who claims that I have merely altered the numbers to fit current events. Especially since I have not myself committed to the theory. In short, any criticism of the view should weigh the evidence fairly rather than dismissing it as "dispensational fantasy."[372]

Conclusion on the Temple Restoration and Trampling

On November 29, 1947 the United Nations voted to partition Palestine and give the Jews a state. On May 14, 1948 a single country became the only country in the history of the world to have been formed and officially recognized in a single day. A prophecy in Isaiah reads, "Who has heard such a thing? Who has seen such things? Can a land be born in one day? Can a nation be brought forth all at once? As soon as Zion travailed, she also brought forth her sons" (66:8). Yet this was done. Jews still reeling from the holocaust were allowed to enter the country unfettered for the first time in decades on that day. They had their parliament and offices and military already awaiting that day. They met officially for the first time that day and they declared independance on that day.

"The future restoration of Israel [is] the common subject of both the Apocalypse and the older prophets."[373] So also is the restoration of the temple. Having argued and debated the points the following conclusions are reached.

Israel was prophesied to return as a nation while still in unbelief as to the true identity of the Messiah (Christ Jesus). Israel will one day rebuild its temple and restore the ancient worship. For some reason, however, the outer court of the Gentiles is deemed unhallowed. Whether the Dome of the Rock will still be standing is open to debate, but the court of Gentiles is to be rejected by God as hallowed ground. Then, after three and a half years of treaty with the anti-Christ he will desecrate the temple (see chapter 6 for more on this portion of the prophecy). Israel will repent and reject the anti-Christ. He will, in turn, revenge himself and attempt to occupy Jerusalem. The holy city will become a battle ground for the last three and a half years of Daniel's seventieth week. This is of what the prophecy speaks.

The Two Witnesses

> "'I will grant *authority* to my two witnesses, and they will prophesy for twelve hundred and sixty days, clothed in sackcloth.' These are the two olive trees and the two lampstands that stand before the Lord of the earth. And if anyone desires to harm them, fire proceeds out of their mouth and devours their enemies; and if anyone would desire to harm them, in this manner he must be killed. These have the power to shut up the sky, in order that rain may not fall during the days of their prophesying; and they have power over the waters to turn them into blood, and to smite the earth with every plague, as often as they desire. And when they have finished their testimony, the beast that comes up out of the abyss will make war with them, and overcome them and kill them. And their dead bodies *will lie* in the street of the great city which mystically is called Sodom and Egypt, where also their Lord was crucified. And those from the peoples and tribes and tongues and nations *will* look at their dead bodies for three and a half days, and will not permit their dead bodies to be laid in a tomb. And those who dwell on the earth *will* rejoice over them and make merry; and they will send gifts to one another, because these two prophets tormented those who dwell on the earth. And after the three and a half days the breath of life from God came into them, and they stood on their feet; and great fear fell upon those who were beholding them. And they heard a loud voice from heaven saying to them, 'Come up here.' And they went up into heaven in the cloud, and their enemies beheld them. And in that hour there was a great earthquake, and a tenth of the city fell; and seven thousand people were killed in the earthquake, and the rest were terrified and gave glory to the God of heaven." (Revelation 11:3-13).

A General Summary of the Two Witnesses

Throughout history men have been intrigued by who these two witnesses are, or will be. Most all commentators agree that these will be two literal individuals, although a number of historicists maintain they are but symbols of the church as a whole.[374] However, the church is one, not two. Some medievals commented that they could represent both the Old and New Testaments,[375] but such allegorizing negates the forceful character of these two "prophets." They are not times, nor dispensations, nor churches, but are "prophets." The miracles they perform are not the miracles of times or nations, but of prophets. Even many medievals recognized this. The prophets are individuals who will come in the last days and "prophesy for twelve hundred and sixty days."

With the majority, it is best to take the Bible at its word and accept these as individual prophets in the last days. Their identity is debated in Appendix C and will not be addressed here, for all that is important to this chapter is the relationship of the two prophets to the nation of Israel and/or the church.

The twelve hundred and sixty days is equal to three and a half Hebrew years or half of Daniel's 70th week. After that time, the beast (who is not introduced in Revelation until two chapters later) will slay them. We are told that they will lay in the streets for three and a half days, after which they will be resurrected for all to see while a great earthquake rips the city and devastates it. Should this too be taken literally? Yes. So sure are most commentators of this, that debate will be reserved for Appendix C, and its literal character assumed here.

The importance of the events is that they are a sign to the Jews. "These Witnesses are not presented to John in a vision. They are described to him by the glorious Angel, who is the Lord Jesus Himself. The account we have of them is not John's account, as in most other instances in this book; but it is *Christ's* account, given in Christ's own words."[376] The witnesses are vital to the repentance of Israel and their coming is foretold in both Zechariah and Matthew.[377] The death of these two witnesses is after three and a half years, thus placing it in the middle of the tribulation, coinciding with the abomination of desolation spoken of in Daniel 9:24, Matthew 24:15, and 2 Thessalonians 2:4. It may also occur in close conjunction with the invasion for Gog and Magog (see Appendix C). One thing is sure. Their resurrection and the earthquake which follows are two of the major signals for the repentance of Israel. Along with the 144,000, Jesus warns those who see the abomination of desolation to flee to the mountains (Matthew 24:15). When these witnesses are slain, the Abomination is at hand, assuming it did not occur immediately prior to their martyrdom. This is the backdrop for the events described in chapter 12.

The Woman Clothed with the Sun

"A great sign appeared in heaven: a woman clothed with the sun, and the moon under her feet, and on her head a crown of twelve stars; and she was with child; and she cried out, being in labor and in pain to give birth.

"And another sign appeared in heaven: and behold, a great red dragon having seven heads and ten horns, and on his heads *were* seven diadems. And his tail swept away a third of the stars of heaven, and threw them to the earth. And the dragon stood before the woman who was about to give birth, so that when she gave birth he might devour her child.

"And she gave birth to a son, a male *child*, who is to rule all the nations with a rod of iron; and her child was caught up to God and to His throne. And the woman fled into the wilderness where she had a place prepared by God, so that there she might be nourished for one thousand two hundred and sixty days.

"... And there was war in heaven, Michael and his angels waging war with the dragon. And the dragon and his angels waged war, and they were not strong enough, and there was no longer a place found for them in heaven. And the great dragon was thrown down, the serpent of old who is called the devil and Satan, who deceives the whole world; he was thrown down to the earth, and his angels were thrown down with him ... and when the dragon saw that he was thrown down to the earth, he persecuted the woman who gave birth to the male *child*. And the two wings of the great eagle were given to the woman, in order that she might fly into the wilderness to her place, where she was nourished for a time and times and half a time, from the presence of the serpent" (Revelation 12:1-14).

Historical Overview

Here lies one of the more controversial passages in Scripture. Like the other issues addressed in this chapter, it is a passage dealing with the question of whether the church is envisioned or whether Israel is envisioned. Unlike the previous passages, however, the answer is not as clear cut. The passage obviously uses symbolism and all accept this fact. As Joseph Seiss remarks, the woman "is said to be *a sign*, a representation or picture of something else - a symbol ... whatever else is literal in this book, the case of the woman is not."[378] Thus all agree that the woman is a symbol. The question remains; a symbol of what?

The early church fathers were divided, as would be later scholars, but the majority saw the woman as a glorified image of the church. Hippolytus saw in her the church and in the twelve stars he saw the apostles. He then depicted the man-child as some form of a representation of the gospel.[379] Victorinus saw the woman as far more than the church. He saw in her all "the ancient church of the fathers and prophets and saints and apostles."[380] In other words, he saw the Old Testament saints, as well as the church, as represented within her bosom. He rightly saw the man-child as Christ.[381] Finally, Methodius saw the woman as the church and the man-child as the faithful within the church.[382]

The medievals followed this popular line of thought. Pierre D'Olivi saw in the woman the church[383] as did Nicholas of Lyra who read his historicism into the text. According to Nicholas the woman was the church, the Sun was Christ, the man-child was the emperor Heraclius, and the dragon was the Persian conqueror Chosroes![384]

In the Reformation John Bale[385] and Joseph Mede continued to identify the woman with the church,[386] as did Isaac Newton.[387] The identification of the man-child varied from Christ[388] to Newton's suggestion that the child was the

Christian empire of Constantine.[389] Later preterists read the Virgin Mary into the vision as well. As has been shown in the trend in history, it was not until the post-Reformation era that scholars began to shed the heavy symbolism for a more literal approach. In this case, since it is a symbol that is being dealt with, the change is almost surprising were it not for the fact that the literal interpretation lends itself to a more systematic interpretation of symbols, as well as the more literal passages.

In the nineteenth century John Darby followed the previous expositors in seeing the man-child as Christ but pointed out that "the Church is in nowise the mother of Christ; she is a Bride."[390] Consequently, he saw the woman as "the Jews."[391] This seemingly flawless logic won over even amillennialists like John Barclay Swete who called the woman the "Jewish Church,"[392] although later attempting to argue that the church is the new Israel.[393] E. W. Bullinger,[394] Sir Robert Anderson,[395] Walter Scott,[396] and Nathaniel West[397] agreed that the woman had to be Israel rather than the church, for the church was given birth to by Christ, not Christ by the church. Many modern expositors have followed this reasoning except for the covenant theologians and partial rapturists who have maintained the older traditional view in some form or other.

The Arguments and Evaluation of the Man-Child
Although the passage is long and complicated, the key figure is the woman. If her identity can be ascertained than the rest of the prophecy follows with relative ease. However, her identification seems to rest largely with the child she carries. Consequently, it is best to start with the man-child. Once his identity has been confirmed, the identity of the woman should follow. Unfortunately, many scholars of past history have done the opposite. They begin with the assumption that the woman is the church, and then must find a way to identify the child in a compatible manner.

The text itself should make abundantly clear that it is Jesus Christ Himself who is depicted as the man-child. He is explicitly said to be the One "who is to rule all the nations with a rod of iron" (vs. 5). This is a quotation borrowed from numerous Messianic prophecies attributed to Christ (Cf. Revelation 2:27, 19:15, and Psalms 2:9). It is an indisputable identification of the child as Christ.

That Christ is apparent in some form in the image of the man-child has escaped few eyes. Of all the commentators throughout the ages most everyone incorporates either Christ or His gospel or some other derivation of Christ within the image of the man-child. Only Nicholas of Lyra seems to deviate from this trend by assigning the child to the Roman emperor Heraclius.[398] Isaac Newton also followed an extreme historicist interpretation, calling the man-child the Christian Empire.[399] Virtually all other commentators, however, depict the child as Christ or His church in various ways. The intriguing aspect is how these authors are able to read the church into both the woman and her child.

Hippolytus assumed the woman to be the church. He, therefore, had to depict the man-child as the product of the church rather than as her originator. He reasoned that the church was to "always bring forth Christ."[400] Thus, Christ, as seen through the gospel, is said to be given birth to by the church. Victorinus rejected this, acknowledging that Christ is depicted in the man-child. In order to explain how the church could be His mother, he merely shifted the woman to the "ancient church."[401] This is a subtle acknowledgement that Israel is the mother, but allows him to read replacement theology into the Scripture. Methodius, on the other hand, simply called the man-child the "faithful" within the church.[402]

Hippolytus' logic is an attempt to justify his identification of the woman, but it does not follow reasonably. Christ is the father of the church, not her son. Despite this fact, Joseph Mede continued to use this line of logic, saying that the child is "mystical Christ, or Christ formed in his members, the sonne not of Mary but of the Church, according to that of the Apostle to the Galatians 4:19."[403] This passage does compare the church to a woman in labor, but does not explain how the imagery here could depict Christ as both father of the church and her child at the same time. It takes the Galatians passage out of context and puts it into a context which would make the church the "one" "who is to rule all the nations with a rod of iron" (vs. 5).

John Bale took a more simple approach, arguing that the church "had Christ in her womb from the beginning."[404] In either case, the logic fails when one examines it closely. If the man-child is Christ, and He is, then no amount of semantic word twisting can equate the church with the man-child. In essence, Hippolytus, Mede, and Bale are all acknowledging that the man-child is Christ. They attempt to read the church into Christ, but the image itself is of Christ. This has become the predominant view since the decline of historicism. Only a handful continue to see the man-child as the "invisible church,"[405] and most of these commentators are partial rapturists (see Appendix A) who attempt to read the "overcomers" into the vision of the man-child.

Govett and Seiss, the originators of partial rapture theory, here deviate from their usual careful logic. Govett says "the Child is the same body as the Great Multitude of chapter vii"[406] but Seiss goes even further. Seiss believes that the child represents the invisible church as opposed to the visible church which he equates with the woman.[407] He even goes to the inexplicable extreme of arguing that "the word ($\check{\alpha}\rho\sigma\epsilon\nu$) which means *male*, has the peculiarity of being in the neuter gender, and so applies to both men and women, and cannot apply to any one individual."[408] This bizarre argument is designed to prove that the word "male" (and Seiss has admitted that is its meaning) actually refers to both males and females. While saying that it is in the neuter gender, he ignores that it is also in the singular form, not the plural as he implies. The fact is that the Greek form of $\check{\alpha}\rho\sigma\epsilon\nu$ merely conforms the proper noun $\upsilon\grave{\iota}\grave{o}\nu$, meaning "son," which it modifies. It is an added emphasis that this is a *male* child. No Greek text will argue that "male" can refer to females. Seiss is merely attempting to justify his assumption that the child is the church.

This vein of interpretation used by the partial rapturists is connected to their belief that the child's being "caught up to God and to His throne" (vs. 5) is a rapture passage. In order to read the rapture in this passage, the partial rapturists declare that the man-child is "not the whole church but are the overcomers within the church."[409] They believe that only these "overcomers" are to be found in the man-child, hence the child is a part of the church, but not inclusive of it. It is the "invisible church" as opposed to the "visible church."[410]

G. H. Lang correctly argued that "there must be some consistency in interpreting symbols"[411] but then suggests that "if the man-child be an individual, Jesus, so must be his mother, and the woman will be Mary. But [there is] no counterpart in the experiences of the Lord's mother and brothers."[412] He presumes that if the child is an individual, so must the woman, but this is not necessarily so. The preterist view that this is Mary cannot hold up, for despite the similarities, there is nothing in Mary's history to coincide with all the events described here. It is unlikely that he would give such an innaccurate depiction of past events in the midst of a prophecy of the future. Moreover, Lang is employing reverse logic to prove that the child *is not* Christ. Rather than beginning with this seemingly easy identification and extrapolating the meaning of the woman, he has argued in reverse, saying that if the woman is not Mary, neither can the child be Jesus; a logically flawed assumption.

This is not unusual for partial rapturists, for they, like those who see the church in this child, begin not with the identification of the child, but with the identification of another passage. Those who see the church in the woman read the child to match. Those who see partial rapture in the "catching up to the throne" interpret the child to match that. In each case, they are beginning with their conclusions. Proper exegesis should begin with the text, and not with our assumptions. Revelation 2:27 and 19:15 explicitly identify the one "who is to rule all the nations with a rod of iron" as our Savior, Jesus Christ. Few Christian scholar seems to refute the identification in 2:27 and 19:15, yet in 12:5 they attempt to shift the iron rod from Christ to His church, or His "overcomers." Both views are false. The man-child is the one "who is to rule all the nations with a rod of iron," and that is the Lord Jesus Christ. He is none other than the the promised Messiah.

The Arguments and Evaluation of the Woman
Having identified the child as Christ "who is to rule all the nations with a rod of iron" (vs. 12:5. Also see 2:27, and 19:15) it is now more practical to identify the woman who gives birth to Him.

The imagery is quite vivid. The woman is said to be "clothed with the sun" with "the moon under her feet, and on her head a crown of twelve stars" (vs. 1). These images are not unique. In Genesis 37 the same imagery is seen in

Joseph's dream. "The sun and the moon and eleven stars were bowing down to me" (vs. 9). According to Jacob, the sun and moon were Joseph's father and mother, and the eleven stars were Joseph's brothers (vs.10). Thus we see the image of twelve stars representing the twelve tribes of Israel. The sun has been variously identified as God the Father and as Christ.[413] However, if Christ is the child, as has been shown, then it is probably best to identify the sun as God the Father. It is possible that the moon is the preincarnate Christ, but the real trouble is not in identifying the sun and the moon, but in the twelve stars. Are they, as in Joseph's dream, the twelve patriarchs as Ironside believes[414] or are they the twelve apostles as Hippolytus[415] and Bale believed?[416]

If one ignores the Biblical imagery found in Genesis then it is imagination which begins to run wild. Watchman Nee argues that moon represents Israel under dispensation of law while the twelve stars represent those under dispensation of the patriarchs.[417] Although borrowing from Genesis, this view goes too far and reads much into the text which is not there. Another view was that of Arthur Bloomfield who declared that the moon is a symbol of "darkness or error."[418] He has, therefore, somehow concluded that this means that the church is "victorious" over error.[419] On the crown with twelve stars he says that "the crown is a symbol of royalty"[420] but does not specify the meaning of the twelve stars. Such reasoning seems common among those who identify the woman with the church. Although the designation of the twelve stars has been made with the twelve apostles,[421] and is conceivable, the problems that such a view creates negates its possibility. One has only to look at the statements of the position's advocates to see its flaws.

Amillennialist Henry Swete admits that Israel is the intended mother but then attempts to shift this to the "larger Israel,"[422] which he calls the church. He believes that "the woman who gave birth to Christ is afterwards identified with her who after its departure suffered for her faith in Him."[423] Thus he admits that Israel is intended as the woman who gave birth to Christ, but he then shifts the woman to the church after Christ's birth. George Ladd gets around the issue by saying the woman "represents the ideal people of God."[424] The same dancing is done by other advocates of the position. They must all explain how the church can be both the offspring of Christ and her mother as well.

Of the more natural interpretations, one unique view has been submitted by Henry Morris. He agrees that Israel is included within the imagery but says that woman's origins must go all the way back to Eve.[425] He believes that the imagery of the chapter is reminiscent of the prophecy of the serpent and the seed of the woman in Genesis 3:15. He, therefore, concludes that the "woman must represent all true believers, beginning with Eve herself."[426] Certainly the prophecy of Genesis 3:15 can bee seen in this passage but the identification of the woman as Eve and her descendants is not as clear. This is evident in Morris' struggle to identify the symbology of the sun, moon, and stars.[427]

Robert Govett seems close to the correct answer when he says that the woman is Jerusalem[428] but if we allow the Bible to interpret itself then the twelve stars appear to represent specifically the twelve tribes of Israel, not the city of Jerusalem. This would be consistent with the application of Christ to the man-child, for the church is referred to as the bride of Christ, not as His mother.[429] Therefore, the mother must be either accepted as the Virgin Mary or as Israel. Preterists have opted for the former, but most others recognize that Mary neither fit the prophecies nor would her inclusion here make sense against the backdrop of the tribulation. The second alternative makes perfect sense, especially given the imagery of the twelve stars as seen in Genesis 37:9.

The Arguments and Evaluation of the Events which Follow

Whether the woman be the church or Israel, as this author believes, verses five through fourteen detail her plight at the hands of the dragon who is all but universally accepted as the devil. That anyone could reject this is inconcevable since verse nine explicitly states that the dragon is "the serpent of old who is called the devil and Satan."[430]

Our question then is what does Satan do to the woman? What is meant by the catching up to the throne (vs. 5), the flight to the desert (vs. 6 and 14), and her time in the desert (vs. 6 and 14)? The rapture (see Appendix A), or rather the "catching up to the throne of God" is the most controversial aspect of this prophecy. Some see in it the rapture of the entire church or a part of the church while others see it merely as Christ's resurrection. Still others read historicism into the passage and even go so far as to identify the rapture with the coming of Constantine![431]

Among the futurist school of thought, the mire of historicism is washed away and the controversies become fewer, although no less heated. The first issue is that of the child's being "caught up to the throne of God" (vs. 5). The imagery is that of rapture or resurrection, so the primary question lies in the identification of the child. Those who see the child as Christ identify the rapture as an allusion back to the resurrection of Christ but others, who see the church in the child, believe this is a rapture passage. This is particularly the view of the partial rapturists. According to Seiss "the instant the Man-child is born, it is *'caught away to God, and to His throne*,'"[432] but he goes on to say that while "the picture is plainly meant to be a summary one ... the fact [is] that not all belonging to the body come to the Birth at one and the same instant."[433] He further connects rapture events with chapters four, five, seven, and fourteen as well.[434] Govett also takes this line of reasoning saying that "the Child ascends as soon as he is born"[435] and connecting him with the "overcomers."[436]

The careful reader will note several critical problems with their exegesis at this point. First, the Bible nowhere says that the child is caught up to God *at the moment* of his birth. This is an assumption which underlies the partial rapture theory but is nowhere stated in this passage or any parallel passage. Secondly, the association of the child with the "overcomers" cannot here be equated with the rapture because verse eleven expressly states, "they overcame him because of the blood of the Lamb and because of the word of their testimony, and *they did not love their life even to death.*" Thus the overcomers of verse eleven do not appear to be raptured, but instead appear to lay down their lives for their faith. It is for this reason that they are called overcomers, not because they are raptured.

Despite the weakness of the partial rapturists' interpretation, there are actually some pretribulationists who follow them in placing the rapture in Revelation 12:5. Arthur Bloomfield is one such author, but how can he place rapture before the tribulation while seeing it in Revelation 12:5? In order to achieve this sleight of hands he actually places the events of Revelation 12 before the 70th week of Daniel but after the seven seals (see Appendix D for more on Bloomfield's unique chronology). According to Bloomfield the idea of being "caught up" "could not possibly apply to Christ," because Jesus "ascended" to heaven.[437] He further states that "the Bible does not use symbols to prophecy past events."[438] His first argument is little more than splitting semantic hairs, but his second argument is better, if unconvincing. That the prophecy itself is about the future is not denied by futurists interpreters. What is denied, is that the Bible cannot make reference to past events, even when those events help to further identify the child.

John Walvoord admits the problem, noting that "the same word is used for the rapture of the church"[439] but points out that "there is no good reason for not identifying the man-child as Christ and interpreting the drama of verse 5 as the panorama of His birth, life, and ascension."[440] As Walvoord has said, "the fact that He is caught up not only to God but to 'his throne' is another indication that Christ is intended."[441] Indeed, how can the partial rapturists believe that we, the church, will all sit on the throne of God? God's throne is for one man only; the Messiah, Jesus Christ.

A final proof of this is the fact that the woman, including the 144,000 (who are still on earth in chapter fourteen – see below), flee the Dragon's wrath *after* the child is caught up to the throne. Partial rapturists must make these as the weak or spiritually immature Christians and deny that the 144,000 are involved. These 144,000 first appear in chapter seven and later reappear in chapter fourteen. Most believe they are one and the same body, although some dispute this. In either case, the issue in chapter twelve is what happens to the woman.

Whether the woman is Israel, the church, or those who have not yet overcome, what is her plight being described in these verses? We are told that she will flee "into the wilderness" where she will be protected by God "for one thousand two hundred and sixty days" (vs. 6). Most futurists take this flight literally. The imagery of the eagle's wings is found in both Exodus 19:4 and

Deuteronomy 32:11. In Exodus the Lord declared, "I bore you on eagle's wings, and brought you unto Myself." Hal Lindsey, on the other hand, believes that the eagle's wings may refer to an airlift by the United States, noting that the bald eagle is the national bird of the U.S.[442] This latter view is suspect, but in either case, the flight itself is held to be literal by most modern premillennialists. The question is then, to where does she fly?

The word for "wilderness" (ἔρημον) actually refers to a desolate area and is sometimes translated as "desert," as the NIV does. Most believe that the desert is what is referred to here. Joseph Seiss believes that the woman flees to the Sinai desert.[443] Robert Govett argues that because the eagle's wings of Exodus 19:4 brought the Jews to Sinai, the eagle's wings of Revelation must also bring them to the same destination.[444] He points out that in the parallel passage of Matthew 24:16 this desert region is also a mountainous regions since Christ said they will "flee to the mountains."[445] This, he believes, further affirms that Sinai is intended. However, there is another mountainous region near Israel.

The majority of modern futurists seem to favor the city of Petra in Jordan, near the Israeli border. The city covers a massive area surrounded by mountains. From the land there is only one narrow entrance which could be easily defended by a handful of people. The city, carved into the rock, is a natural fortress. While it had changed hands many times over the centuries, it is believed never to have been taken by force.[446] Because it resided in the middle of the desert it had become abandoned when trade caravans stopped travelling upon that route, but never had it been taken by siege.[447] This is the view taken by people like Norman Harrison[448] and, more recently, Hal Lindsey[449] and Robert Van Kampen.[450]

Van Kampem even believes that the Bible identifies this area by its ancient name. Recalling the words of Isaiah 16:1-4 Van Kampen suggests that this is a prophecy of the woman's fleeing and a parallel passage.[451] The capital of Edom, Sela, is the city mentioned and is believed to be an ancient name for Petra. However, it is by no means clear that this is a prophecy of end times at all. Walvoord gives no hint that this is an end times propechy.[452] Grogan also sees it as a prophecy long ago fulfilled in history,[453] as does John Martin.[454] The fact is that the Bible does not specifically identify the desert mountainous region. Sinai and Petra are both possibilities, but neither can be proven within the Scriptures themselves. Nevertheless, of the two theories, Petra seems the stronger because of its strong protective nature. Still, critics note several problems with the theory.

First, it is argued that if Petra is the location, then the anti-Christ would know where they are and feret them out. It is suggested that the location must be secret. However, it is unlikely that such a massive number of people would be able to keep their location a secret at all. There will be a minimum of 144,000 people and possibly as many as 5,000,000 Jews included in the flight.[455]

How could they keep their location a secret at all? Norman Harrison states that Petra can easily hold 250,000 people,[456] and others have even implied that it can hold 5,000,000 people.[457] Regardless of which number is more accurate, the fact is that these Jews will escape in massive numbers. Nowhere does the Bible say that the anti-Christ cannot find them, only that he cannot reach them since they are protected by God. In other words, there is nothing in the Bible to indicate that the anti-Christ does not know where they are hiding. He is merely unable to reach them. A greater problem with the theory is that while Petra was invulnerable to ancient sieges, modern warfare could be a different thing. It would not be hard to send thousands of paratroopers into the city from the sky or to attempt to bomb the city with air power. Nevertheless, even this is suspect. To begin with, the anti-Christ will be in the midst of World War III and cannot waste too many valuable resources on dissidents, no matter how much he hates them. Moreover, even with military air power, Petra could still put up a solid defense because of its geography. However, one other reason negates this argument altogether. When we remember that God is protecting these people, the problem disappears. Whether the people hide in Petra, or elsewhere, *they are protected by God.*

Now whether these Jews flee to Petra or Sinai, it is obvious that they are not the only believers. Verse seventeen makes it clear that once the anti-Christ finds himself unable to stop the woman, or rather Israel, he "went off to make war with the rest of her offspring, who keep the commandments of God and hold to the testimony of Jesus." These are the Gentile believers, and future martyrs, of the last days. Are Jews among these martyrs? Possibly. Nevertheless, the woman is the faithful of Israel and will be protected during this time. Some assign to her only the 144,000 while others assign all Jewish Christians. These Jews will survive unto the coming of the Lord.

So if they survive to the second coming, when do they flee? The chronological considerations are important. The Bible says first that they will be "nourished for one thousand two hundred and sixty days" (vs. 6) and later that she will be "nourished for a time and times and half a time" (vs. 14). Nathaniel West has commented "in Daniel and John, we find *one and the same measure of time represented by four different forms of expression,* viz. (1) 'time, times, (dual number) and the dividing (or half) of a time,' Den. vii:25, xii:7; Rev. xii:14; (2) 'half week,' Dan. ix:27; (3) '42 months,' Rev. xi:12; xiii:5; and (4) '1260 days' Rev. xi:3; xii:6."[458] That these four expressions all refer to a period of three and one half year can be demonstrated within the text themselves. Daniel 11:13 speaks of the expression of "times" as synonymous with "years." Likewise, the seven "times" of Nebuchadnezzar's madness is usually agreed to have been a period of seven years during which Nebuchadnezzar was demented. Thus, "time, times, and half a time" equals three and a half years. The half of a week a years is obviously three and a half years. So also, forty-two months according to the ancient Jewish calendar is

91

exactly 1260 days or three and a half years. Moreover, Daniel divides the 70th week into two separate halves by declaring that the abomination of desolation (cf. Matthew 24:15) will occur in the middle of the week (9:27).

We, therefore, have a declaration that the time of the woman's protection is exactly three and a half years located somewhere in the final 70th week of Daniel, but is this the first half of the week, the second half, or an overlapping period? Most agree it is synonymous with the second half of the tribulation. Contextually, this flight follows the murder of the two witnesses from chapter eleven (see Appendix D) which appears to occur at the middle of the tribulation in connection to the abomination of desolation. The pieces fit together quite well. The time of the Dragon's persecution of the woman appears to follow the abomination of desolation and the breaking of the peace treaty. It is inconceivable that the anti-Christ could actually persecute the Jews while the treaty was still valid, hence this flight and the period of the woman's protection begin at the middle of the tribulation immediately following the abomination of desolation, as Christ Himself forewarned, saying, "when you see the abomination of desolation which was spoken of through Daniel the prophet, standing in the holy place (let the reader understand), then let those who are in Judea flee to the mountains" (Matthew 24:15-16). Whether the mountains are in Petra or Sinai, the Lord Himself will watch over these men and woman for the last three and a half years of the tribulation.

Conclusion on the Woman Clothed with the Sun
Most commentators begin with an assumption and build their interpretations around them. The covenant theologians assume the church to be the woman, and build the imagery of the rest of the passage around it. Likewise, partial rapturists see the rapture in the child's being "caught up" to the throne of God and interpret the rest of the passage to fit that assumption. If the reader begins with the identification of the man-child, which is clear enough by a comparison of 12:5 with 2:27 and 19:15, the rest of the passage follows without much difficulty.

The proper meaning is that the woman depicts Israel's faithful. Israel gave birth to Christ, the Messiah, who was caught up to the throne of God in what is probably a brief "flashback" to the resurrection. The scene then shifts back to the tribulation where the woman (the faithful of Israel) is being persecuted by the anti-Christ. The faithful Jews, almost certainly including the 144,000, will flee Jerusalem after the abomination of desolation and hide in the desert for three and a half years where they will be protected from God. When the anti-Christ discovers that he cannot destroy these faithful Jews, he then turns to persecute the rest of the faithful, both Jewish and Gentile Christians throughout the world empire.

The 144,000 on Zion

"I looked, and behold, the Lamb *was* standing on Mount Zion, and with Him one hundred and forty-four thousand, having His name and the name of His Father written on their foreheads. And I heard a voice from heaven, like the sound of many waters and like the sound of loud thunder, and the voice which I heard *was* like *the sound* of harpists playing on their harps. And they sang a new song before the throne and before the four living creatures and the elders; and no one could learn the song except the one hundred and forty-four thousand who had been purchased from the earth. These are the ones who have not been defiled with women, for they have kept themselves chaste. These *are* the ones who follow the Lamb wherever He goes. These have been purchased from among men as first fruits to God and to the Lamb. And no lie was found in their mouth; they are blameless" (Revelation 14:1-5).

Their Relationship to Chapter Seven Debated
Are these the same 144,000 mentioned in chapter seven? Are they to be treated as a distinct group separate from the first? Most throughout history have agreed that these are one and the same who were first seen being sealed in chatper seven. However, a constant minority, penetrating every school of thought and every age, has maintained that they are separate from this group and must be interpreted distinctly.

Tim LaHaye has joined the ranks of those who see these as separate entities. Although he believes that the 144,000 from chapter seven are literal Jews, here he insists they are "Christians from all ages,"[459] later reasserting that they are *not* Jews.[460] LaHaye then comments that this "has for some reason eluded many."[461] In defense of his position he list numerous "differences" bewteen the "two" groups as shown below.[462]

The 144,000 from Chapter 7	The 144,000 from Chapter 14
vv. 1-3 : a scene on earth	v. 1 : a scene in heaven; the Lamb is with them on Mount Zion
v. 3 : "Servants of our God" is written on their foreheads	v. 1 : The name of God *and* Jesus are written on their foreheads
v. 4 : 144,000 from all the tribes of Israel	They are redeemed from the earth
vv. 5-8 : 12,000 from each tribe of Israel	They are not defiled with women
	The follow the Lamb
	They are purchased among men
	They are the first fruits of God and the Lamb
	There is no lie in their mouths
	They are blameless

Many of these alleged discrepancies are merely descriptive and do not constititue proof of sererate classes. We are told that the ones in chapter fourteen are blameless. Are the ones in chapter seven? Since the Bible is silent, so must we be. Chapter fourteen could be easily describing the 144,000 of chapter seven as well as the ones fourteen *if* they be one and the same. It must be proven *first* whether or not they are the same before this kind of distinction can be made. Nonetheless, LaHaye has brought up several points that are worthy of debate. Are the ones from chapter fourteen in heaven, as opposed to the earthly 144,000? Even many of those who believe the 144,000 are the same in each chapter, believe that the scene in chapter fourteen is one in heaven.

Since the Bible states that the 144,000 were on Zion, one might question why so many believe this is a scene in heaven. The appearance of the Lamb with the 144,000, apparently before His coming in chapter nineteen is doubtless the main reason for this charge. Charles Ryrie thinks that "since Zion is used of the heavenly Jerusalem (Heb. 12:22) and since these 144,000 are before the throne (v. 3), it seems more natural to understand Zion as the heavenly city."[463] However, Hebrews 12:22 reads, "you have come to Mount Zion *and* the city of the living God, the heavenly Jerusalem." "And" is in addition to, not synonymous with. Zion *is not* the heavenly Jerusalem, it is a destination of the Hebrews along with the ultimate goal of the heavenly Jerusalem.

Despite this, Walter Scott believes that the 144,000 of chapter fourteen are solely from the tribe of Judah as opposed to those from every tribe in chapter seven.[464] This is based on the assumption that Zion refers to the heavenly city where Judah is believed to reside.[465] To this Dwight Pentecost responds that "there is no proof given that those in chapter fourteen are from Judah,"[466] and one must concur. With Pentecost we should take this as literal Zion[467] unless there is good reason to believe it is not. In fact, there is reason to believe that this is the earthly Zion. In verse two John says, "I heard a voice *from* heaven." The Greek *ek* (ἐκ) literally means "from" our "out of."[468] This seems to imply that if the voice came "out of" heaven, then John and the 144,000 were not "in" heaven.

Ignoring, for the time being, those who believe these are a separate class of people, the question might asked of those who accept that these are the same as the 144,000 in chapter seven; how can they be in heaven? Were they not sealed with the seal of the Living God? Are they not protected? Edward Hindson believes these are the same 144,000[469] but argues that the sealing is for protection from wrath of God only, not from Satan wrath.[470] He, therefore, concludes that they have died a martyrs death at the hands of the anti-Christ.[471] Charles Ryrie also accepts this view saying, "their work of witnessing must now be finished, for none will be able to slay them until then."[472] Hindson, however, denies that witnessing is even a purpose for the 144,000. He claims that "they are never specifically called 'witnesses' ... nor are they called 'preachers' as many evangelicals assume."[473] Robert Gundry is adamant about this. He says, "nothing in these passages says that they'll replace *Christians* as preachers of the gospel during the Tribulation"[474] and "who's to say anyway, that Christians couldn't live on earth at the same time as the 144,000, and even preach the gospel at the same time they do – *if* they do."[475] Of course Gundry's remarks echo his strong anti-dispensational attitude since no one denies that Christians will exist and witness the gospel along with the 144,000. Nonetheless, the idea of the 144,000 being worldwide evangelists is a popular one. While it is not explicit anywhere in Revelation, the Great Commission (Matthew 28:19-20) should be sufficient proof that this is at least one of their duties, while it may not be their primary purpose. G. B. Caird believes that the counting "was a military roll-call, like the census of 1 Chronicles iv-vii. This [144,000] is the army of the Lord."[476] In either case, the real debate is whether or not their seal protects them from martyrdom.

Hindson and Ryrie deny that their seal grants them protection from being slain by the anti-Christ, but both agree that the woman depicted in chapter twelve represents Israel and includes the 144,000. Now chapter twelve depicts the flight of the woman who is escaping the wrath of the anti-Christ and it also depicts divine intervention on her behalf (vs. 16). We are explicitly told that she will "be nourished for one thousand two hundred and sixty days" (vs. 6). In other words, these Israelites, and the 144,000, will be *"nourished"* and protected for the last three and a half years of the tribulation. This excludes her death at the hands of the anti-Christ. Certainly, many Christians will be slain during this time period, but woman is specially protected so that she will survive unto the end and may inherit the Millennial Kingdom. If she dies before then, she would not be able to inherit the Kingdom as mortals. This is the crux of the problem with posttribulationism (see Appendix A) and it is the crux of the problem in seeing these 144,000 as martyrs. In short, if these are the same 144,000 as seen in chapter seven then they *must* be on the literal Zion in Israel, not in heaven.

So are these the same class of people? It has been demonstrated that this Zion cannot be proven to be a scene in heaven. Thus, of LaHaye's four main arguments, three remain. The seals in chapter seven were said to be the "the seal of the living God" (vs. 2), but in chapter fourteen we are told that "His name and the name of His Father written on their foreheads" (vs.1). Is this a different seal as LaHaye contends? No. Although LaHaye believes that the "first group" had "Servants of our God" is written on their foreheads[477] the actual text reads, "we [the angels] have sealed the bond-servants of our God on their foreheads" (vs. 3). "Sevants of our God" is a description of those sealed, not the exact words which are placed on their foreheads. The fact is that we are not told what the seal says until chapter fourteen. There is no proof that these are different seals.

The last two evidences LaHaye makes can be addressed as one. He believes that the 144,000 of chapter seven cannot be the same as in fourteen because the 144,000 of seven are said to be from each of the tribes of Israel while the ones in fourteen are said to be "redeemed from the earth" and "purchased among men."[478] He takes the "earth" and "men" as a reference to the Gentile world and not Israel,[479] but Walter Scott, who also sees these as a separate class, takes the opposite view here. He believes that "earth" is a reference to Palestine[480] and hence identifies these as Jews.[481] Thus we must now question whether these 144,000 are Jews or Gentiles. If they be Jews, then they must assuredly be the same as in chapter seven. While LaHaye saw those as Jews, he sees these as believers from all ages.[482] This is, however, impossible for in verse three the 144,000 stand opposite the Elders in whom most see the church. As Joseph Seiss says, "the sealed ones are one company, complete in itself; and the Elders and Living ones are another company complete itself. John beholds them both at the same time, the one in the presence of the other, but each with its own separate place, character, and blessedness. The 144,000 therefore can by no possibility 'represent the glorified company of the whole church.'"[483]

Still others have presented alternate theories. Watchman Nee says "the 144,000 standing on Mt. Zion are the best overcomers of the church."[484] Govett calls them "the heavenly elect."[485] Hindson believes "the 144,000 represent the whole nation or a specific group (male virgins) within the whole nation."[486] All are speculating. The only clear reference to their identity is in chapter seven; a parallel chapter. There is no evidence to disconnect the two. As one author comments, "chapter seven told us of a body of people consisting of this precise number, of which we can hardly suppose two, unless specially instructed to that effect."[487] It is not logical to take the two as separate for "the history of the 144,000 in chapter VII is incomplete taken by itself."[488] We would be left having two separate classes of 144,000 with the purpose for each being a mystery. It is best to reject the view that these are separate people and concur with William Newell,[489] and the majority of other expositors, that these are one and the same people as spoken of in chapter seven.

If this is so then one last question remains. What of the throne in verse three? Does this not conclude that they are in heaven? If not, what does it mean? What are the 144,000 doing on Zion? The answer depends largely on the chronological considerations. If the scene occurs years prior to the second coming then this almost certainly must be a scene in heaven, casting doubt on whether or not the 144,000 will truly be preserved from death to the coming of the Millennium. If, on the other hand, it is a foreshadowing of Christ at His coming then all the problems are elimiated. As Nathaniel West says, "it shows us elect Israel, now safe, *after* the Antichrist's 1260 days are over, and the Trumpet-Judgments are gone. Contrasted with another company in Heaven, they stand on the earthly Mount Zion singing a 'New Song.'"[490] Whether the throne is Christ's newly established throne in Jerusalem or the throne in heaven opened for all on earth to see, the 144,000 can be viewed as literally standing on Zion awaiting their inheritance of the land.

Concerning this chronology it is important to note that chapter fourteen is viewed almost universally as an interlude, not in time sequence with the rest of the events of Revelation. Nathaniel West calls it "proleptic," or anticipatory.[491] This is nowhere more obvious than in commentators' all but universal belief that verses fourteen through twenty refer to the final days and the Battle of Armageddon. Indeed, the winepress of God is almost always accepted by premillennialists as referring to the blood spilt at Armageddon (see chapter 7). Tim LaHaye's own Prophecy Study Bible says, "these verses describe a scene of Jesus Christ in heaven just before He descends to the earth for the Battle of Armageddon and His glorius appearing,"[492] yet this battle does not occur until several chapters later.

It must, therefore, be concluded that this passage describes the one and same 144,000 elect sealed by God. They are at Mount Zion with the Lord after He descends to establish the Millennial Kingdom and give the land to His people as their promised inheritance.

On Their Virginity

Yet another controversy concerning these 144,000 is the nature of their chasity or virginity. Most translations read "they were virgins." However, the NAS and RSV both read "chaste," while the NIV reads "they had kept themselves pure." The Greek word *parthenoi* (παρθένοι) is correctly translated as "virgins," so the issue is not so much the meaning of the word, as the meaning of the passage. Those who read "chaste" or "purity" tend to interpret the meaning spirutally. They suggest that "there is not more impurity in marriage than in abstinence from marriage. Celibacy is no the subject or virtue in this description, but *purity*, freedom from contamination by the corruptions which prevail in their time."[493]

Some prefer to read the passage as "chaste" rather than "virgins"[494] while others believe that "to be undefiled with women would be synonymous with being a Christian."[495] Still others are noncommital saying "perhaps" it is spiritual for not prostituting themselves with the anti-Christ.[496] Perhaps, as some suggest, the virginity represents a refusal to bow to idoloatry.[497] A number maintain that this passage should be read quite literally as "virgins." It should be said at the outset that this passage has created unnecessary tensions. Some consider this to be a divisive issue despite the fact that it has no bearing on any other passage. Robert Gundry arrogantly protest that the literal view is a "pretribulation view,"[498] but nowhere is there a scholar, and such he is, more identified with literal pretribulationism, nor more derided, than Hal Lindsey. Does Lindsey say these are literal virgins? He says, "the celibacy of these men refers not so much to *sexual* purity (although this is important) but to separation from *spiritual* fornication and adultery (James 4:4)."[499] Another famed pretribulationists is John Walvoord, former chancelor of Dallas Theological Seminary back in its heyday. He argues that "'virgin' is used of both men and women as in II Corinthians 11:2 in reference to the church as a bride."[500] He then cites numerous passages which refer to the "virgin daughter of Zion" (Lamentataions 2:13) and the "virgin of Israel" (Jeremiah 18:13; 31:4; 21; Amos 5:2) as proof that spiritual virginity may be intended.[501] Thus Gundry's agenda against pretribulationists is misplaced in this discourse. Many dispensationalists accept the spiritual application of this passage, and to do so is not to deny the literal. However, the view may be misplaced.

All protestants are in agreement that there is no impurity in marital relationships. Nevertheless, the apostle Paul does speak of celibacy as both good and as a gift (1 Corinthians 7:1; 7:7). Protestants should not overreact to the Catholic dogma of celibacy of the priesthood, for there is good reason to believe that literal virginity is intended here. The passage states not only that they were virgins, but that they "have not been defiled with women" (vs. 4). This seems to imply a direct cause and effect relationship which would loose its force if the passage were to be spiritually understood. Of course, it is responded that chasity is sufficient to fulfill this requirement. Indeed, a chaste man is not defiled by having sex with his wife. The question then falls back to the word *parthenoi* (παρθένοι) or "virginity." Govett states that "these words exclude the married; the married may have chasity, but not virginity."[502] If chasity were intended then John would have used the word *agnai* (ἁγνὰι), not *parthenoi* (παρθένοι). The fact that the chaste are not included in this passage should not disturb anyone. Each man will receive his reward. Would anyone suggest that because Moses was married, his exclusion from these 144,000 is prejudicial? There is nothing in virginity which proves spiritually superiority, but neither is there reason to reject the literal reading of the passage. Were it not for the explicit mention of defilement with women, the spiritual application would be valid, but it appears to be misplaced here.

Summary of Israel and the Church

The critical passages cited in this chapter give the reader an overview of Israel, or more specifically of the 144,000 elect, throughout the 70th week of Daniel. They first appear in chapter seven and are sealed for protection against both the wrath of God and the anti-Christ. Some believe the sealing does not occur until after the six seals are opened while others maintain that the passage is a flashback to the beginning of the tribulation. Arthur Bloomfield believes that the sealing was not needed in the early tribulation because "it would not be supposed that the Antichrist would be killing Jews in Palestine at the same time he is confirming a covenant with them."[503] While such is valid reasoning Hal Lindsey believes that "Revelation 7 gives us a parenthetical panorama ... by flashing back to the very *beginning* of the seven-year period, where God sends

144,000 evangelists out with the gospel message *before* any judgments at all are permitted to fall upon the earth."[504] In either case, it is apparent that the 144,000 are chosen and sealed before they are in harms way.

In chapter eleven we are now told that Israel has rebuilt its temple and worship has been restored during the evangelism of the two witnesses, if not the whole company of 144,000. When these two men are slain and when the abomination of desolation has occured, the faithful of Israel, including but not exclusive to the 144,000, will flee to the desert mountains where they are protected by God. There they will reside until the judgments of God are finished and until the coming of Christ. The anti-Christ will be unable to feret these men out and will thus turn his hatred to the Christians throughout the world that are within his grasp.

In chapter fourteen we have a picture of the end, when Christ returns to the earth and these 144,000 receive their reward. They are on hand for the inauguration of the Millennial Kingdom. They are the pure and undefiled elect of Israel who will lead their people back into the promised land and the Millennial Kingdom. They are the "first fruits" of God and receive a special blessing. These are the true children of Israel. They and the surviving Israelites will make literally true the words of the apostle Paul, "and thus all Israel will be saved; just as it is written, 'the Deliverer will come from Zion'" (Romans 11:26), where the 144,000 are also.

CHAPTER SUMMARY

Chapters 7, 11:1-2, 12, and 14:1-5 are interludes in the story of the tribulation. They revolve around the people of God; specifically, the people of Israel. In these chapters the follow is revealed.

1. The 144,000 sealed by God are special elect believers from the tribes of Israel. The tribes of Dan and Ephraim are omitted because of past sins with idolatry, but they will receive their blessings and allotment in the kingdom to come. They are excluded only from these select group of believers.
2. The temple of Jerusalem will be rebuilt. For some reason, debated by many, the outer court is held to be unhallowed and will be trampled by the gentiles. It is in the middle of the tribulation that the anti-Christ will defile the temple and commit the abomination of desolation.
3. There are two witnesses who are prophets of God. One of these two will be Elijah (see Appendix C). They boldly proclaim the gospel during the first half of the tribulation but are murdered in the middle of the tribulation in close proximity to the abomination of desolation. There their bodies are left out for all to see, but after three and a half days they are resurrected from the dead. It is at this time that an earthquake shakes the city, and the 144,000 flee for the mountains as Jesus forewarned (Matthew 24).

4. The woman clothed with the sun is believing Israel. The anti-Christ will attempt to slaughter them but they will flee for the mountains. An earthquake will prevent the anti-Christ from killing them, and they will be protected by God until He returns. As a result, the anti-Christ will persecute all the remaining believers and vent his wrath upon them.
5. The 144,000 of chapter fourteen are the same 144,000 as in chapter seven, but here is a glimpse of them on Mount Zion after the return of the Lord.

Study Charts on the 144,000

Hippolytus	Chiliast	Apparently sees the 144,000 as literal Jews.
Ephraem the Syrian	Chiliast	Apparently literal Jews.
Victorinus	Chiliast	Sees them as literal Jews.
Adso of Montier	Medieval Chiliast	Literal Jews.
Nicholas of Lyra	Medieval Millenarian	Sees the 144,000 as the Church.
John Bale	Historicist amillennialists	Literal Jews.
Robert Maton	Historicist amillennialists	Literal Jews.
Joseph Mede	Historicist premillennialist	Sees them as "surrogated Israel."
John Darby	Dispensational premillennialist	Sees them as literal Jews but sees the number as symbolic.
Samuel Kellogg	Futurist premillennialist	Sees them as literal Jews.
Sir Robert Anderson	Futurist premillennialist	Sees them as literal Jews who will be restored the land of Palestine.
Robert Govett	Futurist premillennialist	Literal Jews.
Joseph Seiss	Futurist premillennialist	Literal Jews.
E. W. Bullinger	Ultradispensationalist	Literal Jews.
Dwight Pentecost	Dispensational premillennialist	Literal Jews.
Norman Harrison	Midtribulational premillennialist	Sees them as literal Jews but sees the number as symbolic.
John Walvoord	Dispensational premillennialist	Literal Jews.
George Ladd	Posttribulational Premillennialist	As symbolic for an indifinite number of Gentile believers.
Hal Lindsey	Dispensational premillennialist	Literal Jews.
Marvin Rosenthal	"Pre-wrath" premillennialist	Literal Jews.

Historical Survey

	Position
Church Fathers	Almost universally sees the 144,000 as literal Jews.
Medieval Theologians	The medievals were split in their view with the symbolic interpretation that the 144,000 refers to the church taking prominence toward the later part of the Middle Ages.
Reformation Scholars	Mixed opinions but with the literal view regaining strong prominence.
Post-Reformation Scholars	Overwhelmingly of the opinion that they are literal Jews but with notable dissenters.
Modern Evangelicals	Overwhelmingly of the opinion that they are literal Jews but with notable dissenters.

Theological Breakdown

	Position
Premillennial Historicists	Opinions are roughly evenly mixed on whether they should be seen as literal Jews or the church.
Dispensational Pretribulational Premillennialists	Unanimously of the opinion that they are literal Jews.
Midtribulational (and "Pre-Wrath") Premillennialists	Mixed opinions.
Covenant Theologians and Postribulational Premillennialists	Predominantly of the view that this is symbolic for the church, and not true Israel.
Progressive Dispensationalists and other variant Premillenial views	Mixed opinions.

The 144,000 as the Church

Tenants of:

The 144,000 are accepted as "spiritual Israel," or Gentile members of the church.

Popular advocates from:

The Church Fathers : None cited (probably Origen).
Medieval Theologians : Nicholas of Lyra.
Reformation Scholars : Joseph Mede.
Post-Reformation Scholars : No premillennialists cited.
Modern Evangelicals : George Ladd, Robert Mounce, and Robert Gundry.

Strengths:

1) Romans 11 makes a connection between the church and Israel.
2) The absence of the tribes of Dan and Ephraem imply there is something different here.
3) Paul said "there is neither Jew nor Gentile" in Christ (Galatians 3:28). Thus, it is supposedly a contradiction to specify these as Jews.

Weaknesses:

1) The repitition of each of the tribes of Israel cannot be symbolized adequately.
2) The passage appear straightforward that these are Jews.
3) These 144,000 are contrasted with the Great Multitude, whom all agree are Gentiles.
4) If John needed instuction on the Great Multitude, why not the twelve tribes?
5) Roman 11 properly read says we are "grafted" *into* Israel, not that we replace Israel.
6) There is nowhere in the Bible where the proper name "Israel," or any of its tribes, is used symbolically of the church. Romans 11 does not constitute a symbolic use.
7) The view that this was the church originated many hundreds of years after the fact, and is not supported by the early church fathers.
8) Paul said "there is neither Jew nor Gentile" in Christ (Galatians 3:28), but he also said "first to the Jews, and then to the Gentile," (Romans 2:10) implying there is still a certain distinction.
9) The absence of the tribes of Dan and Ephraem is also an argument against the symbolic use, for why exclude the tribes if they were merely symbolic.

The 144,000 as Literal Jews

Tenants of:

The 144,000 are accepted as literal Jews from the tribes of Israel.

Popular advocates from:

The Church Fathers : Victorinus, Hippolytus, Ephraem the Syrian.

Medieval Theologians : Adso of Montier.

Reformation Scholars : John Bale and Robert Maton.

Post-Reformation Scholars : John Darby, Samuel Kellogg, Nathaniel West, Sir Robert Anderson, Robert Govett, Joseph Seiss, Walter Scott, and E. W. Bullinger.

Modern Evangelicals : C.I. Scofield, H. A. Ironside, William Newell, Watchman Nee, J. Dwight Pentecost, Arthur Bloomfield, Charles Ryrie, Tim LaHaye, Hal Lindsey, Robert Thomas, John Walvoord, and Marvin Rosenthal.

Strengths:

1) The repitition of each of the tribes of Israel screams literal.

2) There is nothing in the context to imply that the proper name "Israel," or any of its tribes, is used symbolically of the church.

3) The twelve stars echoes Genesis 37 which is clearly a symbol of Israel, not the church.

4) The view that this was the church originated many hundreds of years after the fact, and is not supported by the earliest church fathers.

5) The absence of the tribes of Dan and Ephraem implies there is something real and literal here. Dan and Ephraem must be excluded for some reason. Their absence cannot be explained if the tribes reference the twelve apostles.

6) John did not need instuction on the twelve tribes because they are clearly Israelites.

7) These 144,000 are contrasted with the Great Multitude, whom all agree are Gentiles.

Weaknesses:

1) The absence of the tribes of Dan and Ephraem is conversly argued to imply that there is something different here, and, therefore, symbolic.

2) Paul said "there is neither Jew nor Gentile" in Christ (Galatians 3:28). Thus, it is supposedly a contradiction to specify these as Jews.

Study Charts on the Temple in Jerusalem

Irenaeus	Chiliast	A literal temple in Jerusalem.
Hippolytus	Chiliast	A literal temple in Jerusalem.
Lactantius	Chiliast	A literal temple in Jerusalem.
Ephraem	Chiliast	A literal temple in Jerusalem.
Victorinus	Chiliast	The temple as a representation of the church.
Adso of Montier	Medieval Chiliast	A literal temple in Jerusalem.
Nicholas of Lyra	Medieval Millenarian	The temple as the church.
Joseph Mede	Historicist premillennialist	The temple as the church.
John Darby	Dispensational premillennialist	A literal temple in Jerusalem.
Nathaniel West	Dispensational premillennialist	A literal temple in Jerusalem.
Samuel Kellogg	Dispensational premillennialist	A literal temple in Jerusalem.
Robert Govett	Futurist premillennialist	A literal temple in Jerusalem.
Joseph Seiss	Futurist premillennialist	A literal temple in Jerusalem.
Samuel Kellogg	Dispensational premillennialist	A literal temple in Jerusalem.
G. H. Pember	Futurist premillennialist	A literal temple in Jerusalem.
H. A. Ironside	Dispensational premillennialist	A literal temple in Jerusalem.
Norman Harrison	Midtribulational premillennialist	A literal temple in Jerusalem.
John Walvoord	Dispensational premillennialist	A literal temple in Jerusalem.
George Ladd	Posttribulational Premillennialist	The temple as the church.
Hal Lindsey	Dispensational premillennialist	A literal temple in Jerusalem.
Marvin Rosenthal	"Pre-wrath" premillennialist	A literal temple in Jerusalem.

Historical Survey

	Position
Church Fathers	Predominantly of the proposition that it was a real rebuilt temple in Jerusalem. A few dissenting voices call it a representation of the church.
Medieval Theologians	A swing toward the allegorical interpretation with the temple as the church, but a number still believed in a literal temple in Jerusalem.
Reformation Scholars	A mix of opinions with the majority still accepting the medieval view that the temple was the church.
Post-Reformation Scholars	Predominantly of the proposition that it was a real rebuilt temple in Jerusalem.
Modern Evangelicals	Predominantly of the proposition that it was a real rebuilt temple in Jerusalem. Covenant Theologians, however, call it a representation of the church.

Theological Breakdown

	Position
Premillennial Historicists	Largely but not exclusively of the view that the temple represented the church.
Dispensational Pretribulational Premillennialists	Almost exclusively of the literal interpretation which accepts this as the real and literal rebuilt temple in Jerusalem.
Midtribulational (and "Pre-Wrath") Premillennialists	Predominantly of the opinion that it is a real and literal rebuilt temple in Jerusalem.
Covenant Theologians and Postribulational Premillennialists	Almost exclusively of the interpretation which accepts the temple as a symbol of the church.
Progressive Dispensationalists and other variant Premillenial views	An increasing mixture on the view but with the tendancy to accept the literal temple in Jerusalem.

The Temple as the Church
Tenants of:
This view believes that the temple merely represents the church as a whole.
Christ is seen as the Altar. It rejects the literal reading of the passage.

Popular advocates from:
The Church Fathers : Victorinus.
Medieval Theologians : Nicholas of Lyra.
Reformation Scholars : Joseph Mede.
Post-Reformation Scholars : None cited.
Modern Evangelicals : George Ladd, Robert Mounce, and Robert Gundry.

Strengths:
1) The word "temple" is used of anywhere where the Lord resides, including the church.
2) "Temple" does have a symbolic usage sometimes.

Weaknesses:
1) If "temple" does equal the church then the altar, worshippers, and court must also be interpreted symbolically, but no consensus can be reached.
2) There are no symbolic uses of the court of the Gentiles found elsewhere in the Bible or apocryphal literature.
3) The temple is expressly said to be in the holy city.
4) The "holy city" is nowhere used symbolically.

The Temple as a Literally Rebuilt Temple in Jerusalem
Tenants of:
This view accepts the natural reading of the text as a literal rebuilt temple of Jerusalem in the last days where ritual sacrifice and offerings will be resumed by the Jews.

Popular advocates from:
The Church Fathers : Irenaeus, Hippolytus, and Ephraem.
Medieval Theologians : Adso of Montier.
Reformation Scholars : Probably Robert Maton and John Bale.
Post-Reformation Scholars : John Darby, Samuel Kellogg, Nathaniel West, Sir Robert Anderson, Walter Scott, Robert Govett, Joseph Seiss, and G. H. Pember.
Modern Evangelicals : William Newell, H. A. Ironside, G. H. Lang, Arthur Bloomfield, Charles Ryrie, Tim LaHaye, Hal Lindsey, Robert Thomas, John Walvoord, Henry Morris, and Marvin Rosenthal.

Strengths:
1) The references to the altar, worshippers, holy city, and outer court all imply a literal temple, and would make little sense symbolically.
2) A literal temple seems apparent in parallel passages like 2 Thessalonians 2:4 and Daniel 9:27.
3) The temple is expressly said to be in the holy city, which cannot be read for anything but Jerusalem. If "holy city" is taken literally, why not the temple in it?
4) The passage does not suggests an allegorical reading.
5) There are no symbolic uses of the court of the Gentiles found elsewhere in the Bible or apocryphal literature.

Weaknesses:
1) The word "temple" is occasionally used of the church.

Study Charts on the Woman Clothed with the Sun

Hippolytus	Chiliast	The church.
Methodius	Chiliast	The church.
Victorinus	Chiliast	The prophets, saints, and apostles.
Pierre D'Olivi	Medieval Millenarian	The church.
Nicholas of Lyra	Medieval Millenarian	The church.
Joseph Mede	Historicist premillennialist	The church.
Isaac Newton	Historicist premillennialist	The church.
John Darby	Dispensational premillennialist	The Jews.
Robert Govett	Futurist premillennialist	Jerusalem.
Sir Robert Anderson	Dispensational premillennialist	The "Jewish church."
Joseph Seiss	Futurist premillennialist	The church.
E. W. Bullinger	Ultradispensationalist	Israel.
H. A. Ironside	Dispensational premillennialist	Israel.
Dwight Pentecost	Dispensational premillennialist	Israel.
Norman Harrison	Midtribulational premillennialist	Israel.
John Walvoord	Dispensational premillennialist	Israel.
George Ladd	Posttribulational Premillennialist	"People of God."
Hal Lindsey	Dispensational premillennialist	Israel.
Marvin Rosenthal	"Pre-wrath" premillennialist	Israel.

Historical Survey

	Position
Church Fathers	Predominantly of the opinion that she is the church.
Medieval Theologians	Almost exclusively of the opinion that she is the church.
Reformation Scholars	A mixture of views begins but with the prevailing view continuing to be that she is the church.
Post-Reformation Scholars	A shift toward the view that she is Israel, but many still clinging the belief that she is the church.
Modern Evangelicals	Mixed opinions but the majority now squarely upon the view that she is Israel.

Theological Breakdown

	Position
Premillennial Historicists	Predominantly of the opinion that she is the church, but with some dissidents accepting that she is Israel.
Dispensational Pretribulational Premillennialists	Almost exclusively of the opinion that she is Israel.
Midtribulational (and "Pre-Wrath") Premillennialists	Mixed opinions but the majority believe that she is Israel.
Covenant Theologians and Postribulational Premillennialists	Predominantly of the opinion that she is the church.
Progressive Dispensationalists and other variant Premillenial views	Mixed opinions.

The Woman as the Church
Tenants of:
The woman is believed to be representative of the church.

Popular advocates from:
The Church Fathers : Hippolytus, Methodius, and Victorinus.
Medieval Theologians : Pierre D'Olivi, Nicholas of Lyra, and most Joachimites.
Reformation Scholars : Joseph Mede, Isaac Newton, and others.
Post-Reformation Scholars : Joseph Seiss.
Modern Evangelicals : G H. Lang, Arthur Bloomfield, Alan Johnson.

Strengths:
1) The twelve stars are viewed as the twelve apostles.
2) The church is elsewhere referred to as a bride.
3) This is the age old view.

Weaknesses:
1) The church did not give birth to Christ.
2) The twelve stars can also be the twelve tribes of Israel as in Genesis 37.
3) Israel is referred to elsewhere as a wife.
4) The rest of Revelation appears to be about Israel and Jerusalem, not the church.
5) The woman is almost certainly fleeing from Jerusalem, hence should be Jews.

The Woman as Israel

Tenants of:

The woman is believed to be representative of the nation of Israel or the Jewish race.

Popular advocates from:

The Church Fathers : Victorinus includes Israel, but also the church.

Medieval Theologians : None known.

Reformation Scholars : None cited.

Post-Reformation Scholars : John Darby, Sir Robert Anderson, Walter Scott, Nathaniel West, E. W. Bullinger, and Robert Govett.

Modern Evangelicals : Norman Harrison, Watchman Nee, J. Dwight Pentecost, William Newell, H. A. Ironside, C. B. Caird, Charles Ryrie, Tim LaHaye, Hal Lindsey, Robert Thomas, and Marvin Rosenthal.

Strengths:

1) The man-child is most certainly Christ, hence the mother must be Israel.
2) The twelve stars is parallel to Genesis 37 which refers to the sons of Israel.
3) Israel is referred to elsewhere as a wife.
4) The rest of Revelation appears to be about Israel and Jerusalem.
5) Matthew 24:15 appears to parallel the account here and echoes the 144,000.
6) The woman is almost certainly fleeing from Jerusalem.
7) Parallel Old Testament prophecies speak of the persecution of Jews, not Gentiles.

Weaknesses:

1) The twelve stars could be viewed as the twelve apostles.
2) The church is elsewhere referred to as a bride.
3) This view was scarcely taught until recently in history.

5

The Trumpet Judgments

The trumpets begin the second series of judgments and are more severe than the first series of seals. Most place them in the second half of the tribulation after most of the events described in the preceding chapter. The abomination of desolation has occurred, the faithful Jews have fled to safety, the anti-Christ has turned on Israel, and war has erupted throughout the empire. Now begins the second series of judgments. Some describe them as natural events which are the outcome of man's own sins and actions, while others emphatically insist that these are supernatural events which are the outcome of God's wrath. Each side had valid reasoning, and each side may be correct in one way or another, but it is best to evaluate those arguments by examining the trumpet judgments themselves. All that is clear is that they are *judgments*. They are the outpouring of God's wrath, whether by His direct intervention or by His permissive will.

The First Trumpet

> "The first sounded, and there came hail and fire, mixed with blood, and they were thrown to the earth; and a third of the earth was burned up, and a third of the trees were burned up, and all the green grass was burned up." (Revelation 8:7).

Historical Overview

The earliest church fathers were silent upon the trumpet judgments. They cited the passages with no commentary. This was usually their custom when they believed a passage to be self explanatory. Of course, today such a remark seems frivolous, but to the church fathers, it was common sense. They did not expound what they did not feel needed to be expounded. They did not elaborate without cause. Most importantly, they did not want to add what was not in the text. For example, Clement of Rome wrote less than a decade after the book of Revelation was written, saying that "all the earth as lead [shall] melt on the fire."[505] It is not clear whether this is a reference to the first trumpet or possibly Peter's description in 2 Peter 3:7. What is obvious is that Clement took the passages literally.

The self explanatory approach is certainly indicative of a literal one, or else the church fathers would have needed to expound and enlighten. Consequently, it can only be assumed that the church fathers saw this trumpet as literal hail and fire. Whether they viewed the earth as the entire planet or merely the "Roman earth," as later expositors argued, is unknown.

With the rise of the Middle Ages, all such literalism was abandoned. Allegorism and historicism began to reign. Joachim believed that the judgments represented the whole of church history, and even human history. Many Joachimites viewed the trumpets as concurrent with the seals, rather than following them. The chronological aspects are debated elsewhere (see Appendix D) and need not be addressed here. The Bible seems explicit enough in that the seventh seal presented the seven trumpets (8:1). How then could the first trumpet sound before the seventh seal had been opened? Such is the plight of allegory. So fanciful were the views of the early historicists that Nicholas of Lyra saw the hail released by the trumpet as the heresy of Arianism.[506]

In the Reformation this highly ambiguous historicist method continued to spawn the wildest imagination. John Bale argued that the grass represented the Jews,[507] Joseph Mede saw the hail as the Gothic invaders,[508] and Isaac Newton related it to the Byzantine Empire.[509]

In the post-Reformation age the more literal views began to reappear slowly. John Darby placed it again in a literal framework and in proper chronological sequence, but still clung to a highly symbolic interpretation. He believed that the earth represented a monarchy, while the trees and grass were a depiction of prosperity.[510] Thus the burning earth and grass was the destruction of the anti-Christ's kingdom. In this he was naturally followed to some extent by Walter Scott[511] and H. A. Ironside[512] but many other premillennialists began to read the more literal aspects into the prophecy. E. W. Bullinger fell back to the church father's method of quoting it with narry a comment.[513] It was literal and need not be elaborated upon. In modern times commentators have become mixed between the Darby methodology and the literal theory.

Evalutaion of the First Trumpet
The historicist method of attempting to find events in history, which can be viewed symbolically as the fulfillment of this prophecy, can be dismissed by the mere fact that no historicist can agree with another. Nicholas of Lyra places it under the rise of Arianism,[514] as if God would cause heresy to arise, while Joseph Mede places it under the Gothic invasion,[515] and Isaac Newton placed it under the Byzantine Empire.[516] Such confusion is common when one abandons even a literal framework. In this respect Darby's view was a vast improvement. Although he still favored a more symbolic approach, he placed it within a workable framework that could be debated more readily.

According to Darby the first four trumpet judgments fall on four separate monarchies; the earth represented the first of these.[517] He believed that "the trees figure that which is elevated, eminent, lofty; the green herb is prosperity."[518] Unfortunately, he offers not a single quote from the Bible to substantiate these assertions. He is offered assistance by Walter Scott and H. A. Ironside. Scott believes that the grass is a depiction of Israel based on Isaiah 40:7.[519] Ironside argues similarly that "grass is used a symbol of man (Isaiah

40:6)."[520] He also argues the Nebuchadnezzar was portrayed as a tree and quotes Matthew 3:10 as proof that men are portrayed as trees in the Bible.[521] An examination of these verses is prudent.

Isaiah 40:6-8 reads, "All flesh is grass, and all its loveliness is like the flower of the field. The grass withers, the flower fades, when the breath of the Lord blows upon it; surely the people are grass. The grass withers, the flower fades, but the word of our God stands forever." Now this is properly an analogy, or as Bullinger prefers, a metaphor.[522] This is an important distinction to make. In a metaphor the one item is compared to another, but not vice versa. In his classic text on the proper use of symbols, Bullinger says, "a *Metaphor* is confined to a distinct affirmation ... the two nouns themselves must both be mentioned ... or else no one can tell what they mean ... for example, 'all flesh is grass.'"[523] In more simple words, man is compared to grass but grass is not compared to man. Solomon might say "your eyes are *like* doves" (Song of Solomon 1:15) but it does not follow that a dove is a symbol for eyes. Metaphors are a distinctive type of symbol and are always used in a comparative sense. Consequently, the Isaiah passage does not prove that grass is a representation of man in Revelation. This is further affirmed by the fact that Scott takes it as Israel, Norman Harrison takes it as man's prosperity,[524] and Ironside as man in general. It remains, at best, a possibility; not a probability.

The dream of Nebuchadnezzar is different. Daniel 4:10-23 definitely compares the king to a large tree. Israel is also compared to a tree and its branches by Paul in Romans 11:17-19. The quotation of Matthew 3:10 is more suspect in context, but the former verses (one of which eluded Ironside) make for the possibility of the symbolic use of tree, but alas, the context cannot support this. If we take the tree in a symbolic use (although it is by no means obvious, as in the aforementioned verses) we must also take grass and earth symbolically. Although the belief that the earth can represent Palestine[525] or the "Roman earth" has become popular, it is nowhere supported in Scripture. As William Newell remarks, "what but your imagination ever told you such a thing? ... Is there a 'Roman' sun?"[526] Another author states, "If earth does not mean earth, then what does it mean? And if earth means earth, then the trees must mean trees and grass grass."[527] The symbolic interpretation of earth and grass are suspect and there is no indication in the passage that the tree, grass, or earth is to be understood outside its normal context. Moreover, even if we accepted these as symbols the question would remain; what does the hail symbolize? Scott declares the the hail represents the judgment of God,[528] but the trumpets themselves are the judgment of God! Can we have a symbol of a symbol?

That the literal view is not so far fetched can be illustrated by the fact that at least one amillennialists has admitted that "blood-red rain is not unknown in nature; in the spring of 1901 the daily Journals contained accounts of this phenomena, which was being witnessed in Italy at the south of Europe, the result, it was said, of the air being full of particles of fine red sand from the Sahara."[529] Seiss also refers to numerous historical sightings of blood-red snow and rain.[530] Are these what are being seen by John? Probably not. The point is that our own experiences should not be the criteria for whether or not we accept the word at face value. Until the advent of Nuclear weapons many refused to accept the literal nature of this prophecy, but now many do accept it. Some even believe that John's "unsophisticated" eyes could be witnessing an ICBM missle attack.[531] This view has actually garnered some stong supporters like David Reagan.[532] Many other theories have been put forth as well. Ladd suggest the possibly of an "electrical display in a fierce thunderstorm."[533] Morris mentions as a further possibility the idea of the earth being caught in the tail of a comet[534] and Robert Thomas speculates massive volcanic activity.[535]

All these suggestions are possibilities, but none should be asserted as the true view until the prophecy becomes history. What should be asserted is that the prophecy has every earmark of being a literal catastrophe. That this judgment is parallel in many ways to one of the ten plagues on Egypt has not escaped the eyes of most commentators. G. H. Lang reminds us that if the plague in Egypt was literal, as evangelicals agree it was, then so also should this be taken literally as well.[536]

The result of this judgment is that a third of the earth, trees, and grass is burned with fire. Bloomfield believes that "the earth itself is hot," although "this heat does not radiate from the sun," but because of the literal hail.[537] The destruction it causes is immense. Nothing in the context suggest that this fire is symbolic, nor that the destruction is wreaks is not real. We are forced to conclude that "a mighty storm of hail and fire mingled with blood means a storm of hail and fire mingled with blood; earth, trees and all green grass means earth, trees, and all green grass, and the burning, and scorching, and destruction means burning, scorching, and destruction."[538] Such is the judgment of the first trumpet.

The Second Trumpet

> "The second angel sounded, and *something* like a great mountain burning with fire was thrown into the sea; and a third of the sea became blood; and a third of the creatures, which were in the sea and had life, died; and a third of the ships were destroyed." (Revelation 8:8-9).

Historical Overview
As with the first trumpet, the history of the interpretation of the second mimics the first. The church fathers were silent, preferring to let the passage speak for itself. The medievals spiritualized it to extremes. Nicholas of Lyra again attributed it to the rise of "great heresy"[539] while the early Reformers followed this pattern. John Darby shifted the prophecy back to its literal time frame and context, but left the figurative interpretation intact.[540] Today many scholars,

armed with the knowledge of science and exegesis, are returning to a literal view, accepting it as a meteorite or similar phenomena.

Evaluation of the Second Trumpet

The figurative interpretation must take both the mountain and the sea as symbols; one will not suffice. It is true that the sea has a symbolic use in Revelation (cf. Revelation 13:1; 15:2), and elsewhere, but is it symbolic here? Joseph Mede declared it was the "sea of politique world"[541] and John Darby saw the sea as the masses,[542] while Dwight Pentecost takes it merely as the nations.[543] That the symbolic use is not intended here should be obvious by the reference to sea life and ships (vs. 9). If sea were merely symbolic for the nations or governments of the world then the mention of ships and sea life would be both unnecessary and confusing. Although sea does sometimes refer to the masses as Darby suggest, it makes no sense here. Consider the text carefully. It states that a third of the creatures "which were in the sea" died. If the sea means the masses, then the repetition of the masses "in the sea" would negate the force of the symbolism. The main problem is that if the sea is taken symbolically, what must the blood mean? Some take it as heresy[544] while others see it as persecution. The former is pure speculation with no justification in Biblical or apocryphal literature. The latter is also suspect. Nevertheless, since the sea can occasionally be used as a symbol it is best to examine the object which falls into the sea to determine if the symbolic interpretation can hold water.

Joseph Mede claims that a "mountain signifying a citie is found of old Babylon."[545] He then procedes to argue that this is Rome under the sack of Alaric in 410 A.D.[546] Such historicist speculations were once rampant. On the question of a mountain signifying a city, there is much debate. It is true that the prophecy of Daniel mentions a kingdom as a mountain, but not Babylon, nor any other earthly kingdom. The only kingdom ever presented as a mountain is that final Kingdom of the Lord God. Daniel 2:31 states that "the stone that struck the statue became a great mountain and filled the earth." The statue was defined by Daniel as representing the kingdoms of the earth (Daniel 2:32-45), *not* the mountain. This mountain is reserved to the Messianic Kingdom alone. Jeremiah 51:25 is a better reference, but the imagery is different. This is the passage which Walter Scott appeals to in his identification of the mountain as the Chaldean/Babylonian monarchy.[547] Ironside also follows this line of thought, saying that a burning mountain was a symbol for the fall of Babylon,[548] yet he does not cite a single passage to prove this.

One of several problems with this line of thinking is that these same people identified the earth in the first trumpet as a kingdom or nation, but now they call the mountain a kingdom which is falling from the sky. They have, therefore, placed a kingdom on earth and one falling from the sky. This is inconsistent. Symbology must, by definition, be consistent. If a symbol is not consistent then it becomes little more than an ambiguous allegory. Norman Harrison says that "a great nation (mountain) burning with zeal for war, cast into the sea of nations, destructive of shipping and sailor life."[549] G. H. Lang sees the burning mountain as a fallen angel,[550] but accepts the blood as literal.[551] Such diverse opinions are to be expected when there is no consistency in interpretation of symbols.

While the symbolic arguments may be plausible, they are not likely. For one thing, the most obvious problem is the passage reads "*something **like*** a great mountain." "Like" a word of comparison. John was describing what it *looked like*. To say it looked "like" a symbolic metaphor is silly. If the mountain were a symbol then the text would read, "I saw a mountain," not "I saw *something like* a mountain." Robert Govett believes it may be "a meteorite stone," [552] Henry Morris suggests "a giant meteorite, or asteroid, or even a satellite,"[553] and Hal Lindsey says said that it is "either an enormous meteor or, more likely, a colossal H-bomb."[554] Now Lindsey's sometimes wild speculations often bring raucous laughter among his critics, but the fair minded individual will notice that Lindsey's speculations are far more reasonable than those of the allegorical school. If faced with choosing between a "colossal H-bomb" and the Gothic barbarians of Alaric, I choose the former. The better choice, however, is that this is a part of a meteor (or asteroid); perhaps even a broken piece of mass from "Wormwood" (which is described in the third trumpet), but which hits shortly before it.

The next question is one of the blood. If the meteorite is literal should not the blood also be? Walvoord points out that Moses turned water to blood.[555] Others believe that the water will merely "look like" blood since the meteorite only "looks like" a mountain. This is a consistent view and, therefore, acceptable, although many prefer to keep the passage as literal as possible. Robert Thomas believes the blood is real and thus believes that the mountain is a supernatural object, since a meteor cannot turn water to blood.[556] Conversely, although accepting the possibility of real blood, scientist Henry Morris believes that this could refer to "poisoned waters, like a great 'red tide,' will spread out soon to the waters of all other oceans so that a third part of the sea 'became blood.'"[557] He states that it may be transformed "chemically or biochemically into blood-red water, poisoned by multitudes of dead microorganism (as in the well-known 'red tides' which occur infrequently in modern oceans)."[558]

The final question is that of the sea. In Greek and Hebrew there is no distinguishing between sea and ocean. Whether one of the oceans is intended or a sea is debated. Tim LaHaye thinks that a meteorite will crash in the Mediterranean Sea.[559] Critics respond to this literalism by asking how a meteorite could destroy a third of the ships in the sea. The answer is all too simple to those versed in science. Govett says the destruction is caused "party by the fall of the meteor, partly by the hurricanes let loose, a third of the ships is wrecked."[560] Morris concurs, saying that Tsunami waves would result from the impact and could destroy many ships.[561]   Since the Mediterranean Sea is the most heavily populated sea in terms of ships, it is easy to see how an impact in that sea could destroy almost every ship in the Mediterranean and result in the literal destruction of a third of the ships in all the seas.

This mention of the ships in the sea is further proof that the sea is to be understood literally. Since the object falling from the sky is merely said to look "like" a mountain, it should be taken as a description and not a symbol. The object, probably an asteroid or meteorite, will fall into the sea, destroy the ships, and pollute the water, thus turning it into either massive "red tides" or literal blood. This is the most natural meaning of the passage and the best.

The Third Trumpet

> "The third angel sounded, and a great star fell from heaven, burning like a torch, and it fell on a third of the rivers and on the springs of waters; and the name of the star is called Wormwood; and a third of the waters became wormwood; and many men died from the waters, because they were made bitter." (Revelation 8:10-11).

Historical Overview

Once again the church fathers are generally silent. They continue their habit of quotation without commentary. The medieval historicists naturally attempted to fit the prohecy into historical events by allegorizing them. The most common theory was to attribute the star to some form of heresy such as Pelagiasm.[562] The Reformers emulated historicism as well. Mede saw it as a description of Odoacer's sack of Rome and called Wormwood, the fall of the Caesars,[563] and Sir Newton said it was the division of the empire between east and west.[564]

Shedding the historicism, but retaining its allegorical qualities, was the renowned John Darby. Rather than attempting to equate the prophecy with some past event, he acknowledged it as future but declared that star's fall was the fall of a future government and the poisoned waters that of the corruption caused by the government.[565] A derivation of this theory was accepted by men such as Walter Scott and H. A. Ironside while men like Norman Harrison and G. H. Lang took the star as a fallen angel.[566] More literal expositors like Govett and Seiss, followed by most premillennialists today, took the passage more at face value, interpreting it as a meteor or comet.[567]

It is not hard to see that even today there is some disparity among the expositors as to the meaning of the third trumpet. Some take it as a symbol of a government or religious dignitary, others as a demon, still others as a meteor or comet, and yet others as a natural weapon such as a thermonuclear device.[568] Nonetheless, modern expositors have returned to the futurist school of thought and the true meaning of the passage may not be as obscure as one might first think. If we interpret it in accordance with the same principles as the preceding prophecies, the answer will come.

Evaluation of the Third Trumpet

The historicist school of thought, which attributes the falling star to a heresy[569] ignores that Christ is the one who sends the star. Christ does not send heresy, He sends truth. As Robert Thomas says, "heresy is hardly a judgment inflicted on men as a penalty for sin."[570] This fact alone dispels much of the medieval thought, and was recognized by those who shifed the star from the heresy to the heretic. However, the number of theories as to what heretic was intended are almost as numerous as there are expositors. The list includes Origen, Simon Magus, Mohammed, Arius, Pelagius, Montanus, Novatus, and many other heretics. Some historicist scholars shift the theory from a heretic to a political leader. Again the names are almost countless; Attila, Eleazar, Odoacer, or others.

The attempt to shift this sort of allegory to futurism has not substantially improved upon the theory. Darby says that the star is "a power in a state of fall."[571] Walter Scott believes that the star is a future high official dignitary.[572] Ironside declares, "stars in the prophetic scriptures symbolize religious dignitaries,"[573] but each fail to cite a single passage to prove it. Ironisde believes that the star is the fall of "an apostate leader" and the poisoned water is the "evil influence" upon the world populous.[574] He believes this world leader is the pope, thus connecting the prophecy to the Harlot of Babylon (see chatper 8), but is not dogmatic.[575] In each of the these cases, the discarding of the historical element does not completely resolve the issue. Not a single quotation from the Bible is given to substantiate the theory that the star represents either a political or religious leader. Consequently, Lang and Harrison once again shifted the allegorical thinking; this time to represent a demon, or even Satan himself.

According to G. H. Lang, the star does not represent a person, but a fallen angel or demon.[576] Norman Harrison goes one step further, stating that the star is none other than Satan himself.[577] These arguments bear closer examination, for there is no doubt that "star" is indeed used as a symbol for angels, both godly and fallen. In fact, Revelation 9:1 specifically calls a "star" "him," implying an angelic being. Revelation 12:4 is also believed by most to represent the fall of Satan's angels from Heaven. The most famous verse, however, is Isaiah 14:12 which has traditionally been viewed as a reference to the fall of Satan. Thus, it is evident that "star" *can* be a symbol for an angel or demon, or even Satan himself. Is that what is spoken of here? The answer must be, "no." First, in contrast to 9:1, where the star is called "him," this verse refers to the star as "it."[578] Furthermore, the results of the star's fall are the natural consequences of its actions, not independant actions, such as those performed by a living being. Mooreover, the description of the star fits the exact description that the ancients gave for meteors, and not the simple imagery of a fallen angel. Finally, to quote Seiss, "when the Scriptures tell us that a thing is a symbol, we are to take it as such; but when they give no intimation that a thing is other than literal, there is no warrant for making a symbol or figure of it."[579] Hence, we are left to examine the more literal interpretations.

The greek word for "star" (ἀστὴρ) properly refers to any astronomical object, not merely a solar star. What is of particular interest that the star is described as "burning like a torch" (vs. 10). Robert Thomas has said "the ancients used 'λαμπὰς' as a description of meteors."[580] Many take it as such. Seiss believes it could also refer to a comet,[581] while Hal Lindsey takes it as "another thermonuclear weapon."[582] All three are feasible, provided they can explain the bitterness of Wormwood.

Wormwood is actually a very bitter and poisonous herb. It is called absinthe, from the Greek word *absinthos* (αψινθος), the very word here translated as "wormwood." The smallest drop is put in liquor to give it a strong taste, but "used freely it produces convulsions, paralysis, and death."[583] The Hebrew word *la'anah* (לַעֲנָה) is sometimes translated wormwood, although the King James translates it as "hemlock" in Hosea 10:4 and Amos 6:12. Thus, the name wormwood does not necessarily mean absinthe, but bitter poison. The apostle tells us that many men died from the bitter waters (vs. 11). Is such a thing possible from an asteroid or meteor strike? Certainly. Meteors and asteroids carry with them much that is deadly and bitter when ingested, such as dangerous microbes. Should a meteor strike the fresh waters of the earth, the pollution would kill many. In addition, many would die of thirst while the governments of the world rush to obtain water from the remaining fresh water reservoirs. The consequences of an asteroid or meteor strike would be global.

In March 1998 an asteroid (named Asteroid 1997 XF11) was discovered heading on what was originally believed to be a collision course with earth.[584] Scientists originally said that the asteroid could hit the earth on October 26, 2028, but following mass hype by the media, calculations were revised to say that the asteroid would only pass within 26,000 miles of the earth.[585] When one considers that the moon is in orbit around the earth at a distance of 238,000 miles[586] the ramifications are enormous. Even if the asteroid misses the earth it could cause tidal waves or even hit the moon, depending on the moon's orbit at the time of the meteor's passing.

As a result of these possibilities some have already begun planning on ways to avert the catastrophe. Some have suggested using nuclear weapons to destroy the asteroid (such as was depicted in a movie entitled *Armageddon*), but if the blast does not "pulverize the asteroid completely" then "large remaining chunks could still cause extensive damage" to the earth.[587] According to CNN, if the asteroid did collide directly with the earth it "would explode with an energy of about 320,000 megatons of dynamite. That equals almost 2 million Hiroshima-sized atomic bombs."[588] Even if the asteroid hit the oceans "all of the coastal cities would be scoured by the tsunami ... where cities stood, there would be only mudflats."[589] Furthermore, "if it struck land, it would blast a crater 20 miles across and so clog the sky with dust and vapor that the sun would be darkened 'for weeks, if not months.'"[590] Do these descriptions not sound familar? Could this asteroid, or part of it, be the "burning mountain" or "wormwood"? We *cannot* say, nor should we. To be definitive would be notoriously close to the sin of date setting (see Appendix E). However, this illustrates the real possibility, and even probability, of something like this occurring in the future. The literal rendering of the trumpets cannot be disregarded for the figurative when there is no logical or exegetical reason for rejecting the literal.

Interestingly enough, another asteroid, much smaller in scale (no larger than a footbal field) was discovered which could hit the earth in February 1, 2019. Although the chances of this asteroid (named Asteroid 2002 NT7) hitting the earth are said to be slim, and the consequences far less severe because of its relative size, it further illustrates the possibility of a meteor, asteroid, or other cosmic object hitting the earth literally as the Bible states. Whether one of these, or some other astronomical object, are the instruments of God's wrath or not, they prove that the trumpets can occur literally at any time.

In summary, the description of the third trumpet is a literal depiction of a meteor or asteroid strike upon the earth. It's impact in the fresh water resevoirs causes the water to become poisoned. The judgment of this bitter wormwood echoes the words of Jeremiah to the unbelieving people of Israel, "I will feed them with wormwood, and give them water of gall to drink" (Jeremiah 9:15). In this case, it is not the Jews who are the targets of this judgment, but the unbelieving Gentile world. Pentecost mentions that water is the "source of life," thus "this may depict judgment upon those whom living water is taken away because they believed a lie."[591] Although Pentecost believes that the prophecy may only be symbolic, it is more likely taken as a literal judgment. It is poetic justice to a bitter world.

The Fourth Trumpet

> "The fourth angel sounded, and a third of the sun and a third of the moon and a third of the stars were smitten, so that a third of them might be darkened and the day might not shine for a third of it, and the night in the same way." (Revelation 8:12).

Historical Overview

Although the relative silence of the church fathers continues with the fourth trumpet, Lactantius believed the actual days would become shorter while Ephraem states that "the stars shall be seen with difficulty in the sky,"[592] implying a literal understanding. Likewise, the common practice of the fathers to allow the Bible to interpret itself also commends itself to this view. Such a view, however, it seems could never be among the medievals. They again continued to interpret the judgments as allegory for some form of heresy.[593] In

122

the Reformation Mede said of this passage that the stars were the "brightness of Rome" diminished by the Ostrogoths.[594] Newton said "the king, kingdom, and princes of the western empire were to be darkened."[595] Such was the chaos of historicism.

With the return to futurism the expositors follow their usual pattern. Men like Darby, Scott, Harrison, and Pentecost interpret the stars as governments of the world.[596] Men like Ironside cling to the belief that heresy is of what is spoken.[597] The more literal expositors, like Seiss, Govett, Bullinger, Newell, Walvoord, Lindsey, Morris, Thomas, and LaHaye, take the passage as referring to literal darkness and sometimes shortened days, as Lactantius believed.

Evaluation of the Fourth Trumpet

The fourth trumpet is a parallel passage to many other prophetic passages on the end days. Isaiah 13:10, 24:23; Ezekiel 32:7; Joel 3:15; Amos 5:20, 8:9; Zephaniah 1:15; Matthew 24:29; and Mark 13:24 all speak of the sun, moon, and stars darkening and not giving their full light. Despite this, many expositors insist upon the figurative meaning. Darby says the sun is a "supreme power" and the moon and stars are those under his authority.[598] Scott likens the darkness to a "crash."[599] Pentecost says the sun, moon, and stars "represent governmental powers and may represent the judgment of God upon the world rulers."[600] The central problem with this interpretation is that Darby, Scott, Pentecost, and like commentators have already applied numerous symbols to the governments of the world. Thus far Darby, Scott, Ironside, Harrison, and Pentecost alone have applied to world governments or nations the imagery of the earth (Darby,[601] Scott,[602] & Pentecost[603]), trees (Darby,[604] & Ironside[605]), grass (Scott[606] & Ironside[607]), mountains (Scott,[608] Ironside,[609] & Harrison[610]), rivers (Darby[611]), the sea (Pentecost[612]), stars (Darby,[613] Scott,[614] Harrison,[615] & Pentecost[616]), the moon (Scott,[617] Harrison,[618] & Pentecost[619]), and now the sun (Darby,[620] Scott,[621] Harrison,[622] & Pentecost[623]). It is inconceivable that if God wanted to represent the governments of the world He would use so many different and diversified symbols. This would only create confusion, and such has been the case with all allegorical interpretations. It is possible to apply one of the symbols to a world government, but to apply all of them to the same meaning is to stretch credibility.

What Joseph Seiss says so uncharitably must, nevertheless, be said. "What are we to understand by the sun, moon, and stars? Ask a child, and it will tell you; but ask our Apocalyptic interpreters, and their answers are as various as their names."[624] Symbolism does exist in Revelation, but when it is used, we are either told or the intimation is demanded by context. Here there is nothing to indicate that the sun, moon, and stars, are anything but the sun, moon, and stars. We are told in many passages (Isaiah 13:10, 24:23; Ezekiel 32:7; Joel 3:15; Amos 5:20, 8:9; Zephaniah 1:15; Matthew 24:29; and Mark 13:24 to name a few) that the sun will be darkened in the last days. In Revelation, at the fourth trumpet, this same statement is made. Either all are symbolic, or all are literal. If the symbolic is accepted here, then Jesus' words in the Olivet Discourse must also be symbolic. If His words were literal there, as most believe, then they must also be literal here.

While we must accept this as literal, and have no reason not to, this does not necessarily answer all the questions. Govett comments that the passage may be taken one of two ways. "(1.) that the light by day and by night was diminished a third *in intensity*; (2.) or that *in regard of duration* the third of the day and of the night *was deprived altogether of light*."[625] Govett, as with most others, prefers the first option, but a number take the second. Charles Ryrie, for example, believes that the duration of the day will actually be reduced to sixteen hours.[626] This was also held by Lactantius, the church father, among others.[627] Those who prefer this option often accept the idea of some form of eclipse, such as John Walvoord suggests.[628] However, one author who accepts the idea that an eclipse is foretold here acknowledges that this is "not a shortening of the duration of daylight and moonlight."[629] Robert Mounce discusses the two alternatives saying, "the first part of the verse, when interpreted in parallel with the other plagues, seems to indicate a decrease in the intensity of available light as a result of a third of the luminaries being darkened. The last two phrases, however, indicate the total absence of light for a third part of both day and night."[630]

In favor of the shortened day theory is the reading of Amos 8:9, for it says, "'it will come about in that day,' declares the Lord GOD, 'That I shall make the sun go down at noon and make the earth dark in broad daylight.'" This would, indeed, imply total darkness for eight hours, but if the night is also shortened by eight hours, then there are sixteen hours unaccounted for. It may be that the darkness is most severe at these hours, but the former is the better understanding. The skies will be filled with darkness throughout the day and night, but for eight hours the skies will be particularly dark.

William Newell reminds us that Genesis says the lights are given "primarily for *signs*."[631] He then points to the Olivet Discourse in which Jesus was asked about the signs of His coming. There is no doubt that the darkening of the days and nights is a sign. It is foretold in both Old and New Testaments. That it is often spoken of in the Old Testament as a sign to the Jews should also serve notice that God is regathering His people, who have repented by this time. That what is spoken of here is far more than an eclipse or a single event that occupies a single day or two should be apparent by the cause and effect relationships of the trumpet judgments. In the first trumpet, either a meteor shower or a nuclear attack occurs. This is followed by the impact of an asteroid or meteor. The larger part of this asteroid strikes the sea, while a smaller portion (wormwood) strikes the fresh water deposits or lakes. Now darkness covers the land. Hal Lindsey believes that the darkness could be caused by radioactive debrit from a nuclear fallout,[632] but the reader should be reminded that CNN has reported that secular scientists believe that the impact of an asteroid would "clog the sky with dust and vapor that the sun would be darkened 'for weeks, if not months.'"[633] This is the better of the two explanations. Following the impact of the "mountain" and "wormwood," the debris covers the land and darkens the sun, moon, and stars.

The Fifth Trumpet

"The fifth angel sounded, and I saw a star from heaven which had fallen to the earth; and the key of the bottomless pit was given to him. And he opened the bottomless pit; and smoke went up out of the pit, like the smoke of a great furnace; and the sun and the air were darkened by the smoke of the pit. And out of the smoke came forth locusts upon the earth; and power was given them, as the scorpions of the earth have power. And they were told that they should not hurt the grass of the earth, nor any green thing, nor any tree, but only the men who do not have the seal of God on their foreheads. And they were not permitted to kill anyone, but to torment for five months; and their torment was like the torment of a scorpion when it stings a man. And in those days men will seek death and will not find it; and they will long to die and death flees from them. And the appearance of the locusts was like horses prepared for battle; and on their heads, as it were, crowns like gold, and their faces were like the faces of men. And they had hair like the hair of women, and their teeth were like *the teeth* of lions. And they had breastplates like breastplates of iron; and the sound of their wings was like the sound of chariots, of many horses rushing to battle. And they have tails like scorpions, and stings; and in their tails is their power to hurt men for five months. They have as king over them, the angel of the abyss; his name in Hebrew is Abaddon, and in the Greek he has the name Apollyon."

"The first woe is past; behold, two woes are still coming after these things" (Revelation 9:1-12).

Historical Overview

Strangely enough, the church fathers continue their seeming silence. Their policy of letting the Scriptures speak for themselves continues even against the backdrop of such a seemingly difficult text. The church fathers may not have understood the passage, but neither did they attempt to speculate wildly upon what they did not know. Such cannot be said for the medieval scholars. Speculation is their forte. According to Pierre D'Olivi, the locusts are the wicked apostate clergy.[634] Nicholas of Lyra said they were Vandals (as followers of heresy), calling Valentenian the star on account of his acceptance of Arianism.[635] With Reformers like Joseph Mede the locusts became the Saracens and Mohammad the fallen star.[636] Newton also attributed the locusts with the Arabs.[637]

Under Darby the fallen star was none other than Satan himself.[638] The locusts remain largely symbolic, but their actions are real and the torment is real. Their tails are said to represent the false prophet.[639] Walter Scott believed that the fallen star was the anti-Christ,[640] followed by men like Ironside and Pentecost. Each of these men, however, were hesitant to take the locusts as real. Most other modern premillennial commentators prefer a more literal approach to the locusts. Bullinger saw the locusts as demons,[641] as do most modern premillennialists. One interesting variant, however, is the notion that the locusts may describe modern technology in some form. Although dating back to the Reformation, this view has gained a small, but notable, group of followers in the modern age.

Evaluation of the Fifth Trumpet

The fifth trumpet is easily the most controversial of all the trumpets. Whereas commentators of like thought were usually in general agreement with one another on the first four trumpets, similar expositors now begin to drift apart. Nonetheless, the patterns are familiar. Historicists continue to seek historical fulfillment in the past, while futurists see these events as literal future judgments, whether they are symbolic of those judgments or not.

Of the historicists, little will be said. Although Mede believes that this prophecy is "long since past,"[642] the historical "fulfillment" does not seem to have cleared up the true meaning of the passage. D'Olivi, Nicholas of Lyra, Mede, Bale, Newton, Poole, Henry, and Napier seem to find no agreement on its historical fulfillment, despite their claim that it has been fulfilled! Some call the star the pope Boniface III,[643] others Arius,[644] and some Mohammad.[645] Some call the locusts the bishops of Rome; others the barbarians invaders of Rome. None of these suggestions can work. The Saracen Muslims slaughtered Christians; the locusts are forbidden to touch the sealed of God. Boniface's heresy has lasted for more than a thousand years; the locusts are to last five months. The barbarians slaughtered men; the locusts are forbidden to kill men, only to torment them. History is filled with men seeking historical fulfillment, and the historicists are still seeking that historical fulfillment. If they wait long enough, they will eventually become united on its meaning, for when that future event becomes past, no one will be able to deny its meaning.

The futurists are united in attributing this prophecy to the last days. Still, we differ as to its meaning. It is, therefore, best to break the prophecy down into sections and examine each individually.

Verses one and two begin by describing a fallen star, which is referred to as "him." While allegorists mock literalism by saying we must take this literally as well, the straw man argument does not hold together. When the Bible speaks of a symbol, that symbol must be literally rendered as a symbol. It is not literal to take parable as a simile, a metaphor as an allegory, a paraleipsis as a hyperbole, an idiom for a type, or a description as a symbol, even as the allegorists do. To take a passage literally means to take it at its face value. In this case, it is obvious that the "star" is a representation of some living being. No one disputes this. E. W. Bullinger openly admits, "that the word 'star,' here, is used for 'angel' seems clear from the personal actions ascribed to it."[646] Robert Govett notes "a star could neither take a key, nor unlock a door."[647] It is, therefore, common sense to take the star as a symbol here, but unjustified to take it elsewhere as a symbol except where context demands it. "This star is an intelligent agent ... a key is given to him. He takes that key. He uses it ... All this argues active and intelligent agency, and furnishes the Divine intimation that we are not to consider this star to be of the same kind as the star under the third trumpet."[648]

Angels are often been compared to stars, and fallen angels to falling stars. Even the phrase, "host of heaven," can refer to either the stars or angels (cf. 1 Kings 22:19 vs. Deuteronomy 4:19). The imagery is plain. Angels are the host of the heavenly abode, while stars are the host of the physical universe as we know it. This is doubtless from whence the imagery of stars for angels originated. Consider Job 38:7 and Isaiah 14:12. Likewise, Daniel 8:10 and Revelation 12:4 appear to speak about the fall of Satan's angels, or rather the demons, as falling stars. Bloomfield correctly believes "any bright object falling from heaven is called a star whether it is a meteor or an angel."[649] This does not justify taking falling stars for demons where the context does not demand it, but to take it as such here is evident. The question is then; what angel? Some have taken it for Satan himself, others for an ordinary demon, and still others for the anti-Christ.

Many authors have noticed that the verse properly speaks of a "fallen" star, rather than a "falling" star.[650] It is a fallen star, or fallen angel. Satan's fall is believed to be referenced in Isaiah 14:12, "How you have fallen from heaven, O star of the morning, son of the dawn!" It is parallel to Luke 10:18, "I saw Satan fall from heaven like lightning." Here, the fallen angel appears again, or so most commentators believe. "John beheld, not a falling star, but a *fallen* star. He had fallen from heaven long ago, though he evidently still was permitted some access to the one on the throne."[651] This is, indeed, evident as depicted in the book of Job. It also answers the greatest criticism made against the view; the question of how Satan can act as an agent of God. Job depicts Satan as being constantly before the throne of God. In Zechariah 3:1 he stands before an angel of God accusing the High Priest, and in Revelation 12:10 the angels rejoice because "the accuser of our brethren has been thrown down, who accuses them before our God day and night." We must remember in Job that Satan could do nothing to Job except what God has expressedly premitted him to do. Here, the case is similar. The locusts, released by the fallen star, are given specific instructions on what they *cannot* do. "They were told that they should not hurt the grass of the earth, nor any green thing, nor any tree, but only the men who do not have the seal of God on their foreheads. And they were not

127

permitted to kill anyone" (vs. 4-5). Consequently, it is obvious that their actions are not carried out by an obedient angel, but from one who must be commanded not to harm those who "have the seal of God on their foreheads." Satan was cast down from heaven in chapter 12, which chronologically predates this judgment (see Appendices B & D), and is permitted to punish those who have rejected Christ, the Messiah.

Some scholars dispute this. Ironside will only say that this fallen star is an apostate leader,[652] but Walter Scott, Dwight Pentecost, and Watchman Nee openly call him the anti-Christ.[653] Scott believes that Isaiah 14:12 refers not to Satan, but to the king of Babylon.[654] He then declares that the anti-Christ is intended by the fallen star,[655] and Satan is the king of verse eleven.[656] This is the reverse of how most would have it, but more will be said of the king momentarily.

Whether this fallen star be Satan, the anti-Christ, or merely a high ranking demon, it is he who is given a key to open the pit. When the pit is opened, smoke pours out and darkens the sky. It should be remembered that in the last trumpet a third of the sunlight, moonlight, and starlight is blocked. Here it is said that "the sun and the air were darkened by the smoke of the pit" (vs. 2). Could this smoke be connected to the fourth trumpet? If so, it would provide a perfect transition from the fourth trumpet to the fifth, and maintain the cause and effect relationship which appears in the first four trumpets. Regardless, it is the designation of this pit that is considered important in the identification of the locusts which come out from it. Govett says that "the Abyss, or bottomless pit, is a place of departed souls. 'Who shall descend into *the bottomless pit?*' Rom. x, 7. It is a dungeon, and a place of punishment, as is manifested by the fear of the demons, lest they should be cast in thither ... Luke viii, 28."[657] We also read of Satan being cast into the Abyss in Revelation 20:3. In that verse there is said to be a "key to the Abyss." Here there is a "key to the bottomless pit." The connection appears obvious. The pit and the Abyss are one and the same.

Most literalists believe that what is released from this pit should be consistent with that pit. It is said that the locusts are demonic creatures. A possible parallel to this judgment may be seen in Joel 1:6 and 2:25. No one doubts that these are not earthly locusts; the question is whether they are demonic locusts, or something else. Among those who accept the demonic locusts are Govett, Seiss, Bullinger, Newell, Ironside, Lang, Bloomfield, Nee, Walvoord, Lindsey, Ryrie, Morris, Thomas, and LaHaye. Others such as Mounce and Ladd believe the locusts represent demonic activity, but they all declare the locusts only symbols thereof.[658] Bloomfield compares them to "infernal cherubim."[659]

The Bible makes clear that these locusts are not allowed to harm the grass or trees, but only to torment men who have rejected the gospel. Many have commented on the fact that normal locusts do the opposite. This is an obvious indication that the locusts are uncommon to this earth, but also raises

128

the possibility of a more rarely advocated, and often ridiculed, view; that the locusts describe modern technology in the only terms that John was capable of using.

The theory of modern technology being depicted in this trumpet (as well as the next) is not really new at all. The Reformers believed that the sixth trumpet in particular described modern weaponry.[660] The view has circulated for some time with most scholars reluctant to take up its cause. Often Hal Lindsey is erroneously accused of being its creator, even though Lindsey actually believes the locusts to be demons. Nevertheless, his popularity, and his willingness to give the view a voice, brought a spotlight upon the theory. After defending the demonic view, which he espouces,[661] Lindsey says, "I have a Christian friend who was a Green Beret in Vietnam. When he first read this chapter he said, 'I know what those are. I've seen hundreds of them in Vietnam. They're Cobra helicopters!' That may just be conjecture, but it does give you something to think about! A Cobra helicopter does fit the composite description very well. They also make the sound of 'many chariots.' My friend believes that the means of torment will be a kind of nerve gas sprayed from its tail."[662]

Those who ridicule Lindsey for including such a statement ignore the fact that well respected scholars such as John Walvoord have given the view due respect even while disagreeing with it. Ed Hindson mentions that chemical warface and nerve agents have been suggested by some[663] and Tim Lahaye mentions the theory that these may be some form of B-29s.[664] Whether the idea is correct or not, it deserves more attention and respect than the speculations which attribute the hair of the locusts to the Muslim turbans or the headdresses of the Zealots of ancient Israel!

According to the Bible, the "locusts were like horses prepared for battle." This implies, as is later evident, that the locusts are an army of some kind. They operate under the instructions of their king (vs. 7) whom many believe to be the anti-Christ. It further says that "they had breastplates like breastplates of iron" (vs. 9). This certainly is compatible with a description of an armored craft of some sort, and is written in descriptive language. Moreover, "the sound of their wings was like the sound of chariots." Again, this is exactly the sound which helicpoter "wings," or rather blades, make. Lastly, the "faces of men" are taken most literally, since men would be piloting the crafts. However, their "crowns of gold," "hair like women," and "teeth of lions" are more difficult to fit into the technological theory. Countless figurative theories have been presented. It is fair to suggest that the crowns of gold might represent authority, but what of the hair and teeth? It is best to take these as descriptive, whether of demons or technology. The demonic locusts theory seems the better fit exegetically, since they come up from the pit, but the technology advocates believe that their theory fits better with the possible identification of their king in verse eleven.

According to 9:11, "they have as king over them, the angel of the abyss; his name in Hebrew is Abaddon, and in the Greek he has the name Apollyon." Who is this king? He is identified as "the angel of the abyss" and named, in English, "the Destroyer." Clearly he is a demon of some sort. Many believe he is none other than Satan. Darby made this assertion[665] along with his protegés Scott and Ironisde. It is also held by men like Walvoord. The problem with this designation is that "the record plainly shows that the star and the king of the locusts are two distinct personages."[666] One is cast down from heaven while the other ascends from the pit.

An alternate view considers Abaddon to be a "chief" demon[667] or, as Bullinger calls him, "one of Satan's superior officers."[668] This would seem to be the best view, but one last view needs to examined; the view that this this angel of the abyss, or demon, is the anti-Christ. Watchman Nee is sure that the locusts' king is the anti-Christ.[669] This is also the view of Dwight Pentecost and others. The basis for their argument is tenative. It is partially based on the demon's title. "Christ is named *Jesus* because He is *the Savior*. The king is named *Abaddon* in Hebrew, and *Apollyon* in Greek, because he is *a destroyer* – the opposite of savior."[670] As Govett explains, "The Savior is 'Christ the Lord:' Luke ii, 11. The Destroyer is Antichrist the False King and Lord."[671] Govett believes that the anti-Christ is called by this name in the Old Testament. He cites possible references as Jeremiah 4:7; 6:26; and Isaiah 16:4. He also attempts to draw allusions in Daniel including 8:25-25 and 11:4, the controversial verses which many attribute to Antiochus Epiphanes.[672] In each case, the reference is questionable at best. However, if this is the army of the anti-Christ, then it would be very consistent with the technology thesis. If the locusts are connected to the army of the anti-Christ, then it would further enhance the cause and effect relationship between the trumpet judgments, as most agree that the sixth trumpet speaks of a human war in conflict with the armies of the anti-Christ. The designation must, however, remain speculative. Even if the army is associated with the army of the anti-Christ, Abaddon is most likely a chief demon, and not the anti-Christ himself. Conversely, Dwight Pentecost associates the locusts army with the Northern Cofederacy (see Appendix C).[673]

While we cannot be sure if the army is in league with the anti-Christ, in league against him, or is led against all unbelievers, we can be sure that their purpose is not to kill but to torment. For five months they will torture men to the extent that they will beg to die (vs. 6)! The torment may serve to chastise men. Since death is not the result, it may be God's last warning to men to repent. In the ensuing chapters we will find that few men are willing to repent. This could be their last true opportunity. Whether the "sting" of these demons is chemical, biological, or demonic in nature, the consequences will either drive men to become bitter and hostile to God, or to repent. So severe is this judgment that it is called the first of three "woes." Two more follow, each more severe than the last.

The Sixth Trumpet

"The sixth angel sounded, and I heard a voice from the four horns of the golden altar which is before God, one saying to the sixth angel who had the trumpet, 'Release the four angels who are bound at the great river Euphrates.' And the four angels, who had been prepared for the hour and day and month and year, were released, so that they might kill a third of mankind. And the number of the armies of the horsemen was two hundred million; I heard the number of them. And this is how I saw in the vision the horses and those who sat on them: *the riders* had breastplates *the color* of fire and of hyacinth and of brimstone; and the heads of the horses are like the heads of lions; and out of their mouths proceed fire and smoke and brimstone. A third of mankind was killed by these three plagues, by the fire and the smoke and the brimstone, which proceeded out of their mouths. For the power of the horses is in their mouths and in their tails; for their tails are like serpents and have heads; and with them they do harm. And the rest of mankind, who were not killed by these plagues, did not repent of the works of their hands, so as not to worship demons, and the idols of gold and of silver and of brass and of stone and of wood, which can neither see nor hear nor walk; and they did not repent of their murders nor of their sorceries nor of their immorality nor of their thefts" (Revelation 9:1-12).

Historical Overview

The church fathers and medieval scholars follow the expected pattern as set by the previous trumpets, but there is a noticable difference. Unlike the interpretations of the previous trumpet, medieval, Reformation, and modern scholars are moderately united in seeing an invading army from the east, armed with modern technology. Certainly, there are a large number who disagree, especially with the latter, but from the ancient to the modern, a majority of scholars agree that an army from the east will invade, armed with destructive powers beyond John's earthly knowledge.

The scholars of the ages disagree on, as to be expected, the other issues. Only recently have commentators begun to take the number 200,000,000 literally. The ancient and medieval scholars merely assumed the number to represent the whole known world, or the vastness of the army without respect to the literal number. Nevertheless, if one ignores the historicists' attempts to place the prophecy into the fold of history, there is a rare consensus among the majority. The nuances, however, have caused the most drastic of controversies; especially in regard to theory of modern technology.

Evaluation of the Sixth Trumpet

This vast army was constrained by four angels, or rather demons, who were bound at the river Euphrates. None doubt that these angels are, in fact, fallen angels, since righteous angels need not be bound.[674] That the angels are bound to the Euphrates stirs more debate. Euphrates has usually been viewed as the boundary between the east and west. It was the easternmost boundary of the ancient Roman Empire and the gateway to east Asia. The ancient city of Babylon was built over the Euphrates, and the Garden of Eden was located where the Tigris and Euphrates cross paths. The Euphrates is, therefore, an important location, but its exact meaning here is greatly disputed. One theory suggest that the Euphrates of Eden is not the same as the current river Euphrates (based on geologic changes during the Flood). It is argued that the fountains under that ancient Euphrates is a literal prison for demons to this day and their release is from the literal Euphrates of Eden.[675] Others take Euphrates as allegory, arguing that the enemies of Israel traditionally came from across the river.[676] The majority take it as the literal Euphrates river which today passes through Iraq.[677]

So we have here a depiction of four demons being released from the Euphrates, and bringing with them a hoard of 200,000,000 horsemen. Three questions arise; (1) who are the four demons? (2) is the number of the army literal? and (3) who are the horsemen?

Victorinus believed that the four angels represented four nations.[678] However, because no complete copy of his commentary exists, we cannot say what nations he believed may have been involved, nor their exact relationship to the horsemen. We know that he believed God assigned an angel to be guardian of each nation, and hence saw the four angels as the release of four nations who would war with one another.[679] Nonetheless, even this thesis admits the angels to be literal beings who are behind the actions of the nations involved. They are demons released to spread death in the last days, but what of the number of their army?

Most ancient commentators found it hard to take the numbers literally. The population of the entire planet is believed to have been no more than 200,000,000 at the time of Christ. Consequently, most scholars before recent times took the number to represent the world at large. The vastness and scope of the war is emphasized rather than the exact number. Even in modern times, many scholars have been reluctant to take the literal stance. Not a hundred years ago, even Henry Swete said that "these vast numbers forbid us to seek a literal fulfillment,"[680] but Nathaniel West believed it indicated the whole of the surviving world.[681] Still, only fifty years ago, men like George Ladd said, "it is difficult to believe that a literal number is intended."[682] Nevertheless, in 1965 *Time* magazine reported that Communist China had an army of 200,000,000 people in back 1961. This fact was reported by John Walvoord,[683] and later Hal Lindsey,[684] to support a literal number. Of course, those, like Lang,[685] who believe the army to consist of demons have no problem with the literal number. As Bullinger said, "spirits are 'legion,'and no difficulties can arise from their number."[686] Certainly, whether the army is human or demonic, there is nothing in the text to imply that the number 200,000,000 is not intended to be literal. In fact, the phrase "I heard the number of them," is a phrase indicative of military roll call; a literal number of soliders.

The main issue is whether the army is demonic of human. The list of those who believe the army is demonic is large and impressive, counting among them, Samuel Kellogg, Robert Govett, Joseph Seiss, E. W. Bullinger, G. H. Lang, William Newell, Arthur Bloomfield, George Ladd, Robert Mounce, Robert Thomas, Henry Morris, and Tim LaHaye. Conversely, a number of well respected scholars believe that the army is human. This includes Victorinus, Joseph Mede, Isaac Newton, John Darby, Walter Scott, Nathaniel West, Norman Harrison, H. A. Ironside, Dwight Pentecost, John Walvoord, and Hal Lindsey. Still others, like Charles Ryrie,[687] are undecided while Watchman Nee says they are men possessed by demons.[688]

Since there is, as its advocates frequently assert, no difficulty in accepting a literal demonic army, the possibility of a literal human army should be addressed. In the third century after Christ Victorinus had no problem believing the army to be of human origin. Although his commentary is incomplete, his clearly associates the angels with nations and their armies. The absence of the rest of his commentary on this section makes it impossible to determine exactly what nations he envisioned, but modern scholars have conencted the army with China, Russia, or even a massive Arabic invasion. The historicists, such as Mede and Newton, argued that the army was that of the Turks. Norman Harrison also believes that a Muslim army is depicted here, but rather than looking for past fulfillment he says that the passage shows a "Holy War breaking loose in the Last Days."[689] John Darby, on the other hand, believes that the Turks assist in the invasion of Gog and the northern confederacy (see Appendix C).[690] Thus, the Turks are a part of this northern confedeacy. In almost every case, Muslim invaders picture into the scenario.

Others argue that the boundary of Euphrates should deliniate an invading army from the east, not the north.[691] Pentecost does not specifically identify the army while Ironside, Walvoord, and Lindsey all see an invasion from China. This would certainly bode well with the fact of China's vast army exceeding the once hard to believe 200,000,000, but the central question is whether or not the description of the horsemen is consistent with a human army, mere symbolism, or demons.

Seiss believes that "John beholds troops of horses of an unearthly order,"[692] but Ironside insist that the horsemen only "seem like unearthly warriors."[693] They are described as having breastplates of fire. The heads of the horses are compared to lions, and fire and brimstone are said to emerge from their mouths (vs. 17). It further describes their tails as being *like* a serpent with its head and capable of harm (vs. 19).

Of the breastplates, there is some dispute as to whether the breastplates are properly worn by the riders or the horses. The NIV, ASV, and King James correctly leave out "riders" as the Greek does not specifically define who is wearing the breastplates. It is naturally assumed that the riders wear armor, but this ignores that horses were often equiped with armor as well. It may be that the passage refers to both the riders and the horses. This is significant because those who believe this is a human army note that armored vehicles could be envisioned here. John Walvoord, who is not prone to idle speculation, presumes that this may be "John's understanding of a scene in which modern warfare is under way."[694] This would fit well with the idea of a tail like a serpent from which devastation may come, for John would doubtless not understand a modern tank. The problem is in the description of the horse's heads. Certainly it is hard to see a modern tank as having a head like a lion, but then again a hundred years ago it would also have been absurd to envision a "horseless carriage" let alone one armored with breastplates for proctetion.

The fire and brimstone, or sulphur as translated by the NIV and others, is presumed by these commentators to be the destructive force of modern weaponry. Although Hal Lindsey again assumes thermonuclear warfare,[695] older commentators from as early as the Reformation have suggested that this might be the description of modern guns to a mind that had never seen gunpowder.[696] Now while this might be "ingenious conjecture,"[697] as Matthew Poole calls it, sulphur and brimstone are one and the same thing. Sulphur is, of course, a primary ingredient in modern weaponry. Consequently, Poole admits the "conjecture" to be the most "literal" of interpretations.[698]

Perhaps the strongest argument for a human army comes from the Old Testament. Appendix C will discuss the controversy over the four armies or confederacies which will compose the war of Armageddon, but it need only be stated here that if there is to be a campaign of Armageddon (as Pentecost calls it),[699] and not just a single battle, then the human armies described in various Old Testament passages, concerning the end times, must find their place here in Revelation. It is, therefore, logical to assume that the armies spoken of in the fifth and sixth trumpet, as well as in the sixth bowl, are those human armies referred to in Ezekiel, Joel,[700] and the other prophets.

Now according to verses fifteen and eighteen, this army slays a third of mankind. Based on the current population, this would mean that nearly two billion people are slaughtered by the army. Of course, many people have already died from the war, pestilence, and death which have previously been meted out against man, but the numbers should be taken literally, and certainly can be, given the advent of modern warfare. Demons may be intended here, but human armies cannot be ruled out, and may even be the preferable interpretation.

Thus it can be said with confidence that this sixth trumpet releases a literal army, whether human or demonic, which slaughters a third of mankind. The judgment itself may seem unbelievable to some, but result of the judgment is what it truly staggering, for we are told that, despite the events unfolding around them, man "did not repent of their murders nor of their sorceries nor of their immorality nor of their thefts" (vs. 21). Men refuse to repent. Their hearts are becoming bitter and cold. No longer are men turning from their sins, but embittering themselves.

One final note might be made here. The greek word for sorceries is *pharmakon* (φαρμάκων) from whence we get the english word "pharmacy." It is not tradional witchcraft, but that breed of religion which utilized potions and drugs. It can rightly be translated "poison," "potion," "medicine," or "drug."[701] Ever since the 1960s drug abuse has become a rampant problem. Whereas alchohol was once the "drug" of choice, modern men have now turned to the more dangerous drugs which were once connected to the sin of sorcery. It is probable that this is the sin of which the Bible speaks, and yet in Joel 2, which many consider a parallel passage, the Lord says, "'*even now*,' declares the Lord, 'return to Me with all your heart'" (vs. 12) and you will be forgiven. "*Even now*" God is prepared to forgive the repentant man, yet they have hardened their hearts against Him. This is the great lesson of Revelation. The judgments both chasten and hasten men's ultimate decision; to accept or reject the Messiah. The choice that many men delay until their old age, is forced upon them in their youth. This is one of the purposes for the judgments of God preceding Christ's return. When He does come, all men will have made up their minds before hand whether to embrace Him or hate Him.

The Seventh Trumpet and Conclusions

The seventh trumpet is not mentioned until chapter eleven, verse fifteen. Even then, the results of this last trumpet are not obvious to all. Is the seventh trumpet the third woe? We are not specifically told. Nor are we specifically told what the seventh trumpet encompasses. What we do know, however, is that after the seventh trumpet is sounded, angels begin to prophecy of God's final wrath and of the victory of Christ. We then read in verse nineteen "the temple of God, which is in heaven, was opened; and the ark of His covenant appeared in His temple, and there were flashes of lightning and sounds and peals of thunder and an earthquake and a great hailstorm." This temple appears again in chapter fifteen where we are told, "the temple of the tabernacle of testimony in heaven was opened, and the seven angels who had the seven plagues came out of the temple, clothed in linen, clean *and* bright, and girded around their breasts with golden girdles. And one of the four living creatures gave to the seven angels seven golden bowls full of the wrath of God, who lives forever and ever. And the temple was filled with smoke from the glory of God

135

and from His power; and no one was able to enter the temple until the seven plagues of the seven angels were finished" (15:5-8). Thus, it seems that even as the seventh seal released the seven trumpets, the seventh trumpet releases the seven bowl judgments.

It is, therefore, best to consider that the entire series of bowl judgments as the third and last "woe." The bowl judgments come under the seventh trumpet, or are at least signalled by it.

In regard to the trumpets, there is an apparent cause and effect relationship between the trumpets. The first trumpet signals either a meteor shower or, as some have suggested, a nuclear strike. The second and third trumpets signal the fall of two pieces of an asteroid, falling respectively in the sea and on the fresh water lakes or resevoirs. These incidents, perhaps all three, doubtless send up smoke and debris which may be related to the fourth trumpet judgment, which results in the darkening of the sun, moon, and stars so that darkness covers the globe. War, which had originally broken loose in the second seal, is now unrestrained. The fifth trumpet unleashes what looks like giant armored locusts who torture and torment men for five months. Finally, after five months of torment, man's release comes in the form of death caused by an army of 200,000,000 horsemen, whose description defies the ancient knowledge of John. Whether these incidents are of earthly origin or the emanations of demons, mankind will know that they are under judgment, but will refuse to repent.

The seven trumpet judgments now passed, seven bowls of wrath are coming. In those bowls "the wrath of God is finished" (Revelation 15:1). Before those bowls are poured out, however, the Bible pauses to explain the background of the tribulation and the 70th week of Daniel. Chapter thirteen describes the rise and rule of the anti-Christ in those last days.

CHAPTER SUMMARY

The trumpet judgments appear to be connected to one another much as a series of chain reactions are connected. Some see human agencies involved, while others see God alone as the agent, but in either case it is God's who is orchestrating the judgments upon man. The trumpet judgments are as follows:

1. Some form of meteoric objects fall to the earth and burn a third of the earth, trees, and grass.
2. A larger meteoric object, "like a great mountain," falls into the sea and destroys a third of the life and ships in the sea, turning the sea blood red.
3. An asteroid or meteor falls into fresh water deposits and poisons the water so that there is no fresh water to drink. This meteor is called "Wormwood."
4. As a result of these catastrophes the sun, moon, and stars, are darkened and there is a third less light, both night and day.

5. An army likened to locusts rises up and tortures men for five months. The effects of their tortures have been likened by some to chemical warfare. This army is led by the demon Abaddon, who may or may not serve the anti-Christ.
6. 200,000,000 soldiers (possibly eastern enemies of the locusts) kill a third of mankind with fire and sulpher.
7. The seventh trumpet releases the next seven judgments, but only after an interlude given in the next few chapters.

Charts on the First Four Trumpets

The Church Fathers	Chiliast	The majority are silent, preferring to let the passages "speak for themselves." Such is the attitude of a literal approach.
Nicholas of Lyra (typifies the medieval view)	Medieval Millenarian	1st Trump: The heresy of Arianism. 2nd Trump: The heresy of Macendonius. 3rd: Pelagian heresy. 4th: Eutyches' heresy.
Joseph Mede	Historicist premillennialist	1st: The gothic invasion of Rome. 2nd: The sack of Rome under Alaric. 3rd: Odoacar's conquest of Rome. 4th: Ostrogothic rule of Rome.
Isaac Newton	Historicist premillennialist	1st: A depiction of the Byzantine empire. 2nd: Depicts the western empire. 3rd: The division of empire after the sack of Rome. 4th: The decline of imperial authority.
John Darby	Dispensational premillennialist	1st: A judgment upon a monarchy. 2nd: The masses are subjected to judgment. 3rd: The state falls. 4th: The political authorities of the world collapse.
Robert Govett	Futurist premillennialist	1st: Literal hail and fire. 2nd: A meteor. 3rd: Another meteor. 4th: Literal darkness.
Joseph Seiss	Futurist premillennialist	1st: Literal hail and fire. 2nd: A meteor. 3rd: A meteor or comet. 4th: Literal darkness.
E. W. Bullinger	Ultradispensationalist	1st: Literal hail and fire. 2nd: Literal. 3rd: Literal but rejects meteor. Refuses to speculate. 4th: Literal darkness.
H. A. Ironside	Dispensational premillennialist	1st: A judgment upon mankind. 2nd: The fall of "spiritual Babylon." 3rd: Fall of the religious leader of Babylon. 4th: Darkness as heresy.
Dwight Pentecost	Dispensational premillennialist	1st: No comment. 2nd: Judgment on Palestine. 3rd: Deprivation of "the water of life." 4th: The fall of governments.

Norman Harrison	Midtribulational premillennialist	1st: War. 2nd: The fall of a nation. 3rd: The ejection of Satan from heaven. 4th: Fall of governments.
John Walvoord	Dispensational premillennialist	1st: Literal hail and fire. 2nd: Literal. 3rd: "Mass from outer space." 4th: Eclipse.
Robert Mounce	Posttribulational Premillennialist	1st: Apparently literal. 2nd: No elaboration. 3rd: Meteor, but not necessarily literal. 4th: Literal darkness.
George Ladd	Posttribulational Premillennialist	1st: "Electrical display" in the sky. 2nd: No comment. 3rd: Possible meteor. 4th: Ambiguous, but appears to rejects literal darkness.
Hal Lindsey	Dispensational premillennialist	1st: ICBM missle attack. 2nd: Either meteor or H-bomb. 3rd: Possibly a thermonuclear bomb. 4th: Literal darkness from radioactive fallout.
Tim LaHaye	Dispensational premillennialist	1st: Literal hail and fire. 2nd: Meteor striking Mediterranean Sea. 3rd: Another meteor. 4th: "Day and night will be reversed."

Theological Breakdown

	Position
Premillennial Historicists	Various contradictory attempts to find historical fulfillments in the past.
Dispensational Pretribulational Premillennialists	Mixed, but usually a literal approach, varying only in speculation as to their exact fulfillment (i.e. will it be a meteor, asteroid, or nuclear weapon?).
Midtribulational (and "Pre-Wrath") Premillennialists	Mixed. Some literal, but others take the more spiritual approach.
Covenant Theologians and Postribulational Premillennialists	Mixed, but generally prefer a more figurative approach.
Progressive Dispensationalists and other variant Premillenial views	Evenly mixed.

The First Four Trumpets as the Spread of Heresies
Tenants of:
Various views attributing the events of the first four trumpets to various heresies spread among the world.

Popular advocates from:
The Church Fathers : None known.
Medieval Theologians : Nicholas of Lyra and most other medieval interpreters.
Reformation Scholars : Numerous historicists.
Post-Reformation Scholars : None cited.
Modern Evangelicals : H. A. Ironside.

Strengths:
1) Stars are sometimes used as symbols for angels or demons.
2) "Earth" is alleged to refer to Palestine or Rome.

Weaknesses:
1) These are judgments from God. Since when as hersey ever been sent by God?
2) The passages often parallel the plagues of Exodus. If the plagues on Egypt were literal, why shouldn't these be?
3) No Biblical proof exist that "earth" refers to Palestine or Rome.
4) The Bible usually identifies symbols as such but does not identify these as such.
5) There is no general consensus as the meaning of these alleged symbols.
6) There is no parallel in the Old Testament or apocryphal literature to show that earth, grass, trees, mountains, the sun, the moon, wormwood, or fire represent heresy.
7) There is nothing in the context to imply a symbolic use of tree, earth, grass, sun, or moon.
8) Historicists must speculate on what heresy is intended.
9) Revelation describes uncommon judgments, but heresy is common.

The First Four Trumpets as the Fall of Governments
Tenants of:
Various views attributing the events to the fall of governents, nations, and political or religious leaders.

Popular advocates from:
The Church Fathers : None known.
Medieval Theologians : None cited.
Reformation Scholars : Joseph Mede, Isaac Newton, and many other historicists.
Post-Reformation Scholars : John Darby and Walter Scott.
Modern Evangelicals : Norman Harrison and J. Dwight Pentecost.

Strengths:
1) Trees are sometimes used as representations of people or kingdoms.
2) "Earth" is alleged to refer to Palestine or Rome.
3) Men are compared to grass in Isaiah 40:6-7.
4) Stars are sometimes used as symbols for angels or demons.
5) Mountain is occasionally used as apparent symbol for a kingdom.

Weaknesses:
1) The passages often parallel the plagues of Exodus. If the plagues on Egypt were literal, why shouldn't these be?
2) If the earth, grass, and trees are symbolic then so must hail, fire, and destruction. No answer as to the meaning of these can be agreed upon.
3) There is nothing in the context to imply a symbolic use of tree, earth, grass, sun, or moon.
4) No Biblical proof exist that earth refers to Palestine or Rome.
5) Isaiah 40:6-7 is a metaphorical use which does not translate to Revelation well. Revelation establishes no metaphor. No other symbolic use of grass exist in the Bible.
6) The Bible usually identifies symbols as such but does not identify these as such.
7) There is no general consensus as the meaning of these alleged symbols.
8) If the sea is symbolic then why are ships and sea creatures mentioned?
9) If the sea is symbolic, what does the blood mean? There is no consensus on this.

Literal Views of the First Four Trumpets
Tenants of:
The passages are taken at face value with debate being reserved as to the exact nuance of the passage or its natural explanation.

Popular advocates from:
The Church Fathers : Most were apparently literal including Lactantius.
Medieval Theologians : None known.
Reformation Scholars : None cited.
Post-Reformation Scholars : Robert Govett, J. A. Seiss, and E. W. Bullinger.
Modern Evangelicals : William Newell, Arthur Bloomfield, Watchman Nee, John Walvoord, Hal Lindsey, Charles Ryrie, Henry Morris, Robert Thomas, and Tim LaHaye.

Strengths:

1) The Bible usually identifies symbols as such, but does not identify these as such.
2) The passages parallel the plagues of Exodus. Since the plagues on Egypt were literal, so should these be.
3) The description of a star burning like a lamp is parallel to numerous ancient references of meteors.
4) "Falling stars" are a common description of meteor showers.
5) The object in the third trumpet is said to be "like a mountain," thereby implying descriptive comparison, not symbolism.
6) The specific mention of ships and sea creatures implies that the sea is literal.
7) There is no Biblical or extra-Biblical symbolic usage of many of the references found in these passages.
8) The literal meaning makes for a cause and effect relationship between at least three of the trumpets.
9) If the trumpets are a sign, then they should not be everyday occurences.
10) The figurative interpreters cannot agree on the meaning of the symbols.
11) The figurative approach requires using various symbols with the same meaning. Logically, if one meaning is intended, one symbol is used.

Weaknesses:
1) Trees are sometimes used as representations of people or kingdoms.
2) Men are compared to grass in Isaiah 40:6-7 in a metaphor.
3) Stars are sometimes used symbolically.

Chart on the Fifth Trumpet

Pierre D'Olivi	Medieval Millenarian	The locusts as apostate clergy.
Nicholas of Lyra	Medieval Millenarian	The locusts as the Vandals.
Joseph Mede	Historicist premillennialist	The locusts as Muslim Saracens.
Isaac Newton	Historicist premillennialist	The locusts as Arab invaders.
John Darby	Dispensational premillennialist	Ambiguous. Apparently symbolic, but possibly demonic.
Robert Govett	Futurist premillennialist	The locusts as a demonic army.
Joseph Seiss	Futurist premillennialist	The locusts as a demonic army.
Walter Scott	Dispensational premillennialist	The locusts as a symbol for the judgment of God.
E. W. Bullinger	Ultradispensationalist	The locusts as a demonic army.
H. A. Ironside	Dispensational premillennialist	The locusts as an occultic army.
G.H. Lang	Futurist premillennialist	The locusts as a demonic army.
William Newell	Futurist premillennialist	The locusts as a demonic army.
John Walvoord	Dispensational premillennialist	The locusts as a demonic army.
Charles Ryrie	Dispensational premillennialist	The locusts as a demonic army.
Robert Mounce	Posttribulational Premillennialist	Symbolic of demons.
George Ladd	Posttribulational Premillennialist	"Symbolic of demonic powers."
Hal Lindsey	Dispensational premillennialist	The locusts as a demonic army.
Tim LaHaye	Dispensational premillennialist	The locusts as a demonic army.

Chart on the Sixth Trumpet

Victorinus	Chiliast	Apparently a literal human army.
Nicholas of Lyra	Medieval Millenarian	Allegorical for the popes and antipopes of history.
Joseph Mede	Historicist premillennialist	The Turkish invasion of Byzantium.
Isaac Newton	Historicist premillennialist	The Turkish invasion of Byzantium.
John Darby	Dispensational premillennialist	A human army of Turk in alliance with Gog. The invasion in last days.
Robert Govett	Futurist premillennialist	A demonic army.
Joseph Seiss	Futurist premillennialist	A demonic army of infernal calvary.
E. W. Bullinger	Ultradispensationalist	A demonic army.
Walter Scott	Dispensational premillennialist	A human army, Gog and the northern cofederacy, invading in last days.
H. A. Ironside	Dispensational premillennialist	Human warriors.
William Newell	Dispensational premillennialist	A demonic army.
Dwight Pentecost	Dispensational premillennialist	A human army in the last days.
Norman Harrison	Midtribulational premillennialist	Islamic warriors invading in last days.
John Walvoord	Dispensational premillennialist	An eastern human army in last days.
Robert Mounce	Posttribulational Premillennialist	A demonic army.
George Ladd	Posttribulational Premillennialist	Symbolic of demonic powers.
Hal Lindsey	Dispensational premillennialist	A Chinese invasion in last days.
Tim LaHaye	Dispensational premillennialist	A demonic army.

6

The Beasts of Revelation

There are several beasts in the book of Revelation. There is also much confusion as to the exact meaning of the beasts, and their relationship to the anti-Christ. Some define the first beast *as* the anti-Christ, some associate the anti-Christ with the second beast, while still others insist that the anti-Christ is but the seventh or eighth head of the first beast. This is the most difficult section of Revelation to discuss, because it involves the discussion of Daniel's prophecies as well. The imagery is intertwined with Daniel's. The two cannot be taken individually, but must be merged together to complete the picture.

The First Beast

> "He stood on the sand of the seashore. And I saw a beast coming up out of the sea, having ten horns and seven heads, and on his horns *were* ten diadems, and on his heads *were* blasphemous names. And the beast which I saw was like a leopard, and his feet were like *those* of a bear, and his mouth like the mouth of a lion. And the dragon gave him his power and his throne and great authority." (Revelation 13:1-2).

This first beast is seen rising up out the sea. This imagery is not difficult. Revelation 17:15 says, "the waters which you saw ... are peoples and multitudes and nations and tongues." In Ephesians 4:14, men are compared to those being "tossed here and there by waves." The imagery is also seen in Jeremiah 47:2 where an invading army is compared to a flood of water. The Bible, therefore, uses the sea, not as an ambiguous allegory, but as a symbol for the multitudes or nations. The beast, thus, rises up out of the troubled nations. G. H. Pember calls it the "sea of anarchy,"[702] and Henry Morris suggest that the peoples of a Mediterranean kingdom in intended.[703] These theories may read too much into the depiction, but it is a sea of troubled nations. That is all we can say. This description is not unique. It appears elsewhere in the Bible, in relation to other beasts. The book of Daniel describes a prophecy wherein four beasts arise from the troubled sea. These four beasts were described as being similar to a lion, a bear, a leopard, and a fourth beast so terrible that it defied description. This is the prophecy of Daniel's beasts, and the last beast is also a foreshadowing of the same beast we have here in Revelation. It is impossible to discuss the beast of Revelation without comparing it to the book of Daniel.

The Relationship to Daniel's Beasts

Part of the key to the identity of the beast lies in its description. The seven heads are important, but equally important is its description as being similar to the attributes of a leopard, bear, and lion. Virtually every commentator agrees that this imagery is drawn directly from a vision to Daniel. In that vision:

"Daniel saw a dream and visions in his mind *as he lay* on his bed; then he wrote the dream down *and* related the *following* summary of it. Daniel said, 'I was looking in my vision by night, and behold, the four winds of heaven were stirring up the great sea. And four great beasts were coming up from the sea, different from one another. The first *was* like a lion and had *the* wings of an eagle. I kept looking until its wings were plucked, and it was lifted up from the ground and made to stand on two feet like a man; a human mind also was given to it. And behold, another beast, a second one, resembling a bear. And it was raised up on one side, and three ribs *were* in its mouth between its teeth; and thus they said to it, 'Arise, devour much meat!' After this I kept looking, and behold, another one, like a leopard, which had on its back four wings of a bird; the beast also had four heads, and dominion was given to it. After this I kept looking in the night visions, and behold, a fourth beast, dreadful and terrifying and extremely strong; and it had large iron teeth. It devoured and crushed, and trampled down the remainder with its feet; and it was different from all the beasts that were before it, and it had ten horns'" (Daniel 7:1-7).

The imagery is obviously similar, right down to the ten horns on the last beast's head. Fortunately, the key to the vision of Daniel is given to him.

"He told me and made known to me the interpretation of these things: 'These great beasts, which are four *in number,* are four kings *who* will arise from the earth. But the saints of the Highest One will receive the kingdom and possess the kingdom forever, for all ages to come.' Then I desired to know the exact meaning of the fourth beast, which was different from all the others, exceedingly dreadful, with its teeth of iron and its claws of bronze, *and which* devoured, crushed, and trampled down the remainder with its feet, and *the meaning* of the ten horns that *were* on its head, and the other *horn* which came up, and before which three *of them* fell, namely, that horn which had eyes and a mouth uttering great *boasts,* and which was larger in appearance than its associates. I kept looking, and that horn was waging war with the saints and overpowering them until the Ancient of Days came, and judgment was passed in favor of the saints of the Highest One, and the time arrived when the saints took possession of the kingdom. Thus he said: 'The fourth beast will be a fourth kingdom on the earth, which will be different from all the *other* kingdoms, and it will devour the whole earth and tread it down and crush it. As for the ten horns, out of this kingdom ten kings will arise; and another will arise after them, and he will be different from the previous ones and will subdue three kings. And he will speak out against the Most High and wear down the saints of the Highest One, and he will intend to make alterations in times and in law; and they will be given into his hand for a time, times, and half a time.

But the court will sit *for judgment,* and his dominion will be taken away, annihilated and destroyed forever. Then the sovereignty, the dominion, and the greatness of *all* the kingdoms under the whole heaven will be given to the people of the saints of the Highest One; His kingdom *will be* an everlasting kingdom, and all the dominions will serve and obey Him'" (Daniel 7:16-27).

The vision is, therefore, parallel not only to this passage in Revelation, but also to Daniel's vision of the giant statue (Daniel 2:31-45). In that vision Nebuchadnezzar had a dream of a statue with a "head of fine gold, its breast and its arms of silver, its belly and its thighs of bronze, its legs of iron, its feet partly of iron and partly of clay" (2:32-33). Daniel's interpretation of that dream was as follows:

"You, O king, are the king of kings, to whom the God of heaven has given the kingdom, the power, the strength, and the glory; and wherever the sons of men dwell, *or* the beasts of the field, or the birds of the sky, He has given *them* into your hand and has caused you to rule over them all. You are the head of gold. And after you there will arise another kingdom inferior to you, then another third kingdom of bronze, which will rule over all the earth. Then there will be a fourth kingdom as strong as iron; inasmuch as iron crushes and shatters all things, so, like iron that breaks in pieces, it will crush and break all these in pieces. And in that you saw the feet and toes, partly of potter's clay and partly of iron, it will be a divided kingdom; but it will have in it the toughness of iron, inasmuch as you saw the iron mixed with common clay. And *as* the toes of the feet *were* partly of iron and partly of pottery, *so* some of the kingdom will be strong and part of it will be brittle. And in that you saw the iron mixed with common clay, they will combine with one another in the seed of men; but they will not adhere to one another, even as iron does not combine with pottery. And in the days of those kings the God of heaven will set up a kingdom which will never be destroyed, and *that* kingdom will not be left for another people; it will crush and put an end to all these kingdoms, but it will itself endure forever" (Daniel 2:36-44).

So the two visions are of the same thing. Both represent the last four great kingdoms of the earth. Babylon is identified as being the first. From ancient to modern times the second kingdom has unanimously been accepted as the Medo-Persia Empire of Cyrus the Great.[704] The two arms of the statue have been suggested to represent the two "arms" of the Medo-Persian empire, which was a conglomeration of Medes and Persians who banded together to defeat the Babylonians.[705] This prophecy was itself fulfilled in Daniel's lifetime as he lived to see Cyrus occupy Babylon.[706] The third kingdom is again unanimously interpreted to be the Greek Empire of Alexander the Great who swiftly conquered the Persian Empire and subjugated it.[707] After Alexander's death, he left no heir, and so the kingdom was divided amongst his four generals,[708] believed to be represented by the "four wings of a bird" and the "four heads" of the leopard (Daniel 1:6).[709] So sure are scholars of the first three empires that liberal scholars, who deny the prophetic element in Scripture, have tried to argue that Daniel was written *after* the rise of Greece.[710] In this way they can repudiate the prophetic element of Daniel and reduce it to a historical allegory. That this is not the case is easily proven by textual criticism, for several passages of Daniel have even been found in the Dead Sea Scroll indicating that Daniel had been around far longer than these critics suggest.[711] The point is that the identification of the second empire with Persia and the third with Greece is undeniable even by critics of the Bible.

It is with the fourth kingdom that contoversy emerges. Even as Daniel was preoccupied with the fourth beast (7:19), the fourth beast has been the subject of debate for over two millennia.

Most every scholar, and all premillennialists, recognize Rome as the last beast.[712] Even the ancient Jews believed Rome to be the last empire,[713] which is one reason many expected the Messiah to come and crush the Roman Empire. The debate is not with its identification, but with its fall. Did not the Roman Empire fall centuries ago? This subject has been the subject of many dissertations,[714] but all historians agree that Rome's fall was not traditional. It was divided and segmented, but it has *never* been replaced by another kingdom. Many commentators have argued that the two legs represent the two branches of the Roman Empire as it divided late in its history. Some believe that "the western leg of iron incorporated the Roman Catholic Church and the eastern leg the Eastern Orthodox Church."[715] Others say they represent the eastern and western empires from Constantine's day.[716] Critics have disputed this, saying "because the Western Empire lasted for a few hundred years, but the Eastern Empire lasted until 1453, you have to make this image stand on one leg for most of the time."[717] However, this is based on the popular, but erroneous, belief that Rome fell in 476 A.D. In fact, days after the sack of Rome, Odoacer stood before the Senate of Rome and accepted the title of Patrician from the Emperor Zeno.[718] Says one historian, "there was only one empire at the time and no one would have dreamed of talking of two."[719] The empire was not truly divided until the time of Charlemagne, and even then, late into the Middle Ages, the two empires (the Holy Roman Empire and the Byzantine Empire) clung to desperate hope that the two halves of the empire would again be united.[720] Thus, it is the Holy Roman Empire and the Byzantine Empire, or the western and eastern Roman empires as they are referred to by the ancients, that are represented by the two legs of Daniel's statue.

What of the statue's ten toes? This is the great debate, for the ten toes are, again, universally seen as a parallel prophecy to the ten horns of the fourth beast of Daniel, and the beast of Revelation. This will be discussed below, and will be addressed there. Nevertheless, the importance of these passages is that the Bible plainly teaches that *Rome* will be replaced by the Messianic kingdom. The medievals had no problem attempting to argue that they were living in the Millennial Kingdom of Revelation 20,[721] but for the more serious scholar, and for the premillennialists, there was only one answer to this prophecy. Rome *must rise again*, and it would rise under the arm of the anti-Christ. The restoration and reunion of the ancient Roman empire has been *the* subject of prophetic interpretation for millennia. Commonly called today the "Revived Roman Empire" or the "Restored Roman Empire," it is believed by most (in various forms) that the beast of Revelation is "the world-power in its final consummation."[722] The beast, in some form, is the portrait of the final stage of the Roman Empire, or the "Revived Roman Empire," under its final ruler, the anti-Christ. This fact shall become evident in the pages to come.

The Heads of the Beast

In addition to Daniel, there is another parallel passage found in chapter seventeen of Revelation. The section deals with a harlot who is said to ride the beast. This harlot will be discussed in another chapter, but the description of the beast in that chapter is essential to understanding the imagery in this chapter. It reads:

> "The beast that you saw was and is not, and is about to come up out of the abyss and to go to destruction. And those who dwell on the earth will wonder, whose name has not been written in the book of life from the foundation of the world, when they see the beast, that he was and is not and will come. Here is the mind which has wisdom. The seven heads are seven mountains on which the woman sits, and they are seven kings; five have fallen, one is, the other has not yet come; and when he comes, he must remain a little while. And the beast which was and is not, is himself also an eighth, and is *one* of the seven, and he goes to destruction" (Revelation 17:8-11).

Thus reads one of the most controversial verses in the Bible. The beast is described as existing the past, but not the present, and returning in the future. The seven heads of the beast are then given a *double* meaning. They represent "seven mountains on which the woman sits," but also "seven kings," five of whom have fallen. Save for the number of the beast (vs. 18), there have perhaps been no more disputed passages than these.

The Seven Heads
Some have argued that the identity of the seven mountains, or hills, are the same as the seven kings. They attempt to discard the difficulties by claiming they are exactly one and the same thing.[723] In fact, this cannot be. The Scripture makes it clear that there is a *double meaning*, even as many prophecies have double fulfillments. The seven heads represent not one thing, but two.

149

The first question involves a debate over whether or not the passage refers to seven mountains or seven hills. "Seven mountains" is supported by translations like the KJV, NAS, and NRSV. "Seven hills" is found in translations like the NIV, Living Bible, NAB, and Amplified Bible. The Greek word is *ore* (ὄρη). Most Greek dictionaries and lexicons lists both "mountain" and "hill" as a possible translation. The *Complete Vocabulary Guide to the Greek New Testament* list "mountain, hill, mount."[724] Even William Mounce's *Basis of Biblical Greek*, which gives only primary definitions, list both mountain and hill as the main translation.[725] The reason is that ancient languages did not distinguish between mountains and hills. It is only in recent times that scientists have attempted to delineate a difference for technical reasons. Even to this day people will argue about what is and isn't a mountain.[726] Mount Zion in Israel is actually considered a large hill by some, but it still a mount or mountain, regardless of whether it has a sharp peak.

Although Henry Morris has argued that the Greek word for "hill" is *bounos* (βουνος), as opposed to *ore* (ὄρη),[727] the word *bounos* (βουνος) is merely an old antiquated word for "hill" or "mound."[728] It is found only twice in the New Testament,[729] and those are direct quotations from the Greek Septuagint (a Greek translation of the Old Testament). Moreover, the word *ore* (ὄρη) is itself found in the Septuagint many times for the word correctly translated as hill by the KJV and others. If one were to had to translate the English word "hill" into *koine* Greek then he would *have* to use the word "*ore*."

The real reason for this debate is that "seven hills" is universally taken as a reference to Rome. Rome has been called the city on "seven hills" for centuries before Revelation was written. Virgil, Horace, Tibullus, Propertius, Ovid, Silius Italicus, Statius, Claudius, Symmachus, and Martial, all of whom were Greeks or Romans, referred to the city of Rome as the city on seven "*ore*" or "*montium*," the Latin word for mountain.[730] Indeed, every year the festival of Septimontium was celebrated. This is literally translated, "the festival of the seven *mountains*."[731] This was the byname of Rome centuries before John wrote Revelation! In fact, during the reign of the Roman Emperor Vespasian a new coin was released featuring Rome as represented by a woman, Roma, sitting on seven hills! When members of the seven Churches in Asia bought food they would have seen the image of a woman on seven hills emblazoned upon the coins with which they purchased. So sure is this identification that one scholar who doubts this is a reference to Rome has had to discount it in this way:

> "No real wisdom beyond that of an ordinary Roman soldier would be required to make such an identification, and we have seen that the perplexing description used before us requires an extraordinary 'mind which has wisdom' ... It is not the common knowledge of the world which will yield up the mystery of the Beast; it is the uncommon knowledge of the Word of God."[732]

So then, even those who reject the view that this is an identification of Rome must admit that "common knowledge" would identify the seven *"ore"* with Rome. So obvious would this be to someone reading John's book in the first or second century that "no real wisdom beyond that of an ordinary Roman soldier would be required to make such an identification." Logically, the only realistic interpretation of this verse, and the one that has endured throughout the ages, is that the seven hills, or mountains, refer to the city of Rome. The only other argument made against this view is a technical one which argues that modern Rome has many more than the original seven hills located within its city limits. Nonetheless, such an argument does not nullify the fact that this city was "the city founded on seven hills" and that the city has been known by that name for twenty five hundred years.[733]

This, the first aspect of the double meaning, will make more sense to the reader in the pages to come. It was, and still is, the location of the beast at the time John wrote, but there is a *second* meaning. The heads are *also* "seven kings." Five had fallen, one "is," and another is to come.

Many commentators through the years have tried fruitlessly to associate these "kings" with the emperors of Rome. The various attempts to identify them have borne little fruit. Victorinus said the five fallen kings were Otho, Vitellius, Galba, Vespasian, and Titus, who preceded Domitian, the emperor at the time John wrote.[734] He counts Domitian, then, as the one who "is," and Nerva as the one who was to stay "a little while."[735] Since Otho was scarcely the beginning of Rome, and seems to have no real relationship to the prophecy, most have sought other emperors as candidates. Some suggest that it was the emperors who sought self deification including Julius Caesar, Augustus, Claudius, Vespasian, and Titus,[736] but, in fact, all the emperors were worshipped. This is not helpful in identifying five pre-Revelation emperors. Others have suggested that it was the emperors who met an unnatural death. Nee list Julius Caesar (who was not an emperor), Tiberius, Caligula, Claudius, and Nero,[737] but ignores that Galba, Otho, and Vitellius were also murdered before Domitian.[738] Joachim identified the five fallen as Herod, Nero, Constantius, Mohammad, and Chosroes, with Saladin as the one who "is."[739] The list of candidates is practically endless. There is simply no way to make the emperor theory work. After Julius Caesar, who was not an emperor, Augustus Caesar became the first emperor of Rome followed by Tiberius, Caligula, Claudius, and Nero. Three emperors followed Nero in quick succession; Galba, Otho, and Vitellius. Next came Vespasian and Titus who were followed by Domitian, the last of the Flavian emperors. There is no way to make Domitian the sixth king.[740]

Obviously, no expositors have been able to come to any sort of consensus upon the identity of these "kings." This is one of many reasons that a number of scholars have abandoned the idea of kings altogether. The problem is that every translation correctly renders *basileis* (βασιλεῖς) as "kings," and a "king" can only be narrowly interpreted, but the passage does not lend itself to this interpretation easily. This problem is only resolved by acknowledging that the Bible is using personification. There are two separate theories which utilize this presupposition. The first of these was popularized in the Reformation age. It is consistent with the line of thinking which associates the anti-Christ with a system rather than a person (see below), and argues that the seven heads are seven "successive forms of government"[741] under Rome. These men argue that kings, consuls, dictators, decemvirs, and tribunes constitute the five "fallen" systems of government.[742] The emperors constitute the one which "is," and the final system is that of the anti-Christ.[743] This theory is weak for a number of reasons. First, to differentiate between the "dictators" and consuls is suspect since many of the "dictators" *were* consuls.[744] Moreover, decemvirs and tribunes were representatives, but not truly heads of state. To argue that these were different systems of government is dubious.

The better alternative is also one of the most ancient views. If the city of Rome is portrayed by a seven headed beast then these kings could also be personification of king*doms*, not individual rulers. In Daniel the kingdom of Babylon was represented by its head of gold and "just as Nebuchadnezzar was the head of gold,"[745] so also the kingdoms were identified by their kings. Says Bullinger, "the terms kings and kingdom are interchageable in Daniel."[746] Seiss observes, "there can be no kingdom without a king, and no empire without and emperor; neither can there be a king without a kingdom."[747] Although Lang does not take a stand on the views, he reminds us that "it does not say five had *died*; but had *fallen*."[748]

The best aspect of this theory is that it matches the parallel passages in Daniel. Even as the beasts of Daniel were kingdoms or empires, so also the seven heads here represent the kingdoms of history. Norman Harrison has reminded us that in Daniel 7 the four beasts had a total of seven heads. The first beast, that of the lion, had one head. The second beast, that of the bear, had but a single head. The third beast, the leopard, however, had four heads. Thus, the last beast's head makes a total of seven heads.[749] The only problem with this comes in determining how "five have fallen." Harrison attempts to argue that the five fallen were the great kings of those empires, rendering them as Nebuchadnezzar, Belshazzar, Antiochus Epiphanes, Herod the Great, and Herod Agrippa.[750] This list, of course, ignores many important kings, and list two kings of Israel. The better alternative is an ancient variant of the model.

The four kingdoms of Daniel cannot be ignored. They are clearly a part of this beast, but three heads remain unaccounted for. Since Revelation discusses the final stage of these kingdoms or beast, the seventh head must, and is commonly agreed to, represent the kingdom of the anti-Christ or the "Revived Roman Empire." The first two heads are believed to depict the two great kingdoms, and antagonists of Israel, which preceded Daniel. This would account for why the kingdoms were not seen in Daniel's prophecy. They are said to be Egypt and Assyria.

Critics have suggested that the identification of these seven kingdoms is as arbitrary as the attempt to identify seven Roman Emperors from among the ten who reigned before Domitian. They argue that China or even the ancient Hittite or Philistine kingdoms could equally qualify as great kingdoms of the earth. Nevertheless, the nation of Israel and the Jews are the focal point of history and the Bible. China obviously had never had any dealings with God's people and could not seriously be considered a great kingdom of the Bible, in which it is never mentioned. The idea that the Hittites could be a great kingdom deserves more credence but falls apart for two reasons. First, this kingdom can scarcely be considered truly "great" since so little was known about it apart from the Bible. So little, in fact, that many Bible critics denied the kingdom ever even existed until archaeologists found the remains of the civilization in 1876.[751] Surely if the kingdom were truly great there would have existed much more information about the kingdom than that little portion found within the Bible and that which was recently unearthed by archaeologists. Secondly, while the Hittites did form an early kingdom they were neither an empire[752] nor a threat to Israel. There was interaction between the Jews and Hittites and, doubtless, occasional conflicts, but the two nations seem to have been neutral to each other and perhaps even allies at certain times.[753] There is no evidence, Biblically or otherwise, to suggest that the Hittite kingdom ever significantly impacted upon the history of the Jews.

This is the same reason that the Philistines and other minor nations that Israel had dealt with can be discounted. True Israel had conflict with the Philistines, but Israel prevailed. Moreover, if this view is correct then the seven kingdoms would have to be empires, not merely single kingdoms, and they would have to have had significant impact upon God's people, and the history of the world itself. Empires are made up of several kingdoms and therefore, by definition, impact upon the history of many people, not merely their own.

Egypt enslaved Israel for centuries, Assyria conquered the northern kingdom of Israel, Babylon conquered Judah, Persia was sovereign over Israel and Haman plotted genocide, under Greece Antiochus Epiphanes desecrated the temple and oppressed the Israelites, and Rome destroyed the temple in 70 A.D.[754] These are the six nations depicted in the first six heads of the beast. This is the acknowledged view of expositors for centuries, with little variance. It was embraced by Joseph Mede, Joseph Seiss, Sir Robert Anderson, George Ladd, Hal Lindsey, Marvin Rosenthal, and many others.[755] Bullinger followed the view closely, but began with Daniel's kingdoms. Hence, Babylon, Persia, Greece, and Rome were the first four.[756] He then made the Muslim Dynasties the fifth head with the kingdom of the anti-Christ as the sixth and Christ's Millennial Kingdom as the seventh.[757] Other ancient derivatives of this view include Pierre D'Olivi's attempt to associate the heads with the kingdom of the Jews, pagans, Greeks, Goths, Vandals, Lombards, and Saracens.[758] Francis Lambert, author of the first Protestant commentary on Revelation, identified the seven heads as the serpent from Eden, Babel's descent into idolatry, the Assyrian/Babylonian kingdom, Medo-Persia, Greece, Rome, and the kingdom of the anti-Christ.[759] This view was echoed by John Bale who interpreted the seven heads of the beast as governors, but the seven heads of the Dragon he saw as identical to Lambert's list.[760] This may also have been the view of Hippolytus, although a complete commentary is lacking from him. We only know that Hippolytus saw the sixth head as the Rome Empire, implying that he also saw the other heads as empires as well.[761]

The final reason that this view should be the accepted view is that it is the only view which can adequately explain the double meaning of the heads. The seven hills must refer to Rome. If the "kings" refer to the kingdoms, then Rome is to be the location of the beast in the last days. In other words, the beast is *properly* interpreted as the kingdoms of Satan. However, his location has changed throughout history. The key to his current location is in the seven hills; Rome. Rome was the sixth head, and the Revived Roman Empire will be the seventh.

The Eighth Head

If the beast is then defined as the kingdoms or empires of Satan in their final manifestation of the last days, then what does the Bible mean when it says; "the beast which was and is not, is himself also an eighth, and is *one* of the seven, and he goes to destruction" (Revelation 17:11)? This is doubtless one of the most confusing aspects of the prophecy and one reason why so many scholars are perplexed. Unfortunately, the problem is exasperated by the misinterpretation of the seven heads. If the seven heads are misrepresented, then the identity of the eighth is impossible to extrapolate. For example, historicists have interpreted the anti-Christ not as an individual, but as a system. Because the historicist methodology stretches the events of Revelation over thousands of years, the systemization of the anti-Christ was a necessity to make their view work. Thus, rather than seeking an individual to reign for 1260 days, they saw the anti-Christ, as an institution, reigning for 1260 years.[762] They saw the *office* of the papacy as the anti-Christ. Since the pope set himself up as the "vicar of Christ," the medieval dissidents and Reformers saw the popes (plural) as anti-Christs. This is true enough, but that is not sufficient proof to make the papal office synonymous with the beast. John himself said, "just as you heard that antichrist is coming, even now many antichrists have arisen" (1 John 2:18). Thus *an* anti-christ does not make *the* anti-Christ, nor does it make the anti-Christ an institution.

That the anti-Christ is an individual who is "the last head of the fourth Kingdom"[763] of Daniel should be evident. The description of the actions of the anti-Christ in 2 Thessalonians 2 is not that of a system, even the papacy, but of an individual. "The *man* of lawlessness is revealed, the *son* of destruction, who opposes and exalts *himself* above every so-called god or object of worship, so

154

that *he* takes his seat in the temple of God, displaying *himself* as being God" (vs. 3-4). This is a person, not an office. Such was the unanimous opinion of all the ancients.[764] Even the early medievals accepted a personal anti-Christ,[765] before the historicists created the anti-Christ as a system theory. It is also apparent in the prophecy of Revelation itself. "The beast which was and is not, is *himself* also an eighth, and is *one* of the seven, and *he* goes to destruction" (Revelation 17:11). In Revelation 20:10 the beast is revealed to be in the Lake of Fire, and one does not throw an empire into hell. One throws an individual, who embodies that empire, into hell. This is the "eighth."

Irenaeus, the earliest of the church fathers who speaks on the subject, affirmed that the anti-Christ was the "eighth."[766] John Darby calls the anti-Christ the head of the beast, but does not specify which head.[767] George Peters and Nathaniel West properly identified the "personal"[768] anti-Christ as the eighth head,[769] which grows out from the seventh. This is not to say that the beast technically has eight heads, for we are told it has seven, but the anti-Christ is *like* an eighth because he is the "head," or ruler, of the seventh and final empire.

It is understandable that the anti-Christ is often confused with the larger beast, of which he is a part (vs. 11). He is integrally connected to it so that the fall of the one is the fall of the other. Says Peters, "he is *the Beast* himself just as Nebuchadnezzar was the head of gold."[770] Even as Nimrod and his kingdom were synonymous and fell at the same time, even as Alexander the Great and his kingdom were synonymous and fell at the same time, even as Napoleon and his empire were synonymous and fell at the same time, so also will the anti-Christ and his kingdom be synonymous and fall at the same time.

In short, the beast itself is properly the final kingdom of Satan, the kingdom of the anti-Christ, who is like an eighth head inasmuch as he is the embodiment of this final kingdom. The beast is, therefore, synonymous with the kingdom of the anti-Christ, but also with the anti-Christ himself. He is the embodiment of the kingdoms of Satan throughout history. He is the Nimrod of the final age. He is also the one who "was and is not, and is about to come up out of the abyss and to go to destruction" (17:8), but what does that mean?

The Wounded Head
The beast "was and is not, and is about to come up out of the abyss and to go to destruction" (17:8). Few words spoken have stirred more controversy, but then the entire subject of the beast has stirred as much. If it is said of the sixth head of the beast that it "is," then how is it that the beast now "is not"? The seeming contradiction has spawned numerous theories, some of which border on the ridiculous. In fact, the answer to the contradiction is easy. The meaning of the passage is not.

155

The beast who "is not" refers to the personal anti-Christ. The sixth head of the beast, which "is," refers to the kingdom of Rome, but there is another curiosity which confuses the issue. Revelation 13:3-5 reads:

> "And *I saw* one of his heads as if it had been slain, and his fatal wound was healed. And the whole earth was amazed *and followed* after the beast; and they worshiped the dragon, because he gave his authority to the beast; and they worshiped the beast, saying, 'Who is like the beast, and who is able to wage war with him?' And there was given to him a mouth speaking arrogant words and blasphemies; and authority to act for forty-two months was given to him."

Thus *one* of the heads of the beast appeared "as if it had been slain" (vs. 3), but when this "fatal wound was healed, the whole earth was amazed *and followed* after the beast" (vs. 3). Many believe the key to the "is not" in verse 17:8 is found here. They are mistaken. Revelation 17:8 refers to the individual anti-Christ whereas 13:3 refers to the kingdom head. There can be no doubt that the anti-Christ is the one who "is not, and is about to come up out of the abyss" (17:8) for verse ten explicitly states that *this* "beast which was and is not, *is*" the eighth. Does the wounded head speak of the eighth? In order to arrive at this conclusion, and in order to properly define the meaning of each passage, it is necessary to look at the passages individually.

It has already been demonstrated that the seven heads of the beast are actually the seven empire of Satan in history. The beast is the final manifestation of these empires, embodied in the kingdom of the anti-Christ. If the sixth head was Rome, then the seventh (which is universally referred to as the Revived Roman Empire by futurists) should naturally be the wounded head. George Peters argued that the beast is currently "headless,"[771] awaiting its final head who is *like* an eighth. Nevertheless, when one misinterprets the proper meaning of the heads, it becomes impossible to correctly interpret the imagery attatched to the heads.

Hippolytus, the early church father, taught that the wounded head was the Roman Empire.[772] According to Hippolytus it is the anti-Christ who "shall with knavish skill heal [the wound], as it were, and restore [the Roman Empire]."[773] Thus the anti-Christ is the healer, not the one healed. However, others, calling the anti-Christ a counterfeit Messiah, have assumed that the wounded head is the eighth, and, therefore, according to Arthur Bloomfield, "it is Satan's counterfeit of the Resurrection."[774] This view, that the anti-Christ is himself resurrected, or at least *appears* to be resurrected, has become very popular in recent years. Its advocates include such notable names as Robert Govett, E. W. Bullinger, Hal Lindsey, Robert Thomas, Tim LaHaye, and Marvin Rosenthal.

Conversely, the older view, that the wounded head is Rome, has notable advocates as Hippolytus, Isaac Newton, John Darby, George Peters,

Walter Scott, H. A. Ironside, and John Walvoord. Acccording to Darby the wounded head was the imperial government of Rome. He, therefore, believed that the anti-Christ would restore that government,[775] and this would be the reason the world marvels; because the Roman Empire has been revived, not because a man has been resurrected.[776] This is the oldest view, and the best. The main appeal of the opposing view is that it seems to fit with the view that the anti-Christ is a "mock messiah."[777] However, it is important to note that the beast is never called a false messiah in the strictest since of the word. He is an anti-Christ, but not necessarily a false messiah. As Pentecost comments, anti-Christ can mean either "over, against, or opposite to" or it can mean "instead of or in place of."[778] He argues for the former partially on the grounds that "the word *antichrist* seems to be contrasted with 'false Christ' in Scripture."[779] He believes that anti-Christ denies Christ, whereas a false Christ affirms himself as Christ.[780]

This is, of course, directly related to the equally controversial topic of whether or not the anti-Christ will be Jewish. This topic and the topic of the religious nature of the anti-Christ are discussed below. Here it need only be said that to attribute the wounded head to the anti-Christ, rather than to the Roman Empire, is based on the assumption that the anti-Christ will mimic the resurrection of Christ. Although tempting, it does not appear to flow from Scripture, but is assumed. The revival of the wounded head is best viewed as the revival of the Roman Empire.

This then bring us back to our first question; what is the meaning of "the beast was and is not" (17:11) and is coming?

The One Who Is Not and Is Coming
The anti-Christ is the embodiment of the beast. He is its final head, and Satan's last hoorah. Since the beginning, minds have imagined what evil this man could be. One movie, *the Omen*, depicts the anti-Christ as a demonic child who could kill a man with a look, yet still appears innocent. The ancients were not immune from this fascination with the character of the anti-Christ. When Nero finally died a popular legend arose, among pagans as well as Christians, that Nero was not truly dead, but sleeping, awaiting the day he return and destroy Rome with fire, as he promised.[781] From this legend, and the horrors of seeing their colleagues burned alive or fed to beasts, some of the church fathers, like Victorinus, conceived of the idea that Nero would, indeed, return to life as the anti-Christ.[782] This theory is called the Nero *redivivus* theory. It has had countless advocates throughout the centuries and remains one of the predominant interpretations of this passage.

It seems clear that the anti-Christ "was" at sometime in the past. It is also apparent that he will come again in the form of the anti-Christ. This has itself led to all kinds of speculation such as the Nero *redivivus* theory, and its counterpart, the Judas *redivivus* theory, but is this what the passage really means? Some have taken the anti-Christ to be none other than Satan incarnate.[783] Hippolytus made a similar argument, suggesting that the devil would occupy what George Peters calls "a phantom body."[784] Accordingly, this view believes that Satan will claim to be born of a virgin. The problem with this hypothesis is that Revelation 20:10 distinguishes between the devil and the beast. They cannot be one and the same. A similar view, presented by men like Lactantius and Bede, believes he will actually be a son of Satan.[785] Others, like Jerome, argue that he will be a man "in whom all Satan shall dwell bodily."[786] Hence, he will be a man, but possessed of the devil.

These later arguments are more compatible with Scripture, but does not bode well with the statement that the anti-Christ "was" and "is about to come up from the abyss" (17:8). That statement seems to imply more than mere possession. This is doubtless one reason that the Nero *redivivus* thesis has been so popular through the ages. Indeed, throughout the ages, there has not ceased to be a barrage of variant theories ranging from the belief that Judas Iscariot will be revived as the anti-Christ or false prophet[787] to Van Kampen's recent implication that Hitler will be reborn as the anti-Christ.[788] Of these, there is no doubt that Nero remains the favorite. The justification for Nero comes, in part, from the argument of G. H. Lang, who says that the "eighth would be one of the former seven" kings.[789] Unfortunately, this is based on the erroneous translation of, the normally excellent, NAS. No other translations renders it as such, nor should they. The Greek says, "*ek tov septa estin* (ἐκ τῶν ἑπτά ἐστιν)" meaning "*from* the seven." It is translated as "belongs to the seven" by the NAB, RSV, NRSV, and NIV. The Rheims New Testament, ASV, NKJV, and KJV all read, "of the seven." The Living Bible, a paraphrase, supports the Nero *redivivus* theory, reading, "having reigned before as one of the seven." Of course, the heads are not emperors, as has been shown, and, therefore, the translation is not particularly helpful. It must be assumed that the heads are emperors, of which Nero must have been one. Still another argument used to support the Nero *redivivus* view is related to the number of the beast. The theory that the number of the beast is actually the number of Nero (discussed below) has been used to support this hypothesis.[790] However, even C. B. Caird, who supports Nero *redivivus*,[791] admits the numerous problems with associating the number of the beast with Nero.[792] In short, the rebirth of Nero is assumed based on tradition. It cannot be proven by Scripture. While the possibility of a reborn individual from the past cannot be exclusivey ruled out, it has many problems and the identity of the individual must be speculative.

What then is the meaning? If the beast is not Nero, Judas, Hitler, or Satan incarnate, then who is he? It does seem that he has to be someone from the past, but it is equally clear that he must come up from the pit. This implies a demon of some sort, like the demons who came out of the pit in the fifth trumpet. Could it be that a chief demon possesses "the man of sin." Perhaps he is a leader from the past, reborn with God's permission, and destined to rule. If

Nimrod was the first "man of sin," the anti-Christ will be the last. Could he be Nimrod? Perhaps he is Nero? Only time will tell. The Bible does not tell us his name, but we know that he will be possessed of the power of Satan and imbued with all his hatred and furor. He will "come up from the abyss" (Revelation 17:8) and will return to the abyss (Revelation 20:4). According to the Bible:

> "He opened his mouth in blasphemies against God, to blaspheme His name and His tabernacle, *that is*, those who dwell in heaven. And it was given to him to make war with the saints and to overcome them; and authority over every tribe and people and tongue and nation was given to him. And all who dwell on the earth will worship him, *everyone* whose name has not been written from the foundation of the world in the book of life of the Lamb who has been slain. If anyone has an ear, let him hear. If anyone *is destined* for captivity, to captivity he goes; if anyone kills with the sword, with the sword he must be killed. Here is the perseverance and the faith of the saints" (Revelation 13:6-10).

He will obviously have great power and authority and will persecute God's children. He is an anti-Christ in that he sets himself up in the place of God. He will be the manifestation of Satan, but is not Satan himself. We can only guess in the present how it is that he comes up from the pit of hell, but we cannot say whether or not he truly is a reborn individual from the past, be it Nero, Nimrod, or another. We only know that he will resurrect the seventh head, and restore the Roman Empire. He will become the last head of Satan's kingdoms and will subjugate all who oppose him. He will also bear "ten horns."

The Ten Horns

The ten horns have not proven to be as controversial as the heads of the beast, thanks to Daniel the prophet. His vision echoes that of Revelation. We were told of the "dreadful and terrifying and extremely strong" beast which had ten horns (Daniel 7:6-7). This beast has already been assocatied with the seven head of the beast in Revelation, but in the ensuing verses Daniel explains the horns in more detail saying, "while I was contemplating the horns, behold, another horn, a little one, came up among them, and three of the first horns were pulled out by the roots before it; and behold, this horn possessed eyes like the eyes of a man, and a mouth uttering great *boasts*" (Daniel 7: 8). Further, this last horn "was larger in appearance than its associates. I kept looking, and that horn was waging war with the saints and overpowering them until the Ancient of Days came, and judgment was passed in favor of the saints of the Highest One, and the time arrived when the saints took possession of the kingdom" (Daniel 7:21-22). Daniel was then given the answer:

"Out of this kingdom ten kings will arise; and another will arise after them, and he will be different from the previous ones and will subdue three kings. 'And he will speak out against the Most High and wear down the saints of the Highest One, and he will intend to make alterations in times and in law; and they will be given into his hand for a time, times, and half a time. 'But the court will sit *for judgment,* and his dominion will be taken away, annihilated and destroyed forever" (Daniel 7:24-26).

Revelation also defines the ten horns:

"The ten horns which you saw are ten kings, who have not yet received a kingdom ten kings who have not yet received their kingdom but for one hour they will receive authority as kings along with the beast. They are of one purpose, and will give their power and authority to the beast. They will wage war with the Lamb but the Lamb will overcome them because He is Lord of Lords and King of Kings. Those who are called with Him are the elect and faithful" (Revelation 17:12-14).

So the answer is easy, or so it appears. They are ten kings, but whose? When do the kingdoms exist? Are they contemporaneous with beast or are they kingdoms supplanted by the last beast? Who are the three uprooted? Why are these three not mentioned in Revelation? These are the questions that have raged for two thousand years.

The Ten Horns Debated
In addition to Daniel 7, there is yet another parallel passage. Daniel's vision of the great statue also depicts these ten kings, or kingdoms, but this time as the ten toes of the statue.

"The toes of the feet *were* partly of iron and partly of pottery, *so* some of the kingdom will be strong and part of it will be brittle. And in that you saw the iron mixed with common clay, they will combine with one another in the seed of men; but they will not adhere to one another, even as iron does not combine with pottery" (Daniel 2:42-43).

That this is parallel, and speaks of the same empire, and the same ten kings, has been universally accepted by premillennialists throughout the centuries. Irenaeus, a second generation disciple from the apostle John,[793] associated the ten toes of Nebuchadnezzar's statue with the ten horns of Revelation 17. He then argues that these ten kings will arise from "from the empire which now rules."[794] So also Hippolytus identifies the Romans as "the legs of the image, for they were strong as iron."[795] Such a view was not, however, restricted to the Jews or the church fathers but continued on to through the Reformation. Says one Reformer, "*the fourth kingdom* is the kingdom of the Romans; and was to last not only to Christ' first coming, but under antichrist to his second coming."[796] This is likewise accepted by most modern scholars such as Dwight Pentecost[797] and C.I. Scofield.[798]

The mixture of iron and clay clearly seems to indicate a kingdom whose unity is precarious. It is reasoned that Rome must revive if Christ is to crush Rome at the second coming. The common view is that the final empire, Rome, shall be partitioned and divided among the ten kings of Revelation. Irenaeus, like the other church fathers, affirmed this:

> "Daniel too, looking forward to the end of the last kingdom, i.e., the ten last kings, amongst whom the kingdom of those men shall be partitioned."[799]

Modern premillennialists have not wavered from this assertion. Says former Scotland Yard inspector Sir Robert Anderson:

> "The Roman earth shall one day be parcelled out in ten separate kingdoms, and out of one of these shall arise that terrible enemy of God and His people, whose destruction is to be one of the events of the second advent of Christ."[800]

On this all premillennialists are united. Even the followers of Origen, the allegorist, agree with the prophetic division of Rome.[801] The debate is upon what form these ten kingdoms will take. The historicists have once again attempted to find the fulfillment of this prophecy in history. Matthew Henry says, "towards the latter end of the Roman monarchy it grew very weak, and branched into ten kingdoms, which were as the toes of the these feet."[802] Along with the historicists, at least one futurist doubts that the ten toes represent a Revived Roman Empire. Arthur Bloomfield argued *"the ten toes do not represent the revival or uniting of the empire.* The toes have already been divided and have now been in existence for 1500 years"* (emphasis in original).[803] However, the historicists have not been able to reach an concordance upon these ten kingdoms. According to Joseph Mede the ten kings were from Britain, Saxony, the Franks, Burgandy, the Visigoths, the Swedes, the Vandals, Alanes, the Ostrogoths, and the Grecians.[804] Sir Isaac Newton's list, however, differs in that Newton disregards the Saxons, Swedes, Ostrogoths, and the Greeks, adding in their place the Suevians, Hunns, Lombards, and Ravenna.[805] The confusion increases with other historicists. In examing these vast and diverse opinions, one finds chaos. As Sir Robert Anderson remarks:

> "The state of Europe at or after the dismemberment of the Roman Empire has been appealed to as a fulfilment of it, ignoring the fact that the territory which Augustus ruled included a considerable district both of Asia and Africa. Nor is this all. There is no presumption against finding in past times a partial accomplishment of such a prophecy, but the fact that twenty-eight different lists, including sixty-five

'kingdoms,' have been put forward in the controversy, is a proof how worthless is the evidence of any such fulfilment. In truth the historical school of interpreters have here, as on many other points, brought discredit upon their entire system."[806]

The most logical answer to this confusion is that the ten nations cannot be agreed upon because they have not yet become history. Certainly the divided nations created by the decay of the Roman Empire may become one of the ten nations, but the nations will all be singularly reunited under the anti-Christ. They are, as Darby states, "contemporaneous with the beast."[807] The ten horns all belong to one and the same head of the beast. Although Joachim says the ten horns were on the sixth head,[808] Joseph Mede, with most others, says "the ten horns do belong to the last head or state of the beast,"[809] that is the seventh; the Revived Roman Empire. As George Peters remarks, "they exist *simultaneously or contemporaneously*. They arise only when the beast for some time – how long it is not stated – had been headless, i.e., has ceased to exist, or is not recognized as an empire."[810]

Nonetheless, futurists have not been exempt from idle speculation. Hal Lindsey says that the European Economic Community or Common Market "may well be the beginning of the ten-nation confederacy predicted by Daniel and the Book of Revelation."[811] He has also observed that the European Economic Community began at a treaty in Rome, which he believes must be the capital of this new confederacy.[812] Phillip Goodman, on the other hand, offers a different scenario. He believes that "the ten parts are equally apportioned, with five parts in the west and five parts in the eastern half."[813] He then suggest that the states may themselves be identified roughly with the regions of Britain, France, Germany, Spain, and Italy in the west and Greece, Egypt, the Balkans, Turkey, and Syria in the east.[814] On the other hand, John Darby believes that the ten nations will be made up only of the western portion of the old Roman Empire.[815] Watchman Nee believes they will be England, France, northern Africa, Spain, Portugal, Romania, Czechoslavakia, Greece, India, and the Persian boundary.[816] One problem with some of these theories is that Ezekiel 38 implies that at least some of these nations will ally themselves with Gog against the ten kings (see Appendix C). Nonetheless, these theories are all plausible, but they are still speculative. All that is clear is that the Roman Empire will rise again in the form of a ten nation confederacy.

These ten nations "have not yet received a kingdom" (vs. 12). When they do, it will be for but "one hour" and will be "of one purpose"; to "give their power and authority to the beast" (17:12-13). In this case, "hour" is used to imply a set period of time. It does not necessitate a literal hour, nor is this disputed. The point is that they exist solely for the purpose of glorifying the kingdom of the anti-Christ. They will assist the anti-Christ and "will wage war against the Lamb" (vs. 14) and slaughter believers for a time. They are the toes mixed of iron and clay. They are "ten independent but confederated kingdoms."[817] Some have argued "from the very earliest days of the church this clay has been interpreted of democracy."[818] Ironside suggest that "it is impossible to mix imperialism and democracy. The one must, of necessity, destroy the other."[819] He believes that the attempt to restore ancient Rome will fail because it is incompatible with democracy. Pember calls it a "democratic monarchy."[820] Whatever the reasons, the ten kingdoms will only remain unified for a short time, and three of the horns will be uprooted.

The Three Uprooted Horns
The uprooting of the three horns is absent from Revelation's prophecies. It is found only in Daniel, but obviously refers to the same time period. It reads, "while I was contemplating the horns, behold, another horn, a little one, came up among them, and three of the first horns were pulled out by the roots before it; and behold, this horn possessed eyes like the eyes of a man, and a mouth uttering great *boasts*" (Daniel 7:8). This little horn is universally recognized as the anti-Christ. Irenaeus acknowleges this,[821] Hippolytus sees it,[822] G. H. Pember knows it,[823] and, indeed, all premillennialists agree upon it. What premillennialists disagree upon is, once again, the details.

G. H. Lang calls the little horn an eleventh horn,[824] but this has caused some confusion. Although the little horn is obviously different from the ten, and therefore, an eleventh, the problem is that this little horn is distinguished from the others. In other words, are there ten nations under the anti-Christ's authority, or does the anti-Christ come with his own kingdom, making eleven nations? Phillip Goodman has argued that there are eleven nations, since the anti-Christ is an eleventh horn.[825] However, the President of the United States is not a fifty-first governor. There are fifty governors, all under the sovereignty of the one President. This is likely the scenario here. The little horn is not said to have an indepedent nation, but to rule the ten under his authority. It is a "ten nation federation,"[826] not an eleven nation one. Nowhere does the Bible paint the image of eleven nations, only ten under the power of the little horn or the eighth head.

These kings receive their power for only "one hour." This is indicative of the short life span of this final kingdom. Whether the term "hour" should be taken to be a year, or some other time frame, it indicates the brevity of the anti-Christ's true power. While too much cannot be made as to the exact time frame implicated by "hour" it may be that this hour begins with the fall of the Whore (see chapter 8), when the anti-Christ claims sole power over all aspects of the empire. The ten rulers side with the anti-Christ in order to solidify their own positions, but the war that erupts soon afterwards will strip them of their dreams. The "hour" could imply a year's time from the fall of the Harlot until their kingdoms fall prey to the War of Armageddon. This could also explain why the anti-Christ is spoken of up to the final battle of Armageddon, but the ten "horns" seem to drop out of the picture rather quickly.

One thing is clear. At some point in the tribulation the power of the anti-Christ and the empire will be threatened. This will most likely be the time in which the anti-Christ chooses to betray the Whore and seize power completely for himself and his ten colleagues. Tim LaHaye concurs with this reasoning. He argues that three of these kings revolt in the middle of the tribulation.[827] This fits well chronologically. However, we cannot go far beyond this. Hippolytus attempted to identify the three who fall as Egypt, Libya, and Ethiopia.[828] Claiming that Isaiah 23:4-5 is a prophecy about the same time period, Hippolytus merged several prophecies and described the war the anti-Christ rages against them, saying, "when he has overmastered three horns out of the ten in the array of war, and has rooted these three out, viz., Egypt, and Libya, and Ethiopia ... his first expedition will be against Tyre and Berytus and the circumjacent territory."[829] This theory is interesting, but merges too many uncertain views of various prophecies. One thing that is clear, however, is that the anti-Christ will overthrow three of the ten kings, probably shortly after the middle of the tribulation.

The Beast from the Earth

> "And I saw another beast coming up out of the earth; and he had two horns like a lamb, and he spoke as a dragon. And he exercises all the authority of the first beast in his presence. And he makes the earth and those who dwell in it to worship the first beast, whose fatal wound was healed" (Revelation 13:11-12).

The first beast came up from the sea, or the troubled nations. This beast comes up from the earth. While the imagery of the sea was easy to understand, the imagery of the earth is less so. Some have mentioned the parallels in Daniel where the "four great beasts were coming up from the sea" (Daniel 7:3), but in Daniel 7:17 it is said, "these great beasts, which are four *in number,* are four kings *who* will arise from the earth." Thus, the empires are from the sea (of nations) while the kings who rule them are from the earth. This is a perfectly accurate comparison, as the two prophecies speak of the same thing, but it still does not define for us what the earth means.

George Ladd claims that "no particular significance is to be seen in the fact that the second beast rises out of the earth"[830] and Alan Johnson says "that the beast comes from the land rather than the sea may simply indicate his diversity from the first,"[831] but if we attach symbolic significance to the "sea," from whence the first beast comes, we cannot ignore that this beast comes from the earth. John Walvoord has suggested that this beast comes from the earth in order to distinguish that it is "a creature of the earth rather than heaven."[832] The problem with this argument is that it looses continuity with the first beast rising from the sea, for the sea is not heaven either. Robert Govett says that the earth is merely in constrast to heaven.[833] An interesting variant of this theory comes from Joseph Seiss. He argues that the "earth means a coming from the under-world,"[834] as opposed to heaven. He then goes on to teach that the false prophet is none other than a revived Judas Iscariot. Of this theory more will be said shortly. Nevertheless, the belief that earth is merely a distinction from heaven is suspect. If the "sea" equalled the troubled nations of the earth, as most agree, then the land must be in conjuction with the same type of symbolism. Daniel showed the beasts coming from the sea, and the kings thereof from the earth (7:3, 17). Any interpretation of Revelation must be analogus to Daniel.

Sir Isaac Newton proposed that the earth was characteristic of Asia and Africa.[835] Robert Mounce generalized to the Asia Minor.[836] Harrison says it is the Near East.[837] However, a number have argued that if sea was Gentile nations then the earth must be the Jewish nation.[838] Darby called it the "prophetic earth,"[839] but does not elaborate. Hal Lindsey says that "earth" could be translated "land" and is therefore a reference to Israel.[840] Since Israel is often referred to simply as "the land," the argument bears some weight, although it is by no means certain. What is certain is that this view has been the most popular theory. Ironside makes the earth a symbol of Palestine,[841] as does Pentecost[842] and many others. Unfortunately, while this theory is in sync with Revelation, it looses cohesion with Daniel, for we know that the kings of Daniel's four beast *did not* come from Israel, or the Middle East.

It is possible, based on both Daniel and Revelation, that the sea is used of nations, while the earth is used of men. The empires grew up out of the troubled nations and these men grew up from out of those empires. Thus, the beast emerges from the sea and creates stability out of the chaos, depicted by stable land or earth. The men then rise up from that newly created earth. The suggestion is tenuous, but any view must be accepted tentatively. All that can be said with confidence is that the empires arise from the masses, and men (as opposed to their kingdoms) arise from the earth.

One thing that is sure is that this beast is called the "false prophet" (cf. Revelation 19:20, 20:10, and also 16:13). The deeds and signs he perform stir up images of an Old Testament prophet, save that this one is conterfeit and wicked. The great debate over this beast is whether this beast is the anti-Christ, or his aid. Although it has been demonstrated that the eighth head should properly be considered the anti-Christ, many have taken the first beast merely as his empire and called this second beast the anti-Christ. This has created much confusion, and makes the clarity of later prophecies murky. To make matters worse, Hippolytus did not see the anti-Christ in either the beast from the sea or the beast from the earth. He argued that the beast from the earth is the final "kingdom of the anti-Christ," and it is the two horns of this beast which represent the anti-Christ and his false prophet.[843]

Although those who interpreted the beast from the earth as the anti-Christ were predominantly from the medieval and Reformation age, modern scholars are by no means united in declaring the false prophet a subordinate of the anti-Christ. Even the famed C. I. Scofield saw the beast out of the earth as the anti-Christ, arguing that the "man of sin" and the "false prophet" are synonyms for this same man.[844] It is, therefore, necessary to begin with a definition of whether this beast is separate from the anti-Christ or synonymous with him.

Anti-Christ or False Prophet?

The first beast clearly represents, by all interpretive views, an empire (if not more than one empire). The anti-Christ, however, is an individual, not an empire. Consequently, it is sometimes difficult to distinguish between the eighth head of the beast and the larger beast. This has led many expositors to see the beast from the earth as the anti-Christ, rather than the eighth head of the first beast. To complicate matters is the confusion between the duties and functions of the anti-Christ and false prophet, assuming they are two distinct individuals. This is exemplified by the title of one of Hal Lindsey's chapters in his commentary. Although he accepts the false prophet as being different from, and subordinate to, the anti-Christ, he entitles his chapter, "The Two Antichrists."[845]

The first question which must be answered is whether or not the false prophet is distinct from the anti-Christ, or whether or not, as Scofield believes, he is synonymous with him.[846] Revelation 19:20 and 20:10 appears to be lucid enough to prove a differentiation of the beast from the sea and the false prophet. Since an empire is not cast into hell, it is only logical that the anti-Christ and the false prophet are two separate individuals who share the same fate. However, many commentators have ignored this, saying that the beast in the abyss does not prove the anti-Christ is not the same as the false prophet.

Among the medievals, Adso of Montier applied the moniker anti-Christ to the beast from the earth.[847] Joachim d'Fiore taught this as well.[848] Eventually the historicists attempted to turn the false prophet into a system, rather than an individual, even as they had done with the first beast. Joseph Mede, accepted the fact that this second beast was an individual, but believes that "the two horned beast is the founder, or erector of that seven headed beast."[849] Hence, he and his successors again recognized the false prophet as an individual, rather than a system or office, but again had trouble deciphering the difference between the false prophet and the anti-Christ. They were not alone. Some modern scholars, like H. A. Ironside, also take that view.[850]

One only has to read the commentaries to see how confused the expositors have been. John Darby acknowledges that the false Messiah is distinct from the anti-Christ,[851] but elsewhere he contrast the second beast with the false prophet.[852] The confusion can be explained, in part, by his acceptance of Hippolytus' theory that the horns represent the anti-Christ and false prophet respectively. This is certainly consistent with the imagery used in Daniel and even the first beast, where the horns represented the kings of the respective kingdoms. It could even be a preferable interpretation except that such a method only serves to further complicate the distinctions between the "corporate" entity of the beast,[853] and the distinct functions of the two leaders (the anti-Christ and false prophet). In other words, there appears to be a civil leader and a religious leader. The "ecclesiastical or spiritual power"[854] is associated with the second beast, while the civil power is inherent in the first beast. If the horns are both on the second beast, how can anyone distinguish between the powers of the two respective leaders? This problem is obvious when Nathaniel West at once calls the anti-Christ both the "mock Messiah,"[855] or false Messiah,[856] and at the same time calls him the "last Gentile ruler."[857] How can a Gentile ruler be the false Messiah?

The same confusion appears in Walter Scott's commentary. He says "some modern expositors regard the Antichrist as the civil head of the Roman empire, but this is not so."[858] He associates the false prophet, or false Messiah, with the anti-Christ,[859] and designates the civil authority of Rome to "the direct control of Satan."[860] Of the beasts he says, "the first is Gentile, the second a Jew."[861] "The first is the Roman power ... the second Beast is the personal Antichrist."[862]

Thus there is a general acknowledgement that two entities, or individuals, exist; the one a Gentile ruler of the Revived Roman Empire, and the other a religious false prophet who compels the worship of the first. Which of these is the anti-Christ? Which is the false prophet? If they are not different, then how can the conflict be resolved? The best way to answer these questions is to examine those roles which we know to be inherent in the anti-Christ and determine if they are, indeed, compatible with the description given of the second beast. In other words, are the descriptions of the anti-Christ or the "man of sin," found in the epistles and gospels compatible with the imagery of the second beast?

We may begin with the controversial question; is the anti-Christ a Jew? Scholars are as divided on whether or not the anti-Christ will be a Jew as they are on whether he is the false prophet. Some of the earliest church fathers associated the anti-Christ with Rome, not Jerusalem. Victorinus, however, argued that Nero would be reborn as a Jew.[863] Later church fathers followed in calling the anti-Christ a Jew, based largely on apocryphal writings such as the *Testament of Dan*.[864] According to Ephraem the Syrian, the anti-Christ would be a Jew from the tribe of Dan.[865] This theory originated from rabbinic tradition which held that the anti-Christ would come from Dan.[866] The popularity of this belief did not subside over the ages. It was held by Haymo of Halberstadt,[867] Adso of Montier,[868] Nicholas of Lyra,[869] and Thomas Aquinas,[870] among many others. Many of the arguments on behalf of this view, however, are based on the association of the false prophet with the anti-Christ. It is prudent, therefore, to examine only those prophecies which we know to explicitly refer to the anti-Christ. The result is a three pronged argument.

The first argument is based on the prophecy wherein the anti-Christ will enter the Holy Temple of Jerusalem and declare himself to be equal with God (2 Thessalonians 2:1-4). It is argued that since only a Jew may enter the Inner Court, the anti-Christ must be a Jew, or else he could not enter. However, by itself this is an unconvincing argument. History has shown that Antiochus Epiphanes, a Greek, entered the temple and defiled it by slaughtering a pig upon the altar, on behalf of the pagan gods. This argument must assume that the Jewish reaction to the abomination of desolation is a good reaction, rather than one of repulsion. This cannot be proved anywhere in the Scriptures.

A variant of this argument suggests that the temple will be rebuilt by the anti-Christ, and thus he again must be a Jew. This reasoning suffers from the same logical flaws. First, it is a fact that the Second Temple was restored by the command of Cyrus, the Persian. Cyrus was not only a Gentile, but a pagan. Consequently, it is not logical to assume that only a Jew can order the restoration of the temple. Moreover, the current political climate would make this virtually impossible. The Arabs have rioted over mere rumors that the Jews might want to harm the al-Aska mosque.[871] Should the Jews attempt to rebuild the temple upon, or near, the site of the Dome of the Rock, war would surely erupt, unless a Gentile leader were to oversee the project. Consequently, it is reasoned conversely that the one who rebuilds the temple *must* be a Gentile. Furthermore, it has always been *assumed* that the anti-Christ would be the one to rebuild the temple, but *nowhere* is the assertion proven in the Bible. He may order the rebuilding of the temple, but it may also be that the temple is already rebuilt before the anti-Christ arrives on the scene.

A second argument on behalf of the Jewish anti-Christ theory is what Randall Price calls a "lexical argument."[872] It is based on Danial 11:37 which says, according to the King James Version, that he shall not "regard the God of his fathers." This would clearly seem to imply that he is a Jew since the "God of his fathers" is a term for the God of the Jews. At the time of Daniel, there was only one true monotheistic religion. Nevertheless, several criticisms of this view exist. The most obvious is that most translations render the passage "gods," rather than God. The NAS, NIV, Living Bible, RSV, NRSV, and the ASV all read "gods." Interestingly, the Jewish translation, Tanakh, reads with the King James in saying the "God of his ancestors." Anecdotally, the Greek *Septuagint* has two readings, one reading "gods" and the other "God." The reason for this confusion is that Hebrew uses the same suffix for plural words as it uses for words which describe the infinite.[873] Thus the *one* and *only* God of the Hebrews uses the *infinite* suffix, even as words like heaven, sky, and water do. It is, therefore, sometimes hard to determine if the plural or inifinite translation of God was intended without context. Consequently, context is the key to this passage.

According to Daniel 11:36-38 "he will exalt and magnify himself above every god, and will speak monstrous things against the God of gods; and he will prosper until the indignation is finished, for that which is decreed will be done. And he will show no regard for the gods of his fathers or for the desire of women, nor will he show regard for any *other* god; for he will magnify himself above *them* all. But instead he will honor a god of fortresses, a god whom his fathers did not know." It seems then that this individual opposes "every god," even the "God of gods." He is said to show no "regard for *any* god," but "he will magnify himself above *them* all." The context does not appear Jewish, but pagan. *Many* gods are mentioned throughout the passage, not merely the God of the Jews. It should also be mentioned in passing that many scholars believe that Daniel 11 is a prophecy about Antiochus Epiphanes, rather than the anti-Christ.[874] While it may well prove to be a legitimate prophecy of the anti-Christ, it cannot provide proof of the anti-Christ's nationality.

The final argument for the Jewish heritage of the anti-Christ comes from the meaning of the word "anti-Christ." If he is the "*anti*-Christ," they argue, then he must be the "false Messiah."[875] The problem with this approach is, as Pentecost remarks, that anti-Christ can mean either "over, against, or opposite to" *or* it can mean "in place of."[876] One meaning cannot be proven over the other without contextual evidence. If Daniel 11 is indeed a prophecy of the anti-Christ, as most premillennialists believe, then the anti-Christ will exalt and magnify himself *above* God, even as 2 Thessalonians 2:4 says. Thus the anti-Christ "opposes" (2 Thessalonians 2:4) God. This fits the primary meaning of "anti" rather than its secondary meaning. He is anti-Christ because he opposes and rebels against God, not because he emulates the real Christ.

This is what is known of the anti-Christ : He will defile the Holy Temple and commit the abomination of desolation (Daniel 9:27, Matthew 24:15, Mark 13:14, Luke 21:20, and 2 Thessalonians 2:4); he will oppose God almighty (Daniel 11:38 and 2 Thessalonians 2:4); he will establish a seven year treaty with Israel (Daniel 9:27); he deny that Christ is Lord (1 John 2:22, 1 John 4:3, and 2 John 7); and he will head the Revived Roman Empire (see discussion above). These are the characteristics which mark the anti-Christ. They are also quite different from those described in Revelation 13:11-12.

Revelation 19:20 and 20:10 make it plain that the False Prophet and anti-Christ are two different beings. Revelation 13:11-12 describe the False Prophet as the religious figure, not the anti-Christ. Thus, it must be said with George Peters, "*the last head of the first Beast is the great leading actor*, under whose leadership the confederation if formed, etc.; and that *this false prophet only occupies a subsidiary position, and one, too, which strives to honor and exalt the power and authority of this last head*" (emphasis in original).[877]

169

The Identity of the False Prophet

Even as there has been much speculation as to the identity, or future identity, of the anti-Christ, there is nearly an equal amount of speculation as to the identity of the False Prophet. Joachim d'Fiore sometimes identifies the first beast with a Saracen emperor,[878] while associating the second with a future antipope.[879] Pierre D'Olivi also believed the False Prophet to be a future antipope.[880] Nicholas of Lyra, however, called Mohammad the False Prophet[881] and was followed in this thesis by other historicists such as John Bale.[882] Both theories fit the identification of the False Prophet with a "religious leader,"[883] but the later is solely a historcists view while the former conflicts with Revelation 17, for as George Peters remarks, "the Papacy is previously overthrown by this Antichrist" [884] (see chapter 8 for more on this theory).

Although some continue to identify the False Prophet with a future pope, or antipope, the most popular theory is a variation of the Nero *redivivus* theory used with the anti-Christ. Watchmans Nee applies the Nero *redivivus* to the False Prophet, rather than the anti-Christ,[885] but also suggest that "the second beast may very well be the return from the dead of the betrayer Judas."[886] The view is supported by G. H. Lang,[887] Joseph Seiss, Robert Govett,[888] and many others. This ever popular Judas *redivivus* theory is based partially on the application of Psalms 109:6 to prophecy. The text reads, "let an accuser stand at his right hand." The passage is thus applied to the anti-Christ, and Judas is identified as the accuser. Of course, the exegesis is suspect. Joseph Seiss presents a far better argument on behalf of the theory.

According to Seiss, the second beast comes up from the earth, because he comes from the underworld.[889] He compares the imagery to that used in 1 Samuel 28:13, wherein the witch of Endor saw Samuel "coming up out of the earth," and to Psalms 10:18.[890] He further argues that both beasts are thrown into the lake of fire alive (Revelation 19:20) because of the prohibition of Hebrews 9:27, which is taken to mean that God forbids a man to die twice.[891] These arguments fit the theory well, but are hardly convincing in themselves. His strongest argument is the fact that both the "Man of Sin" and Judas are referred to as the "Son of Perdition."[892] Judas is called the "son of perdition" in John 17:12 and the "man of sin" is called the same in 2 Thessalonians 2:3. Although sometimes translated as "son of destruction," the Greek word is the same in both passages (ἀπωλείας). He says, Judas "and the Man of Sin are the only two to whom the title 'Son of Perdition' is applied ... a son of perdition is rather one begotten and born of perdition, one that comes forth from hell, which would be most eminently true if they both are Satanically resurrected men, after having been in hell."[893]

As attractive as the *redivivus* theories may be, they are suspect. They cannot be exclusively ruled out any more than they can be proven from natural exegesis. It is tempting to declare that the betrayer of our Lord will return to serve the anti-Christ, as he once served the true Christ, but such conjectures must rely on assumption. The Bible itself does not exclude such a view, but neither does it teach such. The *redivivus* theories remain an option to be taken tentatively, but not authoritatively. It may well be that the False Prophet, like the anti-Christ, will be a new man, never before seen on the earth.

A False Messiah?

It has been shown that if the anti-Christ is not the religious leader spoken of as the beast from the earth, then this beast must be, as most modern scholars agree, the False Prophet who gives honor and glory to the anti-Christ. Some have compared them to an unholy Trinity. G. H. Pember refers to Satan as the anti-Father, the anti-Christ as the anti-Son, and the False Prophet is the "antispirit,"[894] a view echoed by Joseph Seiss.[895] Of course, this would again confuse the anti-Christ with the false Messiah, which is the role of the False Prophet, but a closer examination is needed to make this determination. Revelation 13:13-14 reads:

> "And he performs great signs, so that he even makes fire come down out of heaven to the earth in the presence of men. And he deceives those who dwell on the earth because of the signs which it was given him to perform in the presence of the beast, telling those who dwell on the earth to make an image to the beast who had the wound of the sword and has come to life."

The description of signs and wonders, like a prophet of old, has given cause for many to believe that the False Prophet, rather than the anti-Christ, is a False Jewish Messiah. Hal Lindsey takes the older view that the anti-Christ comes from the tribe of Dan, and applies it to the False Prophet.[896] Dwight Pentecost also believes that the False Prophet will be a Jew,[897] followed by other scholars like Robert Thomas[898] and Tim LaHaye.[899] This view is also accepted by most Messianic Jews (or Jewish Christians). It is based on many of the same arguments as are used to identify the anti-Christ with Judaism, but it has one advantage over that view. The beast from the earth, the False Prophet, has "horns like a lamb." Since Christ was the "Lamb of God" (John 1:29, 36; Revelation 5:6, 8, 12-13; 6:1, 16; 7:9-10, 14, 17; 12:11; 13:8; 14:1, 4, 10; 15:3; 17:14; 19:7, 9; 21:9, 14, 22-23; and 22: 1 and 3), Charles Ryrie had argued that this could refer to the False Prophet as a false Messiah.[900] Were it not for the fact that Christ is referred to as a sacrificial Lamb no less than 25 times in Revelation, the argument might be specious, but the religious character of the False Prophet and imagery of a lamb make it a hard view to reject. Interestingly enough, Norman Harrison has a unique deriviative view.

According to Harrison, the False Prophet must be "a Mohammedan Jew"[901] because only a Mohammedan Jew could unite the Arabs and Jews. Of course, Harrison is speculating. We do not know in what exact form the peace treaty will take, but we do know that the Arabs will among the first to break the treaty (see Appendix C). Moreover, it is worth noting that most Israeli Jews do not even consider Christian or Messianic Jews to be "real" Jews, much less an Islamic one. It is seems farfetched to assume that an Islamic man of Jewish descent could ever be accepted as a Messiah by the Jewish people.

Whether he is a Jew or a Muslim or something else, it is clear that he worships the first beast, and compels others to do so. Victorinus, as with most premillennialists, believed the signs and wonders to be literal. He associated them with black magic.[902] This seems consistent with the straightforward reading of verses 13-14, for "he even makes fire come down out of heaven to the earth in the presence of men. And he deceives those who dwell on the earth because of the signs which it was given him to perform." Although it has become popular to assign all black magic and arts to trickery and sleight of hand, Joseph Seiss comments that the "lying wonders" of 2 Thessalonians 2:9 "does not mean *unreal* wonders, mere trick, jugglery and legerdemain; but wonders *wrought for the support of lies*, that is, *devil miracles* ... They are genuine miracles, wrought in the interests of Hell's falsehoods."[903] He mentions the competition which the False Prophet will enter into against the two witnesses of Revelation 11. If the witnesses' miracles are real, and if the language used is the same, then are not the miracles of the False Prophet real as well? Seiss' point is well taken. In Exodus, we are not told that the magicians of the Pharaoh used sleight of hand, but rather that they imitated the miracles of Moses (and some cases failed), but their miracles were always inferior. They were, however, real. If this was so of Egypt, why not the last days?

The purpose of these miracles is to win people over the beast, and to compel the worship thereof. The False Prophet does not require self worship, but rather the deification of the beast. Is he a prophet to the Jews alone? It seems not. Whether the False Prophet is a Jew or a Gentile, the scope of his power goes far beyond that of Israel and Palestine. We are told that "he causes all, the small and the great, and the rich and the poor, and the free men and the slaves" (13:16) to worship the beast. This obvious implies a global appeal. While the Bible does not say that the False Prophet is successful in this venture, the scope of the language certainly extends far beyond the borders of the Middle East. The False Prophet may be a Middle Eastern character, but his power is not exclusive to that region.

It is of passing interest to note that, while most Jews would never accept a Gentile as Messiah, the ancient Jewish scribes and tradition have variously debated men who might have been the Messiah. Among these men was the Gentile ruler Cyrus the Great.[904] Although he certainly came to be rejected as *the* Messiah, Cyrus was seen as *an* Annointed One (Messiah) because he permitted the Holy Temple to be rebuilt.[905] It is, therefore, not completely infeasible that the False Prophet could be a Messianic counterfeit, even if he is not a Jew. Since his appeal is worldwide, this could well be the case. He is the spokesman and minister for the anti-Christ who will administer his will.

Summary on the False Prophet
The relationship of the False Prophet to the anti-Christ is one so closely intertwined that scholars have often confused the two persons. Nonetheless, the Bible does make it clear that they are two separate individuals. The False Prophet is the minister of the anti-Christ. It is he who serves the anti-Christ and does his bidding. While some historicists scholars have attempted to identify the False Prophet with Mohammad,[906] or some other historical figure, the Bible is clear that "the ten horned beast ... and the two horned false prophet are not separated from the other, either in their rising or in their falling."[907] They are intergrally interwoven. They stand together, and they fall together.

The False Prophet is just that; the false prophet for the anti-Christ. He is the spokeman for, and prophet for, the beast. He performs miracles, which appear beyond mere magic tricks. His role is to deceive not only Jews, but the whole world. Many believe that he will be a Jew. H. A. Ironside even suggests that his Jewish heritage might explain his hatred for Catholics[908] (see chapter 8 for more on this theory). Jewish author Marvin Rosenthal is silent on the issue, but does believe that the anti-Christ will make Jerusalem the capital of his empire,[909] thus implying a close relationship with the chosen race. Nonetheless, while it is clear that Jerusalem figures prominently in the end times and the political climate of the anti-Christ's kingdom, there is no conclusive proof that either the anti-Christ or the False Prophet will be a Jew. While this will doubtlessly continue to be debated, the role of the False Prophet will not. He is to administer the will of the anti-Christ and his kingdom throughout the world, and in Israel. He is to attempt to compel the world to receive the mark of the beast.

The Mark of the Beast

> "And there was given to him to give breath to the image of the beast, that the image of the beast might even speak and cause as many as do not worship the image of the beast to be killed. And he causes all, the small and the great, and the rich and the poor, and the free men and the slaves, to be given a mark on their right hand, or on their forehead, and *he provides* that no one should be able to buy or to sell, except the one who has the mark, *either* the name of the beast or the number of his name" (Revelation 13:15-17).

Here we are told that the False Prophet will attempt to compel all men to receive a mark upon their hand or forehead. Economic sanctions are even imposed on those who refuse the mark. Without regard for the number of the beast, which will be addressed separately, the larger question is what the "mark" itself is, and what is its purpose? Moreover, what is the image to which the prophecy refers?

The question of the image is often forgotten amid the controversies and speculations of the mark and number of the beast. It is not merely the worship of the beast, but the worship of the beast's *image*. It is the sin of idolatry as well worshipping a false god. What is this image? Many insist that it an actual statue of the anti-Christ.[910] We are reminded that the ancient Roman emperors set up statues of themselves and required the worship thereof under pain of death.[911] It is suggested that this is what is envisioned in the last days. G. H. Pember even declared that the "Abomination of Desolation" requires that a literal image of the beast will be set up in the temple of Jerusalem.[912] He further suggest that it is the literal worship of Satan which is required by the False Prophet.[913] Nevertheless, most believe that only the worship of the beast is intended. Literal Satan worship may not necessarily be taught here.

Still, other options include E. W. Bullinger's theory that the image is an "automaton"[914] or that of Jack Van Impe who believes that the image is a three dimensional computer image.[915] Such theories, while possible, are purely speculative. Indeed, some even doubt that a statue, whether physical or computer animated, is what is meant by the image of the beast. Govett, arguing on behalf of the statue view, says, "the Greek word means a 'likeness.' ... It accords with the belief that the Wild Beast is a man; not an empire ... Men could not make the image of an empire."[916] However, this is not necessarily true.

Nelson Darby held to the view that it was the worship of empire, and not a man, which is to be compelled by the False Prophet and anti-Christ.[917] Darby's view is probably best. The image need not be a statue of the beast, but merely, as Walvoord states, "a symbol of his power and majesty."[918] Certainly, neither Thessalonians, nor the Gospels, nor Daniel describe the erection of a statue in the Holy Temple, only the desecration by the anti-Christ, and his blasphemy. The idea of a statue cannot be ruled out, but neither can it be proven from the text. The Roman Standard, a golden eagle, was used as a symbol for the Roman Empire. A similar standard may be what is intended here. If this is true, then the "mark of the beast" could easily be the same as the image itself.

A final remark upon the image might encompass the question of the meaning of giving "breath" to the image, and of its ability to "speak." Joseph Seiss insist that "this arch magician [shall] have power to give animation and speech to this dead statue."[919] Walter Scott also seems to accept this view,[920] along with Henry Morris[921] and others. Still, some, like John Walvoord, whom no one can claim to be non-literal, believed that the passage may only infer "the impression" of life and speech.[922] Charles Ryrie remarks that "the word for breath is *pneuma* ('spirit') ... or the word may be translated 'wind' and indicate some technological feat,"[923] such as perhaps television. Van Kampen goes one step further. He says, "the Greek term here rendered 'breath' is rarely translated that way, but is usally rendered as 'spirit' ... the meaning of his passage, then, is

... some form of spirit or life will be put in these 'images' or idols."[924]   He further believes that demons will actually inhabit these inanimate idols, acting as spies. He thus envisions an Orwellian mightmare wherein the statues watch over all men.[925]

It is difficult to determine the exact meaning of the "breath" which is given to the image. It would not be unjustified to side with Walvoord in assigning a symbolic meaning to the phrase were it not for the word "speak." The phrase "the image of the beast might even speak" does not fit well with a systematic ("literal") use of symbols. However, it should be mentioned that the word "to speak" is found in the subjunctive form.   In Greek, the subjuctive mood is usually translated with the word "might."[926]   It means that the word is not necessarily true, but is a "possibility."[927]   While this does not solve the problem, it does leave the exact meaning open. Is it a sort of propaganda billboard? To the ancients might this be called magic? It is likely that the true meaning of the "breath" and "speech" will not be known until it occurs. The question of the mark is equally difficult.

The early church fathers, as with modern premillennialists, were in general agreement that the mark was literal. Even some medievals continued this belief. Ephraem the Syrian believed that a "serpentine sign" [928] would be branded on the followers of the anti-Christ. Adso of Montier likewise suggested that it was brand,[929] even as the ancients often branded their slaves. Scholars like Charles Ryrie follow this belief,[930] while Henry Swete takes a strictly historicist view and call it an "imperial stamp."[931]   Although the prophecy is clearly future, and not the past or present of John's day, such marks have historically been required. The ancient Romans branded their slaves, often on the forehead, while Roman soldiers received a mark of the emperor on their hand.[932]   So even as God has sealed the 144,000 believers, the anti-Christ requires a seal of his disciples. The mark is a literal mark of some kind, although more recent suggestions have echoed the technology of the modern age. Rather than merely being a brand or tatoo, Hal Lindsey popularized the belief that this was actually a "smart card" implanted under the skin.[933]   In other words, it would be a sort of universal credit card permanently implanted upon the individual. This leads to the second question.

Is the refusal to buy or sell an economic sanction placed on those who refuse the mark, or is the mark itself intergrally related to economics? Walter Scott reminds us that the mark is "commerce and trade controlled."[934]   The economic aspect could be viewed as either a sanction used to punish those who do not bear the mark, or it could be that the mark is the source of identification for ecomonic purchases. Ultimately, they are one and the same thing, but recent theories concerning the mark raise the question. According to one author, quoting from *U.S. News and World Report*, a new technology is being developed to intergrate all personal data information into a single computer chip.[935]   This computer chip has been tested over the years since that book brought the theory to popular attention and has even been tested for implantation under the skin. The argument is that the chip cannot be stolen or lost if it literally *on* the person, or under his skin. It would incorporate credit, banking information, medical records, Social Security data, and all other useful personal information.[936] Henry Morris believes that "the social security card, the draft registration card, the practice of stenciling an inked design on the back of the hand, and various other devices are all forerunners of this universal branding."[937]

The possible implementation of such a universal chip can no longer be considered mere conjecture. Chuck Missler has shown how the internet and other modern technology has paved the way for an Orwellian society,[938] such as that envisioned by John two thousand years before the invention of the computer, credit card, or internet. Indeed, only thirty years ago even personal computers were all but unheard of.

One final note on the mark of the beast is the actions taken against those who refuse. We know that true believers will resist the mark and be persecuted for it. We also know that the world at large will not all bow to the anti-Christ, but that a world war will erupt. Nevertheless, some have arqued that the prophecy teaches the universality of this system. There is no doubt that the False Prophet will attempt to cause "all" to bow to the system, but it is important to note that the word "killed" is in the Greek subjunctive mood. This "mood" is used to identify words in which the verb is "a possibility, supposition, or desire rather than a fact."[939] In other words, as Darby comments, "it is not said, he had them all killed, but he had power to cause all this."[940] This is an important distinction, for many people have assumed that what is spoken of here is the establishment of a global religion (see chapter 8). In fact, while the False Prophet may seek to establish such a global religion, he fails. Not only do true believers rebel against the False Prophet and anti-Christ, but the entire world is plunged into a world war, thus the anti-Christ and False Prophet are not entirely successful in their venture. We are told that the False Prophet has the authority to kill as many as do not accept the mark, and he will doubtless exercise that authority to furtherest extent possible, but he *is not* entirely successful. This can be proven by the wars that erupt in the second half of the tribulation and by the destruction of Mystery Babylon, discussed in chapter 8. It is also important to examine Revelation 14:9-11:

> "If anyone worships the beast and his image, and receives a mark on his forehead or upon his hand, he also will drink of the wine of the wrath of God, which is mixed in full strength in the cup of His anger; and he will be tormented with fire and brimstone in the presence of the holy angels and in the presence of the Lamb. And the smoke of their torment goes up forever and ever; and they have no rest day and night, those who worship the beast and his image, and whoever receives the mark of his name."

This critical passage seems to imply, if not openly state, that those who have received the mark are *beyond* repentance. For these individuals, it seems that it is too late for repentance. We are told "if anyone worships the beast and his image, and receives a mark on his forehead or upon his hand ... he will be tormented with fire and brimstone in the presence of the holy angels and in the presence of the Lamb." This seems to mean that the acceptance of the mark is an act in which God is absolutely rejected once and for all. If this passage is taken at face value, then *no one* who has received the mark can or will repent. While it is possible to see this as hyperbolical, the essential message of the verse best fits the literal application. Consequently, we must assume one of two things. Either the acceptance of the mark of the beast is *not* universal, as often presumed, or that *no one* repents in the second half of the tribulation.

The second option is not a good one. One of the whole points of the judgments is to chastise man and lead many to repentance. The very scope of the persecutions against believers teaches that men will be repenting and turning from their sins, at least during the early judgments. While it is true that man's heart hardens as the more severe judgments are meted out, it is hard to conceive that there are to be no converts during the Great Tribulation. To suggests this, is to minimize both God's mercy and His patience. Given these facts, the first option is best. The instigation of the mark of the beast will be accepted by those whose hearts have been hardened against God, but many, including unbelievers, will oppose the tyranny of the anti-Christ. It will be at this time, after the abomination of desolation and the mandating of the mark, that the kingdom of the anti-Christ will begin to fall. This fall is described in chapters 16 and 17, but its beginning starts here in chapter 13. It will begin when the anti-Christ is revealed in the temple, which he desecrates, and in the wars which follow.

The Number of the Beast

"Here is wisdom. Let him who has understanding calculate the number of the beast, for the number is that of a man; and his number is six hundred and sixty-six" (Revelation 13:18).

There is unquestionably no passage in the whole of Revelation, and perhaps the entire Bible, more controversial than the number of the beast. Perhaps, this should not be too surprising for the verse begins with the phrase, "Here is wisdom. Let him who has understanding ..." These phrases indicate that the meaning is not easily understood. Tim LaHaye may be correct to take the cautious approach by declaring that the meaning of the number will not be revealed until the middle of the tribulation.[941] Nevertheless, this has not stopped the "endless and fruitless ... enquiries to determine the number of the beast, the cryptic meaning of 666."[942] Dozens of popular theories have circulated throughout time, and innumerable lesser ones. Although it is advisable to avoid fruitless hypothesis, man's fascination with the number cannot be denied. Therefore, the various theories will be addressed and refuted where necessary.

Germatrian Theories

Revelation makes a strange remark about the number. It says that the wise man may "calculate the number of the beast." This statement lends credence to one of the oldest methods of "calculating" a name. In the ancient languages, there were no distinct symbols for numbers (like 1, 2, 3 ... etc.). Instead, the actual alphabet was used (like Roman Numerals I=1, V=5, X=10, etc.). Consequently, an individual's name could be assigned a numerical value based on the letters in it. This method of calculation is called *germatria*.[943] Its use in determining the number of the beast is one of the oldest theories, and one of the most abused. Using various *germantrian* calculations there have arisen countless attempts to identify historical figures with the beast, via his name. It has been noted that the name of Jesus Christ in Greek totals 888.[944] The number of the beast is 666. Thus, scholars and laymen alike have sought a man whose name numbers 666. The result is a massive list of candidates. Examples of this include various popes, Napoleon, and Mussolini,[945] not to mention Nero and many others.

Among the most popular of these theories is the identification of the number with Nero. Although promoted largely by preterists, many premillennialists who accept the Nero *redivivus* theory also buy into the belief that Nero's name equals 666 in Hebrew. According to G. H. Pember, Nero will enter the body of a dead leader to mock the resurrection of Christ.[946] The number of the beast is, therefore, said to be the number of Nero. These advocates claim that Nero's name written in Hebrew is "נרון קסר"[947] and is added together to come to 666. Thus, נ=50 ר=200 ו=6 נ=50 ק=100 ס=60 ר=200 equals a total of 666.

Oddly enough, Robert Govett suggests that this is the spelling of Nero found in the Jewish Talmud,[948] but Henry Swete notes that the Rabbinal writings and the Talmud spell Caesar not as "קסר" (q-s-r), but as "קיסר" (q-y-s-r).[949] He is correct. Even modern Hebrew dictionaries, such as Ben-Yehuda's, spell Caesar, "קיסָר",[950] as does the Zilberman's.[951] Yet another problem is the spelling of Nero itself. The nun (n) ending to his name does not properly exist in Hebrew. In fact, it is not even the proper spelling in Greek. Greek uses various consonantal endings to reflect how a noun is used in a sentence. These are called declensions.[952] For example, the ν (n) ending usually represents that the noun is the direct object of a sentence.[953] A proper name, however, will usually use a sigma ending, hence Nero's name in Greek is properly shown as Νερως (Neros), not Νερων (Neron). In either case, Hebrew does not use declensions, but is closer to modern English. Thus, Nero's name is correctly written in Hebrew merely as נרו (Nero).

Still other problems with this hypothosis exist. "John was writing in Greek and could not count on a knowledge of the Hebrew alphabet among his readers."[954] If *germatria* is used in Greek then "Caesar Neron" would equal 1005. In Latin it would equal 616. Of course, some advocates have argued that the variants found in some ancient texts read 616, rather than 666.[955] Despite this, the evidence is overwhelmingly in favor of 666, and is attested by those who studied under John personally. Moreover, the equation of Nero's name with 616 in Latin suffers from the same problems as the transliteration into Hebrew, since Latin uses entirely different declensions.[956] The assumption that the variant of 616 was intentional, based on this Nero germatria theory,[957] does not help, for the Nero hypothosis is not mentioned by any of the church fathers. Polycarp was the apostle John's disciple and makes no mention of the Nero theory. Ireneaus studied under Polycarp and lists no fewer than six theories on the number of the beast, but not one of them mentions Nero.[958] Even if the hypothesis did date back to the church fathers, it does not prove the theory correct. This thesis simply cannot be accepted with impunity, and hinges upon the legitimacy of the Nero *redivivus* view.

After Nero's name, the most popular *germatrian* postulation involves the word *Lateinos*.[959] The Latin word totalling 666 in its native tongue is taken to refer to the final Roman kingdom, or the Revived Roman Empire. It was mentioned by Irenaeus,[960] Hippolytus,[961] and Victorinus;[962] the early church fathers. The view was accepted by Isaac Newton and many others down through the ages.[963] Despite its popular attestation, it is suspect. Robert Govett reminds us that "it is not the number of a people, or of a state of men, as 'the Latin kingdom.' It is no title of honor, but the number of an individual."[964]

Equally popular is the Latin word "*teitan*." The name is taken from the Greek myth of the Titans who rebelled against the gods. The Titans are, therefore, the Greek mythological renditions of demons. The idea is that the demons have returned to the earth, calling themselves the Titans. This view also dates back to the time of the church fathers and is mentioned by both Irenaeus[965] and Victorinus,[966] although with less enthusiasm.

Other Latin names or titles connected the anti-Christ and his number include *antemos*, *genserikos*,[967] and *arnoume* which means, "the one who denies."[968] All of these names are associated with the number 666, and the title of the anti-Christ. None of these names can be proven to be correct. Still other suggestions include Balaam when written in Hebrew, Satan when written in Aramaic, and even *Vicarius fili dei* in Latin.[969] One final offering is the Hebrew spelling of Saturn, the "hidden god." According to some, the name of Saturn is connected to the mysteries of the Catholic Church. As head of the Catholic Church, the pope is given this title, which is transliterated into Hebrew as סתור (s-t-u-r), whose number likewise equals 666.[970] One curious variant of the *germatrian* theories is the fact that the words το μεγα θηριον ("the great beast") equal 666 as is shown; τ=300, ο=70, μ=40, ε=5, γ=3, α=1, θ=9, η=8, ρ=100, ι=10, ο=70, ν=50.[971]

All of these *germatrian* theories can be summed up best by Arthur Bloomfield. He says, "here is a formula by which any man's name may be made to add up to 666. It is this : first try it in Latin. If that does not work, try it in Greek. If that does not work, try it in Hebrew. If that does not work, add a title. If that does not work, do not be too particular about the spelling."[972]

Non-Germatrian Theories

The failure of the *germatrian* theories has led many to take a more practical approach to the number of the beast, without completely abandoning the numerical system. For example, Irenaeus, borrowing from the ancient belief that the earth would end in its 6000th year, suggested that the number of the beast was "a summing up of the whole of that apostasy which has taken place during the 6000 years ... that is, 6 X 100, 6 X 10, 6 X 1."[973] He also offered the views that connect the number 666 with the days of Noah and even the state of Nebuchadnezzar.[974]

According to the Nebuchadnezzar thesis, the statue represents the desire for self worship. Because Nebuchadnezzar required everyone to worship his image, the statue is a forerunner of the image of the beast. It is said that Nebuchadnezzar's image was sixty cubits heigh, six cubits wide, and six musical instruments were used in its worship[975] Following this view, Norman Harrison calculates the number as follows : "normal man : 6, Nebuchadnezzar : First man to deify self : 66, the Superman : Last Man to Deify Self : 666"[976] It should be obvious, however, that the statements are suspect. To begin with, Nebuchadnezzar was hardly the first man to deify himself. In fact, the ancient Egyptian Pharaohs were considered the incarnation of the god Ra,[977] and the ancient Babylonian king Hammurabi was called a god.[978] The same can be said of most all the ancients, long before Nebuchadnezzar.[979] It is possible to see Nebuchadnezzar's statue as an archetype for the image of the beast, but too much cannot be read into this. Others have also build giant monuments to themselves. This includes Nero, who sought to erect a 120 foot tall statue of himself in the Golden House.[980]

Certainly far weaker views exist. For example, among the medieval historicist school of thought, the number 666 was sometimes taken as the duration, in years, of the rule of the anti-Christ, or even the reign of Islam on earth.[981] Another has pointed out that all the Roman numerals added together, except for M, which equals 1000, come to 666. Thus, D=500, C=100, L=50, X=10, V=5, I=1 or 666.[982] While interesting, this is not particularly helpful.

A far better theory borrows from *germatria* without attempting to associate the number with an individual's name. Dating back to the church fathers was the belief that the mark of the beast would be a "serpentine sign."[983] According to Govett, "χ represents the cross, ξ the crooked serpent, χϛ is a contraction for Christ."[984] The contraction is formed by dropping the middle letters from the name Χριστος. By placing the ξ between the χ and the ϛ, χξϛ is formed. This sequence, *Chi Xi Sigma*, is suppose to equal 666 in Greek *germatria*,[985] thus "χξς" is both the mark and number of the beast. One other interesting argument on behalf of this thesis is mentioned by E. W. Bullinger. In Greek, the letter *sigma* is made like "σ." However, when it is placed at the end of a word, it is drawn differently like "ς." The word for this "final *sigma*" is *stigma*. The word for "mark" in Greek is *stigmata*.[986] The drawback to this piece of evidence, is that the Greek New Testament uses the synonym, *charagma* (χάραγμα), rather than *stigmata*.

One final theory should be addressed. Perhaps the least presumptuous of the views, is the belief that the number 666 merely represents a mock unholy trinity.[987] The number seven is often equated with divinity since God rested on the seventh day. The number six is, therefore, "one digit short of divinity."[988] We are told that "six is the number of evil. This triple six represents a trinity of evil."[989] Some have called it the symbol of apostate Christianity.[990] On this, most agree. The question is whether or not this is *all* that was intended, or whether or not there is to be in the future a more literal application. Walter Scott warned that "beyond what is signified in this trinity of evil –666– man cannot go."[991] This is, perhaps, the best view to take.

Summary on the Number
The flurry of guesses as to the number of the beast are surely premature. The early church father Hippolytus suggested several favorable views, but ultimately admitted that "it is not in [our] power to explain it exactly ... only to give a conjectural account."[992] John Darby was honest when he said, "I confess my ignorance as the number 666,"[993] and elsewhere, "I do not pretend to wisdom."[994] Such refreshing honesty is the best policy. The exact literal meaning of the number of the beast will probably not be revealed until the middle of the tribulation, as LaHaye suggest.[995] As Robert Thomas said, "if [the number] was not discernable to [John's] generation and to those immediately following him – and it was not – the generation to whom it will be discernable must have lain (and still lies) in the future."[996]

Summary of the Beasts

Chapter thirteen is one of the most difficult chapters in Revelation. It is debated to this very day, and yet there is unison agreement on many aspects; particuarly among premillennialists. The first beast, which rises from the sea, is the final stage of the Roman Empire, often called the Revived or Restored Roman Empire. It is the same as the ten toes of the statue in Daniel 2. The kingdom will be made up of ten separate states under the authority of the anti-Christ. Eventually, three of those states will be overthrown and subjected to the direct rule of the anti-Christ.

Below the anti-Christ will be a religious apostate prophet, known as the False Prophet. He will attempt to compel the earth, and all who live in it, to worship the beast and its image. In addition to worship, the False Prophet will attempt to require all men to receive a mark on their hand or forehead. No one will be allowed to buy or sell without mark, but many will refuse. The False Prophet will persecute those who do not bow to the anti-Christ and will perform many miracles in hopes of deceiving the world.

These are the things upon which premillennialists are agreed. The specifics will be debated until the time comes for the prophecies to be fulfilled. Will the anti-Christ undergo a false resurrection? Will the anti-Christ be Satan incarnate? Will he be the revival of the ancient dictator Nero? Will he be Judas Iscariot? Will the False Prophet be a False Jewish Messiah? What is the mark of the beast? Will the mark be a computer chip implanted under man's skin? Does the number of the beast represent Nero's name? Perhaps it represents the name of the Roman Kingdom. Or maybe it is the mark, "χξϛ." All these questions will be answered in time. Some are valid. Others are not. None can be said with impunity. We cannot rule these views out, but we must be careful and heed the apostle Paul when he said, "do not go beyond what is written" (1 Corinthians 4:6). If we heed these words, we will not be disappointed.

As Sir Robert Anderson once remarked, "prophecy is not given to enable us to prophesy,"[997] so let us "not go beyond what is written," by presuming to prophesy that which John did not prophesy.

CHAPTER SUMMARY

Revelation 13 gives us background and the rise of the anti-Christ and his kingdom. It also shows us that the ancient pagan kingdoms of the world have been nothing but puppets to Satan who war against God and His people. The following can be gleaned from this chapter.

1. The beast is properly the kingdoms of Satan from Babel to the final Kingdom of the anti-Christ.
2. The seven heads are seven kingdoms which rose in conflict to God's people and Israel; Babylon, Assyria, Egypt, Persia, Greece, Rome, and the Revived Roman Empire or kingdom of the anti-Christ.
3. The "eight" is only said to be "like" a head, and is the anti-Christ himself or perhaps Satan. It is he who will guide the final kingdom of the beast.
4. The wounded head is the Roman Empire itself. It is resurrected under the anti-Christ.
5. The ten kings compose the states under the dominion of this final kingdom. Three of the kings are overthrown by the anti-Christ, probably in the middle of the tribulation.
6. The Beast from the earth is the False Prophet. The False Prophet is a subordinate under the anti-Christ and is not synonymous with him.

7. It is the False Prophet who will attempt to compel people to worship the beast and receive the mark of the beast.
8. The mark of the beast is compelled through economic sanctions. Only the anti-Christ will have the number of the beast. All others will merely have the mark of the beast, but many people will resist the mark and war will ensue.

Charts on the Beasts of Revelation

Hippolytus	Chiliast	The sixth, or possibly seventh, head as the Roman Empire.
Lactantius	Chiliast	Kings as 1) Egypt 2) Persia 3) Babylon 4) Assyria 5) Greece 6) Rome 7) Divided Rome
Victorinus	Chiliast	Mountains as the city of Rome. Kings as 1) Galba 2) Vitellius 3) Otho 4) Vespasian 5) Titus 6) Domitian 7) Nerva
Joachim of Floris	Medieval Millenarian	Kings as 1) Herod 2) Nero 3) Constantius 4) Chosroes 5) Mohammad 6) Saladin 7) anti-Christ
Pierre D'Olivi	Medieval Millenarian	Kings as 1) Jews 2) Pagans 3) Greeks 4) Goths 5) Vandals 6) Lombards 7) Saracens
Francis Lambert	Historicist	Kings as 1) The serpent in Eden 2) Nimrod of Babel 3) Assyria and Babylon 4) Media and Persia 5) Greek 6) Roman 7) kingdom of the anti-Christ
Joseph Mede	Historicist premillennialist	Mountains as city of Rome, but also 1) kings 2) consuls 3) tribunes 4) decimvirs dictators 5) Caesars 6) 7) Christian emperors Kings as 1) Babylon 2) Persia 3) Greece 4) Divided Greece 5) Selucid Greece 6) Roman Empire 7) The Roman Catholic Empire
John Bale	Historicist	Seven heads of the Dragon as 1) The serpent in Eden 2) Nimrod of Babel 3) Assyria and Babylon 4) Media and Persia 5) Greek 6) Roman 7) Papal Rome
Isaac Newton	Historicist premillennialist	Kings as seven emperors, but also connects the first four to the first four horsemen of the apocalypse.
John Darby	Dispensational premillennialist	Mountains as Rome. Kings as seven forms of government.
Robert Govett	Futurist premillennialist	Mountains as Rome. Kings as 1) Julius Caesar 2) Tiberius 3) Caligula 4) Claudius 5) Nero 6) Domitian 7) the anti-Christ

George Peters	Futurist premillennialist	Kings as 1) kings 2) consuls 3) dictators 4) decemvirs 5) tribunes 6) emperors 7) the final stage of the anti-Christ
Joseph Seiss	Futurist premillennialist	Mountains and kings as 1) Egypt 2) Assyria 3) Babylon 4) Persia 5) Greece 6) Rome 7) the kingdom of the anti-Christ
Sir Robert Anderson	Dispensational premillennialist	Mountains and kings as 1) Egypt 2) Ninevah (Assyria) 3) Babylon 4) Persia 5) Greece 6) Rome 7) the kingdom of the anti-Christ
E. W. Bullinger	Ultradispensationalist	Mountains and kings as 1) Babylon 2) Medo-Persia 3) Greece 4) Rome 5) Mohammedan 6) Beast's kingdom 7) Christ's kingdom
H. A. Ironside	Dispensational premillennialist	Mountains as the city of Rome. Kings as seven forms of government.
Arthur Bloomfield	Quasi-dispensational	As the "world empires of all time."
Dwight Pentecost	Dispensational premillennialist	Mountains as Rome. Kings as 1) kings 2) consuls 3) dictators 4) decemvirs 5) tribunes 6) emperors 7) final stage
Norman Harrison	Midtribulational premillennialist	Mountains as 1) Babylon 2) Medo-Persia 3-5) the four heads of Daniel's Greek beast 6) Rome 7) the final kingdom Kings as 1) Nebuchadnezzar 2) Belshazzar 3) Antiochus Epiphanes 4) Herod the Great 5) Herod Agrippa 6) Domitian 7) "the modern Caesar"
John Walvoord	Dispensational premillennialist	Has fluctuated between each of the views throughout his writings
Robert Mounce	Posttribulational Premillennialist	Says the heads are "symbolic" and does not explain their meaning.
George Ladd	Posttribulational Premillennialist	Mountains as "fulness of power." Kings as seven kingdoms.
Hal Lindsey	Dispensational premillennialist	Mountains as Rome. Kings as 1) Assyria 2) Egypt 3) Neo-Babylonian 4) Persia 5) Greece 6) Rome 7) Revived Roman Empire
Marvin Rosenthal	"Pre-wrath" premillennialist	Uncommited but favors 1) Egypt 2) Assyria 3) Babylon 4) Medo-Persia 5) Greece 6) Rome 7) kingdom of the anti-Christ

The Seven Heads of the Beast as Seven Kings
Tenants of:
The belief that the seven heads of the beast represent seven individual kings or emperors.

Popular advocates from:
The Church Fathers : Victorinus.
Medieval Theologians : Joachim of Floris.
Reformation Scholars : Isaac Newton.*
Post-Reformation Scholars : Robert Govett.
Modern Evangelicals : Norman Harrison,* William Newell,* Watchman Nee,* Charles Ryrie,* and Tim LaHaye.

* Sees a dual meaning to the heads; hence, holds to more than one view.

Strengths:
1) Appears on the surface to be the most straightforward view.
2) Makes the eighth head easily identifiable as the anti-Christ.
3) Is an ancient view.

Weaknesses:
1) It cannot accord with history.
2) Domitian can in no way be made the sixth king as ten emperors preceded him.
3) No agreement on the kings has been reached among the view's advocates.

The Seven Heads of the Beast as Seven Forms of Government
Tenants of:
The seven heads represent seven governmental forms; kings, consuls, tribunes, decimvirs, dictators, Caesars, and Christian emperors.

Popular advocates from:
The Church Fathers : None known.
Medieval Theologians : No known advocates.
Reformation Scholars : Joseph Mede,* and some amillennial historicists.
Post-Reformation Scholars : John Nelson Darby,* Walter Scott, and George Peters.
Modern Evangelicals : H. A. Ironside,* Dwight Pentecost.

* Sees a dual meaning to the heads; hence, holds to more than one view.

Strengths:
1) Maintains the representation of kingly authority.
2) Is popular among evangelicals.
3) It makes the Caesars the sixth head.

Weaknesses:
1) The governmental forms are suspect; e.g. tribunes existed throughout most history, including the Imperial days, but were never the absolute authority.
2) The identification of seven governments is somewhat subjective (see above).
3) The view does not seem to have been taught until the Reformation.
4) Looses continuity with the eighth head.

The Seven Heads of the Beast as Seven Kingdoms
Tenants of:
The heads are kings, as representative of their kingdoms. Hence, the seven heads are seven kingdoms, or empires, of the Dragon; usually identified with Egypt, Babylon, Assyria, Persia, Greece, Rome, and the Revived Roman Empire.

Popular advocates from:
The Church Fathers : Hippolytus.
Medieval Theologians : Pierre D'Olivi and some Joachimites.
Reformation Scholars : Francis Lambert, Joseph Mede,* and John Bale, among others.
Post-Reformation Scholars : Joseph Seiss, Sir Robert Anderson, and E. W. Bullinger.
Modern Evangelicals : Arthur Bloomfield, Norman Harrison,* George Ladd,* Hal Lindsey,* Marvin Rosenthal, Robert Van Kampen, Henry Morris, and Robert Thomas.

* Sees a dual meaning to the heads; hence, holds to more than one view.

Strengths:
1) Kings are often used as the representatives of their kingdoms in prophecy.
2) Rome naturally becomes the sixth kingdom, and the kingdom of the anti-Christ becomes the seventh.
3) It is one of the most ancient views, accepted throughout history by premillennialists.
4) It can best explain the double meaning implied in the passage, as Rome is the sixth kingdom and the seat of the Dragon's kingdom in John's day.
5) The identification of the empire is not subjective, for only these came into prominent conflict or interaction with the Jews.
6) It makes the seven heads of the beast in perfect unison with the seven heads of the Dragon, who is Satan. If they are empires, they are Satan's kingdoms.

Weaknesses:
1) The word is properly "kings," not "kingdoms."
2) The anti-Christ is an individual, so this view must closely associate his empire with him as an individual.
3) It is alleged that the kingdom lists is subjective (but see above).

The Seven Hills of Rome
Tenants of:
The belief that the seven "hills" or mountains represent the "seven hills" of Rome; hence identifying the final king, kingdom, or government with Rome.

* Sees a dual meaning to the heads; hence, holds to more than one view.

Popular advocates from:
The Church Fathers : Hippolytus and Victorinus.
Medieval Theologians : Waldenses, Hussites, and most Joachimites.
Reformation Scholars : Joseph Mede, Isaac Newton, and most others.
Post-Reformation Scholars : John Nelson Darby, Sir Robert Anderson, and Walter Scott.
Modern Evangelicals : William Newell, H. A. Ironside,* G. H. Lang,* Watchman Nee,* Hal Lindsey,* Charles Ryrie*.

Strengths:
1) A Roman coin in John's day depicted the Roman goddess as seated on seven hills.
2) The seven hills of Rome are mentioned by Virgil, Horace, Tibullus, Propertius, Ovid, Silius Italicus, Statius, Claudius, Symmachus, and Martial.
3) This would be the most natural understanding of the city on seven hills to anyone living in John's day.
4) The Greek does not distinguish between a mountain and a hill.
5) It is the most ancient of views, accepted throughout history.

Weaknesses:
1) It is alleged that the Greek word refers only to mountains, not hills (see above).
2) It is alleged that the hills are merely a synonym for the seven heads.
3) It is *assumed* that this cannot be Rome because ancient Babylon must rise again (see chapter 8).

The Anti-Christ as a Jew

Tenants of:

The belief that the anti-Christ will be a Jew and present himself as the Messiah.

Selected popular advocates from:

The Church Fathers : Victorinus and Ephraem the Syrian.

Medieval Theologians : Adso of Montier, Thomas Aquinas, and many others.

Reformation Scholars : A few. Most saw pope as anti-Christ.

Post-Reformation Scholars : Nathaniel West and G. H. Pember.

Modern Evangelicals : H. A. Ironside, Norman Harrison, and possibly Marvin Rosenthal.

Strengths:

1) If the anti-Christ is a false Messiah, then he must be a Jew.
2) The absence of the tribe of Dan is supposed to lend support this view.
3) The ancient Rabbinical tradition supports this view.
4) The anti-Christ will enter the temple where only Jews may enter.

Weaknesses:

1) There is no proof that the anti-Christ will be a false Messiah, only that he will oppose the true Messiah.
2) The association of the anti-Christ with the tribe of Dan is based solely on tradition, not solid exegesis.
3) How could a Jew create a peace treaty with Arabs.
4) Gentiles have desecrated the temple before, so the anti-Christ does not need to be a Jew to enter the temple.
5) The anti-Christ will be the last ruler of Rome, so he should be a Gentile.

The Anti-Christ as a Gentile
Tenants of:
The belief that the anti-Christ is the last Gentile ruler of the world, and the Revived Roman Empire.

Selected popular advocates from:
The Church Fathers : Lactantius and probably many others.
Medieval Theologians : Pierre d'Olivi.
Reformation Scholars : Joseph Mede along with most historicists.
Post-Reformation Scholars : Walter Scott.
Modern Evangelicals : Dwight Pentecost and Hal Lindsey.

Strengths:
1) The false Messianic imagery applies to the False Prophet, not the anti-Christ.
2) The anti-Christ will be the last ruler of Rome, so he should be a Gentile.
3) The anti-Christ will initiate a treaty with Israel and bring peace with the Arabs. It is argued that only a Gentile would be trusted by the Arabs to do this.
4) The association of the anti-Christ with the Gentile Roman empire is as ancient a view as the association of him with the tribe of Dan.

Weaknesses:
1) Ancient Rabbinical tradition says that he will be a Jew.
2) It is argued that only Jews may enter the temple, as the anti-Christ will (see above).
3) It is argued that the title anti-Christ implies that he will be a false Messiah.

7

—

The Bowls of Wrath

Ancient, and even modern, commentaries on the bowls are sadly lacking. This is in part because the bowls appear to speak for themselves, but it is also, in part, because the historicists of the Middle Ages, and even some chiliasts, saw the bowls as identical to the trumpets. Similarities between the trumpet judgments and the bowls have led many to assume the description of the bowls are merely expansive and elaborative of the trumpets. John Bale stated that the first bowl coincided with the first seal, as was taught by the concurrent view of chronology (see Appendix D).[998] According to this once popular view, the first seal, the first trumpet, and the first bowl are all different aspects of one and the same thing. Although most now reject the concurrent view, preferring to see the bowls as sequential, following the trumpets, the similarities in judgments have left many commentators to say little on the bowls, believing it would be repetitious. Others have let the passages speak for themselves, as is perhaps prudent. That the bowls are separate from, and following, the trumpets will become obvious. Although similarities can be identified, the differences are too great. Closer similiarities exist between the bowls and plagues of Egypt. Even as God punished the Egyptians for their sins, so God shall punish the world in the last days. These bowls are the last and final "wrath of God" upon man. When they are finished, so also "the wrath of God is finished" (Revelation 15:1).

The First Bowl

> "The first *angel* went and poured out his bowl into the earth; and it became a loathsome and malignant sore upon the men who had the mark of the beast and who worshiped his image" (Revelation 16:2).

The description of the first bowl appears self explanatory, and as such it was treated by the early church fathers. Only with the Middle Ages did the malignant sores become a symbol for "the excommunication of heretics"[999] or the persecution of Christians by Jews.[1000] Later, Joseph Mede assigned historicism to the prophecy, saying that it symbolized the preaching of the Waldenses, Albigenses, Wycliffs, and Hussites.[1001] Thus he envisioned the gospel as a sore upon the Catholic Church.

As has been the case previously, Darby and his followers returned to the early chiliastic interpretations, but did not entirely abandon the heavy symbolic approach. Darby argued that the sun, which he believed caused the sores, represents governmental authority,[1002] even as he had similarly assigned the earth as a symbol of the world government.[1003] Walter Scott said that these were "moral sores" representing a struggle with "soul and conscience."[1004] H. A. Ironside, who normally follows Darby and Scott, is here somewhat reluctant to assign an entirely symbolic view to the bowl. He says that it is "perhaps"[1005] symbolic, but goes on to explain that "the literal judgments may be intimately linked with the symbolic ... both interpretations coalasce."[1006] Ironside, therefore, reluctantly emulates his mentors while acknowledging that a literal meaning may also be intended.

Most evangelical commentators, with the chiliasts of old, agree that literalism is intended here. The attempt to associate the sores with a symbol of government cannot be taken seriously. Those who assign this sort of symbolism to the bowls have equated far too many symbols to earthly governments. They have lacked the judicious approach by assigning earth, grass, trees, water, seas, sky, and even the sun to the world governments. One is a possibility, but too many lacks credibility.

What then of the literal? The comparison to Exodus 9 and the plague of the boils has been made by nearly every commentator. Does not the similarity suggest, as some say, that this is symbolic of the former? On the contrary, it is as literal as the plague of Egypt. In fact, the very same language is used.[1007] It is inconsistent to accept the Egyptian plague as literal while calling this one symbolic. It is, in fact, "the Egyptian plague of ulcers intensified."[1008] Just as God cursed the Egyptians for their rebellion against God, the Lord shall inflict similar punishments upon those who bear the mark of the beast.

Some have tried to decipher the material means through which this judgment will be wrought. Hal Lindsey suggests that the sores are caused by radioactive fallout from a Nuclear war.[1009] While this cannot be rejected as a possibility, the theory suffers one major flaw. How does nuclear fallout target only those who bear the mark of the beast? John Walvoord has said, "there is a notable contrast between the first vial and the first trumpet, in that the first trumpet (8:7) burns up a third part of the trees and all the green grass. Here the judgment is specifically upon men and is directed to a particular group of men, namely, the beast worshipers who have received the mark of the beast."[1010] Henry Morris offers a variant theory which takes this specific targeting into account. He believes that:

> "The very process by which men had received this mark had rendered them susceptible to these unique sores. The mark had been permanently affixed to the skin, like a tattoo, and something in the chemicals or in the marking process (possibility a process of irradiation, because of the government's mandate to mark billions of people rapidly and permanently) may have entered the bloodstream. The angel with the plague, knowing the nature of this poison, could then release some other agent into the atmosphere which would specifically and quickly react with all human bodies so affected, causing them to break out in these 'loathsome and penetratingly painful' sores."[1011]

Certainly, no one on earth today can tell for sure. The method by which the Lord will cause these boils or sores is not told to us. What is told to us is that those who have accepted the mark will be tormented, and they will be tormented in the same way that the Egyptians were. They will suffer from these "loathsome and malignant" sores, but only them. Apparently, even those who have not accepted Christ will be spared this torment, if they have resisted the mark of the beast. The mark is, therefore, a sort of Rubicon. Once anyone has accepted the mark, there is no turning back. God's wrath has been restrained in hopes of leading some to repentance, but against these followers of the beast, there is no restraint. They have crossed the point of no return and are tormented as a warning to others not to give in to the anti-Christ or his False Prophet.

The Second Bowl

> "The second *angel* poured out his bowl into the sea, and it became blood like *that* of a dead man; and every living thing in the sea died" (Revelation 16:3).

The similarities between this judgment and the second trumpet judgment have been pointed out by many, but it is clear that here the judgment is far greater and effects far more than the previous. Whether this is an expansion of the second trumpet or an entirely different judgment is open to debate, but that it follows the trumpets and the first bowl in sequence should not be disputed (see Appendix D). What is contested is the literalness of the passage.

The medieval allegories need not be taken seriously. Whether it is alleged to be an allegory for Charlemagne's conquest of the Saxons[1012] or the intrusion of false teachers into the church[1013] or even Joseph Mede's attempt to associate this judgment with the Reformation, by calling it a judgment on the "pontificall sea,"[1014] this type of high allegory cannot be sustained. The very diverse nature of these speculations illustrates that ambiguous allegory cannot identify the meaning of the prophecy. Having said that, a symbolic level is not without justification. It has been shown that "sea" can sometimes be a symbol for the nations or people of the earth. Following this line of argument John Darby suggest that the blood represents the death of masses of people.[1015] Walter Scott, however, makes death a symbol of moral or spiritual death[1016] while Ironside says that the death may be "physical or spiritual or both."[1017]

If we, for the sake of argument, acknowledge that the blood and sea are symbolic of death and the masses, it does not follow that "the result of this judgment is spiritual death,"[1018] as Pentecost believes. He says that the blood makes all life in the sea "become lifeless,"[1019] but this is exactly the problem. If the blood represents death, then death becomes both the cause and effect. Biblical imagery is never haphazard. It is the blood which *causes* the death of all life in the sea. Pentecost would make both blood *and* death symbolic, despite the fact that the later is the result of the former. This is one major argument for the literal interpretation. Joseph Seiss provides another. "If it is not literal, then were not the plagues of Egypt literal"?[1020]

The similarity to the Egyptian plague is obvious. The language is the same. If we accept that the plague on Egypt was literal, as is plainly taught, then it is inconsistent to make this plague symbolic, "nor is any other sort of fulfillment possible."[1021] We have been told previously that many people will die, so why would the second bowl judgment merely symbolize the same prophecy as a previous judgment in a different way? Some would have *all* the bowls representing spiritual death, but this would be redundant. The judgment must be literal. The blood does not represent death, for it causes death. The blood is real, or at least looks "like" the blood of a man. This is accepted by Joseph Seiss,[1022] William Newell,[1023] G. H. Lang,[1024] Watchman Nee,[1025] John Walvoord,[1026] Charles Ryrie,[1027] Robert Thomas,[1028] Tim LaHaye,[1029] and most other modern evangelicals.

Some questions still remain. First, if the blood is real, then so should be the sea. Henry Swete believes that it is the Aegean Sea,[1030] but it is impossible to tell. Greek does not differentiate between sea and ocean, so it may be that an even greater body of water is intended. Still more interesting is how does such a thing occur. Hal Lindsey proposes some "unknown weapon,"[1031] but Henry Morris provides a more simle solution.

> "Chemically speaking, the composition of sea water is almost identical to that of blood, so that only a relatively small modification would be necessary ... it is merely a chemical solution, water containing iron and other chemicals which give it a blood-red appearance .. (and) brings death to every living creature in the sea."[1032]

Once again it must be said that the methodology is open to debate. The meaning should be obvious. Although "sea" and "blood" do sometimes have symbolic value, that cannot be the case here. The prophecy is as literal as the plague on Egypt. The sea itself is turned into blood, or at least appears like blood, killing what lives in the sea. Whereas the previous plagues showed restraint, the bowls show no restraint and effect one and all. *Everything* that is in the sea dies; not merely a third, but all.

The Third Bowl

> "The third *angel* poured out his bowl into the rivers and the springs of waters; and they became blood. And I heard the angel of the waters saying, 'Righteous art Thou, who art and who wast, O Holy One, because Thou didst judge these things; for they poured out the blood of saints and prophets, and Thou hast given them blood to drink. They deserve it.' And I heard the altar saying, 'Yes, O Lord God, the Almighty, true and righteous are Thy judgments.'" (Revelation 16:4-7).

194

This judgment parallels the second bowl, save that rivers and springs are targeted rather than the seas and oceans. The targets in this judgment are the sources of drinking water. It is poetic justice. The angels say, "they poured out the blood of saints and prophets, and Thou hast given them blood to drink." The punishment is the just dessert for the wicked, but some will argue that such poetic justice indicates that symbolism is intended here. Such remarks are naive. Poetic justice does not mean poetic license. History is full of poetic justice, for God is a God of justice. To argue that this is evidence of allegory or symbolism is trivial. Are we to believe that Haman was not truly hung on his own gallows? Or that the assassins of Caesar did not die unnatural deaths, often by the hands of assassins? Or that Commodus, unbeaten in the arena, did not die by strangulation at the hands of a wrestler? Perhaps Leon Trotski was not really betrayed by his fellow Communist conspirators? No, these are all historical events, and proof that there is a God of justice. Poetic justice is just that. It is justice administered poetically, it is not poetry administered allegorically.

The church fathers, such as Lactantius, call the passage literal.[1033] While Nicholas of Lyra may say that it is symbolic of Chalemagne's war against the Huns[1034] and John Bale that it represents the delusion of true believers,[1035] such allegory can no more be proven than Joseph Mede's theory that the rivers are the Jesuit and ecclesiastical orders fulfilled in the Elizabethian age.[1036] Even Walter Scott's more reasonable belief that the death is "spiritual" rather than physical[1037] is unwarranted. Dwight Pentecost says that this prophecy indicates "removing the possiblity of finding life."[1038] All these ideas, however, conflict with the context of the passages. If Egypt's curses were real, if the trumpet judgments were literal, if the second bowl was literal, if God's punishments are real, then this passage too must be real and literal. The only level upon which a non-literal view can be sustained is the suggestion that the rivers merely appear as blood, rather than being literal blood, but in either case, the rivers cause literal death as people are unable to drink it.

The third bowl is, therefore, a continuation and expansion of the second. Even as the sea was turned to blood, God now turns the drinking waters into blood, so that water is scarce and death is common. Outside of natural water sources, few drinking sources exist. Most every drink readily available uses water as a primary ingredient. It is possible that various plant or fruitjuices, as well as milk, could provide an alternative. The problem is that these sources are much more rare than water. Only the very rich could afford to buy enough of these products to keep themselves from dehydrading. Rain could provide temporary relief, and one can envision people placing buckets outside their homes to catch the life preserving water as it falls to the earth. However, even this resource will be rare, as will be shown in the succeeding judgments.

The Fourth Bowl

"The fourth *angel* poured out his bowl upon the sun; and it was given to it to scorch men with fire. And men were scorched with fierce heat; and they blasphemed the name of God who has the power over these plagues; and they did not repent, so as to give Him glory." (Revelation 16:8-9).

Elsewhere the sun and moon were darkened, yet here the sun scorches men in a fierce heat wave. Some scholars have noted possible parrallels in Old Testament prophecies, including Isaiah 24:6, 30:26, and Malachi 4:1. These are strong possiblities, although the verses in question may actually refer to other events in Revelation. What is not questioned is that those passages cannot be allegorized. They speak of a literal intesity and burning. Here too, there is nothing in the context to imply figuratively language. Despite this, Nicholas of Lyra says that this is a prophecy of the wicked Roman dictator Crescentius.[1039] John Bale says that the "sun of righteousness" is to be blotted out in the fourth age.[1040] This remark is particularly weak. Would a judgment of God restrict the the *Son* of righteousness? Would God ever "blot out" the Word of Christ?

More reasonable figurative interpretations follow Joseph Mede who suggests that the stars are "Princes, Dukes, Prelates, Lords of countries, and Kings,"[1041] but where does he read of "stars" at all in the passage? It speaks only of the sun, whom Darby makes a collective symbol of all rulers. The scortching he says is "intolerable" oppression.[1042] However, the judgment is upon the wicked. It is not the anti-Christ and his minions' "intollerable tyranny"[1043] but God's judgment upon them because "they blasphemed the name of God who has the power over these plagues; and they did not repent, so as to give Him glory"! Nevertheless, Dwight Pentecost insists, "that an individual is envionsioned is seen in that the sun is referred to as 'him'"[1044] In fact, only the King James translates the Greek word αὐτῷ (*auto*) as "he." The word can actually be translated as "he, she, or it."[1045] Accordingly, it is impossible to draw any conclusions from this word. "It" is the sun. Nothing in the text says otherwise.

What the Bible speaks of here is literal scorching heat.[1046] It is a "sun induced heat wave."[1047] Some say that this contrast with the fourth trumpet[1048] and with the next bowl, both of which bring darkness. However, such a contrast does not imply a contradiction. The light from the sun does not necessarily have to be increased in order for the heat from the sun to be increased. Hal Lindsey believes that this could be caused by an expansion in the ozone hole, cause by nuclear fallout.[1049] Such a possibility is but one of many. The sun's heat rays, and ultraviolet rays in particular, do not need to be visible to burn with fire. The Bible is obviously speaking of a dramatic heat wave. A heat wave which is compounded by the fact that men do not have water to drink as a result of the last bowl of wrath. God's judgments are increasing in both frequency and severity.

Another peculiarity about this judgment, and the bowls judgments in general, is the reaction which it produces in men. Rather than bringing men to repentance, men are becoming bitter. We are told that "they blasphemed the name of God who has the power over these plagues; and they did not repent, so as to give Him glory" (vs. 9). Far from turning away from sin, men are now refusing to repent. This fact should not be overlooked. The judgments of God are a dividing sword. All men have a lifetime in which to accept Christ Jesus or turn their hearts to stone and reject God. The tribulation accelerates the process. When Jesus returns every man will have already made his choice. No one can claim not to have known. No man can claim to be ignorant. Every man will have made his choice. The bowl judgments are the last judgments. In the last half of the tribulation the False Prophet will be attempting to compel men to worship the image of the beast. All who resist will be persecuted. All who give in will suffer God's wrath. By the time the bowls are spilled out, it appears as if most men, if not all, have already chosen. They have either accepted Christ or rejected him. When these plagues are brought forth, men do not act surprised or remorseful, but bitter and hateful. They blaspheme "the name of God who has the power over these plagues" and they do not repent or "give Him glory."

The Fifth Bowl

"The fifth *angel* poured out his bowl upon the throne of the beast; and his kingdom became darkened; and they gnawed their tongues because of pain, and they blasphemed the God of heaven because of their pains and their sores; and they did not repent of their deeds." (Revelation 16:10-11).

Although some, including great scholars like Sir Robert Anderson,[1050] have tried to argue that the bowls are an elaboration of the trumpet judgments, the fifth bowl bears no resemblance to the fifth trumpet at all, but rather to the fourth trumpet. This similarity is not unusual since the event is also prophesied throughout the Bible. Isaiah 13:10, 24:23, 60:2; Ezekiel 32:7; Joel 2:1-2, 2:31, 3:15; Amos 5:20, 8:9; Zephaniah 1:15; Matthew 24:29; and Mark 13:24 all speak of the sun darkening and not giving its full light. This first began under the fourth trumpet, but its light still shown, albeit less brightly. Here, there is total darkness.

Some scholars have tried to argue that the darkness is figurative of "spiritual darkness."[1051] John Bale said that it was figurative of the dark empire[1052] and Walter Scott called it the moral darkness of the government.[1053] Dwight Pentecost even went so far as to say that it "may be a reference to the judgment of God that imposes blindness upon the Beast's followers."[1054] Ironically, H. A. Ironside deviates from his usual attempt to associate the sun with the world government and here acknowledges that a literal darkening of sun is envsioned by John.[1055] Doubtless, he made this decision because he had no other choice. Neither is Ironside alone among the less literal interpreters. Henry Swete often mixes historicism with futurism and allegory with literalism, but here he sees the darkness as a literal judgment on the city of Rome.[1056] Joseph Mede, the early historicist, also takes a slightly more literal view by declaring that the prophecy is of the future destruction of Rome.[1057] He does not elaborate, but admits that it refers to the future, and places it in a literal context. Only Nicholas of Lyra, the medieval Joachimite, maintains his extreme historicism, calling it a symbol of the Saracen persecutions.[1058]

That the literal interpretation is preferred, even by those who do not normally incline heavily in that direction, should not be surprising. The only way that one could consistently make this passage figurative would be to make Isaiah 13:10, 24:23, 60:2; Ezekiel 32:7; Joel 2:1-2, 2:31, 3:15; Amos 5:20, 8:9; Zephaniah 1:15; Matthew 24:29; and Mark 13:24 figurative as well. All these passages speak of darkness over the earth in the last days. They speak of a time of judgment when God will darken the skies and God's wrath will be upon men. The plague, like many of the bowls, is reminiscent of the ninth plague of Egypt where darkness fell upon the land.

Darkness does not cause pain, but the intensity of the sun's rays, even though they cannot be seen, do. The boils and sores caused by the first bowl cause pain. The lack of water further aggravates the pain caused by the boils and the sun's heat. Two things are significant in this. First, the sores have not yet dissipated. While most of the judgments of the seals and trumpets were limited in their duration, the bowls do not quickly diminish. Their punishments are prolonged. "The effects of these judgments overlap each other."[1059] Even though darkness does not physically hurt, it always sends an ominous message. While they still cry out in pain from their sores and while they still suffer from thirst and heat waves, darkness will encompass the "throne of the beast," and the world will know that God is the judge.

This knowledge will not bring about repentance. Like the last bowl, man's heart has already been hardened. John Darby argues that it is man's "conscience" that gnaws at them,[1060] but in fact the Bible is clear that they "gnawed their tongues *because of the pain*," not because of conscience. Their conscience does not lead them to repent for the Bible says explicitly, "they did not repent of their deeds." Instead, they "blasphemed the God of heaven because of their pains and their sores."

The Sixth Bowl

"And the sixth *angel* poured out his bowl upon the great river, the Euphrates; and its water was dried up, that the way might be prepared for the kings from the east. And I saw *coming* out of the mouth of the dragon and out of the mouth of the beast and out of the mouth of the

198

false prophet, three unclean spirits like frogs; for they are spirits of demons, performing signs, which go out to the kings of the whole world, to gather them together for the war of the great day of God, the Almighty. 'Behold, I am coming like a thief. Blessed is the one who stays awake and keeps his garments, lest he walk about naked and men see his shame.' And they gathered them together to the place which in Hebrew is called Har-Magedon" (Revelation 16:12-16).

Here we find the most controversial of the bowls of Wrath. We are told that the great river Euphrates is dried up to make way for the armies of the east, and immediately following we see the armies of the world gathering together *at Armageddon*. The whole world, secular or religious, is aware of Armageddon. Its significance in literature and language has made it virtually identifical with the end of the world. It is identified as the place of the final battle, yet among Biblical prophetic interpreters, these issues are not quite so simple. The river Euphrates, the armies of the world, the place of Armageddon, and the final battle are all subjects of contention and debate to this very day.

The Euphrates
This the second mention of the Euphrates found in Revelation. The first occurs in the sixth trumpet, and is one reason that some scholars have attatched a close relationship between the sixth trumpet and the sixth bowl. In the sixth trumpet there were four angels, or demons, bound to the Euphrates awaiting the day of their release. In this judgment the Euphrates is dried up so that the armies of the east may pass. While it is fair to draw a relationship, on account of the Euphrates, it is not fair to draw too close a parallel. In the sixth trumpet the fallen angels release an army of destruction upon mankind. In this judgment, an obstacle is removed from the human armies ability to pass en route to Armageddon. Joseph Seiss actually compares this to the dividing of the Red Sea or the Jordan.[1061] Since that was literal, so must be this be literal, but he also draws another parallel. He believes that even as the Egyptian armies drowned in the Red Sea, these armies "availing themselves of the easy passage thus afforded to come forth, they come to a scene of slaughter from which they never return."[1062] These comments, however, only spark the more controversy and beg the questions asked by scholars throughout the ages. Who dries up the river? Why do they pass? Is this the real Euphrates? If not, then what does it represent?

The first question is properly whether or not this refers to the real river which passes through Iraq and Syria. Historically, the river has served as the imaginary boundary between the east and the west. It was the frontiers of the Roman Empire, and Solomon's domain once stretched to touch the Euphrates in the north. The medieval scholar Nicholas of Lyra believed that this boundary signified the limits of the Roman Empire itself, and was, therefore, symbolic of the fall of Rome.[1063] John Bale applied it to the Holy Roman Empire, or more specifically to the Holy Roman Church, and said that it represents the drying up of papal possessions.[1064] John Darby was equally confused. He saw the possiblity of a double fulfillment referring to both the "drying up of the Turkish power," but also "prosperity to Babylon was dried up." Nonetheless, Darby did not exclude the possibility of a literal application as well.[1065]

The church father Lactantius makes a probable reference to this judgment, saying that rivers and fountains will literally be dried up.[1066] Even some historicists, such as Jospeh Mede, believed that the Euphrates would literally dry up in the future, so that the Turks might overrun Rome,[1067] while Henry Swete believed that drying up Euphrates was reference to when Cyrus dammed the river to enter Babylon, hence "the drying up of the river marks the removal of the last obstacle to [Mystery Babylon's] fall"[1068]

While the Euphrates may well be seen as a boundary between east and west, and as the limits of the Roman Empire, there is nowhere in the Bible where the Euphrates means anything other than the Euphrates. Figurative language cannot be applied here. It is the literal drying up of that great river which is prophesied here.[1069] It is no more a spiritual boundary than it is a spiritual army which passes through it. It is as real as the armies of the east, which are doomed to destruction.

If the real river is intended, then the next question is who dries the river up, and for what purpose? Hal Lindsey believes that the Russians will dam the Euphrates for the specific purpose of allowing the armies to pass[1070] while Joseph Seiss prefers to see God alone as the instrument in the drying up of the Euphrates.[1071] Either theory is possible, but the later is preferable for one reason. The drying up of the Euphrates may be only one of many rivers which will be dried up in the last days. Due to the drought and heat waves, combined with the waters which had previously turned to blood, many rivers may dry up. Several Biblical prophecies imply that this will be the case, at least in Egypt. Zechariah 10:10, Ezekiel 29:10-11, and Isaiah 11:15-16 are all suggested to be parallel passages and a couple describe the drying up of the rivers of Egypt, even naming the Nile. Several scholars believe that these two events are identical. Arthur Bloomfield argues that the drying of the Euphrates is a reference to a destruction of Egypt and Iraq based on Ezekiel 29:10-12.[1072] Bullinger[1073] and Govett both connect the sixth trumpet with Zechariah 10:10-11,[1074] the latter saying, "it seems to be connected to the taking of Babylon."[1075] Tim LaHaye also says that the kings of east "may be preparing to oppose Antichrist, whose capital lies in Babylon."[1076] Unfortunately, even if Govett and LaHaye are right about the capital of the anti-Christ's kingdom (see chapter 8 for this subject) we are not told that they did battle at the Euphrates, but they procede to Megiddo! Let us consider the passages in question. Ezekiel 29:10-12 reads as follows:

> "I am against you and against your rivers, and I will make the land of Egypt an utter waste and desolation, from Migdol *to* Syene and even to

the border of Ethiopia. A man's foot will not pass through it, and the foot of a beast will not pass through it, and it will not be inhabited for forty years. So I shall make the land of Egypt a desolation in the midst of desolated lands. And her cities, in the midst of cities that are laid waste, will be desolate forty years; and I shall scatter the Egyptians among the nations and disperse them among the lands."

Isaiah 11:15-16 reads:

"And the LORD will utterly destroy the tongue of the Sea of Egypt; and He will wave His hand over the River with His scorching wind; and He will strike it into seven streams, and make *men* walk over dry-shod. And there will be a highway from Assyria for the remnant of His people who will be left, just as there was for Israel in the day that they came up out of the land of Egypt."

Finally, Zechariah 10:10-11 says:

"I will bring them back from the land of Egypt, and gather them from Assyria; and I will bring them into the land of Gilead and Lebanon, until no *room* can be found for them. And He will pass through the sea *of* distress, and strike the waves in the sea, so that all the depths of the Nile will dry up; and the pride of Assyria will be brought down, and the scepter of Egypt will depart."

The reader will note that not one of these passages mentions either Babylon or the Euphrates. It is granted that this may refer to events in the end times, but the connection to the Euphrates and the kings of the east is forced. Ezekiel itself does not specifically mention the drying up of the Nile, but could possibly allude to it by saying "I am against you and against your rivers." It does mentioned Egypt's desolation for a period of forty years. Some believe that this refers to the conquest of Egypt by Nebuchadnezzar.[1077] John Walvoord seems to favor this view.[1078] There is good reason. Verse fourteen speaks of the Egyptians return from exile after forty years, and the kingdom of Babylon fell forty three years after the conquest of Egypt.[1079] Moreover, the Bible says that as result of this judgment, Egypt "will be a lowly kingdom. It will ... never again exalt itself above the other nations ... Egypt will no longer be a source of confidence for the people of Israel but will be a reminder of their sin in turning to her for help" (Ezekiel 29:14-16). There seems to be a connection between Israel's alliance with the Egyptians and her judgment. Nebuchadnezzar captured both Israel and Egypt. Both were subjugated to his kingdom. Both were taken captive. The prophecy, therefore, seems to relate to the time of Nebuchadnezzar, not the end times.

Zechariah's passage is the one most frequently cited, since it specifically mentions the drying up of the Nile, but the context of the passage makes this a more difficult interpretation. Walvoord believes that this is a prophecy of Israel's restoration.[1080] Indeed, the passages in question all speak of Israel's return. "I will bring them back from the land of Egypt, and gather them from Assyria; and I will bring them into the land of Gilead and Lebanon, until no *room* can be found for them" (Zechariah 10:10). Verse eleven is, therefore, placed against the context of the Israelites' return to their homeland. It is important to note that "all the depths of the Nile will dry up" is coupled with "the pride of Assyria will be brought down" and "the scepter of Egypt will depart." In Hebrew poetry, this is called parallelism,[1081] or a chaism which Kenneth Barker believes is present here.[1082] In other words, the Egyptian's pride of the Nile is compared to the "the pride of Assyria" and the "scepter of Egypt." Consequently, if the passage is poetic, then the drying up of the Nile, does not refer to a literal historical event, but to the drying up of the Egyptian pride. This is further hinted at by the description of the sea as a "the sea of distress." If the sea represents distress rather than the Red Sea, then the Nile is Egyptian pride, and not the great river. Furthermore, there is, once again, no mention of the Euphrates. The application to last days is suspect, as it appears to prophesy the Jews return to Israel, and not the war of Armageddon.

Isaiah's prophecy is a more likely reference to last days, although the allusion to Assyria still leads some to believe this also refers to Nebuchadnezzar's conquest. Unlike Ezekiel, this passage specifically mentions the rivers and seas of Egpyt drying up so that men may walk over them "dry-shod." It also mentions "a highway from Assyria" indicating that Egypt would be ravaged by the Assyrian armies, but the sixth bowl dries the Euphrates for the armies *east* of Assyria. The armies of the sixth bowl *are not* the armies of Assyria. Walvoord believes this prophecy may relate to the war of the end times and notes that the Russians have built several dams on the Euphrates,[1083] as Hal Lindsey earlier had said.[1084] This brings us to the question of the armies. If the Euphrates, the Nile, and the Red Sea have dried up, then the question arises as to whose army devastates Egypt and whose army crosses the Euphrates?

The Armies
Dwight Pentecost has said that the phrase "battle of Armageddon" is misleading. It "is not an isolated battle, but rather a campaign that extends through the last half of the tribulation."[1085] Robert Gundry, however, vehemently disagrees. He states that "the Battle of Armageddon is just that – a battle, not a war taking place over a more or less prolonged period of in the last part of the tribulation (as taught by some pertribulationists)."[1086] Whose account is true? The greek word *polemos* (πόλεμος), found in Revelation 16:14, is translated battle by NIV, NRSV, RSV, and the King James, but war by the NAS, ASV, and others. The primary definition of the word is "war,"[1087] followed by "battle" or "campaign." The normal word for battle is *mache* (μαχη).[1088] It is naive to believe that the wars described in the seals and trumpets are not in any way related to this final

battle. Pentecost is correct to point out that Armageddon is not a single battle, but the culmination of a war.[1089]   There are many battles mentioned in Revelation and in parallel Old Testament passages. It is impossible to deny that these battles do not in any way relate to a single war; to a final great world war. This war likely begins soon after the abomination of desolation and after the instigation of the Mark of the Beast, but only the army which crosses the Euprhates is of concern here.

The army is defined in verse twelve as the army belonging to the "kings of the east." In the sixth trumpet we are shown the vision of a vast army of 200,000,000, which is connected to the Euphrates. Many believe that these are one and the same army. Their campaign began in the east with the unleashing of the sixth trumpet judgment, but culminates here in their crossing the Euphrates into the west. Nathaniel West believes that this army signifies that literally the "whole world," or at least the surviving remnant, will converge. Here he sees the eastern armies of the world crossing the Euphrates some time after the destruction of "Mystery Babylon" (see chapter 8).[1090]   Others, as aforementioned, connect the crossing directly to the fall of the "Mystery Babylon," even though Revelation describes them as heading directly to Armageddon. There is no mention of a battle at the Euphrates, nor of an attack against Babylon. The army is merely described as having come from the east. Ironside calls them the "mongolian races."[1091] Ed Hindson believes they are the eastern Islamic states such as Iran and Afghanistan.[1092] Others do not take the term "east" literally at all. It is probably best to take them as the far eastern powers.

Joseph Mede said that the "kings" were Jews. Still other historicists associate the armies with those of emperor Henry against Pope Gregory VII[1093] or even the Parthian invasion of ancient Rome.[1094] John Walvoord has estimated that the historicist school of thought has devised no less than fifty different interpretations.[1095] None of these views can fit the context. These armies obvious meet at Armageddon and none of the historcists have been able to fit history into the events described here. This is to be the final battle in the last war. It is literally the armies of the east. Some believe that it is the same 200,000,000 found in the sixth trumpet, or at least the surviving number of that army.[1096] Others believe that this army is separate from that one, which they hold to be composed entirely of demons.[1097] In either case, the army is the literal remnant of the Asian armies, but why do they come? What draws them to their final destruction? The answer is two fold. There is the divine reason, and the human reason. The divine reason is told to us in verses thirteen and fourteen.

> "And I saw *coming* out of the mouth of the dragon and out of the mouth of the beast and out of the mouth of the false prophet, three unclean spirits like frogs; for they are spirits of demons, performing signs, which go out to the kings of the whole world, to gather them

together for the war of the great day of God, the Almighty"
(Revelation 16:13-14).

The divine reason is obvious. God is bringing the wicked to their own destruction. He allows deceiving spirits to come out from the Dragon, who is Satan. We are reminded that a similar incident took place with King Ahab. 1 Kings 22:23 records that "the LORD has put a deceiving spirit in the mouth of all these your prophets" in order to deceive Ahab into going up to Ramoth-Gilead where he was defeated. Says Seiss, "a spirit of hell was allowed to go forth to inflame and deceive him to his ruin."[1098] Here the "spirits of demons" go forth in order to lead the wicked kings of the earth to their destruction. Govett believes the reference to "frogs" is an allusion to the plague upon Egypt,[1099] but this cannot be sure. What is sure is that Satan, by the permissive will of God, is luring the armies of the world to their destruction.

The human reason for the gathering is more confusing. Some believe that the armies gather to war with one another. As the final battle in the war of Armageddon, the forces are believed to meet for a deciding critical battle. Other scholars believe that the armies are converging together against Irsael. Still others prefer a variant of this view, suggesting, with George Ladd, that the kings of the east join with other armies for the specific reason of doing battle against the Messiah,[1100] whom they know will return at Armageddon. This last view is intriguing, particularly in light of the suceeding verse, "Behold, I am coming like a thief. Blessed is the one who stays awake and keeps his garments, lest he walk about naked and men see his shame" (vs. 15). This passage is often used as a rapture passage (see Appendix A). The parallel passages are used by pretribulationists to indicate that the rapture will occur when no one expects it to, but posttribulationists imply that its appearance here disproves this. George Ladd, a posttribulationist, believes that the verse indicates that Christ's return will be "unexpected,"[1101] and yet he favors the idea that the armies come to Armageddon "to do battle with the Messiah."[1102]

Such arguments benefit pretribulationists who believe that the second coming will not be the unexpected event as rapture, which occurs in connection with "peace and safety" (cf. 2 Thessalonians 2:1-10). Nevertheless, this does not explain how the thief imagery is applied here, at the gathering of armies to Armageddon. John Walvoord, a pretribulationist, believes that "the underlying factor in all these [thief] passages is that the coming in view results in the loss for those who are not ready."[1103] In other words, the thief imagery does not explicitly refer exclusively to either the rapture or the second coming, but to both. The imagery is of preparedness. Christ is coming to take possession of the earth. The armies of the world are to be robbed of their dominion. Although they know He is coming, they are still unprepared. They cannot prevail.

204

Armageddon

Strangely enough, despite the historical identification of Armageddon with the last battle, there is actually much controversy over Armageddon. Not only what the battle of Armageddon is, but where is it? It has historically been identified with the Valley of Megiddo, but some believe it cannot be.

The apostle John tells us that the name of the place in Hebrew is הַר מְגִדּוֹן. Armageddon, or Har-Megiddon, is transliterated from the Hebrew into Greek as Ἁρμαγεδών. It literally means the mount of Megiddo. Megiddo is a city located approximately sixty miles north of Jerusalem. It surrounded by mountains which enclose a huge valley known as the plain of Esdraelon or the plain of Jezreel. The area is mentioned in 2 Chronicles 35:22, Zechariah 12:11, and Hosea 1:5. Napoleon once said, "this is the ideal battleground for all the armies of the world."[1104] Indeed, many great battles have been fought upon the vast valley. Kings who led battles in the valley include Tutmose, Ramses, Sargon, Sennacherib, Nebuchadnezzar, Ptolemy, Antiochus Epiphanes, Pompeii, Titus, Chosroes, Omar, St. Louis of the Crusades, Saladin, and the Ottoman battles.[1105] Nonetheless, critics have argued that the plains of Megiddo could not possibly hold all the vast armies of the world.[1106] They often deny that Armageddon is a physical location, but a title given to the last battle. Some say that Armageddon means "mount of slaughter."[1107] Others have attempted to argue etymologically that the term means the "mount of troops" or "soldiers,"[1108] or even the "destroying mountains."[1109] Still other historicist scholars have argued that World War I was the prophesied War of Armageddon.[1110] Finally, some historicists have even gone to the extreme of claiming that Armageddon refers to the Crimea or even a battlefield in France.[1111]

George Ladd summarizes the alleged problems, saying, "Megiddo is not a mountain, but a plain located between the Sea of Galilee and the Mediterrean, part of the valley of Jezreel (Esdraelon) ... Why John calls it the mountain of Megiddo is not clear."[1112] Some believe that the application of "mountain" to Megiddo is because of the prophecy of Ezekiel 38:8 and 39:2-17, which speak of a great battle in the last days as occuring at the "mountains of Israel."[1113] Ed Hindson, and others, however, believe that Mount Carmel may be intended, for the mount extends to the base of the valley.[1114]

All these arguments seem almost trivial. John plainly states that the area is referred to in the Hebrew tongue as Har-mageddon (Ἁρμαγεδών). The mere fact that he transliterated the word from Hebrew indicates that this is an actual place, not merely an etymological title. If it is a place, then it is connected to the valley of Megiddo, regardless of whether it refers to the surrounding hills, to Mount Carmel, or to the mountains of Israel. It refers to the plains of Megiddo.

So if the region is the valley of Megiddo, or Jezreel, then what of the argument that the armies of the world could not possibly fit into valley?

Hindson is correct to note that the battle "spreads over two hundred miles from north to south (cf. Rev. 14:20)."[1115] The picture of the battle extends far beyond the valley itself. The Bible does not say, nor does it imply, that the entire battle occurs within the confines of the valley, but that "they gathered them together to the place which in Hebrew is called Har-Magedon." There are a number of scholar who do not even believe that the battle takes place in Megiddo. They hold that Megiddo is merely the staging ground for the troops who will advance and move toward Jerusalem,[1116] where the final battle will occur.[1117] In any case, the battle takes its name from the plain where the armies of the world will assemble and converge; Armageddon.

The Reaper and the Final Battle
What will actually happen at this last great battle? Many believe that this final battle is foreshadowed in Revelation 14. It reads:

> "And I looked, and behold, a white cloud, and sitting on the cloud *was* one like a son of man, having a golden crown on His head, and a sharp sickle in His hand. And another angel came out of the temple, crying out with a loud voice to Him who sat on the cloud, 'Put in your sickle and reap, because the hour to reap has come, because the harvest of the earth is ripe.' And He who sat on the cloud swung His sickle over the earth; and the earth was reaped
> "And another angel came out of the temple which is in heaven, and he also had a sharp sickle. And another angel, the one who has power over fire, came out from the altar; and he called with a loud voice to him who had the sharp sickle, saying, 'Put in your sharp sickle, and gather the clusters from the vine of the earth, because her grapes are ripe.' And the angel swung his sickle to the earth, and gathered *the clusters from* the vine of the earth, and threw them into the great wine press of the wrath of God. And the wine press was trodden outside the city, and blood came out from the wine press, up to the horses' bridles, for a distance of two hundred miles" (Revelation 14:14-20).

It is from this passage that the phrase "grapes of wrath" originates. The deaths are strung out over two hundred miles. According to Joel 3:12-13 the armies will "come up to the valley of Jehoshaphat, for there I will sit to judge all the surrounding nations. Put in the sickle, for the harvest is ripe. Come, tread, for the wine press is full." The imagery is obviously the same, and speaks of the same event. So where does the Valley of Jehoshaphat lay in relation to the Valley of Megiddo? This valley lays near Jerusalem itself, by the Kidron Valley. Megiddo is approximately sixty miles north of Jerusalem. These passages indicate that the slaughter will reach as much as two hundred miles to the south of Megiddo. According to Ed Hindson, "it covers and area of 200 miles, which is the distance from Bizra (Edom) to Megiddo."[1118]

Although some, like Alan Johnson, contend that the battle is merely symbolic of a battle between good and evil,[1119] most premillennialists are agreed that a literal battle is intended. The wine is a symbol of blood. That is clear. If we then symbolize the blood we are guilt of symbolizing a symbol. Such a thing is absurd. A symbol represents something literal, or it becomes meaningless. Too many have taken the route of claiming that symbol "A" represents symbol "B" which in turn must refer to symbol "C," which finally equals symbol "D." The entire battle becomes nonsense if we strip it from future history. It is real, or will be real. It is a literal battle, as the context affirms. It is the "decisive battle between Antichrist and his God-hating forces of the earth and Christ."[1120]

If this is so, then we are reminded of the earlier argument. "Some have interpreted this as a gathering of forces in anticipation of the second coming of Christ."[1121] Others believe that "it reflects a conflict among the nations themselves in the latter portion of the great tribulation ... the armies of the world contending for honors on the battlefield at the very time of the second coming of Christ do all turn, however, and combine their efforts against Christ and His army from Heaven."[1122] There are arguments in favor of both of these views. In favor of the former is the choice of location for the battle, the use of deceiving spirits to gather the armies together, and the fact that all the armies of the world are astonishingly converging to a single spot. In favor of the later, however, is Matthew 24:22. "Unless those days had been cut short, no life would have been saved." This implies that the Lord actually intervenes in the battle for the very purpose of preserving some life on the planet; His elect and the 144,000. Moreover, it is obvious that a world war has been going on for several years, at least since the opening of the second seal (Revelation 6:3). This may well be the continuation of that war, and the troops from the east may be the very same 200,000,000 soldiers, or at least the survivors thereof, released in the sixth trumpet (Revelation 9:13-19).

Regardless of the reasons for the battle, the outcome is described in vivid detail. The bodies of the dead are piled up as high as a horse's bridle and are strewn across a battlefield two hundred miles in length. The blood spilled by them is likened to a wine press where the grapes are crushed and the blood is spewed out of the press into the wine buckets. In this case, however, the blood reaches as high as the head of a horse. It is Christ Himself who crushes these armies. This sixth bowl, therefore, carries over into the seventh and final bowl, which will occur even while this battle is raging.

The Seventh Bowl

"And the seventh *angel* poured out his bowl upon the air; and a loud voice came out of the temple from the throne, saying, 'It is done.' And there were flashes of lightning and sounds and peals of thunder; and there was a great earthquake, such as there had not been since man came to be upon the earth, so great an earthquake *was it, and* so mighty.

And the great city was split into three parts, and the cities of the nations fell. And Babylon the great was remembered before God, to give her the cup of the wine of His fierce wrath. And every island fled away, and the mountains were not found. And huge hailstones, about one hundred pounds each, came down from heaven upon men; and men blasphemed God because of the plague of the hail, because its plague was extremely severe." (Revelation 16:17-20).

"It is done." With the release of this bowl the wrath of God is finished (Revelation 15:1). Although the second coming is not specifically referred to until chapter nineteen, it is agreed by most all that Christ returns as the seventh bowl is released. The events described in this bowl coincide with the triumphant return of Christ and the destruction of the armies of Armageddon. It is the end of God's wrath and the final end of all those who have rejected the Lord God. The Messiah, Jesus Christ, now returns to His elect to establish the Millennial Kingdom, but first this last plague is unleashed, and upon this plague there is, once again, great debate.

The Earthquake and the Great City

Most premillennialists view the earthquake as real and literal. Some historicists have allegorized the passage, making it a symbol of the Crusades[1123] or "the return to faith."[1124] Nevertheless, even a historicist such as Joseph Mede acknowledged that this was the final judgment which coincides with Christ's return.[1125] Although John Darby again saw the earthquake as a symbol for a great "disruption of all the elements of organized social existence,"[1126] even most of Darby's most loyal disciples admit that the earthquake must be real. Some even believe that the earthquake spoken of in Ezekiel 38:18 is the same earthquake spoken of here. Not only does the apostle describe it as "such as there had not been since man came to be upon the earth," but we are told that it causes "the great city" to be "split into three parts." Such language does not cater to symbolism. How could a social upheaval, such as that viewed by Pentcost,[1127] divide a city into three parts? Why would John compare a symbol to the earthquakes of history? The earthquake is as real as the city it hits.

What city is this "great city"? On this scholars are deeply divided. Three views are suggested; Jerusalem, Rome, and Babylon. In reality, the last two views are similar in nature, for "Mystery Babylon" is what meant, and "Mystery Babylon" (see chapter 8) is either Rome or the Babylon of Iraq. The real debate is, therefore, between Jerusalem and the city of "Mystery Babylon." The phrase "the great city" occurs twelve times in the Bible. Eight of those references are found in the Book of Revelation. Unfortunately, the occurrences are insufficient to define "the great city." Revelation uses the term for both Jerusalem and "Mystery Babylon." The first reference in chapter eleven where the Bible says that the two witnesses "*will lie* in the street of the great city which mystically is called Sodom and Egypt, where also their Lord was crucified"

(11:8). "Where also their Lord was crucified" can refer *only* to Jerusalem. In chapters seventeen and eighteen, however, the New Babylon is referred to as "the great city." A number of scholars believe that New Babylon is intended by the immediately succeeding remark, "Babylon the great was remembered before God."

Tim LaHaye believes that this "great city" is a rebuilt Babylon of Iraq.[1128] Certainly Babylon's remembrance here might indicate that there is a relationship between the "great city" and the remembrance, but this is inconclusive. Walvoord rejects the belief that this is Jerusalem, because he says there is no "clear evidence that Jerusalem is destroyed with the judgments which overtake the earth."[1129] However, the passage indicates not only that the "great city" is divided but that all "the cities of the nations fell." As Henry Morris remarks, "Babylon, like the other cities of the Gentiles, is to be completely destroyed,"[1130] but this "great city" is not. Seiss, like his mentor Govett, agrees that this is Jerusalem. "The great city is rent into fractions, but it does not utterly fall; 'the cities of the nations' are universally ruined."[1131] He says that the great city "is specially distinguished from the cities of the Gentiles, which are entirely ruined."[1132] Moreover, the prophecy is consistent with Zechariah 14:4, which is universally agreed to be a prophecy of the second coming of Christ.

According to Zechariah, "in that day His feet will stand on the Mount of Olives, which is in front of Jerusalem on the east; and the Mount of Olives will be split in its middle from east to west by a very large valley, so that half of the mountain will move toward the north and the other half toward the south." It is obvious that "such an occurrence must necessarily affect the foundation and topography of the city itself."[1133] The Mount of Olives lies within the city of Jerusalem. If the return of Christ splits the very mountain in two, as all agree, then it is perfectly consistent to believe that this is the same earthquake spoken of in Revelation 16:18. Finally, this judgment coincides with the battle of Armageddon, which occurs in Israel, surrounding and besieging Jerusalem. It would, therefore, seem that this earthquake is related to the second coming and the destruction of the armies that encompass Jerusalem.

The evidence may then be summarized as follows. Those who believe that "the great city" refers to Mystery Babylon support it by declaring that Jerusalem will not be destroyed and that Babylon's remembrance is mentioned shortly after the description of the "great city." In favor of Jerusalem is the fact that the "great city" is not completely destroyed, that it coincides with the splitting of the Mount of Olives when Christ returns, that New Babylon is to be completely and utterly destroyed previously (see chapter 8), and that the battle of Armageddon encompasses Jerusalem, not Mystery Babylon. The evidence seems to overwhelmingly favor Jerusalem, not Babylon. Thus when the Messiah, Jesus Christ our Lord, returns to crush the armies of Armageddon, He sets foot on the Mount of Olives, which splits into two, and the city of Jerusalem itself is shaken and split into three parts. Jerusalem survives, but the cities of the Gentiles universally fall.

The Mountains and Hail

Alongside the earthquake which rocks the great city of Jerusalem, there are two other cataclysmic events which occur around the globe. John says that "every island fled away, and the mountains were not found." He also reveals that "huge hailstones, about one hundred pounds each, came down from heaven upon men." The early church fathers took these prophecies literally. Lactantius says "the loftiest mountains will fall, and be levelled with the plains."[1134] It was not until the Middle Ages that plain meaning was abandoned, followed by some modern scholars like Walter Scott who saw the mountains as representing fallen governments.[1135] This figurative approach has been debated earlier and will not be repeated. The mountains are just that; mountains. Most evangelical scholars, like Tim LaHaye,[1136] agree that a literal physical catastrophe is intended.

If the geological catastrophe of the flood of Noah was literal, why should not the geological catastrophe of this event? Even as the mountains were raised in the flood (cf. Psalms 104:5-9),[1137] there are here levelled. Such geologic castrophes are referenced throughout the Bible in connection with the coming of the Lord (Isaiah 24:18, 41:15, 42:15; Ezekiel 38:20; Micah 1:4; and possibly Isaiah 54:10; Hagai 2:6-7, 21; Nahum 1:5; Habakkuk 3:10). Thus it seems that a real catastrophe is spoken of in monumental proportions.

The question is then, how can the mountains flee? How can they be levelled so? Hal Lindsey "leans toward" a massive nuclear strike,[1138] but this cannot be so. Although critics have been overly harsh upon Hal Lindsey's speculative notions, there is no doubt that Lindsey errs in this respect. This last great judgment is not through the medium of men, but directly from God Himself. The Bible does not say here that stars fell to the earth, nor that object "like" huge hailstones fell, but that *huge hailstones* fell to the earth. These objects cannot be taken here as a description of modern technology, as is possible elsewhere. The objects are exactly what John describes them as; huge hailstones weighting one hundred pounds. On the mountains, the question is more difficult. Henry Morris reminds us that "under the judgment of the sixth seal (Revelation 6:12-14), the earthquakes were so great that 'every mountain and island were moved out of their places.' The earth's crust became so unstable that, for a time at least, it was slipping across the deep mantle."[1139] Now these same mountains fall completely. "The great masses of granite and limestone and sandstone broken up and transported to the bottom of the sea. The deep ocean basins, conversely, will be built up."[1140] The result of this cataclysmic events, although disasterous to those living at the time, is actually a restoration of the ancient topography in the days before God's curse. Isaiah 40:4-5 reads:

210

"Every valley be lifted up, and every mountain and hill be made low; Let the rough ground become a plain, and the rugged terrain a broad valley; Then the glory of the LORD will be revealed."

"The gentle rolling topography of the world as originally created will be restored ... the physical environment of the millennium will be, in large measure, a restoration of the antediluvian environment."[1141] In other words, before the flood of Noah, when God cursed man and restricted his life span, the earth was more uniform and less harsh. In the Millennial Kingdom these conditions will be restored (see chapter 9). So what is terrifying and destructive in this age, results in the restored glory of the Millennial Kingdom. God's final judgment brings not only an end to the wicked, but a new dawn to the righteous.

Summary of the Seventh Bowl of Wrath
These events coincide with the battle of Armageddon and the second coming of Christ. The cities of the earth are completely annihilated, save the great city of Jerusalem which is shaken when the Mount of Olives is split assunder. The armies of the anti-Christ fall and those wicked left alive in the world succumb to the giant hailstorm which obliterates what is left of the wicked.

All that remains are the 144,000 believers and their followers. How many believers survive cannot be said, but they inherit the earth afresh and anew. The topography of the earth is radically changed, and the Millennial Kingdom will soon be established after a period of mourning and restoration (see Appendix D). This judgment ends the wrath of God and the current dispensation. With their last dying breath the wicked curse God, and do not repent. The picture is far different from that presented by some posttribulationists, who believe that men will repent upon seeing Christ return. Far from repenting, those who do not repent have already hardened their hearts. When they see the Lord with their own eyes, they will "blaspheme" God. The tribulation has accelerated man's choice. Those who repent and trust the Lord have already done so. Those who reject Christ have already hardened their hearts. When the Lord is seen on the Mount of Olives, the wicked blaspheme Him. There is no repentance in their heart. Only the faithful will rejoice in the Lord's coming, and the new world which He brings; one of peace and love.

CHAPTER SUMMARY

The bowls of wrath are the last judgments dispensed by God and are fairly straightforward so that many commentators of old felt they were self explanatory. As opposed to earlier judgments of a similar nature, there are no limitations to the harm that the bowls cause. They are as follows:

1. The first bowl causes great sores to come upon only those who bear the mark of the beast.

2. The second bowl turns the sea into blood and kills everything that lived in it.
3. The third bowl turned fresh water deposits into blood so that there is no fresh water to drink at all.
4. The fourth bowl causes the sun's rays to burn men. This is probably caused by increased radiation from the sun from which men will have no protection.
5. The fifth bowl will cause darkness to cover the land but this will not effect the sun's radiation which will continue to burn men.
6. The sixth bowl causes the Euphrates river to dry up so that the armies of the east may procede to Armageddon for the final battle.
7. The last bowl will unleash lightning, thunder, and a great earthquake. All the remaining cities of the world will fall and Jesus will return to the Mount of Olives.

Study Chart on "the Great City"

The "Great City" as Mystery Babylon
Tenants of:
The "great city" divided into three parts is Mystery Babylon, variously ascribed to either Rome or Iraq.

Popular advocates : G. H. Pember, Walter Scott, E. W. Bullinger, George Ladd, Robert Mounce, John Walvoord, and Tim LaHaye.

Strengths:
1) Babylon's remembrance is cited shortly after the city is mentioned.
2) The context implies judgment upon the nations.
3) The next two chapters of Revelation deal with Mystery Babylon.

Weaknesses:
1) Zechariah 14:4 mentions a devastating earthquake when the Lord returns to the Mount of Olives.
2) The battle of Armageddon encompasses Jerusalem, not Babylon.
3) "The great city" *is not* completely destroyed as are the cities of the Gentiles.
4) Many believe that Babylon had fallen previously (see chapter 8 and Appendix D).

The "Great City" as Jerusalem
Tenants of:
The "great city" divided into three parts is Jerusalem.

Popular advocates : Robert Govett, Joseph Seiss, Charles Ryrie, Henry Morris, and Robert Thomas.

Strengths:
1) Zechariah 14:4 mentions a devastating earthquake when the Lord returns to the Mount of Olives.
2) The battle of Armageddon encompasses Jerusalem, not Babylon.
3) "The great city" *is not* completely destroyed as are the cities of the Gentiles.
4) Judgment must come to Jerusalem, though it is spared complete destruction.
5) Many believe that Babylon had fallen previously (see chapter 8 and Appendix D).

Weaknesses:
1) The "remembrance" of Babylon appears to coincide with this passage.
2) The passage speaks of judgment upon the Gentiles.

John Martin – The Great Day of His Wrath – 1852

8

The Whore of Babylon

Chapters seventeen and eighteen provide an interlude in the story. It is a flashback of the great harlot whose remembrance is brought to mind when the earth falls (Revelation 16:19). Some scholars have been confused concerning the timing of this harlot's fall, given her appearance so late in the events described, but the Harlot is mentioned previously in Revelation. Revelation 14:6-8 mentions the same Babylon where this woman resides. The verses are parallel, for 14:8 speaks of the "wine" of her "immoralities" just as this verse speaks of "the wine of her immorality." These two chapters are, therefore, designed to give a retrospective of the Whore, not to provide a chronological device.

Oddly enough, the Harlot was one of the least controversial passages in the whole of Revelation until the late nineteen century. The early chiliasts, the early medieval chiliasts, the medieval Joachimites, the Augustinians, and the Reformers, the historicists, and the early futurists were all in unified agreement that the Whore was an apostate Church in Rome. Then upon the approach of the twentieth century, Robert Govett and Joseph Seiss insisted that the ancient prophecies of Babylon's fall had not been fulfilled as promised.[1142] They argued that both Babylon and Ninevah would have to rise again and be rebuilt upon the plains of Iraq.[1143] This theory quickly rose to become the dominant view, replacing the age old view which had stood unopposed for eighteen hundred years. This is the great debate of the twentieth, and twenty-first, century.

Two predominant theories have prevailed in this generation. The one says that the Harlot is an apostate church, usually associated with Romanism. The other says that the Harlot is an apostate religion associated with the worship of the anti-Christ. The former views the city "Mystery Babylon" as Rome. The latter sees it as a future rebuilt Babylon in Iraq.

The Harlot

"One of the seven angels who had the seven bowls came and spoke with me, saying, 'Come here, I shall show you the judgment of the great harlot who sits on many waters, with whom the kings of the earth committed *acts of* immorality, and those who dwell on the earth were made drunk with the wine of her immorality.' And he carried me away in the Spirit into a wilderness; and I saw a woman sitting on a scarlet beast, full of blasphemous names, having seven heads and ten horns. And the woman was clothed in purple and scarlet, and adorned with gold and precious stones and pearls, having in her hand a gold cup full of abominations and of the unclean things of her immorality, and upon her forehead a name *was* written, 'Mystery, Babylon the Great, the Mother of Harlots and Abominations of the earth' (Revelation 17:1-5).

Here is the initial description of the Whore or harlot. Although she is referred to earlier in Revelation, her identification is found here. She is said to be a harlot with whom the kings of the earth have committed *"acts of immorality."* However, the word translated *"acts of* immorality" by the NAS is variously translated. The Greek word ἐπόρνευσαν (*eporneusan*) is translated by the King James and NRSV as "committed fornication," by the NIV as "committed adultery," by the NAB as "had intercourse with," and "had immoral relation" by the Living Bible. The Amplified Bible list both "idolatry" and "joined in prostitution" as possible translations as well. Common to all these translations is the notion of unfaithfulness and immorality. The central definition of ἐπόρνευσαν (*eporneusan*) is "unlawful sexual intercourse."[1144] In this case, however, the choice of the NIV to translate the word as "adultery" is significant.

In Biblical imagery, unfaithfulness to God is compared to adultery. In Ezekiel 6:9, the Lord laments over the "adulterous hearts which have turned away from Me." He mourns that "I have been hurt by their adulterous hearts." In Ezekiel 16:38 God warns that "I shall judge you like women who commit adultery" and in 23:37 He says that "they have committed adultery with their idols." Thus, idolatry is compared to adultery against God. This same imagery is also found in the New Testament where Jesus speaks of "an evil and adulterous generation" (cf. Matthew 12:39, 16:4, Mark 8:38). The vision, therefore, seems to speak of professed believers who have turned their backs on the true faith. It speaks of an apostate church. This is agreed by most all commentators throughout the ages. Even a number of scholars who favor the belief in a rebuilt Babylon, acknowledge that this harlot professes to be Christian. However, there is at least one author denies the connection. He says "the angel never uses the term 'adultery' – a more restricted term implying a previous marital relationship – in connection with the woman, she need not be representative of apostate Israel or the apostate Church."[1145]

The problem with this argument is that the Biblical imagery does not distinguish technically between "adultery" and "fornication," but instead talks of "playing the Harlot." To argue that the word should properly be translated "fornication" *does not* change the meaning of the text, for the imagery remains identical to that used of rebellious children of God. In Exodus 34:15-16 the people of Israel are commanded to destroy their idols "lest you play the Harlot with their gods." Leviticus 17:7 compares sacrificing to other gods as "playing the Harlot." Leviticus 20:5-6 also speaks of allegiance to Molech using the very same words. This exact phrase is again repeated for the unfaithful in Numbers 15:39, 25:1, Judges 2:17 and 8:27. In Judges 8:33 it is lamented that "the sons of Israel again played the Harlot with the Baals." The phrase "playing the Harlot" is further found in 1 Chronicles 5:25, 2 Chronicles 21:11, 21:13, and

216

Psalms 106:39. In Isaiah 1:21 the prophet mourns that "the faithful city has become a harlot." Jeremiah also laments of Israel saying, "she was a harlot" (3:6 & 8). Still other prophets called Israel a harlot, most notably Ezekiel.

Israel is first compared to a harlot in Ezekiel 6:9 and in chapter sixteen a long passage ensues in which Israel's sins of following after false gods are listed in detail. She is called the "harlot" who has fornicated with Egypt, Assyria, the Philistines, and others. God declares "I shall stop you from playing the Harlot, and you will also no longer pay your lover" (16:41). Ezekiel 20:30 repeats the charge, as does 23:30 in which it is said, "these things will be done to you because you have played the Harlot with the nations, because you have defiled yourself with their idols." The book of Hosea contains another long list which further chastise Israel for "you, Israel, play the Harlot" (Hosea 4:12-15).

This is by no means an exhaustive list. The children of God are always compared to a harlot when they rebel against Him and sin with the worldly nations. This imagery is found in Revelation, but refers to Gentiles (as she is the enemy of the Jews). Consequently, the Harlot must refer to an apostate church. Whether ἐπόρνευσαν (*eporneusan*) is correctly translated "adultery" or "fornication" is irrelevant. She is a whore, and the image used of whoredom is always of the unfaithful. After all, if the woman truly belongs to those with whom she has copulated then she is their bride. The fact that she is a whore proves that she does not belong to them.

Those who wish to argue that a harlot is not married, and therefore, not a bride, as the church is the bride of Christ, ignore the vast evidence cited above, but also *assume* that the church in question *really is* a bride. Many scholars maintain that the true Church is merely betrothed and that the marriage ceremony does not occur until the second coming.[1146] If this is the case then "fornication" would be the appropriate translation. In either case, the fact is that this church, like Israel, professed to trust to in God. Harlotry is always the image used of apostate believers. Thus, as scholars have believed for 2000 years, the Whore is an apostate church, or at least religion, who wields power and authority over both kings and commoners. The people and the very nations themselves seem to have fellowship with her. Exactly *who* she is, and what her relationship to the anti-Christ may be is what follows.

What's the "Mystery"?

One of the most critical elements in the determination of the Harlot's identity is the designation of "mystery." The name tattooed upon her forehead reads, "Mystery Babylon the Great: Mother of Harlots and Abominations of the Earth," but what is "Mystery Babylon"? Some hold that "mystery" is an adjective describing Babylon. Others believe that "mystery" is an intergral part of her title. The difference could be important. If "mystery" describes her name then Babylon should probably be read literally, but if "mystery" describes Babylon, then Babylon should be read as "mystical Babylon."[1147] If the latter is true then

Babylon is a moniker, designating another city and/or religion, that is compared to Babylon in iniquity. Even as we call Las Vegas or Hollywood "Sodom" and refer to homosexuality as "sodomy," the Bible sometimes uses "Babylon" as a comparative phrase. This was particularly true of the ancient Jews and Christians. Even before John penned Revelation, "in Jewish and Christian circles Babylon was already an accepted synonym for Rome."[1148] Indeed, the famed Catholic father Jerome himself spoke of Rome by saying, "I dwelt in Babylon, and was an inhabitant of the purple-clad harlot, ... [and subject to] the pontiff of that city."[1149] It is therefore necessary to see how the term is intended in these passages.

Modern english translations are mixed. Even the two most literal translations, the NAS and King James, differ. The NAS reads, "upon her name was written, a mystery, BABYLON THE GREAT." The King James, however, reads "upon her head was a name written, MYSTERY, BABYLON THE GREAT." If, as the NAS translates, "mystery" is merely an adjective describing the Harlot's name, and not Babylon, then Babylon is most likely taken as the literal city. This is obviously preferred by those who see a revival of the literal Chaldean City. However, if "mystery" is a part of the title, as with the King James, then "Babylon the Great" speaks of something more than a city in the desert. It speaks of the mystery cult and religion of ancient Babylon; a religion which has survived, absorbed into other cultures and religions, for forty-five hundred years. It speaks of "Mystery Babylon."

That the word "mystery" is best taken with "Babylon" and not "name" is proven by verse seven which openly speaks of "the mystery of the woman." It is not the "mystery of her name" but "of the woman." Nevertheless, given the indecisiveness of the translators, a brief examination of the Greek is prudent. While this does not provide as much help as we might expect, it does provide us with some clues. First, in Greek the normal way to determine what an adjective describes is by insuring that the adjective uses the same "case tense" as the noun it modifies.[1150] In this case, however, the adjective agrees with both "name" and "Babylon." Where the noun is in the same case as other nouns in the sentence, the Greek falls back to sentence structure, like English. In other words, one must examine how John would have phrased the sentence had he desired to make "mystery" an adjective of "name" or had he wanted it to be an adjective for "Babylon."

Had John desired to make "mystery" an adjective of "name" then he most likely would have structured the sentence to clearly read "mysterious name." For example, he might have written; "καὶ ἐπὶ τὸ μέτωπον αὐτῆς ὄνομα γεγραμμένο καὶ ἐπὶ τὸ μέτωπον αὐτῆς ὄνομα γεγραμμένον, □μυστήριον, Βαβυλὼν ἡ μεγάλη, ἡ μήτηρ τῶν πορνῶν καὶ τῶν βδελυγμάτ ων□τῆς γῆς (*kai epi to metopon autes mysterion onama gegrammenon. Babylon he megale*)" or something similar. Critics might argue that word order is unimportant in Greek, but this is not always true. Greek does not stress word order like English but where it is necessary, it *is* necessary. The choice of what word an adjective describes in not left open to chance. The Greek *is not* ambigious. "Mystery" should indeed, modify "Babylon" and not "name." Consequently, the choice of "Mystery Babylon" over "mysterious name," justified in verse seven, leads to the conclusion that Babylon is not a location, but the mystery religion of ancient Babylon. It is the spiritual successor of Babylon. It is a mystery religion.

The Religion of the Beast?
It is generally agreed upon that the Harlot is apostate. Various different theories have arisen as to the specifics of her apostacy. In ancient Rome, Christians saw the Harlot as the Roman religion of the last days when the anti-Christ will rule. In the Middle Ages this view continued. Medieval scholars envisioned a future apostate pope, some even equating the Harlot with a specific antipope of the future. Joachim suggested that a future antipope, or "quasi universal pontiff," would arise to fulfill the prophecy.[1151] Even loyal Catholics, such as Friar Michael of Cesena, general of the Grey Friars, declared that "the church of Rome is the Whore of Babylon, drunk with the blood of saints."[1152] This view, and the derivations of it, naturally became unacceptable to the Catholic Church and soon became equated with heresy. Nicholas of Lyra provided an alternative by suggesting that the Muslim Turks were the embodiment of the Harlot,[1153] but few accepted this view. Even loyal Catholics, especially the Franciscan Spirituals, continued to believe that a future apostate Romanism was the true interpretation.

It is only natural that the Protestant Reformation continued in this line of thinking. Ironically, most Catholics' answer to the Protestants' charge was not to claim that the Reformers were the Harlot (although a few did pursue this route) but to declare that Rome was indeed the Harlot, but only the Rome of the past or future. One famous Jesuit theologian named Alcazar is known for the creation of the theological interpretation known as "preterism."[1154] This view held that Revelation was a prophecy about the past, not the future, and that all its visions had long been fulfilled. Thus, up until the late 19th Century scholars of virtually every position were united in attatching Rome to the Harlot in some way.

In recent years, however, this view has become challenged. Beginning with the late 19th Century the great scholar Joseph Seiss began to argue that Rome was not alone intended. He argued that the Harlot extends far beyond Romanism. "She began with Nimrod, bears the name of Babylon, and is not destroyed until the day of judgment."[1155] In the 1970s, led by Hal Lindsey, the popular New Age religion was accepted as the beginnings of the final religion of the anti-Christ. Authors such as Constance Cumbey, an expert on New Age cults, and Tex Marrs, identified the Harlot as the New Age teachings, even calling it "the New Age World Religion."[1156]

219

Other modern scholars prefer to accept the Harlot only as a universal apostate religion governed by the anti-Christ without specifically attatching the New Age movement to it. Thus the various theories can be broken down into two basic groups, with a few variants. The first group sees the Harlot associated with Rome in some way. The preterist variant, which is not compatible with premillennialism, argues that it is pagan Rome. Some maintain that it is a future apostate Rome, believing Romanism to be faithful in this day. Others, indeed the majority throughout the ages, believe that the Harlot is specifically the Church of Rome, either past, present, or future.

The second group believes that the Harlot represents a global apostate church which will rise to power in the end times under the anti-Christ. Variants of this view attempt to attach it directly to the New Age movement, but most prefer to remain ambiguous.

Which of these views is best? We must first examine the Scriptures and determine how the pieces fit. When we do this we come to several inescapable conclusions, too often ignored by advocates of each view.

First, the relationship of the Whore to the anti-Christ is an adversarial one. Far from the Harlot representing the religion of the anti-Christ, she actually represents an apostate religion *at odds* with the anti-Christ's power. According to Revelation 17:16, "the ten horns which you saw, and the beast, these will hate the Harlot and will make her desolate and naked, and will eat her flesh and will burn her up with fire." The anti-Christ therefore betrays the Harlot. She is seen riding the beast in verse three, in verse seven the beast is then said to be *carrying* the Harlot, and in verse sixteen the beast burns her with fire. Thus the relationship of the Harlot to the beast is changing one. It is an adversarial one, not unlike politics. This creates some problems for both views. This completely eliminates the possibility of the Harlot being the religion of the anti-Christ. It also, however, creates problems for those who see the pope as the False Prophet or anti-Christ, as some have believed.[1157] As Sir Robert Anderson noted, "the woman is destroyed by the agency of the Beast. How then is he going to separate the Pope from the apostate Church of which he is the head."[1158] This is also affirmed by George Peters, "however much the Beast out of the sea may have sustained the Papacy in the past (as taught in Re. 17), it will, under the last head of this same Beast, be its *deadly enemy*."[1159] It is possible that the Harlot is Romanism, but only if the pope is neither anti-Christ nor False Prophet. He must be a third party.

The second point that is garnered is that this harlot is not young, but ancient. She is said to be drunk with the blood of saints. Some have argued that this refers only to the saints slaughtered during the tribulation, but this is not likely, for the Harlot most likely falls in the middle of the tribulation, before the great persecution has been instigated (see Appendix D). The saints whom she has murdered are the saints of history, as well as of the future. This means that the Harlot must have existed in the past, as well as in the future.

The third point, which is most important, is that she has Christians among her flock. Revelation cries out, "come out of her, *My people*" (18:4). Although the church is agreed by all to be apostate, God's people can be found among her flock! This is a point lost upon those who call her the religion of the anti-Christ, or some New Age cult. God's people *cannot*, and will not, ever worship the anti-Christ, nor his image, nor the gods of the New Age. Consequently, this creates severe difficulties for the global apostate church theory. It can only mean that the cult of the Harlot is one which still deceives some believers. This is one of the arguments for those who hold that the Harlot is none other than the Catholic Church (i.e. there are evangelical believers within the Catholic Church). The strongest arguments, however, come from the identification of Babylon itself and John's decree, "the woman whom you saw is the great city, which reigns over the kings of the earth" (17:18). These points must be addressed separately.

The Babylonian Religion

It has already been demonstrated that the title, "Mystery Babylon" is most likely a reference to the ancient Babylonian religious system, rather than to a rebuilt city (as will be discussed below). If this is true then the religion of the Harlot must mimic the religion of the ancient Babylonians. Of the two systems of thought, each have tried to account for this. Constance Cumbey argues that reincarnation must be a fundamental part of this new religion saying, "the Vatican never taught reincarnation – this is a New Age or mystery teaching."[1160] In fact, the ancient Babylonians did not teach reincarnation either. Reincarnation is an eastern belief and is not explicitly taught in any western religion, including western paganism. While it is possible that a new religion (which may or may not be influenced by the New Age movement) could incorporate the ancient Babylonian mysteries, the fact is that many other long accepted religions have already done so.

Authors such as Alexander Hislop have written long theses in an attempt to prove that Roman Catholicism incorporates all the ancient mysteries of Babylon. In his book *The Two Babylons* Hislop goes into great detail into similarities between the two religions. Unfortunately, he often goes to extremes by comparing the Trinity to the three headed gods of Babylon.[1161] Since Hislop believes in the Trinity as well, one is left to wonder if Protestants would be equally guilty. Nevertheless, despite the occassional exagerrations, the similarities are striking.

The ancient Babylonian religion served as a basis for the religion of each of the great empires of history. If, as aforementioned, the seven heads of the beast represent the seven kingdom of Satan on earth, then the religion of Babylon must be apparent in all seven; not merely the final kingdom. A survey of history shows that this is so. All of the kingdoms (Babylon, Assyria, Egypt, Persia, Greece, Rome, and the Holy Roman Empire) show similarities in religious doctrine. Each of the religions of these great empires taught some variation of the following:

1) *The belief that salvation could eventually be attained after death.* The afterlife was usually composed of a purgatory like abode where the dead existed. Although the ultimate means varied from culture to culture, the basic belief remained that deliverance from this purgatory like state was possible. Usually salvation was attained by good works and deeds, by the purity of the heart, or in cases of the wicked, salvation could be attain by the purging of sins through torture. Sometimes the living may aid the dead in their quest for salvation by prayer or some other substitutionary means, but in each and every case, the dead may be redeemed.

2) Another commonly held belief was *the necessity of repetitive and incessant sacrifices.* Sacrifices may have taken different forms but always it was required. The idea that a single sacrifice was sufficient for all was foreign to the mystery of Babylon's religion and none of the great empires could truly accept this.

3) All the great empires held that *the King and/or the High Priest were the spokesmen for the gods.* In some cases it was held that he was himself a manifestation of god while others held that he was merely divinely appointed and accountable only to the gods. In each and every case the authority of the pagan religions resided not in their Scriptures, but in an individual. It was man who spoke for God, not God who spoke for man.

4) Along with the belief that the High Priest or King spoke for the gods was *an inevitable form of hierarchy.* Various forms of the hierarchy occurred and in some cases the priests even had the power to forgive sins or to damn men to punishment. The Presbyterian form of government was unheard of, and always the priestly government took on a hierarchical form.

5) From the time of Nimrod there was some form of *idolatry.* This idolatry took its most prominent and common form in the context of polytheism which existed in the first six great empires of history. In each and every empire, and religion thereof, idolatry and the use of icons or idols, was a prominent fixture in their religious worship. Prayer to gods or even to the dead was also an integral part of this worship.

That all of these teachings were present up to and including ancient Rome is denied by none. That the Roman Church absorbed these teachings in the Middle Ages should not be denied. When Constantine became a Christian, he did not, nor could he, change the hearts of the people. Those who once worshiped Diana, "the virgin goddess" and "the immaculate one,"[1162] now revered the Virgin Mary. Says historian Kenneth Latourette, "the worship paid to Diana may have been transferred to the Virgin Mary."[1163] That Diana herself is an extension of the ancient Babylonian "cult of the virgin goddesses"[1164] cannot be denied. The Babylonian goddess Ishtar "while being a virgin-goddess, is sometimes addressed as a mother."[1165] From this there "seems to emerge the conception of a virgin-mother."[1166] It is then little wonder that when the Church Council at Ephesus first proclaimed Mary should be called "the Mother of God," the populace who "celebrated the deification of Mary reproduced in such essentials as smoking censers and flaming torches the processions which for so many centuries had been an important part of the worship of Diana."[1167] The parallel "between the Mother of God and the Mother of the gods"[1168] was too much for many of the early church fathers, as well as the Reformers. Some of the early church fathers believed that the Virgin Mary was being transformed from a godly Christian mother and wife into a goddess.

More striking, however, are the other parallels. Like the ancients the Roman Church is notorious for the veneration of icons. The argument that the icons were to be "adored" rather than worshipped[1169] has not lifted the stigma of men and women bowing down before images in prayer. Moreover, many maintain that the teachings of the "sacrfiice of Mass" also reek of perpetual sacrifices. Although the Bible says that Christ died "once for all" (Romans 6:10; Hebrews 7:27, 9:12, 10:10; and 1 Peter 3:18) Romanism teaches that Christ is re-sacrificed at Mass. This is affirmed by Vatican II council which declared that the Mass must "perpetuate the sacrifice of the Cross throughout the ages until he should come again."[1170] According to Council of Trent the "sacrifice" of Mass "is identical with the sacrifice of the Cross."[1171] They teach that every sin that is committed since the time of conversion must be atoned for and expiated thereafter. The *Catechism of the Catholic Church* states "the Eucharist is also offered in reparation for the sins of the living and the dead."[1172] This leads to an even more disturbing revelation: the teaching of purgatory and prayer for the dead.

Since the most ancient of times the belief in a purgatory, or the "Land of the Dead," was taught and practiced.[1173] Prayers for the dead and offerings were often presented at the graves of the deceased in hopes that they might attain liberation from the dark subterranean underworld.[1174]

Thus, like the ancient Babylonians, Assyrians, Egyptians, Persians, Greeks, and Romans, the Catholic Church teaches that the dead must be purged of their sins in a Purgatory where the dead reside awaiting judgment. The living may offer prayer for the dead and even obtain indulgences to assist the dead in their quest for ultimate salvation. As with the ancient empires there is no single sacrifice for one and all. The sacrifice of Mass must occur routinely and the believer must participate in the sacraments in order to obtain remission for the sins he has committed in the course of the week. The pope, or pontifex maximus, like his ancient Roman predecessor, is said to speak for God alone. He is the High Priest and spokesman for God. Below the pope lay a number of subordinates who form an intricate hierarchy as detailed and complex as any in the ancient pagan empires. Lay preaching is discouraged and was once forbidden. Finally, icons, or rather idols, continue to occupy a prominent position in Romanism today and the Saints are offered prays in much the same way as the gods of old.

So apparent are these similarities that the identification of Romanism with the Whore of Babylon was once *the* predominant view of all ages. Whether the ancients, medievals, or Reformers, the Church of Rome was the only Christian religion to teach such doctrines. Says John Walvoord, "the description of the woman as arrayed in purple and scarlet and decked with gold, precious stones, and pearls is too familiar to one acquainted with the trappings of ecclesiastical pomp today and especially of high officials in the Roman Catholic and Greek Orthodox churches."[1175] Critics argue that the Church has reformed itself and that a new church will arise with the ancient teachings. Nevertheless, the ensuing passages will cast doubt on this.

The Betrayal of the Whore
The betrayal of the Whore is essential to understanding her relationship with the anti-Christ. The woman is seen at first to ride the beast. She is in control. However, this changes with time. Later the beast is said to be "carrying" the woman, and eventually the anti-Christ and his ten kings destroy her utterly. There are several factors to consider in this picture. First, it has been pointed out previously that the anti-Christ is technically not the beast, but the eighth head of the beast (Revelation 17:11). It is true that he is called the beast (cf. Revelation 19:20) but they are technically differentiated. If this is so then the Whore is not only shown to have authority over the anti-Christ, but the beast itself. Now it has been argued that the Whore technically represents the apostate religious tradition of Babel and the beast is technically the empires of Satan throughout history. In Revelation, however, they are more specifically identified, in the last days, with an apostate church and the Revived Roman Empire. Therefore, the relationship between the Whore and the beast is one of a church and of the empire.

History has shown that the Roman Empire did not fall, but was swept up into a Papal Empire (the Holy Roman Empire). The kingdom was divided and crumbled awaiting the anti-Christ to resurrect it, but how can the anti-Christ resurrect a kingdom which no longer exist? The kingdom must still linger or else the kingdom of the anti-Christ cannot truly be called Rome. The final kingdom is a part of the fourth empire of Daniel 2 and not separate from it (see chapter 6). So it seems that it is the Harlot who restores the Roman Empire and gives authority to the beast. It is only when the beast believes that he has solidified power and no longer needs the Harlot that he turns on her, and devours her.

Those who believe that the Harlot promotes the worship of the anti-Christ cannot explain this. Charles Ryrie says, "many groups will form together under the one harlot in a kind of federated church. She will incorporate

224

various denominations and religious groups without necessarily amalgamating them."[1176] This reasoning is followed by C.I. Scofield[1177] and Dave Hunt who even declares that "the Antichrist needs the false church"[1178] yet none can give a sufficient account for the betrayal of the Harlot.

C.I. Scofield believes that Babylon is "the apostate world-church"[1179] but admits "it is the Beast and his associated kings who turn upon and rend 'Babylon."[1180] To this he can only suggest that "the Beast will brook no rival worship, even though it be but a form."[1181] However, Scofield does not explain how the Whore becomes a "rival." Obviously, the Harlot can only be a rival if she is not the church of the anti-Christ and is not actively promoting the worship of him.

This same problem also plagues George Ladd who believes that the Harlot causes the "enticement of the peoples to worship the beast."[1182] This confusion arises from those who mistake the False Prophet for the Whore of Babylon. The Bible is quite clear that it is the False Prophet who "causes all, the small and the great, and the rich and the poor, and the free men and the slaves, to" worship the beast (Revelation 13:16). There are not two entities, but three. There are the anti-Christ and the False Prophet, but there is also a third; the Harlot. Any correct view must take the Harlot into consideration as a third power; a religious power, but one with political power as well.

John Walvoord mistakenly argues "the fact that the woman is riding the beast and is not the beast itself signifies that she represents ecclesiastical power as distinct from the beast which is the political power."[1183] How does the image of riding the beast create such a distinction between "ecclesiastical power" and "political power?" Walvoord does not sufficiently explain this line of reasoning other that the fact that the beast wields political power. He must therefore assume that the power the Harlot wields is different from that, but cannot prove it from the text. Conversly, Walter Scott provides a better explanation:

> "The subserviency of the Beast to the Harlot is expressed by the Seer, 'I saw a woman sitting upon a scarlet beast.' The action intimates the thorough and complete subjugation of the civil power. The rule and supremacy of the woman over the vast imperial and apostate power is a singular sight. The woman not only sits upon, or beside, the nations and peoples comprised within the prophetic area (v. 1), but also rules the Beast, the then dominating civil and political power on earth (v. 3)."[1184]

So, whatever the religious and apostate character of the Harlot, her control over the anti-Christ appears to be political. She is not the church of the anti-Christ, but a church who wields vast political power over the anti-Christ. It is not her apostasy that draws the anti-Christ to the Harlot, but the fact that she holds the key to the power that the anti-Christ seeks. As John Darby put it, "she may be the beginning of his kingdom. He comes in here, as the eighth head of the beast, supplanting the woman. The kings lay her waste to give their power to him."[1185] It is not her that the anti-Christ wants, but her kingdom and her authority. She alone has the authority to restore the Roman Empire and to make the anti-Christ emperor thereof.

This the key to the betrayal by the anti-Christ. The role of the Harlot is not one in sync with the role of the anti-Christ, but rather in competition with that role. Any survey of the fall of the Roman Empire will show that the papacy holds the key to the Roman Empire. Even as each and every Holy Roman Emperor from Charlemagne to Napoleon was supposed to be coronated by the pope, so also the anti-Christ needs the blessing of the pope to become the Last Roman Emperor. Even as Napoleon sought the crown from the same pope he later imprisoned, so also the anti-Christ seeks his authority from the church he hates. Just as Napoleon betrayed the pope, once gaining the imperial diadem, so also the anti-Christ will turn on the papacy, once he gains his prize. It is therefore little wonder that Walter Scott compares the conqueror of Revelation 6:2 to Napoleon.[1186]

It thus appears that the answer is not to be found in modern commentators, but in the old writings of the early dispensationalists such as Darby and Scott. To be sure, the Roman Church cannot be proven to be the Harlot on account of the betrayal, but it alone fits the pattern. No other church wields such control over the city of Rome, and it is the *Roman* Empire that the anti-Christ must restore. This is denied by none. Most importantly, however, is the statement of the apostle John himself. "The woman whom you saw is the great city, which reigns over the kings of the earth" (Revelation 17:18).

The "Great City which Reigns"

"The great city, which reigns over the kings of the earth." What city is this? Some argue that it is nothing less than the ancient city of Babylon rebuilt from its ruins. They have argued that it is not "mystery Babylon," but a mystery; that mystery being the revival of ancient Babylon. Others argue that "the great city, which reigns over the kings of the earth" can be nothing more than Rome, which reigned over the earth in John's days.

There was only one city which could have been said to be reigning of over the kings of the earth in John's day. That city was Rome. Thus the great mystery of the woman is that she is not only an apostate church, but also a city. What city could be so closely identified with a church that the two are held to be synonymous? What city has been identified as "the city on seven hills" (cf. Revelation 17:9-10) for twenty-five hundred years?[1187] Is it not said, "the seven heads are seven hills on which the woman sits"? Did not an ancient Roman coin from the very day that John lived show the goddess Roma seated upon seven hills?[1188] Only Rome can fit the bill. No other city can fit the criteria. Nevertheless, critics argue that "the great city, which reigns over the kings of the earth" is future. Since John's visions were future, so, they argue, must the "reigning" be future. This argument, however, is inherently weak. The vision was of the future, but the angel was speaking to John in the first century and identifying the Harlot. The word "reigns" is in the present active indicative. If it wasn't, then the angel's words could mean nothing John. If John had understood who the Harlot was, the angel would not have needed to tell him. If the city was not then reigning over the kings of the earth, then John could not have understood the answer anyway. Rome alone is both a city, an economic capitol, and the head of the largest religion on the planet. Rome must be that city.

Despite this, a new view has arisen in recent days. For approximately 1800 years no commentator had expressly stated that the Babylon of Revelation was the same as Babylon of the Old Testament. Prophecies of ancient Babylon's destruction were universally believed to have been fulfilled in the centuries past and at no point does any extant commentary suggest that Babylon of Iraq would rise from the desert and rule the world again until the great commentators Robert Govett and Joseph Seiss first clearly issued the suggestion at the close of the 19th Century. The arguments cited in favor of Iraq are discussed below.

The Fall of Babylon
Babylon's fall occurs in verse 17:16, but chapter eighteen describes the reaction of the word to her downfall. Some disupte this, arguing that the fall of the woman is distinct from the fall of Babylon, despite the fact that the woman is expressly stated to be the city. Despite this, some, like Joseph Seiss, argue that the phrase "fallen fallen" indicates "two separate parts or stages of the fall."[1189] This assumption, however, is unfounded. As Walvoord admits, "the repetition of the phrase 'the fallen' is for emphasis."[1190] The Bible uses the exact same repetition in Isaiah 21:9 in regard to the fall of Babylon under the Medo-Persians. It is not good exegesis to draw too great a conclusion from a simple repetitive phrase when the most likely explanation is simply one of emphasis. This is seen in the phrase "woe, woe" found six times in the Bible, and is also evident in Jesus' use of the phrase "truly truly," found twenty-five times in the Bible. Bullinger is correct when he states that there are "many who see Rome in some form in chapter xvii, yet find Babylon, literal in chapter xviii. But where is the authority for making such a vital separation between the subjects of the two chapters? There is no indication of such a marked distinction, either in the text, or in the context."[1191] The theory that there are two separate Babylons will be addressed separately. Here, only the fall of the great city of Babylon is of concern, but is this the "new Babylon"[1192] of Rome, or a rebuilt city in Iraq?

Robert Govett and his protege, Joseph Seiss, first created and popularized the belief that Babylon must be resurrected from the grave. Charles Dyer speaks for most advocates of this position when he claims that this is the only real "literal" interpretation.[1193] From Seiss to Bullinger to Dyer, the cry that this is the literal view has convinced many of its virtue, yet this view actually allegorizes or minimizes far more verses than the other. To say that "*mystery* Babylon" *must* be literal Babylon is not only an oxymoron, but it ignores the literal interpretation of "shipmasters" and "harbormasters," as well as the "gold, silver, precious stones, pearls, fine linen, silk, citron wood, ivory, costly wood, bronze, iron, marble, cinnamon, spice, incense, perfume, frankincense, wine, olive oil, fine flour, wheat, cattle, sheep, horses, chariots, and slaves." These things must be accepted for what they are; literal. However, the "literal" Babylon theory must at least minimize these. Consider the lamentations of the merchants.

> "The merchants of the earth weep and mourn over her, because no one buys their cargoes any more; cargoes of gold and silver and precious stones and pearls and fine linen and purple and silk and scarlet, and every *kind of* citron wood and every article of ivory and every article *made* from very costly wood and bronze and iron and marble, and cinnamon and spice and incense and perfume and frankincense and wine and olive oil and fine flour and wheat and cattle and sheep, and *cargoes* of horses and chariots and slaves and human lives" (Revelation 18:11-13).

This great city is obviously rich; rich in "gold, silver, precious stones, pearls, fine linen, silk, citron wood, ivory, costly wood, bronze, iron, marble, cinnamon, spice, incense, perfume, frankincense, wine, olive oil, fine flour, wheat, cattle, sheep, horses, chariots, and slaves."[1194] Despite this long list of riches, Charles Dyer argues that the city is rich because Iraq has "50% of the proven oil reserves in the world."[1195] Thus gold and silver and linen and ivory and incense and wine are said to be "oil reserves." Therefore, Dyer is "literal" in one area and symbolic in another. In fact, it is best to take the gold and riches literally. We must accept "mystery," rather than Babylon, as literal.

Another example is the great sea port mentioned in Revelation 18. We are told that "all who had ships at sea became rich by her" (vs. 19). Again, some argue that the river Euprhates will hold a harbor and that it is this harbor of which Revelation speaks, but this cannot be. Although Seiss points out that the Bible never mentions "a ship of Rome,"[1196] he ignores that the Bible also fails to mention a "ship of Babylon." This is doubtless because Babylon has no sea port. The idea that the river Euphrates could become a huge "*sea*" port seems an inadequate argument. Even if such a port were made it is illogical that merchants would sail around Africa or Asia and up the Gulf to dock at port when air plane freights would be for more cost effective. This is not so of Rome.

Although E. W. Bullinger erroneously states "Rome was never either 'great' or commercial"[1197] and that "it is no Port; and no 'shipmaster' goes thither"[1198] he is sorely mistaken. That Rome "was never great" need not be addressed since any historian could easily refute the remark. That Rome has no port is also a fallacy. The great *Lida de Roma* has been a commercial site for ages. That the port lies just outside the city limits is irrelevant. Trade with Rome has occurred for several millennia and continues to this day. Unlike Babylon, Rome is unique in that ships can carry cargo more than air freights. Consequently, because of its location in the Mediterranean trade ships are usually preferred to air freights; something which would be all but inconceivable in Iraq. Thus, despite Donald Barnhouse's claim that "if Rome should sink into the sea tomorrow, the commerce of the rest of the world would go on as though very little had happened,"[1199] Rome remains one of the largest commercial cities in the world, listed in travel guides a "a major financial and commercial city."[1200] Its riches are well known and extend far beyond "oil reserves," something which is not even included in the list of Revelation 18:11-13. Says H.A. Ironside, "commercialism has always flourished under the patronage of the popes."[1201]

The literal view is then that the great sea port and the riches of the city are just what they are said to be. It is not a river port and oil, but a vast sea port and the wealth of ages.

Only one last New Testament argument remains. Robert Thomas believes that Revelation 17:3 proves that the city resides in a desert. He claims that the definition of the Greek word ἔρημον *"eremon"* is best translated "desert" rather than "wilderness."[1202] In fact, the word is translated as "wilderness" by the King James, the NAS, the ASV, the NRSV, and the Living Bible. Only the NIV accepts "desert" in its translation. The actual meaning of ἔρημος *"eremos"* is a "desolate" or "uninhabited" region[1203] and does not provide any geographic clues.

The fact that John was taken to an "uninhabited" place should serve notice that this verse is not intended as a geographical identification of Babylon, for the Babylon of Revelation is anything but uninhabited. It is a "great" city of the world and a commercial city of great stature. Nevertheless, Thomas carries the argument even further by attempting to draw a parallel between the "many waters" upon which the woman sits. Thomas suggests that "the 'many waters' interestingly corresponds to Babylon's situation on the Euphrates."[1204] Nonetheless, this view blatantly contradicts the explicit statement of Revelation 17:15, "the waters which you saw where the Harlot sits, are peoples and multitudes and nations and tongues." The waters do not refer to a river, or even a sea (which would better fit Rome), but to a "multitudes and nations and tongues."

If it is not obvious yet, it will soon become obvious that the strength of the Iraq theory lies in Old Testament interpretations, not New Testament. Nothing in Revelation can be made to prove that a rebuilt city in Iraq is intended. The prophecies of the Old Testament, however, may be a different matter, and it is these prophecies that have won over many converts. It is, therefore, necessary to deviate temporarily from Revelation and examine the prophecies of Isaiah in order to determine whether or not, as these theorists claim, Babylon must rise again.

Shall Babylon Rise Again?
It is indeed ironic that advocates of the Iraqi theory often quote Jeremiah 51:64 which reads, "Babylon shall sink down and *not rise again*." Phillip Goodman states that Babylon's "reappearance today in Iraq means either (1) the prophecy of the final destruction was mistaken; or (2) its final destruction is reserved for a future rebuilt city of Babylon."[1205] In other words, they argue that Babylon has not yet fallen. They sometimes go to extremes to prove that Babylon has never become uninhabited or barren. Charles Dyer states that "even in this modern era, there are villages *around* Babylon" (emphasis added)[1206] and goes on to declare "I can find no time in history when it can be said conclusively that Babylon ceased to exist."[1207] In this regard, Dyer is sorely mistaken, as will be demonstrated. Nevertheless, referring to Revelation 18:21 and 22 Dyer says, "because music and building and wedding celebrations continue in the city of Babylon, we know that ... the violent destruction of the city has not yet occurred."[1208]

At first glance this appears a solid argument, but in reality it is very presumptive. It exaggerates Saddam Hussein's failed attempt to build a replica of the ancient city (for it is not a reconstruction) and it misinterprets the prophecies of Babylon's fall.

Here is the controversial prophecy:

> "Behold, I am going to stir up the Medes against them,
>   Who will not value silver or take pleasure in gold,
>   And *their* bows will mow down the young men,
>   They will not even have compassion on the fruit of the womb,
>   *Nor* will their eye pity children.
>   And Babylon, the beauty of kingdoms, the glory of the Chaldeans' pride,
>   Will be as when God overthrew Sodom and Gomorrah.
>   It will never be inhabited or lived in from generation to generation;
>   Nor will the Arab pitch *his* tent there,
>   Nor will shepherds make *their flocks* lie down there.
>   But desert creatures will lie down there,
>   And their houses will be full of owls,
>   Ostriches also will live there, and shaggy goats will frolic there.
>   And hyenas will howl in their fortified towers
>   And jackals in their luxurious palaces.
>   Her *fateful* time also will soon come
>   And her days will not be prolonged" (Isaiah 13:17-22).

230

The older commentators were unanimous in saying that this prophecy was fulfilled in the ancient past. Matthew Henry states, "it is foretold that it should be wholly destroyed like Sodom and Gomorrah, not so miraculously, nor so suddenly, but as effectually ... in the process of time it went all to ruin."[1209] Another Reformer affirms that this "was fulfilled by degrees, as is confessed by historians, and appears this day."[1210] Seiss and his proteges, however, have objected to this argument. Seizing upon the comparison to Sodom and Gomorrah they have maintained the destruction of Babylon must be as sudden and complete, with fire, as Sodom and Gomorrah.[1211] The specifics of this prophecy, however, call this into question, for Isaiah says that "their houses will be full of owls." If the Babylonian's homes are to become the abode of owls then they cannot have been consumed with fire. The imagery is of Sodom and Gomorrah's inhabitability and barrenness, not the mode of destruction. Moreover, if Dyer is correct in his exegesis then one is puzzled as to why Dyer does not apply this same exegesis to Ninevah and Assyria for Zephaniah makes a similar prophecy saying, "surely Moab will be like Sodom, and the sons of Ammon like Gomorrah – A place possessed by nettles and salt pits, and a perpetual desolation" (Zephaniah 2:8).

There is a lesson to be learned here, for E. W. Bullinger appears to have believed that Assyria would rise from the grave even as he believed Babylon would rise from the grave. He said, "the Kaiser has undoubtedly scored. When in December, 1899, it was announced that the German Anatolian Railway Company had received a concession from Abdul Hamid for the construction of a railway from Konieh to Bagdad ... it is a favorite thesis with the people who ponder over prophetic mysteries that *both Babylon and Ninevah are to be resuscitated in more than the ancient glories of Nebuchadnezzar and Sennacherib.*"[1212] Of course, the Kaiser was not successful. He lost World War I. The "German Emperor"[1213] never restored Ninevah nor Babylon, for had he succeeded, the prophecies would not have been accurate. Ninevah and Babylon are "a perpetual desolation" (Zephaniah 2:8) just "like Gomorrah" and "like Sodom." Nowhere in the Old Testament is there a declaration that they will fall in ball of fire from heaven. On the contrary, the imagery is one of "sinking" (cf. Jeremiah 51:64) down over time. History has born this out.

While Dyer claims that Babylon never fell,[1214] history records something quite different. No fewer than ten conquest of Babylon have been recorded since Alexander the Great first took the city, without violence, in 331 B.C. After Alexander's death in Babylon, the city "changed hands several times."[1215] Perdiccas was the first regent until he was killed by Seleucus in 321 B.C.[1216] Seleucus, however, lost the city to Antigonus in 316 B.C.[1217] only to retake the city four years later.[1218] Nevertheless, Antigonus would not give up and "a fierce and bitter war brought terrible suffering upon Babylon."[1219] So great was the destruction and terror that the Babylonian chronicles themselves describe "weeping and mourning in the land."[1220] The eventual victory of

231

Seleucus over Antigonus would not end Babylon's woes. As prophecy demanded, Babylon was sinking down slowly. Historian Georges Roux speaks about the "half-ruined city"[1221] of this time, noting that "it was already partly deserted, a great number of its inhabitants having been transferred to Seleucia."[1222] Babylon was "no longer the seat of royal government"[1223] but it was a prize which conquerors still sought. In the wars that would ensue between the Parthians and the Greeks, and later the Parthians and Romans, Babylon would again trade hands many times, with each successive attack and sack of the city making it more and more desolate and barren. Babylon was becoming weaker and weaker with each successive year. In 126 B.C. the Parthians took control of Babylon[1224] but they would also have trouble keeping the city. Crassus of Rome was the first to threaten the Parthians in Babylon, and under Roman conquest Babylon would again change hands several times until the Roman Emperor Trajan sacked Babylon yet again. By the time Dio entered the city he was able to say that Babylon was "nothing but mounds and stones and ruins."[1225]

Now, "twenty-three centuries after Herodotus visited Babylon, however, the great temple of Marduk lay buried under more than twenty metres of earth and sand."[1226] The "barren mounds and heaps of crumbling brickwork"[1227] alone took eighteen years to excavate.[1228] So desolate was Babylon that Marco Polo did not even mention the ruins, although he trod over them. In the fourteenth century another explorer, the friar Odoric, wrote about the ruins of Persepolis, but was unaware that he had ever passed over the ruins of Babylon.[1229] The Roman Emperor Septimus Severus had once entered Babylon, but found it deserted.[1230] So barren had the great city become that even Dyer is forced to quote the famous poet who said "the Great City has become a great desert."[1231]

It would then seem that at first glance that the prophecies of Babylon were fulfilled *literally*, for Babylon has not been "inhabited or lived in from generation to generation" and no "Arab pitches *his* tent there," nor do "shepherds make *their flocks* lie down there." Instead "desert creatures will lie down there, and their houses will be full of owls, Ostriches also will live there, and shaggy goats will frolic there. And hyenas will howl in their fortified towers and jackals in their luxurious palaces." All this has been fulfilled.

Another significant aspect of the prophecy, too often overlooked by Seiss and Dyer, is the fact that this prophecy appear to be of *the Babylonian Empire* and not the city of Babylon alone. As Jeremiah says, "the time when I shall punish you and the arrogant one will stumble and fall with no one to raise him up; and I shall set fire to his *cities*, and it will devour all his *environs*" (50:32). The subject of this prophecy is then the "cities" and "environs" of Babylon. Dyer, in particular, takes the prophecies to apply solely to the city.

One final argument against the Iraqi view is that, despite the fact that this view seems to be promoted mostly by pretribulationists (see Appendix A), it flies in the face of consistent pretribulational theory. Charles Dyer declares that Babylon *must* be rebuilt before the tribulation.[1232] As a pretribulationist, however, he should know that there can be no "signs" which must precede rapture. Tommy Ice, Vice-President of Tim LaHaye's Pre-Trib Research Center, says, "the rapture is a sign-less event."[1233] Signs may precede the second coming, but there are *no* signs of the rapture. Says James Brookes, "we of this church dispensation have nothing to do with signs and dates."[1234] Consequently, if Dyer is correct that Babylon must be rebuilt before the tribulation, then it must also be rebuilt before the rapture. Although Henry Morris has tried to argue that "with modern construction equipment and unlimited wealth at his disposal, the beast can rebuild mighty Babylon almost overnight,"[1235] such is not the case. The rebuilding of the Twin Towers in New York alone has scarcely even begun over a decade after they fell, and that despite modern equipment and billions of dollars from the Federal government. The idea of rebuilding an entire city overnight, and of the seven great wonders of the ancient world at that, is not feasible. It must be remembered that the initial excavations of Babylon themselves took *eighteen years*.[1236] On top of this is the fact that this "new" city must, according the Iraqi theorists, rise to become the economic capitol of the world.

Dyer's sub-title "Sign of End Times" is a contradiction of his pretribulational beliefs, and his title, "the Rise of Babylon," is a contradiction of Jeremiah 51, "Babylon shall sink down and *not rise again*" (vs. 64). Iraq cannot be the current location of "mystery Babylon." After twenty years of trying, Saddam Hussein's vein attempt to restore Babylon failed. In contrast to the inflated claims of some, the tourist trap that Saddam Hussein attempted to build can scarcely be said to be the "reappearance" of ancient Babylon. It features a half sized replica of the old Ishtar gate and other replica buildings, but it is no more Babylon than the Sphinx of Las Vegas is the Sphinx of Egypt. Even if one were to believe that Babylon must be revived in order to fulfill Old Testament prophecies, it has yet to be shown that this is the same Babylon spoken of in Revelation. The Babylon of Revelation is a "mystery" seated upon seven hills. The Babylon of the Old Testament has fallen, and will "*not* rise again."

Double Meaning?
The evidences for the Harlot not being located in Iraq are so great that even many who believe Babylon will rise again accept that the Harlot is not from Iraq. They argue that the Harlot is separate from, and distinct from, the city of Babylon. This view, despite the explicit claim of Revelation 17:18, has quickly become the most popular view in recent years. It is support by, and promoted by, men such as William Newell, Norman Harrison, John Walvoord, and Tim LaHaye. It may be called the "both/and" view inasmuch as it holds that both the ancient view and the modern Iraqi theory are correct. They not only declare that

233

the Harlot and Babylon are separate, but also that the "fall of the Harlot" is separate from the "fall of Babylon the city."

The arguments these men use to separate chapters seventeen and eighteen are as follows:

1. The double usage of "fallen" in Revelation 14:8 and 18:2.
2. The emphasis on "ecclesiasticism" in chapter 17 is contrasted with the "economics" of chapter 18 (the argument that the woman is not a city but a church).
3. The hatred of the ten kings and anti-Christ in chapter 17 is contrasted with the mourning of the kings in chapter 18.
4. The destruction of "physical Babylon" is said to be by divine wrath in contrast to that of "religious Babylon."

The first argument says that the double usage of "fallen fallen" in Revelation 14:8 and 18:2 "require a two-stage destruction of Babylon."[1237] They suggests that the word "fallen" is mentioned twice, because there are actually "two separate parts or stages of the fall."[1238]   Unfortunately, this reasoning is severely flawed.   Although John Walvoord agrees with the "both/and" view he himself admits that "the repetition of the phrase 'the fallen' is for emphasis."[1239] More importantly, the Bible uses the exact same repetition in Isaiah 21:9 in regard to the fall of Babylon under the Medo-Perisans.

The predominant argument used is that chapter seventeen's emphasis is upon religion in contrast with that of chapter eighteen. According to Donald Barnhouse "the one [Babylon] is described under the symbol of a harlot woman, seated upon the beast of government, the other is presented as a mighty city."[1240] In fact, this alleged contrast cannot hold up for chapter seventeen explicitly states that "the woman whom you saw is the great city, which reigns over the kings of the earth" (Revelation 17:18). Chapter seventeen then clearly states that the woman *is the great city* which is discussed in the following passages. Despite this, another author says, "we must insist that the *city* and not the woman, is before us in the 18th chapter. Moreover, the city, with which the woman is identified, is not Babylon, but Rome."[1241] This statement errs in that it assumes its own conclusions. To say "the city, with which the woman is identified, is not Babylon" clearly contradicts the statement of Revelation. The author is merely assuming that the term Babylon in eighteen does not refer to the city mentioned in seventeen as the abode of the Harlot. It is not drawn from logical exegesis. In short, if the Whore *of Babylon* resides in a city with which she is identified, then this city should be viewed as one and the same as that of chapter eighteen.

Still others have suggested that the "reactions of the kings of the earth are different" in these two chapters.[1242] Goodman elaborates:

"When Harlot Babylon is destroyed, it is accomplished by the eleven most powerful kings on earth. The [anti-Christ] and his associate kings from the ten nations of New Rome are the perpetrators ... However, in chapter 18, the reaction of the kings of the world to the sudden blotting out of physical Babylon, the great city, the capitol and commercial center of the later-day earth, is one of sorrow and distress. The kings are anguished and terror stricken. The destruction of physical Babylon *(Rev. 18)* obviously must be a different event than the destruction of its occupant, religious Babylon."[1243]

Goodman has erred in assuming that the ten kings, or eleven as he assumes, are representative of the "kings of the world." Certainly he not alone in this. G. H. Pember has also said, "we find these same Ten Kings – for they are the 'Kings of the Earth.'"[1244] However, the Bible explicitly states "the ten horns which you saw, and the beast, these will hate the Harlot and will make her desolate and naked, and will eat her flesh and will burn her up with fire" (Revelation 17:16). The "ten horns" and the "beast" *alone* betray the Harlot. There is no indication that the "kings of the world" are consulted or are partners in this destruction. On the contrary, the world is, by all commentators acknowledgment, plunged in a world war. How can we assume that the "kings of the world" are at one with the "ten kings," if they are at war with each other? Instead, the shock with which the world reacts illustrates that ten kings and the anti-Christ are losing their support. The world is disintegrating along with the anti-Christ's kingdom.

Another argument levied is that the destruction of the Harlot is clearly described as being at the hands of the beast and the ten kings, whereas Babylon is prophesied to fall by the judgment of God Almighty. However, the fact that Babylon falls at the judgment of God does not exclude using human agencies. As a matter of fact, Revelation specifically states that "God has put it in their hearts to execute His purpose" (17:17). Clearly the anti-Christ and the ten kings are executing "God's purpose." They are merely tools oblivious to the fact that they are achieving God's will. There is no contradiction in this. Most theologians agree that God's will is divided into two separate categories. These are God's "sovereign" or "efficacious" will[1245] and God's "permissive will."[1246] Babylon does fall by the wrath of God, and the beast and his ten kings are the instrument by which God achieves judgment. No differentiation can be made on this basis.

Although this view is popularized by such well respected scholars as Tim LaHaye and John Walvoord, it lacks strength. While it presumably takes the strengths of "both" arguments, it also takes the weaknesses of both. Thus separating chapters seventeen and eighteen does not solve the problem, but magnifies it. The Harlot is clearly associated with "the great city" in Revelation 17:18 and cannot be separated from it. "The identity of Babylon the woman (Ch. 17) with Babylon the great city (Ch. 18) is so unmistakable that it would be inappropriate to make them different entities."[1247]   The context of chapters 17 and 18 require that they be kept together. Robert Thomas, who attempts to separate the two chapters, confesses that "the distinction between the two chapters is that between two systems or networks that have the same *geographic headquarters*" (emphasis added).[1248]

Conculsion

It has been argued that the beast is properly the kingdoms of Satan with Rome being the final kingdom ruled by the eighth head, the anti-Christ. This kingdom arises from the nations of the earth, but it is the Harlot, who in these last days resides in Rome, that harnesses her. She is that mystic, or rather Satanic, power through which all the empires of history have been carried. If the anti-Christ wishes to revive the Roman Empire then he must cater to, and accede to, the authority of that mighty church which alone has the authority to bestow the crown of the emperor.

Throughout world history the six great empires of history have failed to distinguish between the religious power and political power of the realm. It is only with the rise of the Holy Roman Empire that the two began to war with one another. The picture that the Bible paints seems to be a continuation of that war, with the anti-Christ as the emperor and the Whore of Babylon playing the role of the papacy. Just as Napoleon and the Holy Roman Emperors had to accede to the pope to gain the crown, the anti-Christ will assent to the Harlot, and just as the emperors turned on the popes once gaining that crown, so also the anti-Christ will turn on the Harlot once he believes his power to be assured; for only the apostate church of Babel, passed down through the generations to Rome, has the authority to restore the Roman Empire.

For the first half of the tribulation the anti-Christ is concentrating on solidifying his power, but in the middle of the tribulation he makes a tragic mistake. He will enter the temple of Jerusalem (cf. Daniel 9:27, 2 Thessalonians 2:4, Matthew 24:15, & Rev. 11:8) and declare himself God. With the support of the False Prophet he hopes to install universal worship of himself, but the plan backfires. The Jews rebel, the peace treaty is broken (cf. Daniel 9:27), and the nations go to war. It is at this time that the anti-Christ attempts to rid himself of the power of the Harlot, who doubtless, as the leader of professed Christianity, denounces the action of the anti-Christ. This is probably the last straw. While the specifics of the betrayal are not told to us, it is logical to assume that this pivotal event, the "abomination of desolation," signals the unraveling of the anti-Christ's kingdom, the final world war, and the instigation of persecution against all who refuse the mark of the beast (Rev. 13:15). It is also at this time that the anti-Christ attempts to rid himself of the papacy by destroying Vatican City, and possibly the city of Rome itself.

The results of this destruction backfire. Rather than solidifying his power, it further unravels his hold upon the world. The merchants and kings of

236

the earth mourn the great city and the economic backlash does the anti-Christ precious little good. It may be at this time that three of the ten kings turn on the anti-Christ, causing him to subjugate them by violence (cf. Daniel 7:24). There are clearly ten kings that participate in the destruction of Babylon, but we are told that at some point the anti-Christ subjugates three of these kings. This may be what is referenced in Revelation 6:2. It is the beginning of the end for the anti-Christ and his kingdom. The Roman Empire was integrally tied to the apostate woman and without her, it will fall.

CHAPTER SUMMARY

The imagery of the harlot is one of the most controversial in the controversial book of Revelation. Nevertheless, the following conclusions should be conceded.

1. The Harlot practices a form of religion that can be traced back to Babel. This should include:
   A. Idolatry.
   B. The belief that salvation can be attained after death.
   C. The belief that the king or high priest speaks for God.
   D. A hierarchy.
   E. Necessity of repeated sacrifices.
2. The Harlot must be an apostate church which still includes some true, but deceived, believers.
3. The Harlot holds the key to restoring the Roman (or Holy Roman) Empire. In this respect she and the anti-Christ will have a political but turbulent relationship.
4. The Harlot is called "Mystery Babylon," not Babylon.
5. Babylon fell exactly as prophesied and "shall not rise again" (Jeremiah 51:64)
6. The Harlot and the city are virtually synonymous and cannot be separated. This city must therefore meet the following criteria.
   A. It must be an ancient city guilty of many evils including slavery.
   B. It must have seven hills or mountains.
   C. It must have a sea port.
   D. It must be a large commercial city, dealing in linen, precious stones, marble, spices, ivory, olive oils, livestock, perfumes, and all other riches.
7. The Harlot and anti-Christ will enter a power struggle and the Whore of Babylon will be overthrown and destroyed by the anti-Christ and his ten kings, probably in the middle of the tribulation.

Study Charts on the Whore of Babylon

Irenaeus	Chiliast	The Harlot and city as Rome.
Hippolytus	Chiliast	The Harlot and city as Rome.
Tertullian	Chiliast	The Harlot and city as Rome.
Lactantius	Chiliast	The Harlot and city as Rome.
Victorinus	Chiliast	The Harlot and city as Rome.
Chrystostom	Chiliast	The Harlot and city as Rome.
St. Jerome	Allegorical	The Harlot and city as Rome.
Tichonius	Allegorical	The Harlot as a world church and the city as Rome.
Augustine	Allegorical	The Harlot as a world church and the city as Rome.
Joachim of Floris	Medieval Millenarian	The Harlot and city as Rome.
Joachimites	Medieval Millenarians	The Harlot and city as Rome.
Pierre D'Olivi	Medieval Millenarian	The Harlot and city as Rome.
Nicholas of Lyra	Medieval Millenarian	The Harlot and city as Muslim Turks.
Waldenses	Medieval Millenarians	The Harlot Roman church and city as Rome.
John Wycliff	Medieval Millenarian	The Harlot as papacy.
Lollards	Medieval Millenarians	The Harlot as papacy.
Walter Brute	Medieval Millenarian	The Harlot as papacy and city as Rome.
John Huss	Medieval Millenarian	The Harlot as papacy and city as Rome.
Hussites	Medieval Millenarians	The Harlot as papacy and city as Rome.
William Tyndale	Historicist	The Harlot as papacy and city as Rome.
John Foxe	Historicist	The Harlot as papacy and city as Rome.
William Fulke	Historicist	The Harlot as papacy and city as Rome.
Joseph Mede	Historicist premillennialist	The Harlot as papacy and city as Rome.
John Milton	Historicist	The Harlot as papacy.
Isaac Newton	Historicist premillennialist	The Harlot as both Catholic and Eastern orthodox churches. The city is Rome.
John Darby	Dispensational premillennialist	The Harlot and city as Rome.

Robert Govett	Futurist premillennialist	The Harlot as Romanism, but more. The city as literal Babylon in Iraq.
Joseph Seiss	Futurist premillennialist	The Harlot as a new global religion. The city as literal Babylon in Iraq.
George Peters	Dispensational premillennialist	The Harlot as papacy and city as Rome.
Nathaniel West	Dispensational premillennialist	The Harlot and city as Rome.
G. H. Pember	Futurist premillennialist	The Harlot as Romanism. The city as literal Babylon in Iraq.
Sir Robert Anderson	Dispensational premillennialist	The Harlot and city as Rome.
E. W. Bullinger	Ultradispensationalist	The Harlot as a new global religion. The city as literal Babylon in Iraq.
Walter Scott	Dispensational premillennialist	The Harlot and city as Rome.
H. A. Ironside	Dispensational premillennialist	The Harlot and city as Rome.
C. I. Scofield	Dispensational premillennialist	The Harlot as "one great world church."
William Newell	Dispensational premillennialist	The Harlot as Romanism. The city as literal Babylon in Iraq.
Norman Harrison	Midtribulational premillennialist	The Harlot as Romanism. The city as literal Babylon in Iraq.
John Walvoord	Dispensational premillennialist	The Harlot as Romanism. The city as literal Babylon in Iraq.
Dwight Pentecost	Dispensational premillennialist	The Harlot and city as Rome.
George Ladd	Posttribulational Premillennialist	Unsure on harlot. Calls the city the capitol city of anti-Christ.
Watchman Nee	Dispensational premillennialist	The Harlot and city as Rome.
Hal Lindsey	Dispensational premillennialist	The Harlot as a New Age church. The city apparenly as literal Babylon in Iraq, although he names Rome as the anti-Christ's capitol.
Tim LaHaye	Dispensational premillennialist	The Harlot as Romanism. The city as literal Babylon in Iraq.

Henry Morris	Dispensational premillennialist	The Harlot as a new global religion. The city as literal Babylon in Iraq.
Robert Thomas	Dispensational premillennialist	The Harlot as a new global religion. The city as literal Babylon in Iraq.
Robert Lightner	Dispensational premillennialist	The Harlot as a new global religion. The city as literal Babylon in Iraq.
Dave Hunt	Dispensational premillennialist	The Harlot as the Catholic church. The city as Vatican City or Rome.
Charles Dyer	Dispensational premillennialist	The Harlot as a new global religion. The city as literal Babylon in Iraq.
Phillip Goodman	Dispensational premillennialist	The Harlot as a new global religion. The city as literal Babylon in Iraq.
Marvin Rosenthal	"Pre-wrath" premillennialist	The Harlot as Romanism.
Robert Van Kampen	"Pre-wrath" premillennialist	The Harlot as a new global religion. The city as Rome.

Historical Survey

	Position
Church Fathers	The church fathers were unanimously of the opinion that Rome was intended by both the Harlot and the city.
Medieval Theologians	Virtually all scholars, including devout Catholics, acknowledged that the Harlot was future Rome. Many saw Rome as already in apostasy.
Reformation Scholars	Virtually all the Reformers saw the Harlot as the papacy and the city as Rome.
Post-Reformation Scholars	Still predominantly of the proposition the Harlot is Rome, but with the initial instigation of the view that literal Babylon in Iraq was intended for the city. Some began to see the Harlot as a universal church not associated with Rome.
Modern Evangelicals	A thorough mixture of views but with the "both/and" view emerging as the predominant view.

The Harlot as the Global Church of the Anti-Christ

Tenants of:
This view believes that the Whore of Babylon is a universal religion that will compel the worship of the anti-Christ.

* Some advocates of the other positions also believe the Harlot is universally accepted.

Popular advocates from:
The Church Fathers : None known.
Medieval Theologians : Bede.
Reformation Scholars : None cited.
Post-Reformation Scholars : Joseph Seiss, E. W. Bullinger, and C. I. Scofield.
Modern Evangelicals : Hal Lindsey, Cosntance Cumbey, Robert Thomas, Henry Morris, Robert Lightner, Charles Dyer, Phillip Goodman, and Robert Van Kampen.*

Strengths:
1) It presumes to explain the relationship between the anti-Christ and the Harlot.
2) It is consistent with the apostasy of 2 Thessalonians 2:3.

Weaknesses:
1) It confuses the False Prophet and the worship of the anti-Christ with the Harlot, who is destroyed by them.
2) It cannot explain the betrayal of the anti-Christ.
3) It is a relatively new view to history making it suspect in terms of the perspicuity of Scripture.
4) It must assume that the beast encompasses all men.

The Harlot as the Romanism

Tenants of:
This view states that the Harlot is an apostate church in Rome, usually identified today with the Roman Catholic Church (identified by the church fathers as merely an apostate religion in Rome).

Popular advocates from:
The Church Fathers : Irenaeus, Hippolytus, Tertullian, Lactantius, Victorinus, and Chrystostom.
Medieval Theologians : St. Jerome, Joachim of Floris, Pierre D'Olivi, the Waldenses, John Wycliff, Walter Brute, and John Huss.
Reformation Scholars : William Tyndale, John Foxe, William Fulke, Joseph Mede, John Milton, and Isaac Newton.
Post-Reformation Scholars : John Darby, Robert Govett, George Peters, Nathaniel West, G. H. Pember, Sir Robert Anderson, and Walter Scott.
Modern Evangelicals : H. A. Ironside, William Newell, Norman Harrison, Dwight Pentecost, John Walvoord, Tim LaHaye, Dave Hunt, and Marvin Rosenthal.

Strengths:
1) Rome is historically known as the city on seven hills (cf. Revelation 17:9).
2) The Harlot is identified with the city which ruled over the earth in John's day (cf. Revelation 17:18).
3) It is the all but universal view of antiquity (in accordance with the doctrine of the perspicuity of Scripture).
4) This view alone can account for the fact that there are believers within the Harlot church (cf. Revelation 18:4).
5) Rome alone can be associated with both a great church and a great city.
6) The description of her riches fits that of ancient, medieval, and modern Rome.
7) Rome is located by the sea, and has a massive seaport (cf. Revelation 18:17).
8) Rome is referred to as Babylon by Peter (cf. 1 Peter 5:13).
9) The imagery of a harlot implies that she was once the finance of Christ (see discussion of Old Testament parallels in chapter above).

Weaknesses:
1) Some argue that 1 Peter 5:13 was not written from Rome, but from a synagogue in Babylon.
2) It is argued that "mystery" does not refer to Babylon and, therefore, Babylon must be interpreted literally as a rebuilt city in the desert.

The City as the Rome
Tenants of:
This view that the city in which the Harlot dwells is Rome.

Popular advocates from:
The Church Fathers : Irenaeus, Hippolytus, Tertullian, Lactantius, Victorinus, and Chrystostom.
Medieval Theologians : St. Jerome, St. Augustine, Joachim of Floris, Pierre D'Olivi, the Waldenses, John Wycliff, Walter Brute, and John Huss.
Reformation Scholars : William Tyndale, John Foxe, William Fulke, Joseph Mede, John Milton, and Isaac Newton.
Post-Reformation Scholars : John Darby, George Peters, Nathaniel West, Sir Robert Anderson, and Walter Scott.
Modern Evangelicals : H. A. Ironside, Dwight Pentecost, Watchman Nee, and Dave Hunt.

Strengths:
1) Rome is historically known as the city on seven hills (cf. Revelation 17:9).
2) The city is identified as the city which ruled over the earth in John's day (cf. Revelation 17:18).
3) It is the all but universal view of antiquity (in accordance with the doctrine of the perspicuity of Scripture).
4) Rome is located by the sea, and has a massive seaport (cf. Revelation 18:17).
5) Rome is referred to as Babylon by Peter (cf. 1 Peter 5:13).
6) Rome alone can be associated with both a great church and a great city.
7) The description of her riches fits that of ancient, medieval, and modern Rome.

Weaknesses:
1) It is claimed that the Old Testament prophecies demand the rebuilding of ancient Iraq, thus negating Rome.
2) Some argue that 1 Peter 5:13 was not written from Rome, but from a synagogue in Babylon.
3) It is argued that "mystery" does not refer to Babylon and, therefore, Babylon must be interpreted literally as a rebuilt city in the desert.
4) It is frivolously claimed that Rome is not a commercial city.

The City as a Rebuilt Babylon in Iraq

Tenants of:

This view that the city in which the Harlot dwells is a rebuilt city of Babylon in modern day Iraq.

Popular advocates from:

The Church Fathers : None known.

Medieval Theologians : None known.

Reformation Scholars : None known.

Post-Reformation Scholars : Robert Govett, Joseph Seiss, E. W. Bullinger, and G. H. Pember.

Modern Evangelicals : William Newell, Norman Harrison, Hal Lindsey, Cosntance Cumbey, Robert Thomas, Henry Morris, Robert Lightner, Charles Dyer, and Tim LaHaye.

Strengths:

1) It is alleged that the Old Testament prophecies demand that Babylon be destroyed instantaniously by fire in the last days.

2) It is argued that "mystery" does not refer to Babylon and, therefore, Babylon must be interpreted literally as a rebuilt city in the desert.

3) It is argued that ancient Babylon never truly fell or was uninhabited (they say that 1 Peter 5:13 was not written from Rome, but from a synagogue in Babylon).

4) Current events are appealed to as proof of Babylon's "resurrection."

Weaknesses:

1) The Old Testament prophecies compare Babylon to Sodom in terms of desolation, not the mode of destruction (cf. Isaiah 13:18-19).

2) The city is identified as that city which ruled over the earth in John's day (cf. Revelation 17:18).

3) This view seems to have been invented in the late 19th Century (thus conflicting with the doctrine of the perspicuity of Scripture).

4) Babylon does not, and cannot, have a seaport as it resides in the desert (cf. Revelation 18:17).

5) The "rise of Babylon" would create a "sign of the rapture" since no city can be built overnight to become an economic powerhouse.

6) Rome, not Babylon, is historically known as the city on seven hills (cf. Revelation 17:9). Babylon cannot be described as being seated on seven hills or seven mountains.

7) Most historians agree that Peter wrote 1 Peter 5:13 from Rome, not Babylon.

8) Current events are a poor method of exegesis.

9) Any fair evaluation of history shows that Babylon was abandoned and desolate for centuries. According to Jeremiah 51:64 Babylon shall "not rise again."

9

The Millennial Kingdom

There is no issue more controversial than the Millennial Kingdom itself. Since Augustine's time, the very idea of the Millennial Kingdom has been divisive. The medievals declared that the Catholic Church was itself the Millennial Kingdom, and that no literal thousand year reign of Christ was ever intended. Chiliasm, or premillennialism, was declared a heresy. To this very day the controversy remains. However, this book is about *premillennial* interpretations. Consequently, the question of whether or not a literal reign of Christ was intended will only briefly be discussed. The controversy in this chapter is reserved not for the question of the existence of the Millennium, but for its nature. What is the Millennium? What is it for? Will immortals intermingle with mortals in everyday life? Will men live a thousand years? Will there be wars or disease? What is the nature of the final rebellion that the end of the Millennium? These are the questions that will be addressed here.

The Second Coming and the Millennium

"I saw heaven opened; and behold, a white horse, and He who sat upon it *is* called Faithful and True; and in righteousness He judges and wages war. And His eyes *are* a flame of fire, and upon His head *are* many diadems; and He has a name written *upon Him* which no one knows except Himself. And *He is* clothed with a robe dipped in blood; and His name is called The Word of God. And the armies which are in heaven, clothed in fine linen, white *and* clean, were following Him on white horses. And from His mouth comes a sharp sword, so that with it He may smite the nations; and He will rule them with a rod of iron; and He treads the wine press of the fierce wrath of God, the Almighty. And on His robe and on His thigh He has a name written, 'KING OF KINGS, AND LORD OF LORDS.'

And I saw an angel standing in the sun; and he cried out with a loud voice, saying to all the birds which fly in midheaven, 'Come, assemble for the great supper of God; in order that you may eat the flesh of kings and the flesh of commanders and the flesh of mighty men and the flesh of horses and of those who sit on them and the flesh of all men, both free men and slaves, and small and great.'

And I saw the beast and the kings of the earth and their armies, assembled to make war against Him who sat upon the horse, and against His army.

And the beast was seized, and with him the false prophet who performed the signs in his presence, by which he deceived those who had received the mark of the beast and those who worshiped his image;

these two were thrown alive into the lake of fire which burns with brimstone. And the rest were killed with the sword which came from the mouth of Him who sat upon the horse, and all the birds were filled with their flesh.

And I saw an angel coming down from heaven, having the key of the abyss and a great chain in his hand. And he laid hold of the dragon, the serpent of old, who is the devil and Satan, and bound him for a thousand years, and threw him into the abyss, and shut *it* and sealed *it* over him, so that he should not deceive the nations any longer, until the thousand years were completed; after these things he must be released for a short time" (Revelation 19:11-20:3).

The second coming brings together many previous passages and illustrates that the Bible is often arranged topically, rather than by strict chronology. We are told that here, at the second coming, "He treads the wine press of the fierce wrath of God" (19:15). The wine press, however, is first discussed in Revelation 14:19-20. That passage was thus a foreshadowing of the judgment at Armageddon. Indeed, Revelation 19 does not even mention Armageddon, but that it occurs at that battle is obvious for the battle occurs *after* the armies have gathered at Armageddon and while the seventh bowl is poured out upon the earth. "There were flashes of lightning and sounds and peals of thunder; and there was a great earthquake, such as there had not been since man came to be upon the earth, so great an earthquake *was it, and* so mighty. And the great city was split into three part" (16:18-19). This passage is, in turn, parallel to yet another second coming passage found in the Old Tesament. Zechariah 14:4 states that "in that day [of judgment] His feet will stand on the Mount of Olives, which is in front of Jerusalem on the east; and the Mount of Olives will be split in its middle from east to west by a very large valley, so that half of the mountain will move toward the north and the other half toward the south." Therefore, all these events occur in this brief time frame. The Lord returns bodily to the earth, even as he left it (cf. Acts 1:11). His army, which includes those who have been raptured (see Appendix A), come with the Lord while the "wine press" of God metes out punishment to the armies of the anti-Christ. When Jesus lands on the Mount of Olives, the mount will split asunder and a great earthquake will shake the Holy City.

On this most scholars are fully agreed. It is with what follows that debate rages. After these events we see the judgment of the anti-Christ and his False Prophet, who are both thrown *alive* into hell. Then an angel came down from heaven, "having the key of the abyss and a great chain in his hand. And he laid hold of the dragon, the serpent of old, who is the devil and Satan, and bound him for a thousand years, and threw him into the abyss, and shut *it* and sealed *it* over him, so that he should not deceive the nations any longer, until the thousand years were completed; after these things he must be released for a short time." Perhaps it is the fact that the serpent is to be released again one day that has led many to question this passage. Perhaps it is the fact that many do not understand the purpose for a thousand year reign. Perhaps many would prefer that the New Heaven and New Earth of Revelation 22 begin instantly after the second coming, or perhaps some have become so worldly that they insist the Millennial Kingdom is here on the earth now, in this age (as the amillennialists contend). In any case, these issues must be examined carefully.

Arguments Against a Literal Millennium

It must first be said that a literal Millennium was held and accepted from the very beginning. Justin Martyr affirmed the doctrine of a literal Millennium.[1249] Irenaeus also held to the literal Millennium and openly refuted allegory, saying, "if any shall endevour to allegorize prophecies of this kind, they shall not be found consistent."[1250] Nevertheless, it has been erroneously supposed that there is only one passage in the whole of the Scriptures which refers to the Millennial Kingdom. This statement, asserted by amillennialists, is unfounded. While it is true that this passage alone describes the duration of the kingdom, the Millennial Kingdom was not only foretold throughout the Bible, but was eagerly anticipated at Christ's first coming. He spoke of it, as did his disciples, and even his enemies. Says Nathaniel West:

> "It is a very common opinion, widely spread throughout Christendom, and in most cases believed to be true, that 'the thousand years' of which John speaks in the Apocalypse, Rev. xx:1-7, are mentioned nowhere else in the sacred Scriptures ... a deeper study of the sacred volume dissipates this false prejudice and reveals the fact that, not only are 'the thousand years' of which John speaks found everywhere in both Testaments, but that next to the eternal state, the millennial blessedness of God's people on earth, and of the nations, is the one high point in all prophecy, from Moses to John, the bright, broad tableland of all eschatology."[1251]

West properly affirms that "what we find in the New Testament as its outcome in respect to the ages and the kingdom, has already lain the bosom of the Old Testament from the beginning."[1252] One must, however, clarify what West means. There is no doubt that the *duration* of this blessed kingdom is found only in Revelation 20, but that there is a kingdom which must be distinguished from both the present age and the eternal state of Revelation 21 and 22 is indisputable to any objective reader. The ancients all anticipated it. Some even believe that this is one reason the Jewish hierarchy accused Jesus (because He did not deliver the kingdom into their hands and free the Jews from Roman bondage as the prophecies promised). That the idea of an earthly kingdom was prominent in the Old Testament cannot be denied. It is this very fact which led the early medievals to *attack* the literal interpretation. Those who held to an earthly millennium, preceding the heavenly kingdom of Revelation 21-22, were accused of being "Judaizers." The idea of an earthly millennium,

247

stemming from the Old Testament, was considered "Jewish." If the literal interpretation were to be accepted, then it would be clear that Gentile rule would have to end. It is said that the early medievals developed a "system of allegories in order to escape Chiliasm."[1253] As Samuel Maitland said, "St. Jerome tells us repeatedly, and with mistaken triumph, that to hold the Millennial doctrine was to '*Judaize*' ... I am glad of such unexceptional testimony as Jerome's to the fact that this was the judgment of the '*Jewish Church*,' and that to hold the Millennarian doctrine was to '*Judaize!*' It would not be difficult to show that this ancient doctrine of the church was maintained, and unimpugned, *until the Christian Church began to* HEATHENIZE."[1254] Thus it is admitted even by the amillennialists that the doctrine of premillennialism existed long before the New Testament was written. As one amillennialists wrote, the thousand years is "saturated with ideas born upon the soil of Palestine anterior to the publication of the gospel."[1255] Perhaps this alleged "reproach" is true, but as George Peters states, "this term of reproach (given in this sense by man) we cheerfully accept, for it is a distinguishing feature of our faith, seeing that we find it in the covenant given *to Jews*, in *Jewish* Prophets, in the teaching of a *Jewish* Savior and *Jewish* apostles."[1256]

If the idea of an earthly kingdom, preceding the eternal state, is found in antiquity and the Old Testament, then the sole objection that the amillennialists can make is to argue that no other passage can define the *duration* of this kingdom as a thousand years. However, it must be responded that there is also not a single passage anywhere in the Bible that uses the number 1000 symbolically for an indeterminate period of time. The amillennialists must *assume* that 1000 is symbolic, but cannot show anywhere where it is used in this manner. 2 Peter 3:8, the often misquoted verse, does not qualify. It is not symbolism, but *comparison*. It is speaking of time in God's sight. "*With the Lord* a day is *as* a thousand years*.*" Nothing in this context implies that a thousand years is symbolic for an indeterminate period of time. The context of the entire statement is that "the Lord is not slow about His promise, as some count slowness" (1 Peter 3:9). Thus, premillennialists must again challenge amillennialists to find a single passage in which a thousand is used *symbolically* for an indeterminate period of time.

Amillennialists deny that the Millennial Kingdom is literal for various reasons. Some have become accustomed to the modern world, and wish to call this sinful age the "kingdom of God." It is ironic indeed that men such as Augustine called the chiliasts "carnal"[1257] when he applied the promises of this kingdom to the Dark Ages. As we shall see, there is no doubt that the Bible speaks of an earthly kingdom, separate from the current age, which precedes the heavenly eternal kingdom spoken of in Revelation 21-22. To deny this is nothing more to cling to the dying refuse of medieval anti-Semitic doctrines. The medieval church was not the promised kingdom, and neither are the modern day churches of the world.

248

Obsolete Millennial Theories

In addition to those who deny the Millennium is an old, now obsolete, theory which should be briefly addressed. The doctrine of "dischiliasm" taught that there were two separate, and successive, Millennial reigns.[1258] They argue that Revelation 20:2 speaks of "a" thousand years while verse three speaks of "the" thousand years. Thus, they believe that there are two separate thousand year periods.[1259] According to this system, the risen saints are not resurrected until after Satan has been released from his prison, and the saints rule from heaven, not from the earth.[1260] This teaching was apparently an attempt to deflect amillennial criticisms of a "carnal Millennium" where the risen saints would live side by side with mortals. It seems to have begun to some extent with the great J. A. Bengel, who was troubled over this.[1261] Amillennialists had long argued that risen saints cannot be physical incarnations without becoming "carnal." While the relation of immortal risen saints to mortals will be addressed later, the issue of resurrected bodies will be discussed here.

Many Augustinians have long claimed that the resurrected saints will have no physical bodies. The imagery of winged angels with harps on clouds developed from this spiritualistic teaching. As one Augustinian argued, "they who rise in the resurrection *neither eat, nor drink, nor marry,* for there is no further need of these ... fleshy functions."[1262] However, this cannot be reconciled with the Bible. Did not Thomas place his hands into Christ's wounds (John 20:27)? Did Jesus not eat with the disciples (cf. Luke 24:43, John 21:12-14)? It is true that Matthew 22:30 says that the resurrected do not marry (cf. Mark 12:25, Luke 20:35), but it says nothing of eating or drinking. In fact, Revelation 2:7 specifically promises the right to eat of the tree of life and Matthew 26:29 promises that Jesus will eat and drink with the disciples in the Kingdom to come. The idea that a spritual resurrected body that contradicts some form of physical incarnation stems from eastern mysticism and the doctrine that the material world is inherently evil in itself.

Thus the theory of "dischiliasm" was created solely to discard the problems created by a "carnal" Millennium, and yet the entire basis for the criticism is mystical, not Biblical. Nothing in the scriptures teaches that man is to become a disembodied ghost floating on the clouds. We will certainly not be bound by the current earthly laws of nature, but neither will we be denied the ability to hug our loved ones, or to eat of the tree of life (Revelation 2:7, 22:2, & 22:14). Dischiliasm is as dead as Augustinism should be.

The Nature of the Millennium

The predominant question asked by those who deny the literal Millennial Kingdom is, "what is the purpose of such a kingdom?" "Did not Jesus say, 'My Kingdom is not of this world'?" These are fair questions and will not be ignored. Indeed, one must wonder why Christ does not merely bring the New Heaven and New Earth of Revelation 21:1 down with Him at the second coming. Of course the rhetorical response is that Christ could have brought it with Him at the first coming, but did not. The more complex answer deals with the very fundamental questions between dispensationalism and covenant theologians (see Appendix F) as well as between amillennialists and premillennialists. It has to do with the question of why God has made history at all. Why create a world where men live but a hundred years to decide their eternal fate? Why not merely create more angels to live in heaven? Much of this is far beyond the scope of this work, but we are told in Colossians 1:20 that it pleased the Lord "through [Christ] to reconcile all things to Himself, whether things on earth or things in heaven, having made peace through the blood of His cross; through Him." In other words, the ultimate goal is to "reconcile all things to Himself." That this is done through Christ is denied by no Christian. How this plan is enacted it what is debated.

Covenant theologians are correct to state that Jesus's death and resurrection is the pinacle of this plan of the ages, but they err when they claim that the church age must be the final age. God could have sent Christ to died on the cross the day after Adam and Eve fell, but Adam and Eve would not have understood. God had to prepare man for the Messiah. Covenant theologians and dispensationalists agree that man had to be prepared. Each agree that the giving of the law unto Moses was not intended as the means to salvation but, as Romans says, "because by the works of the Law no flesh will be justified in His sight; but through the Law *comes* the knowledge of sin" (3:20). The law was, therefore, given to convict men of sin. It was given to show man that we need a savior. Dispensationalists and covenant theologians have agreed on this, but differ as to what happened before the law. These disputes are discussed elsewhere (see Appendix F). What is of concern are not the early dispensations, or ages, but those which follow the first coming of Christ.

We now live in the church age. This is often called the age or "dispensation of Grace."[1263] All Christian agree that grace is not indiginous to this age alone, but it is the age in which God's grace was manifested through Christ's sacrifice. So what is the purpose of the Millennial age? Why does there need to be a Millennial age? The dispensations previous to the church age were designed in various ways to prepare man for the coming of Christ. The dispensations following Christ's coming are designed to prove that man cannot live without Christ. The rebellion which occurs at the end of the Millennium (Revelation 20:7-10) is proof that the eternal age has not yet begun. Even after seeing the glory of Christ's rule, some men will rebel. Some, like Robert Govett, have suggested that this rebellion may occur to demonstrate that man will sin even with full knowledge of God or to justify eternal punishment of the wicked.[1264] Even George Ladd, a covenant theologian, says that "this [event] makes it plain that the ultimate root of sin is not poverty or inadequate social conditions or an unfortunate environment; but it is the rebelliousness of the human heart."[1265] Many other theories could be offered as well. The point is that there is a point to history. Whether God *could* introduce the New Heaven and New Earth without an earthly kingdom (as He promised to the Jews) is irrelevant. The Bible is *clear* that there *will* be an earthly kingdom which precedes the New Heaven and New Earth. The best rebuttal to their arguments is to examine the prophecies of this earthly kingdom, to weigh them, and to evaluate them. It may be summarized, however, that the Millennial age is the time when God will fulfill His unconditional promises to the nation of Israel, prove that He alone is a just ruler, and discount every argument that critics have ever levied against God. It is the age in which God's promises are fulfilled on earth, before the eternal age begins. It is a prototype of the eternal age, but contains mortal sinners whose hearts have not yet made their eternal choices. It is a return to Eden, but with the Tree of Life absent.

Life in the Millennium

The character of the Millennium is different from both the current age and the eternal age, but there are similarities to each. Like the eternal state, the Millennium will be marked by the direct rule of God, where justice and peace will prevail. However, like the modern age, there will be both sin and death.

The Millennium will be characterized by peace and justice. Disease, pestilence, and war will be absent during the Millennium. Men will once again live for many hundreds of years as they did in the days before Noah. Nature will no longer be man's enemy, but man and nature will coexist in the proper manner, with nature in subjugation to man. Israel will be restored to its rightful place and the promises to the Jewish people will be kept. Christ will rule the earth visibly from Jerusalem and all men will worship the One True God.

Nature in the Millennium

The Millennial Kingdom will be marked by the restoration of nature to its antediluvian state. Ever since the fall of man nature has been under a curse. In the current age nature is often brutal and cruel (far from the image presented by pantheists and New Agers). Jungles breed disease and death. Animals prey on one another and men suffer malnutrition. Deserts make life hard and food is difficult to grow. Such was not the case in the early days of man.

In the Garden of Eden all animals were herbivores (cf. Genesis 1:30), but following the curse of fallen man some animals were made carnivorous (cf. Genesis 9:2). In the Millennial Kingdom animals will once again become herbivorous. According to Isaiah 11, "the wolf will dwell with the lamb, and the leopard will lie down with the kid, and the calf and the young lion and the fatling together; and a little boy will lead them. Also the cow and the bear will graze; their young will lie down together; And the lion will eat straw like the ox.

And the nursing child will play by the hole of the cobra, and the weaned child will put his hand on the viper's den" (vs. 6-8). This same promise is found in Isaiah 65:25 and Ezekiel 34:25 & 28. Man will no longer have to kill for his food, nor fear the animal attacking him.

In addition, the land itself will be restored to its antediluvian state. In the Adamic age the land was fertile and yielded fruit easily. After the curse the land no longer brought forth fruit easily. God told Adam, "you shall eat the plants of the field by the sweat of your brow" (Genesis 3:18-19). The land becomes parched if not properly maintained, or its nutrients are sapped if man does not rotate crops properly. The toil of man's labors will be reduced to that of the Adamic age. Says Ezekiel 34:27, "the tree of the field will yield its fruit, and the earth will yield its increase." Zechariah 8:12 reads, "*there will be* peace for the seed: the vine will yield its fruit, the land will yield its produce, and the heavens will give their dew." Isaiah 30:23-24 also affirms "He will give *you* rain for the seed which you will sow in the ground, and bread *from* the yield of the ground, and it will be rich and plenteous; on that day your livestock will graze in a roomy pasture. Also the oxen and the donkeys which work the ground will eat salted fodder, which has been winnowed with shovel and fork." Ezekiel 36:29-30, Joel 2:22, and Isaiah 35:7 also speak of the earth yielding its fruit and of the bringing forth springs. On account of this, Isaiah 65:21-22 teaches that each man will provide his own food. No longer will stock yards raise foods for others, because each man will be able to provide his own.[1266]

In addition to this, there is an apparent change in the topography and ecology of the earth. Much of this debate involves science and the effects of the antediluvian "vapor canopy" or "water canopy."[1267] Genesis 2:6 says that "a mist rose from the earth and watered the whole surface of the ground." According to scientist Dr. Henry Morris "waters apparently existed in the form of a great vapor canopy around the earth."[1268] Most creation scientists believe that this is what is described in Genesis 1:6-8. They believe that this canopy created a sort of beneficial greenhouse effect which would shield the earth from the sun's harmful rays. The result would be longevity and a uniform climate.[1269] Winter and summer would not vary in great ammounts, but the entire earth, including the Antartica would be habitable. This is born out by the archaeological finds of a large ancient city by the Artic Ocean,[1270] as well as fossils of tropical plants found in Siberia and Alaska.[1271] This condition apparently remained until the flood of Noah. Because there is no rain with condensational nuclei, and because condensaional nuclei does not rise in heat, there was no rain before the Flood (cf. Genesis 2:5). Creationists assume that the waters which once enveloped the earth fell as rain when God dropped the temperature, and those waters sank into the ocean basins, causing the mountains to rise. This is apparently what is alluded to Psalm 104:8-9 where it says of the Flood, "the mountains rose and the valleys sank down to the place which You did establish for them. You did set a boundary that they may not pass over; that they may not return to cover the ear."

The events of Revelation reverse these past events, and apparenly restoring the antediluvian topography and ecology. "Great land movements will also have eliminated the great mountain ranges and islands of the world, filling up the ocean depths and restoring gentle, globally habitable topography and geography all over the world, as it had been in the antediluvian age."[1272] Moreover, Morris asserts that "the redistribution of earth's topography and restoration of its vapor canopy will soon result in an elimination of many, if not all, of its wastelands and deserts."[1273] Another result of the possible restoration of the vapor or water canopy will be the return of longevity.

Death in the Millennium

According to Isaiah 65:20, "no longer will there be in it an infant *who lives but a few* days, or an old man who does not live out his days; for the youth will die at the age of one hundred and the one who does not reach the age of one hundred shall be *thought* accursed." From this premillennial scholars have concluded that the longevity of the antediluvian world (cf. Genesis 5:4-32 & 6:3) will be restored. Even as men used to live nearly a thousand years, men will, once again, live to be many hundreds of years old.

Critics have disputed this on the grounds that Isaiah 65 speaks about the New Heaven and New Earth (vs. 1) rather than the Millennial Kingdom. However, this is an unfounded argument. There are three reasons to doubt that the entire chapter concerns the New Heaven and New Earth. First, the Bible is often arranged topically rather than chronologically. Hence, Isaiah 65 is speaking generally of the times when Christ will rule. This includes both the Millennial Kingdom and the New Heaven and New Earth. Second, the New Heaven and New Earth is actually an extension of the Millennial Kingdom. Thus most of the passages are applicable to both. Most importantly, however, is the third point. The Bible is quite explicit that there is *no death* in the New Heaven and New Earth (Revelation 21:4). Men will *never* die. Consequently, the passage *must* refer to the Millennial Kingdom, and not the New Heaven and New Earth.

Thus, the day when men lived nearly a thousand years will once again be the norm. However, some have erroneously supposed that only the wicked will die in the Millennium. Thus they also believe that all the righteous will live to see the New Heaven and New Earth established. Walter Scott says that "they shall reign with Christ for a thousand years" (Revelation 20:4) means that "saints on earth shall live a thousand years and shall *not* die."[1274] Even Tim LaHaye has erroneously remarked:

> "This verse [Isaiah 65:20] suggests that believers will live after birth to the end of the Millennium ... it also indicates that if a person reaches a hundred years of age and is not a believer, he or she will be accursed, or

253

die. In other words, those living during the Millennium are given a hundred years to make a decision to receive Jesus Christ as Savior and Lord."[1275]

In regard to Scott's assertion, it should be noted that the passage does not refer specifically to the mortal saints on earth, but to the resurrected saints. It says "they came to life and reigned with Christ for a thousand years" (20:4). Thus, it is they who "came to life" who reign for a thousand years. Certainly, the saints on earth will reign with Christ, but it cannot be asserted that they will live for the entire thousand years. LaHaye's statement actually goes one step further, and is equally unjustified. First, nothing in the passage suggest that all unbelievers will die before a hundred years. If so, then who rebels at the end of the Millennium? Is it to be supposed that it is a revolt of children? Moreover, it is debatable whether or not the passage even says they "will be accursed" (cf. KJV, ASV, RSV), as opposed to, they "will be thought accursed" (cf. NAS, NIV, NRSV, Tanakh). In either case, the idea that believers will not die in the Millennium cannot be supported in the Scriptures. Even Methuselah lived only 969 years (Genesis 5:27). How can "the youth will die at the age of one hundred" prove that men will live longer than Methuselah? On the contrary, Isaiah implies that the old man will "live out his days," but does not "live out his days" imply that he does die when his days are complete?

The conclusion that must be reached is that longevity will be restored to man, and that the phrase "the good die young" will no longer have meaning. Instead, they might say, "the bad die young." Men will live to reach the ages of the antediluvians, but there *will* be death. Death will not be abolished until the establishment of the New Heaven and the New Earth. Only there is it declared that "there shall no longer be *any* death."

Israel in the Millennium

In Acts 1:6 the disciples asked Jesus, "Lord, is it at this time that You will restore the kingdom to Israel?" It should be important for covenant theologians and amillennialists to note that Jesus *did not* say that he would not restore the kingdom to Israel, but that "it is not for you to know times or epochs which the Father has fixed by His own authority" (1:8). Nowhere in the Bible does the Lord deny that the promises made to *the nation* of Israel will be fulfilled. Covenant theologians, and amillennialists, have argued that the church has replaced Israel (see Appendix F), but the reader will be reminded that Romans 11:25-26 states that "a partial hardening has happened to Israel until the fulness of the Gentiles has come in; and thus all Israel will be saved." Indeed, *all* surviving Israel will literally be saved. This does not imply that Israel is not Israel, but that at the second coming all Jews who have survived to the end will be saved. When the Millennial Kingdom is ushered in, it will be to Jews, because the "the gifts and the calling of God *are irrevocable!*" (Romans 11:29). The idea that God's covenants to the Jews have been revoked is not Biblical. It is true that some covenants were conditional, but many of the covenants were *unconditional*. The God of Abraham does not lie. He is not a lawyer who tries to find loopholes or manipulate the meaning of a contract. Dwight Pentecost has written extensively upon each of the covenants God made to the Jews. He has shown that most of these covenants are indeed unconditional.[1276] James Brookes also insisted that the fact that these promises were unconditional meant that these covenants *will* be fulfilled in the future.[1277] Those who argue that the church will be the recepients of these promises are allowing their pride to fool themselves, even as the pride of the Jews once denied them eyes to recognize the Messiah. When the Millennial Kingdom begins, the "times of the Gentiles" will be passed. Gentiles will exist in the Millennial Kingdom (see below), but the Jews will have the seat of govenment and power.

The city of Jerusalem and the nation of Israel will be greatly enlarged in the Millennium. Ezekiel goes into great detail as to the size and dimensions of the new city and state (c.f Ezekiel 45 & 48). Isaiah 26:15 further attests to the enlarged boundaries of Israel's national borders. According to Merrill Unger the dimensions which Ezekiel records for the "holy oblation," a sacred portion of Jerusalem, would encompass over a thousand square miles for itself.[1278] Randall Price has similar calculations which would enlarge the "Prince's portion" of Jerusalem to over 2500 square miles![1279] The New Jerusalem, which will not exist until the Millennial age is passed, will actually be nearly as large as the entire continent of Europe (cf. Revelation 21:16). This Jerusalem of the Millennial age will not be as large, but it will far exceed the limits that it has ever known in this age.

Of course, such boundaries do indicate that separate nations will still exist in the Millennial age. Gentiles (surviving believers converted after the rapture) will enter the Millennial Kingdom along with the 144,000 and the believing Jews. We know this because Gog and Magag (Gentile hoards) are those specifically named as rebelling after the release of Satan (Revelation 20:8). These Gentile nations will exist beyong the enlarged boundaries of national Israel, and will willingly serve both God and Israel. This leads to the question of government. What kind of government will the Millennial Kingdom consist of?

Government in the Millennium
First and foremost the government of the Millennium will be a theocracy. Christ himself will rule over man (cf. 2 Samuel 7:16; Psalms 89:20-37; Isaiah 2:1-4, 9:6-7, 11:1-16, 16:5, 24:23, 32:3, 40:1-11. 42:3-4, 52:7-15, 55:4, Jeremiah 33:19-21; Daniel 2:44, 7:27; Micah 4:1-8, 5:2-5; Zechariah 9:9, 14:16-17; Revelation 19:16). It will, however, be a benevolent theocracy where justice, peace, and mercy will reign.

There has, however, been some debate to the role of King David. Many prophecies seem to imply that David himself will rule (cf. Jeremiah 30:9,

33:15-17; Ezeikiel 34:23-24; 37:24-25; Hosea 3:5; Isaiah 55:3-4; and Amos 9:11). Some believe that the "son of David" is intended. George Peters argues that the Messiah, or Christ, is to rule from the Davidic throne from the Davidic line. He cites, as proof of this assertion, the fact that "the immediate disciples and apostles held to this Messianic idea (i.e. Kingship over the restored Theocratic-Davidic Kingdom)."[1280]   Others, such as William Newell, take this literally, saying that the resurrected King David will rule Israel himself. According to William Newell, "David is not the son of David. Christ, as Son of David, will be King; and David, His father after the flesh, will be *prince*, during the Millennium."[1281] This difficulty is more easily resolved than might, at first, be presumed. As John Walvoord has noted, the title, "King of Kings, and Lord of Lords" "would certainly imply other rulers."[1282]   Indeed, the Bible is clear that the resurrected saints will rule *with* Christ during the Millennium (Revelation 20:4). Consequently, it is entirely possible that the resurrected David will rule Jerusalem as regent under Christ the King. This view is accepted by Dwight Pentecost, among many others, who lists its strengths. "(1) It is most consistent with the literal principle of interpretation. (2) David alone could sit as regent in the millennium without violating the prophecies concerning David's reign. (3) Resurrected saints are to have positions of responsibility in the millennium as a reward (Matt. 19:28; Luke 19:12-27)."[1283]

This leads to the next logical question. If believers are to reign with Christ, then how do mortals interact with immortal administrators. George Peters, in discussing the risen saints role in the Millennium, states, "the Theocratic king will also have His associated rulers assuring the most perfect administration of the laws, and securing the most perfect government, productive of peace, prosperity, and happiness, such as the world has never yet witnessed."[1284]   We shall then be the governors, judges, magistrates, and administrators, as well as other important positions in a just government. Some of us will be teachers, and some have suggested that we will also occupy the role of priests. Peters, for example, believes that if the saints are to be "kings and priests" (cf. Revelation 1:6) then both must be literal in the Millennium.[1285] However, others believe that the Levite Priesthood, made up of mortal Jews, must continue in the Millennium. Randall Price maintains that "the ancient promises to the Levitical priesthood cannot have a literal fulfillment unless Ezekiel's prophecy is eschatological."[1286]   In other words, the Levitical priesthood must be restored in the Millennial Kingdom itself. Of this, there seems little doubt. The religious practices of the Millennium, described below, show the Levitical priesthood serving in their traditional roles. It is possible that immortals may also serve some function within the priesthood (perhaps in Gentile countries), but more than likely the main role of immortals will be governmental.

There are several reasons for this. First, the government must be free from corruption. Peters even suggests that "the Kingdom is itself purposely delayed for thousands of years (long to man, but brief to God), in order to raise up this body of rulers to sustain it when manifested with a purity, dignity, power, stability, and glory worthy of a Theocracy."[1287]   The government, therefore, will be free from corruption and the abuse of power seen so prevalent today. Mortals, however, will not be free from the bondage of sin, even in the Millennium.   This is one reason that the priesthood will continue to offer sacrifices for sins in the Millennium (see below). If mortal man sins, then it is mortal man who must repent of those sins.   In this function, the Levitical priesthood must remain composed of mortals, yet it is this very fact creates the most controversial issue of all ... how can there be sacrifices in the Millennium when Christ's sacrifice was sufficient for all?

Religion in the Millennium
Ezekiel 40-48 has created more contention than most any other issue in the Millennial debate. The problem is that Ezekiel's descriptions of the Temple and the sacrifices do not fit history, and, if future, appear to conflict with Christian theology, inasmuch as it depicts animal sacrifices long after Christ's death atoned for man's sins, "once for all" (Romans 6:10).

That the vision of Ezekiel cannot, and should not, be applied to history is granted by virtually all premillennialists. The temple dimensions described therein are far different from the dimensions of any of the previous temples built by Solomon, Zerubbabel, or Herod.[1288] Moreover, the geographical description does not fit history either. For example, Ezekiel describes a river flowing from the temple, but a river "has never flowed from any of the three historical temples."[1289] Some have argued that the vision of Ezekiel is what the Jews were supposed to have built following their return from Babylon, but that the plans of Ezekiel were not followed as they were supposed to have.   Price admits that "although it is reasonable to assume that the builders of Zerubbabel's Temple would have employed these plans, it is obvious that they did not."[1290]   In fact, they *could* not because "geographical changes will be necessary prior to the fulfillment of chapters 45, 47-48."[1291] Finally, Ezekiel's prophecy is just that; a prophecy. It is not a suggestion, but a vision of the future. Consequently, only three choices remain.

The first argues that the temple is mere allegory for the church. Arno Gaebelein says of this, "this is the weakest of all and yet the most accepted."[1292] Doubtless, it is so easily accepted because it is the easiest out, but it offers no explanation for the specifics of the prophecy. To say that the temple is a symbol of the church might be feasible, but only if an adequate explanation can be given for the elaborate measurements and details.   A symbol, by definition, is one thing representing another. If there is a desciption of the one item, then each part described must also represent a part of the item it is representing. Any cursory examination of Ezekiel's prophecy shows that the descriptions are of a real and literal temple. No symbolism can be found for statements like, "so he measured the thickness of the wall, one rod; and the height, one rod. Then he went to the gate which faced east, went up its steps, and measured the threshold of the gate, one rod in width; and the other threshold *was* one rod in width. And the guardroom *was* one rod long and one rod wide ..." (Ezekiel 40:5-7). These precise measurements and descriptive phrases continue on for chapters. Symbolism is not intended here. Says Jon Levenson, "the highly specific nature of the description of the Temple, its liturgy and community bespeaks a practical program, not a vision of pure grace."[1293] Two views remain.

Some have suggested that the temple is a vision of a heavenly temple in the New Jerusalem. This view is most obviously flawed in that the Bible explicitly states there is no temple in the eternal state "for the Lord God, the Almighty, and the Lamb, are its temple" (Revelation 21:22).

One view thus remains. This is a literal temple in the Millennial Kingdom. "Ezekiel sets forth two major purposes for the millennial temple. First, the temple will provide a throne for God among his people (43:6-7), the residency of his glory (43:1-12) from which he will rule over his people. Second, the temple complex will reflect God's holiness."[1294] The *sole* objection which is levied against this view is that it would negate the sacrifice of Christ. Certainly, if true, then the view should be completely discarded and considered "blasphemy" as many have claimed.[1295] As one critic remarked, "Jesus Christ is the only Mediator, His blood the final sacrifice. There can be no going back. If there is a way back to the ceremonial law, to the type and shadows of what has now become the bondage of legalism, then Paul labored and ran in vain – more than that, Christ died in vain."[1296] Such stark words must be addressed.

This author correctly states that Hebrews calls the ancient sacrifices shadows and types of the coming sacrifice of Christ, but fails to see that the statement, "for it is impossible for the blood of bulls and goats to take away sins" (Hebrews 10:4), is *not* new to the New Testament. He implies that animal sacrifices are no longer valid, but ignores that they were *never* sufficient for the remission of sins (cf. Isaiah 1:11, 34:6; Jeremiah 11:15). Nowhere does the Bible teach that animal sacrifices were sufficient to atone for man's sins. That is precisely why the author of Hebrews makes his remark. He does not presume to contradict the Old Testament, but to explain it. More importantly, the similarities to Old Testament sacrifices are not as meaningful as the differences. The differences are many.

As Nathaniel West demonstrates, in the Millennial Temple "there is no Ark of the Covenant, no Pot of Manna, no Aaron's rod to bud, no Tables of the Law, no Cherubim, no Mercy-Seat, no Golden Candlestick, no Shew-bread, no Veil, no unapproachable Holy of Holies where the High-Priest alone might enter, nor is there any High-Priest to offer atonement to take away sin, or to make intercession for the people."[1297] Instead, the Prince will be present during the sacrifices (Ezekiel 45:16). It is has been debated whether or not this prince is Jesus, David, or a representative of the Lord. Since the prince is said to present a sin offereing in Ezekiel 45:22, it is probably best to take the prince as a subordinate, whether David or another. In either case, there is no sacrifice offered *as* the remission of sins in the Millennial temple. Christ's sacrifice was sufficient, and *no* Christian denies this. "The sacrifices *will be memorial* in character."[1298] If memorial, is this not a "retrogression" as some argue? No, "if the system is planned by God as a memorial of Jesus Christ, it can no more be said to be a retrogression to the 'weak and beggarly elements' than the bread and wine can be said to be weak and beggarly memorials of the broken body and shed blood of Christ."[1299]

There is no doubt that the sacrificial system that is recorded in Ezekiel creates difficulties, but those difficulties apply mainly to this age or dispensation.[1300] To argue that memorial sacrifices *cannot* take place, is presumption. Furthermore, it assumes that the Millennial Kingdom is a continuation of the church age, when it is, in fact, a new dispensation for the restoration and purification of the nation of Israel. Each dispensation looks for the same result, but they do not require the same system. Each acknowledges that Christ's blood *alone* was given *as* a sacrifice of atonement, but each memorializes it in its own way. Christ Himself will be present in the Millennium. It is therefore natural to assume that a memorial to Him will be more real. When the blood of an animal is poured out, the realness of the blood will emphasize all the more the realness of His sacrifice; far more than wine and bread.

The End of the Millennium

"And when the thousand years are completed, Satan will be released from his prison, and will come out to deceive the nations which are in the four corners of the earth, Gog and Magog, to gather them together for the war; the number of them is like the sand of the seashore. And they came up on the broad plain of the earth and surrounded the camp of the saints and the beloved city, and fire came down from heaven and devoured them. And the devil who deceived them was thrown into the lake of fire and brimstone, where the beast and the false prophet are also; and they will be tormented day and night forever and ever." (Revelation 20:7-10).

The most disinguishing feature of the Millennial Kingdom is that it ends in revolt. Despite a thousand years of peace and harmony and justice, man will again rebel against God after Satan's release. It is the grand proof that man, in his heart, is still rebellious. While Satan is bound, the one who has not accepted the Lord in his heart will continue to live accordingly at peace with his brother, but when Satan is released, and these men have a leader to follow, they will rebel.

259

How much time elapses between the release of Satan and the final rebellion is not known. This rebellion might occur within a year of Satan's release, or it may be many decades later. If history is any gauge then it is apparent that Satan's deceit does not require long periods of time, but neither is there reason to believe that the rebellion is immediate. There is likely to be a period of time during which Christ will continue to rule with justice and mercy, but during which crime and sin will progressively increase. Satan will blame God, convincing the faithless that God cannot protect them, and stirring up the hearts of the faithless against the Lord.

One question is the identity of Gog and Magog, who are specifically identified with the rebels (Revelation 20:8). They are by no means the only tribes who participate in the rebellion, but they do seem to be the predominant tribes. There has been much confusion as to Gog and Magog (see Appendix C), but some facts remain. Since the Millennial Kingdom will be predominantly Israeli, and since the geography of the earth will change dramatically, Gog and Magog must here be different from the Russian tribes spoken of elsewhere in the Bible (see Appendix C). There will be Gentiles in the Millennium, and some will be from the stock of Gog and Magog. Their descendants are, therefore, those to whom this passage refers. This means that the Gentile tribes will lead the revolt. It does not mean that some Jews do not participate, or other Gentile tribes for that matter, but Gog and Magog appear to be the main group. This is both ironic and just, for even as Jews have traditionally rejected Christ as Messiah in the church age, Gentiles will reject Jesus the Messiah in the Millennial age where Israel is given prominence. This is further attested by the fact that Satan goes out "to deceive the nations" (Revelation 20:8). The word "nations" is, in fact, the meaning of "Gentile." The Greek word ἔθνη (ethne) can be translated as either Gentiles or nations, and is used for both words in the New Testament. The Hebrew word וֹי (goy) is also synonymous with either nation or Gentile.

Of course, it cannot be assumed that only Gentiles revolt, but it is clear that the rebels are gathered from across the globe, beyond the boundaries of Israel. When the rebels reach the city of Jerusalem their destruction is both immediate and complete. With their destruction the Millennial Kingdom ends, and God introduces the New Heavens and the New Earth.

The New Heaven and New Earth

Contrary to those who argue that so-called "apocalyptic literature" invented the idea of a New Heaven and New Earth,[1301] the New Heaven and New Earth were anticipated in Isaiah (65:17 and 66:22). It is also mentioned in 2 Peter's controversial passage:

"The day of the Lord will come like a thief, in which the heavens will pass away with a roar and the elements will be destroyed with intense heat, and the earth and its works will be burned up. Since all these things are to be destroyed in this way, what sort of people ought you to be in holy conduct and godliness, looking for and hastening the coming of the day of God, on account of which the heavens will be destroyed by burning, and the elements will melt with intense heat! But according to His promise we are looking for new heavens and a new earth, in which righteousness dwells" (3:10-13).

This passage has presented problems for some scholars. It appears here that the very *elements* will melt away and the very heavens will pass away. This would imply that Revelation 21:1 is to be taken literally when it says, "the first heaven and the first earth passed away." The apostolic father, Clement of Rome, may have accepted this view when he connected the day of judgment with "the earth as lead melting on the fire."[1302] However, some insist that the earth will never pass away. Arthur Bloomfield had said, "there is no record or suggestion here that the earth is to be destroyed by fire at the end of the Millennium. It is God's purpose to redeem the earth, not to destroy it. That which is redeemed is not destroyed."[1303] These scholars offer Solomon's words as proof; "A generation goes and a generation comes, but the earth remains forever" (Ecclesiastes 1:4). They also believe that God's promise to Noah, "I will never again destroy every living thing" (Genesis 8:21), negates this.

Joseph Seiss says that "in those passages which speak of the *passing away* of the earth and heavens (see Matt. 5:18, 24, 34, 35; Mark 13:30, 31; Luke 16:17, 21, 33; 2 Pet. 3:10, Rev. 21:1), the original word is never one which signifies termination of existence, but παρερχομαι, which is a verb of very wide general meaning, such as *to go* or *come* to a person ... as a ship through a sea; to pass from one place or condition to another."[1304] He admits, however, that "some texts, particularly as they appear in our English Bible, express this change very strongly, as where the earth and heavens are spoken of as *perishing*, and being *dissolved, flying away* (Is. 34:4; 54:10; Rev. 6:14; 20:10)."[1305] This he discounts by quoting Peter's reference to the antediluvian world which "perished."[1306] Arthur Bloomfield also supports this theory, saying, "some have supposed that the references to fire and the destruction of the earth in II Peter 3 teach that the earth is to be destroyed at the end of the Millennium. But everything that Peter says in this chapter is fulfilled by the seven last plagues."[1307]

Are these arguments legitimate? It is true that 2 Peter 3 speaks of the Day of the Lord coming like a thief (vs. 10), and this phrase is often found in relation to the tribulation. However, it has already been demonstrated that the "Day of the Lord" may be understood as any time of judgment; not merely the tribulation. That it comes like a thief is obvious by the fact that the armies of Gog and Magog are destroyed in an instant after surrounding the great city. Had they known, or realized, what was awaiting them, they might have chosen a better tactic. Nevertheless, Satan has deceived them, and fire reigns down on them (20:9). Is this the same fire that 2 Peter 3 talks about? Is this fire that is spoken of in the last seven plagues as Bloomfield believes. The key is in the destruction of the very "elements." Seiss has said that "there is no evidence that a single atom of matter has ever been annihilated,"[1308] but scientist Henry Morris interprets the elements as refering to atomic structure. Whether a single atom has ever been annihilated in the past or not, "second Peter 3:10 prophesies that ... all the atomic structure of the earth [is] permitted to disintegrate instantly into other forms of energy – sound, heat, and fire."[1309]

In respect to the arguments against the complete destruction of the earth it may be said that these same elements may be used in the creation of the new earth. Norman Harrison argues "a new creation God does not necessarily start *de novo;* ... It will be made 'new' in every essential respect. New laws will rule the universe. Great changes will result."[1310] Henry Morris also believes that the new earth is a "renewal" of the old:

> "The first heavens and earth had been contaminated by sin, with the very elements in bondage to God's curse. The only way they could be completely cleansed was to be completely renewed. 'All these things' had to be 'dissolved,' with the elements melting in fervent heat (2 Peter 3:10-12). By the principle of mass/energy conservation, however, nothing had been really lost, except the effects and evidences of sin. After terrestrial matter had been converted either into the vapor state or, more probably, into pure energy, God had once again exercised His mighty powers of creation and integration, and the new heavens and new earth had appreared out of the ashes, so to speak, of the old."[1311]

Thus, the old earth has truly passed away, but the elements, or atoms, of the old have been renewed to form the New Earth. This earth will doubtless be similar in character, save that the laws of the universe will be altered. Death and sin will no longer reign (Revelation 21:4), and this final Kingdom, which many consider an extension of the Millennial Kingdom, will never end. One other unique distinguishing feature, however, is the absence of the sea. The Greek and Hebrew words for sea can be translated as either ocean or sea (since the ancients did not distinguish between them). James Brookes insist that "the sea here is to be understood literally."[1312] It may be remembered that creationists believe that before the flood of Noah, the oceans were not as large as they now are. Over two thirds of the earth's surface are now covered with water. Although populous control advocates claim that the earth is overpopulated, conservative estimates believe that the current earth could easily sustain 20 billion. With the addition of over two thirds of the earth's surface made available for population and colonization, the New Earth could easily hold every believer who has every lived on earth with no crowding whatsoever (it is said that there were as many people living in the 20th century as had lived in the whole of human history).

In addition, the New Heaven and New Earth lack the sun and the moon, for "the Lord God shall illuminate them" (Revelation 22:5). Finally, and most importantly, is the New Jerusalem; the great city of gold and glass, where the tree of life will reside, and were access is granted to all (Revelation 21:10-27). The city itself will be as large as Europe and all believers will come there to eat of the tree of life, and drink from the river of life (Revelation 22:1-2).

CHAPTER SUMMARY

The critic notes that Jesus said "my kingdom is not of this world" (John 18:36), but ignores that the kingdom of which is here spoken is not of this world, but the world to come. It is ironic that those who reject a literal kingdom on the basis that it would be materialistic are the same ones who see the kingdom of God here on earth right now! Is this world not materialistic? They can say that the kingdom is only "spiritual" but this is the old Platonic myth that pretends the spiritual realm has no bearing on the physical. The kingdom of God is both spiritual and physical, but not in this world; in the world to come. That is the hope of man. Revelation 20 teaches us the following:

1. In the Millennial Kingdom nature will be restored to a state similar to that of Eden. Animals will no longer be carnivorous but will leave in harmony with man and other animals. The ground will be fertile and grow crops more easily. The deserts of the world will disappear.
2. Man's longevity will be restored to the ante-diluvian state, but he will not live a full thousand years. He will live many hundreds of years and "live out his days", but both the righteous and unrighteous will die as sin will still exist.
3. The Millennial Kingdom will be a true theocracy ruled by Christ and his ministers who will include the resurrected and raptured saints. As such immortal saints will rule with Christ over mortal men in the Millennium.
4. The Temple of Jerusalem will exist and offer memorial sacrifices honoring Jesus and His one true sacrifice. The Millennial Kingdom is not the New Heaven and New Earth.
5. At then end of the thousand year kingdom Satan will be released from prison and will deceive the faithless. Those who had formerly been obedient but not faithful in their hearts will now rebel in the same way that Satan and his angels rebelled, but they will be destroyed.
6. The old world will then be destroyed with fire and God will create a New Heaven and a New Earth where there will be no more pain, or suffering, or death.

Appendix A

—

Rapture Theories

Implicit in the discussion of Revelation have been references to one of the most controversial of issues: the rapture. Not only is the rapture contested, but its chronology features prominently into many of the views presented throughout this book. It is a prophecy which most believe is not found in the book of Revelation itself, but which is connected to its prophecies so directly that the very word "rapture" is associated with the beginning of the tribulations described therein.

Christians have readily recognized that many Jews at the time of Jesus failed to recognize Him as Messiah because they had misinterpreted the Old Testament prophecies of the Messiah. The Old Testament describes the Messiah coming to redeem man, coming to judge man, and to establish the Davidic Kingdom. Many Jews saw this as one event, but as Christians we know that there are actually two separate events: the first and the second coming. This same problem appears in the New Testament in regard to prophecies of the second coming. Are their actually two separate events; the rapture and the return?

There is no single issue more controversial in premillennial studies than the issue of the rapture. This is not a surprise since the rapture itself is "a mystery," first clearly revealed by Paul in 1 Corinthians and later in 1 Thessalonians. Although many believe it was taught by Jesus, it was often confused with the second coming. Indeed, it is for this very reason that Paul calls it a mystery and revealed its nature to the Thessalonians who had been misled by false teachers concerning the prophecy of the second coming. Nevertheless, it would seem that many modern day scholars would have wished that Paul could have been a tad more lucid in his description of the rapture, or rather the time of the rapture. It will be observed, however, that it is not Paul's, or Christ's, lack of clarity that is the source of the problem, but the nature of prophecy and mystery.

What Is The Rapture?

The first question may rightly be: what is the rapture? Literally, the rapture refers to Christ taking living Christians from the earth and transforming our mortal bodies into immortal resurrected bodies. It is what happens to those who are alive when the Lord comes for them; to those who will not experience death. This much is generally agreed upon. Even early Protestant commentators such as Matthew Henry acknolwedge this event and call it "the rapture,"[1313] although he was not a true premillennialist. Saint Augustine also referred to the rapture.[1314] There is no doubt of its existence in the Bible, only of its exact timing and meaning.

The first explicit reference to the rapture occurs in 1 Corinthians. Paul debates with those who denied the resurrection of the dead. He emphatically states that the dead will be raised and given immortal bodies. He then follows this discussion up by saying:

> "Behold, I tell you a mystery; we shall not all sleep, but we shall all be changed, in a moment, in the twinkling of an eye, at the last trumpet; for the trumpet will sound, and the dead will be raised imperishable, and we shall be changed. For this perishable must put on the imperishable, and this mortal must put on immortality" (1 Corinthians 15:51-53).

It should be noted that the term "sleep" here is used by Christ and the apostles to refer to death. Just as some today use respectful terms such as "pass away" or "his final rest," so the apostles referred to death as "sleep," for the dead are awaiting Christ, who will awaken them and give them a resurrected, immortal body. This statement alludes to a rapture from the body, but while it does say that the rapture is connected to the "last trumpet," it does not clarify exactly when this trumpet sounds.

In Paul's first letter to the Thessalonians he takes issue with those who are confused about, or deny, the second coming of Christ. Some were worried about their dead friends, believing that they might never see them again. Paul comforts them by the following assurance:

> "We do not want you to be uninformed, brethren, about those who are asleep, so that you may not grieve, as do the rest who have no hope. For if we believe that Jesus died and rose again, even so God will bring with Him those who have fallen asleep in Jesus. For this we say to you by the word of the Lord, that we who are alive, and remain until the coming of the Lord, will not precede those who have fallen asleep. For the Lord Himself will descend from heaven with a shout, with the voice of *the* archangel, and with the trumpet of God; and the dead in Christ shall rise first. Then we who are alive and remain will be caught up together with them in the clouds to meet the Lord in the air, and thus we shall always be with the Lord. Therefore comfort one another with these words." (1 Thessalonians 4:13-18)

For the first time Paul seems to give some indication of *when* this rapture or change occurs outside of the trumpet blast. It is apparent that this will occur in connection with the Day of the Lord. Indeed, this was the very question that the Thessalonians were struggling with, for some were teaching that the Day of the Lord had already come,[1315] leaving them to wonder when and how the resurrection would occur.

When Paul says "we who are alive and remain until the coming of the Lord," he is contrasting with those Christians who have died in centuries past. Nevertheless, he states that we "will not precede those who have fallen asleep," but rather, we "will be caught up together with them in the clouds to meet the Lord in the air." In other words, those of us who are still alive will receive our immortal bodies immediately after Christ has resurrected the dead, for "the dead in Christ shall rise first."

This event is universally called the "rapture." This Latin term was used even by the Reformers in reference to this verse, although few at the time developed any sophisticated theology concerning the rapture. What is pertinent here is that the doctrine of the rapture itself is denied by very few, and even mentioned by the allegorist Saint Augustine.[1316] Those who hold to a literal interpretation of Scripture are in full agreement as to the general meaning of this verse. The fundamental question that has arisen in recent years is not "what is the rapture," but "when is the rapture?"

It is certain that this event is said to occur in connection with the coming of our Lord Jesus, but other Biblical passages lead the reader to believe that this rapture is separate from the second coming. This is most evident in Jesus' Olivet Discourse where He sometimes speaks of His return as "coming at an hour when you do not think He will" (Matthew 24:44) while at other times it is said that "the sign of the Son of Man will appear in the sky, and then all the tribes of the earth will mourn, and they will see the Son of Man coming on the clouds of the sky with power and great glory" (Matthew 24:30). In other words, does Christ return specifically at Armageddon or is it that the "day and hour no one knows, not even the angels of heaven, nor the Son, but the Father alone" (Matthew 24:36)? Certainly there *appears* to be a disparity in Jesus' discussion of His second coming, but can this be explained by the fact that Jesus was speaking of two separate events: rapture and the second coming?

The ultimate debate concerning the rapture is, therefore, *when* does it occur. Is the rapture a second event of the second coming? Is it an early "phase"[1317] of the second coming?

The book of Revelation is usually considered to cover a seven-year time frame.[1318] This period is generally referred to as the "tribulation" based on Jesus' statements in Matthew 24:21 and other parallel passages. The predominant views of the rapture are 1) the "pretribulational" rapture view which believes the rapture will occur *before* this tribulation begins, 2) the "posttribulational" rapture which holds that the rapture will occur at the *end* of the tribulation, 3) the "pre-wrath" rapture theory which supposes that the rapture will occur sometime in *the latter half* of the tribulation, 4) the "midtribulational" rapture theory which places the rapture in the *middle* of the tribulation, and 5) the "partial rapture" theory that presumes that different people will be raptured

267

at various times *throughout* the tribulation. In addition to these views, there are a few slight variant views that will also be discussed.

Is There A Rapture?

The reality and existence of rapture is accepted by virtually all premillennialists. Since it is not the purpose of this book to debate those who are not premillennialists, there will not be a substantial amount of space devoted to refuting those who deny the reality of the rapture. However, the confusion surrounding the rapture demands at least a brief response.

There are those who deny the very existence of rapture. They hold that 1 Thessalonians is either allegory, a reference to the second coming itself, or a vague description of the resurrection. These scholars argue that the doctrine of the rapture was never taught or believed in until the 1800s, and many claim that rapture was invented by John Darby, a prominent theologian who helped coin the term "dispensational theology" (see Appendix F). Is this argument true? If it were then one might well question its validity. Nonetheless, this argument is fallacious. Indeed, even these critics argue amongst themselves as to whom they say really invented rapture. There are those who attribute the rapture to Margaret MacDonald, Emmanuel Lacunza, or Edward Irving.[1319] This in itself indicates that the rapture was diversely taught at this time or else critics could at least come to an agreement as to who invented it! A more detailed study, however, will show that rapture studies have their origins many centuries before.

First, *specific* references to *a pre-Armageddon rapture* can be found as far back as the fourth century A.D. The church father Ephraem the Syrian said "all saints and the Elect of the Lord are gathered together before the tribulation which is about to come and are taken to the Lord, in order that they may not see at any time the confusion which overwhelms the world because of our sins."[1320] Ephraem gives a detailed explanation of the tribulation which parallels much of pretribulational premillennialism. Nevertheless, others have argued that Ephraem's statements are midtribulational or even pre-wrath. In either case, it must be accepted that at least one church father anticipated a rapture *before* the second coming.

It is also argued that the other church fathers taught something similar to rapture under the term "imminency." Nonetheless, this is a controversial argument and will be left for later discussion. Only clear references to a pre-Armageddon rapture will be cited here. Two such references are from the time of the American Revolution. Renowned theologian John Gill's commentary on Thessalonians is clear. Gill's comments may not be pretribulational, but they certainly teach a rapture distinct from the second coming.[1321] Since he was a historicist, who stretched the events of Revelation over thousands of years, the problem is compounded, but Baptist Minister Morgan Edwards rejected traditional historicism and explicitly taught that the

268

rapture spoken of in Thessalonians "will be about three years and a half before the millennium."[1322]   Although some might suggest this is a midtribulational view, which is possible, there were a number of scholars who believed Revelation was about a three and a half year period, not seven. In either case, rapture was clearly taught before Darby popularized the view.

While it is true that specific references to a pretribulational or midtribulational rapture are rare, it must be remembered that the Catholic Church burned and destroyed many of writings of those who opposed the church throughout the dark ages. The Reformation is often considered a "rediscovery"[1323] of many of the Biblical doctrines that had taken back stage over the centuries. Certainly the pre and/or midtribulational rapture positions did exist *at least* in the fourth century and were "rediscovered" by *at least* the 1700s.

More importantly, without regard for the time issue, which is the predominant controversy of the rapture, there can be no doubt to the objective observer that the rapture was clearly taught throughout history and in the writings of the Reformers. Famed Reformer and expositor Matthew Henry says of 1 Thessalonians 4:17, "this *rapture* into the clouds, those who are alive will undergo a mighty change" (emphasis mine).[1324] The Reformers' interpretation of the verse was identical to that held by premillennialists today *except* in respect to the time question. Matthew Henry says of the rapture, "this change is so mysterious that we cannot comprehend it."[1325] Henry did not attempt to define the time period in which the rapture would occur simply because he saw no need of it. To the Reformers it was a mystery which was a part of the prophecies of the second coming, and, therefore, considered folly to attempt to clarify the mystery of God. They believed that only God could answer the question when the event itself occurred.

It may also be observed that the very term rapture could be found as far back as Augustine. According to Reformer Matthew Poole, "Augustine imagined that the saints that are found alive shall in their rapture die, and then immediately revive."[1326] This unique interpretation of the rapture shows that even in the early Middle Ages, the rapture was already a controversial subject. What is relevant is that the doctrine of the rapture itself, without reference to time, can be traced back *by name* at least to Augustine if not before.

Finally, even in the time of the church fathers, it cannot be said with objectivity that they did not teach the rapture. Critics of the rapture will argue that there is no reference to the rapture made by the church fathers. However, their argument is that because the church fathers did not use the word "rapture" they did not believe in the rapture. This is an illogical argument. To begin with, the argument that their failure to use the word "rapture" proves that they did not believe in it is specious for this would be attempting to prove an assumption using that very assumption. This is especially true since the word "rapture" is derived from the Latin, and not the Greek. Moreover, many of the writings of the church fathers have not survived, and few complete Bible commentaries by the church fathers exist, so that those critics do not really have sufficient evidence to make their claim.

Many authors have shown that the church fathers preached the doctrine of "imminence" which they believe is only compatible with a rapture belief. There can be no doubt that the church fathers taught and believed in this doctrine. Whether or not this doctrine of imminence is an allusion to the rapture will be discussed in the critique of pretribulationism. Nevertheless, it must be confirmed that the church fathers did speak of Christ's return in two manners. They speak of Christ returning *for* the church and of Christ returning *with* the church,[1327] just as the Bible does. Moreover, at least one, Ephraem the Syrian, appears to make an explicit reference to the rapture.

So if the church fathers taught rapture, what happened to the teaching? Did the medieval scholars abandon it altogether? No, even the medievals accepted a variant view of the rapture.

A Medieval Rapture

Reformer Matthew Poole makes a reference to an ancient view of rapture which he attributed to St. Augustine.[1328] Such an interpretation is brought up to show that the doctrine of the rapture has evolved, but not substantially changed over the centuries. It is only because interest in end times prophecy has been generated over the past two hundred years that studies in the rapture have developed to an intricate level. While it is possible that the church fathers had a better understanding of the rapture than is often attributed to them, their surviving texts only attest to the rapture in terms of the doctrine of imminency. That the medievals spoke of the rapture in a non-controversial manner is further attestation to the fact that this was not a new doctrine. Nevertheless, some medieval scholars did understand the rapture in a different manner than is usually attributed to it today.

According to Poole, some Augustinians believed that when the rapture occurs, our mortal bodies would not be taken with us. Rather than our mortal bodies being transformed into the immortal, he took it to mean that our souls will leave our bodies, leaving them dead in the streets, and we will immediately be given new immortal bodies in heaven with Christ.[1329] Such an event would certainly be as dramatic and earthshaking as the rapture of the body, for the earth would see countless millions of people evidently dropping dead for no apparent reason. Such an event would have as great a political and social impact on the governments of the earth as would the sudden disappearance of millions of people.

270

This was view also held by some of the Protestant Reformers although many were already subscribing to the doctrine that our bodies will themselves be changed. One argument for this view might be the Biblical edict "it is appointed for men to die once" (Hebrews 9:27). Since some believe that this edict cannot be altered, the passages in question, it is argued, must refer to the snatching of our souls out of bodies, and leaving the bodies behind; dead.[1330] The central problem with this exegesis is that it cannot be viewed as an absolute. Obviously, Lazarus and the little girl were resurrected by Jesus (Matthew 9:24, Mark 5:39, Luke 8:51, and John 11:11), thus destined to die a second time, while Elijah and Enoch did not die. The passage must be taken as a general statement, not a universal and unalterable edict for each and every man.

The real problem with Augustine's view is that Paul clearly states "we shall not all sleep" (1 Corinthians 15:51). Sleep is universally seen as a synonym for death. As we might say someone has "passed away" or is "at rest," the apostles and Jesus referred to death as "sleep" (cf. Matthew 9:24, Mark 5:39, Luke 8:51, and John 11:11). Paul then continues, "we shall all be changed, in a moment, in the twinkling of an eye, at the last trumpet; for the trumpet will sound, and the dead will be raised imperishable, and we shall be changed. For this perishable must put on the imperishable, and this mortal must put on immortality" (1 Corinthians 15:51-53). Thus, the *mortal* flesh will be transformed to *immortal* flesh. Is the mortal flesh discarded on the earth? Not if it is literally transformed. So the question is then what does "changed" ($\dot{\alpha}\lambda\lambda\alpha\gamma\eta\sigma\acute{o}\mu\epsilon\theta\alpha$) mean? William Thayer list the root meaning as "to exchange one thing for another"[1331] or "to transform."[1332] Another dictionary list a possible meaning as "alter."[1333] Consequently, we are not left with a firm answer.

Despite the compatibility of Augustine's theory, it has been rejected by all modern premillennialists. It is universally accepted today as a transformation, not an exchange. One support for this is the empty tomb of Jesus. Jesus received His new immortal body at His resurrection but the old decaying body did not remain behind. In fact, His resurrected body even contained the scars from the nails which pinned Him to the cross. While Jesus certainly could have eliminated the scars, He left them as a reminder to men of what He did for them. Nevertheless, the point is that Jesus' old body did not remain behind.

Others might argue, however, that such a teaching is steeped in old mysticism. In all fairness, one reason that the bodies of "heretics" were burned in the Middle Ages was precisely because they believed there would be no body to be resurrected. They felt that if the body was burned and the ashes scattered then the body could not be reassembled for resurrection. However, this was simply a medieval myth and was not held by most theologians, even in the dark ages. It does, however, beg the question. If we do not really need our old

271

bodies to be glorified with immortal ones then does Christ need to take our bodies with us at the rapture? The answer is simply that Christ has no *need* of anything but what He chooses is what will be done. The mystery of the rapture is just that, a mystery. It has been revealed to us so that we might have hope. The promise of rapture seems to imply a transformation, rather than discarding of our old bodies. Whether our bodies remain behind or are transformed is largely irrelevant. All that is essential is that Christ will keep His promise and give us a glorified resurrected body that will be immortal and free from decay and sin. This promise He will keep.

Thus it has been thoroughly demonstrated that the rapture has been taught throughout the ages. That there is a rapture taught in Scripture is not disputed among evangelicals. Indeed, the fact that rapture is a logical conclusion based on a straightforward, or literal, interpretation is born out by amillennial critics. Over a hundred and fifty years ago, one amillennial critic attacked premillennialism on the basis of the order of resurrections found in Revelation. He stated that premillennialism cannot work because "there can be no further resurrection or translation after the Advent, except there be still two Advents of the Lord in the future."[1334] Thus, the critics must themselves admit that two comings, called the rapture and the return by evangelicals, must occur if the Bible is to be taken literally.

The only real question concerning the rapture is when it occurs in reference to the tribulation. Premillennialists are all agreed that there is a rapture but the dividing point is when it will occur. It has been stated that there is no eschatological issue more agreed upon than second coming.[1335] It is, therefore, ironic that there is arguably no one issue more disagreed upon than the rapture and when it will occur.

Pretribulation Rapture

Pretribulationism maintains that the second coming of Christ occurs in two separate phases. The first phase concerns Christ's coming *for* the church to spare them the coming wrath. The second phase is when Christ returns *with* the church in order to judge the world and establish the Millennial Kingdom. The first phase occurs at the *beginning* of the seven-year tribulation. The second, obviously, occurs at the end of the tribulation when the battle of Armageddon is raging on Earth.

The most fundamental issue for most rapturists is the presupposition that the Bible speaks of two separate events in regard to the second coming. This presupposition is fundamental to pretribulationism, midtribulationism, and the pre-wrath view. In each case, the rapture must be seen as a clearly distinct event from the second coming with some time laying between the two events.

Edward Hindson has summarized the prominent differences (with their corresponding passages) which show the distinctions between the rapture and the second coming:[1336]

Rapture	The Return
Christ comes *for* His own (John 14:3, 1 Thess. 4:17, 2 Thess. 2:1)	Christ comes *with* His own (1 Thess. 3:13, Jude 14, Rev. 19:14)
He comes in the *air* (1 Thess. 4:17)	He comes to the *earth* (Zech. 14:4, Acts 1:11)
He *claims* His bride (1 Thess. 4:16-17)	He comes *with* His bride (Rev 19:6-14)
Removal of *believers* (1 Thess. 4:17)	Manifestation of *Christ* (Mal. 4:2)
Only His own see Him (1 Thess. 4:13-18)	*Every eye* shall see Him (Rev. 1:7)
Tribulation begins (2 Thess. 1:6-9)	Millennial Kingdom begins (Rev. 20:1-7)
Saved are *delivered from wrath* (1 Thess. 1:10; 5:9)	Unsaved *experience the wrath* of God (Rev. 6:12-17)
No signs precede rapture (1 Thess. 5:1-3)	*Signs* precede second coming (Luke 21:11, 15)
Focus: *Lord and the Church* (1 Thess. 4:13-18)	Focus: *Israel and the kingdom* (Matthew 24:14)
World is deceived (2 Thess. 2:3-12)	*Satan* is bound (Rev. 20:1-2)

Certainly a few of the passages could be debated but the above chart is as accurate and complete as this author has seen. The differences shown cannot be resolved flippantly. If these verses all referred to the same event rather than two distinct events then these differences would be irreconcilable and the prophecies of Christ would be filled with contradictions.

Thomas Ice has charted the various second coming verses as follows:[1337]

Chart on the Passages for Rapture and the Return

Rapture Passages		Passages of the Second Coming	
John 14:1-3	2 Thessalonians 2:1	Daniel 2:44-45	Acts 1:9-11
Romans 8:19	1 Timothy 6:14	Daniel 7:9-14	Acts 3:19-21
1 Corinthians 1:7-8	2 Timothy 4:1	Daniel 12:1-3	1 Thessalonians 3:13
1 Corinthians 15:51-53	Titus 2:13	Zechariah 14:1-15	2 Thessalonians 1:6-10
1 Corinthians 16:22	Hebrews 9:28	Matthew 13:41	2 Thessalonians 2:8
Philippians 3:20-21	James 5:7-9	Matthew 24:15-31	2 Peter 3:1-4
Colossians 3:4	1 Peter 1:7,13	Matthew 26:64	Jude 14-15
1 Thessalonians 1:10	1 John 2:28-3:2	Mark 13:14-17	Revelation 1:7
1 Thessalonians 2:19	Jude 21	Mark 14:62	Revelation 19:11-20:6
1 Thessalonians 4:13-18	Revelation 2:25	Luke 21:25-28	Revelation 22:7, 12, 20
1 Thessalonians 5:9	Revelation 3:10		
1 Thessalonians 5:23			

Again, one could argue with some of these decisions for, indeed, it is sometimes hard to distinguish between the two events. This is the very problem. The rapture is what Paul called "a mystery" (1 Corinthians 15:51). By its very definition, one cannot see the difference unless he looks for it by faith. The rapture is a mystery and a promised hope for the church.

Why is it a "blessed hope," as it is often called? The answer is another critical defense of the pretribulational interpretation. One must ask why is there a rapture separate from the second coming at all. There are actually several answers to this question, but the one which seems to be the most critical is God's promise to spare the church from coming wrath.

Pretribulationism and the Coming Wrath

Many passages of Scripture promise believers that they will not be the recipients of wrath. 1 Thessalonians 1:10 says that we "wait for His Son from heaven, whom He raised from the dead—Jesus, who rescues us from the coming wrath." The first question that comes to mind is, "whose wrath?" Ultimately, there can only be three possible answers; man's, Satan's, or God's. That the first is not the one from which God promises deliverance is plain from the Scriptures themselves as well as history. Christians have almost always been the victims of persecution, torture, and death by unbelievers. Satan's wrath is restricted by God, and he can touch none but those whom God permits. The obvious answer is, therefore, that the coming wrath from which the church will be exempt is the wrath of God. This is the accepted view of most all premillennialists. The issue in regard to the rapture is one of the relationship of God's wrath to the tribulation and the rapture to that promised deliverance.

The first question in regard to deliverance from this wrath is one of whether or not the entire tribulation is the wrath of God or whether only part of the tribulation is the wrath of God. Pre-, mid-, and pre-wrath tribulationists all agree that the rapture will be a means of protecting believers from wrath, but they all disagree as to when God's wrath is poured out, and therefore, when the promised deliverance will occur. Pretribulationists point out that Revelation 6:16 mentions wrath as part of the seal judgments.[1338] Pretribulationists believe that the Bible clearly teaches that the entire tribulation is a time of wrath and, therefore, rapture is the means of deliverance from God's wrath.

One criticism made against this view that is that the rapture cannot be the method by which God will deliver the church from the time of wrath since there will be believers throughout the tribulation including the 144,000 evangelists of Revelation 7.[1339] It is generally agreed by all that these men will be protected by divine means other than the rapture, so why cannot all Christians be delivered from God's Wrath by the same means? They ask why rapture must be the method for deliverance. The latter question only begs the question since God may choose to do as He wishes. In fact, the real answer to these questions lie in whether or not deliverance from wrath *is the sole purpose* for the rapture. It is true that pretribulationists have put too great an emphasis on this aspect of the rapture and failed to back up other points of pretribulationism. If deliverance from wrath is the exclusive reason for rapture then the posttribulationists would probably be correct. Deliverance from wrath is *one* reason for rapture but *not by any means* the only reason. Posttribulationists are right in that there will be believers in the tribulation, there will be divine protection aside from rapture, and believers are not promised deliverance from persecution by the anti-Christ. There will be believers during the tribulation and these believers will be spared God's wrath through various means. Nevertheless, many of them will not be spared persecution. Why?

275

Pretribulationists must return to their dispensational roots to adequately answer this question or else they will eventually lose support for their position.

Pretribulationism and Imminency

Along with the promise to be delivered from divine wrath, the most central issue to the acceptance of the pretribulational view is the doctrine of imminency. The pretribulational rapture position can stand firm if one rejects some of the other arguments, including the question of wrath, but if one rejects the doctrine of imminency then pretribulationism falls with it.

The doctrine of imminency means that the coming of Christ for the church (the rapture) can occur *at any time*. There is no clear sign or event that will precede the rapture. According to imminency, Christ could come today, tomorrow, or a thousand years from now. *No one but God in Heaven knows exactly when it will occur.* This is based primarily on passages like Matthew 24:36 which state that "of that day and hour no one knows, not even the angels of heaven, nor the Son, but the Father alone" (cf. Mark 13:32). Since Revelation distinctly depicts Christ returning at the battle of Armageddon, many believe that this verse *must* refer not to the return, but to the rapture. Indeed, this would seem to be the only logical answer for in the Olivet Discourse, Jesus Christ Himself refers to the imminent return, while at the same time clarifying all the events which must *precede* the second coming.

If pretribulational rapture is true, then the apparent discrepancies between verses concerning the second coming can easily be rectified. Nevertheless, there are many scholars who deny the doctrine of imminence truly exists in the Bible. They maintain that the attitude of expectancy is nothing more than that. It is an attitude that Christians are to maintain, but it should not be taken as a literal hope that He *really could* return at any moment. These scholars deny that the church ever had any real hope of Christ's return in their lifetimes.[1340]

Is imminency Biblical? From the Biblical standpoint, the answer must be "yes." To discount the many passages which speak of Christ's return as possible at any time is not acceptable. We are specifically told to wait and watch for the coming of Christ, but the day and time are a mystery (cf. 1 Thessalonians 5). There may be several reasons for this. Not the least of which is that we must live our lives as if Christ is returning soon. Doubtless God in Heaven knew He would not return in the first century, but He did not tell the apostles this. Indeed, the purpose for the letters to the Thessalonians and 2 Peter was to instruct believers who were eagerly anticipating the coming of Christ. They were told to be patient, and counseled that it may or may nor happen in their lifetime. Some had actually quit their jobs in anticipation of Christ's return. Paul instructed them that they should continue to work and labor for their families since Christ may not come presently, but that they should be prepared lest He does come forthwith. This cannot be construed to simply be an attitude of expectance if, in fact, Christ's return were not possible. This would mean that we are to expect what is not expected and this would be living a lie. Granted, the apostles did not say that Christ *would* return in their lifetime, but they did hold that it was a possibility. Indeed, this very fact is used by critics of prophecy to suggest that the apostles were wrong. One critic says, "Matthew believed that Jesus had taught that he would return in glory sometime within the years 30-110 [A.D.]"[1341] Some of these critics claim that since Christ did not return in their lifetime, as the apostles had hoped, they must have been wrong. Obviously, this is a misrepresentation of the facts. Peter did allude to the fact that Christ may not return for a thousand years or more (2 Peter 3:8), but he also held that it *could* happen in their generation. This was the point of his letter, and Paul's in Thessalonians. Christ could come today, tomorrow, or a thousand years from now, but be watchful and obedient lest it does happen today!

Critics of imminency claim that this is untrue. Specifically, they argue that some of Jesus' statements precluded an imminent return. One such example is allegedly in John 21:18 in which Peter is told a prophecy of how he would die. This supposedly excludes Peter from believing in the imminent return of Christ. However, Peter did not understand this prophecy until he was crucified. Nowhere in history, or in his epistles, does Peter speak of his future crucifixion. One pretribulationists responds, "as [the early church] looked for the Savior they certainly did not run around asking, 'I wonder if Peter is dead yet?'"[1342]

Another argument is that Acts 1:8 declares that the gospel must be preached to the whole world first and, therefore, Christ could not have returned in the first century. Again, such a statement is made from the hindsight of history, and not valid in excising the doctrine of imminency. Again "with the size of the then inhabited world (grown yet smaller by the unifying influence of Roman rule and Roman roads), it must be confessed that world evangelism was a greater possibility in Paul's day than in ours."[1343] In any case, such remarks are made from the hindsight of history and only prove what God *chose* to do, not what He *could* have done.

If these critics hope to argue against imminency then they must do so based on actual prophetic passages. This they do attempt, but fail; for they argue that several prophecies *must* occur before the rapture, making imminency impossible. Christ's prophecy of the destruction of the Temple, the restoration of Israel as a nation, and the peace treaty that the anti-Christ must make with Israel supposedly preclude the rapture occurring at any time. However, in each of these cases, the critics have *assumed* that the rapture must occur after these things. Nowhere is it stated that Israel had to be restored *first*. Nowhere does it say that the peace treaty must be signed *first*. And nowhere does it say that the temple must be destroyed *first*. Indeed, some now argue that the temple must be *rebuilt first.* In each of these cases, these events *must* happen but they no not *have* to happen before the rapture, although they *may*.

Another proof of imminency is that the fact that it was the widespread belief of the church fathers. This is generally accepted by most historians, although critics of imminency maintain that this is a distortion of the facts. In essence, they use the same arguments that are used to deny imminency in the Bible and apply those to the church fathers, but church historians who have nothing to say on Biblical prophecy agree that the church fathers did believe in imminency. Imminency was taught by Clement of Rome, Ignatius, Irenaeus, Hippolytus, Tertullian, and Cyprian,[1344] just as it is taught in the Scriptures.

The fact is that those who deny imminency ultimately point to the fact that God knew He would not return in the early church, but does this preclude the doctrine of imminency? An example from daily life proves this fallacy best. We do not know when we will die. We *assume* that it will be many many years off, but when we realize that we *could* die today or tomorrow it profoundly changes *how* we live our lives. This is one reason that persecution of Christianity has always accompanied a growth in the church. Christians rarely compromise the faith when they know they may die tomorrow. It is when we are free and we succumb to the world, and compromise Christ's decrees, that we become comfortable in the world, and our evangelism is diminished as a result. The Father in Heaven knows exactly when Christ will return, but we *do not*. If the rapture referred to Christ's coming at Armageddon then this would not be true. We could safely know that Christ will not return until the armies gather in the Valley of Armageddon. Surely, imminency can only refer to the rapture of the church, which can occur anytime.

The Days of Noah

I discuss the "days of Noah" prophecy (Matthew 24:32-41) in detail under the posttribulational rapture section because there are a number of pretribulationists (too many) who reject the notion that the "days of Noah" is a prophecy of rapture. However, I did not want to omit it here, for I can honestly say that the prophecy of the "days of Noah" is the primary reason that I am pretribulational. Ultradispensationalists (see below) have rejected the idea that Jesus could refer to anything in the church age, despite the fact that Jesus mentions the church twice in Matthew's gospel (16:18, 18:17). Consequently, they have sided with posttribulationists in regard to the prophecy of the "days of Noah." In fact, it is not logical to assume that because something is a "church mystery," it cannot be referenced in the gospels. It is the answer to the mystery that is a secret, but mystery itself can exist for ages. If this were no so, then how could Jesus have mentioned the "church" to His apostles (cf. Matthew 16:18, 18:17)? It is sufficient to say that not all dispensationalists take this extreme view, and the prophecy of the "days of Noah" is perhaps the strongest evidence that rapture will take place at a time of peace and safety when the world is seemingly at rest, as opposed to the wrath and destruction that is taking place during the tribulation.

Pretribulationism and Israel

Perhaps the most forgotten element of pretribulational rapture is its distinct purpose in relation to God and Israel. Arnold Frutenbaum once said that God can fulfill His promises to Israel regardless of whether or not God has removed the church,[1345] but is this entirely true? In most respects this is true, but Frutenbaum may have forgotten one of the most crucial elements that cannot occur if the church remains. This is the question of "priesthood."

Part of the central confusion on this issue is the fact that the church is considered synonymous with Christianity. This is true, in *this* generation. Nevertheless, the church is something more. This is one reason why Peter was confused in the early days of the church. In Galatians 2 we read that Peter had at one time taught that Gentile Christians had to be converted to Judaism. Paul sternly rebuked Peter for this and Peter eventually backed down from this stance, but why did he ever hold to it? The answer involves the question of "priesthood." The Bible makes clear that the original purpose for Israel was to be a "kingdom of priests" (Exodus 19:6). Israel was to be a nation of priests (Isaiah 61:6) in order that all the nations of the earth would come to know God *through* Israel. When Israel rejected the Messiah, Jesus Christ, that lot fell on the church, not as a nation, but as a priesthood. In speaking to the seven churches John says that they have been made "priests to God and His Father" (Revelation 1:6). Does this, however, preclude God from keeping His promise to the Israelites? Pretribulationists correctly reject "replacement theology" which suggests that the church has permanently replaced Israel. Israel's rejection was not permanent. God has promised the conversion of Israel as a nation, and that requires the restoration of Israel as a nation of Priests. There will indeed many millions (perhaps billions) of believers in the tribulation but they will believe *through* Israel, and not through the church. Christianity will once again be synonymous with *true* Judaism, the words will no longer be mutually exclusive. The church was predominantly a Gentile priesthood, Israel is the true promised priesthood. The church will be removed, in part, so that Israel will once again be the focus of history. This may be what Sir Robert Anderson meant when he declared that the church "can have no corporate existence" until the rapture "unites us."[1346]

All world history has proven that Israel and the church have been the primary factors in the course of history. Ever since Moses led the Jews out of the mighty Egyptian nation, the tiny nation of Israel has been a plague upon all the wicked pagan nations that have arisen. It is impossible to read about ancient history without encountering Israel and the Jews in some fashion. Even during the Jewish exile in Babylon, King Nebudchanezar's legacy is integrally tied to Israel's. After the fall of Jerusalem in 70 A.D., however, a shift occurred in history. The church *appeared* to replace Israel in world history. The influence of Judaism in world history since then, although not absent, had been seriously rescinded. Even a cursory examination of history shows the church as the main driving force in global history since the fall of Israel. Democracy, science, literature, the arts, and even modern civilization can all be traced back to the church in some fashion.[1347] When the rapture finally occurs, Israel will once again be the focus of world history. The nations will look to Israel to see God, but many will oppose it. This is the forgotten reason for the rapture. The "time of the Gentiles" must come to a close (cf. Romans 11:25). Only then will God "restore the kingdom to Israel" (cf. Acts 1:6), for "it is clear that the church is not the promised and anticipated Messianic Kingdom."[1348]

Circumstantial Evidence from Silence

In addition to the previous arguments, there are a number of circumstantial evidences for a pretribulational rapture. These arguments are sometimes leaned upon too heavily, but they are circumstantial evidence that add weight to the overall strength of pretribulational rapture position. By themselves they are unconvincing, but compiled with all the other evidences, they do help provide the bulk of evidence in favor of this position. Other positions must *explain* the circumstances and problem passages, but pretribulationism *fits* the circumstantial events and evidences very well.

The most touted circumstantial evidence is the intriguing fact that Revelation, save the first three chapters addressed to seven churches (and the postscript in chapter twenty-two), the word "church" is completely *absent*.[1349] Why? All are agreed that there are many believers spoken of in the tribulation but nowhere is the church referred to. Are they not one in the same? Not necessarily. As aforementioned, Revelation sees Israel's return to prominence and the absence of the church. While Israel and the Jews are mentioned repeatedly throughout Revelation there are *no* references to the church after chapter three.

Pretribulationists are quick to point out that such a strange nuance fits in perfectly with a pretribulational rapture. Much is made of the apparent absence of the church in John's description of the tribulation. Again, this is convincing circumstantial evidence, but lacks merit by itself. It is, however, very significant that all other tribulational positions must read the rapture into Revelation, but it is nowhere mentioned in Revelation. Certainly not in any clear terms! Why? Once again, the inferential evidence suggest that it is *because the rapture already occurred before the tribulation began!* Strangely enough, pretribulationists place such an inordinate amount of emphasis upon the missing church of Revelation that they have ignored this obvious fact that goes

280

hand in hand with the church's absence. *The rapture cannot be found in Revelation because it has already occurred.*

Conclusions on Pretribulationism

Pretribulationism was at one time *the* evangelical position. In recent years a trend has moved away from pretribulationism. Doubtless one reason for this is the trend away from traditional dispensationalism and the resulting weak defense for pretribulational rapture. Pretribulationists have held on to the doctrine of imminency but have over-emphasized the lesser arguments for a pretribulation rapture while ignoring the main reason. The church currently serves as priests to God and His Father (Revelation 1:6) but the time *will come* when God will remember His promise to *His* people and Israel will once again become a *nation of priests* and convert the world in the end times. The tribulation is for the conversion of the Jews and for the unbelieving world to be converted by the repentant Israelis.

Pretribulationism's position has been weakened, not by attacks from without, but from within. Pretribulationism is the only position that can adequately account for the complete teachings of the Scripture in regard to the tribulation, the promises to Israel, the rapture, the doctrine of imminency, the promise for deliverance from wrath, the nature and purpose of the church, and circumstantial events described in Revelation.

Posttribulation Rapture

The posttribulational rapture position is the second most popular interpretation of rapture. Its popularity has risen in recent years as evangelicals have drifted further away from traditional Dispensationalism. It is a view quite popular with covenant theologians, or "replacement theologians," and consequently takes most of the passages about Israel to be a symbol for the church.

This view argues that the rapture is virtually synonymous with the second coming. It is believed that as Jesus returns at Armageddon. He first raptures the church to meet Him in the air and then the church returns immediately with Him to the earth. The advocates of this position call themselves "historical premillennialists" because they claim that posttribulationism is the "historical" view. This is refuted by the advocates of other postions who maintain that posttribulationism is not the historical view. Nevertheless, posttribulationists attempt to make their strongest arguments by claiming that the church fathers did not teach imminency but, instead, did not distinguish between rapture and the second coming.

The Historical View?

Posttribulationists have placed a great deal of emphasis on the fact that this is allegedly the view of the church throughout history. This is, however, largely an argument from silence. The posttribulationists deny that the doctrine of imminency was taught by the church fathers. They interpret passages of imminency to mean eagerness, but not necessarily imminence.

It is not imperative to repeat the discussion made on imminency, but a careful examination of some of the church fathers will show that, even if they did not teach imminency, they cannot be viewed as posttribulationists. Church historian Larry Crutchfield prefers to designate the views of many of the church fathers as "imminent intratribulationism."[1350] By this, he means to say that it is impossible to designate the exact timing for which the church fathers placed the rapture, but that most of the church fathers saw it as "imminent" and possibly occurring *during* the tribulation, but not *after* the tribulation. This would be, at best, a midtribulational belief, but nowhere is posttribulationism explicit in the writings of the church fathers. Take, for example, the Byzantine Church. One secular historian notes that they believed that Christ would come for the church "prior to the tribulation that is to come."[1351]

The truth is even Millard Erickson, a posttribulationist, admits that the early church "may have included belief in a pretribulational rapture of the church."[1352] The fact is that the church fathers gave few systematic theologies of the rapture and no such text has survived to give us a clear picture of their views. Some were doubtless midtribulationists and some pretribulationists. Might some of them have been posttribulational? Certainly, but posttribulationism was *not* the view of the early church. The fact is that most of the church fathers mimicked the Bible itself. They often quoted the Biblical passage saying "we do not know the day or hour of His coming" and thus warning their followers to be alert. So the parable of the Ten Virgins sets the pattern for the church fathers' teachings. It is, therefore, not surprising that posttribulationists make the same arguments in regard to the church fathers as they do in regard to the Biblical passages in question. They say that the attitude of expectation is not to be taken as a literal expectation. Their arguments for posttribulational support from the church fathers are arguments from silence. They claim that the church fathers were not pretribulational and, therefore, must have been posttribulational. There is simply no proof whatsoever that the church fathers taught a posttribulational position.

What of the Middle Ages and the Reformation? Were they not posttribulationists? This argument is common but it not sound. The dominant views of the Middle Ages and Reformation were amillennialism and historicism. Posttribulationism is one of several *premillennial* interpretations. The doctrines of historicism stretch the events of Revelation out over thousands of years. Consequently, to argue that they did not place the rapture at the beginning of the tribulation is disingenuous, for they did not see Revelation as a seven year period, but a two thousand year period. If one were to ask Joseph Mede whether or not the rapture would occur seven years before Christ's return, he would probably answer that he did not know for, according to the historicist view, there could be any number of years, or decades, or even centuries, between any two events in Revelation. Only futurist premillennialists place rapture in the seven year duration of Revelation and there is no doubt that when chiliasm, or futurist premillennialism, was popular, the rapture was taught as a separate event in time. In short, it is spurious to argue that posttribulationism was the dominant view of history. In fact, it was not until the mid-twentieth century that posttribulationism became prominent.

Signs of the Rapture?

Another critical argument for posttribulationism is the assertion that "signs" of the second coming referred to in Matthew 24 preclude a pretribulational, or presumably midtribulational, rapture position. This is a critically flawed argument, however, for it relies on a crucial assumption. They assume that the signs precede the rapture rather than the second coming. Since posttribulationists assume the second coming and rapture are virtually identical, they are using that assumption to prove their conclusion. This is circular reason. Douglas Moo, for example, says that 2 Thessalonians 2:1-10 contains statements "where the *church* is told of events to be expected *before* the rapture."[1353] However, a cursory reading of the passage makes it clear that it is the "Day of the Lord" to which Paul is referring. Since pretribulationists believe that the rapture occurs before the Day of the Lord, Moo's argument is based on the assumption that rapture occurs *after* or *on* the Day of the Lord. Again, this is circular reasoning and a logical fallacy.

There is no doubt that there are clear signs of the end times given in both the gospels and the epistles. That these signs refer to events in the tribulation has been accepted by most premillennialists, including many pretribulationists. In itself, this assumption does not prove anything concerning the rapture.

A more serious question is the debate in regard to the parables of the ten virgins and the fig tree. Do these passages refer to rapture or the second coming? Ironically, posttribulationists are joined in their chorus here by many ultradispensationists who believe that these passages cannot be taken as references to the rapture. Matthew 24:32-41 reads;

> "Now learn the parable from the fig tree: when its branch has already
> become tender, and puts forth its leaves, you know that summer is near;
> even so you too, when you see all these things, recognize that He is
> near, *right* at the door. Truly I say to you, this generation will not pass
> away until all these things take place. Heaven and earth will pass away,

but My words shall not pass away. But of that day and hour no one knows, not even the angels of heaven, nor the Son, but the Father alone. For the coming of the Son of Man will be just like the days of Noah. For as in those days which were before the flood they were eating and drinking, they were marrying and giving in marriage, until the day that Noah entered the ark, and they did not understand until the flood came and took them all away; so shall the coming of the Son of Man be. Then there shall be two men in the field; one will be taken, and one will be left. Two women *will be* grinding at the mill; one will be taken, and one will be left."

This passage teaches four things. First, as the figs grow, so also you will know the time is near by the "signs." Second, no one but the Father in heaven knows the day or hour. Third, this coming will be like the days of Noah when men are eating and drinking and giving in marriage. Finally, the parable mentions one being taken while another is left. Is this not the rapture? If so, will not, as the posttribulationists insist, the "signs" spoken of in the Olivet Discourse precede it? If not, then of what does the "one taken" and another left behind refer?

There are actually three interpretations of this passage. Posttribulationists believe that this refers to rapture at the end of the tribulation, immediately before the second coming. They argue that all the "signs" spoken of in the Olivet Discourse apply to the fig tree and must occur first. Some ultradispensationalists believe that this refers to the second coming, but not the rapture. They argue that because the church was still a "mystery" this cannot refer to an event in the church age such as rapture. Most pretribulationists, however, see this as a rapture passage and proof that the rapture will occur at a time of peace, not during the horrors of the tribulation.

The first issue what is meant by "here shall be two men in the field; one will be taken, and one will be left. Two women *will be* grinding at the mill; one will be taken, and one will be left"? Some posttribulationists and most pretribulationists are generally agreed that the passage is speaking about rapture. One is taken to the clouds to meet Jesus while the other is left behind for judgment. Just as Noah and his family were rescued from wrath by the Ark, so also those taken will be rescued from wrath. However, Mal Couch, and some ultradispensationalists, argue with many posttribulationists, that the "taking" refers not to rapture, but destruction. He likens the analogy of the Flood to the destruction and death caused by the Flood. He does not see that the one being taken is being taken aboard the Ark, but being taken by death.[1354]

The problem is that these men must ignore the statement, "they were eating and drinking, they were marrying and giving in marriage, until the day that Noah entered the ark, and they did not understand until the flood came and took them all away." Couch must suggest that this is cursory information indicating that the unbelievers were merely caught unaware, but, in fact,

Revelation makes it clear that by the time of the end *no one* is unaware and *no one* can claim ignorance. In Revelation 6:16-17, the wicked are crying out to the rocks, "fall on us and hide us from the presence of Him who sits on the throne, and from the wrath of the Lamb; for the great day of their wrath has come; and who is able to stand?" There is no doubt that they know what is happening to them. The "Flood" has already begun and they were *not* taken. If one is to take the analogy as one of destruction then he cannot ignore that the "Flood," and the destruction of Sodom found in Luke 17:34 (a parallel passage), occur *without* warning. The passage makes clear that these men were unaware whereas the destruction that awaits men at Armageddon is clearly forewarned and foretold so that men are crying out to the rocks. The weight of evidence then seems to favor that this is a rapture passage.

So if this passage does refer to rapture, as held by many pretribulationists and posttribulationists, then what of the "signs?" Douglas Moo maintains that "there is no basis for any transition from the posttribulational aspect of the Parousia of Matthew 24:32-35 (or -36) to its pretribulational aspect in verses 36ff."[1355] Fortunately, Moo is honest enough to admit that "*all* interpreters, whether they believe the discourse is addressed to the church or to Israel, face the difficulty of explaining how an event heralded by specific signs can yet be one of which it said 'no one knows the day or hour'" (emphasis in original). This is particularly so since the analogy to the Flood emphasizes that the world "did not understand," and was caught off-guard. Surely, this is inconsistent with the world war that is taking place in the tribulation.

The most likely explanation is that Jesus has finished His discussion of the end times events and is now giving instructions to the believers on the expectations and imminency of His Return. In the Greek the use of the word *de* (δε) is often used to initiate a shift in thought. According to a Greek text, "Δε often marks a contrast between two elements ... in narrative discourse δε often introduces a shift or change in thought."[1356] Hence when Jesus says, "*now* learn the lesson ..." a shift has occurred from the "signs" of the end to the "lessons" that we must learn. The relationship is indirect, not direct. This is further proven by the very statements that Moo admits cause "difficulty" to "*all* interpreters."

The events spoken of in this parable are said to occur at a "day and hour no one knows, not even the angels of heaven, nor the Son, but the Father alone." Moreover, we are told that "the coming of the Son of Man will be just like the days of Noah. For as in those days which were before the flood they were eating and drinking, they were marrying and giving in marriage, until the day that Noah entered the ark, and they did not understand." This imagery cannot possibly be of the final battle at Armageddon when the world has been laid waste and the armies gather for one final battle. Posttribulationists who argue that marriage and everyday life will continue until the end are fooling themselves. One only has to read of the death tolls spoken of in Revelation to see the folly of such an assumption. Indeed, at least 70% of the population of the planet has already been decimated before that final battle. Can the survivors "not understand"?

The second parable, that of the ten virgins, creates the same problems for posttribulationists. It is clear that the parable is speaking of those who are anticipating His Return, and yet His Return surprises many for they "do not know the day nor the hour." It is a warning to be alert since the day and hour are unknown. Again, this is the teaching of imminency and is not consistent with the signs of the second coming, for the whole world will know when the Messiah is returning on the day of Armageddon.

Is the Church in the Olivet Discourse?

Another argument made by advocates of posttribulationism is that the entire teaching of the Olivet Discourse is directed at the church. They argue that if the church is the recipient of the message, then the church must be on the earth at the time of the events described or else the message would be irrelevant. If true, this could be a compelling argument. However, before addressing the logic of the argument one must determine whether or not the allegation is true.

According to Douglas Moo, the church must be included in the Olivet Discourse because of the use of the word "elect."[1357] He further argues that the disciples were the recipients of the message and should, therefore, be viewed as representatives of the church. The problem with this argument is that the very assumption is crucial to the interpretation itself. Dispensationalists have argued that the Olivet Discourse applies to Jews and that it was to the Jews that Jesus was speaking, for the Chuch had not yet been created.[1358] Replacement theologians or covenant theologians argue conversely. Each side uses their own assumption as proof of their position, and yet one wonders what the relevance of their arguments is. Why can the church not be taught about end times, if we are not in it? Who is to receive this message of end times? The church is the harborer of God's Word until as such time as Israel, *as a nation*, repents. This repentance is the predominant subject of the end times. Moreover, the term "elect" literally means the "chosen." It is used repeatedly throughout the Scriptures for just that, those "chosen" by God. Is the church chosen? Yes. Is Israel? Yes again. The chosen are seen in Revelation. This term cannot be proof that either the church or Israel is in the tribulation for it is consistent with both. To suggest that it is proof of the church's involvement is not a valid argument.

Once again, this whole argument boils down to an argument between covenant theology and dispensational theology. The argument is actually a side issue that cannot prove posttribulationism. Covenant theologians hope to exclude Israel, as a nation, from God's prophecies. They have attempted to weave this assumption together into their posttribulational views, but this is another example of one's presumptions governing their interpretations. The truth is that the Olivet Discourse does not, in itself, give any true indication of whether or not the church is involved. If we are true to the text then we must look elsewhere to determine whether or not the church is in the tribulation and not read our own assumptions into the text.

A Critique of Posttribulationism

The main advantage of this view is that it creates an easy explanation for the Bible's association of the rapture with the second coming. If the rapture and second coming are two aspects of the exact same event, then it is easy to see why the two are often confused and should be referred to in the same language. Unfortunately, this assumption ignores many verses that clearly show these events, although linked, are not the same.

Much of posttribulationists' arguments are offensive rather than apologetic. Many of the arguments for posttribulationism are inherently weak because they proceed from assumption. As a result, a great deal of posttribulational commentary is actually a critical evaluation of pretribulationism. They attempt to support posttribulationism by default. If pretribulationism falls, then they assume that posttribulationism is all that is left, although midtribulationists and pre-wrath advocates will disagree. Despite this view's popularity it is by far one of the weakest of views. Its major problems can be outlined as follows:

1. Perhaps the biggest problem with posttribulationism is that it is in reality a virtual denial of rapture all together. If one accepts posttribulationism at face value, then one can find no real difference in posttribulational interpretation of the second coming and the interpretations of those who deny the very existence of rapture. In fact, one of the posttribulationists' arguments is that their position can be supported by the false allegation that no one allegedly ever taught the rapture before the 19th century, and yet they claim that posttribulationism is the traditional teaching of the church. This very argument implicitly admits that posttribulationism is a virtual denial of rapture. Moreover, the very acceptance of posttribulationism creates many problems which do not even exist for those who deny the rapture's existence altogether. The most obvious problem created by this view in the interpretation of the second coming is point number two.

2. This view has inordinate difficulty in explaining who inherits the thousand year reign. When Christ returns to the earth He is said to establish a thousand year reign (Revelation 20:6) in which He will reign and rule over mortal believers. Since Christ destroys all His adversaries at Armageddon, then there would be no one left on earth to inherit the kingdom, for this view holds

287

that all believers were raptured merely seconds before Christ returns. This view cannot adequately explain this contradiction. Indeed, when asked about this seeming flaw, one posttribulational professor responded that many of the people among the armies of Armageddon will repent *as they see* Christ coming.[1359] Since the church would have been raptured only seconds earlier, this is the only explanation that he could give.

This explanation is unacceptable for several reasons. First, a careful study of the bowls of wrath described in Revelation 16 shows that those who assemble at Armageddon have already hardened their hearts. Repeatedly, we are told by the apostle John that men "blasphemed God" and "did not repent." There was a great deal of repentance described throughout the seven seals and the seven trumpets, but by the time the seven bowls are poured upon the earth, men have already either repented or hardened their hearts. Indeed, this is one of the major purposes for the seals, trumpets, and bowls: to provoke men to either repent or harden their hearts. By the time Christ returns, men have already made their choice.

Another indication that these armies have hardened their hearts may be in the interpretation, although unsure, that the armies gather for the express reason of fighting God. Even if they do not assemble for this specific reason, the Bible is explicit that when the armies of the world see Christ coming they do not repent, but "make war against Him" (Revelation 19:19). The Bible gives no picture of repentance at the second coming, but instead gives a grisly picture of birds feasting on human flesh as the rebellious unbelievers are devoured and slain.

The idea that men repent only seconds before the second coming is unfeasible. The only other answer offered by posttribulationists is that of Robert Gundry, who says that unbelievers inherit the Millennial Kingdom![1360] Posttribulationism cannot adequately answer this fundamental question. Posttribulationist commentator Robert Mounce completely ignores the question in his commentary as he discusses who will reign *with* Christ, but nowhere answers who Christ will reign *over*.[1361] If the church is raptured seconds before the second coming then there can be no believers left on earth to inherit the thousand year reign of Christ. Posttribulationism then fails to account for the Millennial reign of Christ.

3. Another problem with posttribulationism is that it must deny the doctrine of imminency. Although posttribulationists deny that imminency is taught in the Bible, or among the church fathers, the teachings are apparent. Matthew 24:32-41 is hard to reconcile with the tribulation. Can a posttribulationists really believe that after holocaust, war, famine, death, and plummeting meteorites people will be eating and drinking and buying and selling and planting and building (Luke 17:28) while the final Battle of Armageddon is raging? Posttribulationism must accept the idea that daily life and routine continues up to Armageddon and interpret both rapture verses and

verses concerning the Return as referring to the same event. This task is much harder than one might first think. Some passages speak of a time of peace and daily routine while at other times the coming is to save the world from complete and utter destruction lest "no flesh would have survived" (cf. Matthew 24:22). If the rapture is not separate from the second coming then there is no way to consistently reconcile such passages.

4. Still another problem is that posttribulationism must generally deny the literal fulfillment of the seventieth Week of Daniel 9:27. Although some posttribluationists do attempt to reconcile the seventieth Week of Daniel with the tribulation, the majority of posttribulationists are covenant theologians or replacement theologians who deny Israel's role in the future prophecy of end times. They insist that the church has replaced Israel and Jews cannot, independent of the Gentile church, find salvation. They must either deny or diminish the fact that Israel is the focus of Revelation. Passages in Revelation that appear to refer explicitly to Israel and the tribes of Israel are taken allegorically to represent the church. Posttribulationism is inexorably intertwined with covenant theology. Of course, posttribulationists will respond that pretribulationism is equally connected to Dispensationalism. Nevertheless, while it is true that many Dispensationalists will be pretribulationists, not all pretribulationists are Dispensationalists, nor are all Dispensationalists pretribulationists. The importance of Israel to Revelation should not be dismissed.

Although many good scholars are counted among the posttribulationists, the theory remains among the weakest of views. It offers little exegesis, few explanations for apparent contradictions it creates, and relies heavily upon criticism of alternate views. It assumes the second coming and rapture are virtually synonymous but reluctantly admits they are different. They appeal to the difficulties of the opposing views, which indeed are many, but ignore the multitude of difficulties created by their own system. In short, posttribulationism ignores the difficult issues presented by rapture via a virtual denial of its existence. They, therefore, compound the problem rather than solve it.

Midtribulation Rapture

In the mid-twentieth century, some scholars began to question the traditional pretribulational timing of Revelation. For a short time, midtribulationism became fairly popular, teaching that the rapture occurs not at the beginning of the seven year tribulation, but in the middle of the tribulation, three and a half years from the end.

In some respects, midtribulationism has the appearance of being the strongest view, but at other times it looks the weakest. This is not too surprising since midtribulationism is, in reality, a compromise between pre- and posttribulationism. It takes the strongest arguments for each, and hopes to discard the flaws of each. In actuality, it does much the opposite. It is largely inconsistent in its exegesis since its interpretations actually come from two opposing methodologies. Pre- and posttribulationism are incompatible systems that contradict one another. Midtribulationism, in trying to establish a middle ground, has caught itself in the crossfire. Nevertheless, midtribulationism cannot be dismissed out of hand. Some of its arguments are legitimate and it cannot be denied that midtribulationism may have been the view held by some of the church fathers.

The basic teaching of midtribulationism is that the rapture occurs in the middle of the tribulation, three and one half years into the Seventieth Week of Daniel, probably coinciding with the abomination of desolation, although its advocates are divided as to the *exact* timing. The emphasis is not on the abomination of desolation, but upon the halfway mark of the tribulation.

Points of Agreement

The discussion of midtribulationism is easier if the points of agreement between midtribulationism and alternate views are defined first. Since midtribulationism takes many of the arguments from the other positions that existed at the time, including partial rapture theory, it is best to begin by defining how midtribulationism agrees and disagrees with each view.

Pretrib Teaching	Points of Agreement	Points of Disagreement
The Church will be spared God's wrath through rapture.	Midtribulationists agree with this statement but ...	Disagree as to when the wrath of God begins.
Israel and the Church are distinct in God's program.	Midtribulationists accept the distinction between Israel and the Church but ...	They reject the traditional dispensational views and believe that the two entities overlap.

Posttrib Teaching	Points of Agreement	Points of Disagreement
Imminency is not true and the Church is given signs.	Most midtribulationists would agree on this point but ...	Not necessarily. Some midtribulationists may accept imminency.
The "elect" of the Olivet Discourse refers to the Church.	Midtribulationists would agree but ...	They do not deny Israel's distinct role in end times.

Partial Rapture View	Points of Agreement	Points of Disagreement
The Church must undergo tribulations.	Midtribulationists generally agree with this statement but ...	Reject the Partial Rapture theorists' conclusions.

One can easily see how midtribulationism has taken the various points of opposing views and tried to take the "strong" points of each, while rejecting the "weak" points. Since pre- and posttribulationism have already been debated, only the points of disagreement need to be addressed.

Tribulation and Wrath in Midtribulationism

Midtribulationists are in agreement with pretribulationists that the church will be spared the wrath of God. They believe that rapture will be the instrument through which God will deliver the believer from wrath. However, they disagree with pretribulationists as to when this wrath begins. Pretribulationism maintains that the entire tribulation, or seventieth week of Daniel, is a period of wrath. Midtribulationists disagree and argue that the period of wrath begins only with the pouring out of the "bowls of wrath" mentioned in Revelation 16. They argue that the rapture occurs before this time, at the sounding of the seventh Trumpet of Revelation 11.

According to midtribulationism, there is a strong distinction between wrath and tribulation. Like the partial rapture theory, midtribulationists argue that believers must suffer tribulation. The various verses that they use to justify this include Matthew 24:9-11, Mark 13:9-13, Luke 23:27-31, John 15:18-19, John 16:1-2, John 16:33, Acts 8:1-3, Acts 11:19, Acts 14:22, and Romans 12:12.[1362] Most of these verses speak of persecution and warn believers of what is to come, but there is nothing within them that affirms that *persecution* is a *requirement*. Tribulation does not necessarily imply persecution. For nearly two thousand years Christians have come under persecution and many will continue to, but there is no proof that persecution is required of all. Indeed, the only verse that seems to imply anything of the sort is Acts 14:22. This verse reads, "through many tribulations we must enter the kingdom of God." Nonetheless, midtribulationists are taking this out of context. The verse in its entirety says that Paul and Barnabas were "strengthening the souls of the disciples, encouraging them to continue in the faith, and *saying*, 'through many tribulations we must enter the kingdom of God.'" This was just after Paul had been stoned and left for dead. Consequently, the context of the passage was a warning by Paul to his disciples that they would suffer persecution. Everyone suffers tribulations, but there is nothing in the context to suggest that the church, or its members, *must* undergo persecution.

Since the midtribulationists distinguish between the "tribulation" of Revelation and God's wrath, they believe that the church is destined for the first half of Daniel's seventieth week, during which it will undergo tribulation, but it will be spared God's wrath. This assumption, of course, not only requires believing in the distinction between tribulation and wrath, but also upon a distinct chronology of Revelation and the belief that the wrath of God begins *only* with the bowls of Revelation 16.

In regard to the chronology of Revelation, little will be said, for an entire appendix will be devoted to that difficult subject. It is, however, worth noting that many people do not place the seventh trumpet of Revelation 11 in the middle of the tribulation, as most midtribulationists do. Indeed, even within midtribulationism, there is some debate as to exactly when, and with what prophecy, the rapture occurs. Nevertheless, Norman Harrison is generally considered the father of the midtribulational view, and most midtribulationists follow his chronology, which places the rapture at the seventh Trumpet, immediately following the abomination of desolation.[1363]

The more important issue is that of the wrath of God. Midtribulationists, and their cousins of the pre-wrath position, argue that the wrath of God only occurs with the pouring of the bowls. Norman Harrison calls the bowls God's method of "Divine Warfare."[1364] That the bowls are indeed a part of God's wrath is denied by none. That the seal and trumpet *judgments* are not a part of wrath is denied by all pretribulationists. Indeed, the first mention of wrath in the book of Revelation is 6:16 under the sixth seal. There is explicitly states that men are hiding from "the wrath of the Lamb." Since pre-wrath rapturists make this argument a central figure in their system, the topic will be addressed in more detail in that section. At this point, it is necessary merely to point out that seals and trumpets are all properly called the judgments of God. His wrath is poured out throughout the tribulation and there is no proof that such a rigid distinction can be made between a period of tribulation, described in Revelation 6-10, and a "period of wrath" that follows. Midtribulationists assume this to be true, but cannot prove it from the text. It is for this reason that some modern midtribulationists, such as Gleason Archer, have attempted to clarify the division by defining the time of wrath as synonymous with the Day of the Lord.

According to Gleason Archer, the Day of the Lord begins at the middle of Daniel's seventieth week, and gleefully notes that some pretribulationists agree.[1365] While the shift from wrath to the Day of the Lord does provide a more sound argument, it still relies on the same assumptions. Since the pre-wrath teachers also echo this teaching, the subject of the when the Day of the Lord begins will be addressed in that section, rather than this section.

So the argument that the church is spared only the wrath of God, but not the "tribulation" which procedes it, is unfounded. It must rely on numerous assumptions as follows;

1. It assumes that the sparing of wrath is the *sole* reason for rapture.
2. It assumes that the church is required to undergo persecution.
3. It assumes that the "wrath of the Lamb" is not the same as the "wrath of God."
4. It assumes that the seals and trumpets are judgments, but not "wrath."
5. It assumes that rapture must *immediately* precede the wrath of God.

These assumptions cannot be proven by Scripture but are inferred. The fact is that the entire tribulation should be considered a part of the wrath of God.

The Emphasis on 3 ½ Years

Another argument made by midtribulationists is that Bible makes a very strong emphasis on a three and a half year division of the seventieth week of Daniel. According to Gleason Archer, the division made between the first and second half of the tribulation, found in both Daniel and Revelation indicates that something important will happen at that time.[1366]

There can be no doubt that both Revelation and Daniel's seventieth Week are divided into two separate periods of three and one half years. There is also no doubt that in the middle of the tribulation there will be a monumental event, but that event, which Archer himself refers to many times, is not the rapture, but the prophecy of Daniel 9:27 which reads, "in the middle of the week he will put a stop to sacrifice and grain offering; and on the wing of abominations *will come* one who makes desolate." This is the prophecy of the "Abomination of Desolation" spoken of by Jesus (Matt. 24:15, Mark 13:14, and Luke 21:20) and the apostle Paul (2 Thessalonians 2:4).

Indeed, throughout Archer's discourse on the middle of the week, he speaks repeatedly of the abomination of desolation, but only once makes a specific reference to the rapture, and that by inference. He says, "whether this indicates that the saints have been removed from the domain of the Beast through the rapture, or whether this phase of this tyrannical rule will prevail during the second half of the week ... the midway point in the seventieth week is given great prominence."[1367] Certainly there is no evidence that rapture occurs at this time. The entire argument is, again, made by inference, not exegesis.

The Last Trumpet

A better argument, made by midtribulationists, and some pre-wrath advocates, is that the seventh trumpet of Revelation is the "last trumpet" of 1 Corinthians 15:52 and 1 Thessalonians 4:16. Certainly, one is tempted to make this correlation, but before that correlation can be made a careful examination of the text is necessary. 1 Corinthians defines this as the "last" trumpet, but J.F. Strombeck pointed out that there are many series of trumpet blast in the Bible.[1368] Having given the long list of trumpet blasts found in the Bible, Strombeck that this trumpet "is God's own trumpet, sounded by the Lord Himself."[1369] This is apparent from 1 Thessalonians 4:16, which clarifies that rapture occurs with "a shout, with the voice of *the* archangel, and with the trumpet of God." The seventh trumpet of Revelation is sounded by a mere angel. As Strombeck states, "remembering that the angels are only a little higher than man, it is just as contrary to the laws of logic to say that 'the last trump,' which is God's own trumpet, is the last of a series of trumpets blown by angels."[1370]

Such sound reasoning should put to rest that the seventh trumpet is the "the trumpet of God," but it is interesting to note that pre-wrath advocates also accept this theory while disagreeing upon the time of its occurance. Midtribulationists believe that the seventh trumpet occurs at the middle of the tribulation while pre-wrath advocates rightly place it much nearer the end of the tribulation. In either case, there is no real reason to associate the trumpet of Corinthians and Thessalonians with the trumpet of Revelation 11. Nevertheless, Norman Harrison suggests not only that the seventh trumpet of Revelation is the signal for rapture, but also argues that the resurrection of the two witnesses (11:12) is "symbolic of the resurrection and rapture."[1371]

That the two witnesses are indeed resurrected is obvious, but the association of this resurrection with the seventh trumpet is as tenuous as is making their resurrection "symbolic" of the church as a whole. Moreover, it is clear from the text that the believers flee for the mountains at this time (cf. Matthew 24:15, Mark 13:14, and Revelation 12:5), but how could believers flee to the mountains if they have been raptured? The only answer is that rapture has not occured at this time. The seventh trumpet of Revelation is the trumpet of an angel. The last trumpet is the trumpet of God Himself (1 Thessalonians 4:16).

2 Thessolonians 2, Apostasy, and Signs of the Rapture?

A similar argument to that made by posttribulationists is that there are clear signs of the rapture. This argument has been refuted earlier and will not repeated save the argument made from 2 Thessalonians. This passage, often used to infer the rapture cannot happen until after the revealing of the anti-Christ, is pertinent to midtribulationists because the passage clearly refers to midtribulational events. It reads;

> "Now we request you, brethren, with regard to the coming of our Lord Jesus Christ, and our gathering together to Him, that you may not be quickly shaken from your composure or be disturbed either by a spirit or a message or a letter as if from us, to the effect that the day of the Lord has come. Let no one in any way deceive you, for *it will not come* unless the apostasy comes first, and the man of lawlessness is revealed, the son of destruction, who opposes and exalts himself above every so-called god or object of worship, so that he takes his seat in the temple of God, displaying himself as being God" (2 Thessalonians 2:1-4).

This clearly refers to the revelation of the anti-Christ as being synonymous with the abomination of desolation. The question then is whether or not "it will not come" refers to "our gathering together to Him" or "the Day

294

of the Lord." The passage definitely says that Paul is referring here to the Day of the Lord. Indeed, all pretribulationists are agreed that the rapture *must* precede the Day of the Lord. Consequently, each rapture view spends much time attempting to define exactly *when* the Day of the Lord occurs. Unfortunately, this creates two problems. First, the Bible does not clarify exactly how long before the Day of the Lord rapture must take place, only that it will occur first. Second, it is not logical to argue that "it will not come" refers to rapture if, in fact, the Day of the Lord has already begun. In other words, Paul's letter explicitly states that the Thessolonians should not be "shaken from your composure or disturbed" by allegations that "the Day of the Lord has come" because *that day* "will not come unless the apostasy comes first, and the man of lawlessness is revealed." Thus, it is agreed that the Day of the Lord follows the abomination of desolation, but that does not prove that rapture occurs at that time, only that it occurs *before* this time. 2 Thessolonians is then consistent with both pretribulation rapture and midtribulation rapture, but not the posttribulation or pre-wrath positions.

Still one other possible answer to this argument is the question of apostasy. According to 2 Thessalonians, the Day of the Lord cannot come unless "the apostasy" comes first, but what exactly is the apostasy? Most believe that the apostasy merely refers to the falling away from the true faith. While this is probably the best answer, the alternatives are worthy of note.

Some of the early church fathers believed that the apostasy was merely a title for the anti-Christ,[1372] others that it is a title for the tribulation,[1373] and still others have suggested that the apostasy refers to a revolt or rebellion.[1374] One lesser known view says that the apostasy is nothing less than the rapture itself. It has been argued that the Thessolonians were "disturbed" because they had been told that rapture had already occurred and they were left behind.[1375] This is also the line of reasoning used by partial rapturists like Joseph Seiss.[1376]

This argument asserts that the correct translation of apostasy is "departure." This is born out by the translations found for fifteen centuries before the King James version.[1377] It was translated as such by John Wycliff and William Tyndale, as well as the many other versions which preceded the Authorized edition, but if this is an accepted translation, the question remains, "departure from what?" Departure is consistent with a departure from the faith, but it could also be consistent with a departure from the earth. In other words, the "departure" could be Paul's word for the rapture. This could be supported by the context since Paul begins his address by saying "with regard to the coming of our Lord Jesus Christ, and our gathering together to Him" but then fails to mention "our gathering together to Him." If apostasy is rapture, then Paul did not make such an omission. If, however, the apostasy refers to the departure from the faith, then one must wonder why he mentioned "our gathering together to Him."

A short examination of the word *apostasia* (ἀποστασία) is prudent. The root meaning of the word is "to draw away."[1378] The Greek word for divorce, a separation, is *apostasion* (ἀποστασίον).[1379] To "draw away" might fit the qualifications for rapture, but "divorce" would not. How then is the word used elsewhere in the Bible? According to H. Wayne House, *apostasia* (ἀποστασία) and its cognates are found 220 times in the Greek *Septuagint*.[1380] Sixty-six times it carries the meaning of physical departure and fifty-three times it carries the meaning of spiritual departure or a "falling away" from the faith.[1381]

Certainly there is nothing conclusive. The meaning "departure" or "drawing away" could support either interpretation. More importantly, if the passage does refer to rapture, then it is support against posttribulationism and pre-wrath rapture, but not pretribulationism or midtribulationism. The position is consistent with both of the latter and neither of the former. Consequently, it must be concluded that 2 Thessolonians is consistent with midtribulationism, but in no way detracts from pretribulationism. It is a useful argument against post- and pre-wrath positions, but is not, in itself, a solid argument for the midtribulational view.

A Critique of Midtribulationism

Midtribulationism attempts to merge the strengths of pretribulationism with the strengths of posttribulationism, but in reality merges their weakness as well. Midtribulationism is arguably the second best position, but only if it were to rectify many of the problems of its own creation. The faulty chronology used in midtribulationism requires its advocates to accept the seventh trumpet as occuring immediately after the abomination of desolation, despite the fact that it belongs much later (see Appendix D). It further must discard, or severely minimize, the doctrines of imminency and the importance of Israel. While midtribulationists argue that the church and Israel can co-exist and overlap in history, they do not clearly define how this system works. It may be accepted that an overlap is possible, but only if the nature and scope of this overlap are defined. If they are not, then it becomes a contradiction. Is a Messianic Jew part of the church or Israel or both? If both, then how does this effect the conversion of Israel? Like postmillennialists, the midtribulationists see the Olivet Discourse as being addressed to the church, but they then attempt to find a place for national Israel after the rapture. However, since they place rapture towards the end of the Olivet Discourse, there is little place left for Israel.

Likewise, if imminency is discarded then midtribulationism suffers from the same flaw as posttribulationism. If imminency is accepted then the seventh trumpet could not possibly fall in the middle of the tribulation. Again, midtribulationists have created a contradiction. Although midtribulationism offers an alternative for those discontent with pre- and posttribulationism, it does not offer a substantially better system. It combines elements from both but discards some of the stronger arguments for pretribulationism while keeping some of posttribulationism's weaker points. It is a stronger position than that of posttribulationism or pre-wrath, but it cannot hold up against solid exegesis.

Pre-Wrath Tribulation Rapture

It has been shown that midtribulationism offers some hope to those who have been discontent with pre- and posttribulationism, but its problems have made the view all but disappear in recent years. Nevertheless, in 1990, Marvin Rosenthal attempted to revise the system and correct some of its difficulties. Although its advocates will deny it, the pre-wrath position is closely related to, and descended from, midtribulationism. Indeed, despite the fact that Rosenthal makes no specific mention of his major influences, it is clear that pre-wrath has borrowed ideas from midtribulationists, posttribulationists, and even some variant pretribulational authors such as Arthur Bloomfield. Like midtribulationism, the result is a mixed view that takes both the strengths and weaknesses of the other positions. It is a variation on midtribulationism with an intense emphasis on Rosenthal's *unique* chronology.

Although pre-wrath rapture has yet to find any number of scholarly advocates, it has steadily increased in popularity among the general Christian public. In fact, its popularity is slowly beginning to challenge posttribulationism in prevalence among evangelicals.

The primary teaching of the pre-wrath rapture position is that rapture must occur on the exact day that the Day of the Lord begins. According to pre-wrath, that day is on the seventh seal of Revelation and occurs near the end of Daniel's Seventieth Week. Arnold Fruchtenbaum has thus dubbed the view the "three-quarter tribulation view."[1382] Thus the pre-wrath position places the rapture between the middle of the tribulation and the end of the tribulation.

God's Wrath and the Day of the Lord

The central argument that Marvin Rosenthal makes throughout his book is that the rapture must occur on the very *day* that the Day of the Lord begins.[1383] He then spends most of the book attempting to justify his chronology for the start of the Day of the Lord. Unfortunately, both his timing and his arguments fall apart on close examination. In essense, Rosenthal does a splendid job of making a subtle assumption and then writing chapter upon chapter based on that subtle assumption. If the assumption is missed or overlooked then he appears on solid ground, but if the assumption is caught and examined, the arguments become virtually irrelevant.

The first of the these assumptions is the rapture *must* occur on the exact day of the Day of the Lord. He begins one chapter with the overly dramatic proclamation that "if the Day of the Lord does not start at the beginning of the seventieth week of Daniel, pretribulation rapturism is fatally flawed. It is not a matter of a hole in the dike that can be plugged-it is a veritable flood that cannot be averted."[1384] He then procedes to spend many pages defending, with some success, the fact that the Day of the Lord does not begin at the start of the tribulation. However, this entire subject is virtually irrelevant if Rosenthal is wrong in this assumption that the rapture and the Day of the Lord must coincide. Despite this, the only evidence he presents is a quotation from the Olivet Discourse. Quoting from the gospel of Luke, he notes that the Flood began on the very day that Noah entered the ark and that Sodom was destroyed on the day at Lot left the city. There are, nevertheless, two problems with this interpretation.

First, no analogy can be carried too far. No one would suggest that there must be an Ark in the last days or that a city named Sodom must exist. The analogy is only relevant as far as the context permits. Although this is a controvertial passage, the majority of scholars believe that the passage is either warning that the rapture will occur when people are not expecting it, or that the second coming will take the unbeliever by surprise. The idea that the rapture must occur on the very day that wrath begins is not clear from the text. At best, it may be inferred, but it is clearly not the point of the passages.

The second problem has just been alluded to. Scholars are deeply divided, even with tribulational viewpoints, as to whether or not the passage is referring to the Day of the Lord or the rapture. Rosenthal has suggested that the two are virtually synonymous and built his arguments from there. This is not to suggest that Rosenthal's assumption does not have merit, for this would clear up some problems with the exegesis of the passage, but it would not prove his chronology, and thus it would not subtantially discredit pretribulationism as he hopes. In other words, even if one believed the entire scope of Rosenthal's arguments, it does not prove that pretribulationism is in error unless he can also prove that the sixth seal does not begin until the latter part of the tribulation as he believes.

This is the greatest problem with Rosenthal's chronology. He often seems to contradict himself. He has build a large scale argument around two assumptions which he seems to contradict. First, he has assumes that the Day of the Lord must coincide with the rapture. Second, he has assumed that the Day of the Lord is the beginning of God's wrath and that if one can pinpoint the time of wrath, he can pinpoint the Day of the Lord, and, therefore, rapture. Unfortunately, Rosenthal then confuses the issue by placing each of the three events at different times! He begins the Day of the Lord with the seventh seal of Revelation, but admits that the wrath of God is revealed in the sixth seal! He attempts to skirt around the problem by saying that God's wrath is revealed "*after* the sixth seal is opened,"[1385] and thus assuming that if the seventh seal is opened immediately thereafter, the contradiction is eliminated. In fact, this cannot be. The sixth seal is quite clear;

> "And I looked when He broke the sixth seal, and there was a great earthquake; and the sun became black as sackcloth *made* of hair, and the whole moon became like blood; and the stars of the sky fell to the earth, as a fig tree casts its unripe figs when shaken by a great wind. And the sky was split apart like a scroll when it is rolled up; and every mountain and island were moved out of their places. And the kings of the earth and the great men and the commanders and the rich and the strong and every slave and free man, hid themselves in the caves and among the rocks of the mountains; and they said to the mountains and to the rocks, 'Fall on us and hide us from the presence of Him who sits on the throne, and from the wrath of the Lamb; for the great day of their wrath has come; and who is able to stand?'" (Revelation 6:12-17).

Again, Rosenthal goes to great lengths to argue that "the great day of their wrath *has come*" should not be taken as past tense,[1386] but he seems quiet on the parallel passage in Revelation 11:18 which also used the same *aorist* Greek verb to say that God's wrath "has come." Moreover, he further contradicts himself when he states "the use of the word *wrath* in Revelation does not occur until the Day of the Lord wrath begins (Rev. 6:17)."[1387]

This debate goes beyond the scope of this book, but it should be pointed out again that any attempt to pinpoint the rapture based *solely* on the time of wrath will again fail. He has argued that if the Day of the Lord does not begin at the beginning of the tribulation then pretribulationism falls apart. Nevertheless, he briefly mentions that some pretribulational scholars start the Day of the Lord in the middle of the tribulation, as this author is inclined to, but discounts them without even reviewing their arguments.[1388] The pre-wrath advocates are thus setting up "straw men"[1389] to tear down. The exact timing of the Day of the Lord is only relevant if Rosenthal's two assumptions are valid, yet he spends virtually no time defending those assumptions. He must prove that the Olivet Discourse not only proves the rapture and Day of the Lord are synonymous, but he must also prove his chronology of the seals is valid and explain his contradictions in the timing of wrath.

The "Shortening" of the Great Tribulation

Another argument upon which pre-wrath advocates place an inordinate emphasis is the alleged "shortening" of "the Great Tribulation." Rosenthal says, "the shortening of the Great Tribulation to less than three and one-half years is one of the most important truths to be grasped if the chronology of end-time events is to be understood."[1390] Like many of his arguments, this is based on several quiet assumptions for which he does not devote much time defending.

In order to even understand his argument, one must first understand how Rosenthal divides the book of Revelation. Unlike most scholars, who divide the tribulation in half (based on numerous passages in Daniel and Revelation), Rosenthal appears to borrow from dispensational pretribulational author Arthur Bloomfield who is known for his unique pretribulational scheme. According to Bloomfield, Revelation actually speaks about three separate periods of three and one-half years each.[1391] He believes that the seals occur in the first three and a half years, after which the dispensation of grace will end and the seventieth week of Daniel will begin. He then divides the seventieth week in half, as most other scholars do. Furthermore, Bloomfield specifically defines these three periods of time. The first is called the "Great Tribulation,"[1392] while the seventieth week of Daniel is divided into two halves; the latter of which is synonymous with the Day of the Lord.[1393]

Rosenthal's three-fold division of Revelation mimics that of Bloomfield in some ways. According to Rosenthal the seventieth week of Daniel must be unequally divided into "the beginning of sorrows," "the Great Tribulation," and "the Day of the Lord."[1394] He begins, like many pretribulationists, by dividing the seventieth week in half, but he then argues that "the Great Tribulation," which he and many others define as the second half of Daniel's week, must be cut short. It is only after that "shortening" that the Day of the Lord is to begin.[1395] This is, as Rosenthal states, "one of the most important truths"[1396] of his system but its very foundations are shaky to say the least.

His defense is based on the text of Matthew 24:22 which reads, "unless those days had been cut short, no life would have been saved; but for the sake of the elect those days shall be cut short." Pre-wrath advocates believe that the "coming of the Son of Man" in verse 27 refers not to the second coming but to rapture, thus they apply this verse specifically to "the Great Tribulation" and argue that this proves the rapture "will occur *after* the Great Tribulation but *before* the end of the seventieth week."[1397] Again, the logic is severely flawed. To begin with, Rosenthal places both the trumpet judgments and the bowl judgments *after* "the Great Tribulation,"[1398] but the text is quite clear that the reason for the "shortening" of these days is that without it "no life would have been saved." Inexplicably, the pre-wrath advocate then take this verse and argue that the majority of God's judgments (which will slaughter as much as 60% of the population) occur *after* this "shortening." It may not be charitable to say that this logic is beyond reason, but such is the case. The "shortening" has nothing to do with a chronological time table for "the Great Tribulation." Its purpose is to clearly state the severity of God's wrath in those days. It is a passage concerning the second coming, *not* the rapture.

Thus the argument from the "shortening" of days is not one built on solid ground. It assumes that the verse in question is designating a chronological key when it is merely stating that the return occurs before all men

300

are slain, for the sake of the elect. The verse is self-explanatory, "unless those days had been cut short, no life would have been saved." To build a complicated chronological scheme on such a verse is not sound exegesis. The "shortening" of days cannot be used to support the pre-wrath position.

More "Signs" of the Rapture

Like posttribulationists and midtribulationists, the pre-wrath advocates believe that there are clear signs which must precede the rapture. While they do not completely disregard the "thief in the night" analogy, they do reject the doctrine of imminency. However, the pre-wrath advocates do place an emphasis upon different "signs." Only those "signs" not rebutted earlier need be discussed here.

The most interesting of "signs" advocated by Rosenthal is his belief that Elijah must come before *the rapture*. It is, of course, well accepted by all premillennialists that Elijah will come before *the second coming*, but in his book Rosenthal takes the coming to refer to the rapture. At no point do the pre-wrath advocates attempt to prove this. They merely assume it. Believing that they have proven that the rapture is synonymous with "the Day of the Lord," they merely cite passages which say that Elijah must come first.[1399] They then proceed to declare that the prophecy of Elijah is a sign of the rapture. The careful scholar, however, will notice another contradiction that they have created. According to Rosenthal Elijah must minister for "precisely three and one-half years."[1400] Since Rosenthal begins Elijah's ministry at the middle of Daniel's seventieth week (rather than the beginning as most scholars do) he has created a contradiction with his "shortening" theory. If "the Great Tribulation" is "cut short," what of Elijah's ministry? Does Elijah not get raptured? This is confused all the more, for in Rosenthal's chart, Elijah's "coming" is shown as being synonymous with the rapture.[1401] Robert Van Kampen, however, provides a better chart which places the death of the two witnesses at the end of the seventieth week but *before* the bowls of wrath are poured upon man.[1402] Unfortunately, this only confuses the issue more for in his large foldout chart "the parousia of Christ," or the second coming, is synonymous with the entire Day of the Lord which extends for 30 days beyond the end of Daniel's seventieth week!

At this point, a debate upon the chronology of Revelation is off topic. A separate chapter will be devoted to chronology in the pages that follow. Nonetheless, the reader will notice that the pre-wrath advocates have sewn an intricate chronology that attempts to resolve the contraditions that it has itself created. Elijah's ministry most likely occurs in the first half of he tribulation and is a sign of the second coming, not the rapture.

The 144,000 and Rapture

Another unique element of the pre-wrath position is their view of the 144,000 saints of Revelation 7:4-8. According to Rosenthal it "is abundantly clear and was obviously important ... that 144,000 Jews must be sealed before the Day of the Lord wrath begins."[1403] He later clarifies that this means that "immediately prior to the rapture of the church, the 144,000 Jews are sealed."[1404] He then goes on to say that these elect are *not* raptured with the church.[1405] They stay behind to be a witness for God during the days of wrath. Is Rosenthal implying that they are converted *after* the rapture or that they are *exempt* from the rapture for some special reason?

Certainly, if Rosenthal is suggesting the latter, which is not clear, he would not be the first to suggests that a certain number of elect Jews would be exempt from the rapture, for purposes of a special evangelism. In fact, this author has mulled the theory and found a handful of other theology students who have tampered with the idea, but it is just that; a theory. It is really a variant of the partial rapture theory. It must, at best, be inferred by Scripture, but nowhere is such a thing clear. Nevertheless, it will be accepted as a possibility, with the understanding that it is not anywhere explicit in the teachings of Scripture. Having said this, Rosenthal's late date for the rapture actually *nullifies* the very purpose of the 144,000 staying behind. According to pre-wrath advocates, the 144,000 stay behind as witnesses to the gospel, but it seems clear from Revelation itself that by the time the bowls of wrath are being poured out on man, it is too late to repent.

Although we read of men repenting throughout the first five or six years of the tribulation, the attitudes of the people change as time passes. As the judgments continue to be poured out, those who have not repented harden their hearts. By the time of the bowls we read that "they blasphemed the name of God who has the power over these plagues; and they did not repent, so as to give Him glory" (Revelation 16:9). However, in the pre-wrath scheme, the 144,000 are left behind in this most terrible of times, which the pre-wrath advocates have emphasized as the worst of all wrath, to witness.

Robert Van Kampen is more clear on his view of the 144,000. According to him, "when the church is raptured, the 144,000 will not be taken along with the saints because, in this writer's opinion, they will not, as yet, have been brought into a saving relationship with their Messiah, Jesus Christ."[1406] Unfortunately, this does not solve the problem for it seems imminently clear from Scripture that the 144,000 play a vitally important role in the last days. Because the pre-wrath view places rapture so close to the end, and because, at least according to Van Kampen, the 144,000 are not converted to the faith until the end, one is left to wonder what kind of impact their evangelism can have in a time when men's hearts have hardened and God is pouring His wrath out unrestrained upon the unbelieving world. The pre-wrath chronology simply does not work logically or Biblically.

Peace and Safety?

One of the most critical flaws in pre-wrath theology is their attempt to resolve their fixing of the date of the Day of the Lord with the text of 1 Thessalonians 5:2-3. It reads, "the day of the Lord will come just like a thief in the night. While they are saying, 'Peace and safety!' then destruction will come upon them suddenly like birth pangs upon a woman with child; and they shall not escape." It seems obvious that this text teaches that the Day of the Lord occurs at a time when the people feel safe and at ease. The world is saying, "peace and safety." Pre-wrath rapturists, however, place the Day of the Lord following cataclysmic events. Rosenthal even places the Day of the Lord *after* the events of Matthew 24:22 which reads, "unless those days had been cut short, no life would have been saved; but for the sake of the elect those days shall be cut short."[1407] Seemingly inexplicably, the pre-wrath advocates resolve the difficulty in this way;

> "It will be a time of such severity that except those days were shortened, no flesh (in context, Jewish) would live. But for the elect's sake, those days will be shortened. At that moment cosmic disturbance will signal the approach of the Day of the Lord. Jews being persecuted by the Antichrist will view this as divine intervention on their behalf in the nick of time. They will proclaim 'peace and safety,' but their cry will be premature."[1408]

Hence, pre-wrath advocates claim that when "there will be a great tribulation, such as has not occurred since the beginning of the world until now, nor ever shall" (Matthew 24:21) the Jews will cry "peace and safety" because they will see "a great earthquake; and the sun" becoming "black as sackcloth *made* of hair, and the whole moon" becoming "like blood; and the stars of the sky" falling "to the earth, as a fig tree casts its unripe figs when shaken by a great wind" (Revelation 6:14). Can we really believe that people will cry "peace and safety" when they see "the sky splitting apart like a scroll when it is rolled up; and every mountain and island" being "moved out of their places" (Revelation 6:14)? This stretches the credulity of the view. Unfortunately, it is this kind of argument which shows that the leading pre-wrath advocates are going to extremes to fit the Day of the Lord into a chronology which cannot work.

The Seals and Man's Wrath

Because pre-wrath advocates weave such an intricate web of chronological schemes, there are many other issues that could be brought up. One example is the choice of the pre-wrath advocates to view the judgments of God as sequential with certain inexplicable exception. They correctly believe that the judgments are chronological, yet in regard to the third, fourth, and fifth seal (Revelation 6:5-11) they break that rule and argue that they must be concurrent.[1409] Part of their reasoning for this is that they believe these seals constitute "man's wrath" as opposed to God's wrath. This type of logic is essential to maintain the view that God's wrath does not begin until the seventh seal but, as Fruchtenbaum states, "the wrath of man may be involved, but not to the exclusion of the wrath of God."[1410] Although Rosenthal argues that pretribulationists are ignoring "the distinction between God's active will and permissive will"[1411] it is Rosenthal who has ignored the distinction for it is clearly *Christ Jesus* who breaks *each and every one* of the seven seals and releases what is within them.

As pointed out earlier, even Rosenthal must attempt to read the *future* tense[1412] into the statement of Revelation 6:17, "hide us from the presence of Him who sits on the throne, and from the wrath of the Lamb; for the great day of their wrath *has come*." Pre-wrath simply cannot accept that God's wrath is being poured out from the breaking of the *first* seal onward. Indeed, Rosenthal has based his entire system on the very assumption that this cannot be true. He has argued that pretribulationism allegedly fall apart if this is not so (although he proves this nowhere) but the converse is all the more true, for if God's wrath does exist in *any* of the first six seals, it is pre-wrath rapturism that falls.

A Critique of Pre-Wrath Rapture

There is no doubt that midtribulationism needed a revision, but the revision created by Marvin Rosenthal is inadequate. Although his sincerity and devotion to detail is appreciated he has a tendency to base an argument on an unspoken, or unjustified, assumption and then spend chapters upon chapters attempting to prove the argument, without ever having proven the assumption underlying the argument. The result is a very complicated chronological scheme which sounds sophisticated to many laymen, but underneath it is a weak foundation built on sand.

One of the many problems with the pre-wrath position is that it creates many contradictions within itself. The most obvious example is the attempt to place the "last trump" of 1 Corinthians under *both* the seventh seal *and* the seventh trumpet. They argue that the seventh trumpet is contained under the mantle of the seventh seal,[1413] thus the "last trump" refers to both the seventh trumpet and to the seventh seal. The problem is that their system clearly shows the trumpets to be played out in sequence of time, *after* the seventh seal is opened. How can they logically place the rapture *before* the first trumpet while at the same time placing it *under* the seventh trumpet? They cannot. Despite this, one pre-wrath advocate states that "pretribulation rapturists do not make strong appeal to Paul's statement that the rapture will occur before the last trump" because "if the rapture occurs before the last trump, pretribulation rapturism has no way, exegetically, to associate a pre-seventieth week rapture with the last trump of God."[1414] By this, he means that rapture cannot occur before the seventh *angel's* trumpet of Revelation 11:15 without destroying pretribulationism. This statement is somewhat disingenuous, even hypocritical, in that the pre-wrath system does not *truly* place rapture under the seventh trumpet either. They claim only that the seventh trumpet is contained within the seventh seal, thus placing the rapture under the banner of that seal, but there is no way to get around the fact that pre-wrath rapture is said to occur *before* the wrath of God which they openly admit is contained in the seven trumpets.

Another problem that the pre-wrath view has created for itself is its attempt to resolve the conflicts created by Rosenthal's failure to clearly distinguish between rapture passages and second coming passages. Rosenthal says that pretribulationists are in error when they attempt to define two separate comings of the Lord Jesus. He correctly states that pretribulationists believe that "one coming, it is suggested, is for the purpose of rapturing the church, and the other refers to His return in Glory."[1415] He then goes on to say that this "logic" "is unproven."[1416] Yet again, he has claimed pretribulationism is in error on a point that his own system fails to properly take into account. If posttribulationism is not correct, and the pre-wrath advocates agree on this point, then how can the passages in question not be refering to two separate comings? Rosenthal's solution is to argue that the "*parousia* is speaking of the totality of that glorious *series* of events."[1417] Thus the pre-wrath position fails to take into account a legitimate method of differentiating between rapture and the second coming. This is, in fact, one reason that the pre-wrath system is full of contradictions. It borrows from posttribulational belief that the two comings are indistinguishable, and yet the pre-wrath view continues to maintain that rapture occurs as much as year or two before the glorious return![1418]

The fact is that pre-wrath rapture brings nothing really new to the table. It takes the arguments of pretribulationists, midtribulationists, and posttribulationists and throws them into a melting pot. Much of Rosenthal's work is useful, but only if it is taken out of the context of his intricate chronological schemes and if the rapture theories are removed. Certainly Rosenthal's attempts to better define the Day of the Lord and its relation to the chronology of Revelation are to be appreciated but the study is convoluted with numerous assumptions. The greatest of these assumptions is one that many pretribulationists, midtribulationists, and posttribulationists are all equally guilty: namely, the assumption that the rapture must coincide with the Day of the Lord. We know only that the rapture precedes the Day of the Lord and that that day will come "like a thief in the night" (Matthew 24:43) when the world is crying "peace and safety" (1 Thessalonians 5:3). If we go much beyond this, we are guilty of attempting to set a date for the rapture and/or the Day of the Lord. Jesus Himself clearly taught us that "the Son of Man is coming at an hour when you do not think *He* will" (Matthew 24:44). This is inconsistent with midtribulationism, posttribulationism, and the pre-wrath rapture theory. It is the major flaw of all three systems.

Partial Rapture

A rather rare interpretation of the rapture is called the partial rapture theory. The theory was created and popularized in the late nineteenth century by the great prophetic scholars Robert Govett and Joseph Seiss. It has found followers in recent years among Watchman Nee and Witness Lee but has fallen out of favor among evangelicals as a whole. According to partial rapture theory, all believers must undergo tribulation at some point in their life and be purified. Individual believers are raptured once they have satisfied the requirements and been purified by fire. Partial rapture theorists believe that the first of the saints will be raptured at the beginning of the tribulation, similar to pretribulationism, but other believers, both new converts and the old believers who had not yet been purified, will continue to be raptured throughout the tribulation.

According to the view, rapture is a reward. The Christian may forfeit his rights to the reward if he has not become sanctified through the Holy Spirit. This view obviously places an inordinate amount of emphasis upon the believer rather than Jesus. As a result, this view has sometimes been accused of being cultic in nature. The participation in rapture is sometimes compared to salvation and, therefore, any attempt to make it dependent on works or deeds or any other facet of *man's* spirituality is seen as a more subtle form of salvation by works. In defense of the partial rapture advocates, they do not see the rapture as essential to salvation, but see it strictly as a reward for those believers who endure and remain faithful to God. Certainly, the Bible does teach that we will all be rewarded by our faithfulness and deeds, and such rewards have nothing to do with our merit for salvation or superiority to other believers. Still, the teaching's emphasis on man's works has left many evangelicals extremely weary of this view. Nevertheless, partial rapture advocates should not be seen as promoting or teaching a man oriented theology or endorsing salvation by works. Its two greatest proponents, and inventors, remain the greatest of nineteenth century prophetic scholars whose dedication and knowledge of the Scriptures remain virtually unsurpassed. In whatever they erred, and all men err, they did so without sacrificing the fundamental principles of the Scriptures. Their arguments for excluding some from the rapture are based not on salvation issues, but santification. Consequently, the partial rapture theory deserves to be critiqued with the same fairness and judiciality as the preceding views.

Rapture as a Reward

One of the fundamental assumptions of the partial rapture position is that rapture should be considered a reward, rather than an unconditional promise. The book of Revelation begins with the epistles to the seven churches of Asia Minor. In each of the epistles there are clear warnings for those who do not heed the Word of the Lord and there are blessings promised for "the overcomer." In partial rapture theory, the "overcomer" is believer who has endured and been sanctified. He is the believer who has overcome the world and is rewarded with a special blessing. It is important to note that partial rapturists do not exclude those who fail to overcome from salvation or the blessings and rewards of heaven. They merely exclude them from certain blessings, which include the rapture.

There are several problems with this line of reasoning. First, if one reads the blessings promised to the seven churches, it is clear that at least *some* of those blessings *cannot* be denied to any believer. Since partial rapturists do not deny the salvation of those who fail to overcome, each of those blessings should be an honor not bestowed on all, but not essential to salvation. It can be shown that this is not the case. In the letter to the church of Ephesus the "overcomer" is given the right "to eat of the tree of life" (2:7), to the church of Smyrna the "overcomer" is promised that he "shall not be hurt by the second death" (2:11), to Pergamun "I will give *some* of the hidden manna, and I will give him a white stone" (2:17), to Thyatira "I will give him the morning star" (2:28), to Sardis "I will not erase his name from the book of life, and I will confess his name before My Father, and before His angels" (3:5), to Philadelphia "I will write upon him the name of My God, and the name of the city of My God" (3:12), and to Laodicea "I will grant to him to sit down with Me on My throne" (3:21). Partial rapturists have argued that this last verse shows that not all believers will rule during the Millennium, but the careful reader will notice some of the blessings include the promise not to "erase his name from the book of life" (3:5) and not to be "hurt by the second death" (2:11). It is obvious that if *anyone* is denied these things, he *cannot* be saved. Thus, the "overcomers" cannot be a select group of Christians, but must instead be synonymous with all true believers.

Other passages used to support the reward view include Matthew 25:1-13, 1 Corinthians 9:24-27, and 2 Timothy 4:8. The first of the these verses, the parable of the Ten Virgins, reads;

> "Then the kingdom of heaven will be comparable to ten virgins, who took their lamps, and went out to meet the bridegroom. And five of them were foolish, and five were prudent. For when the foolish took

their lamps, they took no oil with them, but the prudent took oil in flasks along with their lamps. Now while the bridegroom was delaying, they all got drowsy and *began* to sleep. But at midnight there was a shout, 'Behold, the bridegroom! Come out to meet *him*.' Then all those virgins rose, and trimmed their lamps. And the foolish said to the prudent, 'Give us some of your oil, for our lamps are going out.' But the prudent answered, saying, 'No, there will not be enough for us and you *too;* go instead to the dealers and buy *some* for yourselves.' And while they were going away to make the purchase, the bridegroom came, and those who were ready went in with him to the wedding feast; and the door was shut. And later the other virgins also came, saying, 'Lord, lord, open up for us.' But he answered and said, 'Truly I say to you, I do not know you.' Be on the alert then, for you do not know the day nor the hour." (Matthew 25:1-13)

Partial rapturists argue that because the virgins are all invited to the wedding, they should all be viewed as Christians. The fact that the virgins who were unprepared were locked out is then presented as proof that only those who are eager, watching, and waiting for the Lord's Coming will be caught up in the rapture. This is actually one of the stronger exegetical arguments for partial rapturists but it is likely a misinterpretation of the analogy for the words of the Lord to the unprepared virgins, "I do not know you," is a denial of them. It does not imply that they are being punished or denied a reward, but that they are lost. Would Christ deny knowing one of His own? On the contrary, the passage parrallels the words of Jesus in Matthew 7:22-23, "Many will say to Me on that day, 'Lord, Lord, did we not prophesy in Your name, and in Your name cast out demons, and in Your name perform many miracles?' And then I will declare to them, '*I never knew you*; depart from Me, you who practice lawlessness.'" The words "I never knew you" is a denial. The unprepared virgins of the parable are not true believers, but nominal ones who do not truly know the Lord.

The other two main verses used by partial rapturists also fail the exegetical test. 1 Corinthians 9:24-27 is an analogy to running a race. Paul declares, "those who run in a race all run, but *only* one receives the prize." He also warns that we should be careful not to be "disqualified." Again, this is said to refer to the promises of rewards for the believers who endure. However, even if this interpretation is accepted, which may be valid, it does not in any way prove that rapture is one of those rewards promised. The partial rapture theorists must jump from one conclusion to another.

Finally, 2 Timothy 4:8 reads, "in the future there is laid up for me the crown of righteousness, which the Lord, the righteous Judge, will award to me on that day; and not only to me, but also to all who have longed for His appearing." Again, it is argued that this crown is given only to "all who have longed for His appearing." While this verse does make a close connection to the return of Christ, it is again nowhere clear that this verse proves that those who do not long for His appearance will be excluded from rapture. At best, it suggests that these men will be denied a crown, but many crowns are mentioned in the Bible as a reward. Nowhere does the denial of one of these crowns indicate an exclusion from the general promises for believers. Partial rapturists must make the connection between rapture and reward, not merely show that believers may be given or denied certain rewards in Heaven. Such a connection has nowhere been proven. Only Matthew 25:1-13 and Revelation 3:10 are given as proof that such a connection exist. Matthew has been debated already but Revelation 3:10 deserves its own section below.

Revelation 3:10

Surely the most controversial of all alleged rapture passages is Revelation 3:10. "Alleged" because even premillennialists cannot agree on whether or not the passage is truly a rapture passage or not. It reads, "because you have kept the word of My perseverance, I also will keep you from the hour of testing, that *hour* which is about to come upon the whole world, to test those who dwell upon the earth."

The passage is directed to the church of Philadelphia during the reign of Domitian. It has been argued by some critics that this is a promise made only to the church of Philadelphia to be protected during Domitian's persecutions. While that may have been a possibility, the problem with this argument is that the persecutions of Domitian had already begun since John was exiled to Patmos by Domitian. Moreover, the phrase "those who dwell upon the earth" is used many times in Revelation and always refers to the tribulation, as does the phrase "about to come upon the whole world." Furthermore, "'those who live on the earth' is repeated in Revelation a number of times and refers not to believers, but to unbelievers who are the object of God's wrath; i.e., the 'beast-worshipers' (6:10, 8:13, 11:10, 12:12, 13:8, 12, 14)."[1419] That the passage at the very least has a double prophetic meaning referring to the last days is acknowledged even by George Ladd, a posttribulationist, who denies that the "hour of testing" refers to deliverance by means of rapture.[1420] Posttribulationists maintain that God can protect believers without rapture (He can). Because the issue here is whether or not the passage supports partial rapture, the posttribulationists arguments will not be debated. The sole question is whether or not all believers are recipients of this promise.

The key to the verse for partial rapturists is "because you have kept the word of My perseverance." It has been confessed that this verse "refers to the condition under which the promise is valid."[1421] However, it is important to note that the passage does not say "*if* you keep the word of My perseverance, I also will keep you from the hour of testing," but "*because you have* kept the word of My perseverance, I also will keep you from the hour of testing." If this is a rapture passage, as many believe, then it is promised to all. Although partial rapturists cling to the idea that it is only promised to those who "have kept the word," it is interesting that Joseph Seiss, a partial rapturists, makes no mention of 3:10 in his excellent commentary on Revelation. Perhaps this fact, in itself, stands as an indictment against partial rapturists' interpretation of the passage. Revelation 3:10 is certainly consistent with partial rapturism but is by no means a convincing passage for proof of partial rapture. Partial rapture must be read into the passage, but does not naturally flow out of the verse. On the contrary, the conditional promises found in the epistles to the seven churches contain some variation of warning usually following the pattern, "I know your deed ... I have this against you ... therefore, repent ... or else." Revelation 3:10 makes clear that the promise will be carried out. There is no warning issued and no "if" found in the passage. By itself, Revelation 3:10 cannot prove partial rapture theory.

The Necessity of Suffering

Another central doctrine of partial rapturism is the belief that all believers must suffer for the faith. They believe that suffering is required either in the present or in the tribulation. By "suffering" they do not mean everyday trials but a severe testing of the faith, usually involving persecution. Suffering, according to them, should not be interpreted as mere trials but as severe tribulation. Their main passages include Acts 14:22, Romans 8:16-17, 2 Thessalonians 1:4-5, and possibly 1 Corinthians 3:12-15.

The Acts passage states, "through many tribulations we must enter the kingdom of God" (14:22) and is the classic text used to prove the necessity of severe suffering, but in context the apostles are "strengthening the souls of the disciples, encouraging them to continue in the faith" (22) amid persecution. The verse does not prove that "tribulations" are a requirement for entry into the kingdom, only that those who were being persecuted must enter through tribulations. The statement was made for comfort.

Romans 8:17 says, "we suffer with *Him* in order that we may also be glorified with *Him*." Again, partial rapturists are making a leap in logic. Suffering has been commonplace among Christians for thousands of years. Few Christians have had the luxury of living in a free society. Consequently, the fact that Christians, as a whole, must suffer for the faith does not prove that every single believer must suffer persecution. The following verse clarifies the context. "I consider that the sufferings of this present time are not worthy to be compared with the glory that is to be revealed to us" (18). The passage addresses sufferings which many Christians undergo, but it does not follow that all believers must suffer tribulation of the stature which partial rapturists suggest.

The other passages offered include Colossians 3:24, 1 Corinthians 3:12-15 and 2 Thessalonians 1:4-5. Colossians promises rewards to believers who endure, but offers no indication that tribulations are required for inclusion in rapture. 1 Corinthians 3:12-15 speaks similarly of the testing of each man's works, but again offers no indication of a connection to rapture, nor of the necessity of persecution on the level that partial rapturists maintain. 2 Thessalonians 1:4-5 reads "we ourselves speak proudly of you among the churches of God for your perseverance and faith in the midst of all your persecutions and afflictions which you endure. *This is* a plain indication of God's righteous judgment so that you may be considered worthy of the kingdom of God, for which indeed you are suffering." There is no doubt that suffering, and often persecution, have been mainstays of the Christian life in this present evil age, but to jump from this fact to the assumption that persecutions are a requirement for rapture can nowhere be found in this verse or others. All these verses serve to comfort believers who are in the midst of persecution, but none of the them prove that believers who have avoided such persecutions must go through the tribulation in the last days.

If everyone must suffer tribulations either in the present or in the tribulation then what of the countless millions of past American Christians who knew nothing more in their lifetimes than to be made fun of? Surely, there have been a number of Christians in free societies who have died without having truly suffered for the faith. The partial rapture theory has taken the idea of the necessity of suffering and projected it upon the rapture. The various passages illlustrate the suffering that Christians will endure in life, but not a single passage connects this suffering to the promise of rapture.

Does Any Believer Get Left Behind?

It was aforementioned that the idea of Christians being left behind at rapture is not entirely new. Indeed, the partial rapture theorists appear to be the first to have presented the argument, over a hundred and fifty years ago. Nevertheless, this brings up more questions than answers. *If* there are believers left behind, will they be, as partial rapturists believe, the spiritually weak, left to test and strengthen their faith? Or will they be the spiritually mature (such as is implied by Marvin Rosenthal and others), who will stay behind to evangelize the world in the wake of rapture? In either case, there are those who believe that born-anew Christian believers will not all be raptured. It is suggested that some will be left behind and whether they be the strong or weak in spirit, they will be witnesses for Christ in the tribulation.

Certainly, this topic is, if nothing else, interesting. The Bible calls rapture "a mystery" (1 Corinthians 15:51), so it is not surprising that there is much mystery concerning its occurrence, as well as the recipients. However, it is for this very reason that we must be careful about being too dogmatic upon the specifics. This is one of the crucial flaws of the pre-wrath theory, which builds a highly intricate chronological scheme around certain passages.

Consequently, the question of who, if anyone, gets left behind must be made by inference. It *cannot* be proven by the Scriptures explicitly.

The partial rapturists have argued that the spiritually immature will be left to be purified and to suffer for the faith. Since much of this has already been answered, and refuted, the alternative views should be briefly addressed. Namely, will the spiritually mature be left behind? If so, who and why? First, let it be said from the outset that one cannot define those left behind in terms of spiritual maturity, whichever end of the maturity spectrum they are on. If there are Christians left behind, they are most probably related to the Dispensation of Israel. Two clear examples are the two witnesses of Revelation 11. As will be discussed in Appendix C, it is believed by most all premillennialists that one of these two witnesses will be Elijah. Some believe that Elijah will descend directly from heaven but the majority believe that he will be born in the flesh again in the last days. If this is so, and if, as pretribulationists and pre-wrath advocates believe, rapture occurs *before* their ministry then we are only left with one of two possible conclusions. Either *Elijah* was *not* a believer at the time of the rapture or Elijah was left behind to fulfill his purpose in the Dispensation of Israel and to lead Israel to repentance. Obviously, the latter is the better choice.

So if, as this shows, there are *some* believers left behind, what will determine who stays and who goes? Could the 144,000 be left behind? Will Jewish believers (as a part of the the Dispensation of Israel) be left behind? Probably not. Messianic Jews are indeed a part of Israel, but they are also, in the church age, a part of the church and will not be denied any promises made to the church. While the possibility of the 144,000 (as part of a special elect group of believers) is open to the same conjecture as that of the two witnesses, the fact is that the 144,000 will probably be converted after the rapture.

Now some have argued that it is impossible to have converts without witnesses. Hence, they say that pretribulation rapture eliminates all witnesses, leaving no one to "convert" or educate the remaining populous. The obvious Biblical answer is that the Holy Spirit will do its own convicting, converting, and teaching. One must remember that the apostle Paul said of his conversion, "I did not immediately consult with flesh and blood, nor did I go up to Jerusalem to those who were apostles before me; but I went away to Arabia, and returned once more to Damascus" (Galatians 1:16-17). In other words, Paul went to Arabia to study and search the Hebrew Scriptures (for the New Testament did not yet exist). In all that time he did not learn from Christian men but from the Holy Spirit and from the Scriptures alone. So it will be with the 144,000.

In fairness, it must be said that this author once had the same questions about these converts without witnesses. Although I easily accepted the fact that the Holy Spirit does not need men, I pondered how these 144,000 could learn the Scriptures so well in such a short amount of time that they would become effective witnesses within (presumably) months of the rapture. This question was answered for me when I visited Israel during the Iraq war of 2003. My tour guide was a Jewish man of faith, but not a Messianic Jew. He loved evangelical Christians and knew we were the allies of Israel, but he did not accept Jesus as the Messiah. What struck me was that he carried around a Christian Bible and knew the New Testament as well as the Old. He knew the premillennial view of end times and was well acquainted with doctrines of Christ. He did not believe for one reason only. He is waiting for the veil to be lifted (cf. Romans 11:25). I met many such people in Israel. These were men who are unknowingly waiting for the fullness of the Gentiles to be completed. It is little wonder that when we jested with him, saying, "you will become one of the 144,000 after rapture," he merely smiled and acknowledged us.[1422]

A Critique of Partial Rapture

In some ways partial rapture theory is consistent with pretribulationism for most agree that rapture *begins* before the tribulation. The comparisons, however, end there. Partial rapturism has been accussed of leaning heavily upon legalism. While such an argument is overly harsh, especially from a society which leans too heavily upon libertinism, there is no doubt that it places too much emphasis upon the believer and his spiritual maturity rather than on God's grace and His promise of deliverance.

In partial rapture exegesis of the Olivet Discourse in Matthew 24:40-41, the one taken and left is likened to two separate believers. This assumption cannot be proven. On the contrary, the one who left is compared to those who drowned in the flood. Consequently, if the one left behind is a believer, he would be drowned. Such a view is inconsistent with the context. The partial rapture theory appeals to those who have tired of the libertine ethics of modern Christians, but it cannot stand up to the test of the Scriptures. Rapture is for all believers.

Conclusions

There is no doubt that the doctrine of rapture is taught in the Bible. The only question is in regard to its time frame. The Bible teaches that rapture is a "mystery." It is not a doctrine easily understood. It requires patience, prayer, and a thorough survey of the Scriptures to decipher. It is, therefore, somewhat arrogant to proclaim that one view has no problems while degrading others. It is clear that there are stronger views than others, but all views have difficulties. Rapture is simply not an easy issue. We must examine the Scriptures with prayer and humility and decide which view is the best, but must be careful in demeaning other interpretations, so long as they do not deny the essential promises of the Lord. Where one view of God's promise conflicts with another promise made by the Lord, that view must be rejected. God does not change His mind, nor lie. So if a rapture view is consistent with all of God's promises, it is worthy of consideration.

It is prudent to examine the views in light of their strengths and weaknesses. The study charts attempt, as fairly as is possible, to highlight these points. The reader may choose to believe that the answer to a criticism has been answered properly or that a strength has been duly refuted, but he should fairly take all points in due consideration.

With all factors considered, it is the opinion of this author that pretribulationism is the strongest. Pretribulationism can be found, or at least a form of teaching consistent with it, in every age except the Middle Ages. It is the only view (along with an amended midtribulational view)[1423] that can adequately explain the beginning of the Day of the Lord in connection with "peace and safety" and it clearly defines the unique role of Israel in last days. Most importantly, it seems the only view that is consistent with the teaching of imminency. The main problem cited against the view is that it offers no clear cut reason why rapture must precede the tribulation short of an alleged dispensational bias. As such, it is argued, the large number of converts following rapture would have no one to teach them the Word, except for the Holy Spirit.

Midtribulationalism remains the second best position, particularly if it is amended in its chronology of some events. Like pretribulationism, it is possible, although by no means clear, that the view, or one like it, was taught by some of the church fathers and possibly by one of the Reformers during the time of the Great Awakening. It provides a fair balance between the arguments for and against pretribulationism as well as offering a better timetable for the beginning of the Day of the Lord (but not necessarily the rapture). Unfortunately, it creates many difficulties. It must take signs of the Day of the Lord and apply those to rapture,[1424] it must either deny or minimize the teaching of imminency, it must overlap Israel and the church, and it must find a way to read rapture in the book of Revelation where it is not clearly taught.

After pretribulationism and midtribulationism the merit of each view drops off significantly. The pre-wrath position cannot be completely discounted, but it has many problems that cannot be easily resolved. It can only appeal to Ephraem the Syrian as a possible advocate before Marvin Rosenthal, who openly calls himself the inventor of the view.[1425] It must assume that the rapture occurs on the *very day* that the Day of the Lord begins, it must assume a specific chronology of the judgments of God, it must assume that the seals do not contain the wrath of God, it must deny imminency, it must have people believing in "peace and safety" amid "cosmic disturbances" and wars, and it must argue that the *parousia* refers to a *series* of events. Until these criticisms are answered, the view must remain a distant third among the rapture positions.

The partial rapture theory cannot be completely discounted either. Like the pre-wrath position, it relies on many dubious assumptions and cannot be traced back further than Robert Govett and Joseph Seiss. It may be fairly stated that the view is based on a systematic, if erring, interpretation of Scripture rather than examing a few select verses. Nonetheless, the view creates many difficulties. It leans too heavily upon man's works and worthiness in conflict with God's grace, it misapplies verses about nonbelievers to believers, and it fails to properly distinguish between wrath and persecution.

Finally, posttribulationism must be considered. Despite the amazing popularity of the view, it is clearly the weakest of the positions. Its appeal is largely in the fact that it avoids the difficulties of rapture passages by ignoring the distinction between rapture and the second coming. Despite the claim that it is the "historic" teaching of the church, the position was first clearly articulated in the mid-twentieth century. Its main problems are that it must completely and utterly deny the doctrine of imminency and it must dismiss or severely diminish the role of Israel in the last days. The greatest problem it has, however, is its inability to sufficiently explain who will inherit the Millennial Kingdom. Since all believers are said to be raptured only seconds before the second coming, there would be no believers left on earth to receive the inheritance. No posttribulationist has even been able to adequately answer this question.

Thus it can be concluded that rapture will happen and will happen in a day when men are caught unaware. The world will be blinded to their coming destruction and Israel will (as will discussed in the ensuing chapters) believe and return to the Lord. Pretribulationism appears to be the strongest view although an amended midtribulation position cannot be completely ruled out. Will anyone be left behind? Will our bodies remain? All these questions, and many more, have only briefly been addressed here. A careful study by all believers is not only prudent, but wise. Here the views have been presented in as fair and judicious a manner as possible. Whether the reader agrees or not, he must address all the issues and be fair to all positions. Only through devout prayer, humility, and a sincere desire for truth will the Holy Spirit make the "mysteries" of God plain.

Study Chart on the Apostasy

Apostasy as Anti-Christ

Tenants of:

The apostasy is seen as a title for the anti-Christ and synonymous with "the Man of Lawlessness."

Strengths:

1) It is a very old interpretation dating back to the church fathers.

Weaknesses:

1) The conjunction proves that the "Man of Lawlessness" is different from the apostasy.

2) Apostasy, if a proper name, should be in the Greek vocative tense, not necessarily the nominative.

3) This is a minority view even in the days of the church fathers and has never been widely accepted.

Apostasy as War and Rebellion

Tenants of:

The apostasy is synonymous with the rebellion and war of the tribulation.

Strengths:

1) It is an adequate description of the rebellion in the last days of the tribulation.

Weaknesses:

1) The apostasy is clearly stated to come *first*, hence the tribulation follows. The apostasy is not a part of the tribulation but precedes it.

2) The anti-Christ also follows this apostasy, he does not lead it.

3) The word "apostasy" is only used for war with specific contextual identifiers. Apostasy does not naturally mean war, although rebellion can be a legitimate translation.

4) Although sometimes translated as "rebellion," this specific interpretation is not well received throughout the milieu of Christian history.

Apostasy as Religious Apostasy

Tenants of:

The apostasy refers to an apostate Christianity and religion, devoid of the true faith in Christ.

Strengths:

1) This is the most common use of "apostasy" in the Bible.

2) This is the most common interpretation.

Weaknesses:

1) Apostasy, when used in this sense, usually specifies, "from the faith." There is no clarification here.

2) The King James was the first translation to clearly give apostasy this meaning.

Apostasy as the Rapture

Tenants of:

The apostasy is "the departure" and is a title for the rapture.

Strengths:

1) The root meaning of apostasy is "to leave" or "depart." All translations can see their root in these meanings.

2) Virtually all translations before the King James translate this as "the departure."

3) This view has no problem with the doctrine of imminency.

Weaknesses:

1) Used simply as a noun, the word is rarely used in this sense.

2) This view does not appear to have been the accepted view of history.

3) It is not a popular view even among pretribulationists.

Study Chart on the Rapture Positions

Leading Scholars

Irenaeus	Chiliast	Advocates Imminency.
Hippolytus	Chiliast	Advocates Imminency.
Ephraem	Chiliast	Possibly pretribulational or midtribulational.
Adso of Montier	Medieval Chiliast	Unclear.
Matthew Poole	Historicist	Refers to rapture but without time frame.
John Darby	Dispensational premillennialist	Pretribulational.
Joseph Seiss	Futurist premillennialist	Partial Rapturist.
Robert Govett	Futurist premillennialist	Partial Rapturist.
H. A. Ironside	Dispensational premillennialist	Pretribulational.
E. W. Bullinger	Ultradispensational	Pretribulational.
Norman Harrison	Midtribulational premillennialist	Midtribulational.
John Walvoord	Dispensational premillennialist	Pretribulational.
George Ladd	Posttribulational Premillennialist	Posttribulational.
Robert Gundry	Dispensational postribulationist	Posttribulational.
Tim LaHaye	Dispensational premillennialist	Pretribulational.
Hal Lindsey	Dispensational premillennialist	Pretribulational.
Marvin Rosenthal	Premillennialist	Pre-wrath position.

General Summary

	Position
Church Fathers	Advocated the doctrine of imminency. Ephraem makes the clearest reference to rapture but it could be either pretribulational (as usually assumed) or midtribulational. It is not consistent with posttribulationism.
Medieval Theologians	As the historicist interpretation became predominant both rapture and imminency faded away. No medieval scholar makes explicit mention of either.
Reformation Scholars	The term rapture was already in use but within the historicist tradition no time frame for the rapture can be fairly given.
Post-Reformation Scholars	Rapture was clearly defined and advocated. Most were pretribulational although a few were advocates of "partial rapture" theory. Midtribulationism was not yet heard of.
Modern Evangelicals	Rapture belief is now commonly accepted but divided as to the time frame. Most evangelicals are pretribulational but a rising number are posttribulational or even pre-wrath. Midtribulationism had a brief stint of popularity in the middle of the 20th century.

Theological Breakdown

	Position
Premillennial Historicists	Historicists accept rapture as an event related to the second coming, but offer no explanation of the time frame since their system drags Revelation out across the centuries.
Covenant Theologians or Replacement Theologians	Almost universally posttribulational. Some may hold to a midtribulational view, but none known to this author subscribe to pretribulationism.
Dispensational Premillennialists	Generally pretribulational, but a few subscribe to an alternate scheme. Only one dispensational scholar professes to be posttribulational.
Progressive Dispensationalists	They are curiously quiet on the issue of rapture. It is probable that they may embrace any rapture position.

Study Charts on the Rapture

Pretribulation Rapture

Tenants of:

The church will be raptured before the tribulation begins and before the anti-Christ signs his treaty with Israel. The tribulation is viewed as the fulfillment of the seventieth Week of Daniel 9:27.

Popular advocates from:

The Church Fathers : Possibly Ephraem the Syrian. Most of the church fathers taught imminency.

Medieval Theologians : No clear advocates.

Reformation Scholars : Probably Morgan Edwards.

Post-Reformation Scholars : John Darby, E. W. Bullinger, Walter Scott, Sir Robert Anderson, Samuel Kellogg, and Nathaniel West.

Modern Scholars : C.I. Scofield, William Newell, Dwight Pentecost, Charles Ryrie, J.F. Strombeck, Hal Lindsey, Tim LaHaye, Robert Thomas, Henry Morris, and Dave Hunt.

Strengths:

1) The inability to find rapture explicitly in Revelation would be because it already happened before the tribulation. Other positions must read rapture into Revelation.

2) Since rapture precedes the Day of the Lord, it accords better with Thessalonians saying the Day of the Lord begins during a time of "peace and safety."

3) Is strongly supported by the doctrine of Imminency found in both the Scriptures and church history.

4) Recognizes the distinctions between Israel and the church.

5) Acknowledges a literal fulfillment of the seventieth Week of Daniel.

6) Fits the "days of Noah" prophecy far better than other views.

7) Gives a consistent view of God's dispensational/prophetic plan for the culmination of the ages.

Weaknesses:

1) No verses can explicitly fix the time of rapture.

2) Has problems explaining the rise of post-rapture Christians in great numbers.

3) The argument that believers will be spared wrath does not necessarily mean they will be spared persecution. Critics asks if the believers in the tribulation will also be spared wrath and how. If by a different method, why is rapture needed?

Posttribulation Rapture
Tenants of:
The rapture is supposed to be virtually synonymous with the second coming. As Jesus returns at Armageddon He first raptures the church to meet Him in the air and the church then returns immediately with Him to the earth.

Popular advocates from:
The Church Fathers : Possible advocates, but none explicit.
Medieval Theologians : None known, although advocates claim historicism is posttribulational.
Reformation Scholars : None known, although advocates claim historicism is posttribulational.
Post-Reformation Scholars : None known, although advocates claim historicism is posttribulational.
Modern Scholars : George Ladd & Robert Gundry.

Strengths:
1) Explains the difficulty in distinguishing the second coming from the rapture as they are seen as virtually one and the same.
2) Explains the relative silence of the early church fathers on the issue of the rapture.

Weaknesses:
1) In practicality it is a denial of the rapture.
2) Has great difficulty explaining who inherits the thousand year reign.
3) Cannot adequately explain the appearance of believers on earth at the second coming.
4) Must deny the doctrine of imminency.
5) Generally denies the literal fulfillment of the seventieth Week of Daniel 9:27.
6) Cannot adequately explain the order of resurrection since the rapture and second coming are synonymous.
7) Must accept the idea that daily life and routine continues up to Armageddon.
8) Must deny or diminish the fact that Israel is the focus of Revelation.
9) Is largely compatible only with Covenant Theology.

Midtribulation Rapture

Tenants of:

The rapture is held to occur at the seventh trumpet of Revelation, which is, in turn, placed in the middle of the tribulation, following the abomination of desolation.

Popular advocates from:

The Church Fathers : Possibly Ephraem the Syrian.
Medieval Theologians : None known.
Reformation Scholars : Possibly Morgan Edwards.
Post-Reformation Scholars : None known.
Modern Scholars : Norman Harrison, James Buswell, Merrill Tenney, and Gleason Archer.

Strengths:

1) It provides a balance between the arguments of pre- and posttribulationists.
2) It is consistent with (although by no means clearly) the teachings of the church fathers.
3) It correctly places the Day of the Lord during the second half of the tribulation.

Weaknesses:

1) It takes the signs of the Day of the Lord as signs of rapture.
2) It borrows elements from pre- and posttribulationists.
3) Generally denies the doctrine of imminency.
4) It must overlap the Israel and the church within Revelation.
5) Why is rapture not clearly mentioned in Revelation if it occurs in the middle of the tribulation?

Pre-Wrath Rapture

Tenants of:

The rapture is said to occur under the seventh seal toward the end of the Seventieth Week of Daniel and before the trumpet and bowl judgments are poured out.

Popular advocates from:

The Church Fathers : Possibly Ephraem the Syrian.
Medieval Theologians : None known.
Reformation Scholars : None known.
Post-Reformation Scholars : None known.
Modern Scholars : Marvin Rosenthal and Robert Van Kampen.

Strengths:

1) It attempts to better define the Day of the Lord and its components.
2) It appears to accept a literal fulfillment of the seventieth Week of Daniel.
3) It acknowledges some differences between the rapture and second coming.

Weaknesses:

1) It must assume that rapture occurs on the very day that the Day of the Lord begins.
2) It must assume that the "shortening" of the tribulation is a reference to rapture/Day of the Lord.
3) It must assume that God's wrath is restricted only to the trumpets and bowls.
4) It fails to disntinguish between rapture passages and second coming passages, arguing instead that the *parousia* refers to a series of events.
5) It must argue that "peace and safety" is uttered during the midst of persecution.
6) It is interwoven into a specific and intricate chronological view.
7) It is an admittedly new view unheard of for 2000 years.
8) It must overlap the Israel and the church within Revelation.
9) Seriously plays down, or denies, the doctrine of imminency.

Partial Rapture Theory
Tenants of:
Maintains that Christians will be raptured at various times throughout the tribulation. According to partial rapturism, a believer is only raptured if he is eagerly anticipating the Return, has suffered for the faith, and has achieved a certain level of sanctification.

The Church Fathers : None known.
Medieval Theologians : None known.
Reformation Scholars : None known.
Post-Reformation Scholars : Robert Govett, Joseph Seiss, and G.H. Pember.
Modern Scholars : Watchman Nee and Witness Lee.

Strengths:
1) It is based on a systematic interpretation rather than the interpretation of select verses.
2) It can explain the reason that the timing of the rapture is not clear in the Bible; i.e. it is not a single event at a single time.

Weaknesses:
1) It leans too heavily upon our own works and worthiness in conflict with God's grace.
2) The need to suffer for the faith is nowhere defined in Scripture as a prerequisite for rapture.
3) A misapplication of verses about nonbelievers being applied to believers.
4) All believers are a part of the body of Christ and the church and will not be treated separately in rapture.
5) Does not distinguish between wrath and persecution.

Appendix B

—

The Resurrections and Judgment Seats

Tied to the controversy of the rapture are the resurrections and judgments which accompany them. Even as the rapture is a form of resurrection (a transformation from life rather than from death), the issues are connected. Since the Bible associates a judgment with each resurrection, these issues must be addressed together.

Traditionally, scholars acknowledged at least two separate resurrections and two separate judgments. Some, such as John Walvoord, differentiate as many as seven different judgments.[1426] Others, like Irenaeus, saw only a single general judgment and two resurrections.[1427] The issue is, therefore, one which needs closer examination.

The First Resurrection

> "And I saw thrones, and they sat upon them, and judgment was given to them. And I *saw* the souls of those who had been beheaded because of the testimony of Jesus and because of the word of God, and those who had not worshiped the beast or his image, and had not received the mark upon their forehead and upon their hand; and they came to life and reigned with Christ for a thousand years. The rest of the dead did not come to life until the thousand years were completed. This is the first resurrection. Blessed and holy is the one who has a part in the first resurrection; over these the second death has no power, but they will be priests of God and of Christ and will reign with Him for a thousand years" (Revelation 20:4-6).

This is how the Bible describes "the first resurrection." The most immediate observation is that, where there is a "first" resurrection, there must be *at least* a second. The reader will also note that those who partake of the first resurrection are given "thrones" and the authority to judge. However, whom they are judging is not explicitly stated. These participants are said to be the ones who will reign with Christ for a thousand years. Hence, many believe that the judgment given to them is that of judges and governors in the Millennial Kingdom itself. Others believe that the judgments of angels are spoken of in 1 Corinthians 6:3. However, the judgment of angels is not what concerns most scholars, but that of men.

Several observation upon the first resurrection may be made. The most obvious observation is that "the second death has no power" over those who participate in the first resurrection. It is for this reason that it has been called "the resurrection of the just."[1428] All those who participate in this resurrection shall be saved believers, but does that mean that all believers shall participate? This is where scholars begin to drastically differ. One problem is that rapture, by most all accounts, precedes the "first resurrection." Save posttribulationists, all premillennialists believe that rapture has occurred previous to the second coming, and is accompanied by a resurrection. This is proven in 1 Thessalonian 4:16-17 where we are told that "the dead in Christ shall rise first. Then we who are alive and remain shall be caught up together with them in the clouds to meet the Lord in the air." Thus, "the dead in Christ" are resurrected immediately before (virtually simultaneously) the rapture of the living saints.[1429] Whether pretribulational, midtribulational, or pre-wrath, the "order" of the resurrection has created a confusion.

One solution to this difficulty is to say that the "first resurrection" is divided to various "phases." According to Hal Lindsey "there are some very unusual incidences of resurrection which at the very least establish a precedent for having more than two phases within the 'resurrection of life.'"[1430] He argues that the Israeli harvest was composed on several phases,[1431] an appropriate analogy since the Bible likens the second coming to harvest several times (cf. Matthew 13:24-30, Revelation 14:14-20). Lindsey also quotes Matthew 27:52-53 in which "the tombs were opened; and *many*" [not all] "bodies of the saints who had fallen asleep were raised."[1432] This occurred at the resurrection of Christ, two thousand years ago. It is therefore probable that the term "first resurrection" is not intended as a technical term, but a general term for the resurrection of the righteous.

According to Lindsey, there are four phases. He believes that the resurrection of Jesus was itself the first phase based on 1 Corinthians 15:20-25. He then says that the second phase occurs at rapture and includes all believers from "the day of Pentecost until the Rapture."[1433] Phase three he says occurs at the second coming and includes both Old Testament saints and the tribulation saints.[1434] Finally, he believes that all believers will be transformed at the end of the Millennium, constituting the final stage of the first resurrection.[1435] Tim LaHaye divides the first resurrection a little differently. He sees only three stages consisting of church age saints at the rapture followed by Old Testament saints and, lastly, tribulation saints.[1436]

Both Hal Lindsey and Tim LaHaye place the resurrection of church age saints along side the rapture, as all agree, but place the resurrection of Old Testament saints at the end of the tribulation. The problem with this view is that at the second coming, Revelation 20 speaks only of "the souls of those who had been beheaded because of the testimony of Jesus and because of the word of God, and those who had not worshiped the beast or his image, and had not received the mark upon their forehead and upon their hand" (vs. 4). This clearly seems to imply tribulation saints who have died throughout the tribulation, but does it include others? Are the saints of the Old Testament times excluded? Watchman Nee believes that the Old Testament saints are not included here and will not be resurrected until the Great White Throne Judgment.[1437] Walter Scott disagrees. He includes the Old Testament saints with the resurrection of rapture.[1438] His reasoning is simple and true. The saints of the Old Testament all anticipated Christ, the Messiah. Consequently, it is not Biblical to say that Moses, David, and the rest are not "in Christ." Nonetheless, many modern scholars have shifted away from this view. John Walvoord says "the expression 'in Christ' is uniformly used in the New Testament, wherever it has theological meaning, as a reference to those who have been baptized by the Spirit into the body of Christ."[1439] He then says that the phrase "in Christ" is a "technical expression."[1440] It seems odd, to say the least, that while Walvoord accepts "the first resurrection" as a general phrase for the resurrection of the just, he believes that "those who are in Christ" is a technical designation which completely negates Moses and David as participants.

Additionally, Walvoord believes that Daniel 12:2 teaches that Israeli believers will be resurrected after the tribulation.[1441] The passage, however, says nothing of the sort. According to Daniel 12:2, "many of those who sleep in the dust of the ground will awake, these to everlasting life, but the others to disgrace *and* everlasting contempt." This passage is associated with "a time of distress such as never occurred" (vs. 1), and hence tied to the tribulation. However, Walvoord is actually contradicting himself here, for he acknowledges that the wicked are not resurrected until the end of the Millennium,[1442] yet Daniel 12:2 talks of "others [being raised] to disgrace *and* everlasting contempt." If Daniel 12:2 is argued to be a technical designation of what occurs at the second coming, then the wicked must be raised at this time as well, but virtually all premillennialists agree this is not so. Daniel 12:2 speaks of "many" being raised. This means that some are not raised. A careful examination of the passage shows that chronology is not what is emphasized here, but the resurrection of the dead. Many will be raised (we are not told whether these are Old Testament saints or Jewish tribulation saints), others will not. The passage is silent on the issue of the rapture.

In conclusion, too many have taken the phrase "in Christ" in 1 Thessalonians to mean that only the church age alone is intended, but to what purpose would Christ make Moses and David wait till the end of the tribulation? Of course, another alternative is that the Old Testament saints were resurrected immediately after Christ's resurrection (cf. Matthew 27:52-53). The only problem with this, is that the passage speaks of "many," but not all. Therefore, at least some Old Testament saints remain in their graves, awaiting the first resurrection. The best view is that the Old Testament saints rise at the same time as the church age saints. "Those who had not worshiped the beast or his image, and had not received the mark upon their forehead and upon their hand" (vs. 4) is a phrase exclusive to the tribulation, and consistent with the belief that Christ will resurrect all believers in order. When He comes at rapture he will resurrect *all* the saints. When he comes at the second coming, he will resurrect those who were not believers at rapture, but who repented and died for their faith. No one will need to wait needlessly.

The *Bema* Seat

The Greek word for a judgment seat, or tribunal, is βημα (*bema*), found in Acts 18:4. It is considered synonymous with the judgment seat of God, but this judgment seat is distinguished from the Great White Throne judgment found in Revelation 20:11-15. It is a judgment seat associated with the judgment of the righteous, usually believed to occur at the time of the rapture.[1443]

The Bible makes clear that Christians will never be condemned before God, but too many have erroneously taken this to mean that we will not be judged before God. This is not so. Romans 14:10 says that "we shall all stand before the judgment seat of God." Paul also says, "we must all appear before the judgment seat of Christ, that each one may be recompensed for his deeds in the body, according to what he has done, whether good or bad" (2 Corinthians 5:10). Thus, while we are not condemned before God, "each one of us shall give account of himself to God" (Romans 14:12). We shall, therefore, be rewarded accordingly.

As Watchman Nee has said, "no Christian will be judged and condemned before God (John 5:24), but no Christian will be exempt from having to stand and be judged before the judgment seat of Christ according to what he has done (2 Cor. 5:10)."[1444] This concept is not new. In fact, the apostles themselves were often found arguing about who would be the greatest in the Kingdom of Heaven (Matthew 18:4, 23:11; Mark 9:34; Luke 22:24-26). Jesus' response was to tell them "if anyone wants to be first, he shall be last of all, and servant of all" (Mark 9:34). He did not, however, discount the doctrine of rewards for service. God's grace saves us all, but his grace will also reward those who have served Him and our fellow man (cf. 1 Corinthians 3:11-15, 1 Corinthians 4:1-5). Some have rejected this doctrine, arguing that it leads to selfish motives and bickering such as the apostles sometimes engaged in, but God judges the heart. He alone knows our motives. Certainly we cannot all be kings in the Millennial Kingdom, nor can we all sit on Jesus' right side. We will all dwell in mercy and peace for eternity with God, but those who have served Christ, whether Moses and Elijah or Peter and John, will not fail to receive their rewards.

The larger debate is when this judgment occurs. Revelation 11:18 says, "the time *has come* for the dead to be judged, and to give their rewards to Thy bond-servants, the prophets and to the saints and to those who fear Thy name, the small and the great, and to destroy those who destroy the earth." Most agree that this verse is anticipatory of the second coming, but H. A. Ironside believes that this actually refers to the end of the Millennium when the wicked will be judged at the Great White Throne.[1445] This assumption, however, is unnecessary. The final judgment of the wicked may indeed occur at the Great White Throne (see below), but the fact that the dead are placed in the confines of the pit, in anticipation of that day, shows that they have already been judged on at least one plane at the second coming. John Walvoord agrees in principle. He says that a judgment of living Gentiles immediately follows the second coming,[1446] usually called the Judgment of the Sheep and Goats. He says, "it is fitting that a judgment of the Gentiles should take place as a preparation for the Millennial Kingdom."[1447] He believes that this is what is spoken of in Matthew 25:31-46,[1448] as does George Peters, who notes that it is the "nations," rather than the "dead," who are judged in those passages.[1449] These men are judged at second coming, but their ultimate fate is reserved for the Great White Throne.

In short, each man is to be formally judged at his resurrection. Whether righteous or unrighteous, the *bema* seat will preside over him at the time of his resurrection. That would mean that the saints who are transformed at rapture (both the living and dead) are to be judged at that time. The tribulation saints and the living wicked will be judged at the second coming, and the rest of the dead will be judged at the end of the Millennium.

The Great White Throne Judgment

> "And I saw a great white throne and Him who sat upon it, from whose presence earth and heaven fled away, and no place was found for them. And I saw the dead, the great and the small, standing before the throne, and books were opened; and another book was opened, which is *the book* of life; and the dead were judged from the things which were written in the books, according to their deeds. And the sea gave up the dead which were in it, and death and Hades gave up the dead which were in them; and they were judged, every one *of them* according to their deeds. And death and Hades were thrown into the lake of fire. This is the second death, the lake of fire. And if anyone's name was not found written in the book of life, he was thrown into the lake of fire" (Revelation 20:11-15).

The Great White Throne judgment is surely the most controversial of judgment passages. Some scholars believe it speaks of a general judgment when both the righteous and unrighteous will be judged. Others insist that only the wicked will be judged at this time. Both views offer strong support, and neither view can be lightly discarded. Sometimes scholars have a tendancy to interpret in *reaction against* other doctrines or teachings which they know, or believe, to be false. The best example is Matthew 16:18. Catholics have used this passage argue that Peter was the first pope, and that Christ was establishing the papacy. Protestants have reacted against this view by saying that the rock is Christ, since He is the cornerstone (1 Corinthians 3:11). However, the Bible also speaks of the foundations of the apostles (Ephesians 2:20). The context best fits the fact that Jesus was making a word play, for Peter is Πέτρος (*Petros*) in Greek and the word "rock" is πέτρᾳ (*petra*) in Greek. "Cornerstone," however, is λιθος (*lithos*). Thus, it appears that Jesus was making a word play and referring to the foundations laid by the apostles (cf. Ephesians 2:20). Consequently, *both* Catholics and Protestants have developed an erroneous interpretation based on their reaction against one another. So also, the Great White Throne judgment appears to stir a certain amount of emotion. A careful examination of both views, however, will show that both are right and both are wrong. A general judgment is inferred, but *not a single* general judgment. The majority of the righteous have previously been judged and will not be judged again, but it is impossible to deny that believers, as well as the wicked, will participate in this final judgment.

Arguments for and Against a General Judgment

The character of this final judgment is dark and depressing. As Seiss remarks, "we read of no white robes, no spotless linens, no palms, nothing but naked sinners."[1450] Nowhere do we read of eternal rewards or crowns of glory. Instead we read about "the lake of fire." For this reason, most dispensational scholars called this the "resurrection of the wicked," or as Arthur Bloomfield calls it, "a resurrection of damnation."[1451] Even some of the ancient church fathers saw this distinction, such as Victorinus who saw the second resurrection solely for unbelievers.[1452] In addition to the negative tone of the passage, Walvoord says, "it may be assumed that these are the wicked dead, who are not raised in the first resurrection (cf. Dan. 12:2; John 5:29; Acts 24:15; Rev. 20:5)."[1453] Of course, it is this assumption which critics scoff at.[1454]

George Ladd believes, "such a scheme of eschatology cannot be proved but rests upon unsupported inferences."[1455] Ladd then presents his own inferences, saying, "the final issue of the judgment of the nations is not the Millennial Kingdom but is either eternal life or eternal punishment (Matt. 25:46). This is clearly the final judgment which decides the eternal destiny of men. The judgment seat of Christ is also the judgment seat of God before which all believers must stand (Rom. 14:10)."[1456] Robert Mounce agrees in principle, but follows a different line of reasoning. Mounce does not see all believers resurrected at the second coming, but only the martyred dead. Therefore, he says, "if the first resurrection is limited to actual martyrs, then the judgment of verses 11-15 involves both believer and impenitent."[1457] So two objections are raised. Do the gospels teach a general judgment as Ladd believers? Moreover, will there be dead believers at the end of the Millennium?

There is no doubt that Matthew 25:31-46 appears to infer some sort of general judgment. John Walvoord has argued that Matthew 25 refers only to the judgment of the living at the second coming,[1458] as does George Peters and many others.[1459] This is called "the Sheep and Goats judgment." Matthew 13:24-29, 36-43 might also be interpreted in a similar manner, but Walter Scott, who rejects the teaching of a general judgment, acknowledges that "it must be

330

frankly conceded that the Lord's words in John 5:28-29 *seem* to teach a general resurrection."[1460] He discounts this by saying that "the 'hour' referred to embraces a thousand years."[1461] Although the passage does not necessitate a concurrent chronology, these answers are not entirely satisfactory.

Consider Matthew 13:38-40 where Jesus explains the meaning of the parable of the wheat and the tares; "the field is the world; and *as for* the good seed, these are the sons of the kingdom; and the tares are the sons of the evil *one;* and the enemy who sowed them is the devil, and the harvest is the end of the age; and the reapers are angels. Therefore just as the tares are gathered up and burned with fire, so shall it be at the end of the age." It is clear from this verse that "at the end of the age" there will be some judgment, which apparently includes believers, for the wheat and tares are reaped *at the same time*; harvest. There are, therefore, two possible answers. The first is that this speaks of a general judgment at the Great White Throne. This view, however, is not acceptable, for the harvest appears to be related to the second coming; not the Great White Throne (Revelation 14:14-20). The second view is therefore the best. This speaks of *a* general judgment at the second coming; a judgment of the living.

It seems then that Ladd's arguments are not sufficient to discredit the view that only the wicked are judged at the Great White Throne. Ladd has criticized dispensationalists for "inferences,"[1462] but created his own inferences. Certainly, a general judgment is taught, but that judgment cannot be proven to be the judgment of the Great White Throne, but what of Mounce's objection? If there are believers who have not been resurrected previously, will they not participate?

Some scholars, mostly posttribulationists, believe that only the martyred dead, or tribulation saints, will be raised in the first resurrection. They, therefore, assume that Moses, David, and most church age believers will all arise at the end of the Millennium along with the wicked. As a result, they must conclude that the Great White Throne is a general judgment. The problems with this line of reasoning are obvious. To begin with, we (believers) are promised the right to reign with Christ (2 Timothy 2:12). By definition, if we are to "reign" then we must have subjects over which to rule. In the New Heaven and the New Earth, we will all be heavenly immortals in resurrected bodies. We will all be equals in the eyes of God. To be sure, we will not have equal rewards, but there is no indication that any of us will be ruled by any king, save Jesus Christ. It is only in the Millennium that we are told the resurrected will "reign with Christ" (Revelation 20:6). It is, therefore, unacceptable to deny that all believers are risen in the first resurrection.

So then the Great White Throne judgment must be solely of the wicked? No. This is where many dispensationalists err, for there is *no doubt* that believers *will die* in the Millennial Kingdom. As has been aforementioned, even Methuselah would not have lived to see the end of the Millennial Kingdom (cf. Genesis 5:27). So it is probable that *all* those who originally inherit the Millennium at the second coming, will die before Satan is released. They will be spared the pain of seeing their childred deceived by Satan and rebelling against the Lord. They will, however, be participants in this Great White Throne judgment. The negative character of the judgment is owed to the fact that the predominant number of those judged will be condemned, but it cannot be denied that believers will be present. This is apparent by the mere fact that the book of life is present at judgment (Revelation 20:12). Why is the book there at all, if none are to be found in it? Indeed, what are the purposes for these books? Perhaps, our answer is found therein.

The Relevance of the Books
"Books were opened; and another book was opened, which is *the book* of life; and the dead were judged from the things which were written in the books, according to their deeds" (Revelation 20:12). We are thus introduced to two books; the book of life and the book of deeds. We know that the book of life records the name of all believers and that "if anyone's name was not found written in the book of life, he was thrown into the lake of fire" (vs. 15), but there is another book present. This book, the book of deeds, records all the works of man and all his deeds, but why are men judged "according to their deeds?" Does not Scripture state that salvation is by faith alone, not by works (Romans 3:20-28, 11:6, Galatians 2:6; 2 Timothy 1:9)? Several answers are offered.

The church father Lactantius does not believe that wicked will be judged, since they already stand condemned, thus he believes last judgment is for reward and punishment and applies to believers.[1463] Others have argued similarly that the book of deeds for the judging of rewards dispensed to believers, but that the guilty are also present. This view obviously comes from those who accept this as a general judgment. Joseph Seiss, however, offers a unique couter theory. He says, "there is just gradation in the sorrows of the lost, as well as in the rewards of the righteous ... though all the finally condemned go into one place, they do not all alike feel the same pains, or sink to the same depths in those dreadful flames."[1464] Seiss' exegesis is then the flip side of those who believe there is a general judgment here, but there is one final view; a neglected view.

We have been taught, correctly, that salvation is by faith alone. All who reject the Messiah, Christ, are condemned. Therefore, it is assumed that all are condemned *for* rejecting Christ. If we are saved *by* accepting Christ, are we not damned *for* rejecting Christ? Technically, the answer is no. God is a just God. We are indeed all saved through Jesus Christ the savior, and those who have rejected Christ will stand condemned, but the relationship is one of cause and effect. Men reject Christ *because* they are wicked. Because God is a just God, every unbeliever will be judged by his own merits, *and found wanting.* In other words, those who reject Christ, one and all, profess that they deserve to go to heaven by virtue of their merits. God will then say, "okay, let us look at your merits." So by examining the works of each man, every man will condemn himself (cf. Job 15:5; Romans 2:1, 3:20; 1 John 3:20-21)! God is, therefore, just in his eternal punishments. No man will be able to claim that he was damned because he was ignorant, for he will condemn himself out of his own mouth (cf. Job 15:5)! Every excuse will be nullified, and Christ will be vindicated.

Conclusion

It is to be freely admitted that the Great White Throne judgment includes the predominant number of wicked men throughout history. It is also confessed that most believers were judged previously at rapture and the second coming, but the Millennial age believers (and possibly antediluvian believers)[1465] will await this resurrection. One indication that believers are present here is in the fact that the resurrected are gathered from different places. "And the sea gave up the dead which were in it, and death and Hades gave up the dead which were in them" (Revelation 20:13). It would seem, that those dead in the "sea" differ from the dead in "death and Hades." Another indication is the presence of the books.

Two books are present at the Great White Throne judgment. Both books are present, because both are needed. If no saved were present at the judgment, then the book of life would not be needed. Should anyone not be convinced, the words of "ultradispensationalist" E. W. Bullinger should prove the point:

> "We need not speculate as to what is written in these books. Nor can we tell whether this other book – the book of life – is mentioned negatively, to exclude those not named in it; or positively, to embrace those who are. What we do know is that 'the first resurrection' is specifically called 'the resurrection of life'; and that those who have part in it will not be reckoned with 'the rest of the dead which lived not again till the thousand years were finished.' The words, 'according to their works' looks as though there may be two classes of these 'dead.' But where the Word is silent, it is better for is to be silent also."[1466]

Summary

Biblically the dead are judged at the time of their resurrection. The *Bema* Seat is the name given to the judgment of believers when they are resurrected. The Sheep and Goat Judgment occurs at the second coming and refers to the judgment of the living who have survived until Christ's return. Finally, at the end of the Millennium, the Great White Throne Judgment will be the final judgment against all the wicked not previously judged, and those relatively few believers who had not previously have been resurrected. Technically, it is a general judgment, but it is intrinsically negative in tone because it encompasses all unbelievers, save those judged at the Sheep and Goat

Judgment. It is unacceptable to deny that the majority of believers have been resurrected previously.

Appendix C

—

Miscelaneous Issues in Revelation

There remain in Revelation a number of controversies that are of no major consequence (save perhaps the timing of Gog's invasion) to the scope of Revelation, but are of acute interest nevertheless. These issues are discussed because of their prominence in debate, but most of these issues must be admitted to be of a secondary nature. Should Elijah not be one of the two prophets in Revelation 11, my ministry is not harmed, nor does the prophet cease to be a prophet. Should the seven thunders be not what I suspect, none will know or care that I was wrong. These issues are important inasmuch as the Lord God's word is *always* important. No one should minimize that the passages exist for a reason, and where the passages exist, the correct interpretation should be sought. Therefore, by saying that these issues are of no "major consequence to the scope of Revelation," it is not intended to mean that it is unimportant. Instead, it is said with caution. These issues should not be divisive, but their study is encouraged, as is the study of all of God's word.

The Little Scroll

Chapter 10 of Revelation is one of the most difficult in the Bible. In it John is given a scroll and told to eat it. "It was in my mouth sweet as honey; and when I had eaten it, my stomach was made bitter" (Revelation 10:10). Many theories have been devised to explain this passage. Nicholas of Lyra applied the little scroll to the controversial medieval Justinian Treatise,[1467] Darby said that the sweetness was truth but the bitterness was "the ruin-state of the church,"[1468] Norman Harrison said that the scroll was symbolic of Daniel's 70th week because the first half is sweet and second half bitter,[1469] and George Ladd argued that the scroll was prophetic commission.[1470]

Although one might be tempted by Harrison's view, or even another, they all fall apart, because they are based solely on speculation. Two main views remain. The first compares the little scroll to the scroll of Revelation 5:1. After the seven seals were broken the scroll was ready to be read. H. A. Ironside believes that this scroll is "the title deed to the earth."[1471] He says that its sweetness lies in the revelation of Jesus Christ, but its bitterness is "self-judgment" when we learn of our unworthiness.[1472] Arthur Bloomfield follows similar reasoning. He also believes that the scroll is the title deed to the earth,[1473] but differs as to the meaning of the sweetness and bitterness. Bloomfield is more consistent in keeping with the "title deed" theory, for he argues that the scroll declares that Christ is to take "possession of the earth."[1474]

335

The sweetness is, therefore, the inheritance of Christ, but bitterness because the current possessors must be purged.[1475]

This "title deed" theory is tempting, but there is no proof that the scroll is the title deed to the earth, and no proof is offered. It may well be that this little scroll is the same as that of Revelation 5:1, although even this is unproven, but what the scroll is, and what it says, remains a mystery. Perhaps some have tried to read too much into the passage. If we are to understand it, we must allow the Bible to interpret itself.

Walter Scott reminds us that a similar passage exist in Ezekiel 2:8-3:3.[1476] In that passage Ezekiel is told to eat a scroll, on which lamentations and woes are written. That scroll too is said to have been sweet in his mouth. Many scholars take this to mean that the word of God is sweet.[1477] Robert Mounce cites Psalms 119:103, "how sweet are they words to my taste, sweeter than honey to my mouth."[1478] He also cites Jeremiah 15:16 which says, "Thy words were found and I ate them, and Thy words became for me a joy and the delight of my heart."[1479] Hence, as Tim LaHaye says, to eat the scroll is to "digest the word of God."[1480]

If the sweetness is the word of God, as parallel passages seem to indicate, then what is the bitterness which John feels? Walvoord calls it the bitterness of persecution,[1481] although there is no indication that persecution is found in this passage. Robert Thomas also offers some speculation, saying that the joys of consummating prophecy is sweet, but the bitterness is in the rebellion of the judges.[1482] Hal Lindsey says that the love of God is sweet, the rejection of God by men is bitter.[1483] The church father Victorinus offers more sober option, suggesting that the eating is "commiting to memory," the sweetness is "pleasant to hearer," but bitter "to those who announce."[1484] Once again, the interpreter is left with conjecture. Owing to the context of Revelation, the best option is probably to take LaHaye's theory that bitterness represents judgment.[1485]

So the little scroll is brought to John during an interlude following the blast of the seven trumpets. Isolated from the surrounding passages, it can be safely said that the scroll is God's word, sweet to the mouth of John, but bitter in the judgment it brings to the word. However, when the context of chapter ten is placed around it, we must still ponder the specifics of the scroll. Is it, as some believe, the title deed to the earth? Is it, as some argue, a commission to the apostle John concerning the statement, "You must prophesy again concerning many peoples and nations and tongues and kings" (Revelation 10:11)? According to this theory, John is to return to the earth in the last days, as one of the two prophets of chapter 11, which this is said to introduce.[1486] More will be said of this theory later. Certainly, there is nothing explicit in the passage to support such hypothesis, but it does pose interesting questions.

More importantly is the relationship of the scroll to the surrounding chapter. The little scroll is integrally tied to one other issue; that of the seven thunders. The scroll is introduced before the voices of the seven thunders, but it is eaten after the thunders are sealed. What are these seven thunders?

The Seven Thunders

The little scroll is not the only section of chapter 10 which has stirred up men's imaginations, and confused readers. The angel who holds the little scroll cries out like a lion, "and when he had cried out, the seven peals of thunder uttered their voices. And when the seven peals of thunder had spoken, I was about to write; and I heard a voice from heaven saying, 'Seal up the things which the seven peals of thunder have spoken, and do not write them.'" (Revelation 10:3-4). Robert Mounce has informed us that this is in stark contrast to the command of Revelation 22:10, "do not seal up the words of the prophecy."[1487] So why are the words sealed? Logically, if the words are sealed to us then "it is idle to enquire"[1488] and "foolish to conjecture."[1489] However, why mention the thunders at all? If we are not to know what they are, why are we teased with their voices? The answer is not as difficult as might at first be believed. We cannot know the specifics, for reasons delineated below, but the fact that we do know something will happen creates terror in the heart of the unbeliever. It is "added terror before the end,"[1490] but how and in what form?

Some have argued that the seven thunders parallel a sevenfold "voice of the Lord" in Psalms 29.[1491] This view can be traced back to the church father Victorinus who said that it was the "sevenfold" voice of the Holy Spirit.[1492] However, it is by no means clear that any "sevenfold" voice is intended in either this passage, or even in Psalms 29, where God's voice is merely described as majestic and powerful, with many illustrations. So what other alternatives exist? Three more remain.

Norman Harrison says that the voices are "agents" designated to carry the command, "let there be no more delay" (Revelation 10:6) into effect.[1493] He connects these agents with the mystery of Godliness, the mystery of the kingdom of heaven, and the mystery of the church.[1494] John Walvoord also believes that the thunders represent revelations of the "mysteries" of God.[1495] Unfortunately, this is an ambiguous way of resolving the problem. What the voices said are obviously mysteries, because we are not told what they said, but it is for that very reason that we cannot say whether or not the mysteries involve the church or the kingdom of heaven. It is not a valid answer.

Henry Morris suggests that this is the final judgment of God. He believes that the words are sealed, because God has, in His mercy, delayed the judgment until Armageddon.[1496] Nevertheless, this assumption is a contradiction of the explicit command in verse six, "there shall be delay no longer." The thunders, therefore, are not the delayed judgment of God. Many believe, however, that they are judgments. Just as the seven seals, seven trumpets, and seven bowls represent God's judgments upon the earth, the seven thunders are believed to be unknown judgments from God.[1497] The judgments are sealed to us,[1498] but are nevertheless "divine wrath."[1499] Bloomfield argues that they are sealed so that Satan will not know in advance.[1500] Whether Satan knows or not, man will not. Men will doubtless have heard from the prophets and saints of the tribulation of many of the coming judgments. The Bible makes it plain that men know that the judgments are the wrath of God (cf. Revelation 6:16). These judgments, however, they will not know beforehand. It is, as Robert Thomas states, "added terror before the end."[1501] The terror is in what is not known, for it is in not knowing that the greatest terror lies.

The Identity of the Two Witnesses

Previously the two witnesses were discussed briefly, almost as an aside. Their importance to the prophetic scheme is not to be diminished, but their identity, and the mystery surrounding them, was deemed unnessarily burdensome to that chapter. We know that they will testify for three and a half years in Israel and that they will be slain by the anti-Christ. We also know that they will be resurrected and signal the repentance of Israel.

The passage is often seen as parallel to Zechariah 4:1-14 where Zerubbabel is shown two olives trees (vs. 11) which represent "the two anointed ones" (vs. 14). The imagery is the same, but they do not prophesy the same events. Most consider that the two olive trees were representative of the governor Zerubbabel and the high priest Jeshua. The symbolism of the olive trees is, therefore, that of annointed witnesses, so in Revelation 11, "they will be the 'two Olive Trees' for their day, as Zerubbabel and Jeshua were in a former day."[1502]

Strangely enough, some deny that these two witnesses witness the gospel. Watchman Nee says "they do not aim at saving souls"[1503] but that "they testify with force, thereby proving they are not preaching the gospel."[1504] He believes they preach judgment, not the gospel. Henry Morris concurs, calling them "prophets of judgment."[1505] In either case, their preaching leads to repentance, and anger from those who reject the word of the Lord. Eventually, after the anti-Christ has established himself in the temple of God and committed the abomination of desolation, he will order the two prophets slain (something which had been attempted many times previous [Revelation 11:7]). After three days, they will rise from the dead, being resurrected for all to see. Arthur Bloomfield suggests that all eyes will see this event, through the medium of television,[1506] an idea later popularized by Hal Lindsey,[1507] but whether this is true or not, their resurrection will signal the repentance of Israel and the beginning of the darkest half of the tribulation.

These facts are generally agree upon by premillennialists, but who are they? They are prophets, and if that were all that were said then nothing more would be said, but numerous prophecies have suggested that the great Old

Testament prophet Elijah must come again before the second coming of Christ (cf. Malachi 4:5). Is Elijah one of the prophets spoken of here? If he is, then is the second prophet another man who once walked upon the planet ages ago? These are the questions which still stir debate to this day. It is best to evaluate each of these options one at a time, beginning with Elijah of whom the Lord said, "Behold, I am going to send you Elijah the prophet before the coming of the great and terrible day of the Lord" (Malachi 4:5).

Elijah

"Behold, I am going to send you Elijah the prophet before the coming of the great and terrible day of the Lord" (Malachi 4:5). This prophecy was anticipated long before Jesus Christ was born of the virgin. It was anticipated in the apocryphal book of Ecclesiasticus, the apostles anticipated it when they asked Jesus "why then do the scribes say that Elijah must come first?" (Matthew 17:10), and the Jews expected it as well when they whispered that Jesus was Himself Elijah (Mark 6:15; Mark 8:28; Luke 9:8, 9:19). The anticipation of Elijah's coming permeated the society. Even when Jesus was crucified it was said, "this man is calling for Elijah" (Matthew 27:47; cf. Mark 15:35), and the eyewitnesses were told, "let us see whether Elijah will come and save Him" (Matthew 27:49; cf. Mark 15:35). So what of this prophecy? Was it fulfilled in Jesus' day, or it is awaiting fulfillment in the future?

Luke 1:17 seems to indicate that John the Baptist was the fulfillment of the prophecy, as does Jesus' remark "if you care to accept it, [John the Baptist] himself is Elijah, who was to come" (Matthew 11:14). However, this is not conclusive for two reasons. First, John the Baptist expressly denied being Elijah (John 1:20). Second, is the answer of Jesus to his disciples. "'Elijah is coming and will restore all things; but I say to you, that Elijah already came, and they did not recognize him, but did to him whatever they wished. So also the Son of Man is going to suffer at their hands.' Then the disciples understood that He had spoken to them about John the Baptist" (Matthew 17:11-13; cf. Mark 11:12-14). This answer has confused many. It certainly implies that John the Baptist was Elijah, but upon closer examintion it says something as well. "Elijah *is coming* and *will* restore all things" (Matthew 17:11). It is been stated that some prophecies sometimes have dual prophetic meanings; the one close and immediate, and the other distant and future.[1508] This is a perfect example of such a prophecy. In one sentence Jesus declares both that Elijah has come and *will come again*. John the Baptist did not know that he was Elijah, and the prophet of Revelation 11 may not know that he is Elijah. Others have suggested merely that John the Baptist came in the *spirit and power* of Elijah, but was not truly Elijah,[1509] thus Jesus' seemingly odd preface, "if you care to accept it" (Matthew 11:14).

Will then Elijah come as one of the two olive trees? The oldest, best attested, and longest standing tradition says "yes." From the church fathers to

339

the present day, the overwhelming majority of scholars have identified one of the two witnesses as Elijah and the final fulfillment of Malachi 4:5. Among the church father there does not seem to have been a dissenting voice. Hippolytus held to this view,[1510] as did Victorinus[1511] and Tertullian.[1512] Ephraem the Syrian adopted it,[1513] along with Justin Martyr, Cyprian, Methodius, Lactantius, Chrysostom, Theophylact, and even Jerome.[1514] It is also found in ancient apocryphal literature such as "The History of Joseph the Carpenter"[1515] and the "Gospel of Nicodemus."[1516]

The medievals did not back down from this proposition either. Although an increasing allegorical application was apparent, most still believed that Elijah would come again. Adso of Montier affirms it.[1517] Joachim d'Fiore taught it.[1518] Peter D'Olivi believed it,[1519] and even Nicholas of Lyra, although allegorizing it, saw Elijah's return as essential to the prophecy.[1520]

No less enthusiastic are the modern scholars. Nathaniel West supports it.[1521] Joseph Seiss,[1522] George Peters,[1523] and E. W. Bullinger favor it.[1524] Robert Govett[1525] and C. I. Scofield promoted it.[1526] Norman Harrison[1527] and G. H. Lang accepted it.[1528] Arthur Bloomfield believed that Elijah would come down directly from heaven itself, not being born anew through the womb of a woman.[1529] Watchman Nee,[1530] Hal Lindsey,[1531] Robert Gundry,[1532] Henry Morris,[1533] Robert Thomas,[1534] Marvin Rosenthal,[1535] Robert Van Kampen,[1536] and Tim LaHaye[1537] all accept it as well.

Their enthusiasm is bolstered by the vast evidences in its favor. The first is, of course, the promise of Jesus that Elijah will come again in the future (Matthew 17:11). John the Baptist could not have been the complete fulfillment of the prophecy, because Malachi says that Elijah will come before "the great and terrible day of the Lord" (Malachi 4:5). That day is the last days. The first coming of Christ was by no means a "terrible day." It was a joyous day, when the savior was born and when our sins were absolved. It was, therefore, necessary for Elijah to come before both the first coming (through John the Baptist) and the second coming. In the former he came "in the spirit and power" of Elijah (Luke 1:17), and the in the latter he shall return again in the flesh. As Seiss remarks, "there was a twofold ministry embraced in the ancient promise to send Elijah, just as there was a twofold advent in the predictions concerning the Messiah."[1538]

Others have noted that Eljiah was one of the few men in history who did not die a mortal death,[1539] but was taken to heaven in a chariot (2 Kings 2:11). This has led many to speculate as to why. Henry Morris says, "God had a ministry for Elijah which requried that he still remain living in his natural body. There he has remained ever since, awaiting the time at the end of the age when he would return to earth to complete his prophetic mission."[1540] This argument is based on the assumption that Hebrews 9:27 forbids anyone from dying twice. However, while many have taken Hebrews 9:27 as technical designation, proving that no man may died twice, we know that Jesus

340

resurrected a few people who were destined to die a second time (cf. Mark 5:41, John 11:43). However, it is true that those individuals were not translated into their immortal flesh, as the saints shall at rapture. Seiss claims "the saints who have once died, and been resurrected and glorified, have put on immortality, and are no longer capable of death."[1541] In this sense, Seiss could be correct. He, therefore, argues that Elijah was not given his immortal body when he was translated "because it was necessary for Christ first to die for their sins and rise again."[1542] It is then reasoned that Elijah was taken in a chariot up to heaven, so that he could return to the earth again some day in the future. It is based on this assumption that some believe that Elijah will come down *directly* from heaven.[1543] Of course, not all believe this. Many believe that Elijah will be born in a new body and raised as any young Jewish boy in Israel. In either case, the fact that Elijah did not die a mortal death in the past has made him unique among the prophets of history, and led to speculation that he may well be one of these two prophets.

Still other doctors believe that Elijah's appearance at the transfiguration in Matthew 17:3, Mark 9:4-7, and Luke 9:30-36 in an indication of Elijah's importance and prominence.[1544] While this is freely granted, it does not prove that Elijah will be one of the two prophets, anymore than it proves that Moses shall be. Nonetheless, it is does indicate Elijah's closeness to the savior and his preeminence among the prophets.

One lesser argument is the assumption that Elijah must return because Elijah's ministry was left unfinished. According to Hal Lindsey, 1 Kings 19:16 indicates that Elijah's ministry was cut short before its completion.[1545] He reasons that Elijah will return so that his ministry may be completed.[1546]

If this was a lesser argument, the similarities between the miracles of the two witnesses and those of Elijah are not. Revelation says that the prophets "have the power to shut up the sky, in order that rain may not fall during the days of their prophesying" (11:6). Some scholars have noticed that this is the same miracle that Elijah performed, or prophesied, in the Old Testament (cf. 1 Kings 17:1-6).[1547] Revelation also says that "fire proceeds out of their mouth and devours their enemies" (11:5) even as fire once rained down from heaven for Elijah (1 Kings 18:38).

Even those who deny that Elijah will return again, believe that this prophecy makes a symbolic comparison to Elijah. Walter Scott believes that the witnesses are merely symbols of the "faithful servants of Christ"[1548] but compares them to Moses and Elijah.[1549] Likewise, George Ladd Ladd sees this as symbolism for the embodiment of Moses and Elijah.[1550] The same is said by Joseph Mede[1551] and H. A. Ironside.[1552] So it would appear that even those who doubt the literal return of Elijah confess to his appearance in this prophecy, albeit "symbolically."

So the evidences for Elijah's return may be summarized as followed. Malachi predicts Elijah's coming before "the great and terrible day of the Lord"

(Malachi 4:5). Elijah never died but was taken straight to heaven in a chariot (2 Kings 2:11). His ministry may not have been completed on earth; suggesting that he will return later to finish the job. Elijah was also at the transfiguration; indicating his prominence. The miracles of Revelation 11 seem very similar to many of those miracles performed in Elijah's ministry (1 Kings 17:1-6, 18:38), but most importantly of all, Jesus indicated that Elijah "*is coming* and *will* restore all things" (Matthew 17:11). Surely, the words of the Lord are sufficient.

Enoch

If it were not for the strong evidence that Elijah is to come again, there would probably be no speculation as to the identify of the second prophet, but because most agree that Elijah will come again, it is natural to wonder; if the first prophet walked the earth centuries ago, shall not the second prophet also have lived in times long past? Thus the search for the second prophet commences.

Among the most popular views is the view that Enoch (Genesis 5:21-24) will be that second prophet. This view seems at first odd, since Enoch is barely mentioned in the Bible, but, in fact, it is one of the stronger views.

Enoch's appeal is largely in the fact that he is one of two men in the Bible who never died. Conservative scholars are universally agreed that Genesis 5:24 teaches that Enoch was raptured, and did not taste mortal death. This was also the view of history and is found in the traditions of the Jews as well.[1553] Most importantly, it is confirmed by the author of Hebrews who states, "by faith Enoch was taken up so that he should not see death" (11:5). This unique fact makes many believe that Enoch is destined to return one day to the earth. Tertullian said of Enoch and Elijah, their death "was postponed, (and only postponed,) most certainly: they are reserved for the suffering of death, that by their blood they may extinguish Antichrist."[1554] Thus, Enoch and Elijah, as the only two men to never die, are deemed the two most likely candidates for the two witnesses.[1555]

Joseph Seiss makes careful use of the fact that the two witnesses are said to be "standing before the Lord" (Revelation 11:4). "It is not said that they *will* stand before the Lord in the time and office of their prophesying, but they were *then*, while the Angel was speaking, *standing* before the Lord."[1556] This, he argues, is proof that "these Witnesses were persons already living in the time of John ... but John's earthly contemporaries have all been dead for ages."[1557] He, therefore, concludes that they must be the two historical figures who never died; Enoch and Elijah. Of course, Seiss may be making too much out of this fact. The present tense of the verb may show that the two witnesses are individuals from the past, inasmuch as then existed in heaven, but there is nothing in the verse to prove that neither one of the men had died.

Critics have disputed that Enoch is one of the two prophets because Enoch was not a Jew. Tim LaHaye has pointed out that Enoch lived before Abraham, and therefore cannot be Jewish.[1558] Since the two prophets are a part of Israel, Enoch is allegedly discounted. However, Henry Morris believes that Enoch is a perfect candidate precisely because he is from the time before Abraham. He says, "Enoch and Elijah are uniquely appropriate selections for this peculiar ministry in the last days. For approximately the first 2,000 years of human history (Adam to Abraham), God was dealing with the world of mankind as a whole. For approximately the second 2,000 years of history (Abraham to Christ), He was dealing primarily with the chosen nation of Israel ... God will send back His two greatest prophets of the two former ages to renew and to complete their respective testimonies."[1559]

As to the allegation that Enoch was not a Jew it must be answered that 1) since Enoch was before Abraham, as so readily pointed out, the application of Jew and Gentile is irrelevant since neither techincally existed, and 2) if Enoch is brought back to the earth in a new body, then he would be born of a Jew regardless of whether he was in his former life. Should Enoch descend directly from heaven, as some suppose, then his heritage before Abraham would be irrelevant.

Some have noticed that Jude 14-15 mentions a prophecy by Enoch concerning the coming judgment of the world. Of course, whether this judgment was the flood of Noah or the day of the Lord cannot be determined, nor does it prove the Enoch will be present at that judgment. It does, however, lend credibility to Enoch's role as a prophet, and his connection to the last days.

Like the supporters of Elijah, Enoch carries with him the strong testimony of godly men throughout the centuries, from the first to the last. The belief that Enoch will return was held by Hippolytus,[1560] Tertullian,[1561] and Ephraem the Syrian,[1562] to name a few. It is found in the apocryphal writings of "The History of Joseph the Carpenter,"[1563] the "Gospel of Nicodemus,"[1564] and appropriately enough, "the Book of Enoch."[1565] It was taught in the Middle Ages by Adso of Montier,[1566] Ambrose, and aluded to be Nicholas of Lyra.[1567] In the modern word it is maintained by men like Robert Govett,[1568] Joseph Seiss,[1569] G. H. Lang,[1570] Watchman Nee,[1571] and Henry Morris.[1572]

So Enoch makes a favorable option, but only an option. In reality, there is only one real evidence in his favor; that being that he never died, even as Elijah never died. Certainly this is strong evidence and it cannot be so easily discarded, but it might be insufficient evidence by itself were it not for the strong testimony of the ages. It seems that the evidence is inconclusive. Enoch could be a valid candidate, but what other options remain?

Moses

That some believed Moses might be one of the two prophets is confirmed by Victorinus,[1573] who doubts this assertion. In fact, according to the first century rabbi Jochanan ben Zakkai, Jewish tradition says that God once told Moses, "if I send the prophet Elijah, you must both come together."[1574] So it seems that a second coming of Moses was taught in the ancient days, but despite this, the view seems to have virtually disappeared until of the nineteenth century when it quickly grew to become the most popular view, behind Elijah. Today it supported by names such as Nathaniel West,[1575] C. I. Scofield,[1576] Norman Harrison,[1577] Arthur Bloomfield,[1578] Hal Lindsey,[1579] Bob Gundry,[1580] Robert Thomas,[1581] Robert Van Kampen,[1582] and Tim LaHaye.[1583]

Moses' appearance at the transfiguration has often been used to support this theory. It has been commented upon that Moses not only appears at the transfiguration (Matthew 17:3), but that Jesus immediately thereafter tells them about the prophecy of Elijah's coming (Matthew 17:10). Marvin Rosenthal argues that both men must return in the last days.[1584] However, Jesus' remarks about Elijah were spawned by the apostles' questions following their having seen Elijah. There is therefore no direct relationship between the transfiguration and the prophecy of Elijah's return. The transfiguration only proves that Moses and Elijah are two of the most prestigous prophets in history.

Yet another argument is that Moses' ministry was unfinished, requiring a second appearance, in order that God might keep his promise to Moses. Hal Lindsey quotes Numbers 20:12 which reads, "because you have not believed Me, to treat Me as holy in the sight of the sons of Israel, therefore you shall not bring this assembly into the land which I have given them." So Lindsey declares, "Moses never set foot in the Promised Land!"[1585] Unfortunately, Lindsey fails to prove that God ever specifically told Moses he would live to enter the land. In fact, in Numbers 14:24 God tells Moses that, of those who came up out of Egypt, only Caleb would live to see the promised land, and this was before God's final prohibition against Moses for the sin at the rock. It is therefore unproven that Moses' ministry is incomplete.

Like the miracles of Elijah, the miracles of Moses bear close resemblance to those of the two witnesses, for both turn water into blood (cf. Revelation 11:6 & Exodus 7:17-21). Thus the miracles provide support for the belief that Moses and Elijah will return,[1586] but unlike Elijah, Moses died.

Although it is not a proven fact that the two witnesses must have been translated without dying, it is assumed by many that this must be the case. So those who believe that Moses will return have noted the "mystery surrounding the death of Moses."[1587] According to Jude, the archangel Michael "disputed with the devil and argued about the body of Moses" (vs. 9). The close proximity of this verse to prophecy of Enoch regarding the coming judgment of the world (Jude 14-15) is also held up as evidence, but if Enoch is mentioned, should that not be evidence in Enoch's favor? Moreover, despite the mystery of Moses' body, the Bible is clear that Moses was buried "in the valley in the land of Moab, opposite Beth-peor; but no man knows his burial place to this day" (Deuteronomy 34:6). So Moses did die, and was buried. If he is to return, he is to return in a different body.

Although there is more evidence presented in favor of Moses, the evidences do not seem as strong, nor carry as much weight. Certainly, the return of Moses is a possibility, but the evidence is far from conclusive. It should be weighed carefully against the other options, before it is accepted or rejected.

New Prophets
That the prophets, or at least one of the prophets, will be righteous men who have never walked the face of the earth before their generation is a surprisingly minority view. Doubtless, it would be the most prominent view, were it not for the insistence that Elijah must precede the second coming of Christ. Nevertheless, one might wonder, if Elijah does come, why does the second prophet also have to have lived in the earth's history. Cannot Elijah's companion be new to the earth?

This is the view of Dwight Pentecost and John Walvoord, two of the most respected of modern scholars. According to Pentecost "they, in all probablity, are not men who lived before and have been restored, but are two men raised up as a special witness, to whom sign-working power is given."[1588] Walvoord says, "it is probably safe to recognize them as two witnesses who will appear in the end time who are not related to any previous historical character."[1589] George Ladd seems to favor it as well.[1590]

No evidence is needed to promote this view, for it is the logical assumption of those who reject the evidences for a historical figure. Certainly, it would be the most popular view were it not for Malachi 4:5. Still, Malachi cannot be discarded. John the Baptist did not completely fulfill the prophecy, although he was part of the dual fulfillment (Matthew 17:11). Since Elijah is to come again, his partner has been the subject of great debate. Could he be Enoch? Perhaps he is Moses? Or perhaps Pentecost and Walvoord are partially correct. Perhaps at least one of the two witnesses will be new to this earth.

Other Candidates in History
Elijah, Enoch, and Moses have been the favorites for centuries, but many other names have been mentioned as well. Some seem almost frivolous. For example, Peter D'Olivi suggesetd that Francis of Assisi might have been one of the two prophesied men.[1591] Nicholas of Lyra considered the medieval figures Silverius and Menus,[1592] but there are several suggestions that are deserving of note. Some believe that Elisha, Elijah's successor in the Old Testament, will accompany him in the last days,[1593] but there are still other views more worthy of consideration.

The first of the rarely heard views is that of the return of the apostle John. Those who hold to this view claim that John was raptured, like Elijah.[1594] They quote Jesus' statement in John 21:22-23 "Jesus said to [Peter], 'If I want [John] to remain until I come, what *is that* to you? You follow Me!' This saying therefore went out among the brethren that that disciple would not die." It is of interest to note, however, that John did not seem to favor this, but followed it up by saying, "yet Jesus did not say to him that he would not die, but *only*, 'If I want him to remain until I come, what *is that* to you?'" Still, they say that

John's death cannot anywhere be confirmed, but also that Revelation 10:22, which immediately precedes the discussion of the two witnesses, is a prophecy about John's return in the last days,[1595] for it says, "you must prophesy again concerning many peoples and nations and tongues and kings."

Lastly, they argue that John would be the perfect complement for Elijah, for Elijah was from the Old Testament, and John was from the New. The two would balance each other out; the one representing the Jews of ancient Israel, and the other representing the church age.[1596] Certainly, the view is intriguing, and yet John has not been the only disciple mentioned. Peter's name has been brought forth,[1597] but only John can be taken with any serious consideration, and even he does not seem to stand the test real well.

So what other persons might be valid candidates? One of the oldest, although by no means the best attested, views is that the prophet Jeremiah will return with Elijah. This seems to be favored by Victorinus, although he was uncommitted.[1598] The strength of this theory comes from the fact that the disciples themselves alude to the return of Jeremiah, for when Jesus asked "who do men say that the Son of Man is?" the apostles answered, "some *say* John the Baptist; and others, Elijah; but still others, Jeremiah, or one of the prophets" (Matthew 16:14). Of course, this really only means that Jews at the time of Christ believed that Jeremiah might return. It certainly does not prove that the disciples, let only our Savior, believed it to be true.

Thus far the serious candidates include Elijah, Enoch, Moses, John, and Jeremiah. Some believe that the prophets need not have lived in the past at all, but some others believe that there will be no prophets in the literal sense at all. This final view needs to be rebutted.

The "Spiritual" View
As has often been the case with Revelation, many have found it far easier to "spiritualize," or rather allegorize, the passages than to accept them at face value. This has been the long standing tradition of the medieval church, and was passed down to the early Reformers, before later Reformers sought to restore the purity of Biblical interpretation.

Joseph Mede made no attempt to clearly identify the witnesses, choosing to compare them to the prophetic duos of the past such as Elijah & Elisha; Zerubbabel and Jeshua; and even Moses and Aaron.[1599] He actually claimed that the two witnesses represented the Reformers themselves.[1600] This allegorical style was followed by Isaac Newton who said that the two witnesses were two spiritual churches.[1601] Henry Barclay Swete[1602] and John Bale also saw them as mere allegory for the church.[1603]

Surprisingly, even the Brethren, who helped restore the "literal" or the straight-forward interpretation, seem to have been reluctant to accept the two prophets are real people. John Darby said that it was "not a question of their persons"[1604] at all, but that, whomever they may be, "the service of the two witnesses is that of Moses against Pharaoh, and that of Elias in the midst of an apostate people."[1605] Thus, he says that Moses and Elijah are representative of the two witnesses, but makes no attempt to identify the witnesses. Darby's proteges, however, declare that the witnesses are a symbol of "a competent number of faithful servants of Christ."[1606] Ironside also jumps on the symbolic bandwagon saying, the witnesses are "symbolizing a much larger company, [and] will be in the spirit and power" of Elijah and Moses.[1607]

It is not surprising that covenant theologians and posttribulationists, whose system requires a certain element of "spiritualizing," also accept this teaching. G. B. Caird says that the *two* symbolize "innumerable" witnessses,[1608] and Robert Mounce says that the church is symbolized by them.[1609]

As is usually the case, there is no evidence given for how "two" equals an "innumerable" number of witness.[1610] No support is offered for how "two" witnesses equal *one* church. No facts are provided to prove that the prophets' miracles, their martyrdom, or their resurrection can in any way relate to the specific plight of "the church" in the tribulation, especially since these same scholars claim that the flight of the woman in chapter twelve *is the same* "church" which the covenant theologians apply here to the two witnesses who are caught up to heaven immediately *before* the woman takes flight! So the allegorists make both the witnesses and the church one and the same thing, even though they face entirely different fates! It is true that some dispensationalists, such as Darby, Scott, and Ironside, also accept this spiritualization, but they are at as much of a loss as the covenant theologians to explain the specifics of the symbolism. If a symbol does not represent something specific, and literal, then it is not a symbol at all, but an ambiguous allegory. This view *cannot* stand.

Conclusion

Were it not for the strong evidence that Elijah is coming again, idle speculation on who the second prophet is would not exist. The fact is that Elijah *is* coming again, as affirmed by Christ Himself (cf. Matthew 17:11), so the question of who Elijah's partner is remains. Many options have been cited. Of those that deserve mention, the evidence for Jeremiah is meager and based almost solely upon an old tradition. John inclusion in this list is intriguing, but no hard evidence exist to support it. Moses is also tempting, but his death seems to exclude him. Only the similarity in the prophets' miracles to those of Moses gives us reason to truly pause. Enoch then might be the favorite, but the proof cited is his rapture into heaven. Is this really sufficient? Does Jude 14-15 prove that Enoch will have a prophetic ministry in the end time? Of these names Enoch seems to the strongest, but the apostle John should not be completely discounted either. Although Moses has become one of the most popular views, there is no clear support to lift him above these two. Any of them could be Elijah's companion, but does Elijah's companion need to have lived in the past?

347

Why must the prophets of old return to the earth in the last days? Why cannot a man from the earth today fulfill the role? This raises an interesting question. We know that in the last days, the apostasy shall be so great that even the elect shall be deceived, "if possible" (Mark 13:22; cf. Matthew 24:24). So if God send two men back to the earth who have before witnessed on the earth, it is an indication that none living on the earth in these last days are worthy of this special mission. No one on earth is righteous enough to do what Elijah and his companion alone can do.

The Invasion of Gog

Ezekiel 38-39 describes a massive invasion of Israel by Gog and Magog in the last days. The events described have nowhere occurred in history and, therefore, must occur at some time in the last days. All but the allegorists admit this, but *when* exactly is this to occur and how do these events fit into the prophetic scheme of Revelation? If they occur in the end times, then surely they must fit in the tribulation somewhere? Most premillennialists agree on this, but no more than this. Premillennialists are bitterly divided as to whether or not the massive invasion occurs shortly before the tribulation begins, in the middle of the tribulation, at the end of the tribulation, or even at the end of the Millennium. Since any one of these scenarios would impact upon the undertsanding of Revelation, the debate will be critiqued.

Gog and Magog have been almost universally accepted as references to the region occupied by modern day Russia and/or its satellite states.[1611] The evidence is undeniable. Ezekiel 38:2 says that Gog is "of the land of Magog, the prince of Rosh, Meshech, and Tubal." According to Josephus, the first century historian, Magog was "by the Greeks called Scythia."[1612] Pliny, the ancient Roman historian, also mentions that "the Scythians, (were) afterwards called Magog."[1613] So Rosh, Meschech, and Tubal are cities within the region of Magog or Scythia. All of these relate to Gog, and all of these can be confirmed to be a part of modern Russia and its satellite states.

Rosh is the ancient name from which Russia is derived. The ancient name for Russia was Rus, or Kiev Rus.[1614] That this came from Rosh has been accepted for ages. According to Bishop Lowth, circa 1710, "Rosh, taken as a proper name in Ezekiel signifies the inhabitants of Scythia, from whom the modern Russians derive their name."[1615] In 1815 an Anglican priest confirmed that "Rosh signifies those inhabitants of Scythia, from whence the Russians derive their name."[1616]

Meschech is the ancient name from which Moscow is derived. According to Wilhelm Gesenius, the famed early nineteenth century Hebrew scholar, "Meshech was the founder of Moschi."[1617] Josephus also confirmed this.[1618] More importantly is the fact that Moschi is translated into the Russian tongue as Moscow.

Tubal, likewise, is connected to Russia. Some believe that Tubal is to associated with the Russian province of Tobolsk.[1619] Archaeology professor Merrill Unger says that Tubal was "a Scythian tribe."[1620] Although the region Unger describes is probably closer to what is now Georgia, it is still part of the ancient Scythian tribes, and was a part of Russia until recently. So Rosh, Meschech, and Tubal all relate to ancient Scythia, or the region of modern day Russia and its satellite states.

The prophecy is therefore agreed by premillennialists to refer to an invasion by Russia and its allies in the end times. In 1864, long before Russia was a world power, Dr. John Cumming wrote, "This king of the North I conceive to be the autocrat of Russia ... that Russia occupies a place, and a very momentous place, in the prophetic word has been admitted by almost all expositors."[1621] In 1866 another scholar said, "the personal coming of Christ, to establish His millennial reign on earth, will not take place until the Jews are restored to their own land, and the enemies of Christ and the Jews have gathered together their armies from all parts of the world, and have commenced the siege of Jerusalem."[1622] Walter Scott believed that the "last Czar of Russia" would invade Israel after it is restored.[1623] However, Russia does not act alone. Other nations are said to participate in what has been termed by some "the Northern Confederacy."

According to Ezekiel 38:5-6, Persia, Ethiopia, Put, Gomer, and Togarmah will be Russia's allies in this invasion. Persia is universally accepted as modern day Iran and Put is defined as Libya by Josephus.[1624] The identification of Gomer is less confident. Dwight Pentecost equates Gomer and Togarmah with Germany and Turkey.[1625] According to most Bible dictionaries Gomer dwelled with the Cimmeranians,[1626] which was possibly in either Georgia or eastern Turkey. The Bible says that Togarmah was one of Gomer's sons (Genesis 6:2), so it is safe to assume that he settled nearby in the same region. So these countries ally themselves against Israel and launch a massive invasion against her in the end times. This is generally agreed by premillennialists, but how this is related to the events of Revelation cannot be determined exactly until the invasion is placed in chronological reference to the tribulation. This is where scholars are bitterly divided.

In order to place the invasion properly into the prohetic scheme of Revelation several chronological keys are necessary. These "keys" are events which may be used to fix the chronology within a certain framework. Ezekiel 38-39 offers several of these. First, Ezekiel 38:19-20 describes a massive earthquake which rocks the land. Furthermore, the invasion will occur when Israel is living "securely" and "at rest" (Ezekiel 38:10). The Bible also describes a time when the Jews will be burying the dead for a period of seven months (Ezekiel 39:12). Ezekiel 39:9 further describes a period of seven years in which the Jews are burning the weapons of the dead. Finally, and most importantly, the defeat of the invaders seems to signal the repentance of Israel

(Ezekiel 39:22). There are the five key factors that must be considered in placing the events into a chronological framework. The four major theories are outlined and debated below.

The Invasion Precedes the Tribulation
There are actually two similar theories, which here are addressed as one, since their differences are largely inconsequential. Some believe that the invasion will take place immediately before the tribulation or Daniel's 70th Week. Others place it immediately after the beginning of the tribulation or Daniel's 70th Week.

Among the arguments in this view's behalf is the assumption that this view alone permits for the period of seven years during which the Jews will be destroying weapons.[1627] However, this is insufficient to explain *why* it takes seven years to burn the weapons and seven months to bury bodies. Randall Price says that "according to Jewish law, the dead must be buried immediately because exposed corpses are a source of ritual contamination. However, because of the vast number of corpses this will take 'seven months.'"[1628] Unfortunately, this is not a sufficient explanation. If the army were a hundred times larger than Israel's it would still only take a month or two at most to bury the dead. Moreover, "ritual contamination" would be the least of Israel's problems. If a body remains exposed for seven months then disease and pestilence will be the natural result. This fits the third seal of Revelation and the idea that war deters Israel from disposing of the bodies and contaminated weapons more quickly. However, if the invasion occurred at the beginning, or previous to, the tribulation then Israel would be in a period of peace when the treaty with the anti-Christ first takes place. This leads to the question of Israel's "security."

It is true that the invasion occurs at a time of Israel's seeming security, but the invasion signals that this security is not real. Advocates of this position believe that the invasion of Gog is exactly the sort of thing that may cause Israel to make a treaty with the anti-Christ,[1629] since he promises them peace and safety (cf. 1 Thessalonians 5:1). Such speculation is feasible, but not probable. First, Israel cannot now be said to be "living securely" when terrorism and threats of war loom constantly. Walvoord believes Ezekiel "was not describing Israel today which is an armed camp and living in fear of its neighbors."[1630] "If Russia should invade the Middle East today, it would not be a fulfillment of this portion of Scripture. That has to take place when Israel is at rest."[1631] Secondly, and more importantly, it is God who protects Israel, not the anti-Christ. It is therefore ironic that Price says, "the outcome of this war results in at least a temporary peace, as the nations are forced to reckon with the divine protection uniquely afforded Israel."[1632] If the nations are forced to deal with "divine protection" then why does Israel need to make a treaty with the anti-Christ? This would imply that Israel believes they need *his* protection, rather than God's. Clearly, this is not the case. The treaty is made with anti-Christ *before*

Israel comes to repent. Since the invasion triggers Israel's repentance, this scenario is unacceptable.

The most important objection to this chronological scheme is the conflict it creates with the pretribulational rapture position, which many of its advocates profess to believe. The Vice-President of the Pre-Trib Research Center has said that "the rapture is a sign-less event,"[1633] and yet a member of the Pre-Trib Research Center not only says that "the Russian invasion of Israel occurs *before* the seven-year peace covenant,"[1634] but that "if it occurs *before* the covenant, then a peace treaty followed by the Russian invasion could *precede the Rapture and could come at any time*" (emphasis added).[1635] In other words, the invasion of Russia would be a *sign* of the rapture. We could safely say that we *cannot* be raptured today, because Russia has not invaded Israel. Moreover, if Russia does invade Israel then we could anticipate the rapture to occur with a few weeks at most! This view is completely untenable for pretribulationists. As a result, some have argued that there could be a transitional period between the rapture and the beginning of Daniel's 70th Week during which the invasion could occur. However, it is unlikely that this transitional period could last as long as seven months, as its advocates seem to imply.

Although by no means conclusive, a comment is necessary on the earthquake which destroys Gog (Ezekiel 38:19). We already know from Revelation that two major earthquakes will occur in Israel, one at the middle of the tribulation and the other at Armageddon (Revelation 11:13; 16:18).[1636] While it is possible that a third earthquake could precede these two, Jerusalem has not experienced a single major earthquake since the establishment of Israel in 1948.[1637] The two earthquakes described in Revelation are each part of the judgment of God so there is reason to believe that the earthquake in Ezekiel may be connected to one of the two in Revelation.

A final remark is the theory of Dwight Pentecost that the "latter days" refers to the tribulation, and cannot refer to the church age.[1638] He reasons that this proves that the invasion cannot refer to any time before the 70th Week of Daniel begins. Certainly the context of the passage proves that Israel must be back in the land, as it now is, and the tribulation is universally referred to as the "end times" or "last days," but this does not prove that "last days" *cannot* refer to any time before the tribulation. It is the old logic flaw, "a Ford is a car, therefore all cars are Fords." Certainly the tribulation is the "end times," but the "last days" could refer to a larger period of time before the end times.[1639]

After reviewing these points, it seems that the invasion of Israel will probably not occur before, or in the early stages of, the tribulation. This view *may* be consistent with Israel being at peace, and it could be compatible with the seven year time frame for the destruction of weapons, but it is wholly incompatible with two important factors. First, the invasion could create a sign of the rapture, which pretribulationists and some midtribulationists, believe is a direct contradiction of the imminency of Christ. Second, this view cannot explain how Israel repents and turn to the Messiah after this event (cf. Ezekiel 39:22), when they would actually be making a treaty with the anti-Christ thereafter! According to Ezekiel "the house of Israel will know that I am the Lord their God *from that day onward*" (39:22). So "from that day onward" Israel will know the Lord. Why then would they ally themselves with the anti-Christ? The more likely scenario is that Israel will "from that day onward" recognize the anti-Christ for what he is, and the nation will repent, only to suffer the anti-Christ's wrath.

The Invasion Occurs in the Middle of the Tribulation

If the invasion does not take place at the beginning of the tribulation, could it take place at the middle of the tribulation? According to Ezekiel, a tremendous earthquake will shake Israel when Gog invades (38:20). Such an earthquake is also seen in Revelation at the middle of the tribulation (cf. Revelation 11:13, 12:16). This earthquake apparently occurs immediately after the abomination of desolation, at the moment of the two witnesses resurrection, and results in the destruction of the anti-Christ's men who are pursuing believing Israel when they flee to the mountains (cf. Revelation 12:16, Matthew 24:15-16, Mark 13:14, Luke 21:21). Although it cannot be said with certainty, these earthquakes may be one and the same. If this scenario is true then the abomination of desolation is the event which triggers the complete collapse of the anti-Christ's empire, and signals the invasion of the anti-Christ's enemies. The anti-Christ will send his army to engage Gog, but it will be God, not the anti-Christ, who actually destroys their army (Ezekiel 38:23). Realizing that Israel has rejected him, and fearing loosing his grip, the anti-Christ will divert his army to pursue believing Israel, only to be swallowed up by the earth (Revelation 12:16). This earthquake would then simultaneously eradicate all the armies that encompass Israel, signal the resurrection of the two witnesses, and inaugurate the repentance of Israel (Ezekiel 39:22).

Critics will suggest that there is nothing in the text to prove that the earthquakes are the same, and this is a valid comment, but the scenario fits perfectly with what we know to be true. First, the anti-Christ's treaty is broken at the mid-point of the tribulation (Daniel 9:27). He looses the trust of Israel at that time, after the abomination of desolation. Second, Israel repents following the destruction of Gog (Ezekiel 39:22). It is only natural that a repentant Israel would not follow the anti-Christ. Third, although Israel was said to be "living securely" at the time of the invasion (38:14), the result is that "every man's sword will be against his brother" (38:21). In other words, a great war will erupt between the Gentile nations. This too occurs at the mid-point of the tribulation (see Appendix D), when the anti-Christ will wage war against all his enemies in order to keep his kingdom together. Finally, Daniel 11:40 implies that the invasion of the North (which most believe to be Gog)[1640] will de directed at the anti-Christ, as well as at Israel, his ally at that time. So all these events appear to tie together.

Nevertheless, several objections to this view have been raised. Ralph Alexander has taken exception to Dwight Pentecost's belief that the anti-Christ will come to Israel's aid, saying "Ezekiel 38-39 clearly points out that it is God who destroys Gog, not the Antichrist."[1641] This is true. Although some claim that the brimstone, which is also translated sulpher, could depict modern warfare, it is indeed obvious that God, not man, destroys the invaders. This, however, does not discount this view at all. In fact, it has already been alleged that some of the anti-Christ's men will fall along with Gog. However, the movement of the anti-Christ's armies into Israel is consistent with Ezekiel 38:21 as well as Daniel 11:40. The details of the battles are not given, only the ultimate outcome; God destroys all the armies and Israel repents.

A second objection is that Israel could not be considered to be "living securely" during the period of "chastisement and punishment."[1642] The tribulation is seen entirely as a time of war and judgment, but this is debatable (see Appendix D). It is clear that the anti-Christ makes a treaty with Israel to secure peace (Daniel 9:27). That this peace is indeed a "false peace"[1643] is obvious, but to argue that this false peace is "contrary to the usual meaning of the phrase 'living securely'"[1644] is frivolous, since it is obvious that this security is not real. If it were real, then there would be no invasion at all. The mere fact that there is such a massive invasion suggests that Israel's security was false, and will always be false without God, whom they do not turn to until after this event.

Yet another objection is the argument that "burning weapons and burying bodies for seven years and seven months respectively would seem invonceivable during the abomination of desolation, when judgment is at its height."[1645] This objection cannot stand up. It is precisely *because* there are wars and judgments occuring in the second half of the tribulation that these things take so long. Although Randall Price believes that the long duration is because of the "vast number of corpes" and weapons,[1646] it is inconceivable that rotting corpses would be left exposed for seven months, resulting in pestilence and disease, unless circumstances, such as war and persecution, prevented them from devoting their full time to this duty. Furthermore, the burning of weapons for fuel suggest that Israel's resources are being tapped unusually heavily. Although Price says, "if this battle were to take place at any point during the tribulation the Jews would run out of time to complete this task,"[1647] there is no reason to believe that Israel cannot continue the burning of weapons "into the early part of the Millennium"[1648] since "even after the Lord returns they will still need fuel for fires in the Millennial Kingdom as life goes on."[1649] Nothing in the Bible implies that God will pamper the inhabitants of the Millennial Kingdom. They will have to work, as men have always worked, and one of the jobs designated is a period of purification between the end of the tribulation and the beginning of the Millennial Kingdom (see Appendix D).

The best answer is, therefore, that Gog will invade Israel and time their attack to coincide with the festivities which the anti-Christ has set up in the new temple (see chapter 4). Immediately after the abomination of desolation, the attack will commence. God's wrath will then smite Gog. This destruction, combined with the blasphemy of the abomination of desolation, and the resurrection of the two witnesses, will spur the repentance of Israel's elect, and inaugurate the Great Tribulation and time of judgment upon the unbelieving world.

The Invasion Occurs at the End of the Tribulation
Although the best view is that the invasion occurs in the middle of the tribulation, two other popular views place the invasion either synonymous with the battle of Armageddon or early in the Millennium. That the battle does not occur early in the Millennium, when Satan is bound and wars are absent (cf. Revelation 20:2), is apparent to most. Moreover, the unbelievers have all been vanquished at Armageddon (cf. Revelation 19). Therefore, *if* the invasion is to occur in this time frame, then it must be synonymous with the battle of Armageddon itself, as many suggest. So it is necessary to evaluate this popular belief.

The strength of this view lies in the similarities between Ezekiel 38-39 and the battle of Armageddon. Both the book of Revelation and Ezekiel 38-39 describe God's "fury," "wrath," "anger," earthquakes, judgments, "mountains thrown down," fire and brimstone, pestilence, and birds feasting on the dead.[1650] Says one commentator, "in his 'great supper of God,' John appears to allude explicitly to the feast on the carnage of Gog's hordes in Ezekiel 39:17-20."[1651] However, there are significant differences which seem to be ignored. For one thing, most of the judgments in Revelation are on mankind as a whole, and not confined to the land of Israel as in Ezekiel 38-39. Second, the armies at Armageddon are described as "all nations" against Israel (cf. Zechariah 12:3, 14; Revelation 19), whereas Ezekiel describes an alliance of nations with Gog. Instead of "all nations," specific nations are mentioned; Russia, Ethiopia, Libya, Egypt, and possibly Turkey, Georgia, Ukraine, and/or Germany.

Despite the similarities, the problems with this view are many. To begin with, there is no plausible way that Israel can be said to be dwelling in security or be "at rest" (Ezekiel 38:10) before the battle of Armageddon. So severe are the circumstances that Christ Himself declared "unless those days had been cut short, no life would have been saved" (Matthew 24:22). There is no way that Israel can be said to be living in security when all the nations of the world gather around her for the last battle.

Another problem is that Israel must have already repented. The time of Israel's repentance coincides with the invasion of Gog, but at Armageddon men have already made their ultimate choices. Israel is already believing and the 144,000 are waiting for the Lord at His coming (cf. Revelation 14:1).

Still another problem is the complete absence of the mention of Gog in Revelation 19. Even one advocate must ask, "why would John not mention Gog in Revelation 19 if this passage is a fulfillment of Ezekiel 38-39?"[1652] His only answer is to say that John wanted to emphasize the destruction of the beast,[1653] yet the Bible does not fail to mention the "kings of the east" (Revelation 16:12) as being present at Armageddon. The reason Gog is not mentioned is because she has already met her fate.

A final problem with this view is the seven month period for burying the dead. Although the Bible does permit a brief period of cleansing before the Millennium (see Appendix D), that period is no more than 75 days at the most. It does not seem likely that the burying of dead will carry over into the Millennium, even though the burning of weapons could.

This view is based largely on the similarities between Ezekiel and Revelation, but most are inconclusive. The differences far outweigh the similarities. Since God's judgment falls on both Gog and the anti-Christ, the similarities may be expected as the natural result of God's wrath. More evidence is needed to connect the destruction of Gog to the battle of Armageddon, and the conflicts with Israel's time of repentance, as well as other issues, must be resolved before this view can be a viable option.

The Invasion Follows the Millennium

Revelation 20:7-10 describes the final rebellion against God, led by Gog and Magog. This is the only place in Revelation where Gog and Magog are mentioned. This has led many great scholars to assume that events of Revelation 20:7-10 are one and the same as those of Ezekiel 38-39. According to Nathaniel West, "the order of the Eschata is the same in both Ezekiel and John."[1654] He claims that the "many days" of Ezekiel is a reference to "the thousand years" and concludes that the invasion of Gog must follow the Millennial Kingdom.[1655]

On the surface, this view has many strengths. It is certainly consistent with the fact that Israel will be at rest, and the explicit mention of Gog in Revelation 20:7-10 makes for a tempting parallel. The weaknesses, however, are many and far outweigh the strengths. There are noticeable differences which cannot be easily discounted. In Ezekiel Gog comes from the north, but in Revelation 20:8 Gog comes from the four quarters of the earth. More significant is the assertion of E. W. Bullinger that Gog must be before the thousand year reign because Israel's blessings do not occur until after Gog's destruction.[1656] According to Charles Dyer, "the effect on the people is different. In Ezekiel the battle is the catalyst God will use to draw Israel to Himself (cf. Ezek. 39:7, 22-29) and to end her captivity. But the battle in Revelation 20 will occur after Israel has been faithful to her God and enjoyed His blessing for 1,000 years."[1657]

355

Other contradictions exist as well. Randall Price has pointed out that some of the nations who assist Gog in the invasion described in Ezekiel are actually blessed in the Millennium.[1658] According to Isaiah, "I will set a sign among them and will send survivors from them to the nations: Tarshish, Put, Lud, Meshech, Rosh, Tubal, and Javan, to the distant coastlands that have neither heard My fame nor seen My glory. And they will declare My glory among the nations" (Isaiah 66:19). So Rosh, Meshech, Tubal, and Put are all allies of Gog in Ezekiel 38:1-5, and yet in Isaiah 66, which discusses Israel's blessings in the Millennium and beyond, these all declare the glory of the Lord.

The most dramatic of problems with this view is its inability to explain the burial of bodies and the destruction of weapons on numerous different levels. As Pentecost illustrates, "in Ezekiel the bodies of the slain require the labor of seven months to dispose of the dead (39:12). In Revelation 20:9 the slain are said to 'devoured' by fire so that no disposal is necessary."[1659] This contradiction is only part of the problem. "In Ezekiel life goes on after the war, requiring months to bury the dead. The war in Revelation 20 is followed immediately by the destruction of the earth and the creation of the new heaven and new earth."[1660] So if the destruction of Gog "is followed by the new heaven and the new earth" then "certainly the new earth could not conceivably be corrupted by unburied corpes for seven months."[1661] This is compounded by the fact that the Great White Throne judgment and the last resurrection also immediately follow the final rebellion. Ralph Alexander can only respond by saying that "a transitional period here is equally plausible,"[1662] but their is no purpose for such a transitional period. We would be forced to believe that God forces seven years between the end of the rebellion and the creation of the New Heaven and the New Earth, for no other reason than to burn weapons which would be burned with fire at the destruction of the old world anyway (2 Peter 3:10). These problems cannot be discounted and form insurmountable problems for this position.

Although at first glimpse this view shows great promise, it is revealed to be the weakest of views. It cannot resolve numerous contradictions, cannot explain the burial of bodies which are said to be "consumed" in Revelation 20:9, cannot explain seven years of burning weapons, and cannot explain how Israel's repentance can be said to follow the Millennial Kingdom. Furthermore, the very names "Gog and Magog" have a different meaning in the Millennial age. In Ezekiel Magog "means a *land* or *country*, of which Gog is the prince; and in Rev. xx. 8, where 'Gog and Magog' appears to be an inclusive term for the Gentile *nations*."[1663] This is logical. After the Gentile nations fall in the battle of Armageddon, the surviving Gentiles will be mixed together and interbred. There will no longer be distinctive "races" as we know them today. Instead, there will be only Jew and Gentile. The Gentile people may still be known by a particular region or land, but it appears that the term Gog and Magog, even if they are distinct from other Gentiles, are no longer confined to the regions north of Israel. Instead they come from all over the globe. These facts, therefore, are sufficient to discount this popular theory.

Conclusion

While premillennialists have sincerely debated these theories, the allegorists and amillennialists have scoffed and ridiculed the entire prospect of a future invasion by Russia. Many historicists, such as Matthew Henry, have taken the view that this is the same invasion of Revelation 20:7-10,[1664] thus acknowledging it as future, but a smaller group of amillennial historicists have seized upon Gog's alliance with Turkey and attempted to connect the prophecy with the Crusades or even the ancient Greeks. They argue that the invasion could not take place in any of these future times because it allegedly describes ancient warfare when it speaks of horses, bows, and spears.

The Bible has always used the imagery of a "sword" for warfare of any kind. The weapons described do not prove that history is envisioned here. Moreover, the brimstone is actually sulpher and has been interpreted by some as describing "atomic warfare."[1665] Whether this is true or not, it is not logical to assume that Ezekiel would speak of guns and rocketlaunchers, when such words did not even exist in his language. Some have also pointed out that Russia still has a significant calvary force in addition to its regular troops.[1666] So the reference to ancient weapons is insufficient to prove a historical fulfillment.

The proof that the events have not been fulfilled in history is undeniable. No record of Russia ever invading Israel has ever been found. Whether any of her allies did, is irrelevant. In addition, John Walvoord has pointed out that the reference to "unwalled villages" (Ezekiel 38:11) cannot have had a historical fulfillment. "The scene described is a modern scene where walls are no longer necessary to protect a village."[1667] Only in the modern age has Jerusalem been free from walls. The most important element, however, is that the invasion *must* follow the restoration of Israel. Consequently, "Ezekiel's prophecy obviously could not have been fulfilled prior to 1945."[1668]

In response to those allegorists who argue that Revelation merely borrowed from Ezekiel, Bullinger's retort is sufficient. "It is absurd to talk about 'John borrowing from Ezekiel,' as so many say. There is no 'borrowing' in the matter. Both prophecies are 'given by inspiration of God.'"[1669]

The invasion of Gog must be considered a future invasion of Israel in the "last days" (Ezekiel 38:16). Although a handful of scholars believe that Gog is one and the same with the anti-Christ,[1670] most are agreed that Gog is the leader of Russia and her confederate allies. Only the timing of the invasion is controversial, and it is, to be sure, not an easy issue. The mass of evidence, however, favors the invasion occuring shortly before, and even coinciding with, the abomination of desolation when the anti-Christ's treaty will fall apart (Daniel 9:27 cf. Matthew 24:15, Mark 13:14, Luke 21:20, & 2 Thessalonians 2:4), when the Jews will repent and flee to the mountains (Matthew 24:15,

Mark 13:14, Luke 21:20), and when a massive earthquake hits Israel (Ezekiel 38:19 cf. Revelation 11:13). These are the events which trigger the Great Tribulation and the wrath of God.

Study Charts on the Identity of the Two Witnesses

Leading Scholars

Hippolytus	Chiliast	Elijah and Enoch.
Tertullian	Chiliast	Elijah and Enoch.
Victorinus	Chiliast	Elijah and possibly Elisha, Moses, or Jeremiah.
Methodius	Chiliast	Elijah mentioned.
Cyprian	Chiliast	Elijah mentioned.
Lactantius	Chiliast	Elijah mentioned.
Ephraem the Syrian	Chiliast	Elijah and Enoch.
Chrysostom	Chiliast	Elijah mentioned.
Theoplylact	Chiliast	Elijah mentioned.
Adso of Montier	Medieval Chiliast	Elijah and Enoch.
Ambrose	Chiliast	Elijah and Enoch.
Joachim of Floris	Medieval Millenarian	Elijah, but does not name the other.
Pierre D'Olivi	Medieval Millenarian	Elijah and possibly Francis of Assisi.
Nicholas of Lyra	Medieval Millenarian	Elijah and Enoch, but also applies it to Silverius and Menus.
Joseph Mede	Historicist premillennialist	Spiritually as Moses and Aaron, Elijah and Elisha, or Zerubbabel and Joshua.
Isaac Newton	Historicist premillennialist	Two spiritual churches.
John Darby	Dispensational premillennialist	Possibly symbolic for Elijah and Moses.
George Peters	Futurist premillennialist	Elijah, but does not name the second.
Nathaniel West	Futurist premillennialist	Elijah and Moses.
Robert Govett	Futurist premillennialist	Elijah and Enoch.
Joseph Seiss	Futurist premillennialist	Elijah and Enoch.
E. W. Bullinger	Ultradispensationalist	Elijah, but unsure if second is Moses or Enoch.

C. I. Scofield	Dispensational premillennialist	Elijah and Moses.
H. A. Ironside	Dispensational premillennialist	Spiritualized symbol of the church, mimicking Moses and Elijah.
Dwight Pentecost	Dispensational premillennialist	Two new prophets.
Norman Harrison	Midtribulational premillennialist	Elijah and Moses.
John Walvoord	Dispensational premillennialist	Two new prophets.
Arthur Bloomfield	Quasi-dispensational Premillennialist	Elijah and Moses.
Robert Mounce	Posttribulational Premillennialist	Symbol of the church.
George Ladd	Posttribulational Premillennialist	Symbol of the church.
Hal Lindsey	Dispensational premillennialist	Elijah and Moses.
Tim LaHaye	Dispensational premillennialist	Elijah and Moses.
Marvin Rosenthal	"Pre-wrath" premillennialist	Elijah, but undecided as to Moses or Enoch.

Historical Survey

	Position
Church Fathers	All but unanimous that they are Elijah and Enoch.
Medieval Theologians	Elijah continues to be all but unanimous but the second person is variously identified with Enoch still the favorite. There is an increasing attempt to spiritualize the two witnesses as well.
Reformation Scholars	The spiritualization of the two witnesses is popular as well as a shift from Elijah and Enoch to the belief that they represent Elijah and Moses.
Post-Reformation Scholars	A mixture of views but with Elijah and Moses gaining prominence.
Modern Evangelicals	A mixture of views but Elijah and Moses have become the predomint view.

Elijah as One of the Two Prophets

Popular advocates from:
The Church Fathers : Justin Martyr, Hippolytus, Victorinus, Tertullian, Ephraem the Syrian, Cyprian, Methodius, Lactantius, Chrysostom, and Theophylact.
Medieval Theologians : Jerome, Augustine, Adso of Montier, Joachim d'Fiore, and Peter D'Olivi.
Reformation and Post-Reformation Scholars : Nathaniel West, Joseph Seiss, E. W. Bullinger, and C. I. Scofield.
Modern Evangelicals : Norman Harrison, G. H. Lang, Arthur Bloomfield, Watchman Nee, Hal Lindsey, Robert Gundry, Henry Morris, Robert Thomas, Marvin Rosenthal, Robert Van Kampen, and Tim LaHaye.

Strengths:
1) Malachi 4:5 says Elijah will come before "the great and terrible day of the Lord."
2) Jesus said Elijah "is coming" (Matthew 17:11).
3) Elijah never died (2 Kings 2:11).
4) The miracles performed by the prophets parallel those of Elijah (cf. 1 Kings 17:1-6, 18:38).
5) Elijah appeared at the transfiguration.
6) Elijah is the all but universal view of history, supported by the doctrine of perspicuity.
7) Elijah's ministry was allegedly incomplete, and must be completed at a later time.

Weaknesses:
1) Luke 1:17 implies that Malachi 4:4-5 has already been fulfilled (cf. Matthew 11:14).
2) Jesus resurrected the dead before (Mark 5:41, John 11:43), showing that Hebrews 9:27 is not a technical verse, but a summary law.
3) The appearance at the transfiguration does not prove that Elijah is one of the two prophets, only that he is important.
4) There is no real proof that Elijah's ministry was incomplete.

Enoch as One of the Two Prophets

Popular advocates from:
The Church Fathers : Hippolytus, Tertullian, and Ephraem the Syrian.
Medieval Theologians : Adso of Montier and Ambrose.
Reformation and Post-Reformation Scholars : Joseph Seiss and G. H. Lang.
Modern Evangelicals : Watchman Nee and Henry Morris.

Strengths:
1) Enoch never died (Genesis 5:24 & Hebrews 11:5).
2) It has the strong support of history.

Weaknesses:
1) It is said that he was not a Jew and is therefore disqualified.

Moses as One of the Two Prophets

Popular advocates from:
The Church Fathers : None cited, but the view did exist.
Medieval Theologians : None cited.
Reformation and Post-Reformation Scholars : Nathaniel West and C. I. Scofield.
Modern Evangelicals : Norman Harrison, Arthur Bloomfield, Hal Lindsey, Bob Gundry, Robert Thomas, Robert Van Kampen, and Tim LaHaye.

Strengths:
1) The miracles performed by the prophets parallel those of Moses (cf. Exodus 7:17-19).
2) There is a controversy surrounding the death of Moses (Jude 9), which some connect to the prophet of end times (Jude 14-15).
3) Moses was at the transfiguration.
4) Moses's ministry was allegedly incomplete, and must be completed at a later time.

Weaknesses:
1) Moses died and was buried (Deuteronomy 34:6).
2) The appearance at the transfiguration does not prove that Moses is one of the two prophets, only that he is important.
3) There is no real proof that Moses' ministry was incomplete.

Minority Views on the Second Witness

1) The Apostle John:

      Based largely on the belief that John would never die (John 21:23) this view has never had a large following but is the most intriguing of the minority views. Advocates also claim that Revelation 10:22 is a prophecy of John's return and that John would best represent New Testament times, as Elijah represents the Old.

2) Jeremiah the Prophet:

      This view is based on the fact that the ancients seem to have believed that Jeremiah would return (Matthew 16:14).

3) John the Baptist:

      Although not mentioned in the text of the appendix, this is a rare view based on the statement of some that John the Baptist might return (Matthew 16:14). Since John the Baptist is often called Elijah (cf. Matthew 11:14), this would really be repetitive of the Elijah theory. They can't both come.

4) The Spiritual View:

      The allegorical view offers no proof of its symbolism, but merely assumes that "two" equals "many." The witnesses are taken as a symbol of the "church." This view was created in the late medieval times and popularized in the early Reformation. It is popular among covenant theologians.

Study Charts on the Invasion of Gog

The Invasion Before the Tribulation
Tenants of:
Two separate views place the invasion of Gog before, or immediately after, the beginning of the tribulation.

Popular advocates : David Cooper, Randall Price, and Phillip Goodman.

Strengths:
1) Allows for seven years for the destruction of weapons (Ezekiel 39:9).
2) Could explain why Israel makes a treaty with the anti-Christ.
3) Present day Israel might be argued to be living securely (Ezekiel 38:10), via its military presense.

Weaknesses:
1) This could be conceived as a sign of the rapture.
2) The destruction of Gog signals Israel's repentance, not a treaty with the anti-Christ (Ezekiel 39:22).
3) Burying the dead should not take seven months if the false peace is established after the invasion ends.
4) Israel cannot realistically be considered to be living securely given terrorism and fear of invasion.

The Invasion in the Middle of the Tribulation

Tenants of:

This view places the invasion of Gog in the middle of the tribulation, in close connection to the Abomination of Desolation.

Popular advocates : George Peters,* J. Dwight Pentecost, Charles Dyer, Hal Lindsey, John Whitcomb, and John Walvoord.

* Peters sees Gog as a synonym for the anti-Christ.

Strengths:

1) Israel will be peace during the first half of the tribulation (Ezekiel 38:10 cf. Daniel 9:27, 1 Thessalonians 5:3).

2) The earthquake of Revelation 11:13 could be the same as that of Ezekiel 38:20.

3) Seven months to bury the dead (Ezekiel 39:12) suggests that they are prevented from devoting full time to this cleansing. This is compatible with the circumstances in the second half of the tribulation.

4) The destruction of Gog signals Israel's repentance (Ezekiel 39:22), as does the abomination of desolation (cf. Daniel 11:32).

5) Luke 21:20 could refer to Gog rather than the anti-Christ.

Weaknesses:

1) The burning of weapons (Ezekiel 39:9) would continue into the Millennium.

2) The tribulation, even the first half, is alleged to be incompatible with "security."

3) Luke 21:20 probably refers to the armies of the the anti-Christ.

The Invasion at the End of the Tribulation
Tenants of:
This view makes the invasion of Gog synonymous with the Battle of Armageddon.

Popular advocates : E. W. Bullinger, H. A. Ironside, Charles Feinberg, and Ralph Alexander.*

* Alexander sees a double fulfillment (at Armageddon and at the end of the Millennium).

Strengths:
1) There are similarities between the feast of birds on the dead (Ezekiel 39:17-20 cf. Revelation 19).
2) The earthquake of Revelation 16:18 could be the same as that of Ezekiel 38:20.
3) Other similarities between the events of Ezekiel 38-39 and the events of Revelation are seen.

Weaknesses:
1) Many of the events of Revelation are upon the world at large, not the land of Israel.
2) The invasion is supposed to come at a time of rest, when Israel is living "securely"; something incompatible with Revelation 19.
3) The time of Israel's repentance precedes Armageddon and must coincide with the invasion of Gog (Ezekiel 39:22).
4) Seven months are alloted to bury the dead, but the Millennium begins no more than 75 days after Armageddon. There is not enough time to cleanse the land before the Kingdom is inaugurated.

The Invasion at the End of the Millennium
Tenants of:
This view places the invasion of at the end of the Millennium and synonymous with Revelation 20:7-10.

Popular advocates : Nathaniel West, Henry Ellison, and Ralph Alexander.*

* Alexander sees a double fulfillment (at Armageddon and at the end of the Millennium).

Strengths:
1) Israel will definitely be at peace during the Millennium (cf. Ezekiel 38:10).
2) Gog is explicitly mentioned as rebelling against God in Revelation 20:7-10.

Weaknesses:
1) The invasion singals Israel's repentance in Ezekiel 39:22 but Jews will obviously have repented before the Millennium.
2) Some of Gog's allies in Ezekiel 38:1-6 are blessed nations in the Millennium (Isaiah 66:19).
3) Gog comes from the north in Ezekiel but in Revelation 20:8 Gog comes from the four quarters of the earth.
4) The bodies of the dead are buried in Ezekiel 39:12 but burned by God in Revelation 20:9.
5) The creation of the New Heaven and New Earth immediately follow Gog's destruction in Revelation 20:7-10, but in Ezekiel there will be seven years of burning weapons for fuel (Ezekiel 29:9) and seven months of burying dead bodies (Ezekiel 39:12).

Appendix D

—

The Chronology of Revelation

Historians are taught from their earliest days in college that "chronology is the backbone of history." Without it, the events of history have no relationship to one another. The cause and effect relationship is lost. The same is true of prophecy. Prophecy is, after all, future history. Without a proper chronology, the prophecies might pass without recognition. Such was the case with Jesus Christ, centuries ago, because many Jews has misinterpreted the prophecies of the Messiah. The Scriptures had prophesied that the Christ would suffer for our sins, but it also prophesied that He would conquer evil and rule the world from Jerusalem. When it became clear that Jesus had no intentions of overthrowing the Roman Empire or to rule in Jerusalem many turned against Him and became unwitting pawns in the fulfillment the former prophecies. In fact, the Old Testament actually spoke of two comings of the Messiah. The first to redeem man from his sins, and the second to vanquish evil and establish His Kingdom. Because the Jews had misinterpreted the chronology of these prophecies, they did not recognize all the prophecies that were being fulfilled in their very midst.

In the book of Revelation there are a series of events which take place in the context of the 70th Week of Daniel. The difficultly among scholars is determining exactly how these events fit into that context. Although some believe this is a fruitless endeavor, or an unimportant triviality, the chronology of Revelation actually allows the reader to better understand the events and the progression of God's wrath, of the repentance of Israel, and of the hardening of man's heart. It also provides clues that can better identify the true meaning of controversial passages such as the identity of Babylon or the timing of Gog's invasion. Lest anyone underestimate the importance of chronology, the reader should be reminded that the essential difference between the literal interpretation (premillennial) and the allegorical methods (amillennial and postmillennial) is the *chronology* of the Millennium. So chronology, tedious as its study may be, is actually a vital aspect of the study of Revelation, and one which is too often ignored.

The Historicist View of Chronology

Before proceding with the various chronological theories, the historicists' chronology must be rebutted. Historicists naturally reject the placing of Revelation within the confines of Daniel's 70th Week. They believe that Revelation stretches out over the entire church age from the first coming of Christ until His return (see Appendix F). This assumption naturally requires the allegorizing of many passages, including the anti-Christ himself. If the anti-Christ was to exist for thousands of years, the anti-Christ had to become a system rather than a man.[1671] Such beliefs illustrate the inherent flaw in the historicist system, but so does their loose chronology. Since historicists cannot themselves agree on when a particular prophecy was fulfilled, it is only natural that their chronology is ambiguous. There are two ways that attempt to stretch the events of Revelation over the centuries. The first way is called the "day/age theory"; the second is called the "concurrent" view of the chronology.

According to the "day/age theory" the days of Daniel and John are not be taken as literal days, but *years*. Thus the 1260 days become 1260 *years*. Using this sytem of thought, the reign of the anti-Christ (as a system, not a person) was said to be 1260 years. The result of this faulty system left many historicists predicting the end of the 1260 years, and the end of the world (see Appendix E). It is based on the assumption that if a "week" equals seven years, then a day must equal a year. However, as one pointed out, if this were the case then "then 'the 1,000 years *must* mean, at least, 360,000 years.'"[1672] The flaws with this system are obvious and are addressed more fully in a later appendix. The days cannot be made into years, nor may individuals be turned into systems. The historicist system requires it, but cannot support it.

The second aspect of historicist chronology is the "concurrent view." This theory was formulated to a large extent by the medieval historicist theologian Joachim of Fiore; whom some credit with the creation of historicism.[1673] According to Joachim the seals, trumpets, and bowls were broad allegorical visions of history representing "types."[1674] Joachim believed that there are seven eras of history, which correspond to the judgments of Revelation. For example, in Joachim's scheme the first seal represented the age of Christ. This period is alleged to stretch from Christ to the death of the apostle John and it is suppose to correspond typologically to the age of Jacob which extended to the time of Moses.[1675] The second seal he believed represented the pagan priesthood. The church age from the time of the apostle John's death to the coming of Constantine he believed corresponded to the days of Moses until to coming of Samuel and King David.[1676] Along this same reasoning then, the third seal represented Arianism which he then equated with the time of Constantine to Justinian in the New Covenant and the time of David to Elijah in the Old.[1677] He then argues that the trumpets were also typological of the same ages and therefore overlapped the seals, just as the bowls allegedly overlapped the trumpets.[1678] In other words, the seals, trumpets, and bowls all represent the same events in different ways.

This typology of the ages is one of the main tenants of historicism and the primary reason that the seals, trumpets, and bowls are connected. Nevertheless, a few modern futurists have argued for overlapping based primarily on the similarity between the trumpet judgments and the bowl judgments. This system of interpretation is also called the recapitulation theory. While the similarity between the trumpet judgments and bowls cannot be denied, neither can they be equated as one and the same, for too many differences exist. For example, George Ladd illustrates that:

> "At the sounding of the second trumpet, something like a mountain was cast into the sea and a third of its waters became blood and a third of the creatures in the sea died (8:8-10). No such limitation is placed upon [the bowl] plague; all the creatures in the sea died ... the third trumpet plague affected the rivers and the fountains of water so that a third of them was turned poisonously bitter. Here [on the third bowl], there is no such limitation."[1679]

The most clear illustration of the folly of such a system can be seen in Revelation 15. There we see God entering His Holy Temple in Heaven. There He is said to remain until the bowls have all been emptied (Revelation 15:5-7). Since God was not in the temple during either the seals or trumpets it is only logical that the bowl judgments are separate judgments that follow the seals and trumpets.

Any straightforward reading of the text shows that the seals, trumpets, and bowls are sequential in nature. That this is the case seems apparent by the mere fact that the opening of the seventh seal describes the dispensing of the seven trumpets which follow. "When He broke the seventh seal, there was silence in heaven for about half an hour. And I saw the seven angels who stand before God; and seven trumpets were given to them" (Revelation 8:1). So the trumpets either follow the seven seals in sequence or, as some say, all seven trumpets are actually to be placed under, and within, the seventh seal. In either case, the result is the same. The trumpets follow the seals, and the bowls follow the trumpets. All futurists agree that "the seventh judgment of the first two series simply introduces the next series."[1680] Charles Ryrie says, "with the opening of [the seventh] seal comes the series of trumpet judgments ... this seems to be the simplest way to understand these judgments."[1681]

A second problem with the historicists' chronology is that the events of Revelation cannot possibly be stretched out over the centuries. Aside from the fact that such a system requires altering the anti-Christ and False Prophet from individuals into systems, it ignores the specifics of the judgments themselves. For example, "the sores of the first [bowl] plague are still felt during the second and third, and even here under the fifth. This proves that these plagues all fall upon the people of one and the same generation, and hence dare not be extended through centuries."[1682] The historicist system requires some way of stretching out the plagues, but this cannot be done without destroying the credibility of the Scriptures themselves. To do so lends itself to the most outrageous and diverse interpretations that the human imagination can conceive. Were it not for amillennialism, historicism, and the other allegorical systems, critics could not say, "no one can agree on what Revelation means." Within the literal futurist system, the differences are relatively few and are containted within this very book. Were I to choose to write an exhaustive comparative analysis including Augustinians, historicism, allegorism, amillennialism, idealism, and postmillennialists (all of which reject a "literal" straightforward understanding of the prophecies) this book would be many thousands of pages in length. Only a straighforward systematic view can make sense of Revelation, and that requires a sequential view of God's judgments.

Historically, the death of historicism, as a predominant view, began with the historicist Joseph Mede. Although a historicist, Mede recognized that the chronology of Revelation could not realistically be read concurrently. He rejected the concurrent view and returned to a sequential interpretation. Even though he maintained most of the traditional historicist interpretations of his day, his *Key to Revelation* unlocked the chronology of Revelation, returned to a premillennial understanding of Christ's kingdom, and paved the way for the return to futurism under Darby.

Mede showed that the 144,000, regardless of whether they be literal individuals, *must* be contemporary with the surrounding events.[1683] He says that the interpreter must come to the realization that "the woman in the wilderness, the domination of the Beast, the treading of the Holy City under foot, and the prophecies of the witnesses, do synchronize each with other."[1684] Mede's chronology, although still stretched out over fifteen hundred years, began to resemble that of futurists. Thus the premillennial historicists rejected the faulty chronology of the medievals, creating a literal framework from which literal interpretation would one day blossom.

Fixing Reference Points

When studying chronology it is necessary to establish certain reference points. Like a marker which you can see for miles, a chronological reference point allows the interpreter to fix the events of which he is reading in relation to that marker. In archaeology this is called "relative dating."[1685] A particular object can be said to older than, or younger than, another object, but its "absolute age" cannot usually be determined with any accuracy.[1686] The same is true in history. For example, the ancients did not measure time in the same way and many merely referenced the duration of a particular ruler. Egypt might refer to "the sixth year of the reign of Amenhotep" while Persia states that an event occurred in "the first year of Cyrus." This also occurs in the Bible (cf. Daniel 1:21). In order to fix these dates according to our modern calendar we must find fixed events that occurred in those histories. In other words we must find an event which occurs in both Hebrew history and Egyptian history, but which is also known by our own calendar. In this example the erection of Solomon's temple in Jerusalem provides one such "fixed" event. We know from archaeology and other sources that Solomon's temple was erected in approximately 966 B.C.[1687] Because the Bible states explicitly that the temple was erected 480 years after the exodus (1 Kings 6:1) we can then tie the majority of the Biblical chronology to our own. The date of the Exodos is, therefore, approximately 1446 B.C. This, in turn, allows us to fix certain points of Israeli history to Egyptian history (e.g. the sack of the Temple by the Pharaoh Neco [2 Kings 23:29-35][1688]).

This same principle applies to prophetic interpretation. Fixed reference points are needed in order to cross reference various prophetic passages. In regard to the end times there are several passages that give us explicit time frames. The most obvious is the 70th Week of Daniel during which the anti-Christ will rule and during which Israel will travail. Revelation itself discusses two separate periods of 1260 days or 42 months (11:2-3, 12:6, & 13:5). The Book of Daniel likewise divides the 70th Week into two separate halves divided by and marked by the abomination of desolation. Because Jesus Himself discussed the abomination of desolation (Matt. 24:15, Mark 13:14), we can then tie some of the events of Revelation together with Daniel's seventieth week in confidence.

So what fixed reference points can futurists agree upon? The first is this dividing of Revelation equally into two separate halves of three and one half years. Although some futurists do dispute this, most cannot help but agree. "In Daniel and John, we find *one and the same measure of time represented by four different forms of expression*, viz., (1) 'times, times, (dual number) and the dividing (or half) of a time,' Dan. Vii:25; xii:7; Rev. xii:14; (2) 'half week,' Dan. ix:27; (3) '42 months,' Rev. xi:12; xiii:5; and (4) '1260 days' Rev. xi:3; xii:6. These numbers are commensurate."[1689] As far back the church fathers this chronology was agreed upon. Although some have assumed that Irenaeus believed the book of Revelation encompassed only one single three and a half year period, followed by the second coming of Christ,[1690] this is not so. Irenaeus does not define what occurs in the second half of Daniel's 70th week, but he affirms that the three and a half years of Revelation are tied to the first half of Daniel's 70th week. He says:

> "[Daniel] points out the time that [the anti-Christ's] tyranny shall last, during which the saints shall be put to flight, they who offer a pure sacrifice unto God : 'And in the midst of the week,' he says, 'the sacrifice and the libation shall be taken away, and the abomination of desolation [shall be brought] into the temple : even unto the consummation of the time shall the desolation be complete.' Now three years and six months constitute the half-week."[1691]

Hippolytus was even more clear in his connection of Daniel 9:27 to the book of Revelation when he spoke of the "final week of the world."[1692] According to Hippolytus the anti-Christ would reign for three and a half years until the abomination of desolation, after which he would persecute the saints for the final three and a half years.[1693] This differs from Irenaeus only in that

Irenaeus places the persecution of saints in the first half of the tribulation, under the rule and reign of the anti-Christ.[1694] In other words, there is agreement that the anti-Christ will reign for 42 months, as Lactantius states,[1695] and that after this the abomination of desolation will occur and the anti-Christ's power will be challenged. Even Adso of Montier, the medieval chilaist, divides Revelation into two separate halves, totaling seven years, with the "Great Tribulation" occupying the second half.[1696] Certainly few modern futurists doubt this scenario. Consequently, the first reference markers are the two separate periods of three and a half years divided by the abomination of desolation.

The second fixed marker is that of the death and resurrection of the two witnesses. Premillennial commentators are overwhelmingly of the opinion that the death and resurrection of the two witnesses is at the midpoint of the tribulation, following the abomination of desolation. Their ministry is said to be 1260 days (Revelation 11:3) and appears to coincide with the forty-two months of Revelation 11:2. Only a handful of scholars question that the ministry of the two witnesses occurs in the first half of the tribulation. Thus the death of the two witnesses constitutes a second reference point which is also in the middle of the tribulation.

Another marker appears, yet again, to coincide with the middle of the tribulation. This is the flight of the woman (Revelation 12:6). She is said to be nourished for 1260 days, or three and a half years, and is almost unanimously believed to be referenced by our Lord in Matthew 24:15-16, immediately following the abomination of desolation. So another marker is found at the mid-point of Daniel's 70th Week. Obviously, the importance of the middle of the week cannot be underestimated. The difficulty is in tying the other events of Revelation to these fixed points.

Only one other marker seems evident. That is the connection of the seventh bowl to the battle of Armageddon and the second coming of Christ in chapter nineteen. From these fixed points of reference all other chronological events must be cross-referenced.

The Sequential Views

Futurists have generally agreed that the judgments of God must be placed sequentially within the confines of the tribulation. The debates between futurists involve the timing of the seals, trumpets, bowls, and the fall of Babylon. Currently there are two views of Babylon's fall, but three dominant theories on the timing of the judgments, as well as a number of variations. It is best to examine each of these individually.

The Pre-Abomination Seal and Trumpet Judgments View
Of the three main views of the judgments, this theory is one of the most popular, being espoused by names such as Nathaniel West,[1697] Walter Scott,[1698] E. W.

Bullinger,[1699] C. I. Scofield,[1700] H. A. Ironside,[1701] John Walvoord,[1702] Henry Morris,[1703] and Tim LaHaye.[1704] According to this theory, the seal and trumpet judgments are released sequentially in the first half of the tribulation beginning soon after the anti-Christ signs the treaty with Israel. This thesis places the bowls of wrath alone in the second half of the tribulation, over a period of three and a half years.

The strength of this view is in the fact that it is one of the most straightforward chronologies. It assumes that that chapters eleven and twelve are not truly parenthetical, as many believe, but placed in correct chronological order with the judgments. Nonetheless, Nathaniel West, an advocate of this position, himself admits that it is "contrary to analysis, to assume that, because events are mentioned in immediate juxtaposition, therefore they are to follow one another in immediate chronological order."[1705] Still, their strongest argument is based on the "woes" of Revelation 8:13.

It is an accepted fact that these three woes relate to the last three trumpet judgments. The angel himself declares "woe, woe, woe, to those who dwell on the earth, because of the remaining blasts of the trumpet of the three angels who are about to sound." Following the fifth trumpet, it is said, "the first woe is past; behold, two woes are still coming" (9:12). However, after the sixth trumpet, nothing is said of the second woe, until Revelation 11:14. This view, therefore, assumes that the events of Revelation 11 are a part of the sixth trumpet. Since Revelation 11:7 is one of the those fixed reference points, which lies in the middle of Daniel's 70th week, it is assumed that the sixth trumpet must coincide with the events of chapter eleven. A closer examination of chapter eleven, however, will show this view flawed.

The textual problem of 11:14 is not as severe as it might appear in English. In fact, "the third woe is not given here at all"[1706] and "is not described."[1707] This may be because the third woe is the seventh trumpet, under which the entire series of bowls are released. [1708] So the third woe actually constitutes *all* the bowls of wrath, which in turn explains why the third woe is never explicitly mentioned. If this so, then is not Henry Morris correct when he assumes that "the second woe had occupied over thirteen months, including the scourge of the 200 million devil-horsemen as well as the continuing judgments of the two witnesses and, finally, the great earthquake that had fallen on Jerusalem"?[1709] Cannot the second woe encompass the events of Revelation ten and eleven? The fact cannot support this. While the English appears to provide a connection to the previous verses, ancient Greek did not have punctuation.[1710] As Robert Mounce states, "verse 14 stands in isolation, separated from the second Woe by the visions of 10:1-11:13."[1711] George Ladd explains that "John introduces the seventh trumpet as though there had been no interruption."[1712] This is why many translations place verse fourteen with verse fifteen. Others leave fourteen as a singular paragraph, but no translation places it with verse thirteen. Robert Thomas explains why:

"A dramatic announcement as a follow-up to those in 8:13 and 9:12 comes at this point to mark the end of the 10:1 – 11:13 interlude: (*He ouai he deutera apelthen; idou he ouai he trite erchetai tachy*, "The second woe has gone away; behold, the third woe comes soon"). Because of this announcement, some would include the interlude as part of the second woe, thereby extending the second woe beyond the end of the sixth trumpet in 9:21. But the announcement of the passing of the second woe in 11:14a does not necessitate this extension. The writer puts the announcement of the second woe's end here to conjoin it with the announcement of the commencement of the third woe in 11:14b, which identifies with the seventh trumpet sounded in the next verse. The material in 10:1 – 11 especially is hardly in the category of a woe. To maintain clarity, the interlude material must not mix with material in the numbered sequences of the book. Revelation 9:20 – 21 clearly marks the end of the sixth trumpet, which is the second woe."[1713]

It is, therefore, acceptable to say that John resumes his argument from whence the interlude began by simply stating, "the second woe has past." While by no means conclusive, this appears to be the best option, for it is impossible to place the seven thunders and the little scroll (10:1-11) within the sixth trumpet. Moreover, one of the biggest problems is that the events of chapter eleven describe periods of 1260 days (11:3), and of 42 months (11:2). They also describe an earthquake which is not found in the sixth trumpet. There is simply no logical way to place these chapters within the sixth trumpet.

Were this the only problem with the theory, then one might be inclined to accept it, but far greater problems exist. If the seals and trumpets are released before the middle of the tribulations then several irreconcilable problems are created. First, Jesus warned his followers in Matthew 24:15, Mark 13:14, and Luke 21:20 to flee to the mountains when the abomination of desolation was at hand. He tells them, "let him who is on the housetop not go down to get the things out that are in his house; and let him who is in the field not turn back to get his cloak" (Matthew 24:17-18). All of this implies that the persecution of believers is about to begin and a reign of terror will commence, but why would Jesus say such a thing if the persecutions, terror, and horrors of the seven trumpets had already been occuring over the past three and a half years? It seems impossible that any believer would even have a house or own a field, if the horrors of the trumpets were already dispensed.

This also conflicts with the statement of Paul in 1 Thessalonians 5:2-3, "for you yourselves know full well that the day of the Lord will come just like a thief in the night. While they are saying, 'Peace and safety!' then destruction will come upon them suddenly like birth pangs upon a woman with child; and they shall not escape." Most scholars agree that the Day of the Lord refers to the Great Tribulation and time of wrath. The context of this passage also relates this passage to the abomination of desolation, for in 2 Thessalonians 2:3-4 Paul

376

clarifies what he meant in his previous letter, telling the Thessalonians that the Day of the Lord will not come "unless the apostasy comes first, and the man of lawlessness is revealed, the son of destruction, who opposes and exalts himself above every so-called god or object of worship, so that he takes his seat in the temple of God, displaying himself as being God." In other words, the Day of the Lord follows the abomination of desolation, and this day comes when people are saying "peace and safety." It is impossible to argue that men are saying "peace and safety" in the midst of the seal and trumpet judgments, yet this is exactly what some argue![1714]

Along this same vein is the problem with the anti-Christ's treaty. According to this theory there is war and death and terror from the very beginning of the tribulation, but the anti-Christ's treaty is not broken until the middle of the tribulation (Daniel 9:27). This would make the treaty useless! How could the treaty be of any value for the first three and a half years when war, pestilence, death, natural disasters, and invasions of Palestine occur during that time! One cannot help but wonder why the Jews honor the treaty if it does them no good at all. The answer is that the treaty brings Israel a false peace (1 Thessalonians 5:3). It will be valid for three and a half years until the abomination of desolation, when the anti-Christ defiles the Holy Temple and the Jews repent. Only then does God's wrath begin to fall upon the earth. Furthermore, it seems clear that the anti-Christ kingdom disintigrates only *after* the abomination of desolation, for the beast is given domination for 42 months (Revelation 13:5) and during that time his power is such that men asks, "who is able to wage war with him" (Revelation 13:4). This does not sound like the situation present during the trumpet judgments, or for that matter the seal judgments.

A final problem is how the view minimizes and diminishes the importance of the Great Tribulation. It places fourteen judgments (twenty one if the thunders are judgments as well – see previous appendix) in the first half of the tribulation and only seven in the Great Tribulation! This theory must stretch the seven bowls over three and a half years! Most scholars, however, insist that God's judgments come with an increasing intensity and rhythm. There is a staccato rhythm that is associated with the bowl judgments, for with each judgment, God's patients diminishes. "Let there be no more delay" cries the angel in Revelation 10:6, but these theorists would have us believe that God does delay, stretching seven judgments over three and a half years despite the fact that the bowls, by all appearances, are poured out in rapid succession and follow closely on the heels of the trumpets.

The facts conclude that this view is untenable. Although the view appears straightforward and benefits from the assumption that the woe speaks of the events of chapter eleven, it is the weakest of views. It cannot account for "peace and safety" in the middle of the tribulation (1 Thessalonians 5:3), it is unable to explain the warning of Jesus (cf. Matthew 24:15) given the terrors of the trumpets, it must stretch the bowls over three and a half years, it makes the anti-Christ's treaty irrelevant, and it ignores the sequence of events which lead to the fall of the anti-Christ's kingdom.

The Pre-Abomination Seal Judgments View

A second view places only the seals in the first half of the tribulation, with both the trumpets and bowls in the second half. Some place only the first four seals in the early tribulation, and others begin the second half of the tribulation with the sixth seal. This position is also advocated by a number of great scholars including John Darby,[1715] Sir Robert Anderson,[1716] Charles Ryrie,[1717] Dwight Pentecost,[1718] and Merrill Tenney.[1719]

Like the previous view, this is a very straightforward chronological view, flawed only by the seeming difficulty with the second woe (discussed above). Unlike the pre-abomination trumpet view, this theory accepts the increasing impatience of God in respect to the unleashing and intensity of judgments. It also softens, although does not completely eliminate, the problems with "peace and safety," the meaningfulness of the treaty, and the timing of the fall of the anti-Christ's kingdom. It also rids itself of the problem with stretching the bowls out over three and half years, since the bowls only occupy the final year or so of the tribulation. The problems with stretching the seals over three and a half year are relatively insignificant, since most of the judgments (war, pestilence, and death) may well be prolonged events, unlike the specific timelines given in the trumpets and bowls (cf. Revelation 9:10).

One line of reasoning that advocates cite in favor of this theory is the connection between the earthquake of the sixth seal in Revelation 6:12 and the earthquake in 11:13. However, there are too many differences in the earthquakes to verify them as being one and the same. The earthquake in 6:12 appears to be part of a judgment upon the world at large and as a result of the sixth seal, "the kings of the earth and the great men and the commanders and the rich and the strong and every slave and free man, hid themselves in the caves and among the rocks of the mountains" (6:15). Chapter eleven is a different story. In it, a limited number of people die (7,000) and the judgment falls on the Holy City of Jerusalem alone. The connection is possible, but by no means certain. Therefore, the sixth seal cannot be tied to any of the fixed reference points with any certainty; so much so that John Darby[1720] and Sir Robert Anderson actually place the fifth seal, rather than the sixth, following the death of the two witnesses.[1721]

Another argument seemingly in favor of this thesis is the connection between the seal judgments and Jesus' discussion of "birth pangs" (Matthew 24:5-9). According to this precept (one held by some advocates of all positions, but most often promoted by the pre-abomination seal theorists), the Olivet discourse follows the events of the first six seals. Matthew 24:5-9 reads:

378

"For many will come in My name, saying, 'I am the Christ,' and will mislead many. And you will be hearing of wars and rumors of wars; see that you are not frightened, for those things must take place, but that is not yet the end. For nation will rise against nation, and kingdom against kingdom, and in various places there will be famines and earthquakes. But all these things are merely the beginning of birth pangs. Then they will deliver you to tribulation, and will kill you, and you will be hated by all nations on account of My name."

Mark and Luke also have parallel passages. Now John McLean believes that this proves that there are "parallels between the synoptics and the seal judgments"[1722] but this is presumed, not proven. For one thing, the connection between false prophets and the first seal is tenuous at best. When we read the context of Jesus' sermon we see several other problems as well. First, Jesus clearly warns his followers, "see that you are not frightened, for those things must take place, but that is not yet the end" (24:6). Instead, Jesus says, "when you see the abomination of desolation which was spoken of through Daniel the prophet, standing in the holy place (let the reader understand), then let those who are in Judea flee to the mountains" (vs. 15-16). This implies that believers will be relatively safe before the abomination since Christ is telling them not to be frightened by the "birth pangs" (vs. 10), but to "flee to the mountains" when they see the abomination of desolation. This leads to the second point; what are "birth pangs"?

The "birth pangs" spoken of by Jesus are not the first seven seals but, according to many scholars, signs that precede the tribulation.[1723] One cannot help but notice that of the "birth pangs" mentioned all have occurred regularly throughout history. They are not the rare judgment events of Revelation, but "birth pangs" which grow more frequent as the time of birth approaches. This is admitted even by many who place the seals in the first half of the tribulation. D.A. Carson has stated that the warning was given so that believers would "not be alarmed by these events. 'Such things must happen'; yet the End is still to come (v. 6). These are only 'the beginning of [the] birth pangs' that stretch over the period between the advents."[1724]

The carfeul reader will notice that verse seven mentions the frequency of earthquakes. This cannot refer to the earthquake of the sixth seal, for the word is plural. Instead it is warning that as the time of the end approaches, "the whole of creation itself groans and travails in labor pains until now" (Romans 8:22). History has proven that the frequency and intensity of natural disasters has progressively increased over the centuries. In the past few years alone the U. S. has been hit by numerous hurricanes and tropical storms which were once relatively rare. Earthquakes in particular have increased dramtically. Over a decade ago, the *Fort Worth Star Telegram* reported that the twentieth century has recorded no fewer than 900,000 earthquakes![1725] This is compared to only 2119 recorded earthquakes in the nineteenth century, and 640 in the eighteenth

379

century.[1726] These are the "birth pangs" of which Jesus spoke, not the judgments of the tribulation.

The greater problem is that this thesis does not resolve the problem with "peace and safety" before the abomination of desolation. According to John, it is the second seal which "takes peace from the earth" (6:4). After this seal is broken there can be no "peace" or "safety." This problem cannot be diminished or ignored. The Day of the Lord is to come like a thief when people are saying "peace and safety" (1 Thessalonians 5:3). No view can stand unless it can resolve itself with this.

This view is thus a vast improvement over the pre-abomination trumpet view, but still suffers from some of the same flaws. It cannot connect any of the events in the seal judgments to the fixed reference markers, as is evidenced by its own advocates failure to identify which seal belongs in the middle of the tribulation. Some place only the first four seals in the first half of the tribulation (John Darby[1727]), others place the fifth at the mid-trib point (Sir Robert Anderson[1728]), some place the sixth seal in the middle of the tribulation (Merrill Tenney[1729]), and some put the first trumpet at the middle of the tribulation (Dwight Pentecost[1730]). None can agree, because there is no strong evidence to fix any of these events at the mid-tribulation point.

The Post-Abomination Judgments View

According to the post-abomination judgments theory, virtually all of the judgments, whether seals, trumpets, or bowls occur in the second half of the tribulation. "Virtually all," because some believe that the first seal represents the coming of the anti-Christ (see chapter 3) and place it alone in the first half of the tribulation. All other judgments are agreed to occur only after the abomination of desolation.

One will perhaps be astounded more than anything by the number of great scholars who have diverged upon the issue of chronology. Many times it not hard to see a pattern among scholars, but here they diverge without respect to dispensationalism, covenant theology, replacement theology, pretribulationism, posttribulationism, or any other theological "bias." Even as the previous views are held by numerous scholars of stature, this view is also held by scholarly men of renown. This theory is held by men as Joseph Seiss, Hal Lindsey, George Ladd, and Dave Hunt.[1731]

As with both of the previous views, this thesis is very straightforward in its chronology; perhaps more so than the others. It makes no attempt to tie any seal or trumpet to mid-tribulational events, because the abomination of desolation has already passed. This is perhaps one reason that it has been so hard to place one of the judgments at the midpoint of the tribulation; because none of them belong at the midpoint of the tribulation. The judgments properly constitute the "Great Tribulation" and parallel the vivid description Jesus gives in the Olivet discourse. Following his warning of "birth pangs" Jesus then describes detailed parallels to the seals, trumpets, and bowls. In Matthew 24:19

Jesus states that in "the tribulation of those days the Sun will be darkened, and the moon will not give its light, and the stars will fall from the sky, and the powers of the heavens will be shaken." This is a clear parallel to the sixth seal of Revelation in which "the sun became black as sackcloth made of hair, and the whole moon became like blood; and the stars of the sky fell to the earth, as a fig tree casts its unripe figs when shaken by a great wind" (Revelation 6:12-13). Now the significance is that Jesus connects this with the "Great Tribulation," which apparently follows the abomination of desolation. That the "Great Tribulation" is properly the last three and a half years of Daniel's 70th Week is agreed by most all. Thus, the best view seems to be that the seals, as well as the trumpets and bowls, belong in the second half of the tribulation. This is supported for several reasons.

Thessalonian is not the only passage to indicate that the abomination of desolation will be preceded by a time of peace. In Daniel 8:25 the King James version reads that the ruler "by means of peace shall destroy many."[1732]   In Revelation 13:4 the people cry out, "who is like the beast and who is able to wage war against him?" Hal Lindsey argues that "the Antichrist will stop war so that the world will extol him because they believe that no one can make war against him."[1733] He also notes that the abomination of desolation cannot take place until the second seal is opened "because the second seal specifically 'takes peace from the earth.'"[1734] This seems the best answer. What better scenario could fit the words of Paul, "while they are saying, 'Peace and safety!' then destruction will come upon them suddenly like birth pangs upon a woman with child; and they shall not escape" (1 Thessalonians 5:3). This destruction is almost certainly tied to the abomination of desolation, for Paul clarifies his previous letter urging believers not to be concerned until "the man of lawlessness is revealed, the son of destruction, who opposes and exalts himself above every so-called god or object of worship, so that he takes his seat in the temple of God, displaying himself as being God" (2 Thessalonians 2:3-4).

There can be no doubt as to the importance of the *peace* treaty which the anti-Christ makes. Even among those who place the seals and trumpets in the first half of the tribulation there is agreement that the anti-Christ will bring peace for a time. How long that peace is, is the question. Dave Hunt believes that this peace treaty will ulimately be a "colossal trap."[1735] Indeed, it is logical to assume that the time period in which the anti-Christ's treaty brings peace to the world will be synonymous with the time when the world will stand in awe of the Revived Roman Empire, marvel at its restoration, and say, "who is able to make war against it?" (Revelation 13:4). According to Revelation 13:5, this period will last 42 months, or three and a half years. This corresponds to Daniel 9:27 in which the covenant is broken after three and a half years.

Therefore, the best scenario is that the anti-Christ brings peace with Israel throughout the first half of the tribulation. The beast is worshipped and revered and the seven-year peace treaty is established, allowing the temple to be rebuilt (if it has not already been rebuilt). However, once the anti-Christ takes his seat in the temple and commits the abomination of desolation, "destruction" and wrath will come upon the earth. It is only then that the seven seals, and the trumpets and bowls which follow, will be let loose upon the world.

This view also allows for the free witnessing of the gospel during the early portions of the tribulation. We know that believers will be brutally persecuted during the "Great Tribulation." We also know that Jesus' warning in Matthew 24:15 implied that persecution would *follow* the abomination, but nothing is said or implied about persecution preceding that day. The fifth seal shows the martyred dead of the Great Tribulation. It is, therefore, natural to assume that the fifth seal follows Revelation 12:14 in which the woman (believing Israel) flees to the mountains (cf. Matthew 24:15, Mark 13:14, and Luke 21:20). Before that time, the 144,000, along with the two witnesses (Revelation 11:3), are free to prophesy and witness.

This thesis is best. It alone can consistently explain the references to peace preceding the abomination of desolation, the relative safety that believers have before that time, and the warnings of destruction that follow that day. No single event in any of the judgments can be tied to the fixed reference markers because none of the judgments coincide with those mid-tribulational markers. The seals are opened only after the anti-Christ has desecrated the temple.

The Minority Positions

Three significant minority theories remain. The one is relatively old. The others new. Each of these views accepts a literal seven year tribulation, but places some of the judgments *outside* the tribulation period. The first argues that the first four seals *precede* the tribulation. The second creates a separate 42 months which *precedes* Daniels 70th week, thus creating a 10 ½ year tribulational period. The third argues that the seven bowls of wrath *follow* the return of Christ.

The first of these views is a derivative of the pre-abomination theories. Its advocates seize upon the claim that the first five seals are the "birth pangs" of the Olivet Discourse, but acknowledging that the birth pangs precede the tribulation, they in turn place the seals before Daniel's 70th week.[1736] According to Norman Harrison, the 70th week does not begin until the fifth trumpet is blown![1737] Watchman Nee is more discreet in his placement of pre-tribulational judgments, seeing only the first four seals as occuring before the tribulation.[1738]

The flaw of this theory is in its subtle historicist influences. For example, Harrison, looking to present day events for the fulfillment of these prophecies, equated World War I with the second and third seals.[1739] He later identifies the Second World War with trumpet judgments.[1740] It is evident, therefore, that Harrison believed he would live to see the abomination of desolation. This did not, however, happen. His exegesis of Revelation was acceptable, but his attempts to identify the "hail and fire mingled with blood" with aerial bombing in World War II[1741] show a distinctinve historicist influence. This view is obviously incompatible with pretribulationism, but it is also incompatible with the facts. A careful examination shows that there are far more points of disagreement with the prophecies, than points of agreement. To place the judgments outside of Daniel's 70th week is not only flawed, but potentially dangerous (see Appendix E). *All* the judgments of God fall during the tribulation and the 70th Week of Daniel. *None* precede it.

Of course, the flaws with this system were obvious to many, which is why Arthur Bloomfield modified it to escape the historcist influences, while clinging to many of the inherent assumptions which underly it. Ironically, Bloomfield was a strong dispensationalist, which meant that he believed the rapture would precede the 70th Week of Daniel. Consequently, Bloomfield created a unique chronology based on his pseudo-dispensational beliefs. He states that chronologically "there are no 'parenthetical chapters' in Revelation. Nothing is out of place; everything is in order."[1742] Such is largely the view of the pre-abomination trumpet view. However, Bloomfield's chronology begins to significantly diverge from most expositors when he assumes that "the 42 months of this chapter [13] have nothing to do with the Jews, or with either half of the seven years mentioned in Daniel. This 42 months is the length of time that the beast will continue to make war with the saints."[1743] He suggests that this domination of the beast *cannot* coincide with Daniel's 70th week because he says that if the saints do not die *before* Daniel's 70th week, then there would be an impossible mixing of dispensations! [1744] He thereby "solves" the problem by placing the 42 months before the 70th Week of Daniel. The seals are said to fall into this first 42 months, then the trumpets occupy the first half of Daniel's 70th week, and the bowls occupy the final half. The rapture he places between the 42 months and Daniel's 70th week.

Obviously, this complicated system of chronology is based largely on Bloomfield's assumption that dispensations can neither mix, nor that the saints of Revelation seven can be Jews. The problems created by this chronology are far too extensive to debate, given that this is a rarely held view. In "resolving" one problem, Bloomfield has actually created many new ones. He would not, however, be the first or the last to make this mistake. Another chronology, based almost solely upon the assumptions of pre-wrath rapture, was developed by Marvin Rosenthal. In his system of thought the bowls of wrath are not poured out on the earth until *after* the return of Jesus Christ! He makes a distinction between the Great Tribulation and the 70th Week of Daniel. He argues that Matthew 24:22 proves that the Great Tribulation must be "cut short" of its three and a half years, but *not* Daniel's 70th week.[1745] Rosenthal says, "the shortening of the Great Tribulation to less than three and one half years is one of the most important truths to be grasped if the chronology of end-times events is to be understood."[1746] According to his scheme the bowl judgments must be connected not with the tribulation but with the 30 and 45 days of Daniel discussed below.

Like Bloomfield, Rosenthal has seized upon a simple, and unprovable, assumption, and devised an intricate chronology around it. To argue that the Great Tribulation is "shortened," but not Daniel's 70th week, based solely upon Matthew 24:22 is unjustifiable. It also fails to prove that the bowls would be unleashed in that time period. It is too much based upon too little. For these reasons, none of these three theories have found substantial followers. They are of interest to examine, but cannot be taken as serious options.

The Fall of Babylon

The fall of Babylon has been previously addressed (see chapter 8), but the specific arguments for the chronology of its fall will be briefly repeated here. Two opinions prevail. The first holds that Babylon falls in the middle of the tribulation after the abomination of desolation. The second argues that Babylon falls at the end of the world during the sixth or seventh bowl, and immediately before Armageddon. It is not surprising that a third view combines the two saying that the fall of "religious Babylon" occurs at the mid-point of the tribulation but leaves "economic Babylon's" fall to the end.

Those who believe that Babylon is the capitol of the empire or its economic center in Iraq naturally tend to argue that it falls at the end of the tribulation. The reasons for this are based largely on the exegetical problems which an earlier fall creates for this theory (see chapter 8). The textual basis is the fact that Babylon's fall is mentioned in Revelation 16:19, apparently in connection with the seventh bowl.

Kenneth McKinley states that the fall of Babylon "is after the seventh vial is poured out, for it is after the earthquake and hail are begun that Babylon receives her judgment at the hands of the beast."[1747] He further argues "the ten kings give their strength and power to the beast to destroy the Harlot, they will also war with the Lamb who shall overcome them. This definitely ties in the destruction of Babylon with the battle of Armageddon and places it immediately before."[1748] However, McKinley neglects to mention that there will not be ten kings at Armageddon, for the anti-Christ has subdued three of those kings before Armageddon (Daniel 7:24).

Despite the assurances of McKinley he is mistaken on two other levels. First, reference to Babylon following the seventh bowl is one of "remembrance." The actual fall is spoken of in Revelation fourteen, not sixteen. Second, the "war with the Lamb" does not explicitly refer to Armageddon, but to the war against Christ and his believers that is waged in the final half of the tribulation.

Babylon is spoken of twice in Revelation apart from the seventeenth and eighteenth chapters. The first reference is Revelation 14:8 reading "another angel, a second one, followed, saying, 'Fallen, fallen is Babylon the great, she who has made all the nations drink of the wine of the passion of her immorality.'" The first angel had urged the people of the world to repent and a third angel who followed the heralder of Babylon's destruction warns those who receive the mark of the beast of their impending doom. The second reference is in Revelation 16:9 following the seventh bowl and during a brief pause before the battle of Armageddon. This verse reads simply, "the cities of the nations fell. And Babylon the great was remembered before God, to give her the cup of the wine of His fierce wrath."

That Babylon's fall probably does not occur at the time of Revelation sixteen should be evident by the fact that God "remembered" Babylon. There are several pauses in the book of Revelation that break from the chronology. One of these breaks is generally accepted to be chapters seventeen and eighteen. This is acknowledged even by many who accept the fall of Babylon shortly before the battle of Armageddon. Another break, and the one that is most pertinent to this debate, is the break between the seventh trumpet and the first bowl of wrath. This includes all of chapter twelve, thirteen, fourteen, and fifteen. It constitutes the longest break in chronology as the Bible goes back and provides background information for the events described in Revelation. During these chapters the Jewish evangelists, the two witnesses, the two beasts, the anti-Christ, the mark of the beast, the abomination of desolation, and the fall of Babylon are all discussed.

If Babylon's fall is first mentioned in Revelation 14:8 then the most logical way to fix the date for the fall of Babylon is to fix the chronology of chapter 14. A brief description of what transpires in Revelation fourteen may help clarify this chronology. In verse one through five the 144,000 Jewish evangelists are mentioned. Most agree that these evangelists are witnessing throughout the tribulation. They are first mentioned in chapter seven but reappear here on Mount Zion with the Lamb. Verses six and seven see an angel warning the men of the earth, saying, "fear God, and give Him glory, because the hour of His judgment has come; and worship Him who made the heaven and the earth and sea and springs of waters." Verse eight then refers to the fall of Babylon followed by a warning to those who have received the mark of the beast. This in turn is followed by an angel who proclaims "'Blessed are the dead who die in the Lord from now on!' Yes, says the Spirit, that they may rest from their labors, for their deeds follow with them." The final verses of chapter fourteen then describe the reaper in what is usually believed to refer to the battle of Armageddon.

This picture then seems to provide a brief scope of the entire tribulation, for the sealing of the 144,000 is almost universally held to occur at the beginning of the tribulation. The fall of Babylon is then mentioned before the warning to those who receive the mark of the beast. Now it is generally held that the mark of the beast is compelled at least by the mid-point of the tribulation, if not earlier. The reference to the fall of Babylon would then appear to fall somewhere between the sealing of the 144,000 at the beginning of the tribulation and the compelling of the mark of the beast, which probably occurs just after the middle of the tribulation, as Tim LaHaye believes.[1749]

Another problem with the late date is found in Revelation eighteen. How can the kings of the earth mourn the fall of Babylon when Christ Himself has destroyed all the cities of the earth (Revelation 16:19) and when they see Christ "coming with the clouds" (Revelation 19)? It makes little sense to argue that the kings of the earth are bewailing the fall of Babylon when their own homes, families, and countries have burned up and been swallowed up in wrath. Even Henry Morris acknowledges this by trying to create a number of "weeks" between the destruction of Babylon and Armageddon[1750] during which some "semblance of normalcy"[1751] would return to the world. Nevertheless, any logical reading must assume that the fall and mourning occurs at a time when the kings' homes were still safe and at relative peace, not weeks before Armageddon. Clearly, this must occur some time before the last of the bowls are poured out.

Nonetheless, the strongest argument against the late date for Babylon's fall is the fact that it is the ten kings who deliver God's wrath. Since we know from Daniel 7:24 that the anti-Christ will subjugate three of these kings, probably in the middle of the tribulation, it is only logical to assume that the fall of Babylon precedes the conquest of those three nations. Says George Peters:

> "The critical student will also notice that the confederation arises after (Rev. 17) the Harlot has been supported, as in the past, by the beast, and yet before the fall of Babylon (in which fall it participates), and (Rev. 14) before the universal demand to worship the beast and his image, and therefore previous to the persecution of the saints."[1752]

The fall of Babylon most logically occurs in the middle of the tribulation, probably quite soon after the abomination of desolation and just before the anti-Christ turns on three of his colleagues. Of course such a chronology creates difficulties for those who hold that this is the economic capitol of the Revived Roman Empire. There is no way to reconcile a destruction of "economic" Babylon in the middle of the tribulation since the anti-Christ would be destroying his own economic capitol! It is, therefore, little surprise that those who believe Babylon of Iraq will be rebuilt (see chapter 8) have attempted to amalgamate the views. In regard to the Harlot, John Walvoord argues:

> "With the beginning of the second half of the week, the ruler of the revived Roman Empire, who is the political head of the world empire and is himself designated also as 'the beast,' is able to proclaim himself dictator of the whole world. In this capacity he no longer needs the help and power of the church. He therefore destroys the world church and

substitutes for this ecclesiastical apostasy the final form of wickedness in this area of religion, the worship of himself."[1753]

However, in regard to city of Babylon in chapter eighteen, which he believes is separate,[1754] he says it will fall "just prior to the second coming of Christ."[1755] Tim LaHaye has also tried to merge the two conflicting views and this confusion is evident by his own "difficulty"[1756] in resolving the apparent contradictions created by such an integration. He admits that "religious Babylon and governmental Babylon are so intertwined that they are presented together,"[1757] and yet he engages in an elaborate argument to separate the fall of the two. He argues:

> "The reason we know this killing of the prostitute of 'mystery Babylon' is done in the middle of the Tribulation is ... [because] from then on the world does not worship mystery Babylon but the image of the beast. The False Prophet will do away with all religion except the worship of Antichrist Satan, which he will enforce. That begins the middle of the Tribulation."[1758]

Because this scenario does not work with the theory that the ancient city of Iraq will be rebuilt, LaHaye then argues that the destruction of the city must be separated from the Harlot by three and a half years despite the clear statement in Revelation 17:18 "the woman whom you saw *is the* great city, which reigns over the kings of the earth."

The only real option is to acknowledge that the one and only Babylon, harlot *and* city, falls in the middle of the tribulation, shortly after the abomination of desolation. Fearing that the church will rebel against the religious pretentions of the anti-Christ, he makes an example of the church, only to see his kingdom begin to disintegrate.

The Interim Period

A final chronological puzzle comes from the book of Daniel. Numerous and repeated times the Bible makes reference to the 1260 day period (or three and one half Hebrew years) following the abomination of desolation. However, in Daniel 12:11-12, an angel says to Daniel, "from the time that the regular sacrifice is abolished, and the abomination of desolation is set up, *there will be* 1,290 days. How blessed is he who keeps waiting and attains to the 1,335 days!" (Daniel 12:11-12). This makes first a thirty day period *beyond* the end of Daniel's 70th week, as well as a second forty-five days mentioned immediately thereafter, yet in neither place is it defined what will happen in these days. If Daniel's 70th week ends after 1260 days, then what does it mean when it says "there will be 1290?" Twelve hundred and ninety days to what? And what is attained at then end of 1335 days? These statement cannot be discarded as glosses or mistakes. They are affirmed in all the ancient text. They form a mystery that scholars have been debating for centuries.

On one point most premillennialists are agreed. These 30 days, or at least the 45 days, occupy an interim period between the second coming of Christ and the final establishment of the Millennial Kingdom. What happens in these 75 days is the mystery that commentators have debated over the years.

On the question of the thirty days there is little harmony. One view put forth is that the thirty days mark the time between the ending of sacrifices and the actual abomination of desolation; the abomination, therefore, is merely "set up" thirty days prior.[1759] Of this view Dwight Pentecost says that there may be "an announcement (about the abomination) made 30 days before the abomination is introduced."[1760] Gleason Archer favors this view, although inexplicably changing the number of days from 1260 to 1278, to equate it with the modern Gregorian calendar. He then says that there are *twelve days* between the setting up of the abomination and the actual desecration.[1761] Whether thirty days or twelve days, this is not likely. If it were so, then it would give believers as much as a full month to prepare for flight in stark contrast to Jesus' warning in the Olivet Discourse (Matthew 24:15, Mark 13:14, and Luke 21:20). The Bible gives no indication of any warning before the abomination other than seeing "Jerusalem surrounded by armies" (Luke 21:20). The thirty days should definitely *follow* the end of Daniel's 70th week, as Sir Robert Anderson insist.[1762]

Another option is to place the judgment of the world in this thirty day time frame.[1763] The separation of the sheep and the goats (Matthew 25:32-33) would take place at this time. This view is strongly supported by many, such as Stephen Miller,[1764] since Matthew clearly implies some time frame here wherein the living will be judged for their worthiness to enter the kingdom, but it is not clear that this is the thirty day time frame, rather than the forty-five day period. In fact, if the judgment occurred at this time, then believers would not be able to enter into the kingdom immediately thereafter, since forty-five days still remain.

Nathaniel West contends that the reason for the thirty days is for "the triumphal Home-Coming of the Sun-clothed Woman from her desert shelter" (i.e. faithful Israel).[1765] Marvin Rosenthal also sees a processional march, but not of the faithful of Israel, but of Christ Himself.[1766] Van Kampen, Rosenthal's protege, calls this the "reclamation period."[1767] It is during this time period in which Rosenthal and Van Kampen incorporate their unique chronology, placing the death and resurrection of the two witnesses (Revelation 11:3), as well as the seventh trumpet judgment.[1768]

One last view presents itself. John Whitcomb says:

> "The answer lies within the verse itself. The additional thirty days are somehow connected with Antichrist's setting up of 'the abomination of desolation' and termination of 'the regular sacrifice' in the Temple of God in Jerusalem in the middle of the seventieth week. When our Lord returns to the earth exactly 1,260 days after that event, He will

presumably initiate a 30-day cleansing and purification of the Temple of God (cf. 2 Thess. 2:4). Similarly, King Hezekiah postponed by one month the celebration of Passover 'because the priests had not consecrated themselves in sufficient numbers, nor had the people been gathered to Jerusalem. Thus the thing was right in the sight of the king and all the assembly' (2 Chron. 30:2-4)."[1769]

Although there is no definitive proof, it seems that Whitcomb's argument is among the stronger. The time of judgment for the sheep and goats (Matthew 25:32-33) also presents itself as a worthy argument, but it may belong with the forty-five days, rather than the thirty.

At the end of the forty-five days premillennial scholars are unanimous that the Millennial Kingdom will be "officially inaugurated."[1770] It is what happens during this final interim period of forty-five days that is, once again, contested. Some believe that this time is used to set up a Millennial government,[1771] but it seems unlikely that God would need such a time period to establish his government.

Nathaniel West believes that this is Israel's day of national sorrow (cf. Zechariah 12:9-14).[1772] Of course, while Zechariah 12:9-14 certainly is connected to the time of Christ's return, there is no proof, or indication, that this mourning will last forty-five days or that it can be fixed to Daniel's chronology. This theory, however, is far preferable to the chronology of Rosenthal and Van Kampen who place the seven bowls of wrath during this time period, when Christ is marching toward Jerusalem.[1773]

If the thirty days is for the cleansing of the temple, then it seems logical to conclude that this must be the time for the separation of the sheep and the goats (Matthew 25:32-33).[1774] John Whitcomb draws a parallel between Matthew 25:46, "you who are blessed of my Father, inherit the kingdom" and Daniel 12:12's statement, "blessed is he who keeps waiting and attains to the 1,335 days."[1775] Although we cannot be confident, it seems then that the best solution is to consider the first thirty days as a cleansing period, during which the mourning, return of the exiles, and other events will take place. The main purpose for this period, however, is the cleansing of the temple. After that the living will be judged at the sheep and goat judgment (Matthew 25:32-33). This will apparently take forty-five days, after which the Millennial Kingdom will be ushered in.

Study Charts on the Chronology of the Judgments

The Pre-Abomination Seal and Trumpet Judgments Theory
Tenants of:
This view claims that both the seal and trumpet judgments *precede* the abomination of desolation, occuring in the first half of the tribulation.

Popular advocates : Nathaniel West, Walter Scott, E. W. Bullinger, C. I. Scofield, H. A. Ironside, John Walvoord, Henry Morris, and Tim LaHaye.

Strengths:
1) The apparent chronology of the three woes would seem to support this view.
2) This is a straightforward chronological view.
3) The 7th seal clearly initiates the 1st trumpet and the 7th trumpet appears to initiate the seven bowls.
4) Correlates the "birth pangs" of Matthew with the four horsemen of the apocalypse.

Weaknesses:
1) Fails to takes into account Jesus' warning in Matthew 24:15 concerning the Abomination of Desolation as believers would already be in fear of persecution.
2) This view fails to adequately explain those passages that speak of "peace and safety" (1 Thess. 5:3) and must relegate them to pre-rapture.
3) Makes the anti-Christ's peace treaty nonsensical sense the world is at war from the beginning of the tribulation.
4) Contradicts or fails to take into account the importance of the abomination of desolation in regard to the destruction of the anti-Christ's kingdom.
5) This chronology stretches the seven bowls over three and a half years, a seeming impossibility.
6) Contradicts or fails to take into account the increasing rapidity of judgments.
7) Advocates must reject or minimize the application of the term "Great Tribulation" as referring only to the second half of the tribulation.

The Pre-Abomination Seal Judgments Theory
Tenants of:
This view claims that most of the seals precede the abomination of desolation, occuring in the first half of the tribulation.

Popular advocates : John Darby, Sir Robert Anderson, Charles Ryrie, Dwight Pentecost, and Merrill Tenney.

Strengths:
1) This is a fairly straightforward chronological view.
2) The 7th seal clearly initiates the 1st trumpet and the 7th trumpet appears to initiate the seven bowls.
3) Permits for the rapid succession of judgments towards the end of the tribulation.
4) Could associate the earthquake from the sixth seal with earthquake in Revelation 11.
5) Allows for the designation of the "Great Tribulation" as referring only to the second half of the tribulation.
6) Correlates the "birth pangs" of Matthew with the four horsemen of the apocalypse.

Weaknesses:
1) Apparent contradiction with the order of the three woes, or the alleged connection between the second woe and the death of the two witnesses.
2) Brings into question the passage that speaks of "peace and safety" (1 Thess. 5:3) which appears related to the abomination of desolation.

The Post-Abomination Judgments Theory
Tenants of:
This view claims that *all* the judgments (with a few excepting the first seal judgment) *follow* the abomination of desolation, occuring in the second half of the tribulation.

Popular advocates : J. A. Seiss, Hal Lindsey, George Ladd, and Charles Ryrie.

Strengths:
1) This is a straightforward chronological view.
2) The 7th seal clearly initiates the 1st trumpet and the 7th trumpet appears to initiate the seven bowls.
3) This view takes into account Jesus' warning in Matthew 24:15 concerning the Abomination of Desolation.
4) This view best seems to take into account passages that speak of "peace and safety" (1 Thess. 5:3) which appears related to the abomination of desolation.
5) This view permits the evangelization of the gospel for three and a half years without obstruction.
6) This view best fits the declaration that the "Great Tribulation" refers only to the second half of the tribulation.
7) This view permits for the rapid succession of judgments towards the end of the tribulation.

Weaknesses:
1) Apparent contradiction with the order of the three woes, or the alleged connection between the second woe and the death of the two witnesses.
2) May allegedly bring up the question of why a pretribulational rapture is needed, as opposed to a midtribulation rapture.

Study Charts on the Chronology of the Fall of Babylon

Mid-Tribulation Fall
Tenants of:
This view claims that Babylon falls relatively soon in the chronology of Revelation, probably in the middle of the tribulation, shortly after the abomination of desolation.

Popular advocates : Joseph Mede,[1776] John Darby, George Peters, Robert Govett,* Joseph Seiss,* Norman Harrison,* G. H. Lang,* Dwight Pentecost, George Ladd, Watchman Nee, John Walvoord,* Hal Lindsey,* Charles Ryrie, and Tim LaHaye.*

* Sees dual prophecy in Babylon's fall.

Strengths:
1) The fall must occur when the ten kings are still allied with anti-Christ (Revelation 17:16).
2) The nations will mourn the fall of Babylon (Revelation 18:9), but no mention is made of mourning the fall of their own cities which occur at the seventh bowl (Revelation 16:19).
3) Acknowledges that the anti-Christ is the agent for Babylon's destruction (Revelation 17:16-17), rather than God, who is the active agent at the end of the tribulation.
4) Make sense since the Harlot would be a rival of the anti-Christ, rather than his economic boon.
5) The destruction of Babylon is first mentioned in Revelation 14:8, not 16:19.
6) The mention of Babylon in Revelation 16:19 is one of "remembrance."

Weaknesses:
1) The mention of Babylon in relation to the seventh bowl implies its destruction is at that time (Revelation 16:19).
2) The destruction of Babylon is said to be in the same manner as that of Sodom and Gomorrah (cf. Isaiah 13:19), although (a) Isaiah 13:20 makes the comparison to Sodom's desolation, not mode of destruction and (b) a nuclear strike could very well be the same type of destruction, thus the anti-Christ would still be the agent.
3) God is supposed to be the active agent in her destruction (Revelation 18:20), but Revelation 17:17 makes clear that God is acting through an intermediary.

Falls at the End of the Tribulation
Tenants of:
This view claims that Babylon falls at the end of the tribulation shortly before the battle of Armageddon.

Popular advocates : Nathaniel West, Robert Govett,* Joseph Seiss,* Sir Robert Anderson, Walter Scott, H. A. Ironside, Norman Harrison,* G. H. Lang,* Arthur Bloomfield, John Walvoord,* Hal Lindsey,* Henry Morris, and Tim LaHaye.*

* Sees dual prophecy in Babylon's fall.

Strengths:
1) The mention of Babylon in relation to the seventh bowl implies its destruction is at that time (Revelation 16:19).
2) The destruction of Babylon is said to be in the same manner as that of Sodom and Gomorrah (cf. Isaiah 13:19).
3) God is supposed to be the active agent in her destruction (Revelation 18:20).

Weaknesses:
1) The fall must occur when the ten kings are still allied with anti-Christ (Revelation 17:16). Three kings will be overthrow before the end of the tribulation (Daniel 7:8).
2) The nations will mourn the fall of Babylon (Revelation 18:9), but no mention is made of mourning the fall of their own cities which occur at the seventh bowl (Revelation 16:19).
3) Cannot explain why the anti-Christ would destroy his own economic capitol.
4) Must either ignore or created a dual prophecy to explain away the fact that the anti-Christ is the agent for Babylon's destruction (Revelation 17:16-17).
5) The destruction of Babylon if first mentioned in Revelation 14:8, not 16:19.
6) The mention of Babylon in Revelation 16:19 is one of "remembrance."
7) Isaiah 13:20 makes the comparison to Sodom's desolation, not to the mode of destruction.
8) A nuclear strike could very well be the same type of destruction as Sodom, thus the anti-Christ would still be the agent.
9) God is the agent, but Revelation 17:17 makes clear that God is acting through an intermediary.

Appendix E
—
When Is Christ Returning?

"**I**n in the last days mockers will come with *their* mocking, following after their own lusts, and saying, 'Where is the promise of His coming? For since the fathers fell asleep, all continues just as it was from the beginning of creation'" (2 Peter 3:3-4). Scoffers, synics, and even professed Christians have often ridiculed the "literal" interpretation of Revelation. Often they asks, "when is His coming? Tell me what day?" They dare scholars to "set a date," knowing that many false prophets have set dates which have come and gone. What they do not know, and what they deny, is that most date setters are not, and *never were*, literalists. Jesus made perfectly clear, "of that day and hour no one knows, not even the angels of heaven" (Matthew 24:36. Cf. Mark 13:32). However, we have been told that we "are not in darkness, that the day should overtake [us] like a thief" (1 Thessalonians 5:4). As scholars increasingly point out the similarity of current events to prophetic scenarios, the interest in prophecy has increased, along with the intensity of critics attacks.

Men such as Hal Lindsey have created enormous interest in prophecy, but have also been misquoted and made into the subject of ridicule for his sometimes fanciful speculation. The purpose of this appendix is to give a balanced understanding of how the Lord wished us to look at the second coming. There is no doubt that we are to be eager and expectant (cf. Hebrews 9:28), but we are not to neglect our duties or forget our purpose or to set dates for an event whose timing even Jesus Christ does not know (Matthew 24:36).

The Historicist Sin

The sin of date setting, or predicting the return of Christ on a particular day or year, is an ancient sin. The uneducated often say, "people have been predicted Christ's return for two thousand years," but this is not entirely accurate, nor is it relevant to literal futurism, for a survey of history will show that it is not the futurists who are most guilty of this sin, but the historicists.

When it comes to date setting, critics often attach ridicule to literal futurists. Misquotes of men such as Hal Lindsey have circulated implying that he predicted the rapture in the year 1988. It is true that Lindsey seemed to *imply* that rapture might happen within forty years of Israel's restoration (which occurred in 1948),[1777] but as the year 1988 approached Hal Lindsey made no public statements that the end was near, nor did he ever say that he expected to be raptured by years end. When the year 1989 came, Hal Lindsey was still making his regular public appearances and speeches. I personally did not know a single individual who anticipated rapture in 1988, nor did Lindsey say this would happen. It is granted that Lindsey's controversial style lends itself to this type of assumption, but what is important is that the non-event was of far less importance than the thousands of secular doomsayers who predicted the dreaded Y2K bug would devastate the economy and cripple the world. Dave Hunt, the noted premillennial futurist, actually wrote a book refuting the Y2K nonsense in the 1999.

There can be no doubt, however, that many "prophets" and "scholars" have predicted the end of the world. Religious cults such as the Jehovah's Witnesses were actually founded by men who had predicted the coming of Christ. When the Jehovah's Witnesses prediction that the return of Christ would occur in 1874 failed to materialize, they eventually changed their statement to claim that Jesus had returned *invisibly*.[1778] They had also predicted that battle of Armageddon would take place before the end of 1914.[1779] So how are we to respond to these events? How do we respond to critics who connect literalism with these religious cults such as David Koresh? The answer is; with the facts. Each of these cults, and their prophetic interpretations, originated from the historicist school of thought, not the futurist school. A survey of history will show why.

For hundreds of years few of the church fathers dared to predict the second coming of Christ. They may have believed that the time was near, but none dared to prophesy a time or date. In the Middle Ages, chiliasm was outlawed. According to the allegorical school of thought, promoted by Augustine, and followed by the historicists, the "days" of prophecy could be properly interpreted as "years."[1780] Consequently, the 1260 *days* of Daniel and Revelation came to be viewed as 1260 *years.* On this basis Joachim believed that the "third age" would begin in the year 1260.[1781] Peter D'Olivi, on the other hand, calculated 1290 "years" (cf. Daniel 12:12) from the destruction of the temple in 70 A.D.[1782] Thus he believed Christ would return in the year 1360. Many other deriviations of this reasoning continued for centuries, often shifting the starting point of the prophecy. For example, many interpreted the 1290 "years" as being from the time of Christ's death.[1783] Others took the entire 2300 days (cf. Daniel 8:14), or "years," from the time of Antiochus Epiphanes' desecration of the temple.[1784]

This mentality did not change under Protestant historicists. Some interpreted the 1260 days of the anti-Christ's reign as 1260 years of papal oppresion. Some dated this from the time of Constantine,[1785] others from the reign of Pope Gregory VII, who first made an emperor bow before him, and other theories were offered as well. Some historicist scholars even developed complicated schemes of mathmatics to calculate the end. John Napier reasoned that the seventy weeks of Daniel could be multiplied mathmatically to prove that the Millennial Kingdom would begin the year 1786.[1786]

The modern historicists have fared no better. Along with the cults such as the Jehovah's Witnesses, there have been some well meaning historicists who have caused great troubles with their date setting. One was William Miller, a Baptist minister. He dated the 2300 "years" of Daniel 8:14 from the proclamation to rebuild the temple, which he dated in 437 B.C. He, therefore, reasoned that Christ would return on October 22, 1844.[1787] His followers backed down from this prediction but founded the Seventh Day Adventist Church. David Koresh had learned many of his beliefs from that church, although he should *not* in any way be associated with them.

The historicist dates have all failed because they are based on faulty assumptions. Critics, however, seizing upon these false prophesies and predictions have scoffed saying, "Where is the promise of His coming?" (cf. 2 Peter 3:4). Ironically, one of the most unmistable signs of the nearness of Christ is the rise of false prophets. Jesus Himself said, "see to it that you be not misled; for many will come in My name, saying, 'I am He,' and, 'The time is at hand'; *do not go after them*" (Luke 21:8. Cf. Matthew 24:4-5 and Mark 13:5-6). If even *Jesus Himself* did not know the day (Matthew 24:36), then why should we? But if we do not know the day, can we know the season (cf. Matthew 24:32-33)?

The Seventh Milliad

Long before the historicists began to set dates for Christ's return, the chiliasts of old believed that the earth would survive in its current state until its 6000th year. Few attempted to set dates for the return of Christ, since they believed that the year 6000 was merely a round number and not to be taken as an exact timing, but this belief was not only prominent among the church fathers, but even among the Jews who preceded Christ.

According to Jewish tradition, "the prophecy of Elijah" declared that the earth would survive for six thousand years.[1788] Later Christians took this as a parallel to 2 Peter 3:8, believing that the earth would mimic the days of creation and "rest" in the Millennium after the 6th "day." They also noticed that a strict chronology places the time of Abraham approximately 2000 years after creation, and the time of Christ approximately 2000 years later. Some, therefore, expected the church age to last approximately 2000 years.[1789] Barnabas was the first church father whose extant writings support this theory, saying, "in as many days as this world was made, in so many thousand years shall it be concluded."[1790] Lactantius was another church father who supported this theory.[1791] Others followed the unique Septuagint chronology which placed creation around 5500 B.C. Hippolytus, for example, wrote in the late second century that the sixth century would probably be the earth's last.[1792]

Among the church fathers who taught this six milliad tradition were Barnabas, Justin Martyr, Theophilis of Antioch, Irenaeus, Hippolytus, Julius Africanus, Cyprian, Commodian, Victorinus, Methodius, and Lactantius.[1793] This teaching obviously holds appeal to those who believe that we are living in the last days, but two observations must be made. First, the dates were never intended be to exact dates for the second coming, only a generalization of the duration of the earth's history. Second, the creation date for the earth is contested even by creation scientists and scholars. It must also be stated, that for these very reasons, the church fathers cannot be placed in the same category as the historicists. None stated an explicit date for the second coming, or prophesied the end of the world in X number of years. The ancient theory, however, does favor the "sign of the times."

Sign of the Times

We can neither know the day, nor the year, but can we know the season? Jesus said, "now learn the parable from the fig tree: when its branch has already become tender, and puts forth its leaves, you know that summer is near; even so you too, when you see all these things, recognize that He is near, *right* at the door" (Matthew 25:32-33 Cf. Mark 13:28 and Luke 21:29-31). Why does Jesus say this? What does he mean?

These remarks were made in response to the question about the signs of the end times. Jesus gave a description of the "birth pangs" which will precede the end, and then warned His disciples not be easily deceived by false prophets, doomsayers, or heretics, but He also told them that they can know the season. His next remark, however, has dumfounded and confused many. He says, "this generation will not pass away until all these things take place" (Matthew 25:34 Cf. Mark 13:30 and Luke 21:32). "This generation," yet the generation in which Christ lived had passed away two thousand years ago! What did he mean? Preterists (see Appendix F) have used this statement to argue that Jesus' prophecies were all fulfilled in His day and spoke only of the destruction of the temple in 70 A.D.[1794] Others, such as Hal Lindsey, argued that "this generation" refered to the future generation who saw all the signs of which Jesus spoke.[1795] There remains, however, one other lesser known view. The Greek word γενεὰ (genea) can be translated as either "generation," meaning a people of one age, or it can be translated "race."[1796] Some NAS and NIV Bibles even footnote this possible translation. It's base root is "family."[1797] Thus, Nathaniel West says with confidence that when Jesus said, "genea," "He meant the '*Jewish race!*'"[1798] Consequently, this is held to be a prophecy of Israel's return to the Holy Land. Since West wrote his book more than fifty years before Israel's restoration, no man can claim that this was a prophetic interpretation made after the fact. *Israel* will *not* pass away. This was the prophecy. James Brookes also held to this teaching, citing as proof Psalms 12:7, 14:5, 73:15, 112:2; Luke 16:8, and 1 Peter 2:9.[1799] Dave Hunt reasons that Jesus meant to say that Israel would not truly be restored "until 'all these things be fulfilled.'"[1800]

The restoration of Israel had been heralded for centuries before it truly occurred. The reader is referred to chapter four for the extensive quotes from authors who wrote forty, fifty, sixty, and even a hundred years before that day, saying that Israel would be restored in the end times. Great scholars such as George Peters, Nathaniel West, Sir Robert Anderson, James Brookes, Samuel Kellogg, Robert Maton, Joseph Seiss, and Robert Govett did not fail to emphasize the importance of that event which still resided in their future.

If Israel's restoration is a sign of the times, what of the other signs of the times? Many have been alluded previously. The increase in earthquakes, two world wars, natural disasters increasing in their frequency and intensity, false prophets, "the cult explosion",[1801] and the decadence of modern society (cf. 2 Timothy 3:1-5) are but a few.

Another sign that is often neglected is the very fact that the prophecies can all occur as promised. When Revelation speaks of a world war, we no longer need to envision it as the "known world" or the "Roman world," as some in the past have.[1802] Likewise, man himself is now capable of the destruction of the earth by fire. According to Josephus, Jewish tradition records that Adam prophesied that the Earth would be destroyed once by water and once by fire.[1803] The ability of man's technology to utterly destroy the earth is one of the strongest arguments for a sign of the times. For example, Joel 2:30 describes a "column of smoke." The Hebrew word for "column," however, is taken from the root word for "palm tree." Translators were at a loss to understand what a "palm tree of smoke" could be, and naturally prefered the word "column," which is also a possible translation. Now some believe that what Joel actually saw was a "mushroom cloud."

These things cannot prove *when* Christ will return, nor *when* the anti-Christ will come, but they can illustrate that "summer is near" (Matthew 25:32-33 Cf. Mark 13:28 and Luke 21:29-31). The time is a mystery, but the season is at hand.

Appendix F

—

The Fields of Interpretation

Critics claim that there are as many different interpretations of Revelation as there are interpreters. This often used criticism, however, is as misleading as those who say that there are five billion different political views. It may be technically true, but no matter how many different political views may exist, each and every one will fall into a category. People are not truly as original as they might suspect. No matter what opinion is offered, the view will fall under the umbrella of communism, socialism, some form of democratic republic, or perhaps one of the various forms of monarchies. Within these system, the views may then be broken down further into, for example, democrats and republicans. Within these parties one may again categorize the beliefs based on a particular issue such as abortion, taxes, or foreign affairs. Most people do not abandon political opinions for fear that "every interpretation is different." They know that politics effects their lives, for better or worse. In the same way, Revelation *will* effect our lives some day in the future.

Just as political views can be broken down into various systems, so also any interpretation known to man can be placed within a handful of systems. In Revelation exegesis is generally broken down into one of four actual systems or methodologies of interpretation and three different millennial views. The chart below shows the different possible interpretations.

	Premillennial	Amillennial	Postmillennial
Literal or futurist	✓	?	-
Symbolic, allegorical, or idealistic	-	✓	✓
Historicism or presentism	✓	✓	✓
Preterism	-	✓	?

This chart shows how the four primary interpretive methods give way to one of three possible views concerning the Millennial Kingdom. Futurism is largely consistent only with premillennialism, although a handful of invididuals may inconsistently deny the reality of a Millennial reign. The allegorical method is inconsistent with premillennialism, but compatible with either amillennialism or postmillennialism. The same is true of preterism. Historicism, on the other hand, is theoretically consistent with any of the three millennial viewpoints. Thus, a scholar may be a premillennial futurist, a premillennial historicist, an amillennial idealist, amillennial historicist, amillennial preterist, a postmillennial idealist, or a postmillennial historicist.

Below each of the methodologies and millennial views are defined in more detail.

Methodologies

Literalism or Futurism

The "literal" interpretation means that Revelation speaks of literal future events and that the symbols (which none deny) represent something specific and literal, which cannot be interpreted as broad ambiguous allegory. When we pass by a building with a cross on it, we know that the cross represents professed Christianity, and that the building is some kind of Church. We do not ponder the deep and mysterious meaning of the building, because the cross represents something specific and literal. Sometimes context may change the meaning slightly. In a horror movie, the cross may take on the symbol of a magic ward, but even then it represents Christianity in some form, and even then the cross still symbolizes something specific and literal. In other words, the "literal" interpretation of Revelation is the most natural reading of the text. Symbols are not taken as allegories or ambiguous symbols, but as representations of specific events or characters. Moreover, there is no attempt to read symbolism into something unless symbolism is intended.

This interpretation of Revelation was the earliest method of interpretation. It is only natural that if John had intended the book as a allegorical fable his own disciples would have known this but his disciples, taught by him personally, interpreted the book literally. Polycarp was John's disciple, Irenaeus was Polycarp's disciple, and Hippolytus was Irenaeus' disciple. All interpreted Revelation literally. Says one scholar, "the doctrine of the Millennium spread so widely in the first three centuries, has reappeared constantly at different epochs, and is supported by more ancient and formal text than many other doctrines now universally accepted."[1804]

Literalism is, therefore, synonymous with futurism. Revelation is a book about the future. It is not seen as a historical allegory, or a fanciful moral fairy tale. The prophecies, and such they are called (cf. Revelation 22:18), are about the events preceding Christ's return. They are prophecies about the "end times," or "last days." They are not prophecies about the *middle* ages (as historicists teach), but the *last* age. Nor are they prophecies about the *beginning* of the church age (as preterists teach), but about the *end* times. Futurism and "literalism" are, therefore, synonymous.

The methods that literalists use to interpret Revelation were discussed in the Introduction, but will be briefly repeated. In literal interpretation, there has become a saying; "where the natural meaning makes sense, seek no other sense." Where the natural meaning fails, several factors are examined.

> 1. The Bible should itself be examined for the answer. In some cases the meaning of a symbol is explicitly given only a passage or two later.

Despite this, there are those that ignore the explicit definition of a symbol for one of their own liking. Not only should the book of Revelation be scoured for definitions to its own symbols, but many symbols have common usages throughout the Scriptures. The entire Bible must, therefore, be referenced.

2. Context must be thoroughly examined itself. Sometimes the meaning is obvious by the context, but ignored by those who want to read something into the passage that is not there.

3. The history and culture of the writer should be examined. Many words have a clear symbolic meaning to one culture, but lose that meaning in another culture. A cross in 33 B.C. meant death. A cross in 33 A.D. meant life eternal. The meaning of the word in the author's culture may be of great value in determining the meaning of a symbol.

This is the usual method used by literal interpreters. Look first at the natural meaning of the text, *then*, and only then, look to symbolism. When looking at symbolism, make sure that the entire Bible is studied and examined to find similar usages of symbols. When these rules are followed, Revelation ceases to be confusing and the Holy Spirit may reveal its prophecies to us.

Idealism or Allegorism
Idealism and allegory are technically different. Allegory is the methodology used in interpretation by many different views, but idealism is the assumption from whence allegory first rose. According to idealism, Revelation is not intended to represent history, whether past, present, or future. Idealism sees Revelation as an allegorical parable. Revelation is deemed to be little more than a moral fable. Although allegorism is used by historicists and preterists, it is the natural outgrowth of idealism and originated from this teaching.

According to Samuel Kellogg, "the first recorded oppenent of the doctrine [of premillennial futurism] was Caius, a presbyter of Rome, about the beginning of the third century."[1805] Allegorism's first true champion was Origen, and later Tyconius. It was, however, Saint Augustine who was the most dominant force in the temporary triumph of this viewpoint. Origen was born in the late second century. He was raised by a Christian father who died in one of the persecutions of ancient Rome.[1806] Eventually he became a prominent theologian whose desire to make Christainity acceptable to the Roman world led him to merge Christianity with neoplatoism.[1807] The only way to do this was to allegorize the entire Bible. According to Origen's system even Satan himself will eventually be saved.[1808] Naturally, his system made Revelation an allegory as well. If even Satan was to be saved, then Revelation could not be taken literally concerning Satan's eternal fate.

Tyconius followed Origen in allegorizing Revelation. Although much of his writings no longer exist, his influence remains through his most emphatic disciple; Augustine. Saint Augustine, although professing to "spiritualize" Revelation, actually brought materialism to the church by arguing that the Millennial Kingdom was not a literal future kingdom, but was, in fact, already present in the world. He argued that the church *was* the Millennial Kingdom. From Augustine's bosom came the medieval church, and his theology became the basis for the so-called theocracy of the Middle Ages. Thus, Augustine became the father of amillennialism, based on a purely allegorical interpretation of Revelation.

Historicism or Presentism

Called "historicism" from "history" or "presentism" from "present," this view is exclusively a medieval outgrowth of the Augustinian interpretation, but with a renewed emphasis upon the *reality* of the prophetic events. Augustinianism made Revelation little more than an allegory. To the objective reader, this was obviously not what Revelation intended. It was intended to be a "prophecy" (cf. Revelation 22:18), not a fairy tale or fable. Joachim of Floris (or Fiore) therefore took Augustinian allegory but attempted to reinstitute the prophetic element. He believed that Revelation was a prophecy about the whole of human history, told in an allegorical manner. Thus, he saw some of the prophecies as having been fulfilled in the past, some of the prophecies as being fulfilled in his day, and some prophecies he saw remaining for the future. Consequently, the term "historicism," or the more antiquated term "presentism," is the name by which this view is called.

Joachim found many followers including the famed Richard the Lion-hearted who sought an audience with Joachim before the Crusades.[1809] The problem for the church was that Joachim's system restored the possibility of a literal premillennial kingdom, which would deny that the medieval church was the kingdom of God. Moreover, the prophecy of the Whore of Babylon was increasingly being recognized to represent an apostate church in Rome. Since only one apostate church in Rome then existed, it became apparent that Joachim's followers were not looking with favor upon the corrupt popes.[1810] Joachimtes soon became outlawed, but it was too late to stem the tide of historicism's popularity, even among loyal Catholics.

Historicism soon rivaled traditional Augustinianism in popularity and was the methodology of choice for the early Reformers. Joseph Mede was among the first historicist scholars to openly promote a literal Millennial Kingdom. From Mede's disciples, including men such as Sir Isaac Newton, premillennial historicism soon became prominent among Protestants. From this, later Protestants would begin to reject the allegorical elements which still remained from medieval influence, and returned to futurism.

Preterism

With the enormous popularity of historicism in the early Reformation period the Catholic church found itself unable to respond to the claims that she was the prophesied Harlot of Babylon. Some Catholic expositors suggested that Rome was once a harlot, but no more.[1811] The desire to fit the prophecies into history was common in both Protestants and Catholics, but one Catholic, a certain Alcazar, suggested that *all* the prophecies of Revelation had been fulfilled centuries before Rome was even Christian. Utilizing allegory, and many of the elements from historicism, the teaching of preterism held that the prophecies of Revelation were allegories about the first century or two after Christ's death and resurrection. The burning of the earth with fire became Nero's burning of Rome. The persecutions of the saints obviously could be interpreted as the suffering of the early martyrs. Ultimately, everything was tied to the early church and, once again, the Millennial Kingdom, if it was accepted at all, referred to converted Rome after Constantine.

Preterism was, thus, created fifteen hundred years after the fact and was largely an attempt to deflect criticism of the Catholic church. Despite this, the view has become enormously popular among some Protestant evangelical Christians. Bruce Metzger is but one prominent name to subscribe to preterism, along with Baptist scholars such as Ray Summers.

The Millennial Views

Chiliasm and Premillennialism

The oldest view was once outlawed in the Middle Ages, only in recent centuries having been resurrected. Chiliasm and premillennialism literally mean that Christ returns to the earth to establish a Millennial Kingdom. *Chilia* is the Greek word for a thousand. *Millia* is the Latin word for a thousand. Premillennialism is from the prefix "pre" and the world Millennium, meaning that Christ returns "pre" (before) the Millennium.

Chiliasm and premillannialism are the natural outgrowth of the literal or futurist school of thought. It is the most natural and straightforward reading of the text. Only by allegorizing the text can one read anything other than premillennialism into the text of Revelation, for Jesus returns in triumph to the earth in chapter nineteen and the narrative immediately picks up with the introduction of the thousand years. There is no shift in topic, no change in subject matter, no altering of the time frame. There is nothing to indicate anything other than the fact that Christ establishes the thousand years *after* His triumphant return.

Premillennialists are usually futurists, and futurists are virtually always premillennialists, but not all premillennialists are futurists. Some espouse historicism. Historicist premillennialism is the traditional view of churches such as the Seventh Day Adventist Church and the Jehovah's Witnesses. Despite the fact that a number of cults do subscribe to this view, the reader should be careful not to call historicist premillennialist churches, such as the Seventh Day Adventist Church, a cult. Most of the Protestant Reformers were historicist premillennialists, including men like Charles Wesley, and many great scholars have subscribed to this teaching. The belief, however, has faded in recent centuries. Today, the majority of premillennialists are futurists, even to the point that most futurists merely identify themselves as premillennialists, with the futurism understood.

Amillennialism

Amillennialism comes from the prefix "a" meaning "no" or "none." Amillennialists deny that there is such a thing as a literal thousand year reign of Christ. Some argue that it is mere allegory, others argue that the reign is symbolic of Christian society, and still others that the thousand years is merely symbolic for an indefinite period of time.

Amillennialism is the natural result of all the symbolical and allegorical schools of thought. All idealist will be amillennial, virtually every preterist will be amillennial, and many historicists are amillennial. In each of these instances, the amillennialists either deny the reailty of an earthly reign of Christ, or "spiritualize" it to mean the rule of the church on earth. Ironically, Paul wrote the Thessalonians to dispel a popular heresy which echoes this now prevalent belief. As Samuel Kellogg said, "what troubled the Thessalonians was *not* the possible imminence of the Advent, which could only have filled them with gladness, but what had been suggested by some teachers, who taught – like some in our own times - that the day of the Lord was '*now present.*'"[1812]

Amillennialism is, therefore, the teaching that there will be no literal future Millennial Kingdom ruled by Christ on earth. It was the official teaching of the Middle Ages and has retained a large number of followers ever since. After the apostles had refuted the teaching, it was unheard of until the third century, when it reared its head again, remaining with us to this very day.

Postmillennialism

Postmillennialism is an outgrowth of amillennial teachings. It accepts a literal Millennium, but not a literal thousand years, nor do postmillennialists believe that Christ will precede the Millennium. Instead, postmillennialists believe that Christ will return *after* ("post") *man* has established the Millennial Kingdom on earth in His name. This view once again grew out of medieval teachings on the church, but has found many followers among the early advocates of American democracy. Some of the early founding fathers in America began to naively believe that they could establish God's kingdom on earth. Daniel Whitby was the first modern postmillennialist, who found favor among such great names as Jonathan Edwards.[1813] Modern "reconstructionists," and "Dominion Theology," also believe that America can establish a worldwide theocracy by converting the world through the democratic process.[1814] Men such as Gary North, Rousas Rushdoony, David Chilton, Earl Paulk, and even Pat Robertson have openly promoted the idea that, as one spokesman said, Christians are "to bring heaven to earth."[1815] Only then, once the kingdom is established, do these men believe Christ will return to the earth.

This teaching is really little more than a contemporary version of medieval Augustinianism, altered and modified for the modern world. Democracy replaces the Catholic Church as the mode for God's rule, and the Millennial Kingdom ceases to be a mere "spiritual" institution, but a modern governmental institution. In most other ways, it is little different; particularly in its interpretation of Revelation, which is obviously rather allegorical.

Hermeneutic Methodologies

There remain four more exegetical methods not mentioned above. These methods do not necessarily relate explicitly to any one prophetic viewpoint, but do effect how Revelation is interpreted. These methodologies (covenant theology, dispensationalism, ultradispensationalism, and progressive dispensationalism) actually relate to how one interprets the whole of Biblical history, not just prophecy. Since prophecy is future history, it is only natural that these methodologies will, in turn, effect prophetic interpretation, but only indirectly. In fact, premillennialists are composed of covenant theologians, dispensationalists, ultradispensationalism, and progressive dispensationalists. It is true that dispensationalists will always be premillennial, while covenant theologians may be either premillennial or amillennial. Nonetheless, all three of these methods are accepted within the evangelical and premillennial communities.

Covenant Theology

Covenant theology, sometimes called "replacement theology," is the belief that God has replaced Israel with the church. There are held to be only two covenants; the old and new. According to covenant theologians, the old covenant, and all the promises made to Abraham, were nullified when the Jews rejected Christ. Based in part on their interpretations of Galatians and Hebrews, they believe that the church has permanently replaced Israel as God's chosen, and no future for national Israel exist. Arnold Fruchtenbaum calls George Ladd "one of the most prolific writers among Covenant Premillennialists today."[1816] According to Ladd, "when Israel's rejection of the offer of the Kingdom had become irreversible, Jesus solemnly announced that Israel would be taken by others who would prove trustworthy."[1817] He, therefore, believes that the church has *permanently* replaced Israel as God's chosen people.

Although the casual reader may, at first, be inclined to believe this, the view has many problems. First, while it is true that the church has *temporarily* assumed *certain* duties of Israel's priesthood during the church age (cf. Revelation 1:6), it is not logical to conclude that Israel has been replaced or forgotten by God. Second, covenant theologians have taken the name of Israel and applied it in a way never used in the Bible. Third, since covenant theologians distinguish only two covenants, they fail to recognize God's unconditional promises to the physical descendants of Abraham.

On the first point, there is no proof that the Lord has abandoned Israel. George Ladd says that "as the inauguration of a new covenant, Christ abolishes the old covenant,"[1818] but ignores that Christ said, "do not think that I came to abolish the Law or the Prophets; I did not come to abolish, but to fulfill" (Matthew 5:17). Moreover, he fails to provide a single reference to show that the abolishment of the law abolishes Judaism along with it. It is true that Christians are no longer bound by the law, but by the Spirit. This does not, however, justify the libertinism of the Corinthians. There are two heresies in various Christian sects; the one legalism, the other libertinism. Galatians and Hebrews do not anywhere say that the law is of no value, let alone that the promises to the Jews have been reneged by God. This is the second major issue.

Covenant theologians use the term Israel in a way never seen in the Bible. As one dispensationalist says, "some have trouble understanding that Gentiles who become 'Abraham's off-spring' refers to spiritual seed, and it is something God accomplishes because of trust in Christ. Equally so, believers become 'adopted sons of God' (Gal. 4:5-6). This is also understood as something spiritual. Nowhere in Scripture is the church seen as the extension of Israel. Neither is the church called Israel!"[1819] Another points out that "Israel is used eleven times in Romans, but in all the instances it refers to Israel proper; and so do it and *Israelites* in every other portion of the New Testament."[1820] So where to the covenant theologians get that the church is "true Israel"?[1821] Mostly from passages in Galatians and Romans 11. They argue that in Galatians 6:16 "the Israel of God" refers to the church,[1822] but in fact the context forbids this. It reads, "peace and mercy *be* upon them, **and** upon the Israel of God." "Them" refers to Gentile believers. The word "*and*" is then inserted between "them" and "the Israel of God," which refers to believing *Israel*; Jewish believers. Covenant theologians assume that the church is the "Israel of God," but the context cannot support this. A better argument comes from Romans 11:16-24. The passage reads:

> "If the root be holy, the branches are too. But if some of the branches were broken off, and you, being a wild olive, were grafted in among them and became partaker with them of the rich root of the olive tree, do not be arrogant toward the branches; but if you are arrogant, *remember that* it is not you who supports the root, but the root *supports* you. You will say then, 'Branches were broken off so that I might be grafted in.' Quite right, they were broken off for their unbelief, but you stand by your faith. Do not be conceited, but fear; for if God did not

spare the natural branches, neither will He spare you. Behold then the kindness and severity of God; to those who fell, severity, but to you, God's kindness, if you continue in His kindness; otherwise you also will be cut off. And they also, if they do not continue in their unbelief, will be grafted in; for God is able to graft them in again. For if you were cut off from what is by nature a wild olive tree, and were grafted contrary to nature into a cultivated olive tree, how much more shall these who are the natural *branches* be grafted into their own olive tree?"

All agree that the tree and root are Israel, but the reader will note that Gentiles are "grafted *into*" Israel. Nowhere does it say that a new tree is planted, and the old is chopped down. Notice that the illustration never says that the tree is uprooted. We are grafted *into* the tree, we *do not* replace it! Covenant theologians have also failed to take Paul's warning, "do not be conceited, but fear; for if God did not spare the natural branches, neither will He spare you" (11:20). Unfortunately, we have become conceited. We have succumbed to the same sin which led the Jewish nation to reject their own savior. We have become proud and arrogant, and the time is coming when God will chastise the Gentile church, even as he chastised the Jews.

The greatest problem with covenant theology is its failure to distinguish between God's conditional promises and His unconditional promises to the natural descendants of Abraham. Covenant theologians conceive of only two covenants; old and new, but Dwight Pentecost notes, "the Biblical covenants are quite different from the theological covenants posited by the Covenant theologians."[1823] He list the Abrahamic covenant,[1824] the Palestinian covenant,[1825] and the Davidic covenant[1826] as preceding the new covenant. On the Abrahamic covenant, the Bible explicitly calls it an "everlasting covenant" (Genesis 17:7). There is no indication that God can or will abolish it. Pentecost affirms that "it is a covenant with no 'if' attached to it whatsoever."[1827] Further, "it is wrong to state that obedience is always a condition of blessing. If this were true, how could a sinner ever be saved?"[1828]

Although covenant theologians have hypocritically called dispensationalists legalists, it is they who have argued that Abraham's covenant was changed or altered for disobedience. God does not lie. He is not a lawyer that he manipulates the meaning of a contract, or voids certain parts which He no longer likes. God will honor what He has promised *regardless* of the worthiness of recipients. This is the irony of covenant theologians. They constantly talk of the legalism of the old covenant and emphasize God's grace in the new, yet they seem to deny that God will show grace in keeping His promises to the Jews. They talk of how unbelieving Jews are unworthy of the promise, yet ignore that we too were unworthy. Indeed, while the Jews sinned by worshiping before idols, the Gentiles of Europe practiced cannibalism, human sacrifice, and barbarism such as was rarely seen in the worst of Israel's day. God did not bring the gospel to the pagans because He abandoned the

Jews, but to fulfill the prophecy of Isaiah 65:1, "I permitted Myself to be sought by those who did not ask *for Me;* I permitted Myself to be found by those who did not seek Me." The gospel came to the pagan Gentiles because, as Jesus often said, "the first will be last, and the last, first" (Matthew 19:30 cf. Mark 10:31, Luke 13:25). The Jews were the first chosen, and they will (as a people) be the last to accept Christ the Messiah. The Gentiles were the last. We were those who did not seek God, but we were the first to accept His grace as a people. This is because of God's mercy and grace; not our worthiness.

In short, covenant theology reads the church into Israel wherever it encounters Israel. In covenant theology, Israel in Revelation is read as the church. Israel is cut out of the Millennial Kingdom, and the contrast between Jews and Gentiles are ignored. Covenant theology is the view which minimizes or completely disregards the role of Israel in prophecy. Even the restoration of the nation of Israel is viewed as incidental.[1829]

Dispensationalism

Dispensationalism is a literal reading of the promises that God made to the nation of Israel. According to dispensationalism, God will keep his promises to the Jewish nation and fulfill those promises in the Millennial Kingdom. Dispensationalists deny that the church has replaced Israel, at least in any permanent fashion.

Arguments against dispensationalism are numerous, and sometime outright slanderous. Some have called dispensationalism "a cult,"[1830] a "most dangerous heresy,"[1831] and a sect "on the fringes of the Christian Church."[1832] Before refuting these frivolous accusations, it is essential to understand what dispensationalism teaches, since its critics often misreprent the view.

According to dispensationalism, God has worked throughout the ages in different ways at different times. Just as covenant theologians acknowledge that God introduced to law to Moses in order to convict man of his sin, so also dispensationalists believe that God acted in the times before Moses in various ways in order to prepare the way for Christ. In covenant theology there are but two general ages of man; the age of works and the age of grace. In dispensationalism, there are many. Dispensationalists do not always agree on the exact number, because the Bible says little on the early days of man on earth, but generally dispensationalists believe that there are roughly seven ages. The first age covers the age of innocent when Adam and Eve were in Paradise. Certainly there was no "covenant of works" in those days. God was not illustrating man's futility to save himself by works, but man's rebellion against God even in Paradise. The second dispensation is the age between the Fall and the flood of Noah. The third and fourth dispensations are in dispute. Some consider the time before Babel to be a distinct dispensation, but others consider the next dispensation to lead to the Abrahamic covenant. Then between Abraham and Moses a fourth (or fifth) dispensation occurs. Dispensationalists are in general agreement with covenant theologians to the extent that the age of the law and the age of grace are distinctive, but dispensationalists deny that the church age is the final age. Some consider the tribulation to actually be a brief dispensation, while others consider it transitory. In either case, the Millennial Kingdom is believed to be the final dispensation before the eternal age.

Critics have bitterly attacked this view, as alluded to above. Some accusations center on the false assumption that dispensationalists believe in different modes of salvation. They say that "the presupposition of the difference between law and grace, between Israel and the church, between the different relations of God to men in the different dispensations, when carried to its logical conclusion, will inevitably result in a multiple form of salvation – that men are not saved the same way in all ages."[1833] However, it is that author who is assuming, not dispensationalists. In fact, covenant theologians and dispensationalists actually agree that, as the apostle Paul stated, the works of the law were designed to convict man of sin and to prepare the way for the Messiah (cf. Romans 3:20). The law was never truly designed to save man. It is therefore hypocritical to claim that dispensationalists teach different ways to salvation since the covenant theologians themselves profess that the law was presented as a means of salvation, even though God knew man could not achieve that salvation. Says Charles Ryrie, "if sins could be forgiven via the ritual law, then covenant theology must be teaching two ways of salvation – on by law and one by grace! Covenant theology seems to teach the very 'heresy' it accuses dispensationalism of teaching!"[1834] Dispensationalists do not deny, nor ever have denied, that salvation, whether Enoch or David or Moses, was achieved by the blood of Christ. Those who lived before Christ lived in anticipation of His sacrifice, but that does not mean that they fully understood it. Certainly Abraham did not understand that Isaac was spared in order that God might sacrifice His own Son for us, but Abraham was saved by the Son nevertheless.

A slightly less frivolous attack on dispensationalism is the belief that this teaching was invented by John Nelson Darby, the same man that some accuse of inventing the rapture teaching. Unlike the rapture, which is indeed a difficult issue, dispensationalism can be proven to have been taught for thousands of years before Darby. Unfortunately, critics tend to play a game of semantics, arguing that the church fathers never used the modern *word* "dispensation," but referred only to ages (although, in fact, Irenaeus *is* sometimes translated as using the word "dispensation.").[1835] Semantics aside, it is clear that the church fathers, and others, down to the time of Darby, believed that God worked in various ages in various ways. They did not see merely two covenants, but many. Irenaeus believed in four different dispensations including the antediluvian age, the time from Noah to Moses, the time of the law, and the current church age.[1836] Even the famed Archbishop James Ussher, an early preterist,[1837] divided earth history into seven distinct ages.[1838] Likewise, post-Reformation scholars, hundreds of years before Darby presented similar proposals. The famed Jonathan Edwards claimed there were six dispensations, as did the equally famous Isaac Watts.[1839]

The real difference between covenant theologians and dispensationalists is not in how many ages God has worked with man to unfold His ultimate plan of salvation through Jesus Christ, but in whether or not God will keep His unconditional promises to Israel. This is the *real* dividing point. Covenant theologians refuse to accept a future for national Israel in any way. Dispensationalists insist that Israel is distinct from the church. Covenant theologians believe that accepting a national Israel distinct from the church is the same thing as denying Christ, since they associate the church alone with Christ. This is the real crux of the issue. Can Israel accept Christ apart from the "church?" Is the church to be understood as all believers or only as that Gentile priesthood which precedes the tribulation and the Millennial Kingdom? These are the issues which divide theologians.

Ultradispensationalism

Ultradispensationalism is a term given to a very rigid, sometimes called "extreme," view of dispensationalism. It creates a very rigid system of distinguishing between dispensations and separating them so that no overlap or confusion is possible. The problem is that in so doing it often eliminates many prophecies of the church and creates an artificial theology which only serves to cause many of the very contradictions and confusions it seeks to eliminate. For example, ultradispensationalists deny that the church is ever mentioned or prophesied even in the gospels since they hold that the church was not established until Acts 2. Since Jesus mentions the Church twice in the gospel of John, the ultradispensationalists must simply point out that John wrote in the church age, but ignore that what John wrote was true and accurate. In other words, Jesus *did* mention the church. Since few openly call themselves ultradispensationalists these theologians are often found among mainstream dispensationalists. This allows critics of dispensationalism to paint the ultradispensationalists as mainstream and has further created dissatisfaction among true dispensationalists, which has led to the compromise system known as "progressive dispensationalism."

Progressive Dispensationalism

As the reader can see, dispensationalism creates many questions. The nature of the church is but one. Covenant theology has often been considered far too simplistic for many scholars to take it seriously, but many of these same scholars have become disenchanted with dispensationalism for various reasons. Many have come to believe that dispensationalism is too rigid and unwielding in certain beliefs. Distinctions between dispensations are sometimes too strident with no possibility of overlap. Likewise, many have been reluctant to accept

Christian believers outside the church, even in a future dispensation. In an attempt to resolve of the problems that discontented dispensationalists have had, the teaching of progressive dispensationalism has arisen.

There are considered three major areas where progressive dispensationalists differ from traditional dispensationalism. The first is in hermeneutics. Covenant theology is generally figurative in its interpretive methods; dispensationalism is generally literal. Progressive dispensationalists constitute a "both/and" view. They are heavily influenced by covenant theologian George Ladd's "already/not yet" hermeneutic. The problem for Ladd was that he needed a figurative interpretation for his covenant bias, but as an evangelical he could not discard the literal. Borrowing from what Pentecost calls the "law of double reference,"[1840] Ladd expanded this law to what he called "eschatological dualism."[1841] According to Ladd the kingdom of God was both "already" present in a spiritual manner, but "not yet" present in its literal form. Progressive dispensationalism, therefore, takes a figurative view of what is "already" present (thus following covenant views on the present age), while maintaining that a literal kingdom and application will follow in the age to come. It is yet another "both/and" view.[1842]

The second major difference is in the understanding of the major covenants. As with their hermeneutics, the progressive dispensationalists take a "both/and" view. In essense they argue that the new covenant is a realization of the old covenants. Finally, they deny that Israel and the church are truly distinct, but rather than saying that the church has "replaced" Israel, Lanier Burns prefers to say that "Israel has been 'incorporated' or 'reconstituted' into the chuch as the 'new Israel.'"[1843]

The central problem with progressive dispensationalism is that it does *not* resolve the difficulties with traditional dispensationalism, but instead blurs the issues and dilutes understanding. This is particularly evident in their treatment of Israel. Paul does not say that Israel has been "incorporated" into the church, but that Gentiles are grafted *into* Israel (Romans 11:11-24)! Furthermore, the Bible *never* uses the phrase "new Israel." To do so would imply that the "old" is no longer valid. It is, therefore, significant to note that progressive dispensationalists use terminology borrowed from covenant theologians that is completely lacking in the Bible. Charles Ryrie has said that this "minimizing of a clear and consistent distinction between Israel and the church results in ignoring the great prophecy of the seventy weeks in Daniel 9:24-27."[1844]

Progressive dispensationalism is essentially a compromise between covenant theology and traditional dispensationalism. Although it is a noble attempt to resolve complicated issues, it in reality blurs the issues with a convoluted mixture of figurative and literal interpretation. The progressives actually ignore some of the most difficult issues in prophecy, such as the rapture and Daniel's seventy weeks. The result is a compromise theology that is insufficient and inconsistent. Advocates of this view are usually premillennial, but not necessarily pretribulational. This may, in fact, be part of the appeal of the view.

Conclusion

It can be seen that only one system of interpretation has any kind of systematic or consistent methodology for interpretation. The other views invariably rely on "one's own interpretation," ignoring that "no prophecy was ever made by an act of human will, but men moved by the Holy Spirit spoke from God" (2 Peter 1:20-21). Literalists are certainly not agreed on all the issues, but we at least have a basis for communication and a standard for interpretation. It is for this very reason that the literal premillennial interpretation of Revelation has shown more unity amid conflict than the allegorists amid their "agreements."

Appendix G

—

Biographies of the Historical Witnesses

The witnesses are those commentators and scholars who have expressed view and interpretations of Revelation throughout the centuries. These scholars are important not because they attempt tell us (or presume to tell us) the true meaning of the text, but rather because they illustrate whether or not a given theory is consistent with the doctrine of perspicuity. The doctrine of perspicuity is an essential doctrine for the sincere Christian, for it teaches that the words of Scripture may be plainly understood and made known to those who earnestly seek to discern them.[1845] In other words, the perspicuity of Scripture means that God's truth is not shrouded in mysteries that must be unfurled by the discoveries of Darwin, Freud, popes, or modern scholars. The essential truth of the Word of God is manifest to all people who have received and read the Word. This does not mean that the truth is fully revealed, for God did not reveal the Law to Noah, nor the church to Moses, but what is revealed can be understood by men of all ages. Nor does this mean that the older view is the correct view or even that the correct view must be the predominant view for popular opinion has rarely been synonymous with truth. It means only that any legitimate interpretation should not be a new invention discovered by some "prophet" or self heralded teacher.

There are two extreme ways in which people have viewed the role of tradition. The one holds that tradition is paramount to any accurate interpretation of the Scriptures. They hold that any view not held throughout the centuries is in error because only tradition, by standing the test of time, holds the key to proper interpretation. The other rejects tradition entirely and completely. They point out that men have often been wrong over the centuries. In fact, the Protestant Reformation broke away from the tradition of the Catholics that had been held for nearly a thousand years. Did not Jesus preach against the heresy of tradition (cf. Mark 7:9, 13)?

For many ancients the former view held true. Antiquity was often seen as proof of truth. For this reason, tradition has, on occasion, become a standard for weighing truth. As a result, the ancients often exaggerated their histories to prove their antiquity among the nations.[1846] If they could prove themselves to be the oldest of cultures, then they thought they should be proven the wisest. This may, in fact, be the reason for the discrepancies between the Greek *Septuagint* and the Hebrew Bible's chronologies.[1847]

At other times in history people have rejected tradition completely. Like the Enlightenment Age, men feel that they had transcended the ignorance and folly of the past. In arrogance they believe that they alone had the answer. For these men "newer" means "better." For them the past was dead. The sixties was such a generation. Ours is such a generation. However, history has shown that these generations die out quickly, leaving a trail of anarchy and desolation.[1848]

The truth lies between the two extremes. Christ did indeed warn His followers of the dangers of tradition but only when that tradition becomes the basis for Biblical interpretation or truth. Traditional interpretations record the views of past men. Its importance is not that it gives us the truth but that it shows us whether or not our perceived truth existed in the past. This is important because it helps shed light on whether or not a given view is consistent with the doctrine of the perspicuity of Scripture.[1849] If a view had never existed in times past, it becomes suspect. Any true and legitimate interpretation of Scripture must show that its beliefs are not the inventions of modern scholars but that they have existed in times past. The view does not need to be the dominant view nor does the view need to be fully developed. All that is necessary is to prove that an understanding of Scripture, compatible with our own, has existed in times past.

It is for this reason that the history of the interpretation of Revelation has been included in this text. It gives us a tool to evaluate our own exposition in light of past commentaries. Nevertheless, a warning is necessary. Just as men drift from the truth and from the purity of the gospel today, so also men of the past, even the great ones, had drifted away from the uncompromising Word of God. It is therefore prudent to give brief biographical data of the witnesses from whom I most often quote so that the reader may better understand that author's opinions in light of that author's background. This is done in order that the commentator may not be merely a name but a person whose opinions carry weight, whether that be a feather or a iron dumbbell.

The Primary Witnesses
(Those witnesses who are cited whenever possible)

Irenaeus (120-202 A.D.) : The earliest of the church fathers whose extant works testify substantially to Revelation, Irenaeus was the student and disciple of Polycarp, who was in turn the disciple of the apostle John himself. Irenaeus was then a second generation disciple removed from the original author's composition by only fifty to ninety years.

He was the bishop of Lyons in Gaul (modern France) where he worked to refute heresies which were growing rapidly in the Christian Church. Although there is speculation that he suffered a martyr's death, the early Christian historians make no mention of it and he was probably relatively safe from the persecution of Septimus Severus in the region of Gaul.

In terms of exegesis Irenaeus was definitely a Chiliast and he was also the most literal of the church fathers in his exegesis of Revelation, holding not only to a literal millennium but also a literal rebuilt temple in Jerusalem.

416

Moreover, he openly refutes those who attempt to allegorize the prophecies of Revelation.[1850]

Irenaeus is, therefore, the most important witness from the early Church Fathers not only because of his closeness to the disciple of John, but his literal application of Revelation indicates that this was the original manner of interpretation by John's disciples. His treatises are therefore referenced whenever possible.

Tertullian (145-220 A.D.) : A pagan educated at Rome, Tertullian became a convert to the Christian faith in 185 A.D. and a presbyter only five years later. A great apologist, he wrote extensively and most of his writings are extant. Unfortunately, he only wrote a handful about prophecy. He was a Chiliast, preferring the literal interpretation, but he did not write enough to be considered a major witness.

Hippolytus (170-236 A.D.) : Hippolytus was himself a disciple of Irenaeus. The bishop of Portus, in Italy, Hippolytus was not afraid to refute the errors of the bishop of Rome and had at times been an outspoken critic of some of them. Like his mentor he sought to refute heresies in the church. In 217 he was elected bishop of Rome, but a Callistus was also elected, creating a rift in the church. He is accepted by the Catholics as one of the great church fathers, and yet he is also listed an antipope, or false pope. He also suffered martyrdom in the persecutions of Maximinus.

Like Irenaeus, his teacher, he was a Chiliast and a literalist, holding to a literal restoration of the Jewish state and temple.[1851] He is the second most important witness among the early Church Fathers.

Victorinus (d. 303 A.D.) : Victorinus was the bishop of Petau in ancient Panonia (modern Austria). His commentary on Revelation is the first true extant commentary available but, unfortunately, the commentary is fragmentary as much of it was lost over the ages. He was martyred under Diocletian's brutal persecutions just years before Constantine would convert to Christianity.

He calls himself a Chiliast, and therefore a literalist, but he was also influenced by the emerging allegorism. On numerous issues he prefers an allegorical approach to Revelation and is the first to clearly apply the temple in Revelation to the church, thus abandoning the idea of a literal rebuilt temple. Likewise, though a Chiliast, he does not seem to take the thousand year reign as a literal thousand years, but only as a literal reign following Christ's return. He, therefore, provides a perfect shift from the literal Chiliast of the early Church Fathers to the allegorism of Augustine and the Middle Ages.

Lactantius (240-330 A.D.) : Lactantius was a famous Christian apologist and rhetorician who came to befriend the newly Christian emperor Constantine. He later became the tutor for Constantine's oldest son. He is considered an Ante-Nicene Church Father even though he lived to see the council of Nicaea. He is, therefore, the perfect transition from the early Church Fathers to the Post-Nicene Fathers and Medieval Commentators. In terms of exposition he wrote only a few chapters on end times but was a literal Chiliast who did not hesitate to predict the fall of Rome, even as Rome was becoming Christian.

Adso of Montier (930-992 A.D.) : Adso was a medieval scholar who was requested by Queen Berberga of France to write to her on the subject of the anti-Christ. She was the wife of Louis IV and the sister of Otto the Great, the great emperor of the Holy Roman Empire. In an age when allegorism flourished Adso promoted the belief in a literal future anti-Christ, a literal rebuilt Jewish temple, and a literal last day. His extant writings do not contain enough information to give a solid view of his exegesis but he clearly represents a minority of Chiliasts, or Millenarians as they were called at that time. His writings also show that there were many, including the family of the devout emperor to be, who maintained a literal interpretation.

Joachim of Fiore (1135-1202 A.D.) : The one time abbot became famous because of his exposition of Revelation. At one time King Richard the Lion-hearted sought his audience. During this time Chiliam had become associated with heresy and was forbidden but Joachim combined elements of literal chiliasm with the high allegory of the day. The result was that Joachim became the father of historicist interpretation. He reintroduced the futuristic-historical element into Revelation while maintaining the high allegory that suited the medieval Church's desire to call itself the kingdom. However, after Joachim's death, his followers, the Joachimites, were eventually condemned for their belief that a future pope would be anti-Christ and for the belief that the medieval Church would one day be replaced by the heavenly kingdom. He is sometimes considered the father of medieval millenarianism and influenced a great many theologians over the next few centuries.

Pierre D'Olivi (1248-1298 A.D.) : A Franciscan monk from southern France, Peter (or Pierre) Olivi was eventually condemned for his opposition to infant baptism and for his rejection of Aristotle's influence on theology. His commentary on Revelation was likewise condemned by Pope John XXII and Olivi's tomb was destroyed. He was a Joachimite and, therefore, a medieval millenarian or historicist. He was also among the first Joachimites to be condemned by the church, showing their increasing disfavor with Joachimite teachings.

Nicholas of Lyra (1270-1349 A.D.) : Nicholas of Lyra was born in Normandy and became a trusted Bible scholar who opposed the allegorical idealism of his day. He was a missionary to the Jews and he was a Joachimite, for which he faced the opposition of the church. Despite this, his commentary is much more favorable to Catholicism than other Joachimites. Martin Luther was influenced by Nicholas as well. In exposition he followed Joachim and held to a pseudo-literal (but still allegorical) interpretation of Revelation.

Joseph Mede (1586-1638 A.D.) :   Called   the   father   of   English premillennialism, Joseph Mede was a Cambridge professor whose commentary on Revelation became an instant best seller and influenced many Reformation age scholars from Isaac Newton to John Milton. He was still, however, a historicist and is representative of that school of interpretation. His importance is that in adopting a clear premillennial view he paved the way for the return to a more literal (or straightforward) interpretation of Revelation.

Isaac Newton (1643-1727 A.D.) : The famous scientist often called the father of modern science was also devoutly Christian (although some have made much of his Unitarian leaning).[1852] He wrote much on theology and was a professor at Cambridge. His little known work, *Observations on the Prophecies of Daniel and Revelation* is representative of the historicist school of premillennialism in which he follows Joseph Mede, often merely referring the reader to Mede without further commentary.

John Darby (1800-1882 A.D.) : The English graduate from Trinity College helped to form the Plymouth Brethren, a group that opposed church formalism and denominationalism. Although referred to as "separationists," they were really forerunner of modern "non-denominational" churches.

Darby's prophetic writings were a dramatic shift back to literal premillennialism and away from the historicism that had flourished in Protestantism. He was also one of the first modern scholars to explicitly define the doctrine of a pretribulation rapture and dispensationalism. Often accused of being the inventor of both, rapture and dispensationalism (under different terminology) both existed long before Darby, but Darby is rightly said to be among the first to systematically explicate the controversial doctrines. Despite his return to a pure futurism, Darby was still influenced by a heavy symbolic interpretation of Revelation. He is representative of the early Dispensational premillennial futurists.

Robert Govett (1813-1901 A.D.) : The famed English expositor was once a member of the Church of England before being baptized and joining an independant congregation. Educated at Worcester College of Oxford, Govett later became a pastor in Norwich. His famed commentary on Revelation was originally written under the pen name of "Matheetes."

He is considered the author of the partial rapture theory, but he was also one of the first futurists to take a stridently literal stance, since the early church fathers. Unlike the Brethren movement, which retained certain elements of "spiritualizing," Govett took everything in Revelation as literally as was possible.

J. A. Seiss (1823-1904 A.D.) : Joseph Seiss was a Lutheran preacher from the nineteenth century. His popularity led to the publication of many books including his commentary on Revelation which is considered one of the most thorough and detailed commentaries ever written. His futurist premillennial exposition was the subject of much criticism since futurism was still a minority view. Neverthless, his exegesis is very solid and the book remains a classic today. He was clearly influenced by Robert Govett. Despite the notion that futurism and rapture were the concoctions of the Plymouth Brethren Seiss differed from the Brethern in two ways. First, he was a partial rapture theorist and second, he was far more literal in his interpretation of Revelation than the early Dispensationalist writers. He is, therefore, referred to as a "futurist premillennialist" in order to distinguish him from the Brethren movement although Dispensationalists are also futurist premillennialists.

George Peters (1825-1905 A.D.) : A Lutheran minister, George Peters is known for his famed multi-volume *Theocratic Kingdom* work. The work cited thousands of footnotes and set forth a clear dispensational view of the coming Millennial Kingdom. His dispensational views drew the wrath and ire of his beloved Lutheran church, but despite this, he received an honorary doctoral degree after his death from the Lutheran Wittenburg College.

Nathaniel West (1826-1906 A.D.) : After receiving his doctorate from Allegheny Seminary he went on to pastor a church in Pittsburg. A popular prophetic teacher of the nineteenth century West espoused dispensational premillennialism. His most famous book is *The Thousand Year Reign of Christ*.

E. W. Bullinger (1837-1913 A.D.) : The archbishop of Canterbury bestowed this English bible scholar with an honorary doctorate. He was, therefore, enormously respected but also criticized, even in conservative circles, for his "ultradispensational" views. He believed in soul sleep and some of his followers even advocated the doctrine of "annihilationism."[1853] Nevertheless, such criticism does not change the fact that he was an evangelical Christian whose works are very influential. He promoted a dispensational, pretribulational, premillennial view of Revelation.

Samuel Kellogg (1839-1899 A.D.) : A leader among the Presbyterians, Kellogg was for a time a famed missionary to India but eventually settled down to teach in a seminary and pastor a Church in Pittsburg. He was a premillennialist who sought to refute postmillennialism, which was extremely popular at the time. He also believed that the Jews would one day return to their homeland.

Sir Robert Anderson (1841-1918 A.D.) : Anderson was a chief inspector at Scotland Yard during the reign of Jack the Ripper. His analytical mind was also used in various commentaries on the Bible, but his views on the seventy weeks of Daniel is what makes him of special note to prophetic interpretation.

Although erroneously accused of inventing the idea that the sixty-nine weeks of Daniel ended precisely at the Passion Week, his book did clearly spell out, with mathematical precision, the age old view. His work on Daniel has been used by countless dispensationalists to prove that the seventieth week of Daniel remains to be fulfilled in the future.

C. I. Scofield (1843-1921 A.D.) : An American Congregational/Presbyterian preacher, Scofield was involved with the Bible conference movement and wrote many books. He was a promoter of the dispensational premillennial perspective and his *Scofield Reference Bible* served to promote the literal interpretation of Revelation. His critics accuse him of being a charlatan on account of his conviction for fraud and his alleged abandonment of his wife, but these were apparently before his conversion and are not relevant to his Christian walk. In any case, he is very influential and is counted among the more important witnesses.

H. A. Ironside (1876-1951 A.D.) : This Canadian bible scholar was largely self-educated although he would receive an honorary doctorate from Wheaton College. He was an evangelist who spoke often at Moody and Dallas Theological Seminary. He is yet another dispensational pretribulational premillennialist indicative of the rising popularity and interest in the literal interpretation of Revelation.

Arthur Bloomfield (1895-1980 A.D.) : Arthur Bloomfield was a popular Methodist minister. His quasi-dispensationalism offers a unique derivative view from traditional dispensational premillennialism. He is not taken seriously by most scholars because of the unorthodox framework in which he places prophecy. In essence, he attempts to read both the church and literal Israel into Revelation without overlapping them as the church fathers often did. This means creating an extra three and a half year period for the church *before* the 70th week of Daniel begins. He, therefore, sees a 10 ½ year period rather than seven.

John Walvoord (1910-2003 A.D.) : The former President and Chancellor of Dallas Theological Seminary Walvoord became one of the most proficient authors on prophecy in the twentieth century. Like his predecessors he is dispensational and pretribulational. His numerous books on prophecy have encompassed virtually every book in the Bible and he was selected to write the ambitious, if somewhat disappointing, book *Every Prophecy in the Bible*.

George Eldon Ladd (1911-1982 A.D.) : A long time professor at Fuller Theological Seminary George Ladd remains the sole posttribulational representative of "traditional" premillennialism to have a profound impact. He was among the first evangelical to argue for posttribulationism against a pretribulational rapture since futurism had revived. He argued a sort of compromise position between covenant theology and dispensationalism which would later influence the rise of progressive dispensationalism. His theology argued, in essence, both a literal and a spiritual meaning. According to his dualistic treatment of prophecy a future literal fulfillment did not dismiss spiritual interpretations. He is the predominant witness to modern covenant theology and posttribulational premillennialism.

J. Dwight Pentecost (b. 1915 A.D.) : Long time professor at Dallas Theological Seminary, Pentecost's *Things to Come* became the standard textbook for prophetic interpretation among dispensational premillennialists. He is influenced by the Brethren movement and his commentaries reflect this.

Robert Mounce (b. 1919 A.D.) : Robert Mounce is President Emeritus of Whitworth College and former head of Arts and Humanities at Western Kentucky University. He has taught at Bethel College and is a graduate of the University of Aberdeen in Scotland and Fuller Theological Seminary in California. Mounce is not so much influential in his commentary as he is reflective of the covenant theology / posttribulational premillennial interpretation. His commentary is popular and was published in F. F. Bruce's commentary series.

Charles Ryrie (b. 1925 A.D.) : A graduate of Harvard, Dallas Theological Seminary, and the University of Edinburgh, Ryrie served as a professor at Dallas Theological Seminary for many years. He is a defender of dispensationalism as well as pretribulational premillennialism.

Dave Hunt (b. 1926 A.D.) : A former missionary who began by writing on the subject of cults was cast into the forefront when he co-authored *The Seduction of Christianity* in which he compared the rising influence of eastern heresies on Christian Churches to the apostasy prophesied by the apostle Paul.

Hunt's book are clearly futurist pretribulational premillennial, but he is reluctant to take solid stances on specific issues, declaring that he is not an expert (he once commented to a man who referred to him as "Dr. Hunt," "I'm not even a nurse"). Despite his reluctance to count himself with the scholars, he remains one of the most proficient and learned authors on the issue of prophecy in the twentieth century.

Hal Lindsey (b. 1929 A.D.) : Hal Lindsey was a simple Texas graduate of Dallas Theological Seminary who worked for Campus Crusade for Christ until his book *The Late Great Planet Earth* hit the shelves. The book became one of the best selling books of all time.

Part of the book's success was due to Lindsey's attempt to illustrate how the prophecies could fit into modern times, thus making it practical to the average person. Nevertheless, this was also the reason for the backlash against Lindsey who was accused of trying to shape prophecy to fit current events. He also suggested that modern technology could be the means of fulfillment for many of the prophecies of Revelation. He has since become the subject of ridicule even in the conservative seminaries from which he came. Despite such criticism, and jealousy, his works remain among the most important of the latter half of the twentieth century and reflect a heavy dispensational premillennialism.

Tim LaHaye (b. 1926 A.D.) : Tim LaHaye is the pastor of one of the largest churches in San Diego, California. He is the founder and president of Tim LaHaye Ministries and the co-founder of the *Pre-Trib Research Center*, a "think tank" for pretribulational scholars. He holds many Bible prophecy conferences throughout the United States and Canada. He has also founded many Christian high schools and the Christian Heritage College. In addition, he assisted Henry Morris in the creation of the Institute for Creation Research. Tim LaHaye has written more than fifty non-fiction books, but is best known for his fiction series about the rapture, the *Left Behind* series.

Minor Witnesses
(Those witnesses cited with infrequency but some regularity)

Justin Martyr (100-165 A.D.) : Justin Martyr remains one of the earliest Church Fathers, only a generation removed from the apostle John who survived until the end of the first century. Unfortunately, Justin Martyr wrote very little on Revelation. He is included only to reflect the Chiliast stance of the earliest Christians.

Cyprian (circa 190-258 A.D.) : Cyprian was the Bishop of Carthage. He survived the persecutions of Decius, only to die under the later persecutions of

Valerian. He was one of the most famed church fathers known for his extensive writings, but he did not write extensively on prophecy. His views are consistent with chiliasm, but offer no deep insight into his beliefs.

Origen (185-254 A.D.) : Origen was raised by a Christian father who died in one of the persecutions of ancient Rome. Eventually he became a prominent theologian whose desire to make Christainity acceptable to the Roman world let him to merge Christianity with neoplatoism. The only way to do this was to allegorize the entire Bible. According to Origen's system even Satan himself will eventually be saved. Naturally, his system made Revelation an allegory as well. If even Satan was to be saved, then Revelation could not be taken literally concerning Satan's eternal fate.

Augustine (354-430 A.D.) : Saint Augustine is the famous theologian who is often considered the father of both the Catholic and Protestant Church. From Hippo in Northern Africa Augustine became a monk. He was a strong advocate of the doctrines of faith and grace as espoused by later Protestants but paved the way for the Middle Ages by his allegorical application of the Kingdom of God to the current age. As a result the Middle Ages would identify the Millennial Kingdom with the Holy Roman Empire, arguing for a merger of Church and State.

Augustine was the first major commentator to reject Chiliasm for a vague allegorical approach to Revelation. He is considered the father of amillennialism although in many ways his approach was consistent with the later postmillennial view. He did believe in a literal second coming of Christ but rejected a literal reading of Revelation.

Augustine is relegated to a minor witness because he offered no exegesis of Revelation, providing instead only vague allegory. This makes it impossible to tell, for example, where he would stand on the interpretation of the sixth trumpet. He is, nevertheless, an important witness because of the profound impact that he had on medieval prophetic interpretation.

John Bale (1495-1563 A.D.) : A graduate of Jesus College at Cambridge, England, Bale was an English dramatist who faced exile for his Protestant beliefs. During exile he wrote his commentary on Revelation which reflects a pre-Darby form of dispensationalism. Despite the pseudo-dispensationalism he is representative of the Reformation age amillennial historicism. His importance lies not only in the fact that he was pseudo-dispensational but also in that he wrote the first English commentary on Revelation.

Matthew Poole (1624-1679 A.D.) : After graduating from Emmanuel College in Cambridge, England, he would go on to pastor a Presbyterian church where he would serve until his death. He wrote a commentary on the entire Bible which is still published. He is representative of the historicist school who was sympathetic towards premillennialisms. Although he was unsure of the issue of the millennium per se, he leaned toward premillennialism and had great respect for premillennialist author Joseph Mede. His commentary is therefore representative of this historistic premillennialism.

Matthew Henry (1662-1714 A.D.) : The Act of Uniformity in England required churches to follow a specific mode of worship which "nonconformist" refused to accept. Because Matthew Henry was one of these nonconformist he was barred from Oxford and Cambridge and instead attended a small academy in Islington. From there he went on to pastor several dissenting churches in England. His commentary on the Bible remains one of the most famous ever written. Although he was technically an amillennialist, the influence from Joseph Mede, of whom he speaks reverently, is obvious. Like most early Reformers, he was representative of the historicist school of thought.

William Whiston (1667-1752 A.D.) : The successor to Isaac Newton at Cambridge, Whiston was known for both science and theology, like his mentor. He is best known for his translation of the complete works of Josephus from the Greek.

Walter Scott (1838-1933 A.D.) : Walter Scott was an evangelist and member of the Brethren movement. He was heavily influenced by John Nelson Darby in his writings.

J. F. Strombeck (1881-1959 A.D.) : A self-taught Bible scholar who attained popularity with his book entitled *First the Rapture* which served to promote the pretribulational view of rapture. He was a solid dispensationalist.

Watchman Nee (1903-1972 A.D.) : Born in China, Watchman Nee translated various theological works into Chinese and ministered throughout Asia. He was influenced by both the Brethren and Robert Govett. In 1952 he was imprisoned for his faith by the Communist and died in 1972. One of his famed proteges was Witness Lee who died in 1997.

Other names worthy of mention who are included in this volume include Norman Harrison, Robert Thomas, and Marvin Rosenthal, among others. Some, however, might inquire as to why some important scholars are omitted.

Where is ... ?
(Premillennial authors conspicuously abscent from this volume)

Andreas of Caesarea (7th Century) – Andreas was the bishop of Cappadocia. The exact time he lived is disputed, but has been pinpointed between the sixth and seventh centuries. He is know largely for the fact that his commentary on Revelation is the first *complete* commentary that has survived to the present. Other volumes appear to have been suppressed and/or destroyed in the High Middle Ages. Unfortunately, his commentary has never been published in English and the Greek copies are rare and unaccessible to this author. In his stead, Adso of Montier is used to represent this particular generation of prophetic interpreters.

The Venerable Bede (673-735 A.D.) : The Venerable Bede is known as the father of English history. His commentary on Revelation is brief and heavily influenced by Tyconius, who in turn influenced Augustine. Nevertheless, he is useful in illustrating the shifting though of the early middle ages.

Rupert of Deutz (Early 12th Century) – A prominent theologian from the time of Bernard of Clairvaux. His commentary on Revelation does not exist in English, and as a typical medieval allegorist, I did not wish to invest the time and effort into translating a work which would contribute little to this volume.

J.A. Bengel (1687-1752) – J.A. Bengel was known for many things. He was one of the first to begin the modern scientific study of Greek textual criticism as it is known today. He is also the author of one of the earliest and most influential premillennial commentaries of the Reformation age. Bengel is deserving of mention in this book, but his work could not fairly be represented within it. A thorough historicist, he was heavily influenced by medieval concepts. Among his unique interpretations was the teaching of "dischiliasm," in which he held there were acutally *two separate* 1000 year reigns of Christ. One was to be in heaven, and the other on earth. Although he was influential, even most later historicist premillennialist believed many of his views to be dated. His inclusion would, therefore, have unnecessarily protracted this already large volume.

Samuel Tregelles (1813-1875) – A renowned Hebrew scholar and bible translator, Tregelles was also wrote on the subject of prophecy, mostly to refute futurism or dispensationalism. Since he did not write a detailed commentary, and since historicism is minimized in this volume for space, Tregelles is not cited.

Charles Maitland (1815-1866) – Best known for a history of prophetic interpretation, Maitland's work was made dispensable by the huge volumous work of Leroy Froom. Although Maitland was futurist, unlike Froom, the history of prophecy should not cater exclusively to any one interpretation.

Therefore, I prefered Froom's material, although the prophetic researcher cannot and should not discount the earlier work by Maitland.

Charles Spurgeon (1834-1892 A.D.) : Famous London pastor who has been nick-named the "prince of pastors." Spurgeon was a premillennialist who has been called both a midtribulationist and a posttribulationist. Because he wrote no Bible Commentary on Revelation his views are not entirely known and often debated.

Dwight Moody (1837-1899 A.D.) : The famed evangelist of the late nineteenth century would found the Moody Bible Institute. He was a premillennialist but the specifics of his views are debated. He is claimed by both posttribulationists and pretribulationists, dispensationalists and covenant theologians. That he was associated with the Plymouth brethren (a dispensationalist organization) is well known but critics point out that Moody never explicitly made his views known on the subject. He is, therefore, somewhat on an enigma since he did not author a full commentary on Revelation but his influence upon the evangelical community is such that his inclusion was required among the witnesses.

Lewis Sperry Chafer (1871-1952 A.D.) : The former Presbyterian pastor who would become the founder of Dallas Theological Seminary. He was also involved in many Bible conferences and became a renowned Bible evangelist. Although a strong dispensational pretribulationists he did not write extensively on Revelation so his influence is limited to the Seminary he founded.

C. J. Ellicott (1819-1905) – C.J. Ellicott's commentary on Revelation is one of the most popular historicist commentaries from the 19th century. Since this volume does not deal extensively with historicistism, the lateness of his writings made it out of date for the purposes of this work.

E. R. Craven (1824-1908) – Craven was a premillennialist who is best known in prophetic studies for his notes in G.H. Lange's Bible commentary on Revelation. Unfortunately, his notes, much like Scofield's, are not sufficient to be able fairly and accurately discern an author's views of the critical issues. Consequently, Craven is ommitted from this volume.

W.A. Criswell (1909-2002) – The famed Texas preacher was a premillennialists but he was not especially known for prophetic studies. Since dispensationalists are already a majority in this volume, Criswell's work is ommitted as repetitive of the works already cited.

John MacArthur (b. 1939) – Certainly MacArthur is worthy of inclusion but the mass of his work is outside of prophetic studies and I was conscious of the accusation that my work leaned too heavily in favor of dispensationalists. Although the large numbers of dispensational writers are reflective of the work that dispensationalists have done, I did not want to include any dispensationalists whose works have not contributed specifically to the field of prophetic studies. MacArthur was, therefore, regrettably excluded.

Other notables absent from this volume include B. H. Newton, Henry Alford, James Buswell, J.H. Raven, Witness Lee, and even Jerry Falwell. Each is regrettably absent for one reason or another, but in each case, the views of these men have been fully present by other others. For example, Witness Lee's work is representative of his teacher, Watchman Nee. James Buswell did not have a full commentary on Revelation, but his prophetic work is repetitive of Norman Harrison from whom he is indebted.

Below is a summary chart of all the witnesses and a brief explanation of their methodology of interpetation.

Author	Generation	View	Methodology
Justin Martyr	2nd Century	Chiliast	Few comments but what he says is literal and futurist.
Irenaeus	2nd Century	Chiliast	Literal and futurist but with an overlapping of the Church and literal Israel. He openly refutes the allegorization of Revelation.
Clement of Alexandria	2nd Century	Chiliast	Says very little but appears to accept a literal futurist view.
Tertullian	2nd Century	Chiliast	Only offers brief quotations but in a literal manner which implies no elaboration is necessary.
Hippolytus	Late 2nd Century	Chiliast	Like Irenaeus he is both literal and futurist but with an overlapping of the Church and literal Israel.
Cyprian	3rd Century	Chiliast	Treats Revelation as self explanatory.
Nepos	3rd Century	Chiliast	Futurist and millennial in view but no extensive commentary.
Victorinus	Late 3rd Century	Chiliast	Mostly literal but show influence of Origen with allegorization of many specifics. He takes the Temple and Israel as symbols for the Church.

Methodius	Late 3rd Century	Chiliast	Says little on Revelation but appears millenarian (chiliast).
Ephraem the Syrian	4th Century	Chiliast	Mostly literal with some emphasis on symbology. Taught a clear rapture view.
Lactantius	4th Century	Chiliast	No extensive quotations but surprisingly literal in a day when allegory was becoming more prominent.
Augustine	Late 4th Century	Amillennial	The first major allegorical expositor after Origen and Tychonius. Offers no exegesis of Revelation but shows extensive allegorizing of it. He is included in this list only because of his importance in prophetic interpretation.
Adso of Montier	10th Century	Medieval Chiliast	Although no extensive commentary exists Adso takes a very literal futurist stance in a day shortly before Chiliasm was outlawed as heresy. His treatise was addressed to the royal family and sister of Otto the Great, Holy Roman Emperor.
Joachim of Fiore	12th Century	Medieval Millenarian	After Chiliasm was outlawed Joachim reintroduced futurist elements while maintaining the highly allegorical view endorsed by the medieval Church. He is considered the father of "historicism."
Pierre D'Olivi	13th Century	Joachimite Historicist	A follower of Joachim, Pierre (or Peter) adopted a highly allegorical historicist interpretation.
Nicholas of Lyra	14th Century	Joachimite Historicist	Heavy allegorism within the historicist tradition. More favorable toward Catholicism than Pierre D'Olivi.
Joseph Mede	16th Century	Premillennial Historicist	Considered the father of English Premillennialism he nevertheless followed the historicist methodology with its heavy laden symbolism. His premillennialism, however, was a step back towards Chiliasm.

Matthew Poole	17th Century	Historicist	Follows the symbolic historicist method but with a leaning toward premillennialism upon which he was undecided.
Isaac Newton	17th Century	Premillennial Historicist	Follows Mede in most of his interpretations. Premillennial but symbolical within the historicist school of thought.
Matthew Henry	Late 17th Century	Historicist	Historicist who rejected premillennialism but was sympathetic toward it. He is listed for his influence.
William Whiston	18th Century	Premillennial Historicist	Isaac Newton's protégé in both science and theology. He follows the premillennial but symbolical historicist school of thought.
John Nelson Darby	19th Century	Pretribulational Dispensational Premillennial Futurist	Although utilizing a very literal framework he nevertheless adopted a symbolic approach to the specifics of Revelation. He does see Israel as Israel and the Temple as the Temple.
Robert Govett	19th Century	Premillennial Futurist	Not a part of the Brethren movement, Govett rejected pretribulationism for a partial rapture theory. Unlike Darby Govett was very literal in his interpretation. He agreed with the Brethren that Israel is Israel and the Temple is the Temple.
J.A. Seiss	19th Century	Premillennial Futurist	Influenced by Govett, Seiss was a Lutheran who took a very literal approach to Revelation. As with Govett and the Church fathers he may have seen the Church and Israel overlapping but maintained that Israel is Israel.
E. W. Bullinger	Late 19th Century	Pretribulational Dispensational Premillennial Futurist	Considered an "ultradispensationalist" Bullinger rejected the symbolism of Darby for the literalism of Govett and Seiss. He often quotes Revelation with no elaboration saying that it is self-explanatory.

Walter Scott	Late 19th Century	Pretribulational Dispensational Premillennial Futurist	A dispensationalist who follows Darby in most ways. He relies on a rather heavy symbolic approach while maintaining a literal futurist framework including Israel and a rebuilt Temple in Jerusalem.
Sir Robert Anderson	Late 19th Century	Dispensational Premillennial Futurist	The famed Scotland Yard detective wrote extensively on Daniel but says little on Revelation. He nevertheless appears literal in method predicting a restoration of the Jews in Israel.
George Peters	Late 19th Century	Dispensational Premillennial Futurist	Wrote a three volume work on the Millennial Kingdom with extensive footnotes. Although taught as a covenant theologian, he came to espouse a literal dispensational view, which he well defended.
Nathaniel West	Late 19th Century	Premillennial Futurist	Wrote a volume that explicitly refutes historicism and defends premillennialism. He strongly supports the restoration of Israel but does not appear to be heavily influenced by Darby. Accepts a literal interpretation.
Samuel Kellogg	Late 19th Century	Dispensational Premillennial Futurist	Wrote books declaring that Israel would be restored in the future. His is both literal and dispensational. Best known for his defense of Israel.
C. I. Scofield	Late 19th Century	Pretribulational Dispensational Premillennial Futurist	He is considered the father of American Dispensationalism. He does not have a commentary on Revelation but appears quite literal in his interpretation.
H. A. Ironside	20th Century	Pretribulational Dispensational Premillennial Futurist	A student of Darby, his work echoes much of the early dispensational writers. Rather symbolical, but within a literal framework.
J. F. Strombeck	20th Century	Pretribulational Dispensational Premillennial Futurist	Wrote a treatise defending a pretribulational rapture. He is literal and dispensational.

John Walvoord	20th Century	Pretribulational Dispensational Premillennial Futurist	Famous Dallas Theological Seminary Chancellor and prophetic author. He is literal and dispensational.
George Eldon Ladd	20th Century	Covenant Premillennial Futurist	Ladd rejected the pretribulationalism of the previous century and argued that "posttribulationialism" was the historical interpretation. He is moderately literal but has a large dose of symbolism especially in regard to Israel and the Temple which he interprets as the Church. He is a covenant theologian.
J. Dwight Pentecost	20th Century	Pretribulational Dispensational Premillennial Futurist	Pentecost is reflective of early dispensational authors like Darby and Ironside. He is very symbolical, but within a strict literal and dispensational framework.
Robert Mounce	20th Century	Covenant Premillennial Futurist	Robert Mounce reflects the covenant premillennial view, or posttribulationism. He rejects Israel's role in prophecy and interprets anything having to do with Israel figuratively.
Tim LaHaye	20th Century	Pretribulational Dispensational Premillennial Futurist	A literal and dispensational author best known for his fictional series on a pretribulational rapture.
Arthur Bloomfield	20th Century	Dispensational Premillennial Futurist	His unique interpretation is a derivative dispensational system that attempts to read both the Church and Israel into Revelation without overlapping them. His methodology is therefore a mixture of symbolism and literalism but mostly the latter.
Robert Thomas	20th Century	Pretribulational Dispensational Premillennial Futurist	A very literal and dispensational commentator.
Charles Ryrie	20th Century	Pretribulational Dispensational Premillennial Futurist	Ryrie is also a productive literal and dispensational author.

Dave Hunt	20th Century	Pretribulational Dispensational Premillennial Futurist	He has written no Bible commentary on Revelation but appears to take a literal methodology in all is books on prophecy.
Hal Lindsey	20th Century	Pretribulational Dispensational Premillennial Futurist	Popular author is largely literal in interpretation but is best known for popularizing the belief that the prophecies of Revelation could be fulfilled through man's technology.
Marvin Rosenthal	20th Century	"Pre-wrath" Dispensational Premillennial Futurist	Offers no full commentary on Revelation but appear dispensational and literal with the exception of his controversial new rapture view, "Pre-wrath," which places the rapture in the last year before Armageddon.
Robert Van Kampen	20th Century	"Pre-wrath" Dispensational Premillennial Futurist	The first major follower of Rosenthal's rapture theory Van Kampen integrates the view into his exegesis of Revelation.

Glossary of Terms

Abomination of Desolation : The phrase is found both in the Olivet Discourse and the book of Daniel and alluded to in the letter to the Thessalonians. It refers to the time when the anti-Christ will stand in the Temple and descrate it by declaring himself equal to God (cf. Daniel 9:27, Matthew 24:15, Mark 13:14, and 2 Thessalonians 2:2-4).

Amillennial : Amillennial literally means "no millennium." Amillennialists believe that the thousand year reign of Christ, in Revelation 20, is merely an allegorical way of talking about Christ's reign on earth through believers. The view was originally formulated by St. Augustine who held that the Christ was reigning through the church. Although Augustine did not rule out that the reign of the church could last a thousand years, he did not believe that the thousand years need be taken literally. Modern Amillennialists treat the reign of Christ, and often His return as well, as mere allegory not to be taken literally.

Chiliasm : Chiliasm comes from the Greek word for a thousand. It is synonymous with premillenniallism. According to this view Christ will literally return to the earth and establish a Millennial Kingdom in accordance with Revelation 20. The term was commonly used throughout the early church and up until it was outlawed in the Middle Ages. In recent years the term premillennialism has replaced it.

Covenant Theology : A theological system in which God's covenants are said to be transferable. According to covenant theology God made two covenants, the Old and New. Covenant theologians believe that when the Jews rejected the New Covenant the promises made to Israel were revoked and transferred to the church. Accordingly, this view does not accept the restoration of Israel as an unconditional promise and rejects the belief that the state of Israel plays an important role in prophecy. Passages in Revelation that refer to the the Jews and Israel are taken by this view as allegorical for the church. This view is virtually synonymous with Replacement Theology.

Dispensationalism : Dispensationalism comes from the latin word for dispensing. The theological application is a dispensing of a plan. Specifically, God's plan for an age. Dispensationalists believe that God has acted throughout history in different ways during different ages or "dispensations." The idea is that God progressively acts in history toward a specific goal. In each age God unfurls a certain aspect of His divine plan which culminates in Judgment Day and the establishment of the New Heavens and New Earth found in Revelation 21. In prophetic interpretation, this view holds that Israel and the church are two entirely separate entities and that God has a different plan for each. Passages in Revelation that refer to Israel and the Jews are treated literally by dispensationalism and Israel is believed to play a prominent role in the last days. They are exclusively premillennialists. Although it is believed that the church Fathers were dispensational, the first universally recognized modern dispensationalists were from the Brethren Movement in England.

Dominion Theology : Dominion Theology is a recent adaptation of postmillennialism. It holds that the church is to take dominion over the earth and establish the kingdom of God through our own efforts. Dominion advocates believe Christ will only return once we have gained dominion over the earth. Dominion Theology is synonymous with the theology known as reconstructionism.

Futurism : Futurism holds that the Book of Revelation is a book about the future. The prophecies of Revelation are generally held literally and are accepted as future events to occur at or near the end of the age.

Great Tribulation : The term was coined by Jesus in the Olivet Discourse but has come to be a technical term applied to the period of God's wrath or testing. There is dispute upon the specifics of what this time period it encompasses but is generally held to represent the last three and a half years of the tribulation, or 70th Week of Daniel.

Hermeneutic : Hermeneutic from the Greek word meaning "to interpret." A hermeneutic is therefore an interpretive method or approach. Different models of interpretation, for example literal and allegorical, are referred to as different hermeneutics. These methods are addressed throughout the book.

Historicism : The doctrine of historicism was invented in the Middle Ages by Joachim of Fiore who combined elements of chiliasm with Augustinian amillennialism. The result was an allegorical interpretation of Revelation which believed that the prophecies spoke about the whole course of human history. Consequently, many of the prophecies were held to be allegorical references to past history while other prophecies remained to be fulfilled in the future. Historicism was the dominant view of the late Middle Ages and the Reformation but has significantly decreased in the past century. Few advocates still remain.

Joachimites : The followers of Joachim of Fiore (see Appendix G). The Joachimites were a sect who believed that the events of Revelation were currently unfolding throughout the course of history. They often saw the pope as an antichrist and identified the Catholic Church as the "whore of Babylon" spoken of in Revelation 17. They came under persecution during the High Middle Ages. Their school of prophetic interpretation is called "historicism."

Idealism : Idealism is the methodology of interpretation utilized by St. Augustine and many amillennialists. According to this view the prophecies of Revelation are to be treated as allegory and should not be accepted as literal prophecies about the end times. Idealism was the predominant view of the Catholic Church from Augustine's day until the Reformation and it is still dominant among liberal churches and scholars.

Imminence : The doctrine of imminence is the teaching that Christ could return at any time. Jesus is said to return "like a thief in the night" so the emphasis is on the idea that Jesus will return when *no one thinks* he will. This doctrine was common among the early Church Fathers and is often used as proof of the pre-tribulational rapture position since it is seemingly inconsistent with Christ's return at Armageddon.

Literal Interpretation : Literal interpretation means that the Bible speaks about literal historical events and symbols, where they occur, should not be taken as ambigious allegory but should be seen as having a specific literal meaning. In prophetic terms, the literal interpretation means that Revelation is speaking about literal events to unfold in the future and that symbolism in Revelation should not become an excuse for allegory. The symbols of Revelation are treated with a careful regard for their intentioned "literal" meanings.

Midtribulational Rapture : The belief that the rapture will occur in the middle of the tribulation, or the 70th Week of Daniel, soon after the abomination of desolation. The view was first clearly promoted in the mid-twentieth century by Norman Harrison and James Buswell and maintains a few advocates today.

Partial Rapture : The teachings that God will rapture believers throughout the tribulation, or the 70th Week of Daniel. According to this view rapture is a reward, not an unconditional promise, and not all believers will be raptured. Thus individuals are said to be raptured at various points throughout the tribulation. This view was first promoted in the late nineteenth century by Robert Govett and J.A. Seiss. It has only a few advocates today.

Pauline : The title given to the distinctive nature of the apostle Paul's theology. Although the word is often used to imply that Paul's theology was different from those of the other apostles, it can, and should, be taken merely as a title to reference the style of Paul's hermeneutic.

Perspicuity : This is the doctrine which states that all men may understand the Bible without the need for doctoral degrees, scientific knowledge, or philosophical presumptions. The Bible was written for all men, not merely men of a particular education or philosophical bias.

Petrine : The title given to the distinctive nature of the apostle Peter's theology. This should not be taken to imply that Peter's theology was different, however. See "Pauline" for more.

Postmillennial : Postmillennialism literally means "after the millennium." According to this view, Christ will return *after* the Church has established the thousand year reign of Revelation 20. Its advocates argue that Christ will only return once we have converted the world and established the kingdom of God on earth through the church's efforts. Postmillennialism is a natural outgrowth of amillennialism and first appeared to be taught in the early eighteenth century. Daniel Whitby and some of the American Forefathers were the leading postmillennial advocates. Modern postmillennialism virtually died out until it was revived under the term Dominion Theology. It treats the prophecies of Revelation very allegorically as a whole.

Posttribulational Rapture : The posttribulational rapture position teaches that rapture will occur at the very end of the tribulation and that it is virtually synonymous with the second coming. Although it is often presented as the historic teaching of the church it was first clearly taught in the mid-twentieth century by men such as George Ladd. It is a very popular view today.

Premillennial : Premillennialism literally means "before the millennium." According to this view, Christ will return before the thousand year reign of Christ discussed in Revelation 20. His return is specifically for the purpose of establishing the kingdom. Premillennialism is the most straightfoward reading of Revelation and usually, but not always, adopts a "literal interpretation" of the prophecies of Revelation. Premillennialism is the dominant view among evangelical Christians.

Preterism : Preterism maintains that the prophecies of Revelation are allegorical for the history of the early Church. The prestists believe that Nero (although some preterists differ) was the anti-Christ and the events of Revelation are mere allegorical references to the Christian persecutions under Nero and the burning of Rome. The view became prominent in the counter-Reformation under Alcazar and was a popular alternative to historicism and futurism. It is an outgrowth of idealism. The view maintains a large presence in the evangelical community and is dominant among liberal churches.

Pretribulational Rapture : Pre-tribulationalism means "before the tribulation." According to this view, the rapture of the church will occur before the tribulation, or Daniel's 70th Week. The Church is, therefore, absent from the tribulation and is said to be replaced by believing Israel. Although it is argued that the church fathers were pre-tribulational, the first universally recognized modern pre-tribulationist was John Darby and the Brethren Movement in England. Pretribulationism is the dominant view among evangelical premillennialists.

Pre-Wrath Rapture : The pre-wrath rapture position believes that the church will only be raptured on the day that the Day of the Lord begins. Its advocates believe that this will occur toward the end of Daniel's 70th Week and, therefore, place the rapture about five to six years into the tribulation. The view was first present by Marvin Rosenthal in the 1990s.

Progressive Dispensationalism : Progessive dispensationalism is an attempt to mediate between covenant theology and traditional dispensationism. The view takes a "both/and" approach to the issues of Israel, the church, the Covenants, and dispensations. It argues that there are overlaps among these and tries to balance the views into a new conglomerate theology. Progressive dispensationalists are quiet on numerous issues such as their view of rapture and their specific exegesis of Revelation.

Rapture : Rapture is the coming of Jesus for the church as opposed to the second coming proper. According to advocates of the rapture, the second coming is to be distinguished from the taking of believers from the earth before the battle of Armaggedon (or perhaps much earlier). It is based primarily on (but not exclusively) 1 Corinthians 15:50-56 and 1 Thessalonians 4:17. Appendix A discusses this theory in depth.

Reconstructionism : Reconstructionism is synonymous with Dominion Theology. It maintains that the church must exercise dominion over the entire globe. See Dominion Theology for a more detailed definition.

Replacement Theology : Virtually synonymous with covenant theology, Replacement Theology maintains that the church has permanently replaced Israel as God's people. According to Replacement Theology all the promises God made to Israel were conditional and were revoked when Israel rejected Jesus. This view, therefore, does not believe that the state of Israel plays an important role in prophecy. Passages in Revelation that refer to the the Jews and Israel are taken by this view as allegorical for the church.

Rorschach Inkblot : A popular psychology test where the patient is shown an blotted inkblot, similar to a cloud formation, and asked what he sees in the inkblot.

70ᵗʰ Week of Daniel : A prophecy in Daniel states that Israel will be allotted 70 weeks of years or 490 years before the consumation of everlasting righteouness. Dispensationalists, and many other premillennialists, believe that the final week, or seven years, is missing and remains to be fulfilled. According to dispensationalists, and many other premillennialists, the final week of Daniel's prophecy is synonymous with the final events spoken of in Revelation. It is, therefore, commonly held that the 70ᵗʰ Week of Daniel is the same as the tribulation. Chapter two discusses this prophecy in detail.

Tribulation : The tribulation is the title given to the seven year time frame depicted in the book of Revelation. It encompasses the time from the signing of a peace treaty with the anti-Christ to the return of Christ seven years later.

Ultradispensationalism : Also called "hyperdispensationalism," this is the name given to an "extreme" view of dispensationalism. The ultradispensationalists maintain very strict lines between various ages or dispensations with no overlap or leeway. They have an intricate view of each and every dispensation. They also believe that certain passages of Scripture were written solely to a particularly dispensation. That is not to say that we cannot read or understand the Old Testament (for example), but they argue that the gospels and most of Acts was written to the older dispensation. According to ultradispensationalism, only the epistles should be seen as having been written directly to the church. The view is attributed to E.W. Bullinger.

443

General Scripture Index

445

ENDNOTES

1 Robert Mounce, *The New International Commentary on the New Testament : The Book of Revelation* William Eerdmans Co. (Grand Rapids, Mich.) 1977 pg. 19

2 Alan Johnson, "Revelation," *The Expositor's Bible Commentary Vol. 12* Frank Gaebelein, ed., Zondervan's House (Grand Rapids, Mich.) 1981 pg. 402

3 George Eldon Ladd, *A Theology of the New Testament* William Eerdmans Co. (Grand Rapids, Mich.) 1974 pg. 59

4 David Wenham, "Appendix," Ibid. pg. 698

5 J. D. G. Dunn, *Unity and Diversity in the New Testament* (London, England) 1977 pg. 350 as quoted in Ibid. pg. 696

6 Wenham, op. cit. pg. 704

7 G. B. Caird, *The Revelation of Saint John* Henrickson Publishers (Peabody, Mass.) 1966 pg. 162

8 Ibid. pg. 289

9 Mounce, op. cit. pg. 20

10 Ray Summers, *Worthy Is The Lamb* Broadman Press (Nashville, Tenn) 1951 pg. 7

11 John Walvoord, *The Revelation of Jesus Christ* Moody Press (Chicago, Ill.) 1966 pg. 24

12 Mounce, op. cit. pg. 21

13 Amillennialists designate the books of Revelation and Daniel as "apocalyptic" literature which they distinguish from true prophecy. In this way, they can interpret Revelation and Daniel in one way, while adopting a more literal approach to Isaiah or Jeremiah. This doctrine must be rejected as it has neither merit nor logic for the book of Revelation openly calls itself a "book of ***prophecy***" (Revelation 22:19 cf. Revelation 1:3). See discussion in my *Introduction*.

14 Stephen R. Miller, *The New American Commentary on Daniel* Broadman & Holman (Nashville, Tenn.) 1994 pg. 252

15 John Walvoord, *Every Prophecy of the Bible* Chariot Victor Publ. (Colorado Springs, Co.) 1999 pg. 248

16 An interesting sidenote is whether or not this should really be "wall," as opposed to "moat." The Hebrew word is חרוץ (harutz) which is best translated "moat" or, preferably, "trench." However, the King James Version borrows from the Greek *Septuagint* which reads "wall." The current reading could be a scribal error from חיץ (hayitz) meaning "wall." The Hebrew yod (י) could have been easily mistaken for a resh (ר), hence the change. In either case, the translation does not effect the interpretation as whole since neither moats nor walls were permitted until the final edict.

17 Dwight Pentecost, "Daniel," *The Bible Knowledge Commentary : Old Testament* John F. Walvoord & Roy Zuck, eds., Victor Books (Wheaton, Ill.) 1986 pg. 1361

18 Alva McClain, *Daniel's Prophecy of the Seventy Weeks* Zondervan Publishers (Grand Rapids, Mich.) 1940 pp. 13-14

19 Randall Price, *The Coming Last Days Temple* Harvest House (Eugene, Or.) 1999 pg. 665

20 Ibid.

21 Charles Pfeiffer, *The Dead Sea Scrolls and the Bible* Baker Books (Grand Rapids, Mich.) 1969 pp. 127-128

22 Cf. Hippolytus, "Treatise on Christ & Anti-Christ," *Ante-Nicene Fathers Vol. V* Alexander Roberts & James Donaldson, eds. William B. Eerdmans Publishers (Grand Rapids, Mich.) 1990 pg. 184

23 Matthew Henry, *Matthew Henry's Commentary on the Whole Bible : Vol. 4* Hendrickson Publishers (Peabody, Mass.) 1991 pg. 857

24 Edward J. Young, *The Prophecy of Daniel* William B. Eerdmans Publishers (Grand Rapids, Mich.) 1949 pg. 203

25 Nathaniel West, *The Thousand Year Reign of Christ* Kregel Publications (Grand Rapids, Mich.) 1993 (orig. 1899) pg. 136

26 Ibid. pg. 184

27 Young, op. cit. pg. 206

28 Ibid. pg. 205
29 Matthew Poole, *A Commentary on the Holy Bible : Vol. II* Hendrickson Publishers (Peabody, Mass.) no copyright listed pg. 839
30 Miller, op. cit. pg. 263
31 Gleason L. Archer Jr., "Daniel," *Expositor's Bible* op. cit. pg. 114
32 Harold Hoehner, *Chronological Aspects of the Life of Christ* Zondervan Publishing (Grand Rapids, Mich.) 1977 pg. 126
33 Hippolytus, *Ante-Nicene Fathers Vol. V* op. cit. pg. 181
34 Archer, op. cit. pg. 116
35 Miller, op. cit. pg. 269
36 There may also be hidden motives behind some who reject the end of the sixty-nine weeks as pertaining to Christ's death and resurrection. Many of these, but not all, are Covenant Theologians who claim that the entire seventy weeks have been fulfilled. In so doing, they eliminate any future for national Israel and reject the role of modern Israel in prophecy. This can only be done, however, by rejecting the sixty-ninth week's end with the crucifixion of Christ (an event they tie into the seventieth week).
37 Hoehner, op. cit. pg. 125
38 Ibid. pg. 139
39 Miller, op. cit. pg. 265
40 Cf. Archer, op. cit. pg. 115
41 Jim Combs, *Mysteries of the Book of Daniel* Tribune Publishers (Springfield, Mo.) 1994 pg. 108
42 Miller, op. cit. pg. 265
43 Merrill Unger, *Unger's Bible Dictionary* Moody Press (Chicago, Ill.) 1957 pp. 163-166
44 Paul A. Zoch, *Ancient Rome* University of Oklahoma Press (University of Oklahoma, Ok.) 1998 pg. 204
45 A.T. Olmstead, *History of Assyria* Charles Scribner's Sons (New York, NY) 1923 pg. 589
46 Unger, op. cit. pp. 163-166
47 A.T. Olmstead, *History of the Persian Empire* University of Chicago Press (Chicago, Ill.) 1948 pg. 209
48 Ibid.
49 Cf. Unger, op. cit. pp. 163-166
50 Archer, op. cit. pg. 115
51 George Steindorff and Keith C. Steele, *When Egypt Ruled the East* University of Chicago Press (Chicago, Ill.) 1957 pg. 128
52 The exile began when the Babylonians took Jerusalem in 587 B.C. The exile was officially ended when Cyrus granted permission for the Jews return to Israel in 539 B.C., 48 years later by the modern calendar but exactly 49 by the 360 day Hebrew calendar!
53 Sir Robert Anderson, *The Coming Prince* Kregel Press (Grand Rapids, Mich.) 1957 ed. (orig. 1884) pg. 75
54 Julius Africanus actually calculates using the 354 day calendar. The point is that he recognized that the Jews used an alternate calendar (Julius Africanus, "Extant Fragments from Chronography," *Ante-Nicene Fathers Vol. VI* Alexander Roberts & James Donaldson, eds., William B. Eerdmans Publishers (Grand Rapids, Mich.) 1999 pg. 135).
55 Isaac Newton, *Observations on the Prophecies of Daniel and the Apocalypse of St. John* Edwin Mellen Press (Lampeter, England) 1999 ed. (orig. 1733) pg. 117
56 Ibid.
57 Ibid. pg. 118
58 Ibid.
59 Hoehner, op. cit. pg. 135
60 Newton, op. cit. pg. 117
61 Miller, op. cit. pg. 265
62 Archer, op. cit. pg. 115

63 West, op. cit. pg. 153
64 Combs, op. cit. pg. 108
65 Miller, op. cit. pg. 263
66 For a complete discussion of the year of Christ's cruficixion, see chapter 5 of Hoehner, op. cit.
67 Young, op. cit. pp. 205-217
68 Ibid. pg. 220
69 Ibid. pp. 205-217
70 Josephus, "Wars of the Jews," *The Complete Works of Josephus* Kregel Publications (Grand Rapids, Mich.) 1981 ed. pg. 602
71 Ibid. pg. 603
72 Combs, op. cit. pg. 109
73 Pentecost, op. cit. pg. 1363
74 Randall Price   as quoted in Thomas Ice & Kenneth L. Gentry Jr., *The Great Tribulation : Past or Future?* Kregel Press (Grand Rapids, Mich.) 1999 pg. 86
75 John F. Walvoord, *The Millennial Kingdom* Zondervan Press (Grand Rapids, Mich.) 1959 pg. 229
76 Ibid. pg. 228
77 Archer, op. cit. pg. 113
78 Irenaeus, "Against Heresies," *Ante-Nicene Fathers Vol. 1* pg. 553
79 Hippolytus, *Ante-Nicene Fathers Vol. V* op. cit. pg. 184
80 Joseph Mede, *The Apostasy of the Latter Times* Macintosh Printer (London, England) 1865 ed. pg. 211
81 Cf. Mounce, op. cit.
82 For a complete discussion of the chronology of Christ, see Hoehner, op. cit.
83 Irenaeus, "Against Heresies," *Ante-Nicene Fathers Vol. 1* op. cit. pg. 493
84 Victorinus, *Ante-Nicene Fathers Vol. 7* op. cit. pg. 350
85 Cf. Tertullian, *Ante-Nicene Fathers* op. cit.
86 Leroy Edwin Froom, *Prophetic Faith of Our Fathers   Vol. 1* Review & Herald (Washington, DC) 1950 pg. 350
87 Ibid.
88 Nicholas of Lyra, *Nicholas of Lyra's Apocalypse Commentary* Medieval Institute Publications (Kalamazoo, Mich.) 1997 (orig. 1329) pg. 82
89 Poole, op. cit. pg. 964
90 George Eldon Ladd, *A Commentary on the Revelation of John* Wm. B. Eerdmans (Grand Rapids, Mich.) 1972 pg. 98
91 Ibid.
92 Cf. Hal Lindsey, *There Is A New World Coming* Harvest House (Eugene, OR) 1973 pg. 84
93 Walter Scott, *Exposition of the Revelation of Jesus Christ* Pickering & Inglis Ltd. (London, England) 1900 pg. 147
94 Joseph A. Seiss, *The Apocalypse* Kregel Publications (Grand Rapids, Mich.) 2001 reprint pg. 126
95 Ibid.
96 Ibid.
97 Walvoord, *Revelation* op. cit. pg. 127
98 Robert Govett, *Govett on Revelation : The Apocalypse Expounded by Scripture Vol. II* Conley & Schoettle Publishing Co. (Miami Springs, FL) 1981 reprint from 1861 pg. 171
99 Ibid. pg. 161
100 Ibid. pg. 164
101 Seiss, op. cit. pg. 129
102 Ibid.
103 Mounce, op. cit. pg. 154
104 Cf. Nicholas of Lyra, op. cit. pg. 82

105 E. W. Bullinger, *Commentary on Revelation* Kregel Classics (Grand Rapids, Mich.) 1984 ed. (from 3ʳᵈ rev. ed. 1935) pg. 253

106 John Nelson Darby, *The Collected Works of J. N. Darby Prophetic Vol. 2 - Vol. 5 in series* Believer's Bookshelf (Subury, Penn.) 1971 reprint pg. 187

107 Scott, op. cit. pg. 147

108 Sir Robert Anderson, *The Vision of the First Six Seals* Prophecy Investigation Society - R.F. Hunger Printer (London, England) 1913 pg. 8

109 Watchman Nee, *Come, Lord Jesus* Christian Fellowship Publications (New York, NY) 1976 pg. 72

110 Arthur Bloomfield, *All Things New* Bethany House (Bloomington, MN) 1959 pg. 114

111 Govett, op. cit. pg. 164

112 Charles Ryrie, *Revelation* Moody Press (Chicago, Ill.), 1996 pg. 55

113 Ibid.

114 Scott, op. cit. pg. 147

115 J. Dwight Pentecost, *Things to Come* Zondervan Publishing House (Grand Rapids, Mich.) 1958 pg. 360

116 G.H. Lang, *The Revelation of Jesus Christ* The Paternoster Press (New York, NY) 1948 pg. 155

117 Froom, op. cit. pg. 696

118 Nicholas of Lyra, op. cit. pg. 83

119 Joseph Mede, *The Key to Revelation   Part II – the Interpretation* Phil Stephens Printer (London, England) 1643 pp. 42-44

120 Ladd, *Revelation* op. cit. pg. 100

121 Johnson, op. cit. pg. 474

122 Lindsey, *New World* op. cit. pg. 85

123 Cf. Froom, op. cit. pg. 696

124 Nicholas of Lyra, op. cit. pp. 83-86

125 John Bale, "Image of Both Churches," *Selected Works of John Bale* Cambridge Press (London, England) 1574 ed. pp. 318-321

126 Mede, *Key to Revelation* op.cit. pp. 42-48

127 Newton, op. cit. pg. 274

128 Norman Harrison, *The End   Re-Thinking The Revelation* The Harrison Service (Minneapolis, Minn.) 1948 pp. 216-218

129 Ibid.

130 Ibid. pp. 220-223 It is important to note that Harrison does not seem to be dogmatic about these inferences. In fact, he has appropriately separated these statements from the exegesis of the passage by way of a "supplement." Nonetheless, he seems to contradict himself. He is known as the founder of midtribulationism and yet he has apparently extended the seals and trumpet judgments over a period of decades, rather than seven years. Consequently, he sees the judgments of God not as confined to the seven year Tribulation. This chronology will be discussed at more length in a subsequent chapter.

131 Lang, op. cit. pg. 159

132 Lindsey, *New World* op. cit. pg. 85

133 Dwight Pentecost does not specifically identify the Invasion of Magog with the second seal but his chronology matches these events. A greater discussion will made in Appendices C & D.

134 Nicholas of Lyra, op. cit. pp. 87-89

135 Bale, op. cit. pg. 322

136 Mede, *Key to Revelation* op. cit. pg. 52

137 Newton, op. cit. pg. 274

138 Ladd, *Revelation* op. cit. pg. 104

139 Scott, op. cit. pg. 157

140 Bullinger, op. cit. pg. 268

141 Johnson, op. cit. pp. 474-475

142 Ladd, *Revelation* op. cit. pg. 104
143 George Peters, *The Theocratic Kingdom Vol. 1* Kregel Publications (Grand Rapids, Mich.) 1884 pg. 413
144 Edward Hindson, *Revelation : Unlocking the Future* AMG Publishers (Chattanooga, TN) 2002 pg. 83
145 Jim Combs, *Mysteries of the Book of Revelation* Tribune Publishers (Springfield, MO) 1994 pg. 74
146 H. A. Ironside, *Revelation* Loizeaux (Neptune, NJ) 1996 ed. (1920 orig.) pg. 81
147 Seiss, op. cit. pp. 140-141
148 The passage in question is omitted from this book because it has no major interpretive impact upon the different interpretive methods of Revelation. Amillennialists, premillennialists, and postmillennialists may all agree on the intrepretations of chapters four and five in Revelation but still disagree on all the ensuing passages. See preface.
149 Walvoord, *Revelation* op. cit. pg. 133
150 Ibid.
151 Arthur Bloomfield, *The Key to Understanding Revelation* Bethany House (Bloomington, MN) 2002 reprint pp. 159-160
152 Seiss, op. cit. pg. 147
153 Govett, op. cit. pg. 200
154 Bullinger, op. cit. pg. 266
155 Ibid.
156 Scott, op. cit. pg. 155
157 Bullinger, op. cit. pg. 268
158 Scott, op. cit. pg. 155
159 Ibid. pg. 154
160 Ironside, op. cit. pg. 81
161 Ibid.
162 Victorinus, *Ante-Nicene Fathers Vol. 7* op. cit. pg. 351
163 Ibid.
164 Ibid. He may have meant this in the context of persecution taking the church away although there is a possibility that he intended to speak here of the rapture of the church.
165 Lactantius, *Ante-Nicene Fathers Vol. 7* op. cit. pg. 213
166 Cf. Froom, op. cit. pg. 696
167 Nicholas of Lyra, op. cit. pg. 89
168 Ibid. pp. 90-91
169 Ibid. pg. 89
170 Bale, op. cit. pg. 327
171 Ibid. pg. 328
172 Mede, *Key to Revelation* op.cit. pg. 54
173 Newton, op. cit. pg. 275
174 Darby, op. cit. pg. 21
175 Ibid.
176 Scott, op. cit pp. 158-160
177 Darby, op. cit. pg. 21
178 Scott, op. cit. pg. 158
179 Henry Barclay Swete, *Commentary on Revelation* Kregel Publications (Grand Rapids, Mich.) 1977 pg. 92
180 Ironside, op. cit. pg. 82
181 Ibid.
182 Nee, op. cit. pg. 79
183 Nee, op. cit. pg. 79
184 Ibid.
185 Nicholas of Lyra, op. cit. pg. 89

186 Ibid.
187 John Nelson Darby, *The Collected Works of J. N. Darby Prophetic Vol. 1 - Vol. 2 in series* Kingston Bible Trust (London, England) pg 188
188 Walvoord, *Revelation* op. cit. pg. 137
189 Ladd, *Revelation* op. cit. pg. 108
190 Ibid.
191 Henry Morris, *The Revelation Record* Tyndale House (Wheaton, Ill.) 1983 pg. 121
192 Lindsey, *New World* op. cit. pg. 96
193 Ibid.
194 Marvin Rosenthal, *The Pre-Wrath Rapture of the Church* Thomas Nelson Publishers (Nashville, Tn.) 1990 pg. 137
195 Ladd, *Revelation* op. cit. pg. 108
196 Seiss, op. cit. pg. 154
197 Joseph Thayer, *Thayer's Greek-English Lexicon* Baker Book House (Grand Rapids, Mich.) 1977 pg. 82
198 Govett, op. cit. pg. 216
199 Seiss, op. cit. 154
200 Robert Thomas, *Revelation 1-7 An Exegetical Commentary* Moody Press (Chicago, Ill.) 1992 pg. 453
201 Morris, op. cit. pg. 122
202 Lindsey, *New World* op. cit. pg. 97
203 Ibid.
204 Ladd, *Revelation* op. cit. pg. 108
205 Govett, op. cit. pg. 209
206 Bale, op. cit. pg. 328
207 Nicholas of Lyra, op. cit. pg. 90
208 Ironside, op. cit. pg. 84
209 Scott, op. cit. pg. 159
210 Ladd, *Revelation* op. cit. pg. 108
211 Harrison, op. cit. pg. 90
212 Thomas, op. cit. pg. 451
213 Ibid. pg. 454
214 Govett, op. cit. pg. 217
215 Morris, op. cit. pg. 122
216 Ibid. pp. 122-123
217 Ibid. pg. 123
218 Ryrie, op. cit. pg. 58
219 Lindsey, *New World* op. cit. pg. 98
220 Bloomfield, *All Things New* op. cit. pp. 122-123
221 Lindsey, *New World* op. cit. pg. 98
222 It seems odd to this author that George Ladd can openly say that the "vault" is an optical illusion (Ladd, *Revelation* op. cit. pg. 108) but deny that any optical illusion could cause what John saw.
223 Victorinus, *Ante-Nicene Fathers Vol. 7* op. cit. pg. 351
224 Swete, op. cit. pg. 93
225 Darby, *Collected Works Vol. 2* op. cit. pg. 22
226 Scott, op. cit. pp. 159-160
227 Govett, op. cit. pg. 217
228 Ibid.
229 Seiss, op. cit. pg. 155
230 Morris, op. cit. pg. 123
231 Walvoord, *Revelation* op. cit. pg. 137
232 Tim LaHaye, *Revelation Unveiled* Zondervan Publishing (Grand Rapids, Mich.) 1999 pg. 117

233 Seiss, op. cit. pg. 180

234 All these views are mentioned by Seiss, ibid.

235 Morris, op. cit. pg. 140

236 Walvoord, *Revelation* op. cit. pg. 151

237 Ibid.

238 Victorinus, *Ante-Nicene Fathers Vol. 7* op. cit. pg. 352

239 Adso of Montier, *Apocalyptic Spirituality* Bernard McGinn, translator Paulist Press (Mahurah, NJ) 1979 pg. 94

240 Froom, op. cit. pg. 709

241 Nicholas of Lyra, op. cit. pp. 96-97

242 Bale, op. cit. pg. 335

243 Robert Maton, *Israel's Redemption or the Prophetical History of our Savior's Kingdom on Earth* Daniel Frere Shop (London, England) 1642

244 Mede, *Key to Revelation* op.cit. 72

245 Darby, *Collected Works Vol. 1* op. cit. pg. 186

246 Darby, *Collected Works Vol. 2* op. cit. pg. 23

247 Samuel Kellogg, *Are Premillennialists Right?* F.H. Revell (Chicago, Ill.) 1885

248 Ladd, *Revelation* op. cit. pp. 112-113

249 Darby, *Collected Works Vol. 2* op. cit. pg. 23

250 Harrison. op. cit. pg. 147

251 Mounce. op. cit. pg. 168

252 Ladd, *Revelation* op. cit. pp. 117

253 Seiss. op. cit. pg. 164

254 West, op. cit. pg. 94

255 Ibid. pg. 96

256 Govett. op. cit. pg. 249

257 Ibid.

258 West, op. cit. pg. 239

259 Martin Kiddle, "The Revelation of St. John," *Moffatt New Testament Commentary* Harper & Row (New York, NY) 1940 pp. 135-136

260 Mounce. op. cit. pg. 169

261 Nee, op. cit. pg. 82

262 Swete, op. cit. pg. 99

263 Ladd, *Revelation* op. cit. pp. 112-113

264 Ibid. pg. 116

265 Ladd, *Revelation* op. cit. pg. 116

266 Ibid. pg. 116

267 Seiss, op. cit. pg. 161

268 Mounce, op. cit. pg. 168

269 Robert Gundry, *First the Antichrist* Baker Book House (Grand Rapids, Mich.) 1997 pg. 91

270 Robert Gundry, *A Survey of the New Testament* Zondervan Publishing House (Grand Rapids, Mich.) 1994 pp. 433-434

271 Merrill Tenney, *New Testament Survey* William B. Eerdmans Co. (Grand Rapids, Mich.) 1985 pg. 264

272 Johnson, op. cit. pg. 481

273 Walvoord, *Revelation* op. cit. pg. 142

274 Govett, op. cit. pg. 250

275 This is the seventh of Govett's points, but the sixth of the seven I have listed. Likewise, I omitted his eighth point. Cf. Ibid. pg. 251

276 Ibid. pg. 251

277 Hindson, *Revelation* op. cit. pg. 90

278 Ironside, op. cit. pg. 90

279 C. I. Scofield, *Prophecy Make Plain : Addresses on Prophecy* The Gospel Hour (Greenville, SC) 1967 (orig. 1910) pg. 127
280 Victorinus, *Ante-Nicene Fathers Vol. 7* op. cit. pg. 352
281 Seiss, op. cit. pg. 161
282 Ibid.
283 Ibid. pg. 162
284 Ladd, *Revelation* op. cit. pg. 115
285 Bullinger, op. cit. pg. 284
286 Scott, op. cit. pg. 166
287 Mounce, op. cit. pg. 169
288 Ibid.
289 Nestle-Aland *Novum Tesamentum Graece* Deutsche Bibelgesellschaft (Stuttgart, Germany) 1898 pg. 645
290 Irenaeus, "Against Heresies," *Ante-Nicene Fathers Vol. 1* op. cit. pg. 559
291 Mounce, op. cit. pg. 169
292 Ironside, op. cit. pg. 91
293 Hippolytus, *Ante-Nicene Fathers Vol. 5* op. cit. pg. 207
294 Froom, op. cit. pg. 554
295 Adso of Montier, op. cit. pg. 90
296 Nicholas of Lyra, op. cit. pg. 97
297 Froom, op. cit. pg. 657
298 Lidnsey, *New World* op. cit. pg. 109
299 Hindson, *Revelation* op. cit. pg. 90
300 Govett, op. cit. pp. 252-253
301 Johnson, op. cit. pg. 482
302 Seiss, op. cit. pg. 163
303 Irenaeus, "Against Heresies," *Ante-Nicene Fathers Vol. 1* op. cit. pg. 553
304 Hippolytus, *Ante-Nicene Fathers Vol. 5* op. cit. pg. 184
305 Lactantius, *Ante-Nicene Fathers Vol. 7* op. cit. pg. 214
306 Ephraem the Syrian, *When the Trumpet Sounds* Thomas Ice & Timothy Demy ed., Harvest House (Eugene, OR) 1995 pg. 113
307 Victorinus, *Ante-Nicene Fathers Vol. 7* op. cit. pp. 353-354
308 Adso of Montier, op. cit. pg. 91
309 Nicholas of Lyra, op. cit. pg. 127
310 Mede, "Part II : The Interpretation" *Key to Revelation* op.cit. pg. 3
311 Ibid. pg. 6
312 Darby, *Collected Works Vol. 2* op. cit. pg. 32
313 Samuel Kellogg, *The Jews, or, Prediction and Fulfillment* A.D.F. Randolph (New York, NY) 1883
314 Anderson, *Coming Prince* op. cit. pg. 211
315 Scott, op. cit. pg. 228
316 Bullinger, op. cit. pg. 348
317 West, op. cit. pp. 18, 23, 72, 81, 380, etc.
318 Mede, "Part II : The Interpretation" *Key to Revelation* op.cit. pg. 3
319 Mounce, op.cit. pg. 220
320 Ladd, *Revelation* op. cit. pg. 152
321 Ibid.
322 Ibid. pg. 153
323 Seiss, op. cit. pg. 237
324 West, op. cit. pg. 380
325 West, op. cit. pp. 437-438
326 James Brookes, *Till He Come* Gospel Publishers (Chicago, Ill.) 1891 pg. 88
327 Kellogg, *The Jews* op. cit. pg. 267

328 Anderson, *Visions* op. cit. pg. 12
329 Ibid.. pg. 13
330 James Brookes, *Marantha* Fleming Revell Co. (New York, NY) 1889 pg. 539
331 Cf. Martin Gilbert, *Israel* Turner Books (Toronto, ON) 1998 pp. 186-208
332 Brookes, *Maranatha* op. cit. pg. 405
333 William Newell, *The Book of Revelation* Grace Publishing Inc. (Chicago, Ill.) 1935 pg. 147
334 Anderson, *Visions* op. cit. pg. 14
335 Nee, op. cit. pg. 115
336 Seiss, op. cit. pg. 239
337 Lindsey, *New World* op. cit. pg. 148
338 Price, *Coming Temple* op. cit. pp. 337-339
339 Ibid. pp. 339-341
340 Ibid.
341 Ernest Martin, "New Evidence for the *Real* Site of the Temple in Jerusalem," *Bible and Spade* Vol. 14, No. 4 Fall 2001 pp. 111-116
342 Ibid.
343 Leen Ritmeyer, "A Response to Dr. Ernest Martin," Ibid. pp. 117-121
344 Cf. Ibid.
345 Price, *Coming Temple* op. cit. pp. 345
346 Ibid. pp. 347
347 Leon Ritmeyer, "Locating the Original Temple Mount," *Biblical Archaeology Review*, Vol. 18, No. 2 (March/April, 1992) pg. 26
348 Ibid. pp. 26-45, 65-65
349 Price, *Coming Temple* op. cit. pg. 688
350 Ibid. pg. 344
351 Asher Kaufman, "Where the Ancient Temple of Jerusalem Stood," *Biblical Archaeological Review*, Vol. 9, No. 2 (March/April, 1983) pg. 43
352 Ibid. pg. 45
353 Ibid.
354 Ibid.
355 Ibid.
356 Ibid. pp. 40-59
357 Price, *Coming Temple* op. cit. pg. 344
358 It is of interest to note that the Third Temple is not to be Ezekiel's temple (Ezekiel 40-48). Consequently, while the Jews desire to build it over the old temples, it is not unreasonable that the temple could be unknowingly built in the wrong area. Only the future will be able to determine for sure when and where the temple will be rebuild, but we do know that it *will* be rebuilt, and for some reason, the court of the Gentiles will be "cast out."
359 Morris, op. cit. pg. 192
360 West, op. cit. pp. 71-72
361 Arthur Bloomfield, *The End of Days* Bethany House (Minneapolis, MN) 1961 pg. 47
362 Walvoord, *Every Prophecy* op. cit pg. 159
363 Henry, *Commentary Vol. 4* op. cit. pg. 607
364 Cf. Ralph Alexander, "Ezekiel," *Expositor's Commentary Vol. 6* op. cit. pg. 770
365 Bloomfield, *End of Days* op. cit. pg. 52
366 Ibid.
367 Ibid. pg. 49
368 Ibid. pg. 53
369 Ibid. pg. 54
370 Sir Robert Anderson, *The Coming Prince* Kregel Press (Grand Rapids, Mich.) 1957 ed. (orig. 1884) pg. 233
371 Bard, op. cit. pg. 68

372   This is a popular phrase by those critics who lack the respect and dignity expected from a Christian "scholar."

373   Cf. West, op. cit. pp. 18, 23, 72, 380, etc.

374   Cf. Newton, op. cit. pp. 278-279

375   Cf. Bale, op. cit. pg. 387

376   Seiss, op. cit. pg. 242

377   Again the reader is referred to Appendix C.

378   Seiss, op. cit. pg. 278

379   Hippolytus, *Ante-Nicene Fathers Vol. 5* op. cit. pg. 217

380   Victorinus, *Ante-Nicene Fathers Vol. 7* op. cit. pg. 355

381   Ibid.

382   Methodius, *Ante-Nicene Fathers Vol. 7* op. cit. pp. 336-337

383   David Burr, *Olivi's Peacable Kingdom* University of Penn. Press (Philadelphia, Penn.) 1993 pg. 166

384   Nicholas of Lyra, op. cit. pp. 139-141

385   Bale, op. cit. pg. 404

386   Mede, "Part II : The Interpretation," *Key to Revelation* op.cit. pg. 37

387   Newton, op. cit. pg. 275

388   Mede, "Part II : The Interpretation," *Key to Revelation* op.cit. pg. 37

389   Newton, op. cit. pg. 275

390   Darby, *Collected Works Vol. 2* op. cit. pg. 38

391   Ibid. pg. 37

392   Swete, op. cit. pg. 148

393   Ibid. pg. 151

394   Bullinger, op. cit. pg. 393

395   Anderson, *Coming Prince* op. cit. pg. 199

396   Scott, op. cit. 247

397   West, op. cit. pg. 156

398   Nicholas of Lyra, op. cit. pg. 141

399   Newton, op. cit. pg. 275

400   Hippolytus, *Ante-Nicene Fathers Vol. 5* op. cit. pg. 217

401   Victorinus, *Ante-Nicene Fathers Vol. 7* op. cit. pg. 355

402   Methodius, *Ante-Nicene Fathers Vol. 7* op. cit. pg. 337

403   Mede, "Part II : The Interpretation," *Key to Revelation* op.cit. pg. 37

404   Bale, op. cit. pg. 405

405   Bloomfield, *All Things New* op. cit. pg. 176

406   Robert Govett, *Govett on Revelation : The Apocalypse Expounded by Scripture Vol. III* Conley & Schoettle Publishing Co. (Miami Springs, FL) 1981 (orig. 1861) pg. 28

407   Seiss, op. cit. pg. 297

408   Ibid. pg. 298

409   Nee, op. cit. pg. 134

410   Seiss, op. cit. pg. 297

411   Lang, op. cit. pg. 198

412   Ibid.

413   Cf. Nicholas of Lyra, op. cit. pg. 139 and Nee, op. cit. pg. 131

414   Ironside, op. cit. pg. 141

415   Hippolytus, *Ante-Nicene Fathers Vol. 5* op. cit. pg. 217

416   Bale, op. cit. pg. 405

417   Nee, op. cit. pg. 131

418   Bloomfield, *All Things New* op. cit. pg. 175

419   Ibid.

420   Bloomfield, *Key to Understanding Revelation* op. cit. pg. 214

421   Hippolytus, *Ante-Nicene Fathers Vol. 5* op. cit. pg. 217

422 Swete, op. cit. pg. 151
423 Ibid. pg. 149
424 Ladd, *Revelation* op. cit. pg. 166
425 Morris, op. cit. pg. 214
426 Ibid.
427 Ibid. pg. 215
428 Govett, *Vol. III* op. cit. pg. 15
429 Pentecost, *Things to Come* op. cit. pg. 215
430 Nicholas of Lyra actually maintained that the dragon was in fact the Persian king Chosroes despite this passage! (op. cit. pg. 141)
431 Mede, "Part II : The Interpretation," *Key to Revelation* op.cit. pg. 38
432 Seiss, op. cit. pg. 301
433 Ibid. pg. 302
434 Ibid. pp. 302-303
435 Govett, *Vol. III* op. cit. pg. 32
436 Ibid. pg. 33
437 Bloomfield, *Key to Understanding Revelation* op. cit. pg. 217
438 Ibid.
439 Walvoord, *Revelation* op. cit. pg. 190
440 Ibid. pp. 190-191
441 Ibid. pg. 191
442 Lindsey, *New World* op. cit. pg. 167
443 Seiss, op. cit. pg. 317
444 Govett, *Vol. III* op. cit. pg. 59
445 Ibid. pg. 60
446 It is debatable whether or not Isaiah 16:4 implies that Israel took the city. The Moabites fled to Petra, or Sela, for safety but may have left when they realized their cause was lost. Cf. Fabio Bourbon, *Petra : Jordan's Extraordinary Ancient City* Barnes and Noble Books (Vercelli, Italy) 1999
447 Ibid.
448 Harrison. op. cit. pg. 132
449 Hal Lindsey, *The Late Great Planet Earth* Zondervan Publishers (Grand Rapids, Mich.) 1977 pg. 142
450 Robert Van Kampen, *The Sign* Crossway Books (Wheaton, Ill.) 3rd revised ed. 2000 pg. 228
451 Ibid.
452 Walvoord, *Every Prophecy* op. cit. pg. 101
453 E. R. Grogan, "Isaiah," *The Expositor's Bible Commentary* Vol. 6 Frank Gaebelein, ed., Zondervan's House (Grand Rapids, Mich.) 1981 pg. 113
454 John Martin, "Isaiah," *The Bible Knowledge Commentary : Old Testament* Victor Books (Wheaton, Ill.) 1985 pg. 1063
455 This would represent the number of converted Jews in Irsael, and is held by Bill Perkins who teaches this on tours of Petra.
456 Harrison. op. cit. pg. 132
457 See above.
458 West, op. cit. pg. 153
459 LaHaye, *Revelation* op.cit. pg. 229
460 Ibid. pg. 231
461 Ibid. pg. 229
462 Ibid. pg. 230
463 Ryrie, op. cit. pg. 101
464 Scott, op. cit. pg. 291
465 William Kelly, *Lectures on the Book of Revelation* G. Morrish (London, England) no copyright date pg. 318

466 Pentecost, *Things to Come* op. cit. pg. 299
467 Ibid.
468 Bruce Metzger, *Lexical Aids for Students of New Testament Greek* Theological Book Agency (Princeton, NJ) 1991 pg. 8
469 Hindson, *Revelation* op. cit. pg. 153
470 Ibid. pg. 154
471 Ibid. pg. 153
472 Ryrie, op. cit. pg. 101
473 Hindson, *Revelation* op. cit. pg. 153
474 Gundry, *First the Antichrist* op. cit. pg. 88
475 Ibid. pg. 89
476 Caird, op. cit. pg. 178
477 LaHaye, *Revelation* op.cit. pg. 230
478 Ibid.
479 Ibid. pg. 231
480 This is a popular argument throughout the ages stemming from the reluctance of most historicists to identify the earth with the entire globe. Earth was often taken as either the inhabited Roman earth or as Palestine.
481 Scott, op. cit. pg. 291
482 LaHaye, Revelation op.cit. pg. 229
483 Seiss, op. cit. pg. 162
484 Nee, op. cit. pg. 154?6?
485 Govett, Vol. II op. cit. pg. 266
486 Hindson, Revelation op. cit. pg. 153
487 Seiss, op. cit. pg. 351
488 Ibid.
489 Newell, op. cit. pg. 209
490 West, op. cit. pp. 406-407
491 Ibid. pg. 406
492 Tim LaHaye, ed., *Tim LaHaye Prophecy Study Bible* AMG Publishers (Chatanooga, TN) 2001 pg. 1520
493 Seiss, op. cit. pg. 352
494 Johnson, op. cit. pg. 539
495 Bloomfield, *All Things New* op. cit. pg. 201
496 Rosenthal, op. cit. pg. 74
497 Gundry, *First the Antichrist* op. cit. pg. 90
498 Ibid.
499 Lindsey, *New World* op. cit. pg. 187
500 Walvoord, *Revelation* op. cit. pg. 216
501 Ibid.
502 Govett, *Vol. II* op. cit. pg. 276
503 Bloomfield, *Key to Understanding Revelation* op. cit. pg. 244
504 Lindsey, *New World* op. cit. pg. 100
505 Clement of Rome, "An Ancient Homily," *The Apostolic Fathers* J.B Lighfoot & J.R. Harmer, eds., Baker Book House (Grand Rapids, Mich.) 1984 reprint pg. 92
506 Nicholas of Lyra, op. cit. pg. 107
507 Bale, op. cit. pg. 344
508 Mede, "Part II : The Interpretation" *Key to Revelation* op.cit. pp. 85-86
509 Newton, op.cit. pg. 287
510 Darby, *Collected Works Vol. 2* op. cit. pg. 26
511 Cf. Scott, op. cit. pp. 183-186
512 Cf. Ironside, op. cit. pg. 102
513 Bullinger, op. cit. pg. 307

514 Nicholas of Lyra, op. cit. pg. 107
515 Mede, "Part II : The Interpretation" *Key to Revelation* op.cit. pp. 85-86
516 Newton, op.cit. pg. 287
517 Darby, *Collected Works Vol. 2* op. cit. pg. 26
518 Ibid.
519 Scott, op. cit. pg. 186
520 Ironside, op. cit. pg. 102
521 Ibid.
522 E. W. Bullinger, *Figures of Speech Used in the Bible* Baker Book House (Grand Rapids, Mich.) 1968 pg. 735
523 Ibid. pp. 735-736
524 Harrison, op. cit. pg. 100
525 Pentecost, *Things to Come* op. cit. pg. 361
526 Newell, op.cit. pg. 124
527 Seiss, op. cit. pg. 193
528 Scott, op. cit. pg. 183
529 Swete, op. cit. pg. 110
530 Seiss, op. cit. pg. 192
531 Lindsey, *New World* op. cit. pg. 117
532 David Reagan, *Wrath and Glory* New Leaf Press (Green Forest, AR) 2001 pg. 71
533 Ladd, *Revelation* op. cit. pg. 126
534 Morris, op. cit. pg. 146
535 Robert Thomas, *Revelation 8-22 An Exegetical Commentary* Moody Press (Chicago, Ill.) 1992 pg. 15
536 Lang, op. cit. pg. 169
537 Bloomfield, *All Things New* op. cit. pg. 139
538 Seiss, op. cit. pg. 194
539 Nicholas of Lyra, op. cit. pg. 108
540 Darby, *Collected Works Vol. 2* op. cit. pg. 26
541 Mede, "Part II : The Interpretation" *Key to Revelation* op.cit. pg. 89
542 Darby, *Collected Works Vol. 2* op. cit. pg. 26
543 Pentecost, *Things to Come* op. cit. pg. 361
544 Bale, op. cit. pg. 345
545 Mede, "Part II : The Interpretation" *Key to Revelation* op.cit. pg. 90
546 Ibid.
547 Scott, op.cit. pp. 186-187
548 Ironside, op.cit. pg. 103
549 Harrison, op.cit. pg. 100
550 Lang, op.cit. pg. 169
551 Ibid.
552 Govett, *Vol. II* op. cit. pg. 336
553 Morris, op.cit. pg. 147
554 Lindsey, *New World* op. cit. pg. 118
555 Walvoord, *Revelation* op. cit. pg. 154
556 Thomas, *Revelation : 8-22* op.cit. pg. 19
557 Morris, op.cit. pg. 147
558 Ibid.
559 LaHaye, *Revelation* op.cit. pg. 167
560 Govett, *Vol. II* op. cit. pg. 338
561 Morris, op.cit. pg. 148
562 Cf. Nicholas of Lyra, op. cit. pg. 109
563 Mede, "Part II : The Interpretation" *Key to Revelation* op.cit. pp. 94-96
564 Newton, op.cit. pg. 287

565 Darby, *Collected Works Vol. 2* op. cit. pg. 27
566 Cf. Harrison, op. cit. pg. 100
567 Cf. Walvoord, *Revelation* op. cit. pg. 155
568 Lindsey, *New World* op. cit. pg. 120
569 Cf. Bale, op. cit. pg. 346
570 Thomas, *Revelation : 8-22* op.cit. pg. 21
571 Darby, *Collected Works Vol. 2* op. cit. pg. 27
572 Scott, op. cit. pg. 190
573 Ironside, op. cit. pg. 104
574 Ibid.
575 Ibid.
576 Lang, op. cit. pg. 170
577 Harrison, op. cit. pg. 100
578   It might be argued that the verse could be translated either "it" or "he," but the lack of a personal pronoun, as in 9:1, indicates that the noun, star, should not be taken outside of its normal usage.
579 Seiss, op. cit. pg. 196
580 Thomas, *Revelation : 8-22* op.cit. pg. 21
581 Seiss, op. cit. pg. 196
582 Lindsey, *New World* op. cit. pg. 120
583 Seiss, op. cit. pg. 197
584 "Collision Course," *Dallas Morning News* March 12, 1998 pp. A1
585 Ibid.
586 Jay Pasachoff, *Contemporary Astronomy* Saunders College Publishing (New York, NY) 1989 pg. 422
587 "Collision Course," *Dallas Morning News* March 12, 1998 pp. A11
588 www.cnn.com/TECH/space/9803/12/asteroid/
589 Ibid.
590 Ibid.
591 Pentecost, *Things to Come* op. cit. pg. 362
592 Ephraem the Syrian, *Trumpet Sounds* op. cit. pg. 113
593 Cf. Nicholas of Lyra, op. cit. pg. 110
594 Mede, "Part II : The Interpretation" *Key to Revelation* op.cit. pg. 97
595 Newton, op.cit. pg. 290
596 Cf. Scott, op.cit. pp. 190-191
597 Ironside, op.cit. pg. 104
598 Darby, *Collected Works Vol. 2* op. cit. pg. 27
599 Scott, op.cit. pp. 190-191
600 Pentecost, *Things to Come* op.cit. pg. 362
601 Darby, *Collected Works Vol. 2* op. cit. pg. 26
602 Scott, op. cit. pg. 184
603 Pentecost, *Things to Come* op. cit. pg. 361
604 Darby, *Collected Works Vol. 2* op. cit. pg. 26
605 Ironside, op. cit. pg. 103
606 Scott, op. cit. pg. 186
607 Ironside, op. cit. pg. 102
608 Scott, op. cit. pp. 186-187
609 Ironside, op. cit. pg. 104
610 Harrison, op. cit. pg. 100
611 Darby, *Collected Works Vol. 2* op. cit. pg. 26
612 Pentecost, *Things to Come* op. cit. pg. 361
613 Darby, *Collected Works Vol. 2* op. cit. pg. 26
614 Scott, op. cit. pg. 189

615 Harrison, op. cit. pg. 100
616 Pentecost, *Things to Come* op. cit. pg. 362
617 Scott, op. cit. pg. 190
618 Harrison, op. cit. pg. 100
619 Pentecost, *Things to Come* op. cit. pg. 362
620 Darby, *Collected Works Vol. 2* op. cit. pg. 27
621 Scott, op. cit. pp. 190-191
622 Harrison, op. cit. pg. 100
623 Pentecost, *Things to Come* op. cit. pg. 362
624 Seiss, op. cit. pg. 197
625 Govett, *Vol. II* op. cit. pg. 356
626 Ryrie, op. cit. pg. 59
627 Cf. Lactantius, *Ante-Nicene Fathers Vol. 7* op. cit. pp. 213-214
628 Walvoord, *Revelation* op. cit. pg. 156
629 Swete, op. cit. pg. 113
630 Mounce, op. cit. pg. 188
631 Newell, op. cit. pg. 126
632 Lindsey, *New World* op. cit. pg. 120
633 www.cnn.com/TECH/space/9803/12/asteroid/
634 Burr, op. cit. pg. 166
635 Nicholas of Lyra, op. cit. pg. 113
636 Mede, "Part II : The Interpretation" *Key to Revelation* op.cit. pp. 100-102
637 Newton, op. cit. pg. 293
638 Darby, *Collected Works Vol. 2* op. cit. pg. 28
639 Ibid. pg. 29
640 Scott, op. cit. pg. 204
641 Bullinger, *Revelation* op. cit. pg. 318
642 Mede, "Part II : The Interpretation" *Key to Revelation* op.cit. pg. 99
643 Matthew Henry, *Matthew Henry's Commentary on the Whole Bible, Vol. 6 Acts to Revelation,* Hendrickson Publishers 1991 ed. pg. 928
644 Matthew Poole, *A Commentary on the Holy Bible, Vol. III* Hendrickson Publishers pg. 971
645 Mede, "Part II : The Interpretation" *Key to Revelation* op.cit. pp. 100-102
646 Bullinger, *Revelation* op. cit. pg. 316
647 Govett, *Vol. II* op. cit. pg. 373
648 Seiss, op. cit. pg. 204
649 Bloomfield, *All Things New* op. cit. pg. 143
650 Ibid.
651 Morris, op. cit. pg. 156
652 Ironside, op. cit. pg. 107
653 Nee, op. cit. pg. 108
654 Scott, op. cit. pg. 202 Technically, this is true, but most believe there is a dual prophetic meaning in Isaiah. The king of Babylon is, thus, being compared to Satan in his fall.
655 Ibid. pp. 202-203
656 Ibid. pg. 206
657 Govett, *Vol. II* op. cit. pg. 377
658 Ladd, *Revelation* op. cit. pg. 131
659 Bloomfield, *All Things New* op. cit. pg. 144
660 Cf. Henry, *Commentary Vol. 6* op. cit. pg. 929
661 Lindsey, *New World* op. cit. pg. 124
662 Ibid. pg. 126
663 Hindson, op. cit. pg. 109
664 LaHaye, *Revelation* op.cit. pg. 171
665 Darby, *Collected Works Vol. 2* op. cit. pg. 28

666 Seiss, op. cit. pg. 208
667 Morris, op. cit. pg. 164
668 Bullinger, *Revelation* op. cit. pg. 322
669 Nee, op. cit. pg. 108
670 Seiss, op. cit. pg. 206
671 Govett, *Vol. II* op. cit. pg. 413
672 For a discussion of this controversial subject the reader is referred to John Walvoord, *Daniel: The Key to Prophetic Revelation* Moody Press (Chicago, Ill.) 1971 and John Whitcomb, *Daniel* BMH Books (Winona Lake, IN) 1985.
673 Pentecost, *Things to Come* op. cit. pg. 362
674 Cf. Thomas, *Revelation : 8-22* op.cit. pg. 43
675 Morris, op. cit. pp. 167-168
676 Johnson, op. cit. pg. 494
677 Cf. Scott, op. cit. pg. 210; Newell, op. cit. pg. 133; & LaHaye, *Revelation* op. cit. pg. 174
678 Victorinus, *Ante-Nicene Fathers Vol. 7* op. cit. pg. 352
679 Ibid.
680 Swete, op. cit. pg. 122
681 West, op. cit. pg. 408
682 Ladd, *Revelation* op. cit. pg. 137
683 Walvoord, *Revelation* op. cit. pg. 166
684 Lindsey, *New World* op. cit. pg. 128
685 Lang, op. cit. pg. 175
686 Bullinger, *Revelation* op. cit. pg. 330
687 Ryrie does "lean" towards the demonic army. Ryrie, op. cit. pg. 75
688 Nee, op. cit. pg. 110
689 Harrison, op. cit. pg. 102
690 Darby, *Collected Works Vol. 1* op. cit. pg. 191
691 Ironside, op. cit. pg. 114
692 Seiss, op. cit. pg. 219
693 Ironside, op. cit. pg. 114
694 Walvoord, *Revelation* op. cit. pg. 167
695 Lindsey, *New World* op. cit. pg. 129
696 First suggsested by Joseph Mede, the idea is repeated by Matthew Henry (Henry, *Commentary Vol. 6* op. cit. pg. 929)
697 Poole, *Commentary Vol. 3* op. cit. pg. 973
698 Ibid.
699 Pentecost, *Things to Come* op. cit. pg. 340
700 Many believe Joel 1 and 2 to be parallel passages to these last two trumpets.
701 Cf. Thayer, op. cit. & Warren C. Trenchard, *Complete Vocabulary Guide to the Greek New Testament* Zondervan Publishers (Grand Rapids, Mich.) 1998
702 G. H. Pember, *The Antichrist, Babylon, and the Coming of the Kingdom* Schoettle Publishing (Miami Springs, FL) 1988 ed. pg. 22
703 Morris, op. cit. pg. 246
704 J. Michael Hiel, "Asia's Armageddon Army," William T. James, ed., *Piercing the Future* Nelson Walker Publishers (Beaton, Ark.) 2000 pg. 116
705 Combs, *Daniel* op. cit. pg. 34
706 Cf. Daniel 10:1
707 Ibid. pp. 34-35
708 Thomas Martin, *Ancient Greece* Yale University Press (New York, NY) 1996 pg. 199
709 Walvoord, *Every Prophecy* op. cit. pp. 265-266
710 Walvoord, *Daniel* op. cit. pp. 66-67
711 Cf. Harold Scanlin, *The Dead Sea Scroll & Modern Translations of the Old Testament* Tyndale House (Wheaton, Ill.) 1993

712 Even a number of amillennialists agree with premillennialists on this matter. This was also the view held by the ancient Jews and the Essenes of the Qumran community.

713 Cf. Josephus, "Antiquities of the Jews," *Complete Works* op. cit. pg. 227

714 Including my own dissertation. See David Criswell, *She Who Restores the Roman Empire* Iuniverse (Lincoln, NE) 2002

715 Combs, op. cit. pg. 37

716 Bloomfield, *End of Days* op. cit. pg. 91

717 Geoffrey King, *Daniel* William Eerdmans (Grand Rapids, Mich.) 1966 pp. 72-73

718 James Viscount Bryce, *The Holy Roman Empire* MacMillan & Co. (London, England) 1950 pg. 25

719 J. B. Bury, *The Invasion of Europe by the Barbarians* W. W. Norton & Co. (New York, NY) 1967 pg. 170

720 Cf. John Julius Norwich, *A Short History of Byzantium* Vintage Books (New York, NY) 1997

721 Cf. Augustine, *City of God* Modern Library (New York, NY) 1993 ed.

722 Seiss, op. cit. pg. 323

723 Philip Goodman, *The Assyrian Connection* Prescott Press (Lafayette, LA) 1993 pg. 79

724 Trenchard, op. cit. pg. 82

725 William Mounce, *Basis of Biblical Greek* Zondervan Publishing (Grand Rapids, MICH) 1993 pg. 431

726 Once my brother began an argument as to whether or not our home state of Texas had any mountains. Since we were in the middle of Big Bend National Park with its mountains I inadvertently laughed only to draw his ire. He stated they those were but large "hills."

727 Henry, op. cit. pg. 336

728 Thayer, op. cit. pg. 104

729 Trenchard, op. cit. pg. 184

730 Froom, op. cit. pg. 159

731 Pember, op. cit. pg. 68

732 Goodman, op. cit. pg. 77

733 Cf. Zoch, *Ancient Rome* op. cit. pg. 25   Interestingly enough, even before Rome had truly encompassed seven hills the ancient Romans celebrated a festival of "Septimontium" which means the festival of Seven Hills (H.H. Scullard, *A History of the Roman World* Routledge Press (New York, NY) 1997 ed. from the 1935 orig. Ed. pg. 45)

734 Victorinus, *Ante-Nicene Fathers Vol. 7* op. cit. pg. 358

735 Ibid.

736 Caird, op. cit. pg. 217

737 Nee, op. cit. pg. 194

738 Cf. Suetonius, *Lives of the Twelve Caesars* trans. Robert Graves, Rain Publishers (New York, NY) 1957

739 Joachim as cited in McGinn, op. cit. pg. 136. Also see Burr, op. cit. pg. 135

740 Attempts to argue that Revelation was written in the reign of Nero do not help either. Even preterists, who believe Revelation to be historical allegory, cannot make Nero the seventh head, nor Domitian.

741 Scott, op. cit. pg. 344

742 George Peters, *The Theocratic Kingdom Vol. 2* Kregel Publications (Grand Rapids, Mich.) 1884 pg. 643

743 Ibid.

744 Cf. the reign of Sulla in H. H. Scullard, *From the Gracchi to Nero* Routledge (New York, NY) 1959

745 Peters, *Theocratic Kingdom Vol. 2* op. cit. pg. 694

746 Bullinger, *Revelation* op. cit. pg. 519

747 Seiss, op. cit. pg. 323

748 Lang, op. cit. pg. 267

749 Harrison, op. cit. pg. 134

750 Ibid. pg. 174

751 Randall Price, *The Stones Cry Out* Harvest House (Eugene, OR) 1997 pg. 83

752 An empire consist of two or more kingdoms united under a single banner.

753 Uriah was a Hittite. Since he was well respected and fought for Israel, it is unlikely that the Hittite were bitter enemies of Israel.

754 H. L. Wilmington, *The King is Coming* Tyndale House (Wheaton, Ill.) 1984 pp. 96-97

755 Another reason I favor the view is that I had believed it the natural interpretation before seeing that it was accepted by others. I did not learn this view from commentaries or from teachers, but from the Bible itself. Only after formulating a similar view did I learn that others had come across this as well. This lends itself to the perspicuity of Scripture and the veracity of the theory.

756 Bullinger, *Revelation* op. cit. pg. 534

757 Ibid. He argues that the king who "is" is intended from the perspective of the future. Hence, the sixth king is said to be future.

758 Burr, op. cit. pg. 134

759 Richard Buckingham, *Tudor Apocalypse* Sutton Courtenay Press (Oxford, UK) 1978 pg. 261

760 Bale, op. cit. pg. 407

761 Hippolytus, *Ante-Nicene Fathers Vol. V* op. cit. pg. 214

762 For a more complete discussion of this theory see Appendix F.

763 Peters, *Theocratic Kingdom Vol. 2* op. cit. pg. 700

764 Cf. Peters, *Theocratic Kingdom Vol. 2* op. cit. pg. 679

765 Adso of Montier, op. cit. pg. 90

766 Irenaeus, "Against Heresies," *Ante-Nicene Fathers Vol. 1* op. cit. pg. 555

767 Darby, *Collected Works Vol. 1* op. cit. pp. 44 & 51

768 Peters, *Theocratic Kingdom Vol. 2* op. cit. pg. 754

769 West, op. cit. pg. 215

770 Peters, *Theocratic Kingdom Vol. 2* op. cit. pg. 694

771 Ibid. pg. 647

772 Hippolytus, *Ante-Nicene Fathers Vol. V* op. cit. pg. 214

773 Ibid.

774 Bloomfield, *Key to Understanding Revelation* op. cit. pg. 232

775 Darby, *Collected Works Vol. 1* op. cit. pg. 218

776 Darby, *Collected Works Vol. 2* op. cit. pg. 59

777 West, op. cit. pg. 215

778 Pentecost, *Things to Come* op. cit. pg. 338

779 Ibid.

780 Ibid.

781 According to the pagan historian Suetonius, Nero wanted fire to consume the earth. His destruction of Rome by fire was incomplete, and the people feared he would return to try again. Years after his death, many cult leaders claimed to be Nero and used his name to wield great power over their followers. Cf. Suetonius, *Lives of the Twelve Caesars* translated by Robert Graves, Rain Publishers (New York, NY) 1957

782 Victorinus, *Ante-Nicene Fathers Vol. 7* op. cit. pg. 358

783 Bloomfield, *All Things New* op. cit. pg. 190

784 Peters, *Theocratic Kingdom Vol. 2* op. cit. pg. 680

785 Ibid.

786 Ibid.

787 Lang, op. cit. pg. 225

788 Van Kampen, op. cit. pp. 113-115

789 Lang, op. cit. pg. 223

790 Nee, op. cit. pg. 149

791 Caird, op. cit. pg. 218

792 Ibid. pg. 175

793 By "second generation disciple" I mean that he was the disciple of Polycarp who was, in turn, the disciple of the apostle John himself.
794 Irenaeus, *The Ante-Nicene Fathers Vol. I* op. cit. pg. 554
795 Hippolytus, "Fragments from Commentaries," *Ante-Nicene Fathers Vol. V* op. cit. pg. 186
796 Poole, *Commentary Vol. II* op. cit. pg. 817
797 Pentecost, "Daniel," *The Bible Knowledge Commentary* op. cit. pg. 1335
798 C. I. Scofield, *What Do The Prophets Say?* The Gospel Hour (Greenville, SC) 1918 pg. 67 & 150
799 Irenaeus, op. cit. pg. 553
800 Anderson, *The Coming Prince* op. cit. pg. 40
801 Peters, *Theocratic Kingdom Vol. 2* op. cit. pg. 671
802 Henry, *Commentary Vol. 4* op. cit. pg. 809
803 Bloomfield, op. cit. pg. 92
804 Mede, "Part II : The Interpretation" *Key to Revelation* op.cit. pp. 92
805 Newton, op. cit. pg. 101
806 Anderson, *The Coming Prince* op. cit. op. cit. pg. 40
807 Darby, *Collected Works Vol. 1* op. cit. pg. 243
808 McGinn, op. cit. pg. 137
809 Mede, "Part II : The Interpretation" *Key to Revelation* op.cit. pp. 5
810 Peters, *Theocratic Kingdom Vol. 2* op. cit. pg. 754
811 Lindsey, *Planet Earth* op. cit. pg. 83
812 Hal Lindsey, *The 1980s : Countdown to Armageddon* Bantam Books (New York, NY) 1981 pg. 103
813 Goodman, op. cit. pg. 33
814 Ibid. pp. 37-40
815 Darby, *Collected Works Vol. 1* op. cit. pg. 244
816 Nee, op. cit. pg. 171
817 Brookes, *Till He Come* op. cit. pg. 70
818 Pember, op. cit. pg. 21
819 Ironside, op. cit. pg. 149
820 Pember, op. cit. pg. 21
821 Irenaeus, *The Ante-Nicene Fathers Vol. I* op. cit. pg. 553
822 Hippolytus, *Ante-Nicene Fathers Vol. V* op. cit. pg. 178, 184, 209, & 215
823 Pember, op. cit. pp. 33-34
824 Lang, op. cit. pg. 222
825 Goodman, op. cit. pg. 45
826 Pentecost, *Things to Come* op. cit. pg. 325
827 LaHaye, *Revelation* op. cit. pg. 217
828 Hippolytus, *Ante-Nicene Fathers Vol. V* op. cit. pg. 178, 209, & 215
829 Ibid. pg. 215
830 Ladd, *Revelation* op. cit. pg. 183
831 Johnson, op. cit. pg. 529
832 Walvoord, *Revelation* op. cit. pg. 205
833 Govett, *Vol. III* op. cit. pg. 152
834 Seiss, op. cit. pg. 334
835 Newton, op. cit. pg. 273
836 Mounce, *Revelation* op. cit. pg. 258
837 Harrison, op. cit. pg. 138
838 Cf. Govett, *Vol. III* op. cit. pg. 152
839 Darby, *Collected Works Vol. 2* op. cit. pg. 42
840 Lindsey, *New World* op. cit. pg. 180
841 Ironside, op. cit. pg. 162
842 Pentecost, *Things to Come* op. cit. pg. 336

843 Hippolytus, *Ante-Nicene Fathers Vol. V* op. cit. pg. 214
844 Scofield, *Prophecy Made Plain* op. cit. pg. 130
845 Lindsey, *New World* op. cit. pg. 168
846 Scofield, *Prophecy Made Plain* op. cit. pg. 130
847 Adso of Montier, op. cit. pg. 96
848 Froom, op. cit. pg. 706
849 Mede, "Part II : The Interpretation" *Key to Revelation* op.cit. pg. 4
850 Ironside, op. cit. pp. 156-164
851 Darby, *Collected Works Vol. 1* op. cit. pg. 44
852 Ibid. pg. 237
853 Ibid. pp. 224-225
854 Ibid. pg. 224
855 West, op. cit. pg. 215
856 Ibid. pg. 118
857 Ibid.
858 Scott, op. cit. pg. 198
859 Ibid. pg. 280
860 Ibid. pg. 201
861 Ibid. pg. 279
862 Ibid. pg. 201
863 Victorinus, *Ante-Nicene Fathers Vol. 7* op. cit. pg. 358
864 Mounce, *Revelation* op. cit. pg. 169
865 Ephraem, op. cit. pg. 112
866 Ironside, op. cit. pg. 91
867 Froom, op. cit. pg. 554
868 Adso of Montier, op. cit. pg. 90
869 Nicholas of Lyra, op. cit. pg. 97
870 Froom, op. cit. pg. 657
871 Howard M. Sachar, *A History of Israel* Alfred A. Knopf (New York, NY) 2003 ed. pg. 173
872 Price, *Coming Temple* op. cit. pg. 478
873 William Gesenius, *Gesenius' Hebrew Grammar* Clarendon Press (Oxford, England) 1910 pg. 399
874 Walvoord, *Every Prophecy* op. cit. pp. 267-271
875 West, op. cit. pg. 118
876 Pentecost, *Things to Come* op. cit. pg. 338
877 Peters, *Theocratic Kingdom Vol. 2* op. cit. pg. 692
878 Froom, op. cit. pg. 709
879 Ibid. pg. 706
880 Burr, op. cit. pg. 146
881 Nicholas of Lyra, op. cit. pg. 152
882 Bale, op. cit. pg. 500
883 Ladd, *Revelation* op. cit. pg. 183
884 Peters, *Theocratic Kingdom Vol. 2* op. cit. pg. 684
885 Nee, op. cit. pg. 146
886 Ibid.
887 Lang, op. cit. pg. 225
888 Govett, *Vol. III* op. cit. pg. 158
889 Seiss, op. cit. pg. 334
890 Ibid.
891 Ibid.
892 Ibid. pg. 335
893 Ibid.
894 Cf. Pember, op. cit. pg. 51

895 Seiss, op. cit. pg. 332
896 Lidnsey, *New World* op. cit. pg. 109
897 Pentecost, *Things to Come* op. cit. pg. 336
898 Thomas, *Revelation : 8-22* op.cit. pg. 173
899 LaHaye, *Revelation* op.cit. pg. 223
900 Ryrie, op. cit. pg. 98
901 Harrison, op. cit. pg. 138
902 Victorinus, *Ante-Nicene Fathers Vol. 7* op. cit. pg. 357
903 Seiss, op. cit. pg. 342
904 Raphael Patai, *The Messiah Texts* Wayne State University Press (Detroit, Mich.) 1979 pg. 23
905 Ibid. pg. 27
906 Nicholas of Lyra, op. cit. pg. 152
907 Mede, "Part II : The Interpretation" *Key to Revelation* op.cit. pg. 5
908 Ironside, op. cit. pg. 162
909 Rosenthal, op. cit. pg. 174
910 Seiss, op. cit. pp. 344-345
911 Govett, *Vol. III* op. cit. pp. 174-179
912 Pember, op. cit. pg. 46
913 Ibid. pg. 45
914 Bullinger, *Revelation* op. cit. pg. 437
915 Jack Van Impe, *2001 : On the Edge of Eternity* Word Pulishing (Dallas, TX) 1996 pg. 123
916 Govett, *Vol. III* op. cit. pg. 169
917 Darby, *Collected Works Vol. 1* op. cit. pg. 224
918 Walvoord, *Revelation* op. cit. pg. 207
919 Seiss, op. cit. pg. 345
920 Scott, op. cit. pg. 283
921 Morris, op. cit. pg. 251
922 Walvoord, *Every Prophecy* op. cit. pg. 586
923 Ryrie, op. cit. pg. 98
924 Van Kampen, op. cit. pg. 239
925 Ibid. pp. 239-242
926 Young, *New Testament Greek* op. cit. pg. 137
927 Ibid.
928 Ephraem the Syrian, op. cit. pg. 114
929 Adso of Montier, op. cit. pg. 96
930 Ryrie, op. cit. pg. 99
931 Swete, op. cit. pg. 173
932 Govett, *Vol. III* op. cit. pg. 210
933 Lindsey, *New World* op. cit. pp. 182-183
934 Scott, op. cit. pg. 283
935 Lindsey, *New World* op. cit. pp. 182-183
936 If enacted, Obama's health care law will take a giant leap toward this by requiring all citizens to be catalogued.
937 Morris, op. cit. pg. 252
938 Chuck Missler, "Your Future and Technology," *Piercing the Future* op. cit. pp. 191-192
939 Young, *New Testament Greek* op. cit. pg. 137
940 Darby, *Collected Works Vol. 1* op. cit. pg. 225
941 LaHaye, *Revelation* op. cit. pg. 227
942 Lang, op. cit. pg. 226
943 Ladd, *Revelation* op. cit. pg. 186
944 Morris, op. cit. pg. 256
945 Harrison, op. cit. pg. 140
946 Pember, op. cit. pg. 31

947 Nee, op. cit. pg. 149
948 Govett, *Vol. III* op. cit. pg. 225
949 Swete, op. cit. pg. 176
950 Ehud Ben-Yehuda & David Weinstein, eds., *Ben-Yehuda's English-Hebrew Dictionary* Pocket Books (New York, NY) 1961
951 Shimon Zilberman, ed., *The Compact English-Hebrew Dictionary* Zilberman (Jerusalem, Israel) 1997
952 Mounce, *Biblical Greek* op. cit. pg. 31
953 Ibid. pg. 32
954 Caird, op. cit. pg. 175
955 Mounce, *Revelation* op. cit. pg. 264
956 Cf. Frederic M. Wheelock, *Wheelock's Latin* R. A. LaFleur, ed., Harper Collins Publishers (New York, NY) 1995 ed.
957 Bruce M. Metzger, *A Textual Commentary on the Greek New Testament* United Bible Society (Stuttgart, Germany) 1971 pg. 676
958 Irenaeus, op. cit. pp. 557-559
959 Peters, *Theocratic Kingdom Vol. 2* op. cit. pg. 706
960 Irenaeus, op. cit. pg. 559
961 Hippolytus, op. cit. pg. 215
962 Victorinus, op. cit. pg. 356
963 Newton, op. cit. pg. 278
964 Govett, *Vol. III* op. cit. pg. 223
965 Irenaeus, op. cit. pg. 559
966 Victorinus, op. cit. pg. 356
967 Ibid.
968 Mounce, *Revelation* op. cit. pg. 263
969 Harrison, op. cit. pg. 140
970 Alexander Hislop, *The Two Babylons* Loizeaux Brothers (Neptune, NJ) 1916 pg. 269
971 Govett, *Vol. III* op. cit. pg. 223
972 Bloomfield, *All Things New* op. cit. pg. 200
973 Irenaeus, op. cit. pg. 557
974 Ibid. pg. 558
975 Bullinger, op. cit. pg. 440
976 Harrison, op. cit. pg. 111
977 Criswell, *She Who Restores* op. cit. pg. 109
978 Olmstead, *History of Assyria* op. cit. pg. 600
979 Criswell, *She Who Restores* op. cit. pg. 96-130
980 Chris Scarre, *Chronicle of the Roman Emperors* Thames and Hudson (London, England) 1997 pg. 52
981 Nicholas of Lyra, op. cit. pg. 156
982 Harrison, op. cit. pg. 107
983 Ephraem the Syrian, op. cit. pg. 114
984 Govett, *Vol. III* op. cit. pg. 223
985 Morris, op. cit. pg. 256
986 Cf. Bullinger, op. cit. pg. 441
987 Lindsey, *New World* op. cit. pg. 184
988 Swete, op. cit. pg. 176
989 Bloomfield, *All Things New* op. cit. pg. 199
990 Johnson, op. cit. pg. 535
991 Scott, op. cit. pg. 287
992 Hippolytus, op. cit. pg. 215
993 Darby, *Collected Works Vol. 2* op. cit. pg. 43
994 Darby, *Collected Works Vol. 1* op. cit. pg. 225

995 LaHaye, *Revelation* op. cit. pg. 227
996 Thomas, *Revelation : 8-22* op.cit. pg. 185
997 Anderson, *Coming Prince* op. cit. pg. 271
998 Bale, op. cit. pg. 478
999 Nicholas of Lyra, op. cit. pg. 177
1000 Bale, op. cit. pg. 478
1001 Mede, "Part II : The Interpretation" *Key to Revelation* op.cit. pg. 114
1002 Darby, *Collected Works Vol. 2* op. cit. pg. 53
1003 Ibid. pg. 26
1004 Scott, op. cit. pg. 323
1005 Ironside, op. cit. pg. 180
1006 Ibid. pg. 179
1007 Walvoord, *Revelation*, op. cit. pg. 232
1008 Seiss, op. cit. pg. 371
1009 Lindsey, *New World*, op. cit. pg. 204
1010 Walvoord, *Revelation*, op. cit. pg. 232
1011 Morris, op. cit. pg. 296
1012 Nicholas of Lyra, op. cit. pp. 178-179
1013 Bale, op. cit. pg. 479
1014 Mede, "Part II : The Interpretation" *Key to Revelation* op.cit. pg. 115
1015 Darby, *Collected Works Vol. 2* op. cit. pp. 53-54
1016 Scott, op. cit. pg. 324
1017 Ironside, op. cit. pg. 180
1018 Pentecost, *Things to Come* op. cit. pg. 363
1019 Ibid.
1020 Seiss, op. cit. pg. 372
1021 Ibid.
1022 Ibid.
1023 Newell, op. cit. pg. 248
1024 Lang, op. cit. pg. 249
1025 Nee, op. cit. pg. 170
1026 Walvoord, *Revelation* op. cit. pg. 233
1027 Ryrie, op. cit. pg. 112
1028 Thomas, *Revelation : 8-22* op.cit. pg. 250
1029 LaHaye, *Revelation* op. cit. pg. 251
1030 Swete, op. cit. pg. 201
1031 Lindsey, *New World* op. cit. pg. 205
1032 Morris, op. cit. pg. 298
1033 Lactantius, *Ante-Nicene Fathers Vol. 7* op. cit. pg. 213
1034 Nicholas of Lyra, op. cit. pg. 179
1035 Bale, op. cit. pg. 481
1036 Mede, "Part II : The Interpretation" *Key to Revelation* op.cit. pg. 116
1037 Scott, op. cit. pg. 325
1038 Pentecost, *Things to Come* op. cit. pg. 363
1039 Nicholas of Lyra, op. cit. pp. 180-181
1040 Bale, op. cit. pg. 482
1041 Mede, "Part II : The Interpretation" *Key to Revelation* op.cit. pg. 116
1042 Darby, *Collected Works Vol. 2* op. cit. pg. 54
1043 Darby, *Collected Works Vol. 1* op. cit. pg. 236
1044 Ibid.
1045 Thayer, op. cit. pg. 86
1046 Lang, op. cit. pg. 249
1047 LaHaye, *Revelation* op. cit. pg. 253

1048 Walvoord, *Revelation* op. cit. pg. 234
1049 Lindsey, *New World* op. cit. pg. 207
1050 Anderson, *Visions* op. cit. pp. 177-178
1051 Johnson, op. cit. pg. 550
1052 Bale, op. cit. pg. 482
1053 Scott, op. cit. pg. 330
1054 Pentecost, *Things to Come* op. cit. pg. 363
1055 Ironside, op. cit. pg. 181
1056 Swete, op. cit. pg. 204
1057 Mede, "Part II : The Interpretation" *Key to Revelation* op.cit. pg. 118
1058 Nicholas of Lyra, op. cit. pp. 181-182
1059 Seiss, op. cit. pg. 373
1060 Darby, *Collected Works Vol. 2* op. cit. pg. 55
1061 Seiss, op. cit. pg. 376
1062 Ibid. pg. 377
1063 Nicholas of Lyra, op. cit. pg. 183
1064 Bale, op. cit. pg. 484
1065 Darby, *Collected Works Vol. 1* op. cit. pg. 236
1066 Lactantius, *Ante-Nicene Fathers Vol. 7* op. cit. pg. 213
1067 Mede, "Part II : The Interpretation" *Key to Revelation* op.cit. pg. 119
1068 Swete, op. cit. pg. 205
1069 Pember, op. cit. pg. 118
1070 Lindsey, *New World* op. cit. pg. 208
1071 Seiss, op. cit. pg. 377
1072 Bloomfield, *All Things New* op. cit. pg. 213
1073 Bullinger, *Revelation* op. cit. pg. 487
1074 Govett, *Vol. III* op. cit. pg. 404
1075 Ibid.
1076 LaHaye, *Revelation* op. cit. pg. 256
1077 Alexander, "Ezekiel," *Expositor's Commentary Vol. 6* op. cit. pg. 891
1078 Walvoord, *Every Prophecy* op. cit. pg. 178
1079 Ibid.
1080 Ibid. pg. 329
1081 David Peterson & Kent Richards, *Interpreting Hebrew Poetry* Fortress Press (Minneapolis, MN) 1992 pg. 24
1082 Kenneth Barker, "Zechariah," *Expositor's Commentary Vol. 7* op. cit. pg. 672
1083 Walvoord, *Every Prophecy* op. cit. pg. 98
1084 Lindsey, *New World* op. cit. pg. 208
1085 Pentecost, *Things to Come* op. cit. pg. 340
1086 Gundry, *First the Antichrist* op. cit. pg. 28
1087 Trenchard, op. cit. pg. 142
1088 Thayer, op. cit. pg. 394
1089 Pentecost, *Things to Come* op. cit. pg. 340
1090 West, op. cit. pg. 408
1091 Ironside, op. cit. pg. 183
1092 Hindson, *Revelation* op. cit. pg. 170
1093 Nicholas of Lyra, op. cit. pg. 183
1094 Swete, op. cit. pg. 208
1095 Walvoord, *Revelation* op. cit. pg. 236
1096 Ibid. pg. 239
1097 Morris, op. cit. pg. 311
1098 Seiss, op. cit. pg. 378
1099 Govett, *Vol. III* op. cit. pg. 406

1100 Ladd, *Revelation* op. cit. pg. 213
1101 Ibid. pg. 215
1102 Ibid. pg. 213
1103 Walvoord, *Revelation* op. cit. pg. 238
1104 LaHaye, *Revelation* op. cit. pg. 257
1105 Ibid. pg. 310
1106 Roy Metz, class notes from Criswell College
1107 Walvoord, *Revelation* op. cit. pg. 238
1108 Cf. Bullinger, *Revelation* op. cit. pg. 490
1109 Mounce, *Revelation* op. cit. pg. 302
1110 Cited in Walvoord, *Revelation* op. cit. pg. 239
1111 Cf. Seiss, op. cit. pg. 380
1112 Ladd, *Revelation* op. cit. pg. 216
1113 Ibid.
1114 Bloomfield, *Key to Understanding Revelation* op. cit. pg. 261
1115 Hindson, *Revelation* op. cit. pg. 171
1116 Pember, op. cit. pg. 55
1117 West, op. cit. pg. 408
1118 Hindson, *Revelation* op. cit. pg. 159
1119 Johnson, op. cit. pp. 550-552
1120 LaHaye, *Revelation* op. cit. pg. 256
1121 Walvoord, *Revelation* op. cit. pg. 237
1122 Ibid.
1123 Nicholas of Lyra, op. cit. pp. 187-189
1124 Bale, op. cit. pg. 489
1125 Mede, "Part II : The Interpretation" *Key to Revelation* op.cit. pp. 120-121
1126 Darby, *Collected Works Vol. 1* op. cit. pg. 238
1127 Pentecost, *Things to Come* op. cit. pg. 364
1128 LaHaye, *Revlation* op. cit. pg. 258
1129 Walvoord, *Revelation* op. cit. pg. 240
1130 Morris, op. cit. pg. 319
1131 Seiss, op. cit. pg. 381
1132 Ibid.
1133 Ibid.
1134 Lactantius, *Ante-Nicene Fathers Vol. 7* op. cit. pg. 214
1135 Scott, op. cit. pg. 338-339
1136 LaHaye, *Revelation* op. cit. pg. 258
1137 Creation scientists believe that this was case when the waters formed the current oceans. The scientific arguments go far beyond the scopes of this book but the author maybe referred to John Whitcomb, Jr. and Henry Morris, *The Genesis Flood* Presbyterian & Reformed (Phillipsburg, NJ) 1961.
1138 Lindsey, *New World* op. cit. pg. 213
1139 Morris, op. cit. pg. 321
1140 Ibid.
1141 Ibid.
1142 Cf. Seiss, op. cit. pp. 405-415
1143 Ibid.
1144 Trenchard, op. cit. pg. 139
1145 Thomas, *Revelation : 8-22* op.cit. pg. 283
1146 Arnold G. Fruchtenbaum, *Israelology* Ariel Ministries (Tustin, CA) 1996 pg. 296
1147 Cf. Mede, "Part II : The Interpretation" *Key to Revelation* op.cit. pg. 107
1148 Swete, op. cit. pg. 183
1149 Jerome, *Patrologue*, as cited in Froom, op. cit. pg. 449

1150 James A. Brooks & Carlton L. Winberry, *Syntax of New Testament Greek* University Press of America (Lanham, MD) 1979 pg. 70

1151 Joachim, *Exposito* as cited in Froom, op. cit. pg. 706

1152 John Foxe, *Acts and Monuments of the Christian Church Vol. 1* Religious Tract Socity (Picadilly, England) 1841 ed. pg. 445

1153 Nicholas of Lyra, op. cit. pp. 193-194

1154 Criswell, *Restores Roman Empire* op. cit. pg. 68

1155 Seiss, op. cit. pg. 392

1156 Tex Marrs, *Dark Secrets of the New Age* Crossway Books (Westchester, Ill.) 1987 pg. 204

1157 Froom, op. cit. pg. 880

1158 Anderson, *The Coming Prince* op. cit. pg. 299

1159 Peters, *Theocratic Kingdom Vol. 2* op. cit. pg. 684

1160 Constance Cumbey, *The Hidden Dangers of the Rainbow* Huntington House (Shreveport, LA) 1983 pg. 80

1161 Hislop, op. cit. pp. 12-18

1162 Gordan Laing, *Survivals of the Roman Religion: Our Debt to Greece and Rome* Cooper Square Press (New York, NY) 1963 pg. 92

1163 Kenneth Scott Latourette, *A History of Christianity : Volume 1* Harper & Row (New York, NY) 1953 (1975 ed.) pg. 209

1164 Lewis Farnell, *Greece and Babylon* T & T Clark (Edinburgh, England) 1911 pg. viii

1165 Ibid. pg. 166

1166 Ibid. pg. 167

1167 Ibid. pp. 93-94

1168 Robert Turcan, *The Cults of the Roman Empire* Blackwell (Cambridge, MA) 1992 pg. 74

1169 J.N.D. Kelly, *Oxford Dictionary of Popes* Oxford Press (Oxford, England) 1986 pg. 97

1170 Austin Flannery, ed., *Vatican Council II* "Sacred Liturgy," The Constitution on the Sacred Liturgy, no. 47 Costello Publications (Northport, NY)

1171 Loraine Boettner, *Roman Catholicism* Presbyterian & Reformed (Phillipsburg, NJ) 1962 pg. 169

1172 *Catechism of the Catholic Church* United States Catholic Conference (USA) 1994 paragraph 1414

1173 Criswell, *She Who Restores*, op. cit. pp. 101-132

1174 Cf. Morris Jastrow, *Religious Belief and Practice in Babylonia and Assyria* Benjamin Blom. Inc. (New York, NY) 1911 pg. 353

1175 Walvoord, *Revelation* op. cit. pg. 245

1176 Ryrie, op. cit. pg. 118

1177 Scofield, *Prophecy Made Plain* op. cit. pg. 129

1178 Dave Hunt, *Global Peace and the Rise of Antichrist* Harvest House (Eugene, Or.) 1990 pg. 131

1179 Scofield, *What Do The Prophets Say?* op. cit. pg. 157

1180 Ibid. pp. 153-154

1181 Ibid. pg. 154

1182 Ladd, *Revelation* op. cit. pg. 222

1183 Walvoord, *Revelation* op. cit. pg. 245

1184 Scott, op. cit. pg. 343

1185 Ibid. pg. 244

1186 Scott, op. cit. pg. 147

1187 Zoch, op. cit. pg. 25

1188 Froom, op. cit. pg. 160

1189 Seiss, op. cit. pg. 407

1190 Walvoord, *Revelation* op. cit. pg. 218

1191 Bullinger, *The Apocalypse* op. cit. pg. 553

1192 So Joachim called it. Froom, op. cit. pg. 697

1193 Charles H. Dyer, with Angela Hunt, *The Rise of Babylon : Sign of the End Times* Tyndale House (Wheaton, Ill.) 1991

1194 G. H. Pember believes that the institution of slavery will have to be revived in the last days in order that this prophecy may be literal (Pember, op. cit. pg. 115).

1195 Dyer, op. cit. pg. 210

1196 Seiss, op. cit. pg. 400

1197 Bullinger, *The Apocalypse* op. cit. pg. 553

1198 Ibid.

1199 Donald Grey Barnhouse, *Revelation* Zondervan Press (Grand Rapids, Mich.) 1971 pg. 334

1200 *Baedeker Italy* Macmillan Travel (New York, NY) 1996 pg. 377

1201 Ironside, op. cit. pg. 307

1202 Thomas, *Revelation 8 – 22* op. cit. pg. 289

1203 Barclay Newman, ed., *A Concise Greek-English Dictionary of the New Testament* United Bible Societies (Stuttgart, Germany) 1971 pg. 72

1204 Thomas, *Revelation 8 – 22* op. cit. pg. 283

1205 Goodman, op. cit. pg. 165

1206 Ibid. pg. 131

1207 Ibid. pg. 130

1208 Ibid. pg. 31

1209 Henry, *Commentary Vol. 4* op. cit. pg. 65

1210 Poole, *Commentary Vol. II* op. cit. pg. 357

1211 Dyer, op. cit. pg. 19

1212 Bullinger, *Revelation* op. cit. pg. 551

1213 Ibid.

1214 Ibid. pg. 130

1215 Georges Roux, *Ancient Iraq* Penguin Books (New York, NY) 1992 ed. pg. 413

1216 Ibid.

1217 Ibid.

1218 Ibid.

1219 Ibid.

1220 Ibid.

1221 Ibid. pg. 416

1222 Ibid.

1223 Ibid.

1224 Ibid. pg. 414

1225 Even Charles Dyer quotes Dio on this matter (Dyer, *Rise of Babylon* op. cit. pg. 128).

1226 Roux, op. cit. pg. 396

1227 Ibid. pg. 390

1228 Ibid.

1229 Robert William Rogers, *A History of Babylonia and Assyria Vol. 1* Eaton & Mains (New York, NY) 1901 pp. 3-5

1230 Roux, op. cit. pg. 421

1231 Dyer, op. cit. pg. 126

1232 Dyer, op. cit. pp. 208-210

1233 Tommy Ice, "Back to the Future," *When Trumpet Sounds* op. cit. pg. 19

1234 Brookes, *Till He Come* op. cit. pg. 95

1235 Morris, op. cit. pg. 349

1236 Roux, op. cit. pg. 390

1237 Goodman, op. cit. pg. 172

1238 Seiss, op. cit. pg. 407

1239 Walvoord, *Revelation* op. cit. pg. 218

1240 Barnhouse, op. cit. pg. 332

1241 Ottoman as cited by Ibid. pg. 333

1242 Goodman, op. cit. pg. 173
1243 Ibid. pp. 172-173
1244 Pember, op. cit. pg. 73
1245 James Montgomery Boice, *Foundations of the Christian Faith* InterVarsity Press (Leicester, England) 1986 pg. 476
1246 Cf. Millard Erickson, *Christian Theology* Baker Books (Grand Rapids, Mich.) 1992 ed. pg. 361
1247 Johnson, op. cit. pg. 554
1248 Thomas, *Revelation 8 – 22* op. cit. pg. 313
1249 Justin Martyr, *Ante-Nicene Fathers Vol. 1* op. cit. pg. 240
1250 Irenaeus, op. cit. pg. 565
1251 West, op. cit. pg. 1
1252 Ibid. pg. 2
1253 Ibid. pg. 382
1254 Cited in Ibid. pg. 388
1255 Cited in Ibid. pg. 381
1256 Peters, *Theocratic Kingdom Vol. 2* op. cit. pg. 260
1257 Stanley Grenz, *The Millennial Maze* Intervarsity Press (Downers Grove, Ill.) 1992 pp. 42-43
1258 West, op. cit. pg. 297
1259 Ibid. pg. 299
1260 Ibid.
1261 Ibid. pg. 296
1262 Quoted in Ibid. pg. 319
1263 Charles Ryrie, *Dispensationalism* Moody Press (Chicago, Ill.) 1995 pg. 56
1264 Govett, *Apocalypse*, op. cit. pp. 506-508
1265 Ladd, *Revelation* op. cit. pg. 269
1266 See discussion of Isaiah 65 below.
1267 Cf. Jobe Martin, *The Evolution of a Creationist* 2nd Ed., Biblical Discipleship Ministries (Rockwall, TX) 2002 pp. 163-168
1268 Whitcomb & Morris, *The Genesis Flood* op. cit. pg. 240
1269 Cf. Ibid.
1270 William Corlis, *Ancient Man : A Handbook of Puzzling Artifacts* The Sourcebook Project (Glen Arm, MD) 1978 pp. 234-235
1271 C. f. John C. Whitcomb, *The World That Perished* Baker Book House (Grand Rapids, Mich.) 1988 pp. 77-80
1272 Morris, *Revelation* op. cit. pg. 409
1273 Ibid. pg. 410
1274 Scott, op. cit. pg. 405
1275 LaHaye, *Revelation* op. cit. pg. 345-346
1276 Pentecost, *Things to Come* op. cit. pp. 65-115
1277 Brookes, *Maranatha* op. cit. pg. 396
1278 Merrill Unger, "The Temple Vision of Ezekiel," *Bibliotheca Sacra* 105 (October, 1948) pp. 427-428
1279 Price, *Coming Temple* op. cit. pg. 528
1280 George Peters, *The Theocratic Kingdom Vol. 3* Kregel Publications (Grand Rapids, Mich.) 1884 pg. 572
1281 Newell, op. cit. pg. 323
1282 Walvoord, *The Millennial Kingdom* op. cit. pg. 301
1283 Pentecost, *Things to Come* op. cit. pg. 500
1284 Peters, *Theocratic Kingdom Vol. 2* op. cit. pg. 570
1285 Ibid. pg. 604
1286 Price, *Coming Temple* op. cit. pg. 524
1287 Peters, *Theocratic Kingdom Vol. 2* op. cit. pg. 589

1288 Alexander, "Ezekiel," *Expositor's Commentary Vol. 6* op. cit. pg. 943
1289 Ibid.
1290 Price, *Coming Temple* op. cit. pg. 513
1291 Alexander, "Ezekiel," *Expositor's Commentary Vol. 6* op. cit. pg. 943
1292 Arno Gaebelein, *The Prophet Ezekiel* Our Hope Press (New York, NY) 1918 pg. 272
1293 Jon Levenson, *Theology of the Program of Restoring of Ezekiel 40-48* Scholars Press (Missoula, MT) 1976 pg. 45
1294 Alexander, "Ezekiel," *Expositor's Commentary Vol. 6* op. cit. pg. 947
1295 Price, *Coming Temple* op. cit. pg. 533
1296 Edmund Clowney, "The Final Temple," Carl Henry, ed., *Prophecy in the Making* Creation House (Carol Stream, IL) 1971 pg. 85
1297 West, op. cit. pg. 430
1298 Pentecost, *Things to Come* op. cit. pg. 525
1299 Ibid. pg. 530
1300 Randall Price devoted many pages to the discussion of Millennial sacrifices. See Price, *Coming Temple* op. cit. pp. 542-557
1301 Summers, op. cit. pg. 7
1302 Clement of Rome, "Ancient Homily," *The Apostolic Fathers* op. cit. 1984 pg. 92
1303 Bloomfield, *Key to Revelation* op. cit. pg. 299
1304 Seiss, op. cit. pg. 484
1305 Ibid.
1306 Ibid. pg. 485
1307 Bloomfield, *Key to Revelation* op. cit. pg. 300
1308 Seiss, op. cit. pg. 485
1309 Henry Morris, *The Biblical Basis for Modern Science* Baker Book House (Grand Rapids, Mich.) 1984 pg. 226
1310 Harrison, op. cit. pg. 205
1311 Morris, *Revelation Record* op. cit. pg. 436
1312 Brookes, , *Marantha* op. cit. pg. 528
1313 Henry, *Commentary Vol. 6* op. cit. pg. 633
1314 Poole, *Commentary Vol. III* op. cit. pg. 746
1315 There are several theories as to why the Thessalonians were questioning the issues of the second coming and the resurrection but none of them can be proven. It may have been that they were taught, as some allegorists teach today, that the second coming of Christ was nothing more than the coming of the Holy Spirit. All that is clear is that they had been told that "the Day of the Lord has already come" (2 Thessalonians 2:2).
1316 Cited in Poole, *Commentary Vol. 3* op. cit. pg. 746
1317 Hal Lindsey refers to the second coming as occuring in separate "stages." Hal Lindsey, *The Rapture* Bantam Books (New York, NY) 1983 pg. 188.
1318 There have been a few scholars and church fathers that believe that Revelation only covers a 3½ year time frame and at least one who believes it covers a 10½ years period. This is be discussed in Appendix D.
1319 Dave MacPherson argued that Margaret MacDonald, who lived in the early 19th Century, was the inventor. See Thomas Ice, "MacDonald, Margaret," Mal Couch, ed., *Dictionary of Premillennial Theology* Kregel Publications, Grand Rapids, Mich. (1996).
1320 Grant Jeffrey, "A PreTrib Rapture Statement in the Early Medieval Church," *Trumpet Sounds* op. cit. pg. 111
1321 Ibid. pp. 120-121
1322 Tommy Ice, "Morgan Edwards: A Pre-Darby Rapturist," http://www.conservativeonline.org/journals/1_1_journal/Morgan_Edwards.htm (8/29/02)
1323 This is somewhat misleading. The truth was never "lost," but the writings of the true believers throughout the dark ages were suppressed leaving new believers to have to start "from scratch" in formulating the more complex doctrines of the Scriptures.

1324 Henry, *Commentary Vol. 6* op. cit. pg. 633
1325 Ibid.
1326 Poole, *Commentary Vol. 3* op. cit. pg. 746
1327 Larry Crutchfield, "The Blessed Hope and the Tribulation in the Apostolic Fathers," *When Trumpet Sounds* op. cit. pp. 85-103
1328 Poole, *Commentary Vol. 3* op. cit. pg. 746
1329 Ibid. This idea is one which had many times crossed my mind before ever having heard of the Augustinian interpretation.
1330 Ibid. pg. 598
1331 Thayer, op. cit. pg. 28
1332 Ibid.
1333 Trenchard, op. cit. pg. 157
1334 Quoted in Kellogg, *Are Premillennialists Right?* op. cit. pg. 69
1335 Erickson, op. cit. pg. 1186
1336 Ed Hindson, *Earth's Final Hour* Harvest House (Eugene, OR) 1999 pp. 114-115
1337 Thomas Ice, "Why the Rapture and second coming are Separate Events," *Pretrib Answers To Posttrib* (Aug-Sept. 1994) pg. 2
1338 Paul Feinberg, *The Rapture : Pre- Mid- or Posttribulational?* Zondervan Publ. (Grand Rapids, Mich.) 1984 pg. 59
1339 Robert Gundry, *The Church and the Tribulation* Zondervan Publishing (Grand Rapids, Mich.) 1973 pp. 44-45
1340 Rosenthal, op. cit. pg. 2
1341 J.C. Fenton, *Saint Matthew* Westminister Press (Philadelphia, Penn.) 1963 pp. 379-380
1342 Gerald B. Stanton, "The Doctrine of Imminence : Is It Biblical?" *When Trumpet Sounds* op. cit. pg. 231
1343 Gerald B. Stanton, *Kept from the Hour* Schoettle Publ. (Haysville, NC) 1991 pg.119
1344 Larry Crutchfield, "The Early church fathers and the Foundations of Dispensationalism," *The Conservative Theological Journal* Volume 3. No. 9 (August 1999) pp. 198-199
1345 Personal notes from a Pretrib Bible Conference 2001.
1346 Anderson, *Visions* op. cit. pg. 12
1347 Cf. David Criswell, *The Rise of the Holy Roman Empire* Fortress Adonai Press (North Charleston, SC) 2003
1348 Mal Couch, *The Hope of Christ's Return* AMG Publishers (Chattanooga, Tn.) 2001 pg. 133
1349 Cf. Mal Couch, *When Trumpet Sounds* op. cit. pg. 2
1350 Larry Crutchfield, "Blessed Hope," *When Trumpet Sounds* op. cit. pg. 91
1351 Paul Alexander, *The Byzantine Apocalyptic Tradition* University of California Press (Berkley, Ca.) 1985 pg. 210-211
1352 Millard Erickson, *Contemporary Options in Eschatology* Baker Books (Grand Rapids, Mich.) 1977 pg. 112
1353 Douglas Moo, *The Rapture* op. cit. pg. 98
1354 Class notes from Tyndale Seminary.
1355 Moo, op. cit. pg. 209
1356 Richard Young, *Intermediate New Testament Greek* Broadman & Holman (Nashville, Tenn.) 1994 pg. 183
1357 Moo, op. cit. pg. 194
1358 Cf. Mal Couch, *A Biblical Theology of the Church* Kregel Publishing (Grand Rapids, Mich.) 1999
1359 Class notes from Criswell Bible College.
1360 Gundry, *First the Antichrist* op. cit. pg. 128
1361 Mounce, op. cit. pp. 354-359
1362 John Fok, "The Rapture of the Church," http://home.hkstar.com/~johnfok1/Eschatology/4.htm (1/24/02)
1363 Harrison, op. cit. pg. 117

1364 Ibid. pg. 154
1365 Archer, *The Rapture* op. cit. pg. 107
1366 Ibid. pp. 139-142
1367 Ibid. pp. 140
1368   J.F. Strombeck, *First the Rapture* Kregel Publications (Grand Rapids, Mich.) 1992 reprint (orig. 1950) pg, 108
1369 Ibid. pg, 109
1370 Ibid.
1371 Harrison, op. cit. pg. 117
1372 H. Wayne House, "Apostasia in 2 Thessolonians 2:3 : Apostasy or Rapture?" *When Trumpet Sounds* op. cit. pg. 263
1373 Irenaeus, op. cit. pp. 553-554
1374 Ibid. pg. 267
1375 Cf. personal notes from Dave Hunt lecture.
1376 Seiss, op. cit. pg. 315
1377 House, *When Trumpet Sounds* op. cit. pg. 270
1378 Trenchard, op. cit. pg. 166
1379 Thayer, op. cit. pg. 67
1380 House, *When Trumpet Sounds* op. cit. pg. 280
1381 Ibid. pg. 280
1382   Arnold Fruchtenbaum, "Is There A Pre-Wrath Rapture?" *When Trumpet Sounds* op. cit. pg. 382
1383 Rosenthal, op. cit. pg. 140
1384 Ibid. pg. 137
1385 Ibid. pg. 169
1386 Ibid. pg. 165
1387 Ibid. pg. 171
1388 Ibid. pg. 139
1389 Fruchtenbaum, *When Trumpet Sounds* op. cit. pg. 389
1390 Rosenthal, op. cit. pg. 111
1391 Bloomfield, *All Things New* op. cit. pg. 205
1392 Bloomfield, *End of Days* op. cit. pg. 177
1393 Ibid. pg. 38
1394 Cf. Rosenthal, op. cit. pg. 147
1395 Cf. Ibid. pp. 109-110
1396 Ibid. pg. 111
1397 Ibid. pg. 110
1398 Ibid. pg. 147
1399 Ibid. pg. 158
1400 Ibid. pg. 159
1401 Ibid. pg. 194
1402 Van Kampen, op. cit. pg. 363
1403 Rosenthal, op. cit. pg. 182
1404 Ibid. pg. 185
1405 Ibid.
1406 Van Kampen, op. cit. pg. 342
1407 Rosenthal, op. cit. pg. 110
1408 Ibid. pg. 174
1409 John Fok, "The Rapture of the Church," http://home.hkstar.com/~johnfok1/Eschatology/4.htm (1/24/02)
1410 Fruchtenbaum, *When Trumpet Sounds* op. cit. pg. 386
1411 Rosenthal, op. cit. pg. 143
1412 Ibid. pg. 165

1413 Ibid. pg. 193
1414 Ibid. pp. 189-190
1415 Ibid. pg. 216
1416 Ibid.
1417 Ibid. pg. 217
1418 It is impossible to determine exactly how much time either Rosenthal or Van Kampen place between the Rapture and the Return but their charts each show the Rapture roughly two thirds of the way into the Tribulation.
1419 Johnson, op. cit. pg. 454
1420 Ladd, *Revelation* op. cit. pg. 62
1421 Johnson, op. cit. pg. 453
1422 It has since come to my attention that this man has since become a born again Messianic Jew.
1423 It will be demonstrated in a later chapter that the seals may not begin until after the abomination of desolation. If this is so, and an amended midtribulational view were to take this into account, then that view would also be able to accurately account for the idea of "peace and safety" preceding the Day of the Lord.
1424 Although there is a close relation between the Day of the Lord and rapture, it is not logical to take signs of the first and offer them as proof second. The relationship between the two does not necessarily mean that they occur at the same time, as is often assumed.
1425 Rosenthal, op. cit. pg. 265
1426 Walvoord, *Millennial Kingdom* op. cit. pp. 276-295
1427 Irenaeus, op. cit. pp. 565-566
1428 Ibid. pg. 567
1429 Posttribulationists consider this a strength for their view, but posttribulationism has already been refuted.
1430 Lindsey, *Rapture* op. cit. pg. 190
1431 Ibid. pg. 291
1432 Ibid. pg. 290
1433 Lindsey, *New World Coming* op. cit. pg. 259
1434 Ibid.
1435 Ibid.
1436 LaHaye, *Revelation* op. cit. pp. 325-326
1437 Nee, op. cit. pg. 222
1438 Scott, op. cit. pg. 403
1439 Walvoord, *Millennial Kingdom* op. cit. pg. 280
1440 Ibid.
1441 Ibid. pg. 281
1442 Ibid. pg. 332
1443 Ryrie, *Revelation* op. cit. pg. 126
1444 Nee, op. cit. pg. 91
1445 Ironside, op. cit. pg. 133
1446 Walvoord, *Millennial Kingdom* op. cit. pg. 284
1447 Ibid.
1448 Ibid.
1449 Peters, *Theocratic Kingdom Vol. 2* op. cit. pp. 372-384
1450 Seiss, op. cit. pg. 479
1451 Bloomfield, *All Things New* op. cit. pg. 245
1452 Victorinus, op. cit. pg. 359
1453 Walvoord, *Revelation* op. cit. pg. 306
1454 Seiss also offers the opinion that the reading of the Codex Sinaiticus is correct (Seiss, op. cit. pg. 480). That text reads, not that "all were judged," but that "all were condemned." In fact, there is no translation which reads this for a very good reason. The Sinaiticus uses the word "κατακρίθησαν," which is based on the same root as "ἐκρίθησαν" and is most certainly an

accidental gloss. No translation accepts this as the authentic reading. Moreover, there is a single other text which supports this reading. It is an obvious gloss.

1455 Ladd, *Revelation* op. cit. pg. 270
1456 Ibid.
1457 Mounce, *Revelation* op. cit. pg. 365
1458 Walvoord, *Millennial Kingdom* op. cit. pg. 284
1459 Peters, *Theocratic Kingdom Vol. 2* op. cit. pp. 372-384
1460 Scott, op. cit. pg. 403
1461 Ibid.
1462 Ladd, *Revelation* op. cit. pg. 270
1463 Lactantius, op. cit. pp. 216-217
1464 Seiss, op. cit. pg. 480
1465 Whether or not antediluvian believers are promised a part in the Millennial Kingdom never actually addressed by dispensationalists. Doubtless, this is because the Bible does not give great details and the dispensation, and there is much confusion in those details. I prefer to believe that they will share the promises of the saints of Israel, but there is a legitimate question as to what role non-Israeli/pre-Christian believers will play in the Millennium, if any at all. I also believe that those who have never heard the gospel will be judged at this time and those who would have accepted the gospel will be vindicated. The rest will be condemned by their works.
1466 Bullinger, *Revelation* op. cit. pg. 642
1467 Nicholas of Lyra, op. cit. pg. 125
1468 Darby, *Collected Works Vol. 1* op. cit. pg. 193
1469 Harrison, op. cit. pg. 111
1470 Ladd, *Revelation* op. cit. pg. 147
1471 Ironside, op. cit. pg. 120
1472 Ibid. pg. 123
1473 Bloomfield, *All Things New* op. cit. pg. 156
1474 Ibid. pg. 153
1475 Ibid. pg. 156
1476 Scott, op. cit. pg. 225
1477 Walvoord, *Revelation* op. cit. pg. 174
1478 Mounce, *Revelation* op. cit. pg. 214
1479 Ibid.
1480 LaHaye, *Revelation* op. cit. pg. 181
1481 Walvoord, *Revelation* op. cit. pg. 174
1482 Thomas, *Revelation : 8-22* op.cit. pg. 73
1483 Lindsey, *New World Coming* op. cit. pg. 146
1484 Victorinus, op. cit. pg. 353
1485 LaHaye, *Revelation* op. cit. pg. 181
1486 Bill Martin & Bill Perkins, "The Second Witness ... Who Is He?", *Digging Deeper Bible Studies* no date pg. 21
1487 Mounce, *Revelation* op. cit. pg. 209
1488 Swete, op. cit. pg. 128
1489 LaHaye, *Revelation* op. cit. pg. 179
1490 Thomas, *Revelation : 8-22* op.cit. pg. 65
1491 Morris, *Revelation* op. cit. pg. 178
1492 Victorinus, op. cit. pg. 353
1493 Harrison, op. cit. pg. 107
1494 Ibid. pg. 108
1495 Walvoord, *Revelation* op. cit. pg. 171
1496 Morris, *Revelation* op. cit. pp. 179-180
1497 Mounce, *Revelation* op. cit. pg. 209
1498 Ironside, op. cit. pg. 120

1499 Ladd, *Revelation* op. cit. pg. 173
1500 Bloomfield, *All Things New* op. cit. pg. 154
1501 Thomas, *Revelation : 8-22* op.cit. pg. 65
1502 Bullinger, *Revelation* op. cit. pg. 355
1503 Nee, op. cit. pg. 118
1504 Nee, op. cit. pg. 119
1505 Morris, *Revelation* op. cit. pg. 193
1506 Bloomfield, *All Things New* op. cit. pg. 163
1507 Lindsey, *New World Coming* op. cit. pg. 155
1508 Penetcost, *Things to Come* op. cit. pg. 46
1509 Seiss, op. cit. pg. 248
1510 Hippolytus, op. cit. pp. 182 & 213
1511 Victorinus, op. cit. pg. 354
1512 Tertullian, op. cit. pg. 561
1513 Ephraem the Syrian, op. cit. pg. 114
1514 Seiss, op. cit. pp. 248-249
1515 "History of Jospeh the Carpenter," *Ante-Nicene Fathers Vol. VIII* Alexander Roberts & James Donaldson, eds. William B. Eerdmans Publishers (Grand Rapids, Mich.) 1990 pg. 394
1516 "Gospel of Nicodemus," *Ante-Nicene Fathers Vol. VIII* Alexander Roberts & James Donaldson, eds. William B. Eerdmans Publishers (Grand Rapids, Mich.) 1990 pg. 437 & 452
1517 Adso of Montier, op. cit. pg. 94
1518 Joachim, *Apocalyptic Spirituality* op. cit. pg. 140
1519 D'Olivi, op. cit. pp. 168
1520 Nicholas of Lyra, op. cit. pg. 128
1521 West, op. cit. pg. 400
1522 Seiss, op. cit. pg. 255
1523 Peters, *Theocratic Kingdom Vol. 2* op. cit. pg. 87
1524 Bullinger, *Revelation* op. cit. pg. 356
1525 Govett, *Vol. II* op. cit. pg. 225-250
1526 Scofield, *Prophecy Made Plain* op. cit. pg. 129
1527 Harrison, op. cit. pp. 114-115
1528 Lang, op. cit. pg. 185
1529 Bloomfield, *All Things New* op. cit. pg. 160
1530 Nee, op. cit. pg. 118
1531 Lindsey, *New World Coming* op. cit. pp. 152-154
1532 Gundry, *First the Antichrist* op. cit. pg. 43
1533 Morris, *Revelation* op. cit. pg. 194
1534 Thomas, *Revelation : 8-22* op.cit. pg. 89
1535 Rosenthal, op.cit. pg. 156
1536 Van Kampen, op.cit. pg. 369
1537 LaHaye, *Revelation* op.cit. pg. 186
1538 Seiss, op. cit. pg. 248
1539 Nee, op. cit. pg. 118
1540 Morris, *Revelation* op. cit. pg. 194
1541 Seiss, op. cit. pg. 244
1542 Morris, *Revelation* op. cit. pg. 194
1543 Bloomfield, *All Things New* op. cit. pg. 160
1544 Cf. LaHaye, *Revelation* op.cit. pp. 186-187
1545 Lindsey, *New World Coming* op. cit. pg. 154
1546 Ibid.
1547 Lindsey, *New World Coming* op. cit. pg. 153
1548 Scott, op. cit. pg. 230
1549 Scott, op. cit. pg. 232

1550 Ladd, *Revelation* op. cit. pg. 134
1551 Mede, "Part II : The Interpretation" *Key to Revelation* op.cit. pg. 7
1552 Ironside, op. cit. pg. 131
1553 Josephus, "Antiquities of the Jews," *Complete Works* op. cit. pg. 197
1554 Tertullian, op. cit. pp. 227-228
1555 Nee, op. cit. pg. 118
1556 Seiss, op. cit. pg. 254
1557 Ibid.
1558 LaHaye, *Revelation* op.cit. pg. 186
1559 Morris, *Revelation* op. cit. pg. 195
1560 Hippolytus, op. cit. pp. 182 & 213
1561 Tertullian, op. cit. pp. 227-228
1562 Ephraem the Syrian, op. cit. pg. 114
1563 "History of Jospeh the Carpenter," *Ante-Nicene Fathers Vol. VIII* op. cit. pg. 394
1564 "Gospel of Nicodemus," *Ante-Nicene Fathers Vol. VIII* op. cit. pg. 437 & 452
1565 Cf. Seiss, op. cit. pg. 252
1566 Adso of Montier, op. cit. pg. 94
1567 Nicholas of Lyra, op. cit. pg. 128
1568 Govett, *Vol. II* op. cit. pg. 225-250
1569 Seiss, op. cit. pg. 255
1570 Lang, op. cit. pg. 185
1571 Nee, op. cit. pg. 118
1572 Morris, *Revelation* op. cit. pg. 194
1573 Victorinus, op. cit. pg. 354
1574 Johnson, op. cit. pg. 504
1575 West, op. cit. pg. 400
1576 Scofield, *Prophecy Made Plain* op. cit. pg. 129
1577 Harrison, op. cit. pp. 114-115
1578 Bloomfield, *All Things New* op. cit. pg. 160
1579 Lindsey, *New World Coming* op. cit. pp. 152-154
1580 Gundry, *First the Antichrist* op. cit. pg. 43
1581 Thomas, *Revelation : 8-22* op.cit. pg. 89
1582 Van Kampen, op.cit. pg. 369
1583 LaHaye, *Revelation* op.cit. pp. 186-187
1584 Rosenthal, op.cit. pg. 156
1585 Lindsey, *New World Coming* op. cit. pg. 143
1586 Harrison, op. cit. pp. 114-115
1587 Rosenthal, op.cit. pg. 155
1588 Pentecost, *Things to Come* op. cit. pg. 308
1589 Walvoord, *Every Prophecy* op. cit. pg. 574
1590 Ladd, *Revelation* op. cit. pg. 155
1591 D'Olivi, op. cit. pp. 120-121
1592 Nicholas of Lyra, op. cit. pg. 128
1593 Victorinus, op. cit. pg. 354
1594 Martin, "The Second Witness," op. cit. pg. 21
1595 Ibid.
1596 Ibid.
1597 Ibid. pg. 20
1598 Victorinus, op. cit. pg. 354
1599 Mede, "Part II : The Interpretation" *Key to Revelation* op.cit. pg. 7
1600 Ibid. pp. 7-17
1601 Newton, op. cit. pp. 278-279
1602 Swete, op. cit. pg. 134

1603 Bale, op. cit. pg. 387
1604 Darby, *Collected Works Vol. 1* op. cit. pg. 197
1605 Darby, *Collected Works Vol. 2* op. cit. pg. 33
1606 Scott, op. cit. pg. 230
1607 Ironside, op. cit. pg. 131
1608 Caird, op. cit. pg. 134
1609 Mounce, *Revelation* op. cit. pg. 223
1610 Caird, op. cit. pg. 134
1611 George Peters is one of a handful who believes that the prophecy of Gog describes "the ravages of this last, great Antichrist," Peters, *Theocratic Kingdom Vol. 2* op. cit. pg. 709
1612 Josephus, "Antiquities of the Jews," *Complete Works* op. cit. pg. 31
1613 Quoted in Louis Bauman, *Russian Events in the Light of Bible Prophecy* The Balkiston (Philadelphia, Penn.) 1952 Cf. Lindsey, *Late Great Planet Earth* op. cit. pg. 53
1614 John Channon, *The Historical Atlas of Russia* Penguin Books (New York, NY) 1996 pg. 14
1615 Quoted in John Cummings, *The Destiny of Nations* Hurst & Blackette (London, England) 1864 Cf. Lindsey, *Late Great Planet Earth* op. cit. pg. 54
1616 Thomas Scott, Rector of Aston Standford, *The Holy Bible, with Explanatory Notes, Practical Observations, and Copious Marginal References* (London, England) 1828 comments on Ezekiel 38 as quoted in Dave Hunt, *Peace, Prosperity and the Coming Holocaust* Harvest House (Eugene, OR) 1983 pg 224
1617 William Gesenius, *Hebrew and Chaldee Lecicon* Baker Books (Grand Rapids, Mich) 1979 pg 516 #4902
1618 Josephus, "Antiquities of the Jews," *Complete Works* op. cit. pg. 31
1619 Walvoord, *Every Prophecy* op. cit. pg. 192
1620 Unger, op. cit. pg. 1120
1621 Cummings, op. cit. as cited in Lindsey, *Late Great Planet Earth* op. cit. pg. 52
1622 James Grant, *The End of Things* Darton and Co. (London, England) 1866 as quoted Ibid. pg 39
1623 Scott, op. cit. pg 16
1624 Josephus, "Antiquities of the Jews," *Complete Works* op. cit. pg. 31
1625 Pentecost, *Things to Come* op. cit. pg. 344
1626 Unger, op. cit. pg. 419
1627 Price, *Coming Temple* op. cit. pg. 454
1628 Ibid.
1629 Ibid. pg. 455
1630 Walvoord, *Every Prophecy* op. cit. pg. 194
1631 John Walvoord, *The Nations, Israel, and the Church in Prophecy* Zondervan Publishers (Grand Rapids, Mich.) 1988 ed. pg. 114
1632 Ibid. pg. 455
1633 Ice, "Back to the Future," *When Trumpet Sounds* op. cit. pg. 19
1634 Phillip Goodman, "Jerusalem's Earthshaking Northern Threat," William James, ed., *Prophecy at Ground Zero* Starburst Publishers (Lancaster, PA) 2002 pg. 52
1635 Ibid.
1636 There is no proof that the earthquake of the sixth seal occurs in Israel. Instead, it is associated with the Gentile nations (cf. Revelation 6).
1637 Based on information from the Geophysical Institute of Israel (http://www.gii.co.il/).
1638 Pentecost, *Things to Come* op. cit. pg. 347
1639 There is reason to believe that "last days" actually encompasses all the days between the first coming of Christ and the second coming (cf. Acts 2:17).
1640 Cf. Pentecost, *Things to Come* op. cit. pg. 355
1641 Alexander, "Ezekiel," *Expositor's Commentary Vol. 6* op. cit. pg. 939
1642 Ibid.
1643 Cf. Hunt, *Global Peace* op. cit.

1644 Alexander, "Ezekiel," *Expositor's Commentary Vol. 6* op. cit. pg. 939
1645 Ibid.
1646 Price, *Coming Temple* op. cit. pg. 454
1647 Ibid.
1648 Renald Showers, "Gog and Magog," Couch, *Dictionary of Premillennial Theology* op. cit. pg. 125
1649 Walvoord, *Every Prophecy* op. cit. pg. 197
1650 Price, *Coming Temple* op. cit. pg. 453
1651 Alexander, "Ezekiel," *Expositor's Commentary Vol. 6* op. cit. pg. 937
1652 Ibid. pp. 937-938
1653 Ibid. pg. 938
1654 West, op. cit. pg. 435
1655 Ibid.
1656 Bullinger, *Revelation* op. cit. pg. 637
1657 Charles Dyer, "Ezekiel," *Bible Knowledge Commentary* op. cit. pg. 1300
1658 Price, *Coming Temple* op. cit. pg. 453
1659 Pentecost, *Things to Come* op. cit. pg. 350
1660 Walvoord, *Every Prophecy* op. cit. pg. 191
1661 Pentecost, *Things to Come* op. cit. pg. 350
1662 Alexander, "Ezekiel," *Expositor's Commentary Vol. 6* op. cit. pg. 940
1663 Bullinger, *Revelation* op. cit. pg. 637
1664 Henry, *Commentary Vol. 4* op. cit. pg. 762
1665 Walvoord, *Nations, Israel, and the Church* op. cit. pg. 113
1666 Walvoord, *Every Prophecy* op. cit. pg. 193
1667 Ibid.
1668 Walvoord, *Nations, Israel, and the Church* op. cit. pg. 110
1669 Bullinger, *Revelation* op. cit. pg. 637
1670 Peters, *Theocratic Kingdom Vol. 2* op. cit. pg. 710
1671 See Peters, *Theocratic Kingdom Vol. 2* op. cit. pp. 670-683 for a discussion of the evolution of this theory.
1672 West, op. cit. pg. 161
1673 Joachim's historicism was actually a vast improvement over the purely allegorical amillennialism of Augustinianism, and was a first step back toward the return to a more literal interpretation.
1674 Froom, *Prophetic Faith Vol. 1* op. cit. pp. 703-705
1675 Ibid.
1676 Ibid.
1677 Ibid.
1678 Ibid.
1679 Ladd, *Revelation* op. cit. pg. 210
1680 Lindsey, *The Rapture* op. cit. pg. 108
1681 Ryrie, *Revelation* op. cit. pg. 65
1682 Seiss, op. cit. pg. 373
1683 Mede, "Part I," *Key to Revelation* op.cit. pg. 8
1684 Ibid. pg. 4
1685 Bill McMillon, *The Archaeology Handbook* John Wiley & Sons, Inc. (New York, NY) 1991 pg. 114
1686 Most archaeology uses relative dating, and not the overhyped, and often misleading, "absolute dating" which the media pretends is so accurate. Ibid. Also see Colin Renfrew & Paul Bahn, *Archaeology: Theories, Methods, & Practice* Thames & Hudson Ltd. (New York, NY) 1991.
1687 Cf. Unger, op. cit. pg. 332
1688 Peter A. Clayton, *Chronicle of the Pharaohs* Thames & Hudson (New York, NY) 1994 pg. 196

1689 West, op. cit. pg. 153
1690 Larry Crutchfield, "The Early Church Fathers and the Foundations of Dispensationalism Part V," *TheConservative Theological Journal* Vol. 3 # 8, April 1999 pg. 50
1691 Irenaeus, op. cit. pg. 554
1692 Hippolytus, op. cit. pg. 213
1693 Ibid. cit. pg. 184
1694 Irenaeus, op. cit. pg. 554
1695 Lactantius, op. cit. pg. 214
1696 Adso of Montier, op. cit. pg. 92
1697 West, op. cit. pg. 213, also see pp. 229, 234, & 390
1698 Scott, op. cit. pg. 9
1699 Bullinger, *Revelation* op. cit. pg. 368
1700 Scofield, *What Do The Prophets Say?* op. cit. pg. 152
1701 Ironside, op. cit. pg. 132
1702 Walvoord, *Revelation* op. cit. pg. 183
1703 Morris, *Revelation* op. cit. pg. 205
1704 LaHaye, *Revelation* op.cit. pg. 13
1705 West, op. cit. pg. 264
1706 Darby, *Collected Works Vol. 2* op. cit. pg. 194
1707 Ibid.
1708 Cf. Swete, op. cit.
1709 Morris, *Revelation* op. cit. pg. 205
1710 Bruce M. Metzger, *The Text of the New Testament* Oxford University Press (Oxford, England) 1992 pp. 8-15
1711 Mounce, *Revelation* op. cit. pg. 229
1712 Ladd, *Revelation* op. cit. pg. 160
1713 Thomas, *Revelation 8-22* op. cit. pg. 99
1714 Rosenthal, op. cit. pg. 174
1715 Darby, *Collected Works Vol. 1* op. cit. pg. 195
1716 Anderson, *Visions* op. cit. pg. 173
1717 Ryrie, *Revelation* op. cit. pg. 70
1718 Pentecost, *Things to Come* op. cit. pg. 187
1719 Merrill Tenney, *Interpreting Revelation* William B. Eerdmanns (Grand Rapids, Mich.) 1957 pg. 74
1720 Darby, *Collected Works Vol. 2* op. cit. pg. 20
1721 Anderson, *Visions* op. cit. pg. 173
1722 John McLean, "Chronology and Sequential Structure of John's Revelation," *Trumpet Sounds* op. cit. pg. 326
1723 Homer Ritchie, Omer Ritchie, & Lonnie Shipman, *Secrets of Prophecy Revealed* 21st Century Press (Springfield, Mo.) 2001 pg. 36
1724 D.A. Carson, "Matthew," *Expositor's Bible Commentary Vol. 8* op. cit. pg. 498
1725 *Fort Worth Star Telegram*, Novermber 23, 1988, A: 14
1726 Ritchie, Rtchie, & Shipman, op. cit. pg. 30
1727 Darby, *Collected Works Vol. 1* op. cit. pg. 195
1728 Anderson, *Visions* op. cit. pg. 173
1729 Tenney, *Interpreting Revelation* op. cit. pg. 74
1730 Pentecost, *Things to Come* op. cit. pg. 363
1731 Hunt actually says that he is unsure of the exact timing, but insist that the treaty of the anti-Christ will be followed by a period of peace. He is not sure when the peace will end but does acknowledge that the abomination of desolation will be the dramatic turning point in Revelation. From a personal letter to the author.
1732 Some dispute whether this prophecy is truly about the anti-Christ or Antiochus Epiphanes. See Walvoord, *Every Prophecy* op. cit. pg. 242

1733 Lindsey, *Rapture* op. cit. pg. 108
1734 Ibid. pg. 110
1735 Hunt, *Peace, Prosperity, & Holocaust* op. cit. pg. 30
1736 Harrison, op. cit. pg. 94
1737 Ibid. pg. 102
1738 Nee, op. cit. pg. 110
1739 Harrison, op. cit. pp. 217-218
1740 Ibid. pg. 220
1741 Ibid. pg. 221
1742 Bloomfield, *All Things New* op. cit. pg. 134
1743 Ibid. pg. 194
1744 Ibid. pg. 167
1745 Rosenthal, op.cit. pg. 109
1746 Ibid. pg. 111
1747 Kenneth McKinley, *The Chronology of Revelation* A dissertation for Dallas Theological Seminary May 1957 pg. 224
1748 Ibid. pg. 225
1749 LaHaye, *Revelation* op.cit. pg. 13
1750 Morris, *Revelation* op. cit. pg. 372
1751 Ibid. pg. 360
1752 Peters, *Theocratic Kingdom Vol. 2* op. cit. pg. 756
1753 Walvoord, *Revelation* op. cit. pg. 256
1754 Ibid. pg. 258
1755 Ibid. pg. 241
1756 LaHaye, *Revelation* op. cit. pg. 276
1757 Ibid. pg. 277
1758 Ibid.
1759 Walvoord, *Every Prophecy* op. cit. pg. 278
1760 Pentecost, "Daniel," *The Bible Knowledge Commentary* op. cit. pg. 1374
1761 Archer, "Daniel," *Expositor's Bible* op. cit. pg. 156
1762 Anderson, *Visions* op. cit. pg. 186
1763 Walvoord, *Every Prophecy* op. cit. pg. 278
1764 Miller, op. cit. pg. 325
1765 West, op. cit. pg. 294
1766 Rosenthal, op. cit. pg. 52
1767 Van Kampen, op. cit. pg. 365
1768 Ibid. pg. 369-398
1769 Whitcomb, *Daniel* op. cit. pg. 168
1770 Archer, "Daniel," *Expositor's Bible* op. cit. pg. 156
1771 Miller, op. cit. pg. 326
1772 West, op. cit. pg. 295
1773 Cf. Van Kampen, op. cit. pg. 369-398
1774 Whitcomb, *Daniel* op. cit. pg. 168
1775 Ibid. pg. 169
1776 Although a historicist, Mede agrees that Babylon's fall is contemporaneous with the challenge to the anti-Christ's authority at the end of 1260 days. Cf. Mede, "Part II," *Key to Revelation* op.cit. pg. 25
1777 Lindsey, *1980s* op. cit. pg. 12
1778 Duane Magnani, *The Watchtower Files* Bethany House (Minneapolis, MN) 1983 pg. 63
1779 Ibid.
1780 Cf. West, op. cit. pg. 161
1781 Froom, op. cit. pg. 714
1782 Olivi, op. cit. pg. 139

1783 Froom, op. cit. pg. 753
1784 Ibid. pg. 776
1785 Hindson, *Earth's Final Hour* op. cit. pg. 52
1786 Ibid. pg. 49
1787 Ibid. pg. 56
1788 Ibid. pg. 36
1789 Cf. Ibid.
1790 Crutchfield, *The Conservative Theological Journal* Vol. 3, No. 8 op. cit. pg. 34
1791 Lactantius, op. cit. pg. 211
1792 Hippolytus, op. cit. pg. 179
1793 Crutchfield, *The Conservative Theological Journal* Vol. 3, No. 9 op. cit. pp. 198-199
1794 Kennth Gentry Jr., *The Great Tribulation* op. cit. pp. 28-32
1795 Lindsey, *1980s* op. cit. pg. 12
1796 Trenchard, op. cit. pg. 135
1797 Ibid.
1798 West, op. cit. pg. 209
1799 Brookes, *Maranatha* op. cit. pp. 225-226
1800 Dave Hunt, *How Close Are We?* Harvest House (Eugene, OR) 1993 pg. 291
1801 Cf. Dave Hunt, *The Cult Explostion* Harvest House (Eugene, OR) 1980
1802 Cf. Bale, op. cit.
1803 Josephus, "Antiquities of the Jews," *Complete Works* op. cit. pg. 197
1804 West, op. cit. pg. 253
1805 Kellogg, *Are Premillennialists Right?* op. cit. pg. 9
1806 Latourette, op. cit. pg. 149
1807 Justo Gonzalez, *The Story of Christianity* Vol. 1 Harper Collins (New York, NY) 1984 pg. 79
1808 Ibid. pg. 80
1809 Robert Payne, *The Dream and the Tomb* Cooper Square Press (New York, NY) 2000 pg. 225
1810 Criswell, *Restores Roman Empire* op. cit. pp. 55-59
1811 Ibid.
1812 Kellogg, *Are Premillennialists Right?* op. cit. pg. 37
1813 Grenz, op. cit. pp. 68-69
1814 See Dave Hunt, *Whatever Happened to Heaven* Harvest House (Eugene, OR) 1988 for a full discussion of modern reconstructionism.
1815 David Ebaugh, *Monarch* Oct./Nov. 1986, pg. 3 as cited in Ibid. pg. 73
1816 Fruchtenbaum, *Israelology* op. cit. pg. 234
1817 Ladd, *Theology of the New Testament* op. cit. pg. 112
1818 Ibid. pg. 629
1819 Couch, *A Biblical Theology* op. cit. pg. 29
1820 Bernard Ramm, *Protestant Biblical Interpretation* Baker Book House (Grand Rapids, Mich.) 1982 pg. 11
1821 Ladd, *Theology of the New Testament* op. cit. pg. 111
1822 Ibid. pg. 584
1823 Pentecost, *Things to Come* op. cit. pg. 65
1824 Ibid.
1825 Ibid. pg. 95
1826 Ibid. pg. 100
1827 Ibid. pg. 68
1828 Ibid. pg. 79
1829 A covenant professor at Criswell College told me that while he was not willing to deny that God had a reason for Israel's restoration, he could not favor Israel in the Middle East, and he did not see Israel as playing a significant role in prophecy.

1830   John Gerstner, *Wrongly Dividing the Word of Truth : A Critique of Dispensationalism* Wolgemuth & Hyatt (Brentwood, TN) 1991 pg. 150

1831   John Wick Bowman, "The Bible and Modern Religions : II.   Dispensationalism," *Interpretation* April 1956 No. 10 pg. 172

1832   David Chilton, *Days of Vengeance* Dominion Press (Fort Worth, TX) 1987 pg. 494

1833   Clarence B. Bass, *Backgrounds to Dispensationalism* William B. Eerdmans (Grand Rapids, Mich.) 1960 pg. 34

1834   Ryrie, *Dispensationalism* op. cit. pg. 193

1835   Cf.   "those things which have been predicted by the Creator ... completing His dispensations with regard to the human race," Irenaeus, op. cit. pg. 555

1836   Crutchfield, *The Conservative Theological Journal* Vol. 3, No. 8 op. cit. pg. 37

1837   James Ussher, *The Annals of the World* Master Books (Green Forest, AR) 2003 ed. pg. 882

1838   Cf. Ibid.

1839   Ryrie, *Dispensationalism* op. cit. pg. 71

1840   Pentecost, *Things to Come* op. cit. pg. 46

1841   Ladd, *Theology of the New Testament* op. cit. pg. 42

1842   "Both/and" views are not rare. They are usually superficial ways of discarding confusing or divisive issues. Examples include theistic evolution, progressive creationism, Christian psychology, and the like.   They ignore the problem by denying there is a problem.   They discard the blatantly anti-Christian, believing that what is left is productive.

1843   J. Lanier Burns, *Contemporary Dispensationalism* Herbert Bateman, ed., Kregel Publishers (Grand Rapids, Mich.) 1999 pg. 271

1844   Ryrie, *Dispensationalism* op. cit. pg. 176

1845   Cf.   Walter C. Kaiser Jr., *Inerrancy* Norman Geisler, ed.   Academic Books (Grand Rapids, Mich.) 1980 pg. 128

1846   Egypt in particular has argued for great antiquity and its arguments have largely been erroneously accepted by modern scholars.   Josephus, however, disputes much of arguments for Egyptian antiquity (Josephus, "Against Apion," *Complete Works of Josephus* op. cit. pp. 617-621) and aptly named his own writing "The Antiquity of the Jews."

1847   Tradition holds that the Septuagint was originally composed for the great Alexandrian Library of Egypt (Josepheus, "Antiquity of the Jews," op. cit. pg. 246). Owing to the age old debate that Egypt had great antiquity than the Jews they may have tampered with the chronology of the Bible to prove that Judaism was older.

1848   Consider, for example, the Reign of Terror which grew out of the Enlightenment.

1849   Kaiser Jr., *Inerrancy* op. cit. pg. 128

1850   Irenaeus, op. cit. pg. 565

1851   Hippolytus, op. cit. pg. 184

1852   The early Unitarians were not as liberal as the modern Unitarians.   In many respects there were strong Protestants except that they differed in their understanding of the Trinity, often accusing Protestants of catering to Catholic polytheism.

1853   Annihilationism is the doctrine that the soul is annihilated and merely ceases to exist.   In the context of many of its advocates it is applied only to the damned, thus replacing hell but many others apply it to all between the time of death and the resurrection (similar to "soul sleep").   While technically a heretical view it is not as heretical as those who teach universalism, or the belief that all men will be saved and go to heaven. Bullinger, then, is wrongly criticized by the very people whose heresies exceed any minor heresy held by Bullinger himself.

WORKS CITED

Books

Paul Alexander, *The Byzantine Apocalyptic Tradition* University of California Press (Berkley, Ca.) 1985

Sir Robert Anderson, *The Coming Prince* Kregel Press (Grand Rapids, Mich.) 1957 ed.

Sir Robert Anderson, *The Vision of the First Six Seals* Prophecy Investigation Society - R.F. Hunger Printer (London, England) 1913

Augustine, *City of God* Modern Library (New York, NY) 1993 ed.

John Bale, *Selected Works of John Bale* Cambridge Press (London, England) 1574 ed.

Donald Grey Barnhouse, *Revelation* Zondervan Press (Grand Rapids, Mich.) 1971

Clarence B. Bass, *Backgrounds to Dispensationalism* William B. Eerdmans (Grand Rapids, Mich.) 1960

Herbert Bateman, ed., *Contemporary Dispensationalism* Kregel Publishers (Grand Rapids, Mich.) 1999

Louis Bauman, *Russian Events in the Light of Bible Prophecy* The Balkiston (Philadelphia, Penn.)

Arthur Bloomfield, *All Things New* Bethany House (Bloomington, MN) 1959

Arthur E. Bloomfield, *The End of Days* Bethany House (Minneapolis, Minn.) 1961

Arthur Bloomfield, *The Key to Understanding Revelation* Bethany House (Bloomington, MN) 2002 (reprint of *All Things New*)

Loraine Boettner, *Roman Catholicism* Presbyterian & Reformed (Phillipsburg, NJ) 1962

James Montgomery Boice, *Foundations of the Christian Faith* InterVarsity Press (Leicester, England) 1986

Fabio Bourbon, *Petra : Jordan's Extraordinary Ancient City* Barnes and Noble Books (Vercelli, Italy) 1999

James Brookes, *Till He Come* Gospel Publishers (Chicago, Ill.) 1891

James Brookes, *Marantha* Fleming Revell Co. (New York, NY) 1889

James A. Brooks & Carlton L. Winberry, *Syntax of New Testament Greek* University Press of America (Lanham, MD) 1979

James Viscount Bryce, *The Holy Roman Empire* MacMillan & Co. (London, England) 1950

Richard Buckingham, *Tudor Apocalypse* Sutton Courtenay Press (Oxford, UK) 1978

E. W. Bullinger, *Commentary on Revelation* Kregel Classics (Grand Rapids, Mich.) 1984 ed.

E. W. Bullinger, *Figures of Speech Used in the Bible* Baker Book House (Grand Rapids, Mich.) 1968

E. W. Bullinger, *The Apocalypse* Kregel (Grand Rapids, Mich.) 1935

David Burr, *Olivi's Peacable Kingdom* University of Penn. Press (Philadelphia, Penn.) 1993

J. B. Bury, *The Invasion of Europe by the Barbarians* W. W. Norton & Co. (New York, NY) 1967

G. B. Caird, *The Revelation of Saint John* Henrickson Publishers (Peabody, Mass.) 1966

John Channon, *The Historical Atlas of Russia* Penguin Books (New York, NY) 1996

David Chilton, *Days of Vengeance* Dominion Press (Fort Worth, TX) 1987

Peter A. Clayton, *Chronicle of the Pharaohs* Thames & Hudson (New York, NY) 1994

Jim Combs, *Mysteries of the Book of Daniel* Tribune Publishers (Springfield, Mo.) 1994

Jim Combs, *Mysteries of the Book of Revelation* Tribune Publishers (Springfield, MO) 1994

William Corlis, *Ancient Man : A Handbook of Puzzling Artifacts* The Sourcebook Project (Glen Arm, MD) 1978

Mal Couch, *A Biblical Theology of the Church* Kregel Publications (Grand Rapids, Mich.) 1999

Mal Couch, ed., *Dictionary of Premillennial Theology* Kregel Publications, Grand Rapids, Mich. (1996)

Mal Couch, *The Hope of Christ's Return* AMG Publishers (Chattanooga, Tn.) 2001

David Criswell, *The Rise of the Holy Roman Empire* Fortress Adonai Press (North Charleston, SC) 2003

David Criswell, *The Rise and Fall of the Holy Roman Empire* PublishAmerica (Baltimore, MD) 2003

David Criswell, *She Who Restores the Roman Empire* iUniverse (Lincoln, NE) 2002

Constance Cumbey, *The Hidden Dangers of the Rainbow* Huntington House (Shreveport, LA) 1983

John Cummings, *The Destiny of Nations* Hurst & Blackette (London, England) 1864

John Nelson Darby, *The Collected Works of J. N. Darby Prophetic Vol. 1 - Vol. 2 in series* Kingston Bible Trust (London, England)

John Nelson Darby, *The Collected Works of J. N. Darby Prophetic Vol. 2 - Vol. 5 in series* Believer's Bookshelf (Subury, Penn.) 1971 reprint

J. D. G. Dunn, *Unity and Diversity in the New Testament* (London, England) 1977

Charles H. Dyer, with Angela Hunt, *The Rise of Babylon : Sign of the End Times* Tyndale House (Wheaton, Ill.) 1991

Millard Erickson, *Christian Theology* Baker Books (Grand Rapids, Mich.) 1992 ed.

Millard Erickson, *Contemporary Options in Eschatology* Baker Books (Grand Rapids, Mich.) 1977

Lewis Farnell, *Greece and Babylon* T & T Clark (Edinburgh, England) 1911

Paul Feinberg, *The Rapture : Pre- Mid- or Posttribulational?* Zondervan Publ. (Grand Rapids, Mich.) 1984

J.C. Fenton, *Saint Matthew* Westminister Press (Philadelphia, Penn.) 1963

Austin Flannery, ed., *Vatican Council II* Costello Publications (Northport, NY)

John Foxe, *Acts and Monuments of the Christian Church Vol. 1* Religious Tract Soticy (Picadilly, England) 1841 ed.

Leroy Edwin Froom, *Prophetic Faith of Our Fathers Vol. 1* Review & Herald (Washington, DC) 1950

Arnold G. Fruchtenbaum, *Israelology* Ariel Ministries (Tustin, CA) 1996

Arno Gaebelein, *The Prophet Ezekiel* Our Hope Press (New York, NY) 1918

Norman Geisler, ed., *Inerrancy* Academic Books (Grand Rapids, Mich.) 1980

John Gerstner, *Wrongly Dividing the Word of Truth : A Critique of Dispensationalism* Wolgemuth & Hyatt (Brentwood, TN) 1991

William Gesenius, *Gesenius' Hebrew Grammar* Clarendon Press (Oxford, England) 1910

William Gesenius, *Hebrew and Chaldee Lecicon* Baker Books (Grand Rapids, Mich) 1979

Martin Gilbert, *Israel* Turner Books (Toronto, ON) 1998

Justo Gonzalez, *The Story of Christianity Vol. 1* Harper Collins (New York, NY) 1984

Philip Goodman, *The Assyrian Connection* Prescott Press (Lafayette, LA) 1993

Robert Govett, *Govett on Revelation : The Apocalypse Expounded by Scripture Vol. II* Conley & Schoettle Publishing Co. (Miami Springs, FL) 1981 ed.

Robert Govett, *Govett on Revelation : The Apocalypse Expounded by Scripture Vol. III* Conley & Schoettle Publishing Co. (Miami Springs, FL) 1981 ed.

James Grant, *The End of Things* Darton and Co. (London, England) 1866

Stanley Grenz, *The Millennial Maze* Intervarsity Press (Downers Grove, Ill.) 1992

Robert Gundry, *The Church and the Tribulation* Zondervan Publishing (Grand Rapids, Mich.) 1973

Robert Gundry, *First the Antichrist* Baker Book House (Grand Rapids, Mich.) 1997

Robert Gundry, *A Survey of the New Testament* Zondervan Publishing House (Grand Rapids, Mich.) 1994

Norman Harrison, *The End   Re-Thinking The Revelation* The Harrison Service (Minneapolis, Minn.) 1948

Carl Henry, ed., *Prophecy in the Making* Creation House (Carol Stream, IL) 1971

Matthew Henry, *Matthew Henry's Commentary on the Whole Bible : Vol. 4* Hendrickson Publishers (Peabody, Mass.) 1991

Matthew Henry, *Matthew Henry's Commentary on the Whole Bible : Vol. 6* Hendrickson Publishers (Peabody, Mass.) 1991 ed.

Ed Hindson, *Earth's Final Hour* Harvest House (Eugene, OR) 1999

Edward Hindson, *Revelation : Unlocking the Future* AMG Publishers (Chattanooga, TN) 2002

Alexander Hislop, *The Two Babylons* Loizeaux Brothers (Neptune, NJ) 1916

Harold Hoehner, *Chronological Aspects of the Life of Christ* Zondervan Publishing (Grand Rapids, Mich.) 1977

Dave Hunt, *The Cult Explostion* Harvest House (Eugene, OR) 1980

Dave Hunt, *Global Peace and the Rise of Antichrist* Harvest House (Eugene, OR) 1990

Dave Hunt, *How Close Are We?* Harvest House (Eugene, OR) 1993

Dave Hunt, *Peace, Prosperity and the Coming Holocaust* Harvest House (Eugene, OR) 1983

Dave Hunt, *Whatever Happened to Heaven?* Harvest House (Eugene, OR) 1988

Thomas Ice & Kenneth L. Gentry Jr., *The Great Tribulation : Past or Future?* Kregel Press (Grand Rapids, Mich.) 1999

Thomas Ice & Timothy Demy ed., *When the Trumpet Sounds* Harvest House (Eugene, OR) 1995

Jack Van Impe, *2001 : On the Edge of Eternity* Word Pulishing (Dallas, TX) 1996

H. A. Ironside, *Revelation* Loizeaux (Neptune, NJ) 1996 ed.

493

William T. James, ed., *Piercing the Future* Nelson Walker Publishers (Beaton, Ark.) 2000

William James, ed., *Prophecy at Ground Zero* Starburst Publishers (Lancaster, PA) 2002

Morris Jastrow, *Religious Belief and Practice in Babylonia and Assyria* Benjamin Blom. Inc. (New York, NY) 1911

Josephus, *The Complete Works of Josephus* Kregel Publications (Grand Rapids, Mich.) 1981 ed.

Robert Van Kampen, *The Sign* Crossway Books (Wheaton, Ill.) 3rd revised ed. 2000

Samuel Kellogg, *Are Premillennialists Right?* F.H. Revell (Chicago, Ill.) 1885

Samuel Kellogg, *The Jews, or, Prediction and Fulfillment* A.D.F. Randolph (New York, NY) 1883

J.N.D. Kelly, *Oxford Dictionary of Popes* Oxford Press (Oxford, England) 1986

William Kelly, *Lectures on the Book of Revelation* G. Morrish (London, England) no date

Geoffrey King, *Daniel* William Eerdmans (Grand Rapids, Mich.) 1966

George Eldon Ladd, *A Commentary on the Revelation of John* Wm. B. Eerdmans (Grand Rapids, Mich.) 1972

George Eldon Ladd, *A Theology of the New Testament* William Eerdmans Co. (Grand Rapids, Mich.) 1974

Tim LaHaye, *Revelation Unveiled* Zondervan Publishing (Grand Rapids, Mich.) 1999

Tim LaHaye, ed., *Tim LaHaye Prophecy Study Bible* AMG Publishers (Chatanooga, TN) 2001

Gordan Laing, *Survivals of the Roman Religion: Our Debt to Greece and Rome* Cooper Square Press (New York, NY) 1963

G.H. Lang, *The Revelation of Jesus Christ* The Paternoster Press (New York, NY) 1948

Kenneth Scott Latourette, *A History of Christianity : Vol. 1* Harper & Row (New York, NY) 1953

Jon Levenson, *Theology of the Program of Restoring of Ezekiel 40-48* Scholars Press (Missoula, MT) 1976

J.B Lighfoot & J.R. Harmer, eds., *The Apostolic Fathers* Baker Book House (Grand Rapids, Mich.) 1984 reprint

Hal Lindsey, *The 1980's : Countdown to Armageddon* Bantam Books (New York, NY) 1981

Hal Lindsey, *There Is A New World Coming* Harvest House (Eugene, OR) 1973

Hal Lindsey, *The Late Great Planet Earth* Zondervan Publishers (Grand Rapids, Mich.) 1977

Hal Lindsey, *The Rapture* Bantam Books (New York, NY) 1983

Duane Magnani, *The Watchtower Files* Bethany House (Minneapolis, MN) 1983

Tex Marrs, *Dark Secrets of the New Age* Crossway Books (Westchester, Ill.) 1987

Jobe Martin, *The Evolution of a Creationist* 2nd Ed., Biblical Discipleship Ministries (Rockwall, TX) 2002

Thomas Martin, *Ancient Greece* Yale University Press (New York, NY) 1996

Robert Maton, *Israel's Redemption or the Prophetical History of our Savior's Kingdom on Earth* Daniel Frere Shop (London, England) 1642

Alva McClain, *Daniel's Prophecy of the Seventy Weeks* Zondervan Publishers (Grand Rapids, Mich.) 1940

Bernard McGinn, translator, *Apocalyptic Spirituality* Paulist Press (Mahurah, NJ) 1979

Bill Mcmillon, *The Archaeology Handbook* John Wiley & Sons, Inc. (New York, NY) 1991

Joseph Mede, *The Apostasy of the Latter Times* Macintosh Printer (London, England) 1865 ed.

Joseph Mede, *The Key to Revelation* Phil Stephens Printer (London, England) 1643

Bruce Metzger, *Lexical Aids for Students of New Testament Greek* Theological Book Agency (Princeton, NJ) 1991

Bruce M. Metzger, *The Text of the New Testament* Oxford University Press (Oxford, England) 1992

Bruce M. Metzger, *A Textual Commentary on the Greek New Testament* United Bible Society (Stuttgart, Germany) 1971

Stephen R. Miller, *The New American Commentary on Daniel* Broadman & Holman (Nashville, Tenn.) 1994

Henry Morris, *The Biblical Basis for Modern Science* Baker Book House (Grand Rapids, Mich.) 1984

Henry Morris, *The Revelation Record* Tyndale House (Wheaton, Ill.) 1983

Robert Mounce, *The New International Commentary on the New Testament : The Book of Revelation* William Eerdmans Co. (Grand Rapids, Mich.) 1977

William Mounce, *Basis of Biblical Greek* Zondervan Publishing (Grand Rapids, MICH) 1993

Watchman Nee, *Come, Lord Jesus* Christian Fellowship Publications (New York, NY) 1976

Nestle-Aland *Novum Tesamentum Graece* Deutsche Bibelgesellschaft (Stuttgart, Germany) 1898

William Newell, The Book of Revelation Grace Publishing Inc. (Chicago, Ill.) 1935

Barclay Newman, ed., *A Concise Greek-English Dictionary of the New Testament* United Bible Societies (Stuttgart, Germany) 1971

Isaac Newton, *Observations on the Prophecies of Daniel and the Apocalypse of St. John* Edwin Mellen Press (Lewiston, NY) 1733 (1999 reprint)

Nicholas of Lyra, *Nicholas of Lyra's Apocalypse Commentary* Medieval Institute Publications (Kalamazoo, Mich.) 1997 (orig. 1329)

John Julius Norwich, *A Short History of Byzantium* Vintage Books (New York, NY) 1997

A.T. Olmstead, *History of Assyria* Charles Scribner's Sons (New York, NY) 1923

A.T. Olmstead, *History of the Persian Empire* University of Chicago Press (Chicago, Ill.) 1948

Jay Pasachoff, *Contemporary Astronomy* Saunders College Publishing (New York, NY) 1989

Raphael Patai, *The Messiah Texts* Wayne State University Press (Detroit, Mich.) 1979

Robert Payne, *The Dream and the Tomb* Cooper Square Press (New York, NY) 2000

G. H. Pember, *The Antichrist, Babylon, and the Coming of the Kingdom* Schoettle Publishing (Miami Springs, FL) 1988 ed.

J. Dwight Pentecost, *Things to Come* Zondervan Publishing House (Grand Rapids, Mich.) 1958

George Peters, *The Theocratic Kingdom Vol. 1* Kregel Publications (Grand Rapids, Mich.) 1884

George Peters, *The Theocratic Kingdom Vol. 2* Kregel Publications (Grand Rapids, Mich.) 1884

George Peters, *The Theocratic Kingdom Vol. 3* Kregel Publications (Grand Rapids, Mich.) 1884

David Peterson & Kent Richards, *Interpreting Hebrew Poetry* Fortress Press (Minneapolis, MN) 1992

Charles Pfeiffer, *The Dead Sea Scrolls and the Bible* Baker Books (Grand Rapids, Mich.) 1969

Matthew Poole, *A Commentary on the Holy Bible : Vol. II* Hendrickson Publishers (Peabody, Mass.) no copyright listed

Matthew Poole, *A Commentary on the Holy Bible : Vol. III* Hendrickson Publishers (Peabody, Mass.) no copyright listed

Randall Price, *The Coming Last Days Temple* Harvest House (Eugene, Or.) 1999

Randall Price, *The Stones Cry Out* Harvest House (Eugene, OR) 1997

Bernard Ramm, *Protestant Biblical Interpretation* Baker Book House (Grand Rapids, Mich.) 1982

David Reagan, *Wrath and Glory* New Leaf Press (Green Forest, AR) 2001

Colin Renfrew & Paul Bahn, *Archaeology: Theories, Methods, & Practice* Thames & Hudson Ltd. (New York, NY) 1991

Homer Ritchie, Omer Ritchie, & Lonnie Shipman, *Secrets of Prophecy Revealed* 21st Century Press (Springfield, Mo.) 2001

Robert William Rogers, *A History of Babylonia and Assyria Vol. 1* Eaton & Mains (New York, NY) 1901

Marvin Rosenthal, *The Pre-Wrath Rapture of the Church* Thomas Nelson Publishers (Nashville, Tn.) 1990

Georges Roux, *Ancient Iraq* Penguin Books (New York, NY) 1992 ed.

Charles Ryrie, *Revelation* Moody Press (Chicago, Ill.), 1996

Howard M. Sachar, *A History of Israel* Alfred A. Knopf (New York, NY) 2003 ed.

Harold Scanlin, *The Dead Sea Scroll & Modern Translations of the Old Testament* Tyndale House (Wheaton, Ill.) 1993

Chris Scarre, *Chronicle of the Roman Emperors* Thames and Hudson (London, England) 1997

C. I. Scofield, *Prophecy Make Plain : Addresses on Prophecy* The Gospel Hour (Greenville, SC) 1910

C. I. Scofield, *What Do The Prophets Say?* The Gospel Hour (Greenville, SC) 1918

Thomas Scott, *The Holy Bible, with Explanatory Notes, Practical Observations, and Copious Marginal References* (London, England) 1828

Walter Scott, *Exposition of the Revelation of Jesus Christ* Pickering & Inglis Ltd. (London, England) 1900

H. H. Scullard, *From the Gracchi to Nero* Routledge (New York, NY) 1959

H.H. Scullard, *A History of the Roman World* Routledge Press (New York, NY) 1997 ed.

Joseph A. Seiss, *The Apocalypse* Kregel Publications (Grand Rapids, Mich.) 2001 reprint

Gerald B. Stanton, *Kept from the Hour* Schoettle Publ. (Haysville, NC) 1991

George Steindorff and Keith C. Steele, *When Egypt Ruled the East* University of Chicago Press (Chicago, Ill.) 1957

J.F. Strombeck, *First the Rapture* Kregel Publications (Grand Rapids, Mich.) 1992 reprint (orig. 1950)

496

Suetonius, *Lives of the Twelve Caesars* trans. Robert Graves, Rain Publishers (New York, NY) 1957

Ray Summers, *Worthy Is The Lamb* Broadman Press (Nashville, Tenn) 1951

Henry Barclay Swete, *Commentary on Revelation* Kregel Publications (Grand Rapids, Mich.) 1977

Merrill Tenney, *Interpreting Revelation* William B. Eerdmanns (Grand Rapids, Mich.) 1957

Merrill Tenney, *New Testament Survey* William B. Eerdmans Co. (Grand Rapids, Mich.) 1985

Joseph Thayer, *Thayer's Greek-English Lexicon* Baker Book House (Grand Rapids, Mich.) 1977

Robert Thomas, *Revelation 1-7 An Exegetical Commentary* Moody Press (Chicago, Ill.) 1992

Robert Thomas, *Revelation 8-22 An Exegetical Commentary* Moody Press (Chicago, Ill.) 1992

Warren C. Trenchard, *Complete Vocabulary Guide to the Greek New Testament* Zondervan Publishers (Grand Rapids, Mich.) 1998

Robert Turcan, *The Cults of the Roman Empire* Blackwell (Cambridge, MA) 1992

Merrill Unger, *Unger's Bible Dictionary* Moody Press (Chicago, Ill.) 1957

James Ussher, *The Annals of the World* Master Books (Green Forest, AR) 2003 ed.

John Walvoord, *Daniel: The Key to Prophetic Revelation* Moody Press (Chicago, Ill.) 1971

John Walvoord, *Every Prophecy of the Bible* Chariot Victor Publ. (Colorado Springs, Co.) 1999

John F. Walvoord, *The Millennial Kingdom* Zondervan Books (Grand Rapids, Mich.) 1959

John Walvoord, *The Nations, Israel, and the Church in Prophecy* Zondervan Publishers (Grand Rapids, Mich.) 1988 ed.

John Walvoord, *The Revelation of Jesus Christ* Moody Press (Chicago, Ill.) 1966

Nathaniel West, *The Thousand Year Reign of Christ* Kregel Publications (Grand Rapids, Mich.) 1993 ed.

Frederic M. Wheelock, *Wheelock's Latin* R. A. LaFleur, ed., Harper Collins Publishers (New York, NY) 1995 ed.

John Whitcomb, *Daniel* BMH Books (Winona Lake, IN) 1985

John C. Whitcomb & Henry M. Morris, *The Genesis Flood* Presbyterian & Reformed (Phillipsburg, NJ) 1961

John C. Whitcomb, *The World That Perished* Baker Book House (Grand Rapids, Mich.) 1988

H. L. Wilmington, *The King is Coming* Tyndale House (Wheaton, Ill.) 1984

Ehud Ben-Yehuda & David Weinstein, eds., *Ben-Yehuda's English-Hebrew Dictionary* Pocket Books (New York, NY) 1961

Edward J. Young, *The Prophecy of Daniel* William B. Eerdmans Publishers (Grand Rapids, Mich.) 1949

Richard Young, *Intermediate New Testament Greek* Broadman & Holman (Nashville, Tenn.) 1994

Shimon Zilberman, ed., *The Compact English-Hebrew Dictionary* Zilberman (Jerusalem, Israel) 1997

Paul A. Zoch, *Ancient Rome* University of Oklahoma Press (University of Oklahoma, Ok.) 1998

Reference Works

Baedeker Italy Macmillan Travel (New York, NY) 1996

Catechism of the Catholic Church United States Catholic Conference (USA) 1994

Frank Gaebelein, ed., *The Expositor's Bible Commentary Vol. 6* Zondervan's House (Grand Rapids, Mich.) 1981

Frank Gaebelein, ed., *The Expositor's Bible Commentary Vol. 8* Zondervan's House (Grand Rapids, Mich.) 1981

Frank Gaebelein, ed., *The Expositor's Bible Commentary Vol. 12* Zondervan's House (Grand Rapids, Mich.) 1981

Moffatt New Testament Commentary Harper & Row (New York, NY) 1940

Alexander Roberts & James Donaldson, eds., *Ante-Nicene Fathers Vol. I* William B. Eerdmans Publishers (Grand Rapids, Mich.) 1999

Alexander Roberts & James Donaldson, eds., *Ante-Nicene Fathers Vol. V* William B. Eerdmans Publishers (Grand Rapids, Mich.) 1999

Alexander Roberts & James Donaldson, eds., *Ante-Nicene Fathers Vol. VI* William B. Eerdmans Publishers (Grand Rapids, Mich.) 1999

Alexander Roberts & James Donaldson, eds., *Ante-Nicene Fathers Vol. VII* William B. Eerdmans Publishers (Grand Rapids, Mich.) 1999

Alexander Roberts & James Donaldson, eds., *Ante-Nicene Fathers Vol. VIII* William B. Eerdmans Publishers (Grand Rapids, Mich.) 1999

John F. Walvoord & Roy Zuck, eds., *The Bible Knowledge Commentary : Old Testament* Victor Books (Wheaton, Ill.) 1986

Magazines, Articles, and Dissertations

John Wick Bowman, "The Bible and Modern Religions : II. Dispensationalism," *Interpretation* April 1956 No. 10

"Collision Course," *Dallas Morning News* March 12, 1998

Larry Crutchfield, "The Early Church Fathers and the Foundations of Dispensationalism Part V," *TheConservative Theological Journal* Vol. 3 # 8, April 1999

Larry Crutchfield, "The Early Church Fathers and the Foundations of Dispensationalism Part VI," *The Conservative Theological Journal* Vol. 3 # 9, August 1999

David Ebaugh, *Monarch* Oct./Nov. 1986

Fort Worth Star Telegram, Novermber 23, 1988

Thomas Ice, "Why the Rapture and second coming are Separate Events," *Pretrib Answers To Posttrib* (Aug-Sept. 1994)

Asher Kaufman, "Where the Ancient Temple of Jerusalem Stood," *Biblical Archaeological Review*, Vol. 9, No. 2 (March/April, 1983)

Bill Martin & Bill Perkins, "The Second Witness ... Who Is He?", *Digging Deeper Bible Studies* no date

Ernest Martin, "New Evidence for the *Real* Site of the Temple in Jerusalem," *Bible and Spade* Vol. 14, No. 4 Fall 2001

Kenneth McKinley, *The Chronology of Revelation* A dissertation for Dallas Theological Seminary May 1957

Leon Ritmeyer, "Locating the Original Temple Mount," *Biblical Archaeology Review*, Vol. 18, No. 2 (March/April, 1992)

Merrill Unger, "The Temple Vision of Ezekiel," *Bibliotheca Sacra* 105 (October, 1948)

Web Sites, Notes, and Letters

www.cnn.com/TECH/space/9803/12/asteroid/

John Fok, "The Rapture of the Church," http://home.hkstar.com/~johnfok1/Eschatology/4.htm (1/24/02)

Personal letter from Dave Hunt.

Personal notes from Dave Hunt lecture.

Tommy Ice, "Morgan Edwards: A Pre-Darby Rapturist," http://www.conservativeonline.org/journals/1_1_journal/Morgan_Edwards.htm (8/29/02)

Roy Metz, class notes from Criswell College.

David Criswell has a Ph.D. from Tyndale Seminary and a M.Div. from Criswell College. He is also a Fellow at Louisiana Baptist Theological Seminary. David spent three years researching and working on *Controversies in Revelation*. This was actually the first of the *Biblical Controversies* series to be written although the last in the series. The volumes include *Controversies in the Pentateuch, Controversies in Scriptures Vol. II, Controversies in the Prophets, Controversies in Gospels*, and *Controversies in the Epistles*. He has also written *The Rise and Fall of the Holy Roman Empire* and the fiction romance, *Valley of the Blind* which is in development as the first mainstream Christian Bollywood film in India. Dr. Criswell was also the editor-in-chief of *the Evangelical Standard* from 2007 to 2010 and was named Goodwill Ambassador to Israel during the Iraq war of 2003.

www.ingramcontent.com/pod-product-compliance
Lightning Source LLC
Chambersburg PA
CBHW060233100426
42742CB00011B/1517